WITNESS OF THE WORD

WITNESS OF THE WORD

A Biblical Theology of the Gospel

Foster R. McCurley
& John Reumann

FORTRESS PRESS   PHILADELPHIA

ACKNOWLEDGMENTS

Art on p. 6: Vickie DeVilbiss, Celebration Art, Annapolis, Maryland.

Extract on p. 35: Copyright 1974 Time Inc. All rights reserved. Reprinted by permission from TIME.

Photograph on p. 67: Courtesy of The Oriental Institute of The University of Chicago.

Poetry on pp. 135–36, 208, 213: James B. Pritchard, ed. *Ancient Near East: An Anthology of Texts and Pictures.* Copyright © 1958 by Princeton University Press. Excerpts pg. 36, 94, 96, 104–5. Reprinted by permission of Princeton University Press.

Poetry on pp. 214–15: James B. Pritchard, ed., *Ancient Near Eastern Texts: Relating to the Old Testament,* 3rd edn. with Supplement. Copyright © 1969 by Princeton University Press. Excerpt, pg. 60–61. Reprinted by permission of Princeton University Press.

Biblical quotations, unless otherwise noted, are from the Revised Standard Version of the Bible, copyright 1946, 1952, © 1971, 1973 by the Division of Christian Education of the National Council of the Churches of Christ in the U.S.A. and are used by permission.

Library of Congress Cataloging-in-Publication Data

McCurley, Foster R.
  Witness of the word.

  Includes bibliographies and index.
  1. Bible—Theology. 2. Jesus Christ—Person and
offices. 3. Jesus Christ—History of doctrines—
Early church, ca. 30–600. I. Reumann, John Henry Paul.
II. Title.
BS543.M42   1986   220.6   85–47721
ISBN 0–8006–1866–1

1723H85   Printed in the United States of America   1–1866

To our students
over two decades at the Lutheran Theological Seminary, Philadelphia,
especially in classes taught together 1975–83, where approaches to
the Bible in this volume were developed and practiced,

and to the twenty-seven hundred pastors and professional leaders, and
over sixty-five thousand adults with whom we have learned and
taught each other in the "Word and Witness" program in the United
States, Canada, Europe, and beyond.

73093

Contents

Contents

II
THE GOOD NEWS JESUS PREACHED
93

III
THE GOSPEL AS GOD'S VICTORY AND KINGSHIP—IN ISRAEL AND IN CHRIST
131

Contents

Contents

V
THE GOSPEL AS HOPE—GOD'S FUTURE REIGN
251

Contents

Contents

Contents

Authors' Preface

Witness of the Word is a book exploring what the Bible says in both the Old and New Testaments, examined in their ancient settings by means of tools from modern scholarship. The focus is not, however, on modern techniques or historical setting or such introductory questions as authorship and dates for books of the Bible, but on what Scripture said and says about God, the human predicament and recurring bad news for the world, and above all about gospel or what God says and does for the good of Israel and all humanity. As such, this book is an exercise in that elusive discipline called "biblical theology." It is also a thoroughly collaborative undertaking by two colleagues in a seminary faculty, tested with thousands of readers—clergy, professional leaders, and laity—in North America, Scandinavia, Germany, and elsewhere as a study text on the Bible.

While we, of course, cannot avoid the impact of modern scholarship and would not want to miss the richness of what it can bring to biblical studies, ours is not another book on "the criticisms." We have mentioned (in chap. 1) some of these available critical methods, many of them widely accepted, others still in a controversial infancy. But at no point is the aim "criticism for criticism's sake." Only where form criticism, for example, is helpful in understanding a passage is it reflected.

Much the same thing could be said about the history of Israel, ancient Near Eastern settings, data concerning New Testament times, and the Greco-Roman world. Here a stronger case could be made for the importance of ancient history, archeology, Hebrew sociology, and Hellenistic culture, because "the word which [God] sent to Israel" (Acts 10:36) came to a very real world—or, better, worlds in a series of historical periods. But we have not been concerned simply to depict the vividness of David's Jerusalem or of Corinth in Paul's day.

What then? What the Bible says—about God, about us, and our salvation, as the Nicene Creed was later to put it—in its world setting, throughout both testaments, has been our concern.

Talk about God is, in the narrow sense, "theology"; about human beings and their plight, "anthropology" and "hamartiology," to use traditional terms; about salvation, "soteriology." But we have not followed such categories from later dogmatics. Nor have we taken up the Bible book by book (for to start with Genesis and close with the Book of Revelation can produce some misleading impressions about the faith of Israel or of New Testament Christianity). Nor have we arranged things always in the supposed chronological sequence which modern scholarship reconstructs with the help of archeology and other resources. We have even rejected the attractive possibility of presenting biblical thought by literary categories, though we do try to pay attention to genre or types of literature such as history, poetry, or wisdom, in seeking meaning.

How then? After an initial treatment of what the Bible is (in chaps. 1–5), we have found it best to plunge right in with a picture of Jesus and what he taught (chaps. 6–7). (Anyone already "up" on such matters as whence our Bible came and how it is "word of God," or anyone who does not need an overview of biblical events might skip these first five chapters, but she or he would then know less about how we approach Scripture.) Jesus' message about "the kingdom of God" drives one back, in turn, to the Hebrew Scriptures where Jesus and people of the day found the theme of God's kingship.

That "the Lord reigns," according to Israelite thought, we have tried to spell out, against the backdrop of ancient Near Eastern thinking generally. How Israel's God, Yahweh, came to be Lord for that nation, we have approached historically (in a rough chronological account from the exodus until the exile), then doxologically (in Israel's worship and assertions about the whole created world and even in secular wisdom), and then eschatologically (that is, in terms of future hope). This structure allows an examination of the past (chaps. 8–12), the present (chaps. 14–17), and the future (chaps. 19–22), in Old Testament faith. A look at the chart on the structure of this book (pp. xviii–xix), sketching the outline of our thirty-five chapters, may help clarify this sequence. It will likely prove advantageous if one returns to this outline often in the course of reading the book.

A glance at the table of contents or at the outline chart will also show that interspersed regularly with this Old Testament material are chapters

(13, 18, 23) on Jesus Christ. Having begun with Jesus of Nazareth (chaps. 6–7), we have sought to show how much of the New Testament picture of Christ gathers together and builds upon (and sometimes reworks or rejects) elements in the Hebrew Scriptures. There is a sense, therefore, in which the Old Testament points to Christ, but this is not to be stated at the expense of the original meaning of the Hebrew Scriptures in their situation and in their own integrity. One may readily see how God's raising Jesus from the dead is a parallel to God's delivering Israel from Egypt. That Jesus Christ was, quite early in the church's faith, given a role in creation may seem more mind-boggling (though probably so also was Israel's assertion when it was first claimed that a God named Yahweh made the heavens and the earth and all the peoples). The question of what the Old Testament said about "the messiah" and how Jesus responded to the messianic options in his day is much more intricate. In any case, we have chosen to address the interplay of the two testaments in these, as well as in other, ways.

The book goes on with a long unit (chaps. 24–33) on New Testament thought. Though only decades are involved, rather than centuries as in the Old Testament, we have used here an approach that is partially chronological (from after Easter to Paul and beyond, especially the period after A.D. 70), partly canonical and in terms of key thinkers like Paul and John, but also one that does justice to genre (like apocalyptic) and to topics like "church" and "ethics" (chaps. 31, 32). Happily, another look at Jesus in each of the Synoptic Gospels of Matthew, Mark, and Luke (chap. 33) brings us back to the figure from Nazareth whom faith confesses as Christ and Lord.

As something of a balance to the opening chapters, we conclude with a unit on "the one gospel" or "good news" which we have encountered in the Bible in so many forms. Chapter 34 attempts a summary, including reference to how different confessional or denominational traditions have handled this variety. Chapter 35 traces the story of the good news of the kingdom of God, which Jesus preached, through some high spots of interpretation over the centuries to our own day.

While christocentric in many ways, this approach always seeks to root each passage in its historical situation so that the result is a God who speaks and acts in specific times and places, rather than one who issues statements of timeless truths. We have regularly tried to deal with biblical texts as they stand—a great deal of the Bible is directly quoted (usually in the *Revised Standard Version*), but readers will do well to keep a Bible nearby to look up other passages noted. Where, on occasion, we probe behind the existing RSV translation and Greek or Hebrew text, we have

THE STRUCTURE OF THIS BOOK

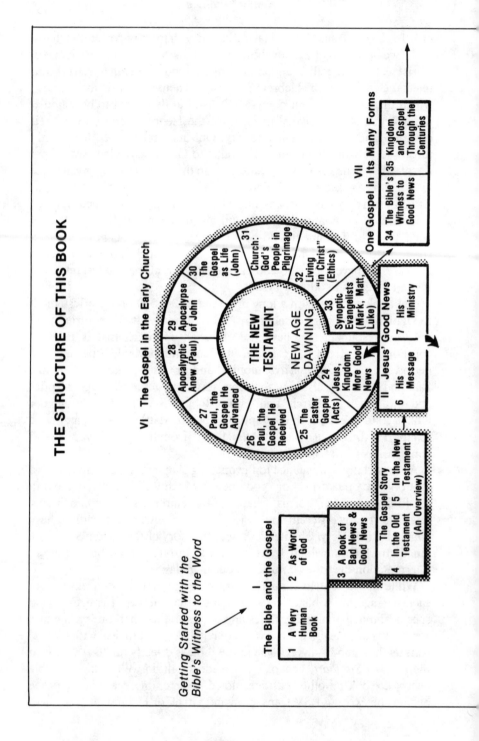

I
The Bible and the Gospel

Getting Started with the Bible's Witness to the Word

1 A Very Human Book	2 As Word of God

3 A Book of Bad News & Good News

4 In the Old Testament	5 In the New Testament
The Gospel Story (An Overview)

VI The Gospel in the Early Church

- 31 Church: God's People in Pilgrimage
- 30 The Gospel as Life (John)
- 32 Living "in Christ" (Ethics)
- 29 Apocalypse of John
- 33 Synoptic Evangelists (Mark, Matt., Luke)
- 28 Apocalyptic Anew (Paul)
- 27 Paul, the Gospel He Advanced
- 26 Paul, the Gospel He Received
- 25 The Easter Gospel (Acts)
- 24 Jesus, Kingdom, More Good News

THE NEW TESTAMENT

NEW AGE DAWNING

II Jesus' Good News

6 His Message	7 His Ministry

VII One Gospel in Its Many Forms

34 The Bible's Witness to Good News	35 Kingdom and Gospel Through the Centuries

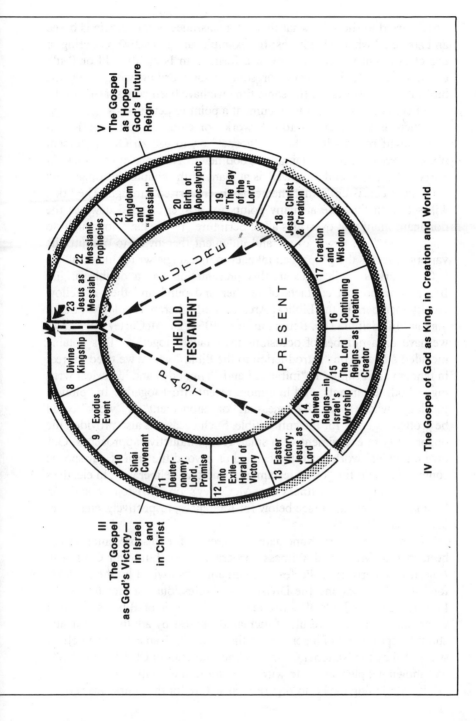

V
The Gospel
as Hope—
God's Future
Reign

21 Kingdom and "Messiah"

20 Birth of Apocalyptic

22 Messianic Prophecies

19 "The Day of the Lord"

23 Jesus as Messiah

18 Jesus Christ & Creation

8 Divine Kingship

17 Creation and Wisdom

9 Exodus Event

FUTURE

16 Continuing Creation

10 Sinai Covenant

THE OLD TESTAMENT

PAST

15 The Lord Reigns—as Creator

11 Deuter-onomy: Lord, Promise

PRESENT

14 Yahweh Reigns—in Israel's Worship

12 Into Exile—Herald of Victory

13 Easter Victory: Jesus as Lord

III
The Gospel
as God's Victory—
in Israel
and
in Christ

IV   The Gospel of God as King, in Creation and World

XIX

usually tried to show on what this reconnaissance of the terrain is based and above all what value it has; for example, an alternative rendering or use of different punctuation or of a form from Israel's world or Paul's environment that is reflected or some prior wording with which the biblical writer works. At the same time we have been very sparing in the use of endnotes, so as not to document a point to death.

If there is a further key to our work—or guiding "hermeneutic," as some might prefer—it is that of "gospel" or, to use an Old Testament phrase, heralding or proclaiming "good news." A glance at the titles for parts 2, 3, 4, 5, 6, and 7, as well as at many of the chapter headings, will show how consistently that theme has been carried through. The book will set forth the case at many points for gospel or good news as the dominant motif that overrides all of Scripture. Yet we have not sought to exclude the "bad news" of sin and judgment thereby or to obscure the variety of forms the gospel can take, even in a single writer like Paul.

Our work as colleagues in this presentation has a double origin. Besides the normal contacts of teacher and pupil and then as fellow faculty members in the Biblical Area of the Lutheran Theological Seminary at Philadelphia (Dr. Reumann since 1951, Dr. McCurley 1964–84), we have on a number of occasions team-taught together. This notably included a course on "Introduction to the Bible," where we tried to treat in tandem such things as "miracles" and "hymnody" and historical writing in both testaments, and in a more recent effort together in "biblical theology" where topics like "messiah" or "atonement" or "work" could be probed together for the entire Bible. Such occasions also provided the opportunity to experiment with small-group, inductive approaches. Our own individual work has often carried us beyond the area of our special competence into the "other testament," and that deliberately, in electives and publications, as witness Dr. McCurley's on Christology and Dr. Reumann's on creation (see below for references, respectively, chap. 8 n. 5, and chap. 16 n. 1).

The other and more immediate background for this presentation has been in the "Word and Witness" program of the Lutheran Church in America. In early 1975 Professor Reumann was invited by the Division for Parish Services and the Division for Professional Leadership of the LCA to serve as biblical consultant for a project of Bible study and witnessing that was a result of increased interest by adults for learning about Scripture and of a perception that "Key '73," an evangelism effort sponsored by the National Council of the Churches of Christ in the USA, had shown people wanted to witness better to their faith.

After designing the basic "figure 8" structure for the course (as revised

for this book, pp. xviii–xix, above), a structure which also had to corre-
late with certain emphases in the witness material at many points, Dr.
Reumann found it impossible to undertake writing all the Bible study
chapters, as then requested, because he had been asked to serve as acting
president of the Philadelphia seminary at an important juncture in its
history—a stint that lengthened to sixteen months of administration
while also teaching full time. Only when it was proposed, to the joy of all
involved, that Dr. McCurley be involved as coauthor, could the project go
ahead. While readers may rightly presume Dr. McCurley is basically
responsible for Old Testament chapters and Dr. Reumann for New (with
"general" chapters like 1–3 and 34–35 in the present numbering divided
between them), there has been a great deal of collaboration and sharing.
If we provided a "source analysis" of authority, readers might be surprised at who wrote what at points.

The biblical material for *Word and Witness* has appeared in three
forms. A field-test edition entitled "The History of the Gospel: Bible
Study for Witnessing" was employed for congregations in the Atlanta,
Georgia; Columbia, South Carolina; and Shenandoah Valley of Virginia
areas in 1976–77. Two paperback editions, *Word and Witness, Understanding the Bible I* and *II* were published (Philadelphia: Lutheran
Church in America, Division for Parish Services), the first in 1977–78
and the second in 1980. The revised second edition included what is here
chapter 3 for the first time. For this present edition we have had the
opportunity to restore in many cases what we originally wrote and what,
for reasons of space, has never appeared before, as well as new material
and corrections and revisions, often based on experiences of ourselves
and others in presenting Word and Witness.

We would pay tribute here especially to staff members of the Division
for Parish Services, in particular the Rev. Lawrence Nelson, who always
had faith in the venture and who lived long enough to see the program
begin nationally; the Rev. Richard Bartley; and as editors, James L.
Barkenquast, Frank W. Klos, and Donald R. Pichaske. We must also
acknowledge the encouragement of friends like Krister Stendahl, then of
Harvard Divinity School, now bishop of Stockholm, an early workshop
leader in Word and Witness, and Norman Hjelm, of Fortress Press, to
revise the material into what, in many ways, is a new book, though the
structure and approach remain the same.

Word and Witness was available from 1977 on, but only by participation on a congregational basis. Pastors and professional lay leaders, as
part of the integrity of the program, were required to attend a nine-day
workshop, usually held in the summer on a college or seminary campus,

before doing the program in their congregation with groups of ten to thirty persons weekly for a one- or multi-year period. These leaders also returned for a three-day follow-up workshop six months later. Professors of Old or New Testament at church-related colleges, universities, and seminaries—like Professor Stendahl or the then-president of the LCA, Dr. Robert Marshall, who gave special support to Word and Witness—served as resource leaders at such workshops. We have learned much from these peers as well as from clergy, directors of religious education, and lay leaders, not to mention people who wrote or phoned us their questions. These insights have been helpful in rewriting this book.

As of 1985, about 65,000 persons in the U.S.A. and Canada have been through the Word and Witness program. While most of them have done so in Lutheran parishes, other Protestant congregations have chosen to use the material, and Word and Witness has been employed in campus ministry, by military chaplains, and for urban clusters of congregations. Some seminaries have employed all or portions of it for orientation or elective courses. We have each met pastors who said their whole ministry has been renewed by participating, and Christians who testified to the deeper faith and more robust witness that has resulted. There have been unexpected blessings in deepened biblical preaching, social concerns, and even arts festivals and other expressions of faith.

A translation into Spanish, *Palabra y Testimonio, Entendiendo La Biblia 1* and *2 (Word and Witness, Understanding the Bible),* has been produced by the Division for Parish Services (Philadelphia, 1983). The Church of Sweden twice sent observers before deciding to translate Word and Witness into Swedish, as *Dialog Ord som förenar (Discussing the Word Together).* Dr. McCurley has twice conducted workshops there as well as in Finland in 1984 when the Lutheran Church of Finland took up the program, entitled *Sanasta Elämä (Life from the Word).* The United Evangelical Lutheran Church in Germany (VELKD) has also begun a translation for use in congregations in the Federal Republic of Germany in 1986, under the title *Wort und Antwort (Word and Answer).* We have also heard of occasional use in Southeast Asia and elsewhere.

Naturally, it is gratifying to have had a hand in a collaborative project that has found a degree of blessing that no one could have programmed in advance and of which we never dreamed. One of the discoveries of Word and Witness is that small-group, corporate study of the Bible—together with a concern for others, for "witness," evangelism, or outreach, call it what you will—makes of biblical study something more than the cerebral, intellectual exercise that it has often become. Readers will at times sense in our pages something of this "setting in the life of the church" that we would not want to lose, even in sending forth this "biblical theology of the gospel" for a wider, often individual, and even more varied audience. We have deep trust, however, that the power of the word is such that the contagion of faith will continue its spread, and others, too, will, each in her or his own way, share insights, helping hands, and witness to God in Christ with others.

Throughout the whole process of writing, teaching, sharing, and revising since 1975 we have not, of course, lost our scholarly concerns that we think people of faith can and should have. But Word and Witness, as a collaborative project, is not the place to develop one's own "pet ideas." Most of what we present here has stood the scrutiny of colleagues of all sorts who hold a variety of views. But in the last analysis, we are responsible for the direction, emphases, content—and errors. Readers should know that early in the development of Word and Witness a decision was made (not by us) to employ two earlier books of ours as supplementary reading:

Foster R. McCurley, Jr., *Proclaiming the Promise: Christian Preaching from the Old Testament* (Philadelphia: Fortress Press, 1974); and

John Reumann, *Jesus in the Church's Gospels: Modern Scholarship and the Earliest Sources* (Philadelphia: Fortress Press, 1968; paperback, 1973).

We have deliberately tried *not* to duplicate what is in print there, nor have we added frequent references to those books here. But our general stance is often elaborated in the two volumes mentioned, and readers will find specific additional information relative to chapters 9–12, 14–17, and 19–22 in *Proclaiming the Promise,* and especially relevant to chapters 6–7, 13, 23, 25, and 33 in *Jesus in the Church's Gospels.*

Our expectations and orientation can perhaps best be perceived by readers—be they people with some biblical knowledge who wish to dig deeper into biblical theology, or persons with virtually no previous study of Scripture who are willing to venture being addressed by the word of God—if we repeat, in introducing this account of "the witness of the word," something of what we wrote at the outset of *Understanding the Bible,* under the heading "Of Spruce Trees and Bible Study."

A friend of ours was having continued bad luck with spruce trees in his yard. One after another he planted them, and with the same regularity they died. Finally the man discussed the problem with the people at the local nursery. They advised him to plant a new tree in the same spot as the others, but with this change: he should tie the tree firmly and tautly from four sides, until the root ball would have a chance to settle in the ground. After a few months the wires should be loosened somewhat. The wind would then rock the tree a little. It seemed like a risk, the people at the nursery admitted. But, they added, the blowing of the wind through the branches would stimulate the roots below ground. In this way the roots would spread out and strengthen the tree.

Bible study can function in a similar way for Christians. One can, of course, study the Bible in many different ways. There can be sharing sessions in which members of a group tell what this or that text has meant to them personally. There are lectures in which a leader goes through a passage verse by verse. One can read about the Bible in books. There are many combinations of methods. All have some value. Whatever the method, one thing is certain: if the study of the Scriptures is easy and comfortable, something is wrong!

The Bible is not easy to understand. It is a collection of writings two to three thousand years old. It was written for people in many different settings. These people viewed many things, including the universe itself, quite differently from the way we view things today. The Bible was written in languages other than English, so it had to be translated to bring meaning to us. Some of the difficulties of this process are obvious when one compares several translations of the Bible. This word or that phrase appears in differing ways.

More important, Bible study can never be easy or comfortable because what is at stake is nothing less than the word of God. That word couched in human speech from people of the distant past speaks to us today as we struggle with the meaning of this passage or that. To be so addressed by God's word is to be met by God. Like Jacob wrestling with God at the Jabbok River (Gen. 32:22–31), we too are challenged to wrestle with God—about love and hate, faith and sin, life and death. It might well happen to us, as it did to Jacob, that life will be different when the wrestling is done. Certainly it is not possible to remain indifferent once God has met us in the word.

We have before us these two factors in Bible study: an ancient history, and the ever-present word of God. The thirty-five chapters of this study are designed to take seriously both these factors. First, because the Bible is thousands of years old, these chapters will attempt to understand what various passages meant when they were written down for people other than ourselves. Second, these chapters will concentrate on God's word as a message of good news, that is, gospel. This message came to the ancients and still comes to us. To be grasped by it means we look for ways of giving the good news to people today.

Thus, we begin to understand the forms that the gospel takes especially as we witness to it today. It is through believing Christians and their witness that God still meets people today. God, with a judging and a cleansing will, meets the lonely, the despairing, and even the confident. We bear the responsibility for bringing such a meeting about, and because of this responsibility we are driven again and again to study the Bible, through which God speaks in surprising ways.

This book of ours is neither easy nor comfortable. Nor *can* it be. It is intended for those in the faith whose roots have settled somewhat and who are ready to spread out and become strong, or who are willing to take root and grow.

And now, if you are ready, loosen the wires a bit, and let the wind blow!

May 29, 1985   FOSTER MCCURLEY
                                                     JOHN REUMANN

"The Beginning of the Gospel"—
Getting Started with
the Bible's Witness to the Word

THE BIBLE IS A COLLECTION of books containing good news, centered in Jesus Christ. This volume is about the Bible—its word, its witnesses, its theology—in light of the gospel or good news of God.

Of course, the Bible does not gloss over calamity and tragedies in its pages, and sometimes those who speak there for God also announce bad news or God's judgment. But what has gripped the hearts and lives of Jews and Christians alike for centuries has been God's lovingkindness and grace proclaimed in the Scriptures, and for Christians this good news comes preeminently in Jesus of Nazareth, the Christ.

But where to begin with so big a book, so many centuries of history, so much theology or talk about God? Our starting point for exploring the Bible's witness to the gospel will be with Jesus himself, as he appeared in Palestine, bringing God's word to people in Galilee in the seventeenth year or so of the reign of the Roman emperor Tiberius (cf. Luke 3:1). To this Jesus we shall return again and again, as we explore the nature of the Bible and its world, the Old Testament literature and its witness, and the epistles, gospels, and apocalyptic sections of the New Testament.

To begin, we shall ask at this point simply how Jesus and the good news intersect and intertwine and to what this points. We shall do so in terms of the Gospel According to St. Mark:

Now after John [the Baptist] was arrested, Jesus came into Galilee, preaching the gospel of God, and saying,
"The time is fulfilled,
and the kingdom of God is at hand;

repent,
and believe in the gospel."
    (Mark 1:14–15)

It is with these words that Mark introduces on the stage of history the man from Nazareth. We may take Mark's to be the first of the four New Testament Gospels to be written and thus the earliest book we have about Jesus' life and ministry. Jesus in 1:14–15 is portrayed as proclaiming God's gospel and exhorting people to believe in it. He and the good news are thus closely related.

In another passage Mark goes further and speaks of Jesus and the gospel in parallel:

whoever loses his life *for my sake* and *for the gospel's* will save it. (Mark 8:35b, to be contrasted with Matt. 16:25 and Luke 9:24; see also Mark 10:29 and pars. in Matthew and Luke for the same phrases.)

In that "for Jesus' sake" and "for the sake of the gospel" are equated, Jesus and the gospel may indeed be said to be the same, for Mark.

Now Mark's theme of "the gospel" has a rich background. Long before Jesus appeared on the scene, there were "good tidings [gospel] from God" for God's people Israel. This extensive heritage prior to Jesus can be explored in the Hebrew Scriptures that we call the Old Testament.

Jesus in his own day spelled out the gospel especially in terms of "the kingdom of God," another phrase that roots in earlier centuries of God's activity in Israel. This Old Testament emphasis, God's kingly reign, covered many aspects of Jesus' teachings and activities.

But later on, Jesus' followers were able to take the good news and cast it in still other terms besides "the kingdom." Over the years, disciples of the Lord Jesus cast and recast the gospel in yet other ways, already in the New Testament period, to reach the hearts of hearers in Syria and Asia Minor, Greece and Rome, eventually in Egypt and Spain, and over ensuing centuries in the northern climes of Europe and the vast continent of Africa, the Indian peninsula, the Americas, the Far East, and the isles of the sea. The gospel marches on.

Today, through the study of Scripture, we can listen to this "gospel of God" as Jesus proclaimed it, or as his predecessors like Isaiah or Moses or the psalmists voiced it, or as his disciples and apostles set it forth. The results of Bible study allow us then to bear our own witness to this same God and Lord yet more informedly and clearly. Plainly the gospel has had a long and varied history, but its heart has always been,

the word God sent to Israel, when he preached good news of peace through Jesus Christ, the Lord of all. (Acts 10:36, au. trans.)

What Jesus preached, coupled with what he taught and did; coupled, indeed, with what he himself was, as an intriguing person to hearers and a figure of compelling power—here for people of many outlooks and persuasions is the center of Christianity. The great creeds of the early centuries are fullest and most detailed when they deal with Jesus Christ. The twenty-seven New Testament books revolve around him. "God" and "the Holy Spirit" are understood in the New Testament christo-centrically, that is, from the point of view where Jesus is the center of things. "Witness" is—in the New Testament books—testimony, first and foremost and above all, to him. Christianity *is* Jesus Christ. Even in the 1960s, when people claimed "God is dead," Jesus still had a lively following among "death-of-God" theologians. In the seventies, "Jesus people" cut across all sorts of social, economic, and racial barriers. The rise of the charismatic movement, stretching on into the eighties, brought the Spirit to the fore, but it was regularly "the Spirit of the Lord Jesus Christ." As the final decades of the twentieth century draw to a close, there seems to be no diminished interest in Jesus. If anything, some people are more alert than ever for his return or "second coming" (1984 having proven wrong) in 2000 or perchance later, if delayed, in 2007.

Jesus is the one of whom people most readily think when "gospel" comes to mind. He is the one Christians for centuries have sung about in the "Te Deum"—"Thou didst open the kingdom of heaven to all believers." In fact, so exclusively do people associate "gospel" and even "kingdom" with him that it may come as a surprise to learn that God's "good tidings" and "kingly rule" had a history for centuries before Jesus' appearance in Palestine. But, obviously, he is the starting point for grasping with our minds and for our lives something of what "gospel" means.

"Jesus—preaching the good news—about the kingdom" is thus the starting point in Mark, our oldest Gospel book. Yet how revolutionary that beginning was in its day is not always appreciated. For what Mark was doing was nothing less than to indicate a new beginning, and climactic recasting, as well as the earlier roots, of the history of God's dealings with his people, compared with the prior assumptions of his day.

Mark's new directions are a bit like the bold beginning in Abraham Lincoln's Gettysburg Address. His rhetorical opening phrase, "Four score and seven years ago our fathers brought forth on this continent a new nation . . . ," was not simply a "cute" way to begin. It was a rewriting of United States history and self-understanding. Previously, American citizens had understood their nation to have begun with the ratification of the U.S. Constitution in 1789—a nationhood that thus began with a legal document and that included slavery, with no Fourteenth or Fifteenth Amendment forbidding it. Lincoln, by his phraseology, pushed the beginnings back eighty-seven years from 1863, not to the conventional date of 1789 (which would have been "three score and fourteen years ago") but to 1776 and the Declaration of Independence. Nationhood, for him, began with a revolution, seeking liberty. (Lincoln had made this point and contrast as early as 1858, in his debates with Stephen Douglas.) It makes a major difference, of course, in one's understanding, to which "foundational event" one looks back—to constitutional law or to a revolution for liberty.

And so with Mark. We may say that his "beginning of the gospel" (1:1) when "Jesus came . . . preaching" (1:14) implies, first, a contrast to all earlier versions of God's good news in Israel and emphasizes the newness to be found in Jesus. Mark certainly sees the person of Jesus, as gospel, to be the foundational event and not some legal document. Jesus frees from the "tradition of the elders" (7:3; cf. 7:1–23). But second, there is in Mark the clear implication that "gospel" was present in and during Jesus' ministry and not just since Easter, after his resurrection from the dead. This point is worth remembering lest we be tempted to make "gospel" exclusively post-Easter. Third, though Jesus' words and deeds go beyond previous good news, it is stated by Mark that Jesus' coming was a fulfillment of what had been spoken as good news previously and thus stands in a certain continuity with Israel's past (compare, e.g., Mark 1:1–4 or 14:49–50). Fourth, Mark suggests that this gospel of Jesus, which begins in Galilee in a new way, goes on and will be heard and responded to far beyond Palestine—in Greece and Rome, in Germany and the British Isles, eventually in Georgia, U.S.A., and Georgia, U.S.S.R., and will indeed be preached to all nations, in the whole world:

> the gospel must first be preached to all nations. (13:10)

> And truly, I say to you, wherever the gospel is preached in the whole world, what she has done [the woman who anointed Jesus in advance of his burial] will be told in memory of her. (14:9)

We must therefore reckon with gospel before and after Jesus' day, as well as during his ministry.

But before we take a closer look at Jesus and the gospel he himself preached, it is important for all our study and use of the Scriptures to get straight about the nature of this collection of books we call the Bible, in its varied historical settings, as a repository of God's good news.

As Dean E. C. Fendt, of Capital University and Theological Seminary, Columbus, Ohio, once put it, "The gospel, yes, but the gospel according to the Scriptures."

4

I
THE BIBLE, IN ITS HISTORICAL SETTINGS, AND THE GOSPEL

SYMBOLS IN THE BIBLE'S GOSPEL STORY:

In God's good creation, there was growth as well as evil.

The butterfly is an ancient symbol of the resurrection.

"A grain of wheat falls into the ground and dies" (John 12:24). "What you sow does not come to life unless it dies" (1 Cor. 15:36). Bread and the fruit of the vine express new life.

ISRAEL was a vine that God brought out of Egypt and planted (Ps. 80:8–18).

David, shepherd-king, "sweet psalmist of Israel" (2 Sam. 23:1), shoot and branch from the stump of Jesse.

JESUS said, "I am the true vine . . . , you are the branches" (John 15:1, 5).

The two tablets of the Ten Commandments, symbolizing covenant at Sinai and God's will.

To abide in the Vine means life, growth, and joy.

Twelve stars, twelve tribes, twelve apostles; the star of Bethlehem looms largest (Matt. 2:2–10, cf. Micah 5:2).

The Bible's story intertwines roots and endings, beginnings and God's goals, pruning and fresh growth, promise and fulfillment.

1

The Structure
of the Bible,
a Very Human Book

THE BIBLE MEANS MANY THINGS to many different people. For centuries, yes, for two or three thousand years, the Bible has held a significant place in the beliefs and lives of Christians and Jews. Yet even among those who love and revere it, its honored pages have not always led to agreement. Today Christians can still divide over how to use Scripture rightly. Reactions run from almost the worship of the Bible to ignorance about the Book and ignoring of it. Meanwhile, in a world of many Bibles and many collections of sacred writings in other religions, even the cultural and literary influence of the Bible may be but a shadow of what it once was. Yet, at least as literature, and certainly for faith, a force it remains, perhaps even, as so often in history, arousing new interest nowadays among many who have not known it well or have not loved it as their grandparents did.

In this chapter we shall examine what is often called "the human side of the Bible," conscious that for most believers there is a further aspect to the story, a "divine side," to be taken up in chapter 2. But whatever one's stance—as a relatively uninformed but interested inquirer or as a person wholly convinced about the Bible's supreme authority and even perhaps its infallibility and inerrancy—we shall not get far in understanding this book unless we are aware of how the volume called the Bible came into existence. We must review and bring into perspective, or for some readers become acquainted for the first time with, some of the many aspects of the very human history of the Book that, for those who believe, is tinged or even shaped by the hand of God.

Unfortunately, this task of gaining clarity about the Bible's history is not always easy, in part because of differences among those who honor it.

7

The French Protestant Huguenots and the First Vatican Council of the Roman Catholic Church agreed, for example, on the importance of the open Bible. The Protestant group regularly put an open Bible on the altars of their churches; the Vatican Council of 1870 kept an open Bible on a table in the transept of St. Peter's Basilica in Rome. Yet in less ecumenical days of the past the Huguenots were persecuted by Catholics, many of them slaughtered in the St. Bartholomew's Day Massacre of 1572, and the First Vatican Council promulgated what many, especially the Huguenots, would regard as a high-water mark of unbiblical doctrine, the dogma of "Papal Infallibility"—this upon the heels of the dogma of the "Immaculate Conception of the Blessed Virgin Mary" (1854). Thus, it matters supremely how you use the Bible, and not simply that you revere it or even have it open!

Nowadays, in happier times when Protestants and Catholics alike treasure Scripture, there is greater common emphasis on the Bible's import and how to use it in the life of the church and the believers. Yet the abundance of denominations and sectarian groups today, each often claiming its interpretation to be the correct view, indeed the *only* correct view, makes clear that how we approach the Bible is no idle academic question. Christians have witnessed with dismay in recent years how various churches have been torn apart, in congregations, seminaries, and even mission work or social action efforts, by disputes over how to interpret Scripture. Denominations have been split into liberal and conservative wings. Getting straight about how the Bible came to be, what it is, and how we are to study it, is therefore a crucial task before going on to trace out the background of Jesus' message about the kingdom and what "gospel" means in other parts of Scripture.

We live in a world where some people have a superstitious awe about the Bible. Such people may be in churches (often of a very Fundamentalist type) or outside (sometimes sharply opposing their Bible to any church). Their views may come from deep, dogmatic indoctrination about Scripture or from inherited ignorance. Other people may live in open disdain or quiet avoidance of the Holy Book—no church, no Scripture, no interest in such things at all. Or they may have other books they regard as "scripture"—*The Book of Mormon,* Hindu writings, or the Qur'an. They may cherish new messiahs like the Reverend Sun Myung Moon or Hare Krishna gurus, or embrace the teachings of a movement like Scientology. Or they may look to the stars and pore over horoscopes for guidance. At best, such people may have but a passing literary acquaintance with some of the Bible's thoughts and terms like "Christ" or "Ten Commandments" or "kingdom," or know only vaguely some of its

8

phrases that live on in popular speech, such as "doubting Thomas" (cf. John 20:24–29); "by the skin of my teeth" (Job 19:20); "like mother, like daughter" (Ezek. 16:44); or "all things to all men" (1 Cor. 9:22). (No, "God helps those who help themselves" is *not* in the Bible!)

Out of the myriad of views possible between these extremes, we seek here to establish an approach to the Bible that does three things: (1) It should reckon seriously with the Bible's long history and use all the abilities we humans have to get at the meaning each passage had for its original hearers and authors. (2) It must at the same time be an approach that allows for the living quality Scripture has as "word of God" for the religious community and that leaves room for the work of God's Spirit accompanying the text from its inception in biblical times to its goal with us today—and tomorrow. (3) It will also be avowedly "evangelical," that is, centered in the *evangel* or gospel, the good news that is the heart of Scripture, whether expressed in Jesus' "kingdom terms" or as tersely as John 3:16 ("God so loved the world that he gave his only Son . . .") or in some other theme.

Accordingly, we shall tackle first what the Bible is, concretely today, in light of its four thousand years of development (chap. 1); then in chapter 2 we shall examine "word-of-God quality"; and last, after a look at aspects of the Bible's "bad news" alongside the good (in chap. 3), we shall seek to sketch the grand historical sweep of its contents (chaps. 4 and 5). All the while we shall be on the lookout for implications for its study and usage today.

At the least, the Bible is a literary gem. For over two millennia it has been significant. It has had a role, and continues to have a key role, as a whole or in its parts, in the Christian and Jewish communities. By any reckoning, the Holy Bible deserves an honored place in the history of world religions. It has had an inestimable influence on literature, thought, and life in most of Europe, the Americas, and the Third World. Recall how, in many African or Asian lands, a large proportion of the leaders there were originally trained in mission schools where the Bible was a staple of instruction. Thus the Bible deserves to be studied as a cultural factor, if nothing else.

Writers of our own day readily come to mind who are deeply influenced by the Bible and its language and thought. Obvious are C. S. Lewis (who, for all the narrative theology in his outer-space trilogy and Narnia novels, argued that "the Bible as literature," and only that, is a pretense which ignores its "remorselessly and continuously sacred" character)[1] and J. R. R. Tolkien (whose *Lord of the Rings* has been read as "good news from Middle Earth," with Tom Bombadil as "not quite Adam" and

Aragorn a "Christ-figure").[2] There are, further, works by Archibald MacLeish (*J.B.*, a Job-like play, 1958), Herman Melville (1819–91; *Billy Budd* and *Moby Dick* are full of biblical overtones), and a plethora of authors who present "Christ-figures" of varying sorts, from Nikos Kazantzakis's *Greek Passion* to the ironic Billy Pilgrim in Kurt Vonnegut's *Slaughterhouse Five* to the characters in Charles M. Schulz's comic strip, "Peanuts" (Snoopy, the "dog God"?). Alan Paton's South African novel, *Cry, The Beloved Country,* is full of allusions to the Bible, "a strangely blended folksong, with elements of Zulu and Xosa speech, and echoes of the rhythm of that Jewish-Christian Bible which speaks with such peculiar intimacy to black men in both America and South Africa."[3]

We can even learn about biblical interpretation from Mark Twain. Jim, in *Huckleberry Finn,* opens up Huck's eyes by claiming that King Solomon's famed proposal in 1 Kings 3:16–28, to divide in two the baby over whom two harlots were disputing, really showed a *lack* of wisdom in "de way Sollermun was raised": one can *afford* to "chop a child in two" when you've got " 'bout five million chillen runnin' roun' de house"! Or one can even master the intricate principles of rabbinic exegesis thanks to Rabbi David Small, in Harry Kemelman's mystery stories.

There is some evidence that the literary side of Bible study is in vogue again. E. S. Bates's old edition of *The Bible Designed to Be Read as Living Literature* is back in print.[4] The University of Indiana Department of Religious Studies has been developing a series called The Bible in Literature Courses, to stimulate in secondary schools the kind of study as a secular subject that the United States Supreme Court decisions of the 1960s encouraged. One volume on curriculum materials lists over three thousand books, articles, recordings, and films suitable for English courses.[5] The teaching of Bible as a literary-critical subject in American colleges and universities has in recent years probably become more widespread than ever before. For all this believers should rejoice; "at the least," God's word is being studied as literature.

Such developments have implications. "Out there," beyond the churches, in the broader community, is a growing number of (often younger) people who have had some literary-historical study of the Bible—study with sometimes quite varying results. For it may have destroyed childhood (or childish) faith. It may have whetted the appetite for more study, but opportunity has been lacking. It may have left these people at the "Bible-as-literature level" (which C. S. Lewis deplored), inoculated, so to speak, against getting infected with any real religious commitment. Two implications are clear: (1) what the churches do with the Bible must take cognizance of all these literary-historical approaches to Scripture, to which people are being increasingly exposed in school or college, to say nothing of the information available in books, magazines (like *Time* and its "Religion" section) and on TV. (2) The church's use of the Bible must go beyond the literary side to religious, ethical, and theological meanings, lest the Bible, though an open book, remain irrelevant for life. The chapters that follow in this book will be aware of such needs and hunger and concerns.

The Bible stands before us today as a single-volume book. It may be stoutly bound in black leather, or be just a cheap paperback with a psychedelic cover. But it appears as one book. Inside, however, really lies a library of sixty-six books, thirty-nine in the Old Testament and twenty-seven in the New. Each book has a story of its own. These books arose during the history of the Israelite (or Hebrew) people and God's dealings with them, especially during the thousand years or so between 1300 and 300 B.C., and during the time after Jesus, when the Christian church arose out of God's dealings then with Jews and Gentiles, the New Testament books appearing in the century between A.D. 30 and 130. But what secrets are hidden in the very structure of this one-volume library? How shall we get at the many things that might be said about this book and its history?

One of the oldest learning devices in the ancient Near East was the "numerical saying" where a number is given and then, often in poetic lines, this literary form goes on to enumerate so-and-so many examples. A famous instance is provided by Prov. 30:18–19,

Three things are too wonderful for me;
    four I do not understand:
the way of an eagle in the sky,
    the way of a serpent on a rock,
the way of a ship on the high seas,
    and the way of a man with a maiden.

Similar is the list at Prov. 30:24–28, citing four things that are small but "exceedingly wise": ants, badgers, locusts, and the lizard.

Such sequences also appeared in other religions and cultures. A Canaanite document refers to two, then three, kinds of sacrifices that the god Baal, "the Rider on the Clouds," hates, namely, those of shame, meanness, and lewdness. In Old Testament examples the number of things enumerated can go as high as six or seven (things which Yahweh hates, Prov. 6:16–19) or even up to ten:

With nine thoughts I have gladdened my heart,
and a tenth I shall tell with my tongue.
(Sir. 25:7–11)

The device continued in Judaism as a means of instructing children (and all who are children at heart) in the counting song for the Passover seder:

Who knows one?
I know one.
One is our God in heaven and on earth.

Who knows two?
I know two.
Two are the tables of the covenant.
One is our God in heaven and on earth.

Then the song went on to tell of three patriarchs, four matriarchs, the five books of Moses, and continued through to the thirteen attributes of God (cf. Exod. 34:6–7). It has been supposed that the song was a catechism for boys, one verse being added yearly until age thirteen (and religious majority) was reached.

A secularized version of this numerical counting device was the endeavor to find religious meaning in a deck of playing cards. The number "1" was said to remind people of the unity of God; "2," of the divine and human natures of Christ; "3," the Trinity. The king was God; the queen, Mary, and so on. Contrived as such devices are, they help organize things and provide a certain unity for disparate facts. With the Bible there are some key numbers that are worth noting in order to sense its structure, and so we shall follow such an outline for presenting some of the data that ought to be noted about Scripture. We shall discuss things about the Bible, 1 to 9. Some statistics, incidentally, such as the number of books and their names and sequence, are even worth memorizing (old-fashioned as that may seem!), for it helps to be able to identify biblical references and be able to look them up easily.[6]

ONE BOOK, TWO TESTAMENTS, THREE LANGUAGES, AND QUESTIONS OF LAW-GOSPEL

We begin with the number "1" in order to remind ourselves that in the Bible we deal first of all with *one book,* a single volume that stands singularly and indeed uniquely apart from all other books, according to the Jewish community and the Christian faith. The following tributes are typical:

Holy Scripture containeth all things necessary to salvation. (Thirty-Nine Articles of Religion of the Church of England, 1571, Article VI)

The sacred and holy ecumenical and general Synod of Trent . . . receives and holds in veneration with an equal affection of piety and reverence all the books both of the Old and of the New Testaments, since one God is the author of both. (Council of Trent, Session 4, April 8, 1546)

We believe, teach, and confess that the prophetic and apostolic writings of the Old and New Testaments are the only rule and norm according to which all doctrines and teachers alike must be appraised and judged. (Formula of Concord, 1580, Epitome 1, *Lutheran Book of Concord*)

The Bible itself on one occasion talks of the so-called seven unities of Christianity—one body (the church), one Spirit, one hope, "one Lord, one faith, one baptism, one God and Father of us all" (Eph. 4:4–6). But to our surprise, perhaps, there is no reference to "one book." This is so because at the time those words in Ephesians were written not all of the New Testament documents were as yet composed, and because the can-onization of the Bible as a collection of sixty-six books into one volume was not fully completed until about three hundred years later. Yet Chris-tians have traditionally added to the seven truths in Ephesians 4 another unity: "one book" as norm for faith.

The number "2" reminds us, however, that this book falls into *two testaments,* the Old and the New. The first thirty-nine books are shared with Jews as sacred writings in what Christians call the "Old Testament" and Jews "the Hebrew Scriptures." The twenty-seven books in the New Testament, on which virtually all Christians agree, are the capstone of the whole Bible; it is in light of them that the Old Testament books are, for Christians, to be interpreted. The total collection of biblical books is thus divided in two by the person of Jesus Christ, just as time itself is divided in the pattern that much of the world has accepted from a Christian confession of faith, the pattern of B.C. and A.D., "*Before* Christ" and "*Anno Domini*" ("in the year of Our Lord"). (Jews prefer to say B.C.E., "*Before* the Common *Era,*" and C.E., "*Common* Era.")

The word "testament" referred originally in Greek use to a "last will and testament," by which a person disposed of his (or, where the law allowed, her) estate after death. But the Greek word involved was also used in the Bible to render the Hebrew term which referred to a "cove-nant" between God and people, for example, in Israel. St. Paul, in Galatians 3, plays with this double sense (v. 15, "will"; v. 17, "cove-nant"). In time the Latin word *testamentum* (which could mean either) began to be applied to the two parts of Scripture, on the assumption that we have here the literary witness to two "covenants" or ways from God

13

for the salvation of human beings. The application of the term, in the sense of "testament," to the two parts of Scripture was strengthened by the fact that Christ had died and thus put his "last will and testament" into effect (cf. Heb. 9:16–17). "Covenant" is, however, really the more common meaning in the Bible for the words involved. (Chap. 10, below, will deal further with the theme.) Some English renderings, like the early editions of the RSV, have tried to restore that term, as on the title page of its 1946–52 edition, which read, "The New Covenant, Commonly Called the New Testament." That title was not well received, however, and generally the traditional name has stuck—*testamentum*/testament.[7] One difficulty with such use of the term "covenant" is that the Bible does not present just two, the Old and the New, but a series of covenants, one with Noah (Gen. 9:8–17), another with Abraham (Genesis 15 and 17), that with the patriarchs Jacob and Isaac (Lev. 26:42), and one with Moses (Exodus 24), not to mention those involving later and lesser figures.

Closely related to the two testaments, but not simplistically to be equated with them, is another pair of much used and abused terms, "law" and "gospel." "Gospel" has already been explained as basically meaning "good news." "Law" is that which commands, enjoins, directs, and orders in life. Some groups, especially Lutherans, like to contrast law and gospel as interpretive keys. They speak of "law" as that in God's word which shows people their shortcomings and sin and need for a savior in contrast to "gospel" as that word of grace and graciousness from God which declares people are forgiven and saved. The difficulty comes when one equates "law" and "gospel" in this sense with the "Old Testament" and the "New," respectively, as the two parts of Scripture. The difficulties are legion when that is done. For the Old Testament at times contains "pure gospel," as Luther himself loved to say (cf. Isa. 40:1–2, "Comfort, comfort my people," or 41:10, "Fear not, for I am with you, be not dismayed, for I am your God"). Some passages in the Old Testament, like Psalm 119 about the law that God gave, do not at all regard it as "bad news," convicting people of sin, but see the law (Hebrew, *torah*) as a good gift from God to guide believers' steps. The New Testament, on the other hand, is by no means all "gospel" but can contain passages which speak as "law" (cf. Rom. 1:18—3:20, especially 3:19–20, about how all have sinned).

One may hold that the law/gospel contrast is a useful one to describe how Scripture is being used, but it is not useful when it is directly and simplistically equated with two testaments, one-on-one respectively, law equated with the Old, and gospel with the New Testament. More useful is a threefold outline that speaks of (1) "law," in the sense of that which

declares God's holy will, in order to show where people fall short and
need deliverance (as noted above, cf. Rom. 3:10–20); (2) "gospel," as
the good news of God's deliverance; and then (3) some term such as "the
imperative," or "God's demand" or "command," to set forth God's
positive will for those who are delivered, how henceforth to live (e.g.,
Romans 12). "The gospel," as what God does to save and aid those saved,
then includes both (2) and (3), as in Jesus' proclamation, "The kingdom
is at hand; therefore believe!" (Mark 1:15, au. trans.).

By and large, however, one should not inflict—and we shall try to avoid
imposing in this book—any arbitrary scheme on Scripture. The aim is to
let the verses speak for themselves. As we shall use the two terms, in light
of verses that will be cited, basically "gospel" means "good news"; the
"law" (*torah*) may at times be part of the good news (sense 3, above), and
at other times function in a negative sense (sense 1, above).

The number "3" might first remind many Christians of *the Trinity*. But,
strictly speaking, the doctrine of the three persons in one godhead,
"equal in glory and coequal in majesty" (the Athanasian Creed), is a
postbiblical development, stating logically, in Greek philosophical terminology, the results of the New Testament experience of the one God. The
statement in older Bibles (KJV) at 1 John 5:7, about "the Father, the
Word, and the Holy Ghost" as three witnesses "that bear record in
heaven," is rightly omitted in the RSV and other translations. It is a late
insertion into the manuscripts, first appearing about A.D. 380, and not
earlier. Other passages do, of course, speak of Father, Son, and Spirit
(Matt. 28:19; cf. 1 Cor. 12:4–6), so that the doctrine of the Trinity was
an inevitable development. But it is not directly stated in the Bible itself,
let alone in the terms that later doctrine came to use.

More in line with actual biblical data, we prefer to let the number "3"
stand here for the *three languages* in which our Bible was originally
written. As is well known, our existing New Testament books are in
Greek (actually a "common dialect" of it used widely throughout the
Mediterranean world in the centuries before and after Christ). Most of
our Old Testament books are in Hebrew, a Semitic language (actually
from its northwest branch, akin to Ugaritic and Canaanite). The third
biblical language was Aramaic, a family of dialects spreading throughout
the Near East from the tenth century B.C. on. Aramaic was in widespread
use in the centuries before Jesus' time. It became the official diplomatic
language during the time of the Persian Empire in the sixth century B.C.
and was the language of everyday speech among Jews in Palestine in New
Testament times. Portions of our Old Testament are written in Aramaic
(chiefly Dan. 2:4b—7:28; Ezra 4:8—6:18, and 7:12–26). A form of

Aramaic was used by Jesus. In a miracle account, he said, " '*Talitha cumi*'; which means, 'Little girl, I say to you, arise' " (Mark 5:41); on another occasion Jesus said to a deaf man, concerning his ears, " '*Ephphatha,*' that is, 'Be opened' " (Mark 7:34); and on the cross he cried out, " '*Eloi, Eloi, lama sabachthani?*' which means, 'My God, my God, why hast thou forsaken me?' " (Mark 15:34), which is Ps. 22:1 in Aramaic (Matt. 27:46 has *Eli,* the Hebrew for "my God"). Aramaic expressions also continued in the early church, such as *Marana tha!* "Our Lord, come!" (1 Cor. 16:22). There were also three languages in which the inscription on Jesus' cross was written (John 19:20)—Hebrew and Greek, but here also Latin. Latin later became the language of Christianity in the West and the means of expressing many developing Christian teachings. Terms like "Trinity" and "redemption" are of Latin origin.

All three biblical languages, Hebrew and Aramaic and Greek, are very different from English. They have their own alphabets, verb systems, rules for grammar, and methods of expression. The transition from the Semitic languages to Greek must have been a major step for Jews who, even before the time of Christ, had settled in the Gentile world and had to learn and use Greek. This step prepared the way for the Christian movement when it advanced outside Palestine. But it was also difficult for early Jewish Christians to shift from Aramaic to Greek. We may compare some of the wrenching effects to those cataclysmic results when people emigrated from some European country to the New World and shifted from German or a Romance or Scandinavian language to the perils of English. We can thus begin to appreciate some of the changes and developments which went into the shift from Semitic thinking (in the Old Testament) to Greek expression (in the New)—not to mention the changes that go into rendering the Bible in other languages, including the type of American English we use today. To make Paul or Isaiah speak to us requires all those transitions.

All this compels raising, at least initially, the much-debated questions of whether or not there is a special kind of "biblical mentality" and whether language is really a key to expressing a people's mind-set. Biblical peoples had a point of view that was, of course, often quite different from ours. They thought of the world, for example, as a "three-story universe," with God above, the dead (and in later views sometimes Satan and demons) below, and human beings on earth's surface—poor humanity a battleground between these two "kingdoms." Later, we shall explore more about their world view (see chap. 3, below, pp. 68–69). But any thought of a "biblical mentality" must not be overdone, for many of the features we find striking in the Bible were actually shared with many other or all cultures in antiquity.

As for "language and mentality," it has sometimes been claimed that "Semitic mentality" is totally different from Greek thought and that the former somehow reflects "revelation" and the latter is "pagan." The truth is that the Old Testament often does have its own particular ways of thinking. In the Old Testament, for example, people are "animated bodies," that is, spirit- or breath-filled bodies, or, in a modern phrase, "psychosomatic unities"; in the Greek world, on the other hand, people were regarded as "immortal souls" that are imprisoned in a body of flesh. In the Old Testament, life is something to be enjoyed in community, with thankful use of all God's gifts (which include sex and the fruit of the vine), though God the creator is not to be confused or identified with what God has made. In the Greek world there were quite different emphases. God and world were sometimes blended together or the visible world was sometimes rejected in deference to a "real" world above so that a false asceticism resulted. Yet even some of the Old Testament views were common Semitic insights, not uniquely Hebrew, and Greek-speaking Christians could share them too. We should look to the language of the Bible to express God's revelation, but not press that language too hard, too esoterically, or univocally, as if it stemmed from a unique world or was filled with hidden meanings. The languages of the Bible are vehicles through which God's word came to speak in the past and for today.

To return to the number "3," we can also call attention to the *three continents* on which the action in the Bible occurs. Palestine is of course the hub of these events, at the juncture of Asia and Africa. A great deal of the action in the Old Testament occurs to the north and northeast of Palestine, in Syria and Mesopotamia (Assyria, Babylonia), and to the east in Persia. But there are also African references, to lands that lie to the south, Egypt and Ethiopia, mentioned in both Old and New Testaments. Europe, the third continent, enters the story only when the Christian mission crosses from Asia Minor into Greece (Acts 16:6–12) and then goes on to Rome.

Some time spent browsing over maps in a good Bible atlas will help readers immensely, as will a check of the proper map, often using a map index, whenever a new place name is encountered. Any of the standard historical atlases[8] will help trace, by means of maps and text, developments in the land at each stage of history. The Israel of the twelve tribes differed from the nation in the days of the monarchy under David or in the time of the divided kingdoms, let alone at the return from the

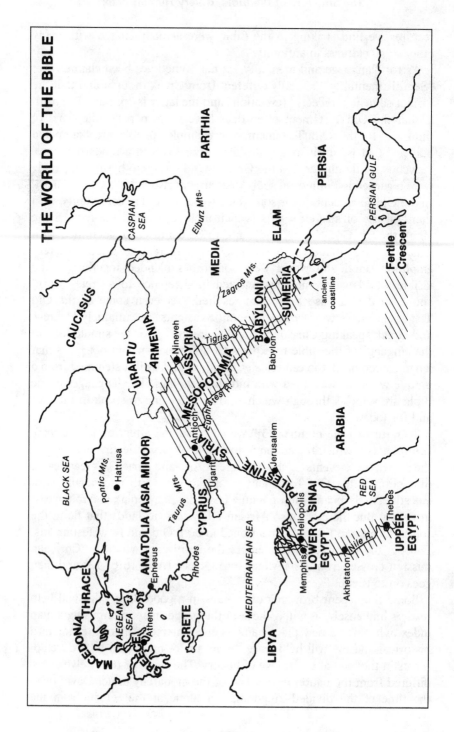

THE WORLD OF THE BIBLE

PARTHIA

CASPIAN
SEA

Elburz Mts.

MEDIA

PERSIA

CAUCASUS

Zagros Mts.

ELAM

URARTU

ARMENIA

Nineveh
ASSYRIA

Tigris R.

BABYLONIA

SUMERIA

PERSIAN GULF

Babylon

ancient
coastline

Fertile
Crescent

BLACK SEA

MESOPOTAMIA

Euphrates R.

pontic Mts.

Hattusa

Antioch

SYRIA

ARABIA

ANATOLIA (ASIA MINOR)

Taurus Mts.

Ugarit

PALESTINE

Jerusalem

THRACE

Ephesus

CYPRUS

MACEDONIA

Rhodes

Heliopolis

SINAI

RED
SEA

Thebes

GREECE

AEGEAN
SEA

Athens

CRETE

MEDITERRANEAN SEA

LOWER
EGYPT

Memphis

Nile R.

Akhetaton

UPPER
EGYPT

LIBYA

18

Babylonian Exile or the period of the New Testament. Photographs and text in such atlases can give some impression of the landscape. Next to visiting the sites oneself, such pictures, with descriptive comments, may be the best means of making biblical places real. To have seen, in person or vicariously, the rugged uphill climb from the tropical oasis of Jericho to the heights on which Jerusalem is built will help a person to appreciate more fully the "songs of ascent," like Psalm 122, sung by pilgrims on the way to the temple, or the reference in Luke 10:30 to going "down" from Jerusalem to Jericho.

Attention to the linguistic-geographical factors in the Bible, symbolized here by three continents and three languages, opens up to us an important portion of the scriptural world.

BIBLE TRANSLATIONS AND THE HISTORY OF INTERPRETATION

From the three languages in which the Bible was originally written we can make a rapid jump to the more than fifteen hundred tongues into which the Bible or portions of it have been translated by our day. Translation provides the specific version of the original in which most people read and study Scripture.

In passing, one ought to note a most ancient translation and one of the most important, the rendering of the Hebrew Old Testament into Greek. The chief Greek Old Testament version is called the Septuagint, meaning "seventy," because it was presumed to be the work of seventy scholars, beginning about 250 B.C. (By way of abbreviation, in Roman numerals for "70," the Septuagint is often referred to as the LXX.) The Greek New Testament, incidentally, has been translated into Hebrew several times, especially in the nineteenth century for missionary work among the Jews.

We can observe what is for us the most relevant part of this same phenomenon—the spread of the word of God into all the languages of humankind—if we look at English translations.[9] We shall single out four major ones, five other current ones, plus six more that may readily be encountered.

English Bible translation has had a dramatic history, centering in the century of efforts that issued in the *King James* or *Authorized Version* of 1611 (KJV), and then in another century or more of activity which began about 1880 and has lasted until our own day. For the number "4" we begin with some major English versions, of somewhat different styles, widely used today. The 1611 Bible (still treasured by many), the *Revised Standard Version* (RSV; 1946 and following), and the *New English Bible* (NEB) are perhaps the most widely used translations in the English-speaking world. What fourth translation fits into the category of widest use is harder to determine. Perhaps one of the fairly recent American translations from Conservative Evangelical auspices or a modern Roman Catholic rendering, such as would be used for vernacular readings in the lectionary at mass, translations which will be discussed below. However, because it not only has had wide import but also reflects a particular translation approach, we shall note here as the fourth *Today's English Version* (TEV) or *Good News Bible* (GNB).

The *King James* (*not* "St. James") *Version* is so well known as to require little comment. Originally the result of efforts by a team of scholars called together by the British monarch James I, it rested on a century of previous translation work. The KJV was, so far as official records go, never "authorized" by crown or church but earned its way into the hearts and minds of all English-speaking peoples by its excellent, often rhythmic, stately cadences. It has often been "modernized" in subsequent printings. The *English Revised* and *American Standard Revised Versions* of 1881–85 and 1901, respectively, were attempts to bring the KJV into greater agreement with more ancient manuscripts available since 1611 and to reflect the philosophy that the same Greek and Hebrew term should regularly be translated by the same English one—an approach resulting in a version often excellent for study but dull for reading aloud. The attraction of the 1611 Bible continues such that between 1975 and 1982 a group of revisers completed *The New King James Version* or KJ II as it is sometimes called. A monument to tradition, the volume is neither 1611 nor 1982 and takes what seem to many the retrogressive steps of printing each verse as a separate paragraph and of following the Greek text known in the sixteenth century, not that available today through discovery of earlier manuscripts.

The RSV is an attempt to keep the language of the *King James Version* as much as possible, but revised for modern comprehensibility and reflective of increasing knowledge about Hebrew and Greek and the recovery of manuscript evidence unavailable in King James's day. The RSV New Testament was completed in 1946, the Old Testament in 1952. There were some revisions in 1959 and 1971. In the pages that follow we shall regularly cite RSV in an edition known as the *Common Bible*, endorsed in 1973 by Protestants, Roman Catholics, and the Eastern Orthodox.

The RSV has attracted considerable publicity in the 1980s because of the use of its text by a task force under the National Council of the Churches of Christ in the USA, specifically under its Division of Education and Ministry, to develop *An Inclusive-Language Lectionary*, based on the RSV. This translation is intended initially for public reading at services in churches that desire not to use "male" terms when women are included in a verse and that do not wish to convey other reflections of exclusivism in language. No translation as yet in English has paid much attention to this problem, let alone achieved success in solving it. A fresh translation effort would be best, which at the least would suggest that women as well as men are included in passages like these:

> Ho, every one who thirsts, come to the waters;
> and *he* who has no money,
>   come, buy and eat!
>
> (Isa. 55:1)

> Behold, I stand at the door and knock; if any one hears my voice and opens the door, I will come in to *him* and eat with *him*, and *he* with me. (Rev. 3:20)

A further problem arises with "God-language," as in John 3:16,

> God so loved the world that *he* gave his only *Son,* that whoever believes in *him* shall not perish but have eternal life.

While the biblical and traditional view of the deity never attributed a sexual nature to God as "masculine," pronouns in Hebrew, Greek, or English do. One would not want to speak of God as an "it" and thus suggest a thing rather than a person. Is the solution to repeat "God" in place of "he" or "him" in John 3:16 and "Child" for "Son," as the *Inclusive-Language Lectionary* suggests? Will it become acceptable one day to say "God self" or even "Godself" instead of "himself"?

The RSV itself is to undergo only modest revision along these lines, chiefly in references to "men" or "he/him." The *Lectionary* endeavor is more far-reaching and should be distinguished from the RSV itself as the work of a different type of committee. (On gender questions in talking about God, there will be further discussion under "Human Talk About God" in chap. 2.)

The *New English Bible,* when it appeared, represented a more radical approach than that taken in the RSV on heritage of translation. After World War II, church leaders in the British Isles conceded that the KJV did not speak clearly enough anymore to people there, especially outside the churches, so a completely new translation was undertaken. The language is intended to be good literary, contemporary British English. The textual basis reflects, especially in the Old Testament, new manuscript and linguistic evidence. The NEB New Testament was completed in 1961, for the 350th anniversary of the KJV, and the Old Testament with Apocrypha in 1970.

Traditionally, the American Bible Society has seen its task as the mass distribution of existing scriptural translations. In 1966, however, it published a modern speech version entitled *Good News for Modern Man* (this was prior to the concern for inclusionist language) and subtitled *The New Testament in Today's English Version.* TEV became its acronym. The ostensible audience was those whose first language is not English, but the version met with resounding response in many quarters. Sales were phenomenal. A fourth edition of the New Testament was published in 1976 (for the United States bicentennial) together with a fresh rendering of the Old Testament, which had been appearing in sections; the whole was called the *Good News Bible.* GNB is now the preferred abbreviation. Its style, in contrast to that of "formal correspondence" (where an English word corresponds to one in the original, preferably the same one each time), is termed "dynamic equivalence." Here the aim is to take the information that the biblical author sought to convey and transform it into a way of speaking in the "receptor language" so that the modern reader responds just as the original writer wanted his or her hearers to react. NEB reflects this philosophy also; TEV and GNB seek to carry it out more fully. The wide usage of this translation suggests considerable popular acceptance, though for study purposes GNB/TEV is sometimes too free to be entirely helpful.

While those four translations are of basic importance, we shall mention, for the number "5," some other renderings that, for certain audiences, may be just as significant or loom even larger. Several times reference has been made to increased interest and contributions by Roman Catholics in scriptural scholarship. The Second Vatican Council, in the wake of a Catholic Bible study movement, made vernacular translations a necessity for reading at mass. While there were earlier Catholic versions in both Great Britain and the United States, two stand out. The first to fill the void was *The Jerusalem Bible* (JB), published by British Catholic scholars in 1966, but based on *La Bible de Jérusalem,* the work of French Dominicans in the Holy Land. The original is especially distinguished by its extensive and learned notes. The British version, while made with reference to the Hebrew and Greek, rests on the French, though not the French version completed in 1974; it is thus "frozen" at an earlier and perhaps more conservative stage of its prototype. J. R. R. Tolkien was a literary collaborator. The existence of JB has served to keep British Catholicism from having a part in a U.S. Bible version for Catholics that began much earlier and took a new turn with Vatican II, so that fresh translation, based on the original languages, into contemporary idiom became the goal. *The New American Bible* (NAB), as this translation was called, was completed in 1970. A revision of the New Testament was nearing completion in 1985. The style has been called that of "dynamic equivalence," but the trend in the revision is toward greater "formal correspondence." *The New Jerusalem Bible* appeared in 1985.

Another major market for Bible translations is that among those frequently called Conservative Evangelicals. Here the KJV long dominated, but there has also been a history of revisions (such as KJ II) and of independent translation attempts. Because of its literalness, the 1901 *American Standard Version* (ASV) was a favorite. A revision of the ASV was published in 1971 as *The New American Standard Bible* (NASB). It is marked by a literal, conservative approach, and cannot be said to have given us much improvement stylistically; indeed, some prefer the old 1901 Bible. In popular appeal, this and other efforts were overshadowed in the conservative market by *The Living Bible, Paraphrased.* Published in sections from 1965 on, *The Living Bible* was completed in 1971. Its author was Kenneth W. Taylor, an Illinois businessman, who did much of the work while on the train commuting from Wheaton to his job at the Moody Literature Mission in Chicago. The result, rightly described as a paraphrase, proved a great commercial success and was sold in supermarkets and written up in *The Wall Street Journal* as a business phenomenon. *The Living Bible* tends to expand the English to express what the author believes the passage to have meant, so as to speak to his audience today. Some have been critical of the lack of careful recourse to the original languages. Perhaps of most lasting significance among "conservative" translations will be *The Holy Bible, New International Version.* The New Testament of NIV appeared in 1973, the Old Testament in 1978. More than 110 scholars from some thirty-four religious groups in the United States, the British Isles, Australia, and New Zealand took part. The project, sponsored by the New York International Bible Society, aimed at creating a team of "scholars who hold to a high view of Scripture as set forth in the Westminster Confession of Faith . . . ," so as to do "for our time what the King James Version did for its day." The result is a dignified, quite accurate translation, not as colorful as *The Living Bible* or even NEB, more literal than GNB, and enough like RSV that some have asked whether the book was necessary.

For the number "6" we shall mention rapidly half a dozen of the many other available translations. Two old favorites that still deserve to be heard are James Moffatt's *A New Translation of the Bible* (1926; revised, 1935) and the Smith-Goodspeed *American Translation.* James Moffatt, a Scotsman of considerable literary gifts, taught New Testament at Union Seminary, New York. He is one of the few people ever to have translated the entire Bible himself. E. J. Goodspeed, a New Testament scholar at the University of Chicago, did a New Testament translation in American idiom in 1923; colleagues completed the Old Testament for a "Chicago translation" in 1927, and the Apocrypha in 1938.

The New Testament in Modern English was begun by J. B. Phillips during the Nazi air blitz on London, while he was a parish rector, for his Anglican youth group. The entire New Testament was completed by 1958 (revised edition, 1972), and he has also translated four prophets (Amos, Hosea, Isaiah 1—35, and Micah) in 1963.

While individual Jewish scholars have occasionally had a hand in Christian translations like the RSV, there are also translations, obviously of the Hebrew Scriptures only, by and for Jews. The old translation of the Jewish Publication Society, *The Holy Scriptures According to the Masoretic Text* (1917), which was KJV-like in tone, has been replaced over the last twenty years by a contemporary, idiomatic rendering of the eternal message. *The Torah: The Five Books of Moses* appeared in 1962. The *New Jewish Version,* as the whole is known, was completed in 1982.

A quite recent undertaking that was greeted with a certain derision by some is *The Reader's Digest Bible Condensed from the Revised Standard Version* (1982). Actually there have been "shortened Bibles" before, including one by E. J. Goodspeed. The RDB aimed at abridgment for the general reader. While keeping the Ten Commandments and Lord's Prayer, for example, intact, the RDB eliminates repetition, some rhetoric, duplication (e.g., 2 Samuel 22 because it duplicates Psalm 18), and such seeming irrelevancies as genealogies.

Finally, a translation known to many because of its being offered door-to-door by Jehovah's Witnesses is the *New World Translation of the Holy Scriptures* (1961). It is the work of an anonymous committee of translators, not without scholarly credentials, from the Watchtower Bible and Tract Society in Brooklyn. But sectarian tenets are often obvious, including the effort to bring the name "Jehovah" into the New Testament. A more recent translation, published by the same group, is *The Bible in Living English* (1972). Actually, it is the work of a man of Congregationalist background, Steven T. Byington (1868–1957). Byington had some odd ideas, such as that in the New Testament "men had nearly the same feelings as we have about addressing God," whereas Old Testament men had no such feelings, and hence he uses "thou" for God in the New Testament but "you" in the Old. What led the Watchtower group to publish his translation, however, was no doubt Byington's use of "Jehovah" for God. Perhaps Byington's review of the *New World Transla-*

tion of the New Testament (in *The Christian Century* 57 [1950]: 1295)
brought his work to the group's attention.

Thus, four, five, six, or more, you have today a wide choice of translations. These vary not only because of the style of English sought by the project and not only because of the outlook and competence of the translators. They vary also, we have noted, because of the manuscripts and text followed. There are problems here, and alternative footnote renderings in modern translations such as the RSV often call attention to these. Examples occur at Mark 1:1 (some "ancient authorities," as RSV puts it, omit the words "the Son of God") and 1:2 (instead of "in Isaiah the prophet," later manuscripts more correctly read "in the prophets") and Matt. 8:7 (instead of "I will come and heal him," the NEB note punctuates so that Jesus asks the centurion, "Am I to come and cure him?"). Sometimes we shall refer to such alternative translations, when important for a point, in the chapters that follow.

It is thus a long and involved story, how the Bible was transmitted to us. Basically, the scribes copied the manuscripts with great fidelity. But there are these variant readings and even occasional gaps in the original. As an example of such a break in the text, Gen. 4:8 in the Hebrew can be cited: "And Cain said to Abel his brother, and when they were in the field, Cain rose up against his brother Abel, and killed him." But what Cain said is not reported in the Hebrew, and translators must fill in from versions in other languages like the Greek Septuagint. Even how to arrange word order, or how to punctuate, can pose problems. Shall 1 Cor. 15:19 be rendered "If for this life only we have hoped in Christ . . ." (RSV, 1959) or "If in this life we . . . have only hope" (RSV, 1946)? Is 1 Cor. 7:1, "It is well for a man not to touch a woman," Paul's own view (RSV), or an opinion of Paul's Corinthian opponents (see, for example, the NEB footnote, punctuating this as a slogan of theirs). Text, punctuation, translation are all part of the story of bringing the Bible to modern readers.

Even when the biblical text is determined in Hebrew or Greek and accurately translated, however, it is then further subject to interpretation. That interpretation stretches from the day a text was written until the present moment. Under the number "7" there can be said to be at least that many eras of interpretation,[10] from biblical to modern times.

1. *Within the Bible itself.* For example, Mark 12:1–9 offers Jesus' interpretive development of Isa. 5:1–7, the Song of the Vineyard. Galatians 4:22–26 allegorizes the story of Sarah and Hagar in Genesis 16 and 21.

2. *Early Jewish interpretation* (and continuing Jewish interpretation to

the present). Rabbinic rules for exegesis, Qumran devices, and allegory (which Jews took over from the Greek world) all appear in New Testament writings and the work of the early church.

3. Christian interpretation in *the church fathers* and other writers during the "church-building" centuries. Here Greek influence became more prominent, and schools, such as those in Alexandria and Antioch, arose. The former school was more given to allegory than the latter.

4. *The Middle Ages.* Here a multiple sense was sought in most texts: literal, allegorical, moral, and mystical or eschatological.

5. *The Reformation* meant a new concentration on the biblical languages and on the literal sense, and a heightened concern for (biblical) theology. It often should be distinguished from what followed in the periods after the Reformers.

6. Post-Reformation developments like *Pietism* (which first developed biblical, in contrast to dogmatic, theology) and *Rationalism* or the Enlightenment, when genuine biblical criticism first began to develop.

7. The *modern period* has many subdivisions and is an area for study all its own. It includes a quest for sources, history "as it really was," liberal and neo-orthodox phases, and an interplay with all the trends in theology generally and secular techniques for the study of texts. Most passages of the Bible have been affected, so far as meaning for us goes, by their history of interpretation over the centuries. Indeed it helps structure the sense for us. At least we must be aware that we are never the first to have inquired what a passage meant.

LITERARY TYPES AND FORMS

We turn to the number "8" as the next device in looking at the structure of the Bible. This number can conveniently apply to the various types of literature, or literary "genres," found in the Bible. In German the word *Gattung* is sometimes used.

In daily life, even just in reading a newspaper, we encounter and readily adjust to different forms like the news story, op-ed page (opinion, editorials), sports columns, stock-market quotations, or obituaries; we read each accordingly. A business letter is one thing, a note to one's son or daughter at college something else, a recipe in a cookbook still a third thing. Each has a genre or literary form. So in the Bible there are types of literature.[11] We list eight possibilities of literary types, book length or longer (as in a collection of books like those of the several prophets or the four evangelists) or shorter than a book but still of some size.

Types of Literature (Genre)
1. Historical narrative
2. Law codes
3. Prophetic materials
4. Poetic compositions
5. Wisdom literature
6. Apocalyptic
7. Gospels
8. Epistles or letters

Each of these has some distinctive characteristics, such as are noted here and will be detailed in later chapters.

Historical narrative is found, for example, in Deuteronomy, 1—2 Chronicles, Ezra, Nehemiah, and Acts. It tells about a series of events, often in chronological order, sometimes with interpretive arrangement or comment.

Law codes can be illustrated by the Ten Commandments or the "Covenant Code" in Exodus 20—23. Colossians 3:18—4:1 and 1 Cor. 3:17 provide New Testament examples of a code for relationships within a household and a saying with divine authority about God's judgment, perhaps spoken by a prophet in the early church.

Prophetic materials often begin with "Thus saith the Lord." They can take the form of "oracles of woe" or "oracles of salvation" (Zephaniah; Jer. 46:1—51:58). The New Testament knows prophets, too (Acts 11:27; 1 Cor. 12:28).

Poetic compositions include hymns, songs, and psalms. Obviously, these include the Book of Psalms and Song of Solomon (or Song of Songs) in the Old Testament. Luke's Gospel contains several hymns (1:46–55, the Magnificat; 1:68–79, Benedictus; 2:29–32, Nunc Dimittis). Colossians 1:15–20 is poetry, a hymn about Christ.

Wisdom literature often consists of short sayings, with some hint of philosophy, and reflections on the human condition (Proverbs; Ecclesiastes; James). See chapter 17, below.

Apocalyptic (literally, an "unveiling," as of the immediate future) is a literary type with distinctive features such as colorful, often mysterious imagery. It requires careful handling, as we shall see below in chapters 20, 28, and 29. It is found, for instance, in Daniel, the Book of Revelation, and Mark 13 (with parallels in Matthew 24 and Luke 21).

The Gospel book—Matthew, Mark, Luke, and John—may well be a Christian invention to tell the Jesus story.

The letter or epistle can be of a very polished, literary kind (Hebrews) or like an everyday note to a friend (Philemon).

In addition to these eight literary types, we must also think of smaller units or "forms" that went into books or longer compositions and helped make them up. Employing the number "9," we can list at least that many types of brief units that probably once circulated orally, rather than in writing, and that had distinctive structure and characteristic uses.[12]

(Oral) Forms
1. Proverb
2. Parable
3. Miracle story
4. Pronouncement story
5. Saying
6. Creed
7. Fable
8. Legend
9. Myth

The proverb is a short bit of advice such as that which is quoted by Jesus at Luke 4:23, "Physician, heal yourself," meaning "Put your own house in order." Proverbs which may once have circulated individually were often gathered into collections in antiquity, for example, those attributed to Agur (cf. Prov. 30:1), Lemuel (31:1), and Solomon (1:1; 10:1; 25:1).

Parables are found in the Old Testament and frequently on the lips of Jesus throughout the Synoptic Gospels. See below, chapter 7 especially, for examples.

Miracle stories, in either testament, usually include a description of some illness, the means of cure used by the miracle worker, and some statement about the effectiveness of the cure. Such stories thus have a distinctive form. See Mark 1:30, then 31a, and then 31b, for an example.

The phrase "pronouncement story" is one term used to describe a tale with little or no setting, where the chief emphasis is on what is said as the "punch line" by the leading character—in the Gospels usually Jesus. See, for an example, the pointed statements about the kingdom of God in Luke 17:20–21.

The saying form covers a great variety of often isolated statements, like Luke 10:18; Mark 9:49 or 50. The "beatitude" (Luke 10:23–24) could be called a variety of saying; some prefer to list it as a separate form.

The fact that confessions of faith or little creeds occur in the Bible is surprising to some. Yet there are such creeds at Deut. 26:5–10; 1 Cor. 8:6; and Eph. 4:4–6, to mention just a few.

There are still more forms. They—or the names scholars have given them—can cause great confusion and even consternation among some Christians. This comes about in all probability because the terms used, such as fable, legend, and myth, can suggest something unreal or that what is reported did not actually happen. Sometimes the terms do carry this implication, but not always. The categories are ways of classifying, and thus of understanding, certain types of expression in the Bible.

The fable is a fictitious story, often involving animals or trees, designed to point up a truth. A famous example is Jotham's "fable of the trees" in Judges 9:8–15. Did it ever "happen" that "the trees once went forth to anoint a king over them" (9:8)?

The term "legend" denotes an edifying story about a holy person (such as Elisha in 2 Kings 7—8), a holy place (like Ophrah in Judges 6:11–24), or a holy institution or cultic custom (cf. 1 Samuel 4:1—7:2 about the ark). Legends are often a blend of folk tale and history. To use the term does not necessarily prejudge the question of whether something actually happened, but the term does alert us to the point that more than historicity is involved. There is meaning beyond historicity, or even beyond what did not happen literally. Genesis 3 may speak profoundly even if we do not think snakes once walked upright instead of crawling on the belly or we do not believe serpents eat dust (3:14).

Myth as a category raises similar flags. Some people, on the basis of warnings in the New Testament itself against "godless myths" (1 Tim. 4:7, cf. 1:4; and Titus 1:14), would prefer to avoid the term entirely. But when many Bible scholars use the word in regard to literary form, they mean a story in which God self speaks or appears. The baptism of Jesus is an example (Mark 1:11). Or the Adam and Eve story in Genesis 2—3, where God speaks and makes clothes (3:21).

All must agree that myths are highly symbolic. They contain deep truths that tax the literal use of words, indeed truths that can be conveyed sometimes in no other way. Compare the way we speak of "the myth of evil"—or is it "of the Evil One"?

Myth always seeks to express some understanding of life, of the existing structures of reality. It seeks to show who man or woman is and what the human condition means (which, in the Bible, is always in relation to God). Myth speaks about such things but in terms we can understand. The idea is sometimes expressed this way: in myth, the Otherworldly and Transcendent is expressed in this-worldly, human terms. To "demythologize"—to use a technical term sometimes employed—means stripping away the alternate form of expression and putting the Bible's message into terms pertinent to people today.

As we study the religions of the ancient Near East and the Hellenistic world, we encounter "mythological themes" (see chap. 8). It is no surprise that some of these are carried over into the Bible (see chaps. 9 and 15, for example), though often with a twist, in changed form. Anyone reckoning with modern biblical scholarship can expect the term "myth" to be used with regard to portions of the Bible. It is a term that alerts us to deeper meanings, not less truth.

One could easily go on, beyond these nine categories, cataloging other "forms" found in the Bible. There are, for example, literary units that are prayers (1 Chron. 6:14–42; Acts 4:24–30), liturgies, sermons, and catechisms. Often these units had a life of usage in the Israelite or Christian community before being incorporated into larger literary structures and books. Literarily speaking, there is a great richness of forms in the Bible, and a vigor of images that speak of God in the Bible, but they are not to be confused with God.

HOW CANONICAL PASSAGES DEVELOPED
AND RESOURCES FOR STUDY

By this time some readers may feel that we have been overemphasizing the parts and components of the Bible far too much. While this procedure may be necessary in getting to see the structure of the Bible, the fear is that the biblical scholar seems here to be acting like a chemist who tries to isolate the elements that make up the compound, or like the zoologist who dissects specimens to understand better the nature of an animal. Only elements or bits and pieces of a "specimen" are left.

The biblical scholar, however, can better be compared to a biologist dealing with living organisms in their setting. The investigator seeks to explain or reconstruct one entity (a passage or unit) within the entirety of the whole structure. Thus, "the theologian," as Israel Abrahams once remarked, "is more akin to the biologist than to the chemist."[13] Hence we seek, in theological Bible study, to put each part in the context of a living whole, moving from the origins of that passage to its understanding for us today within the setting of the overall message of the Bible.

A rough-and-ready outline of the course of development for any passage in the Bible might then involve the following stages, after the incident, event, or saying involved occurred:

1. Brief or elaborate *oral account;* here the *form* and how it arose is of concern; for example, a saying, proverb, or miracle story.

2. Incorporation of that unit and of others like (or unlike) it into what we call a *"source,"* and then, possibly with other sources, into *one of the sixty-six books* of the Bible. There must often have been this intermediate step of collections of materials into sources, which were then used in making up a book; for example, the collections of individual proverbs that underlie our canonical Book of Proverbs.

3. *The collection of books,* usually of the same literary type or genre, into a *"corpus"* or "body" of related books; for example, the four Gospels together, or the Pauline corpus. Our canonical Book of Psalms is really a collection of five "books" of Psalms; cf. Pss. 41:13; 72:18–20; 89:52; and 106:48 with 107:1. Possibly Psalm 150 is a closing doxology for the entire Psalter. In the *Common Bible* Apocrypha, then note Psalm 151; the LXX in some manuscripts heads the collection "The 151 Psalms of David." The five-part structure in the Psalter is probably an imitation of the five books (of Moses) put together in the Pentateuch (Genesis-Deuteronomy).

4. The gathering of these collections of books into a *"testament"* (discussed above) or "canon" (see below).

5. The combining of two testaments into the Christian *canon of sixty-six books,* which thus include many more sources than are preserved (e.g., "The Book of the Acts of Solomon," 1 Kings 11:41; "The Book of the Chronicles of the Kings of Israel," 1 Kings 14:19 and sixteen other references; or the "Book of Jashar," 2 Sam. 1:18) and innumerable form units.

Each step includes in some shape or form what preceded it. We have inherited the results of these stages of development from centuries ago.

But when we look with historians' eyes at the biblical text as it has come down to us, we are often able to reconstruct many of the steps in the series of developments that led to the passage as we have it. We start with one Bible whose division into two testaments and sixty-six books shows up clearly. Working back further, we can imagine how editors put together what they had heard or had by way of sources, and how what they had heard and received must have once consisted of smaller units of material originally transmitted by word of mouth.

Thus, starting at the other end, historically in the beginning there existed the (reconstructed) form-unit; then the source; next, the book involving genre or literary type; thereafter, chronologically, corpus, testament, and Bible. And always at each stage there was some purpose—such as witness, or use as a guide, standard, or norm, for a religious community, Israel, or the church—in the material.

One term that still requires comment is "canon." The word means literally a "measuring rod." It came to be applied to the group of books that, it was agreed, were normative for a religious group. The thirty-nine books accepted most widely by Christians in the "Old Testament" are those also employed by the Jews as canonical (though the Jewish arrangement of these books differs).

In addition, however, there are three other collections of Jewish writings outside this canon. They stem chiefly from the three centuries or so preceding the New Testament or from the first century A.D. They are (1) the Old Testament Apocrypha; (2) the Pseudepigrapha; and (3) the Dead Sea Scrolls. Most of the books in the Apocrypha were, in the light of prior use, accepted by the Roman Catholic Church into its canon officially in 1546. Reformers like Luther termed these writings "interesting to read" but "not to be used as a basis for doctrine." Some Bibles like the RSV *Common Bible* and all Catholic translations include the fifteen books or portions of books in this collection. Many do not. The term "Pseudepigrapha" means literally "falsely written," that is, presented under assumed names. Involved is an even larger collection than in the case of the Apocrypha.[14] The Pseudepigrapha has perhaps proved more influential on the New Testament than has the Apocrypha on these Christian canonical writings, but the pseudepigraphal books are not counted as Scripture by any major group today. To the Apocrypha and Pseudepigrapha might now be added the Dead Sea Scrolls or Qumran writings, another collection of documents very helpful for the study of Judaism in the century or two before Jesus and in his own day, but not treated as canonical scripture by any religious group today.[15]

For the New Testament a similar picture develops. Twenty-seven books are accepted as canonical by almost all Christians. In addition, there are (1) a New Testament Apocrypha[16] and (2) a collection of writings from the "Apostolic Fathers."[17] None of these today receives canonical status, though some of the latter are as old as some books in the New Testament and in some cases once circulated in the same manuscripts as canonical books. To these may now be added (3) the considerable library of "gnostic" literature found at Nag Hammadi (Chenoboskion) in Egypt beginning in 1945.[18] Some of the documents found there, like the *Gospel of Thomas,* may preserve quite early or even original versions of what Jesus said. But by and large this library of writings reflects later gnostic views of those who felt they possessed special "knowledge" by revelation and insight into God's plan, beyond the New Testament.

In table form, the bodies of literature concerning Hebrew and Christian origins include the following:

Writings	Number of "Books"	Language	Use in New Testament?
Old Testament	39	Hebrew, Aramaic	Quoted or alluded to over 1300 times
OT Apocrypha	15	Hebrew, Aramaic, Greek	Reflected (never cited explicitly)
Pseudepigrapha	15 or more	Hebrew, Greek, Ethiopic, etc.	Cited
Dead Sea Scrolls	20–40	Hebrew, Aramaic	Occasional links
New Testament	27	Greek	_____
NT Apocrypha	80–100	Greek	_____
Apostolic Fathers	16	Greek	_____
Nag Hammadi Library	40–50 treatises	Coptic	_____

The Christian church has, over the years and out of long experience and testing, drawn a line, in effect, around the Old and New Testaments. (Catholics would add the Old Testament Apocrypha; so also do the Orthodox, with minor variations such as the addition of Psalm 151.) Those books inside the fence are "authoritative" and "canonical" for each respective religious community. The thirty-nine Old Testament books follow a canon developed within Judaism perhaps as early as the late first century A.D. The New Testament collection of twenty-seven books reached canonical status by the latter half of the fourth century.

Criteria that were involved included the tests of widespread usage, acceptance by councils and church authorities, often the notion of authorship by an apostle, evangelist, or prophet, and, overall, conformity with the gospel or basic Christian message.

Needless to say, with such a vast amount of literature in the Bible and surrounding it, a host of disciplines and specialized skills are needed to get at various aspects of the meaning of these texts.

Some tools like textual criticism—the science of determining, insofar as possible, the best possible and earliest text of the Bible, based on the analysis of ancient manuscripts and versions—are obvious in their importance and are respected and accepted by almost all.

Other tools, like form criticism, are newer and more controversial. "Form history," as it is sometimes called, seeks to recover the earliest brief units behind certain biblical passages. It assumes there were set "forms" used for various community purposes in Israel and the early church during an oral period when data were spread by word of mouth, before being written down. The form critic tries not merely to recover the early form of the material but also to determine how it was used around Israelite campfires or in the courts of the Jerusalem temple or, for the New Testament, by a Christian assembly in Galilee or Corinth.

A very recently developed tool is "structuralism." It involves insights from linguistics, literature, philosophy, psychology, anthropology, and communications theory combined in an attempt to get at the "deep meaning" of a passage. Structuralism goes far beyond the sort of attention to the general structure of the Bible that we have been exploring in this chapter. Its concern is not with history or developing interpretations of a topic over the years but rather with the structure of language itself and the text as an entity determining the meaning of its parts. As yet, structuralism cannot be said to have produced many lucid, agreed-upon results, and only time will tell whether it will be a helpful tool for interpretation. It can lose even the expert in its details.

Archeology, which often expands our knowledge of the biblical world, has an enormous power of attraction for people inside and outside the church, professionals and amateurs alike, in Bible study. We shall from time to time need to draw on this and other disciplines in understanding the Bible's message.

As these techniques and disciplines are applied to Scripture, remember that the Bible also has, for the religious community, a "word-of-God" quality (see chap. 2). It claims to be God's word to humankind, its full power beyond the abilities of any human skill or discipline to ferret out completely. A traditional way to speak of this is to refer to the work of the

Holy Spirit in interpreting Scripture. Still another way is to hold the assumption that God has revealed something of the divine will and plan and ways in the history of Israel and in Jesus Christ, and that what God revealed is witnessed to in the Bible's pages by Israel and its ancestors from Abraham and Sarah onward, by prophets, apostles, and evangelists. For all the human aspects of the Bible, Scripture tells of God what would not otherwise be known. That is the reason why no effort is too great, for those who believe or seek God's message, to study Scripture with infinite care, employing all the range of human techniques available today.

Over the doorway of the main reading room in the New York City Public Library are inscribed these words from John Milton's *Areopagitica:* "A Good Booke is the pretious Life-Blood of a Master Spirit, embalm'd and treasur'd upon Purpose to a Life Beyond Life." That fits the Bible, preeminently—from a Master Spirit, God's, for a "Life beyond life," for those who read its words. An essay on the Bible as "The Believer's Gain," in *Time* magazine's Christmas issue, once caught well the eternally valid side of this intensely studied book:

> The miraculous can be demythologized, the marvel explained, but the persistent message of the Bible will not go away. Both in the Jewish and Christian Bibles it is irreducible: some time, some where, God intervened in history to help man. Whether it was at the time of the Exodus, the giving of the Law, the Incarnation or the Resurrection, or any of those smaller interventions that are still so cherished, ordinary human history was interrupted, and has never since been the same.[19]

NOTES

1. *The Literary Impact of the Authorized Version,* Facet Books Biblical Series 4 (Philadelphia: Fortress Press, 1963), 33, cf. 4, 29–34; reprinted in *They Asked for a Paper: Papers and Addresses* (London: Geoffrey Bles, 1962), 49, cf. 27, 46–50.

2. Cf. Gracia Fay Ellwood, *Good News from Tolkien's Middle Earth* (Grand Rapids: Wm. B. Eerdmans, 1970).

3. Lewis Gannet, Introduction to Alan Paton's *Cry, The Beloved Country* (New York: Charles Scribner's Sons, 1948), xix.

4. This shortened edition of the Old and New Testaments in the King James Version originally appeared in 1936 (New York: Simon & Schuster) and has been reprinted by the same publisher in 1965 and as a Touchstone paperback in 1972.

5. *Bible-Related Curriculum Materials: A Bibliography,* ed. Thayer S. Warshaw and Betty Lou Miller, with James S. Ackerman (Nashville: Abingdon Press, 1976).

6. Basketball star Jerry Lucas developed a Bible memorization system, with cartoons, in his book, *Remember the Word* (Los Angeles: Acton House, 1975).

7. The matter is by no means closed, however. The "Introduction to the New Testament," in *The New Oxford Annotated Bible with the Apocrypha* (= RSV; New York and Oxford: Oxford University Press, 1977), insists "A more appropriate word than 'testament' to designate the character of these books is 'covenant' " (p. 1167).

8. For example, Herbert May, ed., *Oxford Bible Atlas*, 3d ed. (New York: Oxford University Press, 1984); G. Ernest Wright and Floyd V. Filson, eds., *The Westminster Historical Atlas to the Bible*, rev. ed. (Philadelphia: Westminster Press, 1956); Y. Aharoni and M. Avi-Yonah, *The Macmillan Bible Atlas*, rev. ed. (New York: Macmillan Co., 1977).

9. On major and recent translations of the Bible, see Lloyd R. Bailey, ed., *The Word of God: A Guide to English Versions of the Bible* (Atlanta: John Knox Press, 1982), on RSV, NEB, NJV, NASB, JB, TEV (GNB), LB, NAB, and NIV; and, more comprehensively, Sakae Kubo and Walter F. Specht, *So Many Versions? Twentieth-century English Versions of the Bible*, rev. and enl. ed. (Grand Rapids: Zondervan, 1983).

10. Cf. the outline in G. W. Anderson, "The History of Biblical Interpretation," in *The Interpreter's One-Volume Commentary on the Bible*, ed. C. M. Laymon (Nashville: Abingdon Press, 1971), 971–77, used as a reference resource in the Word and Witness program. More detailed are the articles in *The Interpreter's Bible*, vol. 1 (Nashville: Abingdon Press, 1952), 106–41; *The Interpreter's Dictionary of the Bible* (Nashville: Abingdon Press, 1962), 1:407–18; and Robert M. Grant, *A Short History of the Interpretation of the Bible* (New York: Macmillan Co., 1963); 2d ed., rev. and enl., with three additional chapters by David Tracy (Philadelphia: Fortress Press, 1984).

11. On genre in the Bible, cf. the articles in *The Interpreter's One-Volume Commentary on the Bible*—Dorothea Ward Harvey, "The Literary Forms of the Old Testament," 1077–81; and R. McL. Wilson, "The Literary Forms of the New Testament," 1124–28—as well as articles on "The Compiling of Israel's Story" (history), and on law codes, prophetic literature, wisdom, and apocalyptic.

12. In addition to the references cited in n. 11, cf. the delightfully illustrated book by Gerhard Lohfink, *The Bible: Now I Get It! A Form-Criticism Handbook*, trans. D. Coogan (Garden City, N.Y.: Doubleday & Co., 1979).

13. I. Abrahams, *The Glory of God* (London: Oxford University Press, 1925), 17.

14. For many years the standard edition in English has been *The Apocrypha and Pseudepigrapha of the Old Testament*, ed. R. H. Charles, 2 vols. (Oxford: Clarendon Press, 1913; reprinted, 1963). A much more recent collection, now superseding Charles, is *The Old Testament Pseudepigrapha*, ed. J. H. Charlesworth, 2 vols. (Garden City, N.Y.: Doubleday & Co., 1983, 1985). It lists fifty-two writings.

15. English translations include those by T. H. Gaster, *The Dead Sea Scriptures*, rev. ed. (Garden City, N.Y.: Doubleday & Co., 1964), and Geza Vermes, *The Dead Sea Scrolls in English* (Baltimore: Penguin Books, 1962).

16. See E. Hennecke, *New Testament Apocrypha*, ed. W. Schneemelcher, Eng. trans. ed. R. McL. Wilson, 2 vols. (Philadelphia: Westminster Press, 1963, 1965).

17. Trans. in *The Apostolic Fathers* in The Fathers of the Church (New York: Christian Heritage, 1947), or in the six volumes of *The Apostolic Fathers: A New Translation and Commentary,* ed. R. M. Grant (New York: Thomas Nelson & Sons, 1964–68).

18. *The Nag Hammadi Library in English,* ed. James M. Robinson (New York: Harper & Row, 1977).

19. "The Bible: The Believer's Gain," *Time* 104, no. 27 (December 30, 1974): 41.

2

The Bible as
the Word of God to Us

AT THE VERY LEAST, the Bible is a literary gem, rich in history and human meaning in many ways, as chapter 1 has suggested. But the Bible, by its own claim, is more than that. For the Bible declares that its words are life, its teachings truth, its contents "able to wise you up to salvation through faith in Jesus Christ," as 2 Tim. 3:15 might be paraphrased. At the most, then, Scripture is a message from God, a witness to God's revelation, indeed a revelation itself.

On the one hand, we may say (and have, in chap. 1), the Bible is a collection of historical documents to be viewed from a historical perspective. This perspective includes seeing the Bible in its setting of world religions, not to mention world history, the law codes in other world religions, and the like. On the other hand, the Bible has a word-of-God quality, for those who hear and believe, within the community of faith.[1] From the Bible's own perspective, the book is "theological," for it is about God and what God says to us. As God's word, the Bible speaks with authority. Its word lasts forever and is the gospel preached to us, as a New Testament author says:

"... the word of the Lord abides for ever."
That word is the good news which was preached to you. (1 Peter 1:25, the first line being a quotation from Isa. 40:8)

THREE BIBLICAL MEANINGS FOR "WORD OF GOD"

But what is "the word of God"? Perhaps no phrase stirs so much emotion, positive, questioning, and critical, in connection with the Bible as "word of God" or (in a frequent synonym) "word of the Lord." And rightly so! For everything said and believed about the Bible depends on what one means by "God's word."

The Gospel of John gives the Bible's own climactic summary from a New Testament point of view when it says that *Jesus Christ is the Word of God made flesh*. The first chapter of the Gospel According to John states that the Word was "in the beginning," that the Word was "with God," and that the Word in fact "was God" (John 1:1). A few verses later this theological prologue to the Fourth Gospel says that the Word "came to his own" (people and home) but with mixed results, for, though some believed, by and large "his own people received him not" (1:10–12)—a possible reference to how this Word intertwined with Israel's history. Then the climax: the author says that the Word "became flesh and dwelt among us" (1:14), and it soon becomes clear that this Word that has been the topic of John 1 is none other than Jesus Christ (see vv. 15, 29–30). This is the testimony of his community of followers (1:14, "*we* have beheld his glory," and 1:16, "from his fulness have *we* all received, grace upon grace"; note the first-person plural verb forms). So in the first place and preeminently, then, Jesus Christ is the Word of God made flesh. (Because "Word of God" is here a christological title for a person, we prefer to capitalize it, in contrast to other uses of the term "word," where no capital letter is called for.) For Christians this reference to Jesus as "the Word" has long been the primary meaning of the term.

But "word of God" has other meanings as well. In the New Testament the word is also *the message* about Jesus Christ and about what God accomplished in Jesus' life, death, and resurrection. It is the message about the identity and work of Jesus to which the New Testament bears witness and for which the Old Testament prepares the way. In this sense "word of God" is synonymous also with "the gospel," the good news, as the passage quoted above from 1 Peter makes clear.

To repeat for clarity and emphasis: in the first sense and preeminently, Jesus Christ is the Word of God made flesh; in the second sense, the word of God is "the gospel" or good news about Christ (or about earlier expressions of God's grace and goodness).

The Epistle to the Philippians makes this identification between "the word of God" and "the gospel" quite clear, for Paul there uses these terms interchangeably:

> I want you to know, brethren, that what has happened to me has really served to advance *the gospel,* so that it has become known throughout the whole praetorian guard and to all the rest that my imprisonment is for Christ; and most of the brethren have been made confident in the Lord

because of my imprisonment, and are much more bold to speak *the word of God* without fear. (Phil. 1:12–14, italics added)

Advancing the gospel and speaking the word of God mean the same thing.

Thus, the word of God is the *message* about Christ—in oral form. (As suggested above and as we shall see later, "the gospel" will take other forms of good news in the Old Testament writings; these messages too are "word of God.") The point applies even to what sometimes is called "law" (Hebrew, *torah*) in both testaments. This becomes clearer when a third sense of the term "word of God" is considered.

In a third sense, "word of God" refers to *the whole Bible,* to Old and New Testaments alike. All the Bible is seen as witness to the gospel and indeed to Christ, his message and role in God's overall plan. If one seeks biblical references for Scripture as the word of God (actually the hardest of the three senses for which to find evidence in the Bible itself), the best supporting passages that refer to a *written* word are probably Mark 7:13 (and pars.) and 2 Tim. 2:15. In the former verse Jesus, in speaking to the Pharisees, contrasts "the word of God" with "your tradition which you hand on" and plainly endorses written *torah* over subsequent oral traditions and interpretations. In the latter, the reference is to the Christian leader, like Timothy, "rightly handling the word of truth." But usually in Scripture "the word" refers not to something written but to what is spoken.

Both testaments contain the phrase "word of God." Fifty-eight of the sixty-six books in the Bible have clear-cut references to God speaking. In the Old Testament, the word is the means by which God speaks to and acts on his people Israel. In the New it is the means by which God speaks and acts even more universally, in gospel message and "in the flesh," in Christ. In most cases "the word" was originally oral proclamation, but subsequently it came to be written down in the Bible. God's people have found the Bible to be that place where God continues to speak to them, and so they have since New Testament times also termed it "word of God."

People become Christians because they hear the scriptural message about Christ and are given faith to believe in Christ's gospel. For many people today this message has been theirs since childhood. Indeed, many of them were baptized into this Christ as infants. At that time they became children of God on the basis of Jesus' death on the cross. Others hear and believe only later in life. In either case, the word—as the message about Christ, as Christ himself, and in its scriptural formulations—is central to everything believed and to their identity as Christians.

From that message and person to which the New Testament Scriptures bear witness, Christians look back to what they call the Old Testament writings. There they see that the word which eventually became flesh, personally, was in various ways the means by which God spoke to and acted upon the people of Israel (and, indeed, faith sometimes asserts, in both testaments, prior to Israel in the very creation of the world). When God speaks, that involves God's word. Whenever God addresses people through the written words of Scripture, there is his word. And so the Bible as a whole is called "word of God."

SPEAKING THE WORD OF GOD

The phrase "word of God" occurs 241 times in the Old Testament alone. Of these instances, an astonishing number (123) appear in the expression "the word of the Lord came to . . ." someone. Immediately thereafter follows a speech from God to that someone, and usually that someone is to deliver the message to another person or to the whole people. This use shows that the word of God is something to be heard; it is a communication from God to persons who should be listening. The message might be devastating to hear, or it might be comforting. A more or less technical theological phrase "law and gospel" (see above, chap. 1, pp. 14–15) has long been used to capture this combination of what judges (with devastating effect) and what comforts (with promise of mercy).

Whether devastating or comforting, the message *does* have an effect that is impossible to predict in advance with precision. That is the nature of speech. When person A speaks to person B, person B cannot know beforehand precisely what will be said. Neither can A know what impact the speech will have. Of course, if B knows A rather well, B might in some cases anticipate what will be said, particularly in recurring settings. (One usually says "Good morning" or "How are you?" at a predictable time! Or in a family, the 5:30 P.M. cry, "I'm hungry!") But for the most part, personal communication lacks such predictability.

What is it that causes human speech to vary?

Two things, at least: the *relationship* of the persons involved, and the *situation* in which the communication takes place.

In regard to relationship, we may suppose that the conversation of two strangers will be different from that of two friends or relatives. Strangers speak more formally and usually about something at hand, like the weather, the score of the ball game, or the time of day. Friends and relatives talk casually about old times, mutual friends, their present lives, or future hopes and plans.

As to situation, we know that conversation during a neighborhood picnic is quite different from that at a church committee meeting. Or the content of a conversation during a period of economic recession will be quite different from that during a time of prosperity; that in battle differs from talk in peacetime.

So it is with proclaiming the word of God! Of the 123 times the Old Testament records the expression "the word of the Lord came to" someone, no two instances are quite identical. God speaks as a person—not as a human, to be sure—but as a person who addresses each situation anew! If God's people are rebellious or proud of their own achievements, God's word takes the form of some particular judgment! When God's people are depressed and feel lost or forsaken, God speaks words of faithfulness and love.

Thus the *content* of God's word varies according to the many situations in which God's people are found. The *form* also varies. For example, whenever the Book of Isaiah wishes to describe the beauties of salvation, there comes a distinctive poetic form. This can be seen especially in Isa. 11:1–9, describing the unbelievably benign conditions which will prevail when the "shoot from the stump of Jesse" comes. A similar poetic proclamation is to be seen in Isaiah 35, describing the restoration of the devastated area at the center of Jerusalem (Mount Zion). Another form that is linked with a certain type of message is the "utterance of woe." Isaiah 5:8, 11, 18, 20, 21, and 22 show this form, beginning "Woe to those who . . . ," a form which appears elsewhere in the Old Testament (Amos 6, for example) and very prominently in Jesus' teachings as given in Matthew (e.g., 23:13, 15, 16, 23, 25, 27, 29) and Luke (6:24–26).

Thus we see an interesting variety in God's word. That variety may even appear to be self-contradictory at times. For example, in the eighth century B.C., in the northern kingdom of Israel, God instructed Hosea to take to himself "a wife of harlotry and have children of harlotry" (Hosea 1:2). In the seventh century B.C., in the city of Jerusalem, God commanded Jeremiah with these words: "You shall *not* take a wife, nor shall you have sons or daughters in this place" (Jer. 16:2). Certainly neither one of these commands can be made into an absolute demand, equally valid for all people in all times and places. Each one was addressed to an individual in a specific situation, and each one must be appreciated in its own right. Jesus and his apostles follow much the same pattern of addressing people personally, with forms and contents that fit the situation.

Let us take a very vivid example of this situational variety from the New Testament. In regard to divorce, the advice is given in different ways. On the one hand, there is the teaching "no divorce." This appears in Mark 10:2–12, depicting a confrontation between Jesus and the Pharisees on this matter. Jesus rules out divorce altogether on the grounds that from the beginning of creation God had ordained an indissoluble unity between husband and wife. But Matthew slips in some "except" clauses at 5:32 and 19:9, suggesting that a man may divorce his wife on the grounds of unchastity (or possibly marriage within forbidden degrees of kinship as listed in Lev. 18:6–18). Paul writes in 1 Cor. 7:10–15 about some other conditions under which separation, and divorce, may occur. Here the context is set within the congregation at Corinth and mixed marriages in which one spouse was a believer and the other not. Do the latter passages suggest decades of actual Christian experience, compared to Jesus' dictum in the face of "easy divorce"?

All this argues that the word of God is not easily codified or put into unchanging form. It is, however, powerful and dynamic, and it is concrete. It takes form and substance according to the situations of people and God's will for their lives.

The preacher or teacher or believer of today must, of course, study the biblical text carefully. One must ask further, What is the concrete situation of the persons to whom the word of God is addressed?

Though the Bible consists of sixty-six books composed by even more authors and editors, each prophet whose speeches are recorded, each theologian who wrote narratives, each priest who contributed to rich cultic material, each evangelist who wrote a gospel account of the life of Jesus, each letter writer in the early church was in effect delivering a sermon, making a witness. In other words, each biblical writer was addressing the word of God to a particular situation in a concrete time and place.

UNDERSTANDING THE WORD OF GOD

To interpret the Bible, then, and all its many parts, to understand each story or law code or letter, we today must attempt in every way possible to learn the situation for which these parts were created. The society of ancient Corinth, the psychological state of the exiled Israelites in Babylon, the conflicts between early Gentile Christians and Jewish Christians—all these and many more concrete situations need to be studied in order to understand the particular situation. Students of the Bible today likewise need to comprehend the various ways of storytelling possible in ancient days, the methods of composing laws and letters, and the ways then in vogue of expressing thoughts. Knowledge of all these concerns—situations, forms, ancient ways of thought and expression—helps the modern reader.

To interpret any biblical text, then, it is appropriate to ask two questions:

1. What is God saying or doing here?
2. What circumstances are being addressed? What is the situation in the life of the people being addressed in which God is saying or doing this?

The answer to the first question will usually have God as the subject of an active verb. The second answer will regularly contain a description of the circumstances in or to which God speaks or acts. In this way modern readers can zero in on the reason the story was told or the letter composed. We can determine the likely meaning of the passage then and thus see how that scriptural passage may speak to lives today.

While a popular contemporary bumper sticker affirms that "Jesus Christ is the answer!" we must ask, What is the question? A question about fighting inflation, winning an athletic contest, or why geese fly south for the winter is *not* the kind of question to which Jesus Christ is the answer. On the other hand, consider these questions: Who is the Lord of my life? By what means do I become right with God? Whom does the church worship? These are appropriate questions.

A sociological question demands a sociological answer. A theological question demands a theological answer. This is not to say the answers are in separate, watertight compartments. It is to say that an answer must fit the question.

Suppose one asks, What was the message of Ezekiel? To such a question, it is not sufficient to give historical data, such as "between 586 and 538 B.C. the people of Jerusalem were exiled in Babylon." That statement is true, but such data give background only. They may help us in a small way to understand Ezekiel's message, but they do not go to the heart of the matter. For that, other questions are needed. The word of God that Ezekiel proclaimed was addressed to theological dilemmas imposed upon the exiles, such as:

Is God dead?

Has God annulled the covenant made with the forefathers?

Why has God punished us?

Can God live apart from the temple at Jerusalem?

Thus, to understand the Bible and appropriate its message for today, the reader must interpret the life and times of the persons addressed in this situation or that in light of the human condition before God (see chap. 3).

To proclaim the word of God today is not essentially different from the

44

witnessing of biblical times. This means at least two things. God's word comes to people in the words of other people. And proclaiming the word of God assumes "inspiration." To explore each point will help us understand further the dynamics of the Bible.

In spite of human prejudices and errors in judgment, in spite of grammatical peculiarities, nasal tones, and geographical dialects, God speaks, addressing other people through human speech. Thus, a "perfect word of God" can never be separated from the imperfect words of people, even in the Bible, for it is precisely through these imperfect words that God chooses to meet us. Words can indeed be ambiguous, but they are the least ambiguous means of communication available (for human beings). So God's word comes in speech—sermons, conversations, dialogues.

As for "inspiration," we encounter in it a much-used and little-understood word. A prophet of biblical times and a preacher or evangelist today have in common what people call inspiration. From God. Without being inspired to speak *God's* word to a particular situation, one will likely not attempt to do so. Why, after all, should a witness of today, or of long ago, speak (and why should we listen) unless he or she is inspired? But how does one become inspired? By hearing the word of God (which is accompanied by God's Spirit)! How does one hear the word of God? Through someone else's words in the Spirit-filled community! And so inspiration comes from God, through God's preachers everywhere. God works through them as "means."

Inspiration in this sense means that *the person* is inspired. Now, as in biblical times, people are confronted by God's word to speak to others. Precisely what they say and how they say it depends on the situation, on the imagination of the speaker, and on the nature of the audience. It is not simply the words themselves that are inspired; it is the speaker! The one who speaks is the one who chooses the words that will best convey God's message in a particular setting, though the message, we say, is ultimately of God. Thus, it is just as important today to ask, What is the concrete situation of the persons to whom the word of God is addressed?

To phrase it another way: God always works through *means*. Or: the Holy Spirit works through *means*. The word of God is accompanied by the Holy Spirit and is the Spirit's means of bringing God to humans. To put it thus reflects not just one verse but the total impact of all the Bible over the years. In terms of specific references, the highest concentration is to be found in 1 Corinthians. Chapter 1 v. 21 in that epistle shows that what is preached actually saves, that is, the word is *the* means of salvation. In chapter 2, vv. 1–5 show how faith rests not in people but in the Holy Spirit who is the power of God. Sacramentally, 10:1–5 links baptism and eating and drinking with early foreshadowings of salvation and of judgment in the Old Testament; 10:16 affirms that the eating and drinking are communion in the body and blood of Christ, who was earlier proclaimed "the power of God and the wisdom of God" at 1:24; and finally 11:23–26 identifies the bread and the cup with Christ and with remembering him and proclaiming his death until he comes. In the light of all this, the later summary formula, "The Holy Spirit works through means, and these means are word and sacrament," gives a useful way of bearing witness to total biblical teaching.

We emphasize that it is the *same* Spirit speaking, whether in the days of the Bible or in our own day. The Spirit who was active in the proclamation and witnessing of the biblical speakers is at work in proclamation today. One does not "canonize" (in the sense of elevating into a collection of canonical books, such as were described in chap. 1, above, pp. 32–34), however, what some modern says—even the most charismatic Christian voice nowadays—in the same way that what Isaiah or Paul said has been canonized. In speaking of the Spirit's work today we do not allow that today's utterances or today's spokespersons have the same authority as those of the Bible or grant them the same universal acceptance, but we do insist that such persons are instruments of the one same Spirit. Thus we wish to stress that God's word comes through the work of the Holy Spirit with persons, and not as decrees "dropped from heaven" or a script that prophets or apostles or Jesus memorized and then delivered with no appreciation of situation or audience. We shall emphasize below that God's word is best seen in its results. That is, we see it best not as something in and by itself but as something at work making things happen.

Such a picture emerges not only from the host of passages in the Bible about God's word or the Spirit but precisely also from the two verses traditionally and most widely quoted about inspiration of the Bible. In describing the "prophetic word," 2 Peter 1:19–21 states that "no prophecy of scripture is a matter of one's own interpretation" and further that "no prophecy ever came by the impulse of man, but men moved by the Holy Spirit spoke from God." Here, clearly, the emphasis is on persons who spoke in the past, "moved by" the Spirit, and on "interpretation" now under the same Spirit. When 2 Tim. 3:16 adds that "all scripture" is, literally, "God-breathed-into" (RSV, "inspired by God"), the emphasis is really on its function, that is, what it does, not the procedures by which it came to be. The functions enumerated here involve four areas where scripture is "profitable": teaching, reproof, correction, and training in righteousness. People in the Bible, moved by the same Spirit that operates today, spoke for purposes both positive (teaching, training) and negative (reproof, correction).

The Bible is thus not automatically word of God; it is word of God when it has a chance to effect the goals for which its original authors spoke. Henry Ward Beecher once went so far as to say, "The Word of God in the Book is a dead letter. It is paper, type, and ink. In the preacher that Word becomes again as it was when first spoken by prophet, priest, or apostle. It springs up in him as it were first kindled in his heart, and he were moved by the Holy Ghost to give it forth."[2]

Such proclaiming of God's word is by no means a lecture about God and divine attributes. Witnessing or preaching means speaking on behalf of God with the result that God meets the listener—by means of God's own word in the mouth of a spokesperson. Then, something happens! Either by way of judgment or reassurance.

THE EFFECT OF GOD'S WORD

The very first chapter of the Bible makes clear the effectiveness of God's word. God's "Let there be . . ." (Gen. 1:3, 6, 14; cf. 1:9, 11, 20, 24) simply does it. And there is perhaps no more beautiful statement about this power of God's word than this:

> For as the rain and the snow come down from heaven,
>   and return not thither but water the earth,
> making it bring forth and sprout,
>   giving seed to the sower and bread to the eater,
> so shall my word be that goes forth from my mouth;
>   it shall not return to me empty,
> but it shall accomplish that which I purpose,
>   and prosper in the thing for which I sent it.
> (Isa. 55:10–11)

In this light we can understand Paul's definition of the gospel as "the *power* of God for salvation to everyone who has faith" (Rom. 1:16). The gospel concerning Jesus Christ actually effects salvation for everyone who has faith; the gospel itself is power.

Lest we overlook how basic is this emphasis, it is necessary to point out how closely "power" and "kingdom" are associated in the New Testament. The "kingdom of God," Jesus' favorite theme, is not just a *declaration* of power; it *is* power (Mark 9:1; Luke 4:36 and 11:20; 1 Cor. 4:20; in the concluding doxology to the Lord's Prayer at Matt. 6:13 in some manuscripts, "power" parallels "kingdom"). God was in Christ, not only *declaring* reconciliation, but *effecting* it; we declare it. Christ did it

47

(2 Cor. 5:19–20). The word of God is not just talk *about* God's power; it *is* God's power.

Such an emphasis is caught in the later nonbiblical phrase "means of grace." Whatever actually conveys God's power is a means of grace. The word and, through its power, baptism and the Lord's Supper fit this category.

> The *word* of the cross is folly to those who are perishing. but to us who are *being saved* it is the *power of God*. (1 Cor. 1:18)

> We preach *Christ crucified*, a stumbling block to Jews and folly to Gentiles, but to those who are called, both Jews and Greeks, Christ the *power* of God and the wisdom of God. (1 Cor. 1:23–24)

The difficulty of the preaching and witnessing task is offset by the presence of the word's power, which effects salvation by grace.

The words found in many baptismal liturgies over the centuries, "I baptize you in the name of the Father, and of the Son, and of the Holy Spirit," actually accomplish, according to the "sacramental realism" of the Bible, the incorporation of the individual into the death and resurrection of Christ. Paul wrote:

> We were buried therefore with him by baptism into death, so that as Christ was raised from the dead by the glory of the Father, we too might walk in newness of life. (Rom. 6:4)

Or elsewhere:

> God our Savior . . . saved us . . . by the washing of regeneration and renewal in the Holy Spirit, which he poured out upon us richly through Jesus Christ our Savior, so that we might be justified by his grace. . . . (Titus 3:4–7)

The words "This is the body of Christ given for you" and "This is the blood of Christ shed for you" effect the forgiveness of sins for the recipient which was worked once for all in Christ's cross:

> As often as you eat this bread and drink the cup, you proclaim the Lord's death. . . . (1 Cor. 11:26)

> Drink of it, all of you; for this is my blood of the covenant, which is poured out for many for the forgiveness of sins. (Matt. 26:27b–28)

These actions—sacraments—do not merely symbolize an idea; nor do they simply recall events in the life of Jesus. They accomplish the very thing they proclaim by their words: the forgiveness of sins. This is in keeping with the entire Old Testament view of the power of God's word, as shown in Isa. 55:10–11.

The same is true of other kinds of proclamation. In a formal sermon or in a personal one-to-one conversation, the speaking of God's word makes God present in order to accomplish the divine will in the lives of people. A Christian's witness to a lost and lonely person does not merely tell about God's forgiveness; it actually effects it!

So it is with the rich and varied witness of the Bible. The prophets and narrators and poets and letter writers whose work has been preserved for us proclaimed the word with power. Their messages effected God's will for one situation after another, and thus their messages can be effective for us today as well.

We cannot, however, overlook the power granted to humans to reject God's word. Certainly this negative strength is still abundantly present among those to whom the word of God would come. All the power of God's word, actually effecting the forgiveness of sins, cannot efface the stubborn human ability to say no, even after an initial yes. But this is no cause for hopeless despair. As Paul says (Rom. 3:3–4, quoting Pss. 116:11 and 51:4):

> What if some were unfaithful? Does their faithlessness nullify the faithfulness of God? By no means! Let God be true though every man be false, as it is written,
> "That thou mayest be justified in thy words,
> and prevail when thou art judged."

Listening to the lessons read aloud during a formal worship service, hearing a family member read a passage from the Bible around the dinner table, or sitting alone to concentrate on the words of the Scriptures—all these settings today provide opportunity for the word of God to address us through the words which once comprised sermons to someone else. Thus, study of the Bible, or use of many portions of it in liturgy and also in private, enables God to speak to us in a personal and effective way.

For this reason Bible study cannot be a matter of idle curiosity for the Christian. To delve into the meaning of the Bible and its parts is to make a commitment of faith to the God who speaks in its various parts. The Bible's smallest bits and pieces and biggest books were all composed by people of faith who saw God at work in their lives. And so, to understand its message, the Bible must be read and studied by people of faith who take the risk that God will indeed address them and affect their lives.

That phrase, "people of faith," brings up one final crucial element in our picture of the word and its effectiveness. Too often Scripture is studied by individuals in lonely isolation, without the thrill of being able to share one's discoveries with others. Thus one loses the opportunity to learn further insights from others who have also been under the word. In reality, the Bible cries out for a community of faith, for committed people, who study this book. The two are reciprocals, each one related to the other:

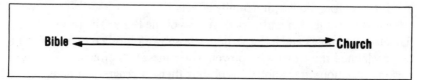

It is the particular emphasis of some Christians—historically in the Reformation but ecumenically today the view is more widespread—that both Bible and church stand under the Word of God (Christ, the message about him) or, as this text stresses, the gospel. Since our concern here is also to see God's word in relation to God's will for Christian witness in God's world, our chart may be completed thus:

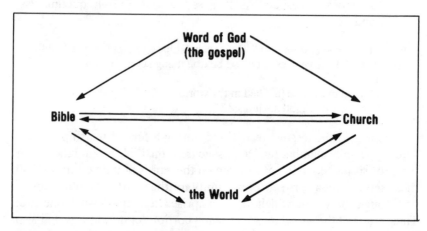

We thus deal in Scripture with:
a library written by human beings, and at the same time,
from the lips and pens of men   God's word to us,
(and women) who are really and   from the personality of God,
totally mortal,   the Lord,
  blind, dumb, deaf sinners,   holy, righteous, and loving,
whose humanity obtrudes   whose presence in the word proclaimed
  again and again ...   resounds again and again.

HUMAN TALK ABOUT GOD

While the word of God is not merely talk about God, nevertheless, the way the biblical witnesses discuss God, God's nature, and God's activity is of utmost importance in understanding how humans witness to God. The obvious fact is simply that humans have no option but to use human words and figures which communicate to other humans. There is no other way to talk about God than in ordinary human terms.

Several of the prophets in the Bible spoke of God as a ravaging beast. Amos said that "the Lord roars from Zion" (Amos 1:2) and elsewhere compares the Lord's speaking to the roaring of a lion (3:8). Hosea, too, uses similar imagery: God will act "like a lion," "like a leopard," "like a bear robbed of her cubs," and "as a wild beast" (Hosea 13:7–8). These images in no way suggest that God is an animal. They are similes used to express the ferocity of God's wrath against human sin, particularly idolatry. Thus, the purpose of this imagery is to describe God in words that human beings use and understand.

Other images are used to describe God's comforting and saving roles. Following the judgment that Hosea prophesies by means of his beastly analogies, the prophet speaks of God in botanical terms. God promises to be "as the dew to Israel," causing it to flourish (Hosea 14:5) and "like an evergreen cypress" from which Israel receives fruit (14:8). Surely God is not identical to morning moisture or to a tree. Each image serves a particular purpose in communicating the ways in which God relates to people—as the vital force which causes the community to flourish and as the provider of food for its nourishment.

Human images are used even more frequently in the Bible to describe God's relationship with people, particularly with the people of Israel. Hosea, who described God by those similes of raging beasts and fruitful trees, is best known for his portrayal of God as a husband of an unfaithful wife, Israel. Hosea's own personal life provides an analogy for the divine relationship which—so broken by infidelity—led the Lord to sue for divorce (Hosea 2:2–13). That same image of God as the husband of Israel was continued by the later prophets Jeremiah and Ezekiel (see Jer. 2:2–3; Ezek. 16:1–14).

Yet Hosea also describes the Lord as the Parent of a son named Israel (Hosea 11:1–2). This device is one of the ways for the prophet to explain to the people that their relationship with God went back in history to the time of the exodus from Egypt. That parental love continued over the centuries in spite of the constant rebellion on the part of the child. The imagery of Parent, first used with Moses before the exodus (Exod. 4:22–23), was continued and masculinized at a later time by Jeremiah. That "weeping prophet" reports God's disappointment that Israel did not call out the words "My Father" to God (Jer. 3:19). Nevertheless, Jeremiah announces that because of the Father-son relationship, God will deliver

Israel once again, this time from exile in Assyria and Babylon (Jer. 31:9). Thus, again and again, the parental analogy provides the motive for God's deliverance of the people from oppression.

In addition to the role of Father of the people as a whole, God is portrayed also as the Father of Davidic kings who ruled from Jerusalem's throne. When the Lord first promised to David that his dynasty would continue in Zion, the relationship that God vowed to have with his successors was this: "I will be his father, and he shall be my son" (2 Sam. 7:14). This relationship was established with each succeeding king on coronation day itself when the priest addressed the new king on behalf of God: "You are my son, today I have begotten you" (Ps. 2:7). By this adoption transaction from the first day of rule, the human king could turn to God in times of trouble and call out "Thou art my Father, my God, and the Rock of my salvation" (Ps. 89:26).

Yet all this masculine imagery, which portrays God as a physically strong advocate to whom the people could look for rescue, cannot lead to the conclusion that God is always portrayed as mighty or male. Often when the biblical writers speak elsewhere of the relationship of God to the people, particularly in terms of intimacy, mercy, or compassion, they compare God to a mother.

One part of the female image is related to the Hebrew word for "mercy" or "compassion." It is the word which in its basic forms means "womb." Ancient folks believed that emotions were based in certain parts of the body. The liver was the seat of joy; the bowels were tied up with agony and distress; the heart was the center of the intellect (what we call the mind). The womb was related to compassion. By this understanding it is virtually impossible to speak of the mercy or compassion of God without using the words related to "womb."

This understanding enables us to comprehend that passage in Jeremiah where the prophet speaks of the loving, intimate relationship between God and the people.

"Is Ephraim my dear son?
  Is he my darling child?
For as often as I speak against him,
  I do remember him still.
Therefore my heart yearns for him;
  I will surely have mercy on him," says the Lord.
(Jer. 31:20)

In the time of the Babylonian Exile in the sixth century B.C., another prophet compared the Lord to a woman. He used the cry of "a woman in travail" to describe the Lord's sudden change from silence at Israel's plight (Isa. 42:14). Just as the long waiting of pregnancy suddenly erupts in labor pains, so does God now change the action suddenly in order to take the exiles home. In yet another passage the same prophet answers Israel's painful belief that the Lord has forgotten her in exile,

Can a woman forget her suckling child,
that she should have no compassion on the son of her womb?
(Isa. 49:15)

In the so-called Song of Moses, an anonymous poet tried his hand at teaching about God. In the process he described Israel's neglect of the intimate relationship between the people and God.

You were unmindful of the Rock that begot you,
and you forgot the God who gave you birth.
(Deut. 32:18)

If this verse provided the only image of God in terms of the relationship with Israel, we would need to conclude that God is female. The verbs used here describe the "bearing" of a child and the travail of labor, completely feminine actions.

It must be said that none of these passages leads us to conclude that God is female. They are human ways of talking about God's relationship to people, about intimacy, and about acts of mercy. At the same time it must be stated that those passages which speak of the deity as Father do not prove that God is male. They are likewise human ways of talking about God's relationship with people and with the Davidic king. While these sexual roles might not be adequate in today's world, they were the expected roles in the Middle East in biblical times. As such they were appropriate to describe the indescribable God.

In the first chapter of the Bible we find the creation of humans is presented as being "in the image of God."

So God created man in his own image,
in the image of God he created him;
male and female he created them.
(Gen. 1:27)

Perhaps the most important concept to remember in Hebrew poetry is the use of synonymous parallelism. That is, the second and even third lines of poetry mean the same as the first line, and parallel meaning is achieved. A process of elimination makes clear that "male and female" are used as synonyms for "in the image of God." Thus, the image of God, that portrayal of God to the world, consists of female and male together, populating the world and ruling over it as responsible queens and kings.

But what of Jesus' way of describing God? Here we need to deal with at least two issues. First, we must recall that Jesus spoke of God in a variety of images. In his parables in particular God appears as a farmer sowing seed, a landowner, a shepherd, and also as a housecleaning woman. Second, we must recall that Jesus, the Son of God, was also a human being who spoke in human terms even about God. He called God his Father and never Mother, but that is precisely the case also in Jesus' Bible, what we refer to as the Old Testament. Jesus was a Jew, and his whole tradition determined the ways in which he spoke about God. If he had not spoken as a Jew, who among the poor and oppressed in Galilee or Jerusalem would have understood him? If Jesus had spoken God's language instead of human language, what would he have communicated? If in that culture Jesus had spoken of God as Mother, no one would have listened to the important message that the reign of God was breaking into history.

Even as we struggle with some of these issues, a new translation of the Bible is being prepared (see above, chap. 1, pp. 20–21). This version will attempt to desexualize or even demasculinize God and simultaneously use more inclusive language for people. To change such expressions as "the sons of Israel" to "the people of Israel" will be welcomed indeed, because such inclusiveness is even demanded by the Hebrew. But is it wise or even helpful to replace "Father" with "Parent" and to refer to Jesus as "Child of God" rather than "Son"? Such changes offer the advantage that we do not thereby give the impression that God is male. Yet such changes deprive us of the rich variety of images by which we can speak about God. In either case it is our responsibility to use the Bible's richness and not isolate one image to the neglect of others.

As a word of conclusion, God is not a lion or a she-bear or a leopard. God is not the morning dew or a fruitful tree. God is neither male nor female. God is God.

"For my thoughts are not your thoughts,
neither are your ways my ways," says the Lord.
(Isa. 55:8)

NOTES

1. For the authors' further views on the word of God and Scripture, see Foster R. McCurley, Jr., *Proclaiming the Promise: Christian Preaching from the Old*

Testament (Philadelphia: Fortress Press, 1974), 20–28, 45–49; and J. Reumann, "The New Testament Concept of the Word," *Consensus: A Canadian Lutheran Journal of Theology* 4 (1978): 15–24, and 5 (1979): 15–22.

2. Cited from Henry Ward Beecher's *Yale Lectures on Preaching* (1871–74) by Edgar DeWitt Jones, *The Royalty of the Pulpit* (New York: Harper & Brothers, 1951), 6.

3

A Book of
Bad News and Good News

THE BIBLE IS A VERY human book which speaks God's word to us. Its basic message is good news such as the gospel Jesus proclaimed about God's coming to reign. But the total message of the Bible also includes bad news. The bad news offers a frank analysis of the human predicament as well as unflattering accounts of human efforts in establishing community, security, and culture that often ended in disaster.

"Sin" is the term traditionally used to sum up all the bad news from God about us and our pretensions. "Judgment," "the wrath of God," "evil," "disobedience" are all related terms. Martin Luther liked to describe the human plight by talking about "the heart turned in upon itself," away from God.

In the Brief Order for Confession and Forgiveness in the *Lutheran Book of Worship* (and it is typical of what one finds in *The Book of Common Prayer* and countless liturgies), there is a frank acknowledgment of the human condition so clearly described in the Bible:

> We confess that we are in bondage to sin and cannot free ourselves. We have sinned against you in thought, word, and deed, by what we have done and by what we have left undone. We have not loved you with our whole heart; we have not loved our neighbors as ourselves. For the sake of your Son, Jesus Christ, have mercy on us. Forgive us, renew us, and lead us, so that we may delight in your will and walk in your ways, to the glory of your holy name. Amen.

During World War II a group of young people in German-occupied Holland found support and excitement in studying the Scriptures. Exposed daily to endless blasts of Nazi propaganda, they paid the Bible this supreme compliment: "It is the only book which does not tell lies about persons." In those all-too-frequent times in human history when truth about the nature of human beings is twisted or suppressed, God's word has the special, often unpleasant task of "telling it like it is." With crystal-clear honesty, the Bible confronts us with bad news about our lives and hearts and the world as God sees it all. Indeed, this is exactly what we find in those Genesis stories that follow the telling of the creation account.

Before we look closely at several of those early Genesis stories about the nature and consequence of sin, we may find it helpful to understand how Jesus and Paul, his greatest interpreter, viewed these matters.

BAD NEWS IN THE NEW TESTAMENT— JESUS AND PAUL

At first glance Jesus seems to have had surprisingly little to say about "sin." Many people do not include him among those who proclaim bad news about the human scene because Jesus seems to concentrate more on heralding good news and painting a word-picture of "great times coming" in the kingdom. As a teacher, Jesus seems more concerned with describing the kind of behavior that is pleasing to God than with pointing out what we have done wrong (see chaps. 6 and 7, below, for details).

But Jesus does not overlook the human predicament. In the course of an argument he refers to people as "evil" (Matt. 7:11; Luke 11:13). He assumes that we commit "trespasses" against God (Matt. 6:14–15). In the Lord's Prayer he teaches the disciples to say, "Forgive us our sins" (Luke 11:4). His parables are often stories about disasters in life or of ultimate judgment, such as the Salt Cast Out (Matt. 5:13), the Rich Fool's Death (Luke 12:16–20), the Fig Tree Almost Cut Down (Luke 13:6–9), or the Ten Maidens, 50 percent of whom are unwise (Matt. 25:1–12). And without question, Jesus' basic message about the kingdom of God assumes something had gone wrong so as to require people to repent (Mark 1:15).

Why did Jesus talk so little about sin as a topic for discussion, yet still believe the human predicament was such even in Israel as to require repentance and forgiveness of sins? An explanation may lie in the background painted in the Hebrew Scriptures and assumed by Jesus. For the Old Testament begins not just with the creation stories (Genesis 1—2) but with a picture of creation flawed and fallen (Genesis 3—11). It is to these opening chapters of the Bible that we must turn shortly if we are to understand the bad news about humanity's desperate plight that runs through the whole Bible. This familiar biblical view, which certain Old Testament and other Jewish writers had developed, Jesus carried on, but he went further. By looking upon sin as missing the mark in *intention* as well as in actual misdeeds, he deepened sin's meaning. What he said in the Sermon on the Mount (Matthew 5—7, esp. 5:21–48) is a much more radical reading of divine demand and human disobedience than that to which many Jews of his day were accustomed; sin could be committed just by thinking, without any outward actions at all.

But the gospel Jesus proclaimed provided the way out of the human predicament. In light of his death on the cross where he did pour out his life, what Jesus said in the upper room about his blood being "poured out for many for the forgiveness of sins" (Matt. 26:28) came to be understood as the good news in the face of the bad news of human sinning.

The New Testament writer and perhaps the person in all of Scripture who most sharply sets forth the bad news as background and necessary foil for the good news is the apostle Paul. In his letters, especially Romans, Paul deliberately and systematically describes how bad the human predicament is so that he can proclaim the gospel more effectively. Put simply, Paul's version of the evil tidings is that "all have sinned and fall short of the glory of God" (Rom. 3:23). The good news is that "they are justified by his grace as a gift, through the redemption which is in Christ Jesus" (Rom. 3:24). Throughout his writings the apostle develops his points on sin and grace not so much in story form but with a kind of relentless logic. For instance, in Rom. 6:5–6 Paul writes, "For if we have been united with him [Christ] in a death like his, we shall certainly be united with him in a resurrection like his. We know that our old self was crucified with him so that the sinful body might be destroyed, and we might no longer be enslaved to sin." (Note also 2 Cor. 5:14–15; 1 Tim. 2:5–7; Rom. 5:6; 14:9.)

As he seeks to force us to see the gravity of the bad news about ourselves, Paul presents the plight of sinful humankind in three ways.

1. In Romans 1—2 he describes how peoples in God's world actually do sin and transgress. The Gentiles are the non-Jewish segment of the world who do not know God's law and fall short because they confuse things God created with the creator God. They end up enthroning someone or something else—even themselves—as God. Romans 1:18–32 details the terrible corruptions into which such idolators, particularly those who worship sex, can then fall. Paul's indictment is much as a Christian—or Jewish—missionary must have indicted the Greco-Roman world of Paul's day. To complete the picture, Romans 2 indicts the Jews also as those who have God's law and who should know better: "You . . . are doing the very same things" (Rom. 2:1). Christians must recognize that Paul's argument also applies to church members who, sinners that

they are, get self-righteous as they view themselves in comparison with others.

2. As we might expect, Paul appeals to his Bible for passages that press home the bad news about all humankind. Romans 3:10–18 is a chain of quotations, chiefly from the Psalms, about how "no one does good, not even one" (Rom. 3:12). The quotations allude to various parts of the body (tongue, feet, eyes) as if to say all of a person has been taken over by sin.

3. Alongside these arguments from experience and from Scripture, Paul advances a third line of thought which is the hardest for us moderns to grasp. In Rom. 5:1–11 Paul talks about how one man, Jesus Christ, died to save (justify) all. Then follows Rom. 5:12–21, which takes us back to the Book of Genesis. Paul says the good news comes as a counterpart to some bad news there, namely, that "sin came into the world through one man [in Hebrew *'ādām* means "man"] and death through sin, and so death spread to all men because all men sinned" (5:12). The final phrase, "all ... sinned," reflects again the argument from actual experience.

The Greek word-phrase translated "because" in this passage in the RSV and most English translations has an interesting history. The Latin Vulgate translated this word-phrase as "in whom," referring to Adam— obviously the "one man" referred to earlier in the verse. From that interpretation, championed by Augustine, developed the idea of "original sin." This concept has it that somehow the whole human race was involved "in Adam" at the outset of human history. Ever after, by virtue of Adam's fall, all people inherit an inevitable inclination to sin and a common status as sinners.

Paul certainly can contrast Christ with Adam (see 1 Cor. 15:45–49) and, like all Semites, think in terms of a "corporate personality." His good news then is that we can be redeemed "in Christ." The bad news is that we are by nature "in Adam." Paul taught that sin and death abound not merely because we commit sinful acts but because this has been so ever since Adam. But Paul never went quite so far as a Jewish contemporary who prayed to God:

> Thou didst lay upon him [Adam] one commandment of thine; but he transgressed it, and immediately thou didst appoint death for him and for his descendants.... For the first Adam, burdened with an evil heart, transgressed and was overcome, as were also all who were descended from him. (2 Esd. 3:7, 21, RSV Apocrypha)

In his discussion of sin Paul frequently referred to the Genesis accounts, and we are again driven back to the opening chapters of the Bible to study the nature of that bad news that is also part of the fabric of God's word. Genesis describes the human situation in narrative form. Chapters 3—11 are composed of colorful yet hard-hitting stories about people who came face-to-face with the bad news about themselves: Adam and Eve, Cain, the Tower-of-Babel builders, and those who drowned in the flood as well as those who sailed on Noah's ark.

THE HUMAN STORY IN GENESIS 3—11:
ADAM AND EVE

In Genesis the first episode about the man and the woman, after the Lord God had created them, begins a story of bad news. This incident is not merely an account involving the first couple; it is the story of every human being. Unlike most of the rest of the Bible (where God is the subject), in the stories in Genesis 3—11 humankind is the subject of the action. Some of the deeds of the people recorded in genealogies are positive cultural achievements, like building cities (Gen. 4:17; 10:11–12), raising cattle (4:20), making music (4:21), doing metal work (4:22), even planting vineyards (9:20). In all these narratives, however, the actions of people are such that the result is always a disaster. So characteristic and pervasive is the negative nature of human action that all humanity brings upon itself the judgment of God. That is the bad news.

One story after another describes the rebellious nature of humans as they attempt to erase the lines that distinguish God from people. Thus the nature of sin, as the stories in Genesis 3—11 explain it, is rooted in the dissatisfaction of people to be what God made them to be. The sin itself is the futile attempt to "play God," and God's response to this universal rebellion is sharp and unambiguous.

Yet while God punishes sinful creatures, God does so in ways that avoid their complete annihilation. In the midst of the bad-news disasters that humans bring upon themselves, God holds out some measure of good news for the rebels. The last word is grace from God, not the self-inflicted judgment of the people. Ultimately the story of human self-glorification in Genesis 3—11 paves the way for a new story to begin in Genesis 12. There, in a series of promises given to Abraham, God becomes the subject of the action; the Lord elects Israel to be a witness in the world so that God might turn the universal curse into a blessing for all the families of the earth.

According to Genesis 1—2, God created everything in his world to serve particular functions and to share in specific relationships. God made it all good, and made it to be free. We human beings under whom the rest of the creation is set were not robots like Artoo Detoo of *Star Wars*. We were made free persons, able to make responsible decisions about our roles in the world and particularly about our relationships to God and to one another. Everything that came from God's hands was good and beautiful and complete.

Yet, as Luther put it, that harmonious scene of good news and joy lasted only until "the afternoon of the first day." The first decision that the first couple made was based on self-interest rather the proper performance of the God-given roles. It happened like this.

Adam and Eve, roaming carefree through the garden together all morning, became separated long enough for a serpent to approach the woman alone with a question: "Did God say, 'You shall not eat of any tree of the garden'?" (Gen. 3:1). Eve answered that such a statement was totally false. The couple could eat of any tree in the garden. Well, there was one exception—the tree of the knowledge of good and evil in the midst of the garden. She explained that if they ate or even touched the fruit of that tree, they would die. The serpent, clever as he was, corrected the order from God. "You will not die. For God knows that when you eat of it your eyes will be opened, and you will be like God, knowing good and evil" (Gen. 3:4–5). With that new information the woman streaked down to the middle of the garden, plucked a luscious piece of fruit, and munched away. Not having any pockets to take one back for her husband, she simply tossed him what she was eating when they met on the path, and he ate too.

The enticing words of the serpent provide the explicit reason for the first couple's disobedience: they wanted "to be like God." And they acted out that desire by eating the fruit from the tree of the knowledge of good and evil. That fruit, the serpent had said, is precisely what would make them godlike.

What does the tree of the knowledge of good and evil represent? It surely has to do with an intellectual desire to know how to distinguish good things from bad things. It might even symbolize the ability to have intellectual awareness of all things that exist. But the Hebrew understanding of knowledge involves much more than intellectual comprehension. It has more to do with experience. The same Hebrew word is used in Gen. 4:1 where we read that "Adam *knew* Eve his wife, and she conceived and bore Cain." The word also occurs in Amos 3:2 where we are told that the Lord said to Israel, "You only have I *known* of all the families of the earth." In both cases, the Hebrew word describes an intimate relationship based on personal experience. Thus, it would appear that the tree of the knowledge of good and evil represents the desire to experience all things, without restriction, and thus to be completely free.

Surely God made humans to be free. They could enjoy all the pleasures of the garden and frolic together in the peace of Eden. They could have anything in the garden which God had made for their benefit—with only one exception, the fruit of that tree of the knowledge of good and evil. The one exception put a limit on human freedom, and that limitation made clear the distinction between Creator and creatures. When the humans sought to experience all things and ate the forbidden fruit, it was nothing less than rebellion against God and against life as God defined it.

As a result of that rebellion, the harmony of Eden was distorted. First, something happened to the beautiful relationship that existed between the man and the woman. They who wanted to experience everything now knew what shame and guilt were like. Recognizing disgrace as they stood naked before each other, the pair covered themselves with fig leaves.

That was only the beginning of the consequences. When the Lord God discovered the man and the woman hiding among the trees, it was clear that the forbidden deed had occurred. In the old pass-the-buck routine, Adam blamed "the woman whom thou gavest to be with me" (Gen. 3:12), and Eve pointed her finger at the snake. In reverse order God spelled out the bad news.

The serpent would be cursed more than all other animals. He was destined to crawl on his belly and to eat the dust through which he slithered. Moreover, hostility would now define the relationship between the serpent and humans.

> I will put enmity between you and the woman,
>   and between your seed and her seed;
> he shall bruise your head,
>   and you shall bruise his heel.
>
>   (Gen. 3:15)

The "he" and "his" of the last two lines are used in the general sense, as some modern translations convey by using the plurals "they" and "their." The curse on the serpent thus speaks of the hostility that will continue for all generations.

With the woman God does not use the word "curse." Instead he announces the bad news in two ways. First, the experience of bringing babies into the world will be painful. Each new "blessed event" will be marred by the travail of labor and the writhing of delivery. Second, the equal partnership which existed from the creation of the woman as the man's counterpart now is distorted into a subjection of the wife to her husband (Gen. 3:16). This resulting hierarchy of the sexes is thus the consequence of human sin rather than the intent in divine creation.

And the bad news for the man is a strained relationship with the ground from which he was taken. The very ground itself is cursed because of his rebellion. So the man shall reap the benefits of the ground only with a great deal of toil and sweat. While from the beginning man had the responsibility to work the ground (Gen. 2:15), now the work becomes a "pain in the neck" because the labor will not produce proportionate benefits (3:17–19).

With that, God's judgment appears at an end—but only for a moment. Since the humans had eaten of the forbidden tree, God decided that something needed to be done to prevent them from eating of the tree of life. There was only one thing to do. God drove both the man and the woman out of the Garden of Eden and set up an impassable barrier to the tree of life. Immortality was reserved for God alone!

The first couple did not die by their rebellion as God had threatened. They walked on their own two feet out of the garden to live separated from its gifts. It seems that, in a sense, the serpent was right after all: "You will not die" (Gen. 3:4).

But in fact they did die! In the Bible life and death are defined by our relationship to God. Life is to be in the divine presence, to relate to God as the creatures we were meant to be. Death is to be separated from God, to exist without that divine presence. Adam and Eve died on the same day they played God, because they were driven out of the garden where they knew and experienced God's presence in an intimate way. They now experienced their death "east of Eden," the phrase John Steinbeck used as a title for a novel that powerfully portrays disharmony and death.

Yet God's love and grace for people even outside this presence continues. While the couple were packing their bags, "the Lord God made for Adam and for his wife garments of skins, and clothed them" (Gen. 3:21). Even east of Eden, in the condition of death, God provided the means to keep their bodies warm.

THE TRAGEDY CONTINUES:
SECOND GENERATION, FLOOD,
AND A TOWER

The story in Genesis 4 is about the two sons of Adam and Eve and shows the continuing rebellion of humans against God. It started at a sacrificial altar, and it ended with brother killing brother. Cain, the firstborn, was a tiller of the ground, and Abel, the second son, was a shepherd. Each offered sacrifices to the Lord that reflected their occupational pursuits. For a reason unexplained in the Bible, the Lord looked with favor on Abel's animal offering but with disfavor on Cain's agricultural gift of first fruits. This seeming unfairness angered Cain, and his feelings were obvious enough that the Lord felt it wise to have a heart-to-heart talk with Cain about mastering emotions and evil thoughts. Unpersuaded by the advice, Cain killed Abel out in the field (Gen. 4:8).

When the Lord asked Cain about his brother's whereabouts, the murderer responded with the familiar lie, "I do not know; am I my brother's keeper?" (4:9). But God already knew what had happened. Cain had played God by giving himself the power over life and death. The bad news was inevitable! Cain, the tiller of the ground, would work it now to no avail. Whereas Adam's punishment for his rebellion involved toil and sweat in producing food from the ground, Cain's judgment was extended to include no food at all. The first murderer was expelled from the land to become "a fugitive and a wanderer on the earth" (4:12). Cain feared that he was destined to be fair game for any would-be slayer.

But in the midst of all that bad news God's grace resounds once again. God promised to protect Cain by putting a certain mark on him—apparently on his forehead (see Ezek. 9:4, 6). Anyone who saw that mark would realize that the Lord would take vengeance if Cain were killed. So even to the first murderer God extends a protective hand and continues a way of grace.

In Gen. 6:1–4 appears a story that on the surface seems rather comical but that really conveys a serious message. One thing is certain: this description of the marriages between "the sons of God" and "the daughters of men" is surely not a historical record of the first visit from outer space! Actually it is an old story from the ancient world used to emphasize the same idea that we find in the previous Genesis stories: the distinction between the divine and the human must be maintained.

The Old Testament contains a number of passages which suggest that at one time the Lord God was viewed as the head of a heavenly court consisting of "sons of God," that is, lesser gods over whom he reigned. These gods were believed to convene in the divine assembly for various reasons related to human affairs (Job 1:6; 1 Kings 22:19–23) and for praising the Lord (Ps. 29:1–2). These views eventually disappeared during the Old Testament period.

According to the original story, these "sons" or divine beings took a fancy to human women and chose marriage partners from among them. This confusion of divine and human, particularly in sexual relations and the begetting of superheroes, resulted in God's unambiguous decree: "My spirit shall not abide in man for ever, for he is flesh, but his days shall be a hundred and twenty years" (Gen. 6:3). What concerned God was the possibility of immortality which would result if the divine beings conveyed their qualities to the human women or to the resulting offspring. It was precisely on the issue of immortality that God drew the line for Adam and Eve, and God's stance here is perfectly consistent.

What follows in Genesis 6 are some short statements reporting the utter corruption of the earth and God's regrets about creating humans, along with a plan to destroy the whole creation by a flood. Only a man named Noah, "a righteous man, blameless in his generation" (Gen. 6:9), was singled out for protection. But that one man and his family were God's means of grace in the midst of the bad news to come. Through Noah and his wife, God would both continue and start anew the creation he was about to destroy.

The story about the great flood is a common one in the ancient world. Several accounts, similar in many respects to the Bible's story, have been unearthed and translated during the past century. Most of them come from ancient Mesopotamia and were written between 2500 B.C. and 1500 B.C. The oldest flood story comes down from the Sumerians.[1] In details strikingly similar to Genesis 6—8, it tells of a man named Ziusudra whom the gods saved from the flood and on whom they conferred immortality. In another such story called the Gilgamesh Epic, the gods selected the human Utnapishtim, whose name means "he found life," to survive the flood, and on him too the gods bestowed immortality.[2]

In the Bible, however, there are no exceptions to mortality. Not even Noah, the hero of the flood, is allowed to live forever. It is not that the issue is avoided by the biblical writers in some conspiracy of silence. On the contrary, the message is clear, "All the days of Noah were nine hundred and fifty years; and he died" (Gen. 9:29).

Thus, while the Old Testament repeats the common tale of the flood, the writers use the story in a unique way. No longer is it a story to explain the one exception to human mortality; it is now a story that portrays the seriousness with which God regards human rebellion and the necessary distinction between God self and human creatures. So serious is God's judgment that creation virtually returns to the watery chaos out of which the earth arose (Gen. 1:2).

But so gracious is God's concern for humankind that with mortal Noah and his family God began creation anew. And to that same Noah God vowed that the earth would never again be destroyed by a flood (Gen. 9:9–17). Once again a crack of light appeared in the darkness of the bad news; a measure of God's grace turned the chaotic scene toward new life.

The final story in our survey of Genesis' history of humankind and sin is the record of the Tower of Babel (Gen. 11:1–9). The biblical writer begins with the announcement that once upon a time everyone spoke the same language. Then something occurred that led to the dispersal of the people and the multiplication of their languages. Here is a report of what happened.

When people migrated westward, they settled in a plain called Shinar, a word used here and elsewhere (Gen. 14:1) for Babylon. There they decided to build a city and a tower so high it would reach into the heavens. By this spectacular construction they would make a name for themselves and thereby gain the means for holding the people together. When God saw what they were doing, the Lord addressed the heavenly court in terms reflecting the concern shown back in the garden (cf. Gen. 3:22).

> Behold, they are one people, and they have all one language; and this is only the beginning of what they will do; and nothing that they propose to do will now be impossible for them. Come, let us go down, and there confuse their language, that they may not understand one another's speech. (Gen. 11:6–7)

Then the Lord scattered the people all over the earth, and because the city was the place where "the Lord confused" (Hebrew, *balal*) their language, it was named Babel (Gen. 11:9).

At first glance the story appears to report an unfair action on God's part. All the people wanted to do was construct some architectural monument. It seemed no worse than eating a piece of fruit. Yet it had the same type of rebellion behind it that led Adam and Eve to their folly. The people living in Shinar set out to play God. Note a couple of things.

In the first place, their attempt to build a tower that reached into heaven presumed that they could penetrate into the penthouse area they believed was reserved for God. Even until the acceptance of the Copernican theory in the sixteenth century, people believed in a three-story universe. God was thought to dwell above in heaven, people below on the earth, and the dead under the earth. Poor human beings! They saw themselves caught between these "two kingdoms." By attempting to enter the realm of God by a tower route, people holding such a view of the world were demonstrating once again their dissatisfaction in being creatures with a variety of limitations. Their piece of construction was a rebellious act against the Creator.

According to many religions of the ancient world, particularly in Mesopotamia where Babylon was located, a sanctuary built upon a hill and reaching high into the sky was the place where the divine and human

The tower of Babylon, named *Etemenanki* ("house of the bond of heaven and earth"), was the structure believed to have been fashioned at the time of creation to converge the divine and the human worlds.

worlds came together. Because it was believed that humans were nurtured by this physical connection with divine beings, such a place was considered to be "the navel of the earth." The idea is reflected in Gen. 28:10–17 where we are told that, when Jacob saw the angels of God ascending and descending on the old familiar ladder (actually it is a ramp or mound), he exclaimed, "How awesome is this place! This is none other than the house of God, and this is the gate of heaven" (v. 17). Actually, in spite of the play on the words *balal* ("confuse") and Babel in Gen. 11:9, the real meaning of Babel is "the gate of the god(s)." We know that in the ancient city of Babylon there was a tower named *Etemenanki* that seems to have been the place of communication between the heavenly and earthly worlds.[3]

According to the biblical storyteller, such a tower was an affront to God, presuming the ability of humans to penetrate into the domain of deity. That attempt is described with delightful irony. Even though the people thought the tower reached to heaven, the Lord had to "come down" to see what they were doing. Such is the illusory nature of human accomplishment.

Note also that the people of Shinar claim that their work will "make a name" for themselves. That illusion is based on the belief that our importance is based on the things we do. Yet it is clear throughout the Bible and in particular in Gen. 12:2 that it is God who makes us important. God makes our names great by bringing to fulfillment the promises given to people and by the divine-human relationship which those promises establish.

In these two ways, by attempting to penetrate God's domain and by thinking that people make themselves great, the people of Shinar brought God's judgment upon themselves. The effect of their self-inflicted punishment is dispersion from the place of communication with God and inability to communicate with one another. Whereas earlier "the whole earth had one language," now the people live in diversity and disharmony arising from their inability to understand one another. Earlier we saw the disruption between husband and wife, then between brother and brother. Now, even in the new creation which God began with Noah, the rebellion goes on and the judgment continues.

"BIBLICAL MENTALITY" AND GOD'S CONTINUING GRACE

In studying these Genesis stories we are forced to recognize that they contain a kind of "biblical mentality" (cf. above, pp. 16–17). The point of view of biblical people was, of course, quite different from our own. Their idea of a three-story universe is a classic example. In those times people also regarded the world as flat, with four "corners" and "windows" above which opened into the heavens to let down rain (Gen. 7:11). We today, of course, can actually see the roundness of the earth via television from the moon. We know something about outer space and earth's core and can seed the clouds to bring rain and do things of which these ancestors scarcely dreamed.

But the idea of a unique "biblical mentality," in distinction from the mind-set of contemporaries in antiquity, must not be overdone. Many of the assumptions in the Bible were not uniquely Israelite or Christian but were shared throughout the entire ancient Near East or the Hellenistic world. Furthermore, some of the assumptions involved were undergoing change during the centuries of the biblical period. Thus, the New Testament can reflect a much more elaborate scheme than that of the three-story universe, namely, a view of at least "three heavens" (2 Cor. 12:2), and the Epistle to the Hebrews has an almost Greek "Platonic" idea of "two worlds," one above and one below (Heb. 8:1–5). Once in the past, people had thought in terms of God as the direct cause for everything (cf. Amos 3:1–8, Yahweh even causes the lion to roar). But in the New Testament times, at least in some quarters influenced by Greek thought, the notion of secondary causes and of natural phenomena as factors had emerged (cf. Luke 12:54–56)—a philosophical view out of which the modern scientific method has developed. People in biblical times may have thought differently from the way we do at many points. They thought in the manner of their times. But we must not confuse this common outlook of all men and women of their day with the essence of biblical faith. The way to empathy with biblical figures is not to try to "play Semite" or accept their world view, but to see ourselves in our situations, and them in theirs, before the same God.

Thus the Tower-of-Babel story should not be used to argue against space exploration as though journeys into space were elbowing in on God's territory. We have a different view of the universe based on scientific exploration. Moreover, we do not describe heaven as spatially "up there" but as life hereafter in the presence of God. As in the stories of the garden, of Cain and Abel, and of the divine-human marriages, we should understand the story of the Tower of Babel as the insistence of God on keeping a clear distinction between God and us, his creatures.

The grace of God continues to offer blessings to people even though they are bringing judgment on themselves. As this universal history of humanity in Genesis 3—11 draws to its close, it seems the whole world is left hopelessly under a curse. But a curse is never God's last word! The sequel to the Tower-of-Babel story is the call to Abraham and God's promise that in him "all the families of the earth shall bless themselves" (Gen. 12:3).

Thus God begins a new story, not a history of bad news in which humans are the subject but a history of good news in which God self works in love to turn curse into blessing for everyone. When that promise is ultimately accomplished in the gospel of Jesus Christ (Gal. 3:8), the way is paved to reverse the effect of the Tower of Babel. After the risen Christ ascended to the Father, the Spirit of God fell on the disciples, and each family of the earth "heard them speaking in his own language . . . the mighty works of God" (Acts 2:6, 11). The final word of good news belongs to God!

NOTES

1. "The Deluge," trans. S. N. Kramer, in *Ancient Near Eastern Texts: Relating to the Old Testament*, ed. James B. Pritchard, 3d ed. (Princeton: Princeton University Press, 1969), 42–44, and in *The Ancient Near East, Volume 1, An Anthology of Texts and Pictures*, ed. James B. Pritchard, 6th paperback printing (Princeton: Princeton University Press, 1973), 28–30.

2. "The Epic of Gilgamesh," translated E. A. Speiser, in *Ancient Near Eastern Texts* (cited above, n. 1), 93–97 (tablet XI); in *The Ancient Near East, Volume 1* (cited above, n. 1), 65–75.

3. For a picture of the *Etemenanki,* the tower of Babylon, within the complex of Babylon's temple, see *The Ancient Near East, Volume 1* (cited above, n. 1), illustration 189.

4

The Gospel Story
in the History of
the Hebrew Scriptures

W HEN GOD SET OUT to change the curses of human sin into the blessings
of divine love, the Lord began a history of promises with Israel that
continue their way into the New Testament. Indeed, as the New Testament writers themselves described the story about Jesus, they often spoke
of his person and his actions as the fulfillment of what God had promised
in the Hebrew Scriptures.

The themes of promise and fulfillment provide one way in which the
two testaments fit together as one Bible. Just as engagement precedes
marriage and a regular baseball season is played out prior to the World
Series, so the promise of the Hebrew Scriptures precedes the fulfillment
of the New Testament story about the act of God in Christ.

To what do the terms "promise" and "fulfillment" refer? The fulfillment of the New Testament is not any single idea or event but a variety of
activities performed by Jesus and by God through Jesus. Sometimes it is
not so much the activities of Jesus but his person as the divine Son or as
God's Messiah that is said to fulfill a former promise.

What then is the promise that is fulfilled in Jesus? A standard dictionary defines "promise" as one's pledge to another to do or not do something specific. Another meaning given is the ground for hope, even
assurance of eventual success. The Hebrew Scriptures are full of promises
that God will do this or that or even refrain from certain acts. Out of all
the promises, which one is *the* promise? In effect, there is one consistent
element throughout these many promises: God will act for and upon
Israel and humanity.

Thus the promise of God which is fulfilled in the person and work of
Jesus Christ is none other than God's faithful presence and activity. God

self is *the* promise, and the divine presence and activity among the people of Israel is the ground of their hope and the assurance that God will one day bring everything to fulfillment.

The Hebrew Scriptures record how this promise worked itself out in many ways throughout the history of the chosen people, and so *the* promise takes the appearance of concrete promises as God's word addresses each situation anew. This record of *the* promise and the many promises is the way of the gospel in the Hebrew Scriptures, a way which spans almost two thousand years of history.

THE PROMISE AS BLESSING, LAND, AND FREEDOM

Genesis 12:1–3 begins the history of God's promise with the people of Israel. Here God promises to Abraham posterity, fame, and blessing for himself, and through him blessing for all the families of the earth. From here on, we are involved in a history that will continue into the New Testament—a history of the unfolding promises of God. The first part of this history, that of God's dealings with the patriarchs and their wives and families, reported in the Book of Genesis, is centered in the promise of blessing and descendants and points to the gift of land that is promised at Gen. 12:7. (See "Appendix: A Chronological Table.")

Historically speaking, Abraham, Isaac, and Jacob are usually dated in the period from 2000 to 1500 B.C. It was a time of vast migrations. That Abraham's family moved from Ur in southern Mesopotamia to Haran in northwest Mesopotamia (Gen. 11:31), and that from Haran Abraham was sent to Canaan (12:5), is typical of Amorite migrations in the twentieth and nineteenth centuries B.C. These Amorites, among whom Abraham is said to have lived for a time (14:13)—perhaps because he was one of them—were spread out from Mesopotamia to the Mediterranean Sea. There are many parallels in the patriarchal stories with customs reported in documents from this historical period. One example is the use of a handmaid to bear children, as in the story about Abraham and Hagar in Genesis 16. Furthermore, the archeological evidence that mass movements of Arameans occurred between 1900 and 1500 B.C. puts into perspective the reference to Jacob as "a wandering Aramean" in the liturgical creed, "A wandering Aramean was my father" (Deut. 26:5).

During these years the patriarchal families grew in the land of Canaan. They mixed with other people who had for a long time lived in Canaan and intermingled with others who were immigrants from elsewhere. God's promise of many descendants was becoming a reality. But because of unpredictable weather conditions in Canaan, many people had moved themselves and their flocks to Egypt where the constancy of the Nile River offered a better chance of survival. Eventually, such a large number of folks settled in Egypt that some enterprising pharaohs, Seti I (1309–1290 B.C.) and his son Rameses II (1290–1224 B.C.), used the foreigners as slaves in building the cities of Tanis (biblical Pithom) and Raamses (Exod. 1:11).

It was in the early part of the reign of Rameses II that God commissioned Moses to serve as the instrument for God in effecting another promise: "I have come down to deliver them out of the hand of the Egyptians, and to bring them up out of that land to a good and broad land, a land flowing with milk and honey . . ." (Exod. 3:8). Through a series of encounters with the pharaoh, God showed superior power and ultimately led the people out of Egypt across the Reed Sea (called the "Red Sea" in many English translations of the Bible). Thus God fulfilled the first part of the divine promise.

The way between Egypt and the promised land was a long one, lasting for forty years according to the Bible (that is, about a whole generation). After this long and troublesome trek through the wilderness, the refugees from Egypt and those who joined them on the way entered Canaan in about 1250 B.C. There, partly by conquest and probably more by peaceful settlement, this group moved in and inhabited parts of the land. They joined others who had remained in Canaan and who had made it their permanent home. Some of the groups living there for years had formed themselves into tribes, and as the new groups entered the land, more tribes were formed. Finally, there were twelve tribes who formed a federation known as Israel. The rules and regulations for this tribal league were laid down by Joshua at the city of Shechem. The primary mandate was to put away all other gods in order to serve Yahweh alone (Josh. 24:14–16).

For two hundred years or more the Lord related to the people through this tribal structure. This period, roughly 1200 to 1000 B.C., is called "the period of the judges," because during this time Yahweh rescued the people from outside threats by raising up charismatic leaders called judges. It was they who led the people, or sections of the people, to battle the enemy. The villains throughout this period were Canaanites (Judges 4—5), Midianites, Moabites, and especially Philistines. (The last mentioned were part of the Aegean "sea peoples.") Around 1200 B.C. these Philistines had ravaged the Hittites of Asia Minor. They then went on to northern Syria, to the coast of Palestine, to Cyprus, and even on to attack Egypt. Battles with these invaders, along with the regular festivals for worship, provided the only real contact among the various tribes of Israel.

Toward the end of the eleventh century B.C. the people attempted to achieve some stability by appointing a king. Because of some impressive victory over the Philistines, a man named Saul became Israel's first king through the Lord's commissioning. During Saul's reign a young hero, David, came into prominence as a warrior against the Philistines. The result was a rivalry between Saul and David that ended in Saul's insanity and in David's flight to the hills of Judah.

THE PROMISE AS DAVIDIC DYNASTY

After Saul had been killed in battle, David was made king over the southern section, which belonged to the tribe of Judah (2 Samuel 2). Over the rest of Israel, Saul's son, named Ish-bosheth, ruled for several years. During this time fighting between David and Saul's successor was constant. When Ish-bosheth (actually his name was Ish-Baal, "the man of Baal") was killed, David became king over north and south and thus of a united monarchy. The date is easy to remember: 1000 B.C.

One of David's first acts as king was to select a new capital. His decision, based on his concern to avoid alienating north or south, was Jerusalem. This city belonged not to any of the tribes but to a group of Canaanites named Jebusites. Settled in the new capital, David prospered. He built a palace of splendor, defeated the Philistines once for all, and brought into the city that most famous sacred object from Israel's past, the ark of the covenant (2 Samuel 5—6). In the midst of all this glamor, David began to feel guilty that he lived in a palace while the Lord, enthroned on the ark, was out there on the windy hill in a tent. At first David's prophet, Nathan, thought it was a good idea to build a temple for God. Later, however, God told David, through Nathan, that the project should be postponed. Rather than have David build a house for God, the Lord would build a house, that is, a dynasty, for David. This dynasty, God said, would endure forever, and it would be left to David's successor to build the temple (2 Sam. 7:13). Now a *new promise* of God was in effect: no longer would God relate to the people through tribal structures or judges or even charismatic kings; now he would deal with Israel through a dynasty.

It was Solomon who succeeded David in 961 B.C., and construction of the temple began shortly thereafter. It was an exquisite structure, which apparently whetted the appetite for beauty and splendor. Thus, all sorts of building projects, as well as international trade and its benefits, brought glory upon Solomon and his ever-expanding empire. Life was not completely rosy for the people or for Solomon, however. To effect many of his international deals, Solomon acquired for himself wives out of various nations. These women brought with them to Jerusalem their idols, their extraordinary tastes for glamor, and an entourage of foreign servants. In addition, Solomon offended many in the kingdom, particularly in the north, by his policy of heavy taxation. He even resorted to forced labor to keep up the building activity.

And so, when Solomon died in 922 B.C., his son Rehoboam could not hold the kingdom together. Northern Israel split off under their own king Jeroboam, who, in order to make the break complete, established sanctuaries at Bethel and at Dan to rival the temple in Jerusalem. Not even for festivals did the Israelites of the north "go up to Jerusalem."

The following two centuries were an unimpressive age. The reigns of the southern kings of Judah are set side by side with the northern kings of Israel in the accounts from 1 Kings 12 to 2 Kings 17. While the dynastic principle continued in the south, northern kings came to the throne by election—or intrigue and even murder.

The middle of the eighth century B.C. was the period of the prophets Amos and Hosea. Now the major problem was not feuding between north and south; it was the terror of the Assyrian Empire which, under Tiglath-pileser III, was expanding westward. An attempt by Israel and Syria to take over Judah in order to make a united effort against Assyria (735–734 B.C.) failed, and so in 722/721 B.C. the northern kingdom crumbled before the new king of Assyria, Sargon II. The normal Assyrian practice followed: the natives of the land were deported to other parts of the empire and foreigners were brought in to settle in Israel (2 Kings 17:24). This policy assured the Assyrians that no surge of nationalism would break out in the various segments of the empire.

At the same time that Israel was falling in ruin, Judah was falling on its knees before the Assyrian king. In this time of the prophets Isaiah and Micah not only was heavy tribute exacted from the vassal Judah, but religious objects such as altars were erected by King Ahaz (2 Kings 16:10–16) in the Jerusalem temple, in order to show that Assyrian sovereignty was all-encompassing. Because of God's promise, however, the Davidic dynasty remained on the throne through this tumultuous period.

A rebellious attempt at freedom by Judah's King Hezekiah (715–687 B.C.) was short-lived, and under his son and successor, Manasseh, vassalage to Assyria was once again in full swing. But when a series of weak kings came to rule the Assyrian Empire, that vast, fearsome power became weaker and weaker until its capital city of Nineveh fell in 612 B.C.

at the hands of the Medes and the Babylonians. The prophet Nahum was active at this time, probably also Habakkuk and Zephaniah.

About 621 B.C. King Josiah of Judah was carrying out impressive reforms. Centralizing all political and religious activity in Jerusalem, Josiah extended his domain northward in a nostalgic attempt to rebuild the Solomonic Empire. But in 609 B.C. this good king was killed at Megiddo by the Egyptian pharaoh Neco, and until 605 Judah was unmistakably a vassal of Egypt. In this period the prophet Jeremiah was very much on the public scene.

In 603/602 B.C. Judah's king, now Jehoiakim, became a vassal of Nebuchadnezzar, ruler of Babylon. Thus began a state of dependency and subjugation that would last more than sixty years. An attempt at rebellion by Jehoiakim resulted in 597 B.C. in a tragic deportation. The leading citizens and skilled craftsmen were carried off to Babylon, along with much of Jerusalem's treasures. A young, eighteen-year-old king, Jehoiachin, reigned briefly (2 Kings 24:6–15) but was carried off captive to Babylon. Then his uncle, Zedekiah, became ruler for ten years. At the end of this period came another invasion by the Babylonian army and another deportation of people. In addition, the suppression of Jerusalem's rebellion in 587 B.C. was marked by the total destruction of the city, including the temple on Mount Zion. Thus did the state of Judah join the fate of Israel one hundred thirty-five years earlier.

THE PROMISE AS RESTORATION

Precisely what was occurring in Jerusalem for the next fifty years is difficult to determine. Most of our written records seem to come from the exiles in Babylon. Against their feeling of Godforsakenness the prophet Ezekiel, who was among the first group of deportees, preached the word of God. To speak against a feeling of hopelessness and despair that God was dead, or at least safely removed from the exiles, the group known as the Deuteronomists compiled a long history of Israel. It included the framework of our Book of Deuteronomy as introduction, and then followed the Books of Joshua, Judges, Samuel, and Kings (i.e., in our Bible, 1—2 Samuel and 1—2 Kings). It may be too that a group of priests worked at this time to present their understanding of the beginnings of the world and the early history of Israel as the touchstones for the lengthy regulations recorded in Exodus, Leviticus, and Numbers. But surely the outstanding witness to God's word in Babylon was that anonymous prophet we call Second Isaiah, whose preaching is recorded in Isaiah 40—55. It was he who announced that the end of the exile had arrived and that the Lord was coming to lead the exiles homeward to Jerusalem.

But all these witnesses in exile continued to proclaim the promise of God. They proclaimed that God was indeed with his people through the words of commissioned mediators and that God would restore them to their land.

It was in 538 B.C. that Cyrus, king of Persia, accomplished his victory over Babylon and issued an official decree which allowed the Israelites to return to Jerusalem. The decree provided the funds for rebuilding the temple and restored the sacred vessels that Nebuchadnezzar had stolen fifty years earlier. That decree, known as the Edict of Cyrus, is recorded in the official Aramaic language at Ezra 6:3–5.

Of course, during the fifty years in Babylon many of the Israelites made homes and established themselves in various ways. The edict that allowed them to go home was not met with overwhelming response. Apparently a small group headed homeward immediately and began work on temple construction, but the progress was painfully slow and without enthusiasm. It was the prophets Haggai and Zechariah who preached in 520 B.C. that completion of the temple was important in the Lord's plans. Finally in 515 B.C. the temple was completed and dedicated. Although it did not match the splendor of Solomon's temple, this (second) temple did provide a focal point for the "remnant of Israel" who could remember God's promise of restoration.

About 450 B.C. word reached the Persian court in Babylon that matters in Jerusalem were bad. There was no security from outsiders; religious practices had given way to laxity and toleration; the people despaired. A Jewish man named Nehemiah was at that time the cupbearer for the Persian king. Upon hearing the plight of his brothers and sisters in Jerusalem, he requested the king to send him as leader of a group to restore order. The gracious king not only complied with Nehemiah's request but appointed him governor over Judah. By about 440 B.C. the new governor was on the scene, tackling one job after another. The most crucial was the rebuilding of Jerusalem's walls. A good, pious man, Nehemiah also worked hard at trying to establish religious principles and practices in the face of such laxity.

It was left to another Jew from Babylon, Ezra, to accomplish in the area of religious purity what Nehemiah had failed to do. A priest in Babylon, Ezra, came to Jerusalem with a commission to right the religious situation by teaching the laws of Moses to the Jews and administering the district in such a way that the laws would be obeyed. One of his most startling acts to purify religious practice and to establish a Jewish identity was to dissolve all marriages of Jews with non-Jews. Toward the end of

View from the ruins of Qumran, looking south along the Dead Sea toward the fresh-water springs at ʿAin Feshkha. In the scriptorium of the Qumran "covenanters" the Dead Sea Scrolls were copied.

the fifth century B.C. Ezra constituted the Jewish community on the basis of the law. Thus, along with Nehemiah he restored order in Judaism.

The beneficent reign of the Persian emperors came to an end in 331 B.C. when Alexander the Great flexed his Macedonian muscles and brought most of the ancient Near East under his control. Now Greek institutions, Greek structures, Greek philosophy, and everything else Greek began to pervade the ancient world, including, of course, Israel.

When Alexander died in 323 B.C., the vast empire which he had created was broken into smaller parts. Ptolemy, who was governor of Egypt under Alexander, occupied Palestine and then had to defeat those who showed particular interest in this area. Thus from 312 B.C. the area of Palestine was under the control of the Ptolemaic state, which was centered at Alexandria in Egypt. There was always some tension regarding the Palestine area, however, because another branch of the empire, that of the Seleucids centered in Syria, constantly sought more influence over Palestine.

During the third century, when Palestine was under the control of the Egyptian Ptolemies, many Jews ended up in Alexandria. There they adopted the Greek language and much Greek thought and culture. These

Greek-speaking Jews in Alexandria attracted converts to the faith, called "proselytes," who knew no Hebrew or Aramaic. Thus there arose the need for some Greek translations of the pericopes (public readings of the Bible) used in the synagogues. Finally, there developed a Greek translation of the Pentateuch, then of the whole Hebrew Bible. We call this Greek version the Septuagint (from the Latin word for "seventy," since it is supposed that seventy scholars produced it; see above, p. 19).

About 198 B.C., the Ptolemies lost their control over Palestine and Phoenicia. In the Seleucid state in Syria there arose a king named Antiochus III (223–187 B.C.) who, after years of fighting, finally secured that part of the empire as his own. Relations between Antiochus III and the Jews were not bad, but in 175 B.C. there came to the Seleucid throne Antiochus IV Epiphanes ("The Revealer"). Jewish life and thought were a menace to the cultural uniformity he had hoped to achieve in his empire. Bred as he was on an easygoing tolerance in religious matters, he increasingly sided with that party in Judaism which was "open" to the all-pervasive Greek, or better Hellenistic, thinking. He was so broad-minded about things religious that he might not have imagined the outcome of his actions in 167 B.C. At that time he defiled the temple in Jerusalem by committing "the abomination of desolation" (something like sacrificing a pig on the altar) and prohibiting thereafter any Jewish sacrifices. In addition, Jewish law was declared illegal (so that one could not own a copy), and so also was Sabbath observance. To enforce his ways, Antiochus established a garrison of troops within the city of Jerusalem. In this setting the Book of Daniel was written to encourage the Jews to be faithful to God.

One such faithful Jew was a man named Mattathias, a priest from a town named Modin. In dramatic fashion, Mattathias struck down both the Syrian officer who had come to enforce the Hellenistic sacrifice commanded on the villagers and the Jew who stepped forward to cooperate. Mattathias and his four sons then fled to the hills to begin guerrilla warfare against the enemy. The family came to be known as the Hasmoneans (after the priest's great-grandfather) or as the Maccabees (a nickname for the oldest son, Judas, which means something like "the Hammerer"). The fighting of this family is described in detail in the apocryphal Books of Maccabees. The Hasmoneans were successful enough in their warfare. Three years after the desecration of the temple, in December 165 B.C., the temple was theirs once again. Their restoration of religious freedom was marked by the Feast of Dedication which has been observed by Jews ever since as Hanukkah, or the Feast of Lights.

As for the Syrians, they had their hands full of internal conflict after the death of Antiochus Epiphanes and were only too willing to grant the Jews religious freedom. While some pious defenders of the faith were willing to settle for this agreement, the Maccabees were in high gear and went on to fight for political freedom as well.

Thus the history of Israel from the eighth century onward was by and large a sorry scene. The chosen people were subjected to one master after another. But in the midst of all this bad news, the good news (the gospel) was that God the Promise continued to act upon and for the people of God, in order to lead the many promises to fulfillment. In spite of one disaster after another, God kept Israel as a people in order to accomplish that promise given to Abraham, namely, that "by you all the families of the earth shall consider themselves blessed" (Gen. 12:3, au. trans.). This promise, fulfilled by God in the event of Christ, was "the gospel [preached] beforehand to Abraham" (Gal. 3:8).

5

The Gospel Story
in the History of
the New Testament

In the New Testament era God's promise is fulfilled: God sends his Son.

> But when the time had fully come, God sent forth his Son, born of woman, born under the law.... (Gal. 4:4)

So much did God love the world he had made, in spite of all its willfulness and perversity (John 3:16)! "The promise to Abraham and his descendants, that they should inherit the world, ... not ... through the law but through the righteousness of faith" (Rom. 4:13), begins to come to fruition through Jesus and the church. Christ Jesus, whom Paul, Silvanus, Timothy, and the other apostles and their helpers preached, is the one in whom "all the promises of God find their Yes" (2 Cor. 1:20). Jesus is called "Emmanuel," that is, "God with us" (Matt. 1:23, in fulfillment of Isa. 7:14).[1] Jesus is designated "Lord," reflecting all the veneration in which ancient Israel held God. God the Promise reaches self-fulfillment in Christ, and Jesus is the very revelation of the Father (John 1:1; Heb. 1:3). He makes God known (John 1:18).

But promises fulfilled beget new promises. The one who fulfills the Emmanuel-pledge in Matt. 1:23 also promises in Matt. 28:20: "Lo, *I* am with you always." In John's Gospel, the one who reveals the Father, Jesus, also promises "another Counselor" like himself, "the Spirit of truth" (John 14:16–17). Even after "the light of the world" (John 8:12) has appeared, people must still walk by faith and not by sight (2 Cor. 5:7). An apostle knows whom he or she has believed, but does not yet behold the Lord face to face; the apostle trusts God to guard what has been entrusted, but Paul knows that even he has not yet attained (2 Tim. 1:11–12; Phil. 3:12). The saints, made righteous by faith, do not yet inherit the earth, but must rest content with a beatitude, which is really a future promise from God, that "they shall inherit the earth" (Matt. 5:5; see chap. 7, below).

That, of course, is why and how the gospel story goes on—old promises are fulfilled, and new ones made, from Israel to Christ to believers today, on into the eternity of God. But the heart of it for Christians is the unique fulfillment attained in Jesus about A.D. 30, and the new patterns toward fulfillment of future promises let loose in the "Christ-event."

Having seen how gospel was preached beforehand to Abraham (Gal. 3:8) and to all the other Old Testament personalities (chap. 4), we now turn to the gospel story par excellence in the New Testament, traced out against the history of its times.

The age of the New Testament is a remarkably brief one, but intense, compared to the Old Testament period. Not two thousand years, but three hundred at best. If we focus on the public ministry of Jesus, that lasted three years at most. If we take the decades when most of the New Testament writings were composed, the time span is fifty years or so (A.D. 50–100). If we extend the time to stretch from Jesus' birth (at the earliest, 7 B.C.) to the writing of the last New Testament book (no doubt 2 Peter, perhaps as late as A.D. 150), it is only a century and a half. We can double that period only by adding the period of Maccabean independence which began about 166 B.C.

MACCABEES AND ROMANS:
WHAT GOOD NEWS?

As noted above in chapter 4, the Maccabean period began when Mattathias and his sons unleashed a struggle for religious and political freedom, a struggle that lasted from the initial guerrilla revolt (166 B.C.) until Simon, a second brother of Judas Maccabeus, succeeded Jonathan and in 142 B.C. secured recognition from Syria of the nation's independence. This Jewish state continued until 63 B.C., when the Romans took control. It was the last time there would be an independent Jewish state until the creation of the modern state of Israel in 1948. (The temple area was not reclaimed by Israelis until 1967.)

The leaders and rulers in the Maccabean period were from the house of Hasmoneus, the great-grandfather of Mattathias (according to Josephus, *Antiquities* 16.7.1; possibly, in turn, from a place name, Heshmon or Hashmonah). They included Judas; two of his brothers, Jonathan and Simon; then Simon's son, John Hyrcanus; and a succession of often short-lived kings, the most remarkable of whom was Alexander Janneus, who expanded the nation's holdings to rival the empire of David almost a thousand years earlier. This list includes an even more remarkable queen, Alexandra, who had been married to a king (Aristobulus I) and then chose the imprisoned Janneus to rule, and finally ruled alone (76–67 B.C.). These Hasmonean rulers managed to achieve something previous Israelite rulers had not attained: the combining of the office of king with that of priest. Even after the Romans came, a Hasmonean high priest continued in office for a time.

During this period of the Maccabean state, what "gospel" was there? People in general and Christians in particular are not normally accustomed even to ask such a question. But there was "good news" which Jews of the Maccabean period vehemently declared to be from God, and promises aplenty, and hopes. The political rulers regarded Jerusalem, Zion, the temple, priesthood and throne, and nationhood as the fulfillment of age-old promises to David—that God

> has made with me [David] an everlasting covenant,
>   ordered in all things and secure.
>   (2 Sam. 23:5)

This meant a nationalistic religion.

Others, the Pharisees, for example, reacted in pious horror to these political claims and centered their religion in a way of life that stressed prayer, fasting, and good deeds. Even more upset at what was happening in Jerusalem, at the alliance between temple and throne, were the extreme Pietists. They left the city and went off in the wilderness, south of Jericho, near the Dead Sea, to establish a community around their own idea of the covenant and new and further revelations from God. This is the group at Qumran who wrote the Dead Sea Scrolls.

Still other Jews in Jerusalem, the Sadducees, held to a conservative view of the law, maintained loyalty to temple worship, and often compromised with Gentile practices. And there were those who treasured wisdom, traditional or new and Hellenistic, as the guide to what was good.

This was the religious situation into which the Roman legions came.

The Romans were, of course, the dominant political power from 63 B.C. onward, throughout the entire period of the New Testament and of the early church, until the fall of Rome in A.D. 476. We need not trace here how the city-state on the banks of the Tiber became a world power, leaving its mark from Scotland to Mesopotamia. Suffice to say, in Maccabean times, during the second century B.C., Rome was expanding eastward, and Judea was just one of many petty states absorbed by Rome in the process. It was a turning point in human history when the Roman general Pompey the Great took Jerusalem and, according to one story, shook his head in amazement that there was no statue of any sort of "the Jewish God" in the innermost shrine of the Jerusalem temple.

Rome's arrangements for Palestine were not really made secure for some years. While many of the desert boundaries on the eastern flanks of the empire were quite flexible, Palestine was a special problem. The reason was that, to the east, beyond the desert buffer zone, lay the one nation that rivaled Rome in this period, namely, the Parthian Empire. The Parthians ruled from the Euphrates to India, and they had inflicted unheard-of defeats on Roman arms in 53 and 36 B.C. Their realm included many Jews from the period of the Babylonian Exile, so there were Jewish links to Palestine. As late as 40 B.C., the Parthians invaded Palestine and briefly seized Jerusalem. They were always a kind of "apocalyptic menace," beyond the frontier, ever a threat to intrude and destroy Roman rule. This fact explains in part why Rome welcomed a militarily effective adventurer from Idumea, Herod by name, in the year 40 B.C., and why the Roman Senate proclaimed him "king of the Jews."

The political history of the New Testament era henceforth falls within the Roman orbit. Rome itself was undergoing transition, of course, but continued as the dominant political fact of the times. This transition took Rome from a republican form of government to a series of strongman rulers, the last two of whom were Julius Caesar (assassinated 15 March 44 B.C.) and his nephew Octavian, who defeated his rivals, including Mark Anthony and Cleopatra, and created a new type of government, called the "principate," with himself a *princeps* ("first" citizen of Rome). Eventually a transition was made to an empire, and Augustus ("august, majestic," the name Octavian took) ruled from 27 B.C. to A.D. 14. He is the ruler mentioned at Jesus' birth (Luke 2:1) as "Caesar" (originally Julius's family name, later a title like kaiser or czar). Thereafter power rested chiefly with the emperor in Rome. We sometimes meet the names of such emperors in the New Testament: the recluse Tiberius (A.D. 14–37; cf. Luke 3:1); the madman Gaius Caligula (A.D. 37–41), whose attempt to have his statue set up in the Jerusalem temple touched off Jewish reactions such as had not been seen since the times of Antiochus Epiphanes and the "abomination of desolation" (see chap. 4); and Claudius (A.D. 41–54), during whose reign there was a famine in Palestine (Acts 11:28).

The emperor, of course, never came to Palestine. Rome ruled through a remarkably efficient and quite just civil service—though one not without corruption. At first, Judea was incorporated into the province of Syria, with a Hasmonean as high priest. When intrigue arose and the Parthian invasion came, Rome turned to the ruthless efficiency of Herod the

Great. He ruled from 37 to 4 B.C. For all the scandals about his ten wives and many offspring, and stories about his cruelty, which the New Testament and secular sources record (cf. Matt. 2:16, the slaughter of the babes at Bethlehem), he was a far more important ruler than history books have generally allowed, for he brought Judea to new prosperity and fame.

Herod's sons and successors, however, did not do as well. Archelaus (Matt. 2:22) lasted only from 4 B.C. to A.D. 6 as "ethnarch" in his father's stead. (An "ethnarch" was a "ruler of the people," lower in rank than a king, usually dependent on appointment by some outside power.) Herod Antipas (Luke 3:1, 19; Mark 6:14; Matt. 14:1; this is the man Jesus called "that fox," Luke 13:32) lasted until A.D. 39 as "tetrarch" of Galilee, but then was banished to France. (A "tetrarch" was, literally, the ruler over one-fourth of a larger area. The title suggests that Herod Antipas too was less than a king.) Herod Philip (Luke 3:1) was given rule over a different fourth or "tetrarchy" of Herod the Great's realm, but died without heirs in A.D. 34.

Archelaus's failure as a ruler led to the imposition of direct Roman rule, through appointed Roman governors or "procurators," A.D. 6 to 41 and then, after a brief interlude, from A.D. 44 to 66. The most famous of these procurators was Pontius Pilate, who governed (26–36) at the time Jesus died.

The only other members of the Herodian family to appear in the New Testament are Herod Agrippa I, a grandson of Herod the Great, who ruled Judea briefly (A.D. 41–44; see Acts 12:1–23), and Agrippa II, his son, who in the fifties and sixties was king over a part of Judea. Agrippa II appears during the legal hearings involving Paul in Jerusalem (Acts 25—26).

What gospel for God's people existed in this period of Roman rule and Herodian princelings? There continued, of course, all the options that had existed in Maccabean times. Law, piety, temple and cult, retreat to the desert and renewal there, and wisdom were all offered as "good news." The Sadducees and those termed "Herodians" found their answers in cooperation with Rome. Elsewhere a new movement was taking shape that was zealous for the law and for the kingship of Yahweh. These Zealots wanted to drive out the Romans by force and have no king but God. Political, violent revolution was their creed.

JESUS AND THE RISE
OF CHRISTIANITY

Into this world came Jesus, preaching his message about the kingdom of God (see above, pp. 1–2, and chap. 6, below). Jesus' gospel (good news), as we have already noted, was an announcement of how God's kingship was breaking in.

At this point, let it suffice to say that after Jesus' death and resurrection, a new and further gospel arose. It told of what God had done in raising Jesus from the tomb and in exalting him to sit at God's right hand as Lord (cf. Ps. 110:1; below, chaps. 13 and 25). We may call this good news "the Easter Gospel." It was the message Paul, along with other apostles, carried far beyond Palestine, to the wider world of Greece and Rome (see chap. 26). Paul, of course, in facing many new needs and situations, found new ways to make explicit the message of Jesus about the kingdom and about what God had done in Jesus Christ (chap. 27).

Few periods of history have been studied as intensively as the brief months of Jesus' public ministry, and the years of mission expansion that followed it after Easter. Since the New Testament rarely tells us about many details we might like to know, only certain segments of this period emerge with any clarity. These include the following.

Jesus was born prior to the death of Herod the Great which occurred in 4 B.C. He was "about thirty years of age" when he began his ministry (Luke 3:23). His predecessor John the Baptist began his ministry "in the fifteenth year of the reign of Tiberius Caesar" (Luke 3:1). Such references suggest that the Baptist appeared on the scene between A.D. 26 and 28, and Jesus between 27 and 29. A great deal in this dating depends on whether one credits Jesus with a one-year public ministry or a three-year ministry—that is, whether one follows the Synoptic Gospels or John. The former imply a one-year ministry, culminating in a final trip to Jerusalem. The latter suggests a three-year ministry, with several journeys to Jerusalem. Related to this is the conflicting evidence over whether there was a neat sequence in Jesus' career of "Galilee-Jerusalem" (so Mark); or a back-and-forth movement between the two (as in John); or was it a "Galilee-Samaria-Jerusalem" sequence as Luke declares? Probably Jesus carried out a ministry of a year or more, but it need not have been so concentrated in Galilee as the Synoptic Gospels suggest. But it was likely a ministry to Jews only, with only occasional Gentile or Samaritan contacts.

After Easter a "Jesus movement" broke out both in Jerusalem and Galilee, where people beheld the risen Christ. We know next to nothing about Galilean Christianity, since Luke has chosen to depict the spread of the gospel as a movement from Jerusalem to Rome in three stages: Jerusalem, then Judea and Samaria, then the regions beyond (Acts 1:8). Jerusalem was probably not as exclusively dominant as Acts suggests, but Paul himself did pay heed to Jerusalem and the leaders there (Galatians

1—2). The outline in Acts shows a steady march from Jerusalem to Rome, first through preachers like Peter and Philip the Evangelist (chaps. 2—12), and then through Paul and his companions (chaps. 13—28). Paul's work is sketched in terms of three missionary journeys, and a fourth to Rome as a prisoner, yet with opportunity to preach the gospel even as a prisoner. The Acts material may be outlined thus:

Journey 1, Paul and Barnabas—

Antioch (in Syria), Cyprus, southern Turkey, and back to Antioch, A.D. 47 or 48 to 49 (Acts 12:25—14:28)

Journey 2, Paul and Silas—

Antioch, Asia Minor, into Europe, touching Philippi, Thessalonica, Athens, and Corinth, with return via Ephesus and Palestine to Antioch, A.D. 49–52 (Acts 15:36—18:22)

Journey 3, Paul—

Antioch, Asia Minor with Ephesus as his center, a trip (or trips) to Greece, and a long sea voyage to Palestine, where he was arrested by Jewish opponents at the temple, A.D. 53–57 (Acts 18:23—21:36)

The Journey to Rome—

After two years' imprisonment in Palestine, A.D. 58–59 (Acts 21:37—26:32), ending with "house arrest" in Rome (Acts 27—28). The curtain falls on Paul in Rome about A.D. 60. According to tradition, he was martyred sometime thereafter.

On all these travels Paul exhibited a knack for enlisting other persons in the cause of the gospel. They included those already believers and some who apparently became believers only upon meeting Paul. In the former category were Apollos (Acts 18:24–28; also mentioned at 1 Cor. 3:4–8, 22) and Timothy (Acts 16:1–3). In the latter category were perhaps Priscilla and Aquila (Acts 18:1–4) and Titus (mentioned only in Paul's letters).

Paul kept in touch with his congregations through letters, some of which are preserved in the New Testament. But there must have been a host of other missionaries, not the least important of whom were Stephen and the Hellenists (Greek-speaking Jewish Christians), who challenged an orientation of the Christian message toward Jewish institutions like the temple and the law and insisted on preaching a more radical gospel to Jews and non-Jews alike. In this connection one should read Acts 6:8—

8:1; 8:4–40, and especially 11:19–26, pondering each line and indeed trying to read between the lines.

The net effect of the work of Stephen and the Hellenists and later of Paul was to expand the Jesus movement from a current inside Judaism to a more universal faith. This transition was not without growing pains. Acts 15 describes it in terms of an effort by unnamed men from Judea to impose circumcision and obedience to the law upon Gentiles as a price of salvation. At a "council of Jerusalem," to be dated about A.D. 49, there is hammered out a decision on this issue. At the insistence of James (the brother of Jesus) and Peter, it is agreed that Gentile converts are to abstain from three or four things, but they need not be circumcised or keep the whole law of Moses. Unfortunately, it is difficult to tell what these three or four requirements were (cf. Acts 15:20, 29, and the summary at Acts 21:25).

The matters prohibited here may be taken in a moral sense, as referring to the chief pagan sins, namely, idolatry, immorality, and murder ("blood"), or they may be taken in Old Testament legal terms as "meats offered to idols" (cf. 1 Corinthians 8), "unchastity" in the sense of marriage within forbidden family relationships (see Leviticus 18), and "things strangled" (omitted in some manuscripts) as a synonym for "blood" in the sense of meat not slaughtered according to kosher food regulations.

The mystery deepens when we note that Paul's letters never refer to any such rules or to any "Jerusalem decree," though he does speak of consultation with Jerusalem over whether Gentile converts like Titus must be circumcised (Gal. 2:1–10).

We may suppose that the transition from a fellowship addressing itself to Jews to a church making a worldwide proclamation was no easy step (see further, below, pp. 391–95). But by Paul's day it was happening. After Paul's death came another event destined to accelerate the process of transition, change Judaism immensely, and leave the church mostly Gentile. That event was the fall of Jerusalem to the Roman armies on 10 August (the 9th or 10th of the month Ab, in the Jewish calendar) A.D. 70.

In the late sixties the whole empire had seemingly gone mad. Nero, on the throne, was scarcely sane. It was whispered he had had part of Rome set on fire in order to clear an area for his building projects. There are stories outside the New Testament about how the blame was foisted on the Christians, and persecutions in Rome and Asia Minor followed. Nero's death in A.D. 68 touched off a scramble for the throne, the Roman legions supporting first one candidate, then another. The fateful year of A.D. 69 saw three would-be emperors occupy Rome. The successful survivor was a general, Vespasian, whose armies were laying siege to Jerusalem at the time he took control of the empire.

For years in Palestine there had been fanatic guerrilla groups opposing Rome. In A.D. 66 these began a full-scale revolt which for a time produced a Jewish state and the dream of another Maccabean age. But the Roman legions swept through Galilee, enveloped Qumran, and eventually took Jerusalem. The last Jewish stronghold at Masada fell in 73. This Jewish war is not directly mentioned in the New Testament. Its results, however, became apparent very soon. Jewish Christians were either wiped out in fighting or fled to the east side of the Jordan Valley where they lived on as a kind of archaic relic. The church became more and more Gentile, Judaism lost its temple and its priesthood, and thousands of its people were slain. Henceforth, the synagogue and study of the law, led by the rabbis, were to be the marks of Judaism's community. A council or academy of rabbis at Jamnia in Palestine reconstructed Jewish life along lines that have lasted into the twentieth century. Its message would be the law (*torah*), from God, to be earnestly studied and daily applied.

Christians in the decades after 70 faced problems too. Chief among these were persecution and coming to self-understanding and community identity, especially in relation to reconstructed Judaism, the world, other faiths, and the Roman government. The emperors of this period varied considerably, one from the other. Titus, the conqueror of Jerusalem, succeeded his father, Vespasian, but ruled for only three years (A.D. 79–81). Domitian (81–96) pushed hard on enhancing his own position as more than emperor: he claimed to be a god. The Book of Revelation is a call to Christians to resist his claim to the point of martyrdom. The five "good emperors" who followed him carry us well into the second Christian century, but even under some of them (for example, Trajan) there could be persecution.

The Christian literature of the period after 70 reflects the new needs of the church. There are epistles which deal, at least in part, with persecution situations—1 Peter especially speaks here. The gospels were written, based on earlier materials, to retell the Jesus story to a new generation. The apocalyptic tendencies of the time of Domitian are reflected in the Revelation of St. John. The needs to settle down in the world, live with a variety of neighbors, get along with government, and develop church structures appear in Christian writings of the period. If Christianity were to be meaningful, it had to be at home in the shops, forum, offices, and petty details of life where people were living.

Gradually a transition was made from the apostolic age to the subapostolic period and to the time of the Apologists and of the church fathers. (The Apologists were well-educated Greek Christians who wrote defenses of the faith to Roman emperors. The term "church fathers" is often used to describe writers and theologians of the patristic period, the second Christian century and beyond.) This transition was gradual, not abrupt. One cannot exactly date such periods. An apostolic father like Clement of Rome can write a letter about A.D. 96 which does *not* get included in the canon. A writing attributed to St. Peter may be written as late as A.D. 150, yet 2 Peter is eventually included in the official canonical list.

History continued apace too. There were more Jewish revolts, in North Africa A.D. 115–17, and a last big one in Palestine in 132–35, under a military leader, Simon bar Kochba, and a rabbi, Akiba. Movements from the Gentile world continued too, some of which threatened Christianity. One such movement was called Gnosticism; it placed an emphasis upon knowledge (saving knowledge at that) that came by occult revelation. There were also radical internal developments within Christianity, such as Marcion's attempt to create a canon consisting only of one Gospel, Luke's (expurgated, to be sure), and a shrunken collection of Paul's letters. Marcion cast aside the entire Old Testament as the product of an unworthy religion and a god inferior to Jesus Christ. Marcion wanted to be more christocentric than God's revelation had been.

THE GOSPEL AND SALVATION HISTORY

In all this development what was at stake—and served as lodestar and guide—was the gospel itself, in its many forms. The fact that there was good news in the Old Testament, then Jesus' announcement of the king-dom, Paul's message about how God justifies sinners, plus Second Isaiah and Revelation announcing hope—all this and more kept the Christian community on the proper course, but with that flexibility and openness that following God in a changing world demands. The task remained, through the decades and the centuries, to discover the Promise, God, and the promise as good news.

To see the unity of Scripture amid its rich diversity, perhaps nothing better can be done than to seek for the various forms the gospel has taken in Scripture, or to trace the Promise, God, amid the biblical promises. But students of the Bible have for centuries attempted to spell out an overall unity of theme in this book in other ways. Many of these take the form of attempting to trace "the history of salvation."

One way of presenting salvation history is to set forth chronologically different "ages" in God's plan, according to the biblical witness. This is a perfectly possible method, though it can run the danger of separating these ages into rigid and even conflicting "dispensations" or schemes of salvation. Or it can be done in terms of "the scope of grace" and the size of the group on whom God's gospel focuses at a given time or with whom it is concerned—the patriarchs and their families; Israel; the southern kingdom of Judah; the remnant of true believers; or the elect Christian community; or humanity in its entirety. One widely held view may be diagrammed as follows (reflecting the writings of Oscar Cullmann):[2]

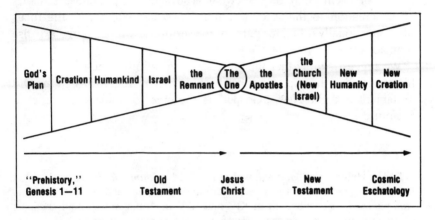

| God's Plan | Creation | Humankind | Israel | the Remnant | The One | the Apostles | the Church (New Israel) | New Humanity | New Creation |

| "Prehistory," Genesis 1—11 | Old Testament | Jesus Christ | New Testament | Cosmic Eschatology |

Others have sought to pick out the seven decisive events in the Bible, as if we were dealing with "The Seven Wonders of the World." One list runs,[3]

Eden, the Flood, Covenant with Abraham, Exodus, Exile,
Christ, and the Parousia ("coming again").

Note that two of these fall into "prehistory," one is "beyond history," three are in the Old Testament, and one in the New, a broad "Christ-event," which surely needs further elucidation.

Still others opt for a briefer list, often more alliterative: Creation, Covenant, Christ, Church, and Consummation.[4] Or shorter still: Sinai, the Savior, the Spirit (as if there were three ages, one for each person of the Trinity).

Still another method is to try to depict the Bible story as a drama, with its acts and scenes played out on the Bible's pages.[5] Another variation is to find a history of three types of institutions: those in general history, those in Israel, and finally, the church.

All of these designs are attempts to secure unity. They may help the reader to see sequence in the Bible, where at first glance no sequence appears. They conform to P. T. Forsyth's dictum, "The analysis of the Bible must serve the history of Grace."[6]

But grace is primarily a Pauline term. Church history shows that it has often all too easily been institutionalized. Any salvation history that treats redemption in institutional terms runs the risk of overemphasizing the structural-and-machinery side of the church, just as any that ends with an "age of the Holy Spirit" as the climax suffers from the likelihood of becoming too "spiritual" and anti-institutional. A list of (seven) people, places, or events may be somewhat arbitrary, and grandiose schemes "from creation to the second coming" may serve to throw the focus disproportionally on minor parts of the scriptural witness at the expense of major ones.

We suggest simply that the "history of salvation" is best viewed as a history of what the good news has been, in its concrete forms, in the Old Testament and the New. "Gospel" is the clue for understanding even Scripture.

NOTES

1. The Hebrew for "God with us" at Isa. 7:14 is *'immānû'ēl;* hence, RSV has "Immanuel" there. But the Greek transliteration there and at Matt. 1:23 is *"Emmanouēl,"* transliterated in KJV and RSV as "Emmanuel." Both spellings continue to this day, as in the names for churches: two parishes in Philadelphia are distinguished among pastors and others as "Eye-manuel" and "Eee-manuel."

2. O. Cullmann, *Christ and Time: The Primitive Christian Conception of Time and History,* trans. F. V. Filson, rev. ed. (Philadelphia: Westminster Press, 1964), esp. 83; and *Salvation in History,* trans. S. G. Sowers et al. (New York: Harper & Row, 1967).

3. Eric H. Wahlstrom, *God Who Redeems: Perspectives in Biblical Theology* (Philadelphia: Muhlenberg Press, 1962).

4. Randolph Crump Miller, *Biblical Theology and Christian Education* (New York: Charles Scribner's Sons, 1956).

5. For example, Bernhard W. Anderson, *The Unfolding Drama of the Bible* (New York: Association Press, 1953).

6. In the *Contemporary Review* (October 1905): 579. as cited in A. M. Hunter, *Teaching and Preaching the New Testament* (London: SCM Press, 1963), 148.

II
THE GOOD NEWS
JESUS PREACHED

Galilee, where Jesus' ministry began, stretches westward from the Sea of Galilee. This scene, near Capernaum, shows stony ground and good soil, as in the parable of the Sower (Mark 4:3–8).

6

The Message:
"Jesus Came Preaching
the Gospel of God"

W E HAVE ALREADY EXPLORED "the beginning of the gospel," as set forth by Mark, in the preaching and work of Jesus (see " 'The Beginning of the Gospel'—Getting Started with the Bible's Witness to the Word"). Having gained an overview (in part 1) of what the Bible is—viewed theologically, as word of God, and historically as seen by modern scholarship; as a book of good news, yet set against a background of sin and the constant bad news that comes from sinning and God's judgment; and its broad sweep as a story of Israel, Jesus, and the church, where gospel is proclaimed—we are now ready to delve into the history of the gospel in Scripture, in all of its grandeur and in some of its detail.

We here begin our story with the historical Jesus, looking at the good news in his message (chap. 6) and ministry (chap. 7). That gospel of Jesus will both drive us back to the Old Testament (parts 3–5) and propel us forward into the New Testament (part 6). As we seek to trace out the story of the historical Jesus, we shall find that each Synoptic evangelist tells of the beginnings of the Jesus gospel enough in his own way that we shall sense the flexibility, as well as the unity, of the biblical records. For when we ask, successively of Mark, Matthew, and Luke, how one starts to tell the story of Jesus and the kingdom message that he preached, we can expect to find a solid common core of preaching about God, but also a variety of narrative methods. These differences reflect the situations of the evangelists and are pointers to the full riches of scriptural witness.

BEGINNING THE GOOD NEWS IN MARK

Mark begins his good news about Jesus with a prologue (Mark 1:1–15) that is as significant, in its own way, as the more famous prologue in the Gospel of John. True, Mark lacks John's imagery about Jesus as the Word who was "with God" and came into the world, becoming flesh, and who "dwelt among us" (John 1:1–18). For Mark chooses to talk solely in terms of Jesus' life from the time he journeyed from Nazareth in Galilee to be baptized by John the Baptist in the Jordan River, thus fulfilling what Old Testament prophets had pointed toward. Mark does not deal with any earlier period, either of Jesus' conception and nativity (as Matthew 1—2 and Luke 1—2) or of when Jesus was "with God" (John 1:1–4). But Mark does emphatically agree with John that no one has made known, as Jesus did, God the Father (John 1:18)— or God's kingdom. Jesus himself thus wraps up in his own message and person the "good news" of and from God.

Mark's "prologue" can be analyzed as follows:

1. Verse 1, if taken by itself as in RSV, is a kind of title, "The beginning of the gospel of Jesus Christ, the Son of God." (The phrase "the Son of God" is present in many, but not all, manuscripts.)

2. There follows a brief preface about John the Baptist, who prepares the way by his preaching and the strange rite of "a baptism of repentance for the forgiveness of sins" (1:2–8). Verses 2–3 quote the Old Testament Scriptures that John's appearance fulfills:

Behold, I send my messenger to prepare the way. . . . (Mal. 3:1)
A voice cries:
"In the wilderness prepare the way of the Lord,
make straight in the desert a highway for our God." (Isa. 40:3)

Verse 4 presents John briefly; v. 6 describes him; vv. 7–8 summarize his message about a mightier successor to come. The tremendous response of the people is indicated in v. 5.

3. Verses 9–11 recount the baptism of Jesus by John, with heaven itself bearing witness (to Jesus) that the man from Nazareth is God's "Son."

4. A brief account of the temptation of Jesus by Satan follows (vv. 12–13). Not mentioned are the three specific temptations which we know from the other Synoptic Gospels (Matt. 4:1–11; Luke 4:1–13). Mark mentions only that Jesus, with the help of heaven (angels), is victorious, besting Satan. Jesus subsequently goes on into Galilee to begin his ministry.

5. Then comes, in vv. 14–15, the summary of his message about the kingdom—about God's rule—as the gospel of God. These two verses should be understood, not as "episode one" in Jesus' public ministry, but as the climax of Mark's prologue and a thematic summation that stands over all that Jesus says and does in the entire book by Mark.

Mark's prologue is not sufficient to answer all our modern questions, or even the queries of Christians in ancient times; that is why Matthew and Luke, to say nothing of John, will begin their witness to Jesus differently. Mark, for example, does not tell us much about John the Baptist (the account of his death is postponed until 6:14–29; his significance will be taken up only at 9:13). Mark's Gospel is scant on details and prompts questions that Mark himself may not even have considered, such as, "If John practiced a 'baptism for the forgiveness of sins,' was Jesus a sinner in that he allowed himself to be baptized?" Mark is interested preeminently in telling us who Jesus is, and his answer is simple and direct: Jesus is the one to whom Scripture points, attested by the Baptist and by heaven itself, who has bested and will defeat at every turn Satan the tempter. Jesus' message is to be heard and heeded.

It is attractive to link vv. 1 and 14–15: "The beginning of the gospel . . ." occurs therefore when "Jesus came into Galilee, preaching . . . , 'the kingdom of God is at hand. . . .' " There is a sense in which there was "gospel" before Jesus, in the Old Testament (cf. Gal. 3:8). There is a sense in which, we shall want to say later, the gospel begins with Jesus' resurrection from the dead and enthronement as Lord (what might be called the "Easter Gospel"). But for Mark, the good news seems linked with Jesus' proclamation of God's kingship during glad days in Galilee.

A different approach in interpreting the beginning of Mark is to link vv. 1 and 4, taking 2–3 as parenthetical (au. trans.): "The beginning of the gospel of Jesus Christ, the Son of God (just as it is written in Isaiah . . .) was John the Baptist, preaching in the wilderness. . . ." This would make John the Baptist "the beginning of the gospel." Or one can push the beginning back another step, to fulfillment of the Old Testament, as J. B. Phillips does, by linking v. 1 with vv. 2–3: "The Gospel of Jesus Christ, the Son of God, begins with the fulfillment of this prophecy of Isaiah—. . . ." Or one can refer "the Beginning of the Gospel" to the entire book as a title, that is, through Mark 16:8. This title, as in the RSV, then refers to what is sometimes called the whole "Christ-event."

All this is to suggest that the very real question of where the gospel begins is already posed for us by the opening verses of Mark. We shall have to return to this topic, by asking more precisely what "gospel" means, throughout our study of Scripture.

Whatever exactly its "beginning" may be, "the gospel of God" is spelled out very precisely by Mark in the four-line message of Jesus. The chronological peg is the arrest of John the Baptist; Jesus is now "on stage" alone. The date: about A.D. 29; the place: the villages, cities, and countryside of Galilee. Jesus came "preaching." The verb in Greek suggests what is a technical term in other parts of the New Testament: *kerygma* or "proclamation." Jesus' kerygma here is the "gospel of God," which can convey the idea of "good news *about* God" or "good news *from* God." It is likely that Jesus' message combines both aspects. It is a message with God as its source and its content.

But what does Jesus say about God?

The first line of his message has to do with time: "Fulfilled has been the *kairos*" (au. trans.; we translate it literally, and transliterate the final Greek word, in order to get at a point over which translators have struggled). It suggests, "The time has come at last" (Phillips; *Living Bible*); "the time is fulfilled" (KJV). "Time" (*kairos*) here means not a period or moment, chronologically (Greek has another word for that kind of time, namely, *chronos*), but a significant point, a turning point, in the plan of God. Jesus' appearance with this message about the kingdom is a turning point, what might be called a "kairotic moment," in the program of salvation from God. (Paul once speaks about the sending of God's Son as "the fullness of time" (*chronos*) in Gal. 4:4, and he knew well the importance of "times and seasons" [literally, *chronoi* and *kairoi*], 1 Thess. 5:1.) In God's time scale, it is striking midnight as Jesus speaks. A new dawn is coming.

The big news is that "the kingdom of God is at hand." God's kingly, sovereign rule is meant. It is an Old Testament theme, the full import of which will be developed in subsequent chapters of this Bible study. It suffices to say here that the phrase means "God is/was/and will be king." God reigns. It has to do more with the *fact* of God's reigning, that is, with God's *kingship,* than it has to do with a territorial *kingdom*—his "reign" rather than his realm. To talk of God's kingly rule was not new. What was startling was Jesus' assertion that the kingly rule now "is at hand"!

The exact meaning of the Greek verb usually translated "to be at hand" is much debated. Does it mean "be near" (but not yet here, as in *The Living Bible*), or that the kingdom may "be upon you already" (as in the NEB)? The exact translation cannot be determined by examination of the Greek word here alone (or the Aramaic behind it, which Jesus may have used). It must be worked out in harmony with other statements of Jesus about the nearness of the kingdom. This we shall do in the next chapter.

Let it be noted at this point that Jesus himself seems to have looked upon God's kingship both as already present during his own ministry, *and* as a power to come. Mark, in 1:15, by presenting the point about the kingdom in parallel with the line about time being fulfilled, seems to be implying for his day and readers that the kingdom is indeed here:

The Jordan Valley (aerial photo, looking south). The river meanders from the Sea of Galilee to the Dead Sea (top of picture), watering the arid "wilderness of Judea." John ministered here.

Fulfilled has been the time,
the kingdom of God has arrived. (au. trans.)

From this (more literal) rendering, the implication is clear: the *kairos* is fulfilled precisely *because* the kingdom has appeared.

Such momentous good news leads, as always in the Bible, to consequences. Because of this fulfillment and the coming of the kingdom, you, the hearer, are to (1) repent and (2) believe in the gospel. Both verbs—"repent," "believe"—are in what is grammatically termed the imperative mood, the form employed to give orders and commands. But theologically one must observe the careful sequence in these lines: first comes a statement of what God has done or is doing; then comes the demand. Here the kerygma comes first, saying that God is fulfilling the times and bringing to pass a "kairotic moment" in his plan; the kingdom is being ushered in. The verbs there—"is fulfilled," "is at hand"—are in the indicative mood, as a statement of fact and reality. Then comes the imperative, "Repent! Believe!" This sequence of "indicative-imperative" is a hallmark of biblical thought in both testaments. Whether in the Pentateuch or Paul, Scripture will often first present what God does for us; then it will call for our faithful response.

"Repent" in Mark 1:15 conjures up a command given to God's people by the Hebrew prophets. It means "Turn around, in a new direction, away from the wrong you have been doing." The verb was common in the Dead Sea Scrolls, and John the Baptist used it too (Mark 1:4). It is a necessary part of new beginnings and of daily reorientation when we go astray. The preachers in the early church liked to close their evangelistic sermons with the call to repent:

> *Repent,* and be baptized every one of you in the name of Jesus Christ for the forgiveness of your sins. . . . (Acts 2:38)

> *Repent* therefore, and *turn* again, that your sins may be blotted out, that times of refreshing may come from the presence of the Lord. . . . (Acts 3:19)

Jesus' own disciples "preached that men should repent" (Mark 6:12). But, perhaps significantly, Jesus himself spoke comparatively little of repentance. This is especially true in Mark, who has no occurrences of the word beyond those already noted. Where Mark 2:17 has "I came not to call the righteous, but sinners," it is only Luke, at 5:32, who adds "to repentance."

All this suggests that Mark has employed "repent!" as an apt imperative in this summary of Jesus' preaching (Mark 1:14–15), but that the emphasis properly is on the other term, "believe." "Have faith" "or "just

The Message

believe" are phrases which Jesus used, and he often said, "Your faith has made you well" (5:34; 10:52; cf. 2:5). Paul's doctrine of justification by faith alone (or being set right with God by faith) is close to Jesus' counsel at Mark 5:36:

> Jesus said to the ruler of the synagogue, "Do not fear, *only believe.*" (Mark 5:36b)

> We hold that a man is justified by faith apart from works of law. (Rom. 3:28)

> You stand fast only through faith. (Rom. 11:20)

Here it is significant that the object of faith is—the gospel. "Believe in the gospel." This concluding phrase of Mark 1:15 points us back to Mark 1:1, and, in turn, to the entire volume by Mark, centering in Jesus' proclamation of the kingdom of God.

Thus does Jesus' ministry begin in Mark with an urgent summary of his message: fulfillment (of God's past promises); the in-breaking of God's ancient kingship, so long sought on earth; and the demand to shape one's life and faith accordingly. Over it all stands the motto: the gospel is beginning.

BEGINNING THE GOSPEL STORY
IN MATTHEW

Mark's pioneer way of beginning to tell the gospel story of Jesus is so impressive that one is almost surprised that any other approach could have developed in the early church. But different situations demand different ways of putting the same truths and even an emphasis on other points.

Matthew's Gospel, it is widely agreed, was composed a decade or two after Mark's, when the times had changed. Jerusalem was in ashes now, destroyed by Roman armies in A.D. 70. Jews were no longer the only target for Christian evangelism (though many Jewish Christians, often in the Jewish ghettoes of eastern Mediterranean cities, continued their faith in Jesus as Messiah). More and more Gentiles were now being attracted into the church, but not without the danger that they would fail to be assimilated to the Old Testament heritage and that they would fail to live up to the imperatives of following Jesus as disciples. They might lose their biblical roots. It was to fit needs in such a situation that the Gospel According to Matthew, as we call it, was put together as a guide and study book for believers.

How did Matthew begin his gospel story of Jesus?

The opening genealogy (Matt. 1:1–17) may bore modern readers, but for Matthew's audience it was a striking opening, legitimating Jesus' role as "Christ, the son of David, the son of Abraham" (1:1). The nativity material (1:18—2:23) charms us, but we perhaps miss the sense it had for ancient readers, as it told who Jesus was (nothing less than "Emmanuel," "God with us," 1:23, who fulfills scriptural prophecy, 1:22; 2:5, 14, 17, 23). Then follows, as in Mark, material about John the Baptist, augmented from other sources. Included, for example, is an effort to show that Jesus' baptism was not necessary because of any sinfulness on Jesus' part but rather because it was a part of God's righteous plan (Matt. 3:14—15). Then, after a temptation account (much fuller in Matthew than in Mark), Matthew presents his parallel to Mark 1:14—15.

It should not surprise us that Matthew's development of how and what Jesus began to preach is longer and a bit different from the summary in Mark. Matthew begins (4:12), "Now when he [Jesus] heard that John had been arrested, he withdrew into Galilee." We can recognize this as Mark 1:14 slightly rewritten. For example, the verb "withdraw" is a favorite Matthean expression, appearing—with varying translations into English—in 2:12, 13, 14, 22; 9:24; 12:15; 14:13; and 15:21. Also, Matthew's version is a bit different from Mark's when Matthew goes on, "and leaving Nazareth he [Jesus] went and dwelt in Capernaum by the sea, in the territory of Zebulun and Naphtali" (4:13). But it is possible to account for these additions.

Whereas Mark merely mentioned that Jesus had gone from Nazareth to be baptized, Matthew has previously, in the chapters about Jesus' childhood, described how, after the flight into Egypt to escape from Herod the Great, Jesus and his parents returned to Palestine. Joseph, to avoid the power of Herod's son, Archelaus, withdrew to Galilee and "went and dwelt in a city called Nazareth" (Matt. 2:23). But now (4:13) Matthew portrays Jesus "leaving Nazareth," in order to dwell in Capernaum, by the Sea of Galilee. Capernaum becomes the center for Jesus' Galilean ministry (Mark 1:21; 2:1). But Matthew sees a particular significance in this move to Capernaum, which will henceforth be "headquarters," except for a single, unsuccessful visit back to Nazareth (Mark 6:1—6; Matt. 13:54—58).

Matthew 4:14—16 presents us with a favorite Matthean device: a quotation from the Old Testament, introduced by a stock formula that can be summed up thus: "(This happened) in order that it might be fulfilled which was spoken (by the prophet), saying. . . ." (See also 1:22; 2:5, 15, 17, 23; 12:17; 26:54; and 27:9, among other passages.) It is Matthew's way of making explicit the idea that Jesus fulfills Scripture.

Here the quotation which follows the formula comes from Isa. 9:1–2. Jesus relocated in Capernaum

> that what was spoken by the prophet Isaiah might be fulfilled:
> "The *land of Zebulun and the land of Naphtali,*
> *toward the sea,* across the Jordan, Galilee of the Gentiles—
> the people who sat in darkness have seen a great light,
> and for those who sat in the region and shadow of death light has dawned."
> (4:15–16, citing a version of Isa. 9:1–2)

This quotation explains why Matthew, in v. 13, has described Capernaum as "by the sea" and "in the territory of Zebulun and Naphtali" (even though, by the time Matthew wrote, these two tribes of whom Isaiah had spoken eight hundred years earlier had long since been scattered by the Assyrian invasion of that time). The phrases fit Matthew's description of Jesus and the center for his ministry.

But Matthew's application has some further subtleties. When he says "the people who sat in darkness [and] death" have "seen *a great light,*" he is understanding Jesus as "the light" who has "dawned" on them. This christological assertion about Jesus is only a step removed from the great claim made at John 8:12 when Jesus says "*I* am the light," not just of Galilee, but "of the world." We may also guess that Isaiah's passing reference to "Galilee *of the Gentiles,*" which originally was a description of the area as "the circuit of the nations," attracted Matthew as a pointer toward the fact that Jesus' message must eventually go to "all nations" (Matt. 28:19). (The word for "Gentiles" is the same in Greek as that for "nations"; cf. Isa. 9:2, RSV.) It fits Matthew's interest in the evangelization of the Gentiles.

Only now comes Matthew's summary of Jesus' proclamation. When 4:17 says,

> From that time Jesus began to preach, saying
> "Repent, for the kingdom of heaven is at hand,"

it might seem that we have a casual introductory phrase. In actuality, it is planned to balance very carefully a similar sentence at 16:21,

> From that time Jesus began to show his disciples
> that he must go to Jerusalem and suffer many things.

The turning point in time at 4:17 inaugurates Jesus' public ministry, when he went about teaching great things openly, teaching, preaching, and healing (4:23; 9:35). According to Matthew's careful outline, 16:21 introduces Jesus' private ministry to the twelve disciples, teaching about the passion. The section 4:17—16:20 deals especially with the kingdom; the contents 16:21—28:20 concern the events of Jesus' death and resurrection. And, we may add, 1:1—4:16 are introductory, for the whole gospel.

Finally, Jesus' message, according to Matthew, can be summarized in two thoughts, not four:

Repent,
for the kingdom of heaven is at hand.
(Matt. 4:17b)

"Kingdom of heaven" is a Jewish way of speaking about the "kingdom of God" so as to avoid using the sacred name, the four-letter Hebrew term *Y-H-W-H,* for the Deity. Matthew especially prefers "kingdom *of heaven*." Jesus himself could have used either term, or both.

Note something seemingly in contrast with what we saw above in Mark (pp. 100–101). There we noted how "indicative" comes before "imperative." Here, in Matthew, the imperative ("Repent") comes before the indicative ("the kingdom . . . is at hand"). A stress on imperatives (here, by putting "Repent" first) will be characteristic of Matthew, to emphasize Jesus' commands for converts who might otherwise seek to avoid all the Lord's imperatives. But any change in the indicative-imperative sequence is only apparent, not real, since Matthew has connected his imperative-indicative sequence with the word "for"; the reason one repents is *because* the kingdom is at hand.

It may also have caught the attention of readers that in Matthew the message of Jesus has appeared earlier, on the lips of a predecessor: John the Baptist came preaching, "Repent, for the kingdom of heaven is at hand" (Matt. 3:2). Thus Matthew calls attention to a continuity between John and Jesus. This continuity is carried still further when Jesus' disciples speak the same message during Jesus' ministry (Matt. 10:7). We see here a favorite Matthean emphasis: the continuity which connects God's spokespersons of the past (like John) with Jesus and with Jesus' disciples.

Continuity, Christology, Old Testament fulfillment more precisely described, a stress on the imperatives—such are some of Matthew's particular nuances, as he begins to tell the story of Jesus.

BEGINNING THE GOSPEL HISTORY
IN LUKE

Luke proves to be, by far, the most different of the first three Gospels in portraying the beginning of Jesus' ministry. (We concentrate here only on the "Synoptic" Gospels—Mark, Matthew, and Luke—which agree in so many ways in giving an overall view of Jesus' career, when printed side by side and examined together. John differs in so many ways that we shall treat the witness of the Fourth Gospel later, in chap. 30, though it is witness to the same Lord.)

And why should not Luke differ from Mark and Matthew? Luke wrote, literally, for a very different world. It is not so much that Luke's Gospel was composed at a later date than Matthew's, though Luke probably is to be dated a bit later. It is rather that he wrote much more for Gentiles. Jewish Christianity was for him no longer significant. Then, too, some of his sources differed, and his writing style showed the polish needed for a Greek audience of some education (compare his preface, Luke 1:1–4). Moreover, he was able to plan and write a second volume, which we call "The Acts of the Apostles," showing in it how "the word of the Lord grew" and moved forward in the early church:

> And the word of God increased; and the number of the disciples multiplied greatly in Jerusalem, and a great many of the priests were obedient to the faith. (Acts 6:7)

> So the church throughout all Judea and Galilee and Samaria had peace and was built up; and walking in the fear of the Lord and in the comfort of the Holy Spirit it was multiplied. (Acts 9:31)

> So the churches were strengthened in the faith, and they increased in numbers daily. (Acts 16:5)

See also Acts 2:41; 12:24; and 19:20. Such factors as this orientation toward the Gentile world and a concern with the growth of the church were already at work in the way Luke tells of the beginnings of Jesus' public ministry.

Luke, as remarked, begins with a preface (Luke 1:1–4; cf. Acts 1:1) such as a Hellenistic-Roman historian might employ. Then comes the infancy material (chaps. 1—2), written in a style akin to the Old Testament Scriptures, not so much in their original Hebrew form as in the translated Greek version. All of Luke's material about John the Baptist is concentrated in a single section, 3:1–20, including a reference to his arrest and imprisonment (3:20), so that Jesus' baptism is described as if John were not even there (3:20–21)! (Is that Luke's way of avoiding any embarrassing implications in Mark's baptismal story?) Luke's genealogy traces Jesus back not just to Abraham (Matt. 1:2) but to Adam, "the son of God" (3:38), the progenitor of all humanity.

After a temptation account that is quite similar to Matthew's (Luke 4:1–13; Matt. 4:1–11), Luke presents his parallel to Mark 1:14–15, about how the public ministry began. It begins similarly enough, but

Luke soon moves into his own distinctive paths. Luke 4:14–15 tells how Jesus, after the baptism, returned to Galilee:

> And Jesus returned in the power of the Spirit into Galilee, and a report concerning him went out through all the surrounding country. And he taught in their synagogues, being glorified by all.

The phrase "in the power of the Spirit" captures a typical Lukan emphasis. Luke's is often called "the Gospel of the Spirit." Luke, at 1:35, has described the role of the Spirit in Jesus' conception; at 3:22, how the Spirit descended "in bodily form" on Jesus at his baptism; and at 4:1, how Jesus was therefore "full of the Holy Spirit."

While there is added emphasis on the Spirit, Luke, though following Mark 1:14–15, omits any summary of Jesus' proclamation. There is no mention of repentance, or of the kingdom, or of the gospel of God. Luke is content to say that "a report concerning him went out. . . ." The reference to his "being glorified by all" again presents a favorite phrase in Luke (cf. 7:16; 13:13; 17:15; 18:43). The reference to *"their* synagogues" seems to distinguish the meeting houses of the Jews from "our synagogues" (those of Christians), as if there has been a break between the two by the time Luke writes.

The key word is that Jesus "taught." But what? Explicit reference to "the kingdom" is postponed until 4:43, where Jesus says "I must preach the good news of the kingdom of God to the other cities also; for I was sent for this purpose." Luke, we shall see, relates Jesus' preaching about the kingdom to a broader theme, "good news" or "gospel."

Accordingly, the key scene that sets forth Jesus' message in Luke and anticipates many perspectives in Luke's Gospel and the Book of Acts is the one which follows, 4:16–30, when Jesus returns to his home town and is thrown out of the synagogue at Nazareth—but not until after he has had something to say.

It might be admitted at the outset that Luke here differs radically from Mark and Matthew, who portray the Nazareth rejection scene only later, well along into the Galilean ministry (Mark 6:1–6; par. Matt. 13:54–58). Luke presents it at the outset of the Galilean ministry, as a kind of dramatic frontispiece. Some scholars have suggested that Luke had a special source at his disposal here, others that he has combined several journeys back to Nazareth into one account.

In any case, 4:16 depicts Jesus attending synagogue at Nazareth on the Sabbath. When it came time to read the lessons, he did what any layman or teacher had the right in Judaism to do, namely, read one of them. It is not clear whether "he found the place" (4:17) means the place *he* selected or the lesson *appointed* for the day in the lectionary system. The Scripture quoted (4:18–19) combines Isa. 61:1–2 and 58:6. After reading about someone on whom the Spirit of God rests and about the functions of a figure like "the servant of the Lord" who is mentioned earlier in Isaiah, Jesus' sole comment is, *"Today* this scripture has been *fulfilled* in your hearing" (Luke 4:21). The people are impressed; they wonder at his "gracious words," since they know him only as "Joseph's son" (v. 22).

Jesus responds to their proverb ("Physician, heal yourself," v. 23) in light of the expectation that people in Nazareth will demand the same miracles of him as those done at Capernaum. Hence the trenchant statement, so true in Jesus' case, "No prophet is acceptable in his own country" (v. 24). (Luke, seemingly, has "painted himself into a corner" here: in Mark and Matthew, by the time the rejection at Nazareth is described, several miracles during Jesus' ministry at Capernaum have been presented; Luke has depicted none of these as yet. But Luke "covers" the situation by making it a prophecy of *future* happenings— "Doubtless you *will* quote to me this proverb. . . .")

The Nazarenes do expect miracles. Jesus picks up their challenge by reminding them in almost poetic fashion that, in God's past dealings, miracles were sometimes reserved for Gentiles, not Israelites (4:25–27):

In truth, I tell you, [a solemn form of assertion; cf. also v. 24] there were many widows in Israel in the days of Elijah,
> when the heaven was shut up three years and six months,
> when there came a great famine over all the land;
>>>>>> (1 Kings 17:1; 18:1–2)

and Elijah was sent to none of them
> but only to Zarephath, *in the land of Sidon,*
> to a woman who was a widow.
>>>>>> (1 Kings 17:8–9)

And there were many lepers in Israel in the time of the prophet Elisha;
> and none of them was cleansed,
> but only Namaan *the Syrian.*
>>>>>> (2 Kings 5:14)

The implication was that God's new miracles through Jesus might be for Gentiles and not just Nazarenes. So the people "were filled with wrath." They sought to kill Jesus, but he escaped (4:28–30).

How shall we assess this moving scene with which Luke begins his account of Jesus' public ministry? We shall not here deal much with details of setting, such as the fact that in Luke Jesus moves from Capernaum to Nazareth, while in Matthew he moves from Nazareth to Capernaum at the onset of his ministry. A theological interpretation of the Matthean detail has been suggested above (pp. 102–3). Luke's account, as noted, may likewise focus on a theological point, rejection at home as a pointer to a ministry later far beyond, even among Gentiles, through Jesus' disciples and their preaching of his word.

For the Lukan passage at hand, there are all sorts of fascinating interpretations. One, for example, holds that what Mark and Matthew have as a "rejection scene" has been made here by Luke into a "success story" (though it really is not). Another interpretation is that Jesus was a success at Nazareth until he refused to go the route of doing miracles as the townspeople desired. Or, more ingeniously, it has been argued that what bothered the Nazarenes was the way Jesus read the Scriptures. He ended with Isa. 61:2a, ". . . to proclaim the acceptable year of the Lord" (Luke 4:19), but they were waiting for him to go on beyond these "gracious words" (or words about God's grace, Luke 4:22) to Isa. 61:2b, about "the day of vengeance of our God" (see below, pp. 178–79) against their enemies. Then Luke 4:22 could be interpreted, "They all protested with one voice *against* him and were furious because he spoke *only* about grace and omitted vengeance." But such a reading depends on so many conjectures that it is not persuasive.

Most of these interpretations see the words from Isaiah as a key. There is something to the point that Isaiah speaks of "the *acceptable* year of the Lord" (Isa. 61:2 = Luke 4:19) and Jesus refers to a prophet "*acceptable* [to God]" at 4:24. We have thus the suggestion that Jesus was speaking of the Old Testament "year of Jubilee," when by God's decree everything changes and life is made new, to begin again. According to the law, estates are to be broken up; ancestral lands returned; those who had sold themselves into slavery, to be set free; the whole agricultural-economic system is given shock therapy, at the fiftieth or Jubilee year:

> You shall hallow the fiftieth year, and proclaim liberty throughout the land to all its inhabitants; it shall be a jubilee for you, when each of you shall return to his property. . . . The land shall not be sold in perpetuity, for the land is mine. . . ." (Lev. 25:10, 23—and generally throughout chap. 25, esp. 25:39–41)

But no doubt the most impressive aspect of this Lukan introduction to Jesus' public ministry is the manner in which literally every line of the Isaiah quotation applies to Jesus as portrayed in Luke's Gospel. (The italics are added below in the following phrases from Isaiah to facilitate comparisons with Luke's contents.)

"The *Spirit* of the Lord is upon me"—cf. Luke 3:22 at the baptism, and 4:1, 14.

"He has *anointed* me"—the verb "anoint" is from the same root that gives us the term "anointed one," Greek *Christos* (or Christ), Hebrew *Messiah*. The implication is that God, *not* John the Baptist, has anointed Jesus. See also, in Luke's second volume, Acts 4:27, about "... thy holy servant [or child] Jesus, whom thou didst anoint ..."; and Acts 10:38, "God anointed Jesus of Nazareth with the Holy Spirit. ..."

"... to *preach good news to the poor*"—to "proclaim gospel" is a favorite Lukan term (see also 4:43; 8:1; 9:6; 20:1; Acts 10:36). Concern for "the poor" is characteristic of his writings (Luke 6:20, contrast 24; 14:13, 21; 16:19–31).

"He has *sent* me [see also 4:43b] to proclaim *release* to the *captives*—here is a reference to the Jubilee idea. The Greek is very vivid: to preach a "kerygma" of "release" or "forgiveness." The word thus translated as "release" in Luke 4:18 is the same as that regularly employed in sermons in the Book of Acts for the "forgiveness of sins" which the gospel offers. One example:

> God exalted him [Jesus] at his right hand as Leader and Savior, to give repentance to Israel and *forgiveness* of sins. (Acts 5:31)

(Other examples in Acts at 2:38; 10:43; 13:38; and 26:18.)

Returning to Luke 4:18, we note that this "release" is "to the captives." These "captives" seem to be those in captivity to sin and Satan; compare Luke 13:16, "a daughter of Abraham whom Satan bound for eighteen years."

"... and recovering of *sight* to the *blind* ..."—Luke will recount healings of the literally blind (18:35–43), but there may also be here the implication of those spiritually blinded.

"... to set at *liberty* those who are *oppressed*, and to proclaim the *acceptable year of the Lord*. ..."—It is Jubilee time, that is, "salvation time," when Jesus comes. It is a "theology of liberation" from Satan and sin. A verse in one of Isaac Watts's hymns in 1719, drawing on Psalm 72, connected this with a scriptural vision of the kingdom, when Jesus' universal reign is realized:

> Blessings abound where'er he reigns;
> The pris'ners leap to lose [not "loose"; God does it!] their chains,
> The weary find eternal rest,
> And all the sons of want are blest.

Luke has here achieved, in dramatic style, in a way far different from Matthew's "formula quotations" or Mark's brief references to "fulfillment," a detailed picture of how Old Testament Scripture and Jesus fit together. This "fulfillment" he finds in that unique period which Luke calls "today," that is, that period when Jesus was here on earth, from his birth to his ascension. That was "Jubilee time" such as humanity had never before known.

Yet in this same scene Luke is foreshadowing Jesus' rejection by Israel, his passion (cf. 4:28–29), his resurrection triumph (v. 30), and the fact that the gospel must go to non-Jews, the Gentiles, as the later volume, Acts, will describe.

Most of all, we may note, Luke has thus presented the beginnings of Jesus' ministry without, in these particular verses, using the term "kingdom." "Good news" or gospel (4:18) is the overarching theme. "Gospel" could take the form of Old Testament assertions in Isaiah and their reiteration in Jesus' life and Luke's own day. Yet "kingdom" was the way in which, as even Luke later shows (4:43), the historical Jesus set forth God's good news.

What was Jesus' "kingdom" theme all about?

7

Jesus' Ministry:
The Gospel
of the Kingdom

JESUS' MESSAGE AND MINISTRY centered in the kingdom (kingship) of God (or "of heaven"). To realize this is no small insight. For to be aware that there is this central, unifying theme corrects the impression held by all too many people, who have only a sporadic, hit-or-miss idea of what the gospels are about or what Jesus stood for.

This lack of unity in our modern picture of Jesus comes about, for one thing, because people do not read the Bible so much anymore or because they hear it only in bits and pieces. Lectionary readings in church consisted for years of a few verses from Matthew one Sunday, a discourse from John the next, and a Lukan scene the third Sunday. In the three-year lectionary in use since 1969, the endeavor is to read selections from one Synoptic Gospel each year, but there are enough intrusions and gaps in the process that it is questionable whether a unified picture has resulted for most parishioners. For the many who do not worship regularly, Jesus is seen as the author of some random, perhaps striking statements— "turn the other cheek," "love your enemies"—but not at the center of God's kingly reign.

There is a second reason why people become confused about any central message on the part of Jesus. That stems from the fact that each gospel has its own way of telling the good news about Jesus. Within the New Testament, there is one Jesus but four Gospels. And so unity is again obscured.

It is important therefore to discern that a "gospel" about "the kingdom" was Jesus' basic message. The first three books of the New Testament, Matthew, Mark, and Luke, make this clear in no uncertain terms. (The Fourth Gospel has references to "the kingdom" also, but it presents

Jesus in such different terms that we shall devote our attention only later, in chap. 30, to the Gospel of John.)

Of course, we need to keep in mind that this message of Jesus about God's kingdom took such a shape that it led to his death in Jerusalem. On that all four Gospels agree; the man who spoke in parables, worked miracles, taught and preached God's kingdom, also gathered followers and posed such a threat that powerful rulers of the day brought him to his death on a cross—a human "achievement" of the rulers which God at Easter worked into even greater good news, beyond the "kingdom" message that had preceded it.

No gospel makes clearer than Matthew that all Jesus did and said centered in the kingdom. Matthew, in chapters 4—10, integrates this theme systematically with all of Jesus' activities and the work of his disciples. It is as if Matthew were framing Jesus' Galilean ministry with two summary verses of his own composition about the kingdom. After Jesus settled in his "headquarters" at Capernaum (Matt. 4:12–17, see above, pp. 102–4) and after the call of the first four disciples (4:18–22), the fishermen Simon Peter and Andrew and another pair of brothers, James and John, the Matthean account goes on:

> He [Jesus] went about all Galilee, teaching in their synagogues and preaching the gospel of the kingdom and healing every disease and every infirmity among the people. (Matt. 4:23)

With this statement should be compared the summary later on, virtually word for word the same:

> Jesus went about all the cities and villages, teaching in their synagogues and preaching the gospel of the kingdom and healing every disease and every infirmity. (Matt. 9:35)

We can recognize here certain reflections of conditions in Matthew's day (note, as we did previously, "*their* synagogues" in contrast to "ours"). The phraseology there is probably Matthew's own choice, as is the threefold outline, "teaching, preaching, healing." For Mark, in a parallel verse, mentions just two activities, "he went throughout all Galilee, preaching in their synagogues and casting out demons" (Mark 1:39). In this way Matthew expands on Mark, who does not stress teaching the way Matthew does or give much of its content. Luke's parallel has simply, "he was preaching in the synagogues of Judea" (Luke 4:44), a singular emphasis which reflects the preceding verse, where Jesus said, "I must preach the good news of the kingdom of God . . ." (4:43). (Luke's reference to "Judea"—occurring in the best manuscripts—not "Galilee," reflects a view that Jesus' ministry was to "all Israel.")

Matthew, seemingly, has taken the activity of preaching (mentioned in all three Synoptic Gospels), augmented it with "healing" (parallel with Mark's "casting out demons"), and added his own stress on "teaching." Indeed, he begins his list with "teaching." This threefold activity is paralleled by the instructions that Jesus gives the Twelve when they are sent out in chapter 10, to preach (Matt. 10:7) and to heal (10:8). Oddly, in Matthew the disciples are not told to teach until after Jesus is risen (28:20); there is only one Teacher in Matthean thought, Jesus himself (23:8). In the same vein, the Great Commission (28:19–20) does not mention healing, which was so prominent during the earthly ministry of Jesus.

In Matthew, then, there are three "kingdom" activities of Jesus. These are neatly spelled out in chapters 4—10. "Preaching" means to proclaim the message, "Repent, for the kingdom of heaven is at hand" (Matt. 4:17), the same prophetic message heard from John the Baptist (3:2), and the same kerygma the disciples are to announce (10:7). Jesus' parables about the kingdom may also be reckoned part of his preaching (as in Matthew 13), for they confront people with God's kingship.

The "teaching" of Jesus about the kingdom is implicit in Matthew 5—7, the Sermon on the Mount. Lest anyone miss the connection, Matthew depicts Jesus "sitting down," the posture of a Jewish teacher, and says "he *taught* them" (5:2). Matthew concludes the sermon with the comment, "He *taught* them as one who had authority" (7:29); people were "astonished at his *teaching*" (7:28).

Just as Matthew has grouped a large block of Jesus' teachings in chapters 5—7, so in chapters 8—9 he has gathered a collection of miracle stories about him. There are ten separate miracle accounts, in addition to which 8:16 says, as a summarizing statement,

That evening they brought to him many who were possessed with demons; and he cast out the spirits with a word, and healed all who were sick.

The ten miracle stories which Matthew groups together, interrupted only by a few verses on "following Jesus" (8:18–23; 9:9–17), are as follows:
1. 8:1–4   A leper healed
2. 8:5–13   Centurion's servant healed
3. 8:14–15   Peter's mother-in-law cured of a fever
4. 8:24–27   Calming of the storm on the sea
5. 8:28–34   Two (Gadarene) demoniacs healed

6. 9:1–8   Paralytic healed
7. 9:20–22   Woman with hemorrhage healed
8. 9:18–19, Ruler's daughter raised from death (the story is inter-
   23–26   twined with the previous one)
9. 9:27–31   Two blind men healed
10. 9:32–34 Dumb demoniac healed

Some of these stories occur in other gospels in completely different settings. The healing of the leper (first in the list above), for example, occurs in Mark during a preaching tour in Galilee, in between residences at Capernaum (Mark 1:40–45); but in Matthew the setting is not so clear. Compare also 8:5–13 above with Luke 7:1–10, or 8:24–27 above with Mark 4:35–41.

We may assume that Matthew has himself systematically grouped these miracle stories here. His hand is also to be detected in the phraseology of 4:23 and 9:35, "healing every *disease* and *infirmity*." That vocabulary comes from 8:17, which is, in turn, a "formula quotation" of Isa. 53:4, "This was to fulfill what was spoken by the prophet Isaiah, 'He took our *infirmities* and bore our *diseases*' " (Matt. 8:17). The wording differs from Isa. 53:4, RSV, because Greek, rather than Hebrew, is being cited. Matthew thus sees Jesus fulfilling this line from Isaiah 53, not at the cross, but by his healing ministry, evidently when he takes disease, infirmity, and the demonic upon himself.

The artful way in which the material is here arranged from 4:23 to 9:35 may be Matthew's contribution to telling the story of Jesus, but the intertwining of preaching, teaching, and healing with the kingdom of God reflects historical fact as borne out in other gospel sources. Jesus did preach God's kingdom; he taught kingdom; and when Jesus healed, people either said, "He casts out demons by the prince of demons [Satan or Beelzebub]" (9:34), or had to allow his claim, "If it is by the Spirit of God that I cast out demons, then the kingdom of God has come upon you" (12:28). We may take these three activities as promulgations of God's kingship coming to pass in Jesus' ministry.

Nowhere, however, does Jesus ever define exactly what he means by the "kingdom of God." He simply announces it. Yet this master theme encompasses many aspects of what he said and did. Before we turn to some passages where Jesus deals with the kingdom in more detail, we do well to highlight certain of the chief aspects of "the kingdom . . . at hand."

SOME CHARACTERISTICS OF THE KINGDOM
IN JESUS' TEACHINGS

One is the aspect of *promise*. If the phrase "kingdom of God" means the Almighty's kingly rule, there is a sense, to worldly eyes, in which this is always a *future* hope rather than a *present* fact. Old Testament voices had long looked forward to a time when their God, Yahweh, would assert his power and reign. For example, there was the hope that "one day" God would do this or that:

On that day the LORD will punish
  the host of heaven, in heaven,
  and the kings of the earth, on the earth.
They will be gathered together
  as prisoners in a pit;
they will be shut up in a prison,
  and after many days they will be punished.
Then the moon will be confounded,
  and the sun ashamed;
for the LORD of hosts will reign
  on Mount Zion and in Jerusalem
and before his elders he will manifest his glory.
                    (Isa. 24:21–23)

(The small capital letters in the word LORD represent an editorial device in some English translations to show that the Hebrew word for the sacred name of God, *Y-H-W-H*, is being translated.) To enemies of God such statements come as threat, but to God's people, often downtrodden and in despair, they come as promises by which people can live. Jesus at times talks of God's kingly rule as a promise relating to the future.

On other occasions, however, he speaks of it as *presence*, already here, exerting its influence now. The kingdom is here or will be very soon. For example, "If it is by the Spirit of God that I cast out demons, then the kingdom of God has come upon you" (Matt. 12:28—involved is one of Matthew's rare uses of "kingdom of God" instead of his usual "kingdom of heaven"). Or, Jesus said, "The kingdom of God is in the midst of you" (Luke 17:21). Again: "There are some standing here who will not taste death before they see that the kingdom of God has come with power" (Mark 9:1).

The last verse quoted calls attention to another aspect of the kingdom: *power*. Whether present or future, it is rooted in Almighty God's power, which has been ever of old. One can scarcely think of Yahweh in the Old Testament without the element of power coming to mind; and it is an everlasting characteristic. This same "power of the Lord" was felt to be with Jesus, to heal (Luke 5:17). The very word "miracle" (which in the RSV New Testament translates the Greek term *dynamis*) means "powerful or mighty deed." Jesus' power and authority, rooted in his relation to God, struck all his contemporaries. Underlying "kingdom," as set forth by Jesus, was a notion of power, from God.

As promise, presence, and power, the kingdom of God in Jesus' teachings thus links past, present, and future, as God's eternal power erupts here and now and is promised for the future. Jesus proclaims this kingdom in various forms of preaching, teaching, and mighty deeds. We add here only that hearers were also challenged to *respond,* and the sequence of "indicative-imperative" will constantly be observed: Jesus declares what God is doing, and enjoins people to respond through various commands (imperatives). In what follows we shall be concerned with some typical passages which go back to the time of Jesus' ministry and illustrate the kingdom's further meaning.

No more intriguing pictures of the kingdom can be imagined than those "blessings" which we call "the Beatitudes" (Matt. 5:3–12). They follow upon the initial announcement in Matthew that the kingdom is "at hand" (Matt. 4:17), and constitute Jesus' first teaching in that Gospel. Luke has a smaller collection of beatitudes as part of his "Sermon on the Plain" (Luke 6:20–23). Mark lacks such verses. Matthew begins his Sermon on the Mount with them.

Matthew 5	*Luke 6*
v. 3 Blessed are the poor in spirit, for theirs is the kingdom of heaven.	v. 20 Blessed are you poor, for yours is the kingdom of God.
v. 4 Blessed are those who mourn, for they shall be comforted.	v. 21b Blessed are you that weep now, for you shall laugh.
v. 5 Blessed are the meek, for they shall inherit the earth.	
v. 6 Blessed are those who hunger and thirst for righteousness, for they shall be satisfied.	v. 21a Blessed are you that hunger now, for you shall be satisfied.
v. 7 Blessed are the merciful, for they shall obtain mercy.	

Matthew 5	Luke 6
v. 8 Blessed are the pure in heart, for they shall see God.	
v. 9 Blessed are the peacemakers, for they shall be called sons of God.	
v. 10 Blessed are those who are persecuted for righteousness' sake, for theirs is the kingdom of heaven.	v. 22 Blessed are you when men hate you, and when they exclude you and revile you, and cast out your name as evil, on account of the Son of man!
v. 11 Blessed are you when men revile you and persecute you and utter all kinds of evil against you falsely on my account.	
v. 12 Rejoice and be glad, for your reward is great in heaven, for so men persecuted the prophets who were before you.	v. 23 Rejoice in that day, and leap for joy, for behold, your reward is great in heaven; for so their fathers did to the prophets.

Matthew thus has eight beatitudes similar in structure (in the third person, "Blessed are those who . . .") and a ninth in the second-person plural (v. 11, "you"). Luke has four, all in the second-person plural.

The beatitude form is ages old, occurring frequently in Scripture, introduced by the word "blessed" or "happy," as in these examples:

Blessed is the person
who walks not in the counsel of the wicked,
nor stands in the way of sinners,
nor sits in the seat of scoffers.
(Ps. 1:1, au. trans.)

Happy is the person who finds wisdom,
and the person who gets understanding.
(Prov. 3:13, au. trans.)

The form, beyond its use in such "wisdom" sayings, became particularly common in "apocalyptic" expressions—those penned in dark times to voice a future hope:

Blessed is he who waits and comes to the thousand three hundred and thirty-five days. (Dan. 12:12)

Blessed are the dead who die in the Lord henceforth. (Rev. 14:13)

Of course, Jesus could have spoken all ten or so of the beatitudes of Matthew 5 and Luke 6, in their varying forms, at different times. Those who have studied them most intensely think, however, that his original utterance most likely was in the second-person form, addressed to those (like Peter, Andrew, James, and John) who had heeded his call, and included as the core beatitudes 1, 2, and 4 in Matthew, those about poverty, mourning, and hungering for righteousness.

The reason for predicating these three as the heart of Jesus' message lies in their affinity with the thought of Isa. 61:1–7 (italics added below to make clear the verbal links):

Jesus	*Isaiah 61*
	61:1 "The Spirit of the Lord GOD[1] is upon me, because the LORD has anointed me to bring good tidings to
1. "Blessed are you *poor.*" (Luke 6:20; Matt. 5:3)	*the afflicted.*" [or *poor,* as a more literal rendering, see RSV footnote]
2. "Blessed are those who *mourn,* for they shall be *comforted.*" (Matt. 5:4; Luke 6:21b)	61:2 "... to *comfort* all who *mourn* ...," 61:3 "... to give ... the oil of gladness instead of *mourning, ...*"
3. Compare Matt. 5:10, "for *righteousness*' sake."	61:3 "that they may be called oaks of *righteousness. ...*"
4. "Blessed are you that *hunger* now, for you shall be *satisfied.*" (Luke 6:21a; Matt. 5:6)	61:6 "you shall *eat* the wealth of the nations. ..."
Compare Matt. 5:5, the meek shall inherit "the *earth*" (or the *land*); also Matt. 5:12, "*Rejoice! ...*"	61:7 "in your *land* you shall possess a double portion; yours shall be everlasting *joy.*"

Isaiah 61, it will be recalled, was the passage Jesus read in the synagogue at Nazareth, at the outset of his ministry as portrayed in Luke (4:17–19). Here it shines forth as the heart of the beatitudes at the beginning of the teaching ministry in Matthew. More important for our purposes is the fact that, however the collection of beatitudes may have developed, they are expressions of the kingdom. Matthew 5:3 and its parallel, Luke 6:20, about the kingdom of heaven or God, stands as the theme over all the beatitudes; Matt. 5:10, with another reference to the kingdom, rounds out the eight Matthean ones that are so similar in structure.

Above all, the beatitudes are to be seen as promises of God, concerning what life under God's kingship will one day be. Note the future tense in so many of the promises, "they *shall be* comforted" (Matt. 5:4; see also vv. 5, 6, 7, 8, 9; Luke 6:21). Finally, we may note, every promise depends on God. Some translations, like TEV (the *Good News Bible*), are right when they render the passive voice form as an active, with "God" as subject: "*God* will comfort them" (Matt. 5:4), or "they will receive what *God* has promised!" (Matt. 5:5). According to the beatitudes, the kingdom of God thus promises comfort (the end of hunger, sadness, grief) to those now cast down and deprived—all this to be wrought by the initiative of God.

Small wonder, then, that Jesus taught his disciples, who had heeded the kingdom-call and knew God's promises, to pray for this kingdom that it would come to them as well. The Lord's Prayer—which, like the beatitudes, exists in two versions, a longer one in Matthew and a shorter one in Luke—centers on God and his kingdom, and its meaning for us.

Matthew 6		*Luke 11*
v. 9 Pray then like this:	v. 2	And he said to them, "When you pray, say:
"Our Father who art in heaven, Hallowed be thy name.		'Father, hallowed be thy name.
v. 10 Thy kingdom come. Thy will be done, On earth as it is in heaven.		Thy kingdom come.
v. 11 Give us this day our daily bread;	v. 3	Give us each day our daily bread;

119

Matthew 6	Luke 11
v. 12 And forgive us our debts, As we also have forgiven our debtors;	v. 4 and forgive us our sins, for we ourselves forgive every one who is in- debted to us;
v. 13 And lead us not into temptation, But deliver us from evil."	and lead us not into temptation.' "
Some manuscripts add: "For thine is the kingdom and the power and the glory, for ever, Amen."	

As with the beatitudes, so here, it is possible that Jesus could have taught and used both versions. The one in Luke is a simpler, disciples' prayer, of just five petitions; Matthew's is more complex, containing seven requests. But even the liturgical ending contained in some later manuscripts of Matthew could have been known in Jesus' day, for it reflects an Old Testament passage:

> Thine, O LORD, is the greatness, *and the power, and the glory,* and the victory, and the majesty; for all that is in the heavens and in the earth is thine; thine is *the kingdom,* O LORD, and thou art exalted as head above all. Both riches and honor come from thee, and thou rulest over all. In thy hand are power and might; and in thy hand it is to make great and to give strength to all. (1 Chron. 29:11–12)

Those who have given years to study of this prayer, even seeking to translate from the Greek of our New Testament back to the Aramaic language that Jesus likely used—a poetic, rhymed Aramaic at that—opt for the shorter Lukan form, sometimes with words from Jesus better preserved in Matthew, like "debts" (Matt. 6:12).[2] In any case, the coming of the kingdom is what disciples pray for, alongside the hallowing (keeping holy) of God's name (God's very Person). From the Old Testament prayer quoted above comes the doxological thought that the "kingdom, power, and glory" are forever God's. Jesus' disciples, secure in the promise that God's kingship will come to be manifested some day, pray that this kingdom may come into their lives. The prayer asserts that a holy God rules, and it petitions God that his rule may break into the existing world order and make new one's relationship with God and relations with others. These (re)newed relationships are spelled out, first with God, as

"Father" forgiving our sins and debts to God (Luke 11:4), and then with others, as we forgive them (Luke 11:4). Such prayer moves us further into the reign of God which Jesus preached.

The best part of Jesus' good news was that he did not merely promise the kingdom and teach his followers how to pray for it: he announced its *presence*. We have already seen how his basic preaching claimed God's reign was breaking in (Mark 1:15). How near the kingdom is can be seen from some of his sayings. We have already cited (above, pp. 114, 115) the Matt. 12:28 passage (par. Luke 11:20): Jesus' exorcisms of demonic spirits from their human victims are a manifestation of God's power as king. Luke 17:20–21 adds that the coming of God's kingdom is not a matter of "signs" or predictions of any sort, nor even of miracles; the kingdom comes suddenly from God. Before you know it, it is already "in the midst of you." Whatever else one of Jesus' most difficult sayings at Matt. 11:12 (par. Luke 16:16) may mean, it clearly states that the kingdom of heaven (God) is now present:

Matt. 11:12	*Luke 16:16*
From the days of John the Baptist until now the kingdom of heaven has suffered violence, and men of violence take it by force.	The law and the prophets were until John; since then the good news of the kingdom of God is preached, and every one enters it violently.

There are numerous interpretations, especially regarding the "violence" associated with the kingdom. We note in Luke the emphasis that the "kingdom of God" is being "preached as the gospel [= good news]." But what of the note of "violence/violently" in both the Lukan and Matthean versions? Some have claimed that behind the saying by Jesus was a charge made by Pharisees that God's kingdom was being violated by sinners trying to get in without obeying all the rules in God's law. Some have tried to explain the phrase in a more pedestrian way: the violence reflects the zeal with which Jesus' hearers sought to wrestle entry into the kingdom for themselves.

It is attractive to take the saying as an announcement that the kingdom is here, since the proclamation by John the Baptist and Jesus of its imminence, "Repent, for the kingdom of heaven is at hand" (Matt. 3:2; 4:17). It can then follow that the rule of God, thus asserted by these spokesmen and their followers, is "suffering violence." The reference could be to the martyrdom of the Baptist (Matt. 14:3–9) and the prospective suffering that Jesus must have seen for himself and for his disciples, reported in such sayings as these:

> I have a baptism to be baptized with; and how I am constrained until it is accomplished! (Luke 12:50)

> But Jesus said to them, "You do not know what you are asking. Are you able to drink the cup that I drink, or to be baptized with the baptism with which I am baptized?" And they said to him, "We are able." And Jesus said to them, "The cup that I drink you will drink; and with the baptism with which I am baptized, you will be baptized." (Mark 10:38–39)

> (See also Matt. 5:10–12, quoted above, pp. 119–20).

Such is the context of the "violence" saying of Matt. 11:12; it follows a discussion of John the Baptist's fate (11:2–11). It is also possible that Jesus' enigmatic saying reflects the Old Testament idea of a war between the kingdom of Satan and the kingdom of God, a conflict found in the apocalyptic visions in Daniel (chaps. 8—9 especially) about warfare against the saints of the Most High. Compare Luke 4:5–6, where "the kingdoms of the world" are thought of as having been "delivered to" Satan for a time. Jesus can talk of this struggle in almost mythological terms; compare the saying of Jesus in Luke 10:18, "I saw Satan fall like lightning from heaven," or the picture of Satan as the "Strong One," in Luke 11:21–22, opposed by a Stronger One (Jesus). In such an interpretation, we have a pointer also toward Jesus' passion—he died because he proclaimed the presence of God's kingdom. The activity of God as king is being felt among humankind, and to be a herald of this King may mean martyrdom.

For all its attendant pains and birth pangs, God's kingdom, according to Jesus, *is* breaking in upon the world. And, for all the apocalyptic overtones, Jesus' view of *the world and nature* was, surprisingly, a quite positive one. Many of his parables are drawn from daily village life. Whole sections of the Sermon on the Mount vibrate with reflections of God's providential care. See, for example, Matt. 6:25–34 about God's care for the birds of the air and the lilies of the field, and you! God who directs the world as Creator and Ruler is good.

Yet the incursion of God's reign in the kingdom which Jesus announces also has the effect of exposing what has become wrong in the creation. There has been a demonic distortion. There exists an alien kingdom, of which Satan is the prince, and this Satan is at work (Matt. 12:24, 26). Such an idea of the forces of evil developed in the late stages of the Old Testament writings and in Jewish history in the centuries just preceding the time of Jesus. The notion of a prince of demons, "Beelzebub" who is "ruler of the house," appears in Jesus' ministry (see Matt. 10:25). That is another reason why, in Jesus' announcement of the reign of the proper God, he must begin "Repent!" (Matt. 4:17; i.e., "Turn away!").

THE MIRACLES AND THE KINGDOM

This background, just sketched above, helps explain too how Jesus' miracles—above all the exorcisms, when a demonic spirit is driven out—are seen as signs of salvation coming and of the kingdom. The mighty deeds of Jesus displayed God's kingly power at work—to heal, help, and restore life—foreshadowing the kind of existence promised in the beatitudes.

A host of such "wonder" stories about Jesus are told in the four Gospels. Modern readers are often offended by some (or all) of them, and pick and choose which ones they most wish to accept, on various grounds. No doubt the miracle stories did develop in the early church along varied lines, and some of them have points to make far beyond the occurrence of a wondrous deed. Yet the fact is that all gospel sources, and also such Jewish references as we have to Jesus, agree that Jesus did work what contemporaries termed "miracles"—though these might also be explained as actions of Satan and his kingdom, not of God's kingdom (Matt. 12:24–37).

Sometimes the miracle stories in our Gospels are long and detailed. The healing of the Gerasene demoniac, Mark 5:1–20, strikes many readers as quite "folksy" or "full of eyewitness details." Other miracle stories are abbreviated. Matthew 8:28–34, for example, about two Gadarene demoniacs—which seems a parallel to the Mark 5 passage—is much shorter. Still others are just a bare outline, as terse as possible (cf. Matt. 8:14–15, on the healing of Peter's mother-in-law; or Matt. 9:32–33, where the exorcism is reduced to a subordinate clause in order to concentrate on the response of onlookers, vv. 33–34). We illustrate how a miracle story may take on a particular message by the second of the ten examples in Matthew 8—9.

Matthew 8	*Luke 7:1–10, summarized*
5 As he [Jesus] entered Capernaum, a centurion came forward to him, beseeching him 6 and saying, "Lord, my servant is lying paralyzed at home, in terrible distress." 7 And he said to him, "I will come and heal him." 8 But the centurion answered him,	Same setting, but the *slave* is said to be "*at the point of death.*" The centurion sends *Jewish elders* to implore Jesus' help—the centurion deserves it because he built a synagogue. Jesus goes with them.

Matthew 8	*Luke 7:1–10, summarized*
"Lord, I am not worthy to have you come under my roof; but only say the word, and my servant will be healed. 9 For I am a man under authority, with soldiers under me; and I say to one, 'Go,' and he goes, and to another, 'Come,' and he comes, and to my slave, 'Do this,' and he does it." 10 When Jesus heard him, he marveled, and said to those who followed him, "Truly, I say to you, not even in Israel have I found such faith.	Next the centurion sent *friends,* telling Jesus not to trouble himself, "for I am not worthy to have you under my roof"; the three examples of authority follow, as in Matthew, "Go," "Come," and "Do this" (quoted by the friends). Jesus marvels and tells the multitude, ". . . not even in Israel have I found such faith."
11 "I tell you, many will come from east and west and sit at table with Abraham, Isaac, and Jacob in the kingdom of heaven, 12 while the sons of the kingdom will be thrown into the outer darkness; there men will weep and gnash their teeth."	(The saying about people from the four corners of the earth eating with the patriarchs of old, while you are rejected, is found in a different context at Luke 13:28–30.)
13 And to the centurion Jesus said, "Go; be it done for you as you have believed." And the servant was healed at that very moment.	7:10 "And when those who had been sent returned to the house, they found the slave well."

Mark lacks this story. There is a similar one at John 4:46–54, about a royal official at Capernaum whose *son* Jesus healed from afar by his powerful word. There are enough variations in John and points of interest to observe in Matthew and Luke that we omit the Johannine version here (cf. under "Miracles as Signs" in chap. 30). It is difficult to try to guess what historically happened at any one incident, though the similarities are so great that some connection in the three accounts is to be assumed. What stands out is that Jesus was asked to heal a Gentile's servant (or slave), and that he did so from far off. In no account does Jesus ever enter the Gentile's house. (The suggestion in the *New English Bible* footnote is likely correct, namely, that we should punctuate Jesus' words in Matt. 8:7

as a question: "Am I [a Jew] to come [into your house] and cure him?")
The emphasis, in any case, is on the centurion's *faith*. This is seen in the
way he asks Jesus, so trustingly, for help; the way he asserts that Jesus can
heal by a mere command (as a soldier, the centurion knows what orders
mean, vv. 8–9); the way Jesus commends him (v. 10, "such faith"; v. 13,
"as you have believed"). The fact he is not an Israelite makes this the
more remarkable, and the saying attached in vv. 11–12 (elsewhere in
Luke) underscores the point: Gentiles, and not the traditional "sons of
the kingdom" (Jews), will sit at the promised future messianic banquet.

This miracle story, about the centurion's servant, has become a vehicle
for showing how Gentiles may be saved—by faith. The story emphasizes
the power of Jesus' word. Originally such power may have been a sign
that the kingdom was arriving, but our Gospels are also interested in
using the story to teach about *faith* and *the word*. Miracles were signs
that conveyed the kingdom. They called forth faith. They were not pegs
on which to hang calculations about exactly when the kingdom would
come. Part of the good news is a call for faith. In effect, abandon
calculations because faith is the absence of human calculation. In terms
of Mark 1:15, "*believe* in the gospel."

MORE ASPECTS OF THE
KINGDOM OF GOD

What else did Jesus call for besides faith in God (Mark 11:22)?
Repentance, we have already seen, is demanded according to summaries
such as Matt. 4:17 and Mark 1:15, but Jesus himself used the term
comparatively little (above, p. 100). A better way to put the meaning of
Jesus' call is in terms of a demand for *decision* and then for *discipleship.*
Again and again, Jesus' words call on hearers to decide for God's kingdom. The coming of the kingly rule of God means "woe" for people who
think they are secure, as in a passage that is the obverse of the Lukan
beatitudes:

> But woe to you that are rich, for you have received your consolation.
> Woe to you that are full now, for you shall hunger.
> Woe to you that laugh now, for you shall mourn and weep.
> Woe to you, when all men speak well of you, for so their fathers did to the
>   false prophets.
>
> (Luke 6:24–26)

These four threats against those who are rich and now "full" contrast to
the promises in the beatitudes. Those who count themselves "righteous"
are special targets (cf. Matt. 23:13–39). Catastrophe is imminent (see the

parable of the Rich Fool, Luke 12:16–20). Judgment awaits (Luke 13:6–9). The call is for firm decision and resolute action, exactly as the unjust steward took in his time of crisis (Luke 16:1–8). Discipleship means a life of building firm foundations (Matt. 7:24–27), particularly in terms of prayer (Matt. 6:5–13), forgiveness (Matt. 6:14–15), and typical pious practices of the day like almsgiving and fasting (Matt. 6:2–4, 16–18). Even when Jesus took over existing styles of life and commands, he regularly enriched them by looking at the real motive (Matt. 5:21–48) and by warning against legalism in life. The Ten Commandments *do* matter. Jesus reviewed them in his encounters with people, as with the rich young man who asked about inheriting eternal life (Mark 10:17–22). But Jesus condemned legalism fiercely. The legalistic interpretations of men and even those attributed to Moses can obscure what supremely matters, namely, God's eternal and kingly will (cf. Mark 3:35; 10:2–9; 7:1–23; Matt. 6:10; 7:21).

Response to Jesus also included participation in his *mission* and his *fellowship*. We have already found several references to Jesus' followers (especially the Twelve) and to the throngs attending him. His followers Jesus sent out to preach the kingdom message, with a ministry much like his own (cf. Mark 3:13–19; 6:7–13; Matthew 10; and Luke 9:1–6, on the evangelistic mission of the Twelve; Luke 10:1–20 describes, in addition, the mission of a band of seventy). "Participation in Jesus' fellowship," while not described with the specific Greek term *koinonia* or related words used for fellowship in early Christian congregations after Easter, does look forward to a "meal with God and/or his Messiah," of which the Old Testament had spoken:

> On this mountain the LORD of hosts will make for all peoples a feast of fat things, a feast of wine on the lees, of fat things full of marrow, of wine on the lees well refined. . . . (Isa. 25:6)

Jesus made a reference to it, in a saying already noted but stunning in its rebuke of Jesus' own hearers who presumed too much on their inheritance of the kingdom as "sons":

> I tell you, many will come from east and west and sit at table with Abraham, Isaac, and Jacob in the kingdom of heaven, while the sons of the kingdom will be thrown into the outer darkness; there they will weep and gnash their teeth. (Matt. 8:11–12; par. Luke 13:28–30)

More specifically, we may say that the feeding miracles of Jesus were a foreshadowing of this banquet (Mark 6:30–44, the feeding of the Five Thousand; 8:1–10, the Four Thousand). Similarly, the meal in the upper room (Mark 14:17–25) was a foreshadowing and a realization in advance of eating and drinking "in the kingdom of God" (Mark 14:25).

Many of these points about the kingdom of God are brought home to us in a most penetrating way by the parables of Jesus. Over fifty are preserved in our Gospels, and modern scholars are convinced that here we hear the authentic voice of Jesus most clearly. For parables were his characteristic way of speech.

The device of telling parables—colorful stories from everyday life to make a point, often by comparison with a more abstract truth—was an old one, to be sure, even in the days of Jesus. In the Old Testament, there was Jotham's story about the trees looking for a ruler (Judges 9:7–21); or the brief reference to the dialogue of the thistle and the cedar (2 Kings 14:9–10; par. 2 Chron. 25:18–19). An excellent example is Nathan's devastating indictment of King David after the latter's adultery with Bathsheba, when Nathan got the king to listen to the story of two men, one rich and one poor, and how the rich man took the poor man's dear ewe lamb (2 Sam. 12:1–15), ending with the climactic cry "You are the man" (v. 7) directed at David. Rabbinic teachers of Jesus' day also used the parable form.

Jesus brought the parable to new literary heights as a vehicle to teach about God's kingship. "The kingdom of heaven is like . . ." (Matt. 13:31, 33, 45, 47); it "may be compared to . . ." (Matt. 13:24); many of his parables begin with a simile, where the kingdom is likened to something familiar in life. Other parables do not mention the kingdom directly, but deal in their content with its growth, or with the crisis caused by its appearing. For an example of a parable of growth, see the Sower, Mark 4:3–9; for one of crisis, the Laborers in the Vineyard, Matt. 20:1–16, where God's goodness reverses human values, a theme found in Jesus' sayings too, for example, Mark 8:35; 10:31.

Thus the parables can be put together to provide a summary of Jesus' message about the kingdom in a variety of its aspects. Many of them talk about its coming; compare the Fig Tree in Mark 13:28: when it is in leaf, you know that summer is near—so with the kingdom, Luke 21:29–31. Others take up the reversal of situations and roles that occurs as the kingdom comes. For example, the invited guests are displaced, new ones are sought for the banquet, as in Luke 14:16–24, paralleled at Matt. 22:1–10. The disciples' response must be to act decisively and then bear fruit (Matt. 21:33–43; 25:14–30). One expositor, D. J. Crossan, has summed it up, on the basis of the sequence in two parables, the Treasure in the Field and the Pearl of Great Price—

Matt. 13:44—"found, goes and sells, and buys"

Matt. 13:45–46—"finding, went and sold, bought"—
as the sequence of *advent* (of a new world and unforeseen possibilities),
reversal (of one's entire past), and *action* (expressing a new world and its
possibilities).[3] One should read and heed Matt. 13:44–52; one who is
"trained for the kingdom" (v. 52) brings forth "what is new and what is
old" from parables like these.

As Jesus spoke them, parables dealt with God's kingdom. As meta-
phors, they have continued to speak down through the years with yet
further meanings, in the early church and down to our own day. Every
parable has had a history in its interpretation. But the aim of the New
Testament writers is to confront us with what Jesus taught—sometimes
interpreted for the evangelists' own day. This biblical meaning stands
sovereign over all later interpretations. The genius of much modern study
of the parables is to take us back to what Jesus himself said. And the
contribution of such study is to show us how the parables revolve around
the kingdom of God. As the Laborers in the Vineyard makes clear (Matt.
20:1–16), God is a gracious God who gives the kingdom—and crosses
up human expectations.

Jesus' parables, the Beatitudes, the Sermon on the Mount, the Lord's
Prayer, his teachings and miracles, the call for decision, faith, discipleship—all these things were intertwined to form his gospel of the
kingdom of God. Ever since then, as a symbol and a reality, the kingdom
of God has moved men and women to dreams and to actions. The
Christian missionary to Africa, David Livingstone (1813–73), wrote,

> I will place no value on anything I possess save in relation to the kingdom
> of God. If anything will advance the kingdom of God it shall be given away
> or kept, only as by the giving or the keeping of it I shall promote the glory of
> Him to whom I owe my hopes in time and in eternity.[4]

Non-Christians too have been inspired by Jesus' gospel. The Sermon on
the Mount made a great impression upon Mahatma Gandhi (1869–
1948), the Indian leader, who was influenced by Matt. 5:38–48 in his
idea of nonviolent revolution, though his specifics went far beyond Jesus,
as when in 1946 Gandhi sought to bring peace in the villages of
Noakhali, east of Calcutta, by the device of getting a Hindu and a Moslem
leader to live together under one roof and each to undertake a fast to the
death if his co-religionists attacked those of another faith. A part of Jesus'
gospel inspired that in a non-Christian land!

But by and large Jesus dealt with no such life-and-death scenes. He
avoided any revolutionist movements, the conventional Jewish religious
parties, the fanaticism of the Qumran desert community, and hairsplit-

ting rabbinic debates—though he seems to have known all of these. He left no legislation, no blueprint for society. He went about Galilee, and later went to Jerusalem, preaching good news, the word which God sent, about God's kingdom (cf. the summary in Acts 10:36–42).[5]

But never did Jesus define "the kingdom." But his audiences knew, at least to the degree they shared his knowledge of what the Hebrew Scriptures said about the reign of God. And we shall fully understand what Jesus meant only after we explore the kingdom of God as gospel in the Old Testament (see part 3).

NOTES

1. Here the RSV, following KJV practice, employs small capital letters for GOD to represent the sacred name Y-H-W-H (see above, p. 115) in the combination in Hebrew of the two names "Elohim" (see below, pp. 148, 206–7) and Y-H-W-H. See further, below, pp. 181–82.

2. Cf. J. Jeremias, *The Lord's Prayer,* trans. J. Reumann, Facet Books Biblical Series 8 (Philadelphia: Fortress Press, 1964).

3. D. J. Crossan, *In Parables: The Challenge of the Historical Jesus* (New York: Harper & Row, 1973), 35–36.

4. As quoted from *Effective Workers in Needy Fields* (Student Volunteer Movement, 1902), 28, in Milo Kauffman, *Stewards of God* (Scottdale, Pa.: Herald Press, 1975), 18.

5. For further reading on the subjects in chaps. 6 and 7, see especially (and the bibliographies there) J. Reumann, *Jesus in the Church's Gospels: Modern Scholarship and the Earliest Sources* (Philadelphia: Fortress Press, 1968), esp. 224–41 (Sermon on the Mount and Beatitudes); 92–106 (Lord's Prayer); chap. 7 (miracles); and the index on specific sayings of Jesus.

III

THE GOSPEL AS GOD'S VICTORY AND KINGSHIP— IN ISRAEL AND IN CHRIST

The body of a lion and the head of the human king Khaf-Re form the Great Sphinx guarding the ancient necropolis of Giza. One of three pyramids built here in the third millennium B.C., that of Khufu is pictured here.

The temple at Karnak, part of the site of ancient Thebes, is reflected in what may have been a sacred pool. This home of the Egyptian god Amon-Re was entered through gigantic pylons, believed to be pillars of the sky.

8

Divine Kingship Among Israel's Neighbors

HERALDING THE GOOD NEWS of God's reign is one of the basic themes in the Bible. To announce that God is king is to confess that God's word and will determine and shape life as a whole. Yet in this very announcement about the reign of God, the biblical writers shared a confession common among other peoples of their times. And so, in trying to understand this theme as well as numerous others in the Bible, it is important to see how Israel lived within its own environment: how the cultural, literary, and historical relationships with its neighbors affected its life and expression. Only in seeing how Israel was part of the world of the day can we discern with clarity how Israel was unique among the nations round about it.

A CYCLICAL VIEW OF LIFE

Israel's neighbors understood the whole world in terms of the cycles of nature, usually the seasons of the year. Basically, the cycle was determined by times of water and times of drought. Through the winter months, the falling rain and the melting snows fill the river beds, and the land becomes enriched and fertile. When the rainy season and the luscious spring are past, the heat of the rainless summer withers the vegetation. In late fall the rains begin again, and the cycle is repeated.

This entire procedure corresponded, the ancients believed, to the fate of the gods in heaven. Water meant that the storm god, the deity of fertility, was alive and well. Drought was the earthly sign that the heavenly battle did not fare well for the beneficent god; indeed, the god of sterility had won—at least until the next season.

Perhaps the clearest example of this seasonal pattern of life can be seen in the New Year Festival of the Babylonians who lived in Mesopotamia (modern Iraq) from about 2000 B.C. until about 500 B.C. According to written sources from the Babylonians themselves, the people acted out the story of creation on the fourth day of their festival. The drama was based upon the recitation of a story known as the *Enuma elish*. In this creation account the god Marduk was commissioned by the other gods to battle against Tiamat ("the Deep"), a mean, watery serpent bent on causing destruction. But because Marduk, the young warrior, was willing to battle the monster, the grateful gods acclaimed him king and conferred on him the royal privileges. The strong, young Marduk mounted his chariot, took with him bow and arrow, a net, and the four winds. Courageously he faced the fearsome Tiamat and her general named Kingu. Marduk and Tiamat exchanged some nasty words, and when Tiamat opened her mouth to devour the hero-king, Marduk sent the wind into her mouth. The air filled her whole body, and she puffed up. When Marduk shot his arrow into her belly, she exploded like a balloon pricked with a pin. After smashing her head, the victorious god split her body into two pieces. Out of half of her corpse Marduk made the sky. He then brought into being the entire universe, organizing all the parts and assigning functions to the many gods. As for Kingu, Tiamat's general, Marduk used his blood to make humans, whose job it was to serve as slaves. The gods, truly grateful to their leader, erected for him a glorious temple in Babylon.[1]

This gruesome story tells of the way the ancient Babylonians understood the origin and structure of the universe. For them creation was the result of a victory of the god of order over the force of chaos. In order to ensure that order would in fact prevail over chaos, the Babylonians believed it was necessary to dramatize the story each New Year's Day. By so doing, they believed, the heavenly battle would take place just as it was enacted in the earthly ritual. Thus, creation occurred annually each New Year's Day, and the highlight of that celebration was the victory of Marduk and his coronation as king of the universe.

In Canaan there existed a similar battle story based on the cycle of the seasons but without any concern for creation of the universe. As recently as 1929, at a seacoast town in northern Syria called Ras Shamra, archeologists unearthed the ancient Canaanite city of Ugarit. Among the most spectacular finds were tablets (dating from 1500 to 1200 B.C.) containing the stories of gods. The longest and most important group of stories was that which told of the god Baal and his sister Anath.

El was the chief of all the gods and in some sense their father. His favorite son was Yamm ("Prince Sea"). Because El so loved his son, he commanded the master craftsman Kothar-wa-Khasis to build a glorious

The Lion Gate guarded the entrance to the ancient Hittite capital called Hattusa. From here the Hittite suzerains ruled the vassal states of their empire from 1600 until 1200 B.C.

palace for Prince Sea. Understandably, El's other children complained, among them Prince Baal, the storm god of fertility.

One day, when Baal was serving in the assembly of the gods, a pair of messengers arrived from the palace of Prince Yamm. They reported that their leader wanted to rule over Baal.

> Surrender the god *with a following,*
>   *Him whom the multitudes worship:*
> Give Baal [to me to lord over],
>   Dagon's son whose spoil I'll possess.[2]

Much to Baal's distress, El granted the request.

One day, however, Kothar-wa-Khasis offered these words of advice to the enslaved Prince Baal:

> I tell thee, O Prince Baal,
>   I declare, O Rider of the Clouds.
> Now thine enemy, O Baal,
>   Now thine enemy will thou smite,
>   Now wilt thou cut off thine adversary.

135

> Thou'lt take thine eternal kingdom,
> Thine everlasting dominion.[3]

With one of the clubs conveniently supplied by Kothar-wa-Khasis, Baal dealt Prince Sea a mighty blow to the head. The wounded Yamm cried out twice, "I am dying, Baal will reign."

Baal was now victorious, but he still had no palace of his own. The god and his sister Anath approached the mother of the gods, Asherah. They convinced her to speak to El about this matter of a palace, and to their delight she succeeded. A palace of gold and silver was built for Baal. He mounted his throne with the pride and dignity of a true and victorious king.

Thus, in Canaan and Mesopotamia, the people believed that the god who represented the frightening and chaotic force of water (Yamm and Tiamat) had to be defeated in battle by the good god of fertility (Baal and Marduk) in order for life to continue. In each case the victorious god was acclaimed king and set upon the throne in a palace.

In Egypt the situation was somewhat different, for there the waters of the Nile River were not destructive but were the life-giving force which provided stability in the land. But in Egypt, too, there was belief in a battle between two opposing gods. The battle occurred not annually or seasonally, but daily—or better, nightly—with the transition from daylight to darkness and back again.

The Egyptians believed that the sun god Re rode across the heavens in his boat throughout the day. Upon entering the western horizon, Re changed boats to enter the realm of darkness. At the end of his night journey, just before dawn, the sun god battled the dragon Apophis. Then as Re peeked over the eastern horizon at sunrise, the Egyptians knew he had once again been victorious. On this basis Re was acclaimed "King of men and gods altogether."[4]

In all these civilizations the stories about the hero-god's victory were far more than stories. They explained for these ancient people the meaning of life itself, the origins and functions of natural phenomena, and above all the name of the god of life who ruled the universe and expected homage.

MONSTER-HUNTING IN THE BIBLE

Not surprisingly, a number of these serpentine monsters and the raging Prince Sea himself appear in some of the poetic sections of the Bible. In a number of these passages, the monsters are portrayed as being opponents of Yahweh, the God of Israel.

Prince Yamm (the sea) rears his head along with Tiamat (the deep) in the hymn preserved in the third chapter of Habakkuk. This ancient poem demonstrates the power of Yahweh against all opposing forces.

Was thy wrath against the rivers, O LORD?
  Was thy anger against the rivers,
  or thy indignation against *the sea,*
when thou didst ride upon thy horses,
  upon thy chariot of victory?
Thou didst strip the sheath from thy bow,
  and put arrows to the string.
Thou didst cleave the earth with rivers.
The mountains saw thee, and writhed;
  the raging waters swept on;
the deep gave forth its voice,
  it lifted its hands on high.
               (Hab. 3:8–10)

In some biblical passages the monster is called by the name Leviathan, an alias used for Yamm in the Ugaritic texts. Like the monster described there, the biblical Leviathan has several heads (Ps. 74:12–19). He is a twisting, fleeing serpent which the Lord will vanquish in the last day (Isa. 27:1), although in other passages Leviathan is portrayed as God's pet (Job 41; Ps. 104:26).

An unnamed serpent is pierced by the hand of God (Job 26:13), and the sea or sea monster—like Tiamat of Babylon—needs to be subdued or even locked up (Job 7:12). A dragon is the portrayal of the pharaoh, king of Egypt, in his hostility against Yahweh, the God of Israel (Ezek. 29:3–6), and even the "waters" seem to be God's adversary at Ps. 104:5–9.

In addition to using the monsters of the neighborhood in order to describe the evil forces with which God must contend, the Bible includes one more not yet found in the ancient literature: Rahab. This uniquely Israelite monster is the serpent of old whom Yahweh defeated (Job 26:12; Isa. 51:9). Indeed, it is the victory over Rahab which resulted in the kingship of Yahweh in the heavenly council (Ps. 89:5–18).

These and other similar passages in the Old Testament seem to indicate that Israel was no different from its neighbors. But such a conclusion is by no means correct. To be sure, the biblical writers used the vivid imagery of their times to describe the glory and power of the Lord who fought and defeated the same monsters as were conquered by Marduk and Baal. In most cases, however, the battles which Yahweh fought were not in the distant past, that is, at creation time, but in the future. According to Isa. 27:1 it is on the future "day of the Lord" that God will defeat the forces of evil in order to establish the kingdom. In other cases, the defeat of the monster is a powerful demonstration of Yahweh's power to deliver the people of Israel from oppression (Isa. 51:2). At other times the monster is nothing more than a metaphor for one of Israel's neighbors (see Isa. 30:7). In no case do the biblical writers use, as their contemporary counterparts do, the monster imagery to interpret the meaning of life or the relationship of Israel to God.

Indeed, against the entire interpretation of life and time so common in the ancient Near East, Israel proclaims something different: it is not the cycles of nature in their rhythmic stability but the dynamic unfolding of history which provides the arena in which God acts; it is not heavenly escapades among the gods which determine life but the involvement of God in human time and space.

ISRAEL'S HISTORICAL CONFESSIONS

Israel bore witness to a God who functions in history according to his own plan and will. This "history" of which we speak is not the modern understanding of events based on cause and effect; rather, biblical history is the story of God.

This story is *personal:* God makes a plan, a promise, which is shared with the people of Israel, and then speaks and acts in order to accomplish that promise. This story is *spread across the millennia:* God speaks to Abraham about 1800 B.C. and continues speaking throughout the biblical period until the first century A.D. and beyond. This story is *filled with meaning:* God's constant and faithful activity makes a difference everywhere: at home, at worship, at work, at play.

The Israelites of the biblical period based everything they did on what God did for them in history. That totality of belief and life can be illustrated in several ways. First, it was the duty of an Israelite father to teach his children how to act properly as God's people. The father was to instruct the child in the laws given by the Lord. And when the son would ask about the meaning of all these teachings and laws, the father was to say:

> We were Pharaoh's slaves in Egypt; and the LORD brought us out of Egypt with a mighty hand; and the LORD showed signs and wonders, great and grievous, against Egypt and against Pharaoh . . . ; and he brought us out from there [to] give us the land which he swore to give to our fathers. (Deut. 6:21–23)

Second, it was the duty of every Israelite to offer as sacrifice to the Lord the first pickings of each year's harvest. This ordinance might seem as though the Israelites were very much like their neighbors. Offering first fruits is a practice one would expect of a Canaanite or a Babylonian at the harvest season. But the Israelites' reason for offering the sacrifice was quite different from a concern to appease the fertility gods. For Israel the motive was based in history. As the worshiper laid down the basket of first fruits, this recital of faith was pronounced:

A wandering Aramean was my father; and he went down into Egypt and sojourned there, few in number; and there he became a nation, great, mighty, and populous. And the Egyptians treated us harshly, and afflicted us, and laid upon us hard bondage. Then we cried to the LORD the God of our fathers, and the LORD heard our voice, and saw our affliction, our toil, and our oppression; and the LORD brought us out of Egypt with a mighty hand and an outstretched arm, with great terror, with signs and wonders; and he brought us into this place and gave us this land, a land flowing with milk and honey. And behold, now I bring the first of the fruit of the ground, which thou, O LORD, hast given me. (Deut. 26:5–10)

A third example occurs in the formation of Israel as a tribal confederation. When Joshua gathered together the twelve tribes at Shechem (Joshua 24), his first words were those of the Lord, in which were recited the great deeds God had done for Israel (vv. 2–13). This entire story forms the basis of the covenant which God made with the people, a covenant which defines their relationship and Israel's responsibilities.

At the same time this history of God with the people constantly reminded the people of their covenant. In their worship the Israelites sang songs of various kinds to express their faith in this God of history. These hymns (at least some of them) make up the biblical Book of Psalms. Several of these psalms (105, 106, 135, 136, in particular) recount the same acts of God which are described in those little summaries in Deuteronomy 6 and 26 and in Joshua 24.

All these brief summaries and songs contain basically the same outline of God's acts in history. They usually tell of God's relationship with Israel's ancestors, of God's rescuing the people from slavery in Egypt, and of God's giving to the people the land of Canaan, promised to Abraham years before. Sometimes they include also some reference to God's leading the people through the wilderness from Egypt to Canaan, and sometimes they mention details about persons and places. But one thing is clear and constant: they tell of God's activity as the reason for what people do—at home, at worship, at community gatherings.

All these examples show that the biblical writers interpreted the meaning of life and of God in a way different from any source known to us from the ancient world. Those who bore witness to God and the impact

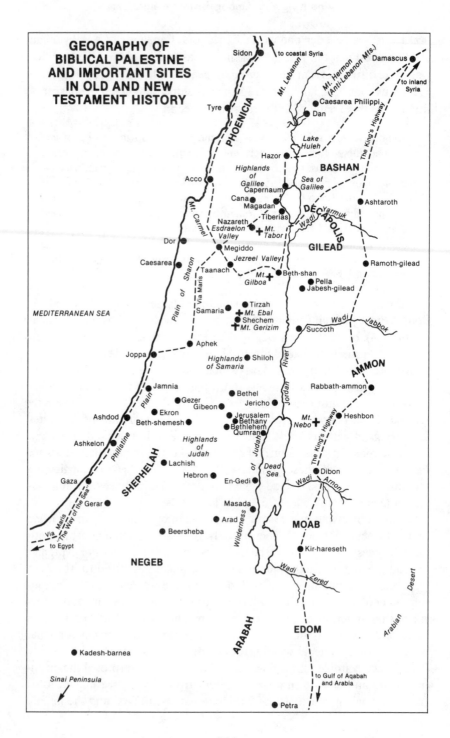

GEOGRAPHY OF
BIBLICAL PALESTINE
AND IMPORTANT SITES
IN OLD AND NEW
TESTAMENT HISTORY

Sidon
to coastal Syria
Mt. Lebanon
Mt. Hermon (Anti-Lebanon Mts.)
Damascus
to inland Syria
Tyre
PHOENICIA
Caesarea Philippi
Dan
Lake Huleh
The King's Highway
Hazor
BASHAN
Acco
Highlands of Galilee
Sea of Galilee
Capernaum
Cana
Magadan
Ashtaroth
DECAPOLIS
Wadi Yarmuk
Tiberias
Mt. Carmel
Nazareth
Esdraelon Valley
Mt. Tabor
Dor
Megiddo
GILEAD
Jezreel Valley
Caesarea
Plain of Sharon
Taanach
Mt. Gilboa
Beth-shan
Ramoth-gilead
Via Maris
Pella
Jabesh-gilead
Tirzah
MEDITERRANEAN SEA
Samaria
Mt. Ebal
Shechem
Mt. Gerizim
Wadi Jabbok
Succoth
Aphek
Joppa
Highlands of Samaria
Shiloh
River
AMMON
Jamnia
Bethel
Rabbath-ammon
Gezer
Gibeon
Jericho
Jordan
Ashdod
Ekron
Jerusalem
Bethany
Mt. Nebo
Heshbon
Beth-shemesh
Bethlehem
Qumran
Ashkelon
Highlands of Judah
The King's Highway
SHEPHELAH
Philistine Plain
Lachish
Dead Sea
Gaza
Hebron
En-Gedi
Dibon
Gerar
Masada
Wadi Arnon
Via Maris
"The Way of the Sea"
Arad
Wilderness of Judah
MOAB
to Egypt
Beersheba
Kir-hareseth
NEGEB
Wadi Zered
Arabian Desert
ARABAH
EDOM
Kadesh-barnea
Sinai Peninsula
to Gulf of Aqabah and Arabia
Petra

of the Divine Presence on their lives saw things differently from their neighbors.

THE MEANINGS OF "MYTH"

The word "myth" can mean many things. To most people it seems to describe something which is not true, a figment of one's imagination. A dictionary defines myth as a story which tries to explain some practice, belief, institution, or even some natural phenomenon. Others define myth as a story about gods, and still others, as a form of poetry which proclaims a truth.

Originally the word meant something which conveyed truth, and that most often meant religious truth. Stories about gods or even the one God can be called myths insofar as they tell of some truth. Part of the reason for needing stories to communicate what is true is simply that there often exists no option. To put it in other terms, myth is simply a storylike way of describing what is otherwise indescribable. How can a human being talk about God except to assign to God certain human characteristics and traits such as joy and sadness, regret and commitment? Even to suggest that God hears and sees and smells is to portray God in terms we can understand. Such stories about God's throwing hailstones from heaven (Joshua 10) or removing the wheels from the Egyptian chariots (Exodus 14) are descriptions of God as myth. They tell about God as defender and savior in story form.

If one asks if there is myth in the Bible, then one must respond affirmatively, provided myth is understood as that which conveys truth. The answer depends, of course, on how one defines myth in the first place.[5]

Whether we use the word "myth" or not, Israel looked at life from the vantage point of history, a word with several meanings. History can be a written and systematic account of events or, as in the Bible, it can recount the story of God as God speaks to and acts upon people. That history was written by people who believed that in this or that event God was at work to carry out his will for all humanity. Therefore, the history of God recorded in the Bible is a record of faith. It is written by those who have been inspired by God to see his judging and saving presence where others are concerned only with presenting a systematic account of events.

Israel's neighbors were highly sophisticated peoples. They left behind records of mathematical genius, monuments of engineering marvel, stories of creative skill. But it was Israel, a rather puny bunch of semi-nomads and farmers, a motley crew of refugees, who interpreted God, life, and history, even time itself, in a totally different way.

141

How could Israel's faith be so different? Many have tried to explain the difference sociologically or historically. However, the origin of faith can only be explained by revelation. Somehow in the midst of historical change and sociological upheaval, God was made known to Israel in a different way.

In short, God reigns as king over Israel and over all creation—not on the basis of a heavenly victory over a monster at creation time but on the basis of victories in earthly time and space.

NOTES

1. For translation of *Enuma elish,* the so-called Babylonian Genesis, see, for example, *The Ancient Near East, Volume 1* (cited above, chap. 3 n. 1), 31–39; or *Documents from Old Testament Times,* ed. D. Winton Thomas (New York: Harper Torchbooks, 1961), 3–16.

2. "Poems about Baal and Anath," trans. H. L. Ginsberg in *The Ancient Near East, Volume 1* (cited above, chap. 3 n. 1), 94. The italics designate an uncertain translation, the brackets a restoration in the text.

3. Ibid., 96.

4. On Re versus Apophis, see *Ancient Near Eastern Texts* (cited above, chap. 3 n. 1), 6–7.

5. See further on myth, Foster R. McCurley, *Ancient Myths and Biblical Faith: Scriptural Transformations* (Philadelphia: Fortress Press, 1983), esp. 1–10.

9

The Exodus Event:
God as King and Deliverer

WITHOUT AN UNDERSTANDING of life based upon a god's victory over the chaotic forces of nature, how did Israel herald the gospel of God's victory? Without a battle against the various monsters, how did the God of Israel become king?

The God of the Bible is revealed primarily in history. It is in history then that God fights battles, wins victories, and is acclaimed king over Israel. It is in history that the God of the Old Testament finds enemies, those who thwart the divine purposes by their treatment of the elected people. God's enemies are not the phenomena of nature but historical kings and nations who oppose the divine will.

YAHWEH VERSUS PHARAOH

The classic battle in the Old Testament is recorded in the first fifteen chapters of the Book of Exodus: the battle between Yahweh ("the LORD") and the pharaoh of Egypt that culminates in the victory of Yahweh at the Reed Sea.

The first chapter of Exodus reports that after the migration to Egypt of the whole family of Jacob in the days of Joseph, the Israelites multiplied in that land beyond belief. They became so numerous that the Egyptians feared for their own security, and with public safety as an excuse the king of Egypt ordered that the Israelites be made slaves to work on his construction projects. Pharaoh's purpose was to build two new cities, Pithom and Raamses, now identified by archeologists as either the modern Tell er-Retabeh or Tell el-Maskhutah and Tanis, respectively. Since no other pharaoh was involved in royal building activity at these sites, it is rather safe to conclude that the pharaoh of Exodus chapter 1 was

143

Rameses II who ruled Egypt from 1290 to 1224 B.C. Thus the classic battle of the Old Testament is firmly rooted in time and place—in history.

To grasp this battle properly, it is necessary to understand that the struggle between God and the king of Egypt was a battle in history between two gods—at least, between God and one who thought he was a god. The pharaoh of Egypt was considered by himself and by his people to be the god Horus. Every king of Egypt, when he was alive and ruling, was thought to be Horus, and then he became the god Osiris when he died. In addition, the king had intimate relations with other gods as well, for in some cases he was called the son of this or that god, especially of Re, the sun god. In fact, the name Rameses itself means "son of Re" or "begotten of Re." Thus the struggle in the Book of Exodus was between Yahweh, the God of the Hebrews, and Rameses, the god of Egypt.

It was to free the people Israel from the oppression of Pharaoh that God revealed identity and promise to Moses at the burning bush (Exodus 3). There God gave the name "I am" and commissioned Moses to go to Egypt and bring out the people. Just as Moses was about to leave on his mission, God told him the words he should speak to Pharaoh: "Thus says the LORD, Israel is my first-born son, and I say to you, 'Let my son go that he may serve me'; if you refuse to let him go, behold, I will slay your first-born son" (Exod. 4:22–23). This is the key to the struggle which follows: Let my people go that they might serve me. In light of the divine aspirations of the Pharaoh, the command might be paraphrased "Let my people go from serving you, O Pharaoh who think you are a god, that they might serve me, the true God."

The first approach of Moses, now joined by his brother Aaron, to the Pharaoh went like this. "Afterward Moses and Aaron went to Pharaoh and said, 'Thus says the LORD, the God of Israel, "Let my people go, that they may hold a feast to me in the wilderness." ' But Pharaoh said, 'Who is the LORD, that I should heed his voice and let Israel go? I do not know the LORD, and moreover I will not let Israel go' " (Exod. 5:1–2). That was Pharaoh's mistake! From that moment on the Lord made quite clear to Pharaoh who the Lord was.

Using Moses and Aaron as instruments of power, the Lord sent upon all the land of Egypt one plague after another. At first it was an almost comical contest. Then it became more and more serious. In front of Pharaoh, Aaron threw down to the ground his shepherd's staff, and it became a serpent. But Pharaoh called his wise men and magicians, and by their secret mumbo jumbo they too turned their staffs into serpents. Apparently Pharaoh thought that the Lord's power was no greater than that of his own magicians. But then the staff of Aaron swallowed up the

144

staffs of the magicians, and the more powerful one was known. Pharaoh would not, however, let the people go.

Even as it is today, the Nile River was then a source of life for the people of Egypt. Because of its importance for the land, the river was almost considered to be a god who brought blessings. But the Lord showed power by changing the water of the Nile into blood. The fish died in the river, and the water became foul. What had been a symbol of life to the Egyptians became a symbol of death by the power of the Lord. The purpose of all this was to show Pharaoh that "I am the LORD" (Exod. 7:17).

The frog, because of its close connection with the life-giving Nile, was especially adored by the Egyptians. But the Lord sent so many frogs upon the land that they were crawling on beds, in cupboards, ovens, and bowls. There were frogs everywhere. Egyptian magicians came along to show that they could do the same trick. They, too, brought frogs upon the land—only to make the whole situation worse! And so the hopping little creatures became despicable to the Egyptians.

Then the Lord sent plagues of gnats, of sickness on livestock, of boils, of locusts, of hail, and of darkness. But Pharaoh remained stubborn and would not let the people go. His land was being devastated, his people were suffering every possible difficulty, his food crops were being damaged. But Pharaoh was stubborn—not strong, not powerful, not able to do anything about the power of God as it affected Egypt's life, but stubborn. The most the "god" of Egypt could do against the Lord was to remain obstinate.

By this time Pharaoh was beginning to regret his initial question, "Who is the LORD?" When the flies swarmed everywhere except on the land of Goshen where the Hebrews lived, God told Pharaoh that his purpose was "that you may know that I am the LORD in the midst of the earth" (Exod. 8:22). Before the hail came, God spoke through Moses to Pharaoh:

> For this time I will send all my plagues upon your heart, and upon your servants and your people, that you may know that there is none like me in all the earth. For by now I could have put forth my hand and struck you and your people with pestilence, and you would have been cut off from the earth; but for this purpose have I let you live, to show you my power, so that my name may be declared throughout all the earth. (Exod. 9:14–16; see also 9:29)

Thus there is no doubt that the plague stories portray a power struggle in which the Lord is superior. But none of these demonstrations led to the release of the Hebrew slaves. Finally, God had to take a severe measure in

An Egyptian god in the form of a hawk (usually the symbol of Horus or Harakhti). The disk on the head represents the sun, and the uraeus (the snake figure) indicates royal sovereignty.

A Canaanite god found in excavations at Hazor, once the capital of northern Canaan (Josh. 11:10). One of the symbols of Canaanite deities found beside this figure is the moon.

order to free the Hebrew people from their bondage to Pharaoh. The Lord sent the final plague: death for all the firstborn of human beings and beasts in the land of Egypt. The children of the Hebrew slaves were saved from the destroying power. They identified themselves as Hebrews by sacrificing an animal and smearing the blood on the doorposts of their homes. Since the plague passed over the Hebrews, they called this night the Passover and celebrate it to this day. But the plague did not pass over the homes of the Egyptians. The people of Egypt cried bitterly as the children died. Pharaoh's own son was among them (Exod. 4:22–23; 12:29–30). Finally, the king summoned Moses and his brother Aaron in the middle of the night and told them to go out from Egypt to serve the Lord.

The people of Israel gathered together all the things that belonged to them, as well as some gifts which the Egyptians had given them. Then they set out for the wilderness where they could worship God and be free from the bondage of Pharaoh. The people arrived at the shore of a certain sea. (This is called the Red Sea in most English translations, but the Hebrew means "the Sea of Reeds"; thus *Reed* Sea is more appropriate.) By this time Pharaoh had changed his mind and had sent war chariots after them. The Hebrews stood at the sea as they heard the thundering of the horses and chariots behind them. The people—by no means prepared for battle—could do nothing. Surely they were about to be destroyed or taken back to slavery. They stood between "the devil and the deep blue sea," completely unable to save themselves from the approaching disaster.

THE DECISIVE BATTLE

What occurs next in the story is the decisive battle in the encounter between Yahweh, the God of Israel, and Pharaoh, the god of Egypt. This battle is recorded in three different versions, two in prose and one in poetry. The reason for such a conglomeration of accounts is the nature of the first four books of the Bible. In Genesis through Numbers there are intertwined at least three different accounts about the patriarchs, the exodus events, and the wilderness wanderings. Sometimes materials from these various sources are set side by side in blocks, while at other times verses and even half verses have been interwoven by skillful editors to present one story of the activity of God in Israel's past.

One can compare this phenomenon to the first three Gospels in the New Testament. Three different writers wrote three accounts of Jesus' life at three different times in three different places. Now if someone were to take these three Gospels and interweave them (as did the "History of the

Passion," read in some churches in Lent, or Fulton Oursler in his book *The Greatest Story Ever Told*), there would be one story. On the basis of characteristic words and concepts, phrases and idioms, someone else then could unravel the story of Jesus in order to discover the three original and separate accounts.

Unraveling the sources of the Tetrateuch (the first four books of the Old Testament) has been going on for over two hundred years. The sources identified have been essentially three. The "J" source (for "Jahweh" or "Yahweh," God's personal name in the Old Testament) is the oldest one, written in the tenth century B.C. in the court of David and/or Solomon. Source "E" (for "Elohim," the Hebrew and generally Semitic word meaning "god") is usually considered to have its origin in the northern kingdom, Israel, in the ninth or eighth century B.C. The source called "P" (for "Priest") comes from the sixth or fifth century B.C. at the hand of a priestly circle of writers who may have been writing for the exiles in Babylon. Each of these sources is better considered as a collection of older material—oral and written—than as an original composition. Of course, the editor's purpose in each case is served by the way he arranged the material handed down to him. Where he places an old story, or the sentence he uses to introduce it, can suggest his own reason for writing. These characteristics of style are clues to his message about God and people in his own time and place.

The battle at the sea described in Exod. 14:10–31 contains the J account interwoven with that called P. Each one by itself presents a complete story with its own emphases addressed to the tenth and sixth centuries, respectively.

EXODUS 14

J	*P*
v. 10 . . . the people of Israel lifted up their eyes, and behold, the Egyptians were marching after them; and they were in great fear.	*v. 10* When Pharaoh drew near, . . . the people of Israel cried to the LORD. *vv. 15–18* The LORD said to Moses, "Why do you cry to me? Tell the people of Israel to
vv. 13–14 And Moses said to the people, "Fear not, stand firm, and see the salvation of the LORD, which he will work for you today; for the Egyptians whom you see today, you shall	go forward. Lift up your rod, and stretch out your hand over the sea and divide it, that the people of Israel may go on dry ground through the sea. And I will harden the hearts of the Egyp-

EXODUS 14

J

never see again. The LORD will fight for you, and you have only to be still."

vv. 19–20 ... and the pillar of cloud moved from before them and stood behind them, coming between the host of Egypt and the host of Israel. And there was a cloud and the darkness; and the night passed without one coming near the other all night.

v. 21 ... and the LORD drove the sea back by a strong east wind all night, and made the sea dry land ... *v. 24* And in the morning watch the LORD in the pillar of fire and of cloud looked down upon the host of the Egyptians, and discomfited the host of the Egyptians, *v. 25* clogging their chariot wheels so that they drove heavily; and the Egyptians said, "Let us flee from before Israel; for the LORD fights for them against the Egyptians."

v. 27 ... and the sea returned to its wonted flow when the morning appeared; and the Egyptians fled into it, and the LORD routed [actually "shook off"] the Egyptians in the midst of the sea.

P

tians so that they shall go in after them, and I will get glory over Pharaoh and all his host, his chariots, and his horsemen. And the Egyptians shall know that I am the LORD, when I have gotten glory over Pharaoh, his chariots, and his horsemen."

v. 21 Then Moses stretched out his hand over the sea; ... and the waters were divided. *v. 22* And the people of Israel went into the midst of the sea on dry ground, the waters being a wall to them on their right hand and on their left. *v. 23* The Egyptians pursued, and went in after them into the midst of the sea, all Pharaoh's horses, his chariots, and his horsemen.

vv. 26–27 Then the LORD said to Moses, "Stretch out your hand over the sea, that the water may come back upon the Egyptians, upon their chariots, and upon their horsemen." So Moses stretched forth his hand over the sea.. .. *vv. 28–29* The waters returned and covered the chariots and the horsemen and all the host of Pharaoh that had followed them into the sea; not so much as one of them remained.

EXODUS 14

J	*P*
	But the people of Israel walked on dry ground through the sea, the waters being a wall to them on their right hand and on their left.
vv. 30–31 Thus the LORD saved Israel that day from the hand of the Egyptians; and Israel saw the Egyptians dead upon the seashore. And Israel saw the great work which the LORD did against the Egyptians, and the people feared the LORD; and they believed in the LORD and in his servant Moses.	

This comparison of the descriptions of the deliverance at the sea by J and by P shows that two somewhat different versions existed. The P account tells of the cry of the people and the answer of the Lord to the effect that God would save the people and show strength over the Egyptians. The Lord also instructed Moses to divide the sea by stretching out his hand. This action Moses performed, and the sea was indeed divided into two walls of water. The Israelites passed through, and when the Egyptians followed, Moses again stretched out his hand and "the walls came tumbling down" upon the Egyptians—drowning every last one of them. This account, supernatural and magical in its description, may have been used by the priestly writers, in a time when the exiles in Babylon were constantly being pressured to worship Marduk for his victory over Tiamat, in order to stress the dramatic victory of Yahweh. By so portraying the victory, the writer was encouraging the Israelites to see the power of the Lord and to be faithful to God.

The J account of the victory at the sea reports that the wind from the east dried up the water for a while. Although the story seems to be quite natural in its reporting, it is nevertheless filled with typical expressions of battle, especially battles in which Yahweh fights a "Holy War." The instruction to the people that they should not fear in the face of the large and overpowering enemy (vv. 10, 13), the promise that "Yahweh will fight for you; you have only to be still" (v. 14), the presence of God with the people (the pillar of cloud in vv. 19, 24), the self-destructive panic of the enemy (v. 24), the flight of the enemy (v. 25), and the eyewitness report of God's victory (v. 30)—all these are characteristics of such Holy War passages as Deut. 7:17–26; 20:1–4; Josh. 10:6–11; 1 Sam. 7:10–11; and Psalm 48. All these details of the story appear to be dictated by a certain outline or formula for reporting Yahweh's wars.

The third account of the sea event is the poem or Song of Moses in Exod. 15:1–18. This song, based apparently on the little song of Miriam at v. 21, celebrates Yahweh as "a man of war" who "has triumphed gloriously" over the Egyptian chariots. In imagery which seems to combine the piling up of waters from P and the wind from J, this song dramatically portrays the victory of Yahweh in vv. 1–12. Then vv. 13–17 indicate clearly that the song as a whole was composed some time after the people of Israel had entered into, and settled in, the land of Canaan, for that guidance into the land by Yahweh is described.

Finally, the last verse of the song—which is also the last verse of the exodus event and the climax of the victory of the sea—acclaims Yahweh as king. "The LORD will reign forever and ever" (v. 18). Now it becomes clear that for the Old Testament, as well as for the ancient neighbors of Israel, God becomes king and establishes enduring reign on the basis of victory! But for Israel this good news of victory and kingship is based on God's activity in the arena of history. It was somewhere on the border of Egypt and sometime in the thirteenth century B.C.—not in some pre-creation myth—that God is established as king over Israel and makes Israel the people of God. This is the good news:

> I will sing to the LORD, for he has triumphed gloriously;
> the horse and his rider he has thrown into the sea.
> (Exod. 15:1)

Therefore, "The LORD will reign for ever and ever" (Exod. 15:18).

151

10

The Sinai Covenant: Indicative and Imperative

AFTER GOD HAD LED the people out of Egypt, he brought them through the wilderness to the foot of Mount Sinai. At this mountain occurred a series of events which occupy one of the largest traditions in the whole Bible. Beginning with the nineteenth chapter of Exodus, the Sinai story runs through the end of that book, on through the entire Book of Leviticus, and down to the tenth chapter of Numbers. Since most of this material consists of legal instructions pertaining especially to the ritual life of Israel, we shall concern ourselves here with the *core* of this Sinai material, Exodus 19—24. These chapters can be outlined as follows:

 I. The Theophany ("God appearance")—chap. 19
  A. Arrival at Sinai (vv. 1–2)
  B. Covenant formula (vv. 3–8)
  C. Instructions and preparations for the theophany (vv. 9–15)
  D. The theophany itself (vv. 16–20)
  E. Further instructions to Moses (vv. 17–25)
 II. The Law Codes—chaps. 20—23
  A. The Ten Commandments (20:1–17)
  B. Moses as mediator (20:18–21)
  C. The Book of the Covenant (20:22—23:33)
 III. Covenant Making—chap. 24:1–11
  A. Covenant by sacrifice (vv. 3–8)
  B. Fellowship meal (vv. 1–2, 9–11)

Positioned at the beginning (19:3–8) and at the end (24:3–8) of this Sinai tradition is *covenant.* What is the meaning of this oft-used word?

THE STRUCTURE OF THE COVENANT
GOD MADE

By standard definition a covenant is an agreement between persons or parties. In general terms such agreements might be of a political, economic, legal, or religious nature, and they might be made between equals or nonequals. They might be personal or official agreements, and one party might be bound to it more than the other.

In the covenant made at Sinai the partners are God and the people of Israel. The partners are thus nonequals, and the nature of this covenant is religious. On what is the covenant based? And who is bound?

The context of the Sinai tradition alone makes clear the basis of this covenant. God had already delivered the people from the bondage of Egypt by victory over the pharaoh (Exodus 14—15). In that decisive encounter the people of Israel did nothing; the Lord did it all. Thus the account of what the Lord did indicates the basis of the covenant relationship that follows. It is no accident, in other words, that chapters 19—24 follow chapters 14—15. The exodus event is the *indicative* (what God did) which forms the motive or basis for the *imperative* (what God demands), in the context of a covenant relationship. In the Bible it is not the other way around: people are not delivered because they keep the imperatives; rather they are given the imperatives as people already saved!

The biblical editor who put together the many separate pieces of Sinai material made the point explicit by positioning the covenant formula as the first event when the people arrived at Sinai.

"Thus you shall say to the house of Jacob,
    and tell the people of Israel:
You have seen what I did to the Egyptians,
    and how I bore you on eagles' wings and brought you to myself.
Now therefore, if you will obey my voice and keep my covenant,
    you shall be my own possession among all peoples;
    for all the earth is mine,
    and you shall be to me a kingdom of priests and a holy nation.
These are the words which you shall speak to the children of Israel."
    So Moses came and called the elders of the people, and set before them all these words which the LORD had commanded him. And all the people answered together and said, "All that the LORD has spoken we will do." And Moses reported the words of the people to the LORD. (Exod. 19:3–8)

The structure of this little passage is the same as that of the entire Book of Exodus. First is reported God's indicative: "what I did to the Egyptians" and "brought you to myself." Then comes God's imperative: "obey my voice and keep my covenant." This time there is added a conditional "if," the fulfillment of which leads to various blessings for Israel. Faithfulness to the God who brought Israel out of Egypt will result in Israel being God's "own possession," "a kingdom of priests and a holy nation," in the midst of the whole earth which belongs to the Lord.

What do these expressions mean? How can we discover the impact these words and phrases had on the audience for which they were written? One obvious way is to see how the same expressions appear elsewhere in the Old Testament, to examine the context in each instance, and thus conclude in a probable way what went through the minds of the ancient Israelites as they heard and read this passage.

A HOLY NATION AND A KINGDOM OF PRIESTS

The phrase "a holy nation" (Hebrew *gôy qādôš*) appears nowhere else exactly as it appears here in Exod. 19:6. However, the expression "a holy people" (Hebrew *'am qādôš*) does appear four times—all in Deuteronomy. In three of those four cases, "a holy people" appears in combination with "own possession" (Hebrew *sĕgullāh*), just as in Exod. 19:5–6, and so the terms deserve some attention. In citing them below, we italicize the key phrases.

> For you are *a people holy* to the LORD your God; the LORD your God has chosen you to be a people for *his own possession,* out of all the peoples that are on the face of the earth. It was not because you were more in number than any other people that the LORD set his love upon you and chose you, for you were the fewest of all peoples; but it is because the LORD loves you. . . . You shall therefore be careful to do the commandment, and the statutes, and the ordinances, which I command you this day. (Deut. 7:6–8a, 11)

> You are the sons of the LORD your God; you shall not cut yourselves or make any baldness on your foreheads for the dead. For you are *a people holy* to the LORD your God, and the LORD has chosen you to be a people for *his own possession,* out of all the peoples that are on the face of the earth. (Deut. 14:1–2)

> This day the LORD your God commands you to do these statutes and ordinances; you shall therefore be careful to do them with all your heart and with all your soul. You have declared this day concerning the LORD that he is your God, and that you will walk in his ways, and keep his statutes and his commandments and his ordinances, and will obey his voice; and the LORD has declared this day concerning you that you are a people for *his own possession,* as he has promised you, and that you are to keep all his commandments, that he will set you high above the nations that he has made, in

Known in Arabic as Jebel Musa, "The Mountain of Moses" has been identified as Mount Sinai since the fourth century A.D. St. Catherine's Monastery (in the foreground) was founded by Emperor Justinian in the sixth century.

praise and in fame and in honor, and that you shall be *a people holy* to the LORD your God, as he has spoken. (Deut. 26:16–19)

Although '*am qādôš* appears in one other place (Deut. 14:21) and *sĕgullāh* occurs elsewhere (at Mal. 3:17 and Ps. 135:4), the combination of the phrases in the above-cited passages is particularly significant. In every case where they appear together, the expressions introduce God's imperatives: do the statutes and ordinances, obey his voice, walk in his ways; do not gash yourselves or make yourselves bald for the dead (according to the mourning rites of the neighboring pagans).

The word *sĕgullāh* is worth one more glance. At 1 Chron. 29:3 the word appears in the same way that it is used in other Semitic languages: to describe a king's personal and private treasure. In that passage King David is willing to give to the building of Solomon's temple not only a grant from the royal treasury but also a portion of "a treasure of my own." This reference helps us to understand that the phrase at Exod. 19:5 indicates what we saw at the end of the last chapter: that on the basis of the victory over the Egyptians, Yahweh is acclaimed as Israel's king.

155

Thus, to be God's own possession and "a people holy to the Lord" is to have the responsibility of obedience to the Lord as to a sovereign king, which God is! To be God's private treasure chest, made so by God's own decision and election, is to have a mission in the world from which Israel is separated.

Separation, in fact, is the basic meaning of *qādôš*, holiness. That which is separated from other things is holy. God is holy because the deity is separated from all else in the world. Objects in the temple were considered holy because they were separated from everyday profane use in order to serve a specific function. The mountain of God was called holy too, not because there was any special quality about its dirt and stones but because God used that place to communicate with people in a certain way. Likewise, Israel is a holy nation (or a holy people) not because of any quality inherent in the nation itself but because God separated it from the rest of the nations for a special task.

That special task in all the passages in Deuteronomy cited above is to keep the laws. The particular responsibility in our passage at Exod. 19:3–8 is summed up by "obey my voice and keep my covenant." Here even one of the blessings indicates the mission which accompanies the privilege of being God's holy nation and God's own possession: Israel is to be "a kingdom of priests."

This phrase means, in the first place, that Israel has some special privilege in being allowed to approach God as priests do. Second, in light of the responsibility placed on Israel as a holy nation and God's own treasure, Israel is called to minister to people everywhere, for God says "all the earth is mine."

The universal mission of Israel can be seen in different ways throughout the Old Testament. Chief among the promises given to Abraham when God called him out of nowhere was this: "by you all the families of the earth shall bless themselves" (Gen. 12:3). The same emphasis on universal hope occurs in the prophecy at Isa. 2:2–4 (identical to Micah 4:2–3): Israel's sanctuary at Jerusalem will be the focal point of all nations who shall proclaim,

> Come, let us go up to the mountain of the LORD,
>   to the house of the God of Jacob;
> that he may teach us his ways
>   and that we may walk in his paths.

Thus, Israel saw beyond itself to a ministering role for all peoples— precisely because Israel had been delivered by God's victory. To keep God's covenant and obey the Lord's voice was to be blessed in this ministry. The people of Israel consented to this responsibility in their response to Moses: "All that the LORD has spoken we will do." In this way Exod. 19:3–8 outlines a covenant that is yet to be made by a sacred rite.

What was introduced in Exod. 19:3–8 comes to completion in 24:3–8. Moses told the people all the ordinances of the Lord, and the people responded as before. "All that the LORD has spoken we will do." The next morning Moses built an altar and twelve pillars at the foot of Mount Sinai and then had young men offer sacrifices. "Moses took half of the blood and put it in basins, and half of the blood he threw against the altar. Then he took the book of the covenant, and read it in the hearing of the people; and they said, 'All that the LORD has spoken we will do, and we will be obedient.' And Moses took the blood and threw it upon the people, and said, 'Behold the blood of the covenant which the LORD has made with you in accordance with all these words' " (Exod. 24:6–8).

Thus was ratified the Lord's covenant with Israel, a covenant in which God, acting as king, laid the obligations on his people, the covenant partner. Clearly there are no obligations placed by Israel upon God. God has already done his part, namely, delivered Israel from the house of bondage. God's act was the basis, the motive, or the reason for making the covenant. And because of the victory at the sea, the indicative, God now issues the imperative within the context of a covenant.

THE TEN COMMANDMENTS AND
"CASE LAW"

The Ten Commandments, or Decalogue, are usually considered to be the imperative of the Sinai covenant. Yet even in this code of law, God's indicative appears—virtually ensuring that no one would think human deeds take priority.

I am the LORD your God, who brought you out of the land of Egypt, out of the house of bondage.

This introduction to the commandments at Exod. 20:2 repeats the historical act of deliverance and of God's victory as the basis for the imperatives and prohibitions that follow. It is as though v. 3 should begin with "Therefore." That is, the reason for the commands is the salvation event that has already occurred.

There are traditionally ten such commands, but the verses have been divided in various ways. In Judaism the statement about the exodus event in v. 2 is considered to be the first "word." Verses 3–6, which prohibit other gods and the making of images, constitute the second word. The prohibitions against covetousness in v. 17 are combined as the tenth word. In most Protestant denominations and in the Greek Orthodox tradition, the First Commandment prohibits other gods, and the Second lists separately the making of images. Verse 17 is considered the Tenth Commandment. In the Roman Catholic and Lutheran traditions, the prohibitions against other gods (v. 3) and against images (v. 4) are combined as the First Commandment, and v. 17 is divided into two prohibitions concerning covetousness, making the Ninth and Tenth Commandments. All traditions, however, end up with ten.

In any case, the commandments laid down here for redeemed Israel reach out to every area of life. They seem to fall into five pairs as a way of making a double impact on the people.

I. The Person of the Lord
   "You shall have no other gods before me."
   "You shall not make for yourself a graven image."
II. What Belongs to the Lord
   "You shall not take the name of the Lord your God in vain."
   "Remember the sabbath day."
III. Family Relationships
   "Honor your father and your mother."
   "You shall not commit adultery."
IV. The Integrity of Persons
   "You shall not kill."
   "You shall not steal" (originally, kidnap).
V. What Belongs to Other Persons
   "You shall not bear false witness against your neighbor."
   "You shall not covet your neighbor's house."

These imperatives from God are unqualified and unconditioned demands. As such they are classified as *apodictic* law, that is, law stated in the second person with no "ifs, ands, or buts" attached. The law code that follows, namely, the Book of the Covenant, at Exod. 20:22—23:33 contains a different kind of legal formulation, known as *casuistic* or "case" law. This type is full of conditions and cases, usually indicating in the third person a possible crime, followed by the punishment to be meted out in various circumstances.

> Whoever strikes a man so that he dies shall be put to death. But if he did not lie in wait for him, but God let him fall into his hand, then I will appoint for you a place to which he may flee. But if a man willfully attacks another to kill him treacherously, you shall take him from my altar, that he may die. (Exod. 21:12–14)

Both these law types—apodictic and casuistic—were well known in the ancient world among Israel's neighbors. But in Israel the codes take on particular meaning, for these and other laws in the Old Testament function as Israel's joyful response to the historical victory of the Lord who brought the people out of Egypt. In its own way, each of these codes serves as a guide for the redeemed people to live under the kingship of the Lord and in society with one another. For this reason the primary meaning of the Hebrew word *torah,* usually translated as "law," is actually "instruction." In the Old Testament, especially in its first five books, the laws instruct and guide the people in their life.

Of course, in the Old Testament's long history—as in other areas of legal development—law codes changed to meet new situations. To take a modern example, there was no need for antipollution laws for automobiles a century ago when the horse was the chief means of transportation, and so new laws had to be made when cars and trucks became common. Likewise, laws governing horse-and-wagon traffic on the streets of towns had to give way to different regulations for automobiles. In other areas, too, some acts which were once illegal are no longer so, and vice versa. It is not surprising then that law codes in the Bible were over the years modified or changed or rewritten. There is sufficient evidence to show, for example, that the Book of the Covenant was written sometime between 1200 and 1000 B.C. At that time there was no king, no royal or monarchical institution, no money economy, and the society was basically agricultural. Several hundred years later the society changed. A king ruled, cities developed, and the economy became money-oriented. At that time a new law code was written in order to replace the older, outmoded one. This revised code is contained in chapters 12—26 of Deuteronomy.

Once again, then, God's will for the people of Israel, the word of the Lord to "his own possession," took a different form and a new content because the situation had changed. The dynamic quality of God's word is thus attested in law, as it is in prophetic preaching and even earlier storytelling.

This Sinai covenant, from beginning to end, is based upon the sovereignty of God. Possessing a treasure of his own, commanding statutes and ordinances to govern life, and continuing promises, God is Israel's king. That exalted position was achieved, we have seen, through the victory over the Egyptians at the sea. On the basis of that indicative, God announced, "I am the Lord who brought you out of the land of Egypt, out of the house of bondage. Now, *therefore,* hear my law and walk in my ways as your response." The indicative-imperative—always in that sequence—is crucial in understanding the good news of deliverance and responsibility.

11

Deuteronomy:
God as Lord,
God as Promise

IN THE TENTH CENTURY B.C. David was acclaimed king over Judah in the south and then over the northern kingdom of Israel. Under his skillful leadership the combined monarchy flourished. David's own personality and ingenuity contributed to his success, but his son and successor, Solomon, did not fare as well. The kingdom would never again flourish as it had under David. Solomon made everything more glorious to be sure. He made an exquisite palace for himself and a magnificent temple for the Lord. The society became more urban and cosmopolitan. Trade flourished with other nations. But Solomon made some harsh internal decisions. Upon his death, they led to the breakup of the monarchy into the Kingdom of Judah in the south and the Kingdom of Israel in the north.

THE TWO KINGDOMS,
ISRAEL AND JUDAH

Side by side these two kingdoms existed for two centuries. But in the second half of the eighth century B.C. there came to the throne of Assyria the powerful ruler Tiglath-pileser III. To expand his empire this Assyrian king needed to control the territory occupied by Israel and Judah, for that land was a crossroads. Egypt lay to the southwest, Asia Minor to the north and northwest, the Mediterranean Sea to the west. With swift abandon Tiglath-pileser made his move, and in spite of some feeble attempts to stop him, his successor, Sargon II, brought the Kingdom of Israel to its end in 721 B.C. Judah was saved for a while because its king, Ahaz, began paying heavy tribute to Assyria as early as 735 B.C.

Ahaz's son and successor, Hezekiah (715–687 B.C.), was a most unusual king in Judah. He was one of the very few kings there who remained faithful to the Lord and did not introduce foreign gods and relics into the temple at Jerusalem. On the contrary, Hezekiah took bold steps to remove all idolatrous objects from the temple in order to keep it pure.

> And he did what was right in the eyes of the LORD, according to all that David his father had done. He removed the high places, and broke the pillars, and cut down the Asherah. And he broke in pieces the bronze serpent that Moses had made, for until those days the people of Israel had burned incense to it; it was called Nehushtan. He trusted in the LORD the God of Israel.... For he held fast to the LORD.... And the LORD was with him; wherever he went forth, he prospered. He rebelled against the king of Assyria, and would not serve him. (2 Kings 18:3–7)

In short, Hezekiah removed all the symbols of Baalism—the high mounds of sacrifice, the phallic and other symbols of fertility—and even the serpent that Moses had made (Num. 21:4–9), because it was becoming an idol. He tried in every possible way to free his land from the power of Assyria and from the heavy tribute Judah was paying to that empire.

But Hezekiah's son Manasseh, who succeeded on the throne, was not "a chip off the old block." Manasseh was only twelve years old when he began to reign; perhaps this explains his defection. Other people may have given the young ruler bad advice in order to meet their own desires. In any case, Manasseh undid all the good that his father, Hezekiah, had accomplished. The biblical historian's account of the reign of Manasseh stands in sharp contrast to that of his father, cited above.

> And he did what was evil in the sight of the LORD, according to the abominable practices of the nations whom the LORD drove out before the people of Israel. For he rebuilt the high places which Hezekiah his father had destroyed; and he erected altars for Baal, and made an Asherah, as Ahab king of Israel had done, and worshiped all the host of heaven, and served them. And he built altars in the house of the LORD, of which the LORD had said, "In Jerusalem will I put my name." And he built altars for all the host of heaven in the two courts of the house of the LORD. And he burned his son as an offering, and practiced soothsaying and augury, and dealt with mediums and with wizards. He did much evil in the sight of the LORD, provoking him to anger. (2 Kings 21:2–6)

Manasseh was not what one would call a model servant of the Lord!

While Manasseh was king of Judah, a new ruler ascended to the throne of the Assyrian Empire. Sargon's successor, Sennacherib, had died, and so the latter's son Esarhaddon became the new king in 681 B.C. From Assyrian documents that have been excavated and translated, it is known that all the vassal states of the Assyrian Empire were summoned to the new king about 672 B.C. The purpose of this meeting was to enable the

Assyrians to reassert their lordship over each vassal. The nations who came were required to pledge their loyalty to the ruler and his successor, Ashurbanipal. Although no mention of this meeting appears in the Bible, it is most probable that Manasseh, as king of one of the many vassal states, would have been required to attend or at least send a representative. Thus it is also probable that there was brought back to Jerusalem a copy of the treaty contract that Assyria imposed on all its vassals. Some of the actual treaties of Esarhaddon which have been preserved show an outline that looks like this, in six parts:

Preamble:	listing the parties involved in the treaty;
Exhortations:	calling for obedience to the treaty code;
Stipulations:	the code of laws which instruct the vassal in what he should or should not do;
Blessings and Curses:	a vivid description of what will happen to the vassal if he obeys or disobeys the stipulations;
Witnesses:	a list of the gods who witness the provisions of the treaty and its signing;
Reading the Treaty:	one copy kept by the king of Assyria, and one copy taken home by the vassal as a reminder of his responsibilities, probably to be read publicly at given intervals.

This treaty arrangement meant that the vassal vowed to serve the king of Assyria and the gods of Assyria, for political domination also involved religious devotion. In particular, this arrangement meant that the king of Judah would have been required to place in the temple at Jerusalem objects which were Assyrian. Some of these were statues of horses which were dedicated to the Assyrian sun god (2 Kings 23:11). But, most seriously, the arrangement meant that Judah had to bow down to a new lord: the king of Assyria and his gods. This requirement was a violation of the Lord's first and basic commandment: "You shall have no other gods beside me."

DEUTERONOMY IN
ITS HISTORICAL SETTING

It seems that the Book of Deuteronomy, or at least the core of that book, was written about this time. The book is presented as "the last will and testament" of Moses, but the outline of the book demonstrates its probable purpose in the early part of the seventh century B.C.

Preamble:	lists the relations of the two parties, the Lord and Israel (1:1—6:3);
Exhortations:	calling for obedience and wholehearted worship, beginning with the command to "love the LORD your God with all your heart, and with all your soul, and with all your might" (6:4—11:25, quotation from 6:5);
Stipulations:	the code of Deuteronomy in which God expresses anew the divine will for all of life (chaps. 12—26);
Blessings and Curses:	vivid descriptions of the Lord's judgment on the people for disobeying the stipulations and of rewards for keeping them (introduced at 11:26–32 and then expanded at chaps. 27—28);
Reading the Treaty:	the code is to be written down and deposited with those who carry the ark of the covenant; it shall be read before all the people at the Feast of Booths every seven years (31:9–11);
Witness:	the code itself shall be placed beside the ark of the covenant in order to serve as a witness against the people of Israel (31:26).

Thus the Book of Deuteronomy has the same outline as the treaties that King Esarhaddon of Assyria imposed on his vassal states. That king demanded loyalty in an absolute sense. But over against his claim, the biblical writers attested to the claim of the Lord who allowed lordship to no one but Yahweh. God and God alone is the object of the people's worship and devotion. No government—no matter how powerful—has the right to demand that this worship be subverted. On such nations and on the people who succumb to such pressure, God announces sure and certain judgment. The Book of Deuteronomy, using the same form and even some of the same content as contemporary political treaties, makes clear there is only one Lord: God!

At the same time Deuteronomy explains to the people of the northern kingdom, Israel, why their land collapsed at the hands of the Assyrians in 721 B.C. They were unfaithful to the treaty God had made with the people in the days of Moses, and so he brought the curse upon them. This same explanation would also apply to the southern kingdom, Judah, when it collapsed in the sixth century B.C. But judgment is not the last word. God holds out hope for the people on whom punishment is inflicted. The Lord gives them opportunity to start all over again, as though they were about to enter the land for the first time:

> I call heaven and earth to witness against you this day, that I have set before you life and death, blessing and curse; therefore choose life, that you and your descendants may live, loving the LORD your God, obeying his voice, and cleaving to him; for that means life to you and length of days, that you may dwell in the land which the LORD swore to your fathers, to Abraham, to Isaac, and to Jacob, to give them. (Deut. 30:19–20)

It is this promise of God to the patriarchs that provides hope for the people. In fact, one of the most dominant themes in Deuteronomy is the promise of land to the patriarchs, and the covenant (*bĕrît*) that God made with them appears at 4:31; 7:9, 12; 8:18.

This covenant in which God promised the land is, of course, a major concern in the Book of Genesis. There in 12:1–3 God promised to bless Abraham and make him a great nation. God promised that through Abraham all families of the earth would experience blessing. A few verses later the Lord promised to give the land of Canaan to Abraham's descendants (v. 7). This J passage is paralleled by P at Genesis 17 where the same promises of posterity and land are set within the context of a covenant (*bĕrît*).

Perhaps the most dramatic—and in some sense, amusing—portrayal of God's unconditional promise of land as the content of covenant occurs at Genesis 15.

> And he [the Lord] said to him [Abram], "I am the LORD who brought you from Ur of the Chaldeans, to give you this land to possess." But he said, "O Lord GOD, how am I to know that I shall possess it?" He said to him, "Bring me a heifer three years old, a she-goat three years old, a ram three years old, a turtledove, and a young pigeon." And he brought him all these, cut them in two, and laid each half over against the other; but he did not cut the birds in two. And when birds of prey came down upon the carcasses, Abram drove them away. . . .
> As the sun was going down, a deep sleep fell on Abram; and lo, a dread and great darkness fell upon him. . . . When the sun had gone down and it was dark, behold, a smoking fire pot and a flaming torch passed between these pieces. On that day the Lord made a covenant with Abram, saying, "To your descendants I give this land. . . ." (Gen. 15:7–12, 17–18)

What a peculiar story! In response to Abraham's question about the assurance of receiving the land, God instructs him to cut animals apart and place them in two corresponding rows. Then when Abraham fell asleep (or was put to sleep), a smoking fire pot (actually "a furnace of

smoke") and a torch of fire moved between the rows. A hilarious sight—
until the seriousness of the act is understood!

The only parallel to this rite in the rest of the Old Testament occurs at
Jer. 34:18–20. Because the people of Jerusalem had reneged on their
responsibility to set free the slaves during the year of liberty, the Lord
promised to bring unrelenting judgment on them. It is described thus:

> And the men who transgressed my covenant and did not keep the terms of
> the covenant which they made before me, I will make like the calf which they
> cut in two and passed between its parts—the princes of Judah, the princes of
> Jerusalem, the eunuchs, the priests, and all the people of the land who passed
> between the parts of the calf; and I will give them into the hand of their
> enemies and into the hand of those who seek their lives. (Jer. 34:18–20)

This account explains the old rite rather well. The cutting up of an animal
was a means of making a covenant. The party who walked between the
rows of dissected animal parts vowed to keep the conditions of the
covenant or else end up like the animals split in two! The leaders of
Jerusalem had violated their oath.

But in Genesis 15 what moves between the rows of anatomical pieces is
a furnace of smoke and a torch of fire. What do they represent? Let the
Old Testament speak for itself. At Isa. 31:9 the Lord is described as one
"whose *fire* is in Zion, and whose *furnace* is in Jerusalem." Again, when
the people stood at the foot of Mount Sinai, they experienced the thun-
derings and the *torches* and trumpet blast and the smoke, because the
Lord was present on the mountain (Exod. 20:18). In other words, the
furnace of smoke and the torch of fire in Genesis 15 represent the
presence of God. It was the Lord who passed between the parts of the
animals; it was God who vowed to keep the terms of the covenant made
with Abraham; it was God alone who was obligated to the promise of
land. And so this covenant is one of grace, of gift, of God's own deed and
faithfulness.

Deuteronomy thus contains two ways of talking about covenant: (1) a
covenant in which God places the obligations on Israel (as we saw to be
true at Sinai and now in the whole outline of Deuteronomy); and (2) a
covenant in which God alone assumes the obligations (a covenant type
attested in the stories about Abraham and, after him, Isaac and Jacob). In
the first instance God is seen as *Lord* over the lives and destinies of the
people chosen; in the second, God is seen as *Promise*, for God vows to be
faithful to the people involved. That both types come together in this
Book of Deuteronomy demonstrates once again the indicative and imperative. The indicative: what God does for people; the imperative: what

God asks of people. These can never be separated without falling off the fence to legalism on the one side or libertinism on the other.

GOD'S CONCERN FOR PEOPLE

It is appropriate then that the laws contained in Deuteronomy demonstrate again and again God's concern for people. Among these is the insistence by God that followers show kindness and dignity to others. These humanitarian laws, grouped in chap. 24, have a profound impact on the people of God.

> When you make your neighbor a loan of any sort, you shall not go into his house to fetch his pledge. You shall stand outside, and the man to whom you made the loan shall bring the pledge out to you. And if he is a poor man, you shall not sleep in his pledge; when the sun goes down, you shall restore to him the pledge that he may sleep in his cloak and bless you; and it shall be righteousness to you before the Lord your God. (Deut. 24:10–13)

Here it is clear that respect for a person's dignity as a human being and for his bodily care are the concerns and commands of God. The following law continues this concern for the poor.

> You shall not oppress a hired servant who is poor and needy, whether he is one of your brethren or one of the sojourners who are in your land within your towns; you shall give him his hire on the day he earns it, before the sun goes down (for he is poor, and sets his heart upon it); lest he cry against you to the LORD, and it be sin in you. (Deut. 24:14–15)

There is no mistake that God's concern reaches out beyond race to include anyone who lives with and works for and with the people who worship this Lord. Next comes the demand for justice.

> You shall not pervert the justice due to the sojourner or to the fatherless, or take a widow's garment in pledge; but you shall remember that you were a slave in Egypt and the LORD your God redeemed you from there; therefore I command you to do this. (Deut. 24:17–18)

And finally the concern for bodily nourishment.

> When you reap your harvest in your field, and have forgotten a sheaf in the field, you shall not go back to get it; it shall be for the sojourner, the fatherless, and the widow; that the LORD your God may bless you in all the work of your hands. When you beat your olive trees, you shall not go over the boughs again; it shall be for the sojourner, the fatherless, and the widow. When you gather the grapes of your vineyard, you shall not glean it afterward; it shall be for the sojourner, the fatherless, and the widow. You shall

167

remember that you were a slave in the land of Egypt; therefore I command you to do this. (Deut. 24:19–22)

These last two laws concerning justice and food for the stranger, the orphan, and the widow are based upon the activity of God in history. Israel is called upon to identify with those wretchedly poor and lost persons who have no security of their own. Israel's former identity as slaves is part of the basis for this identification. Yet it was God's redemption of the people of Israel from Egypt which gives the laws their particular punch: "Just as God cared for you when you were slaves, so now it is your responsibility to care for those who are defenseless in society." In other words, the understanding of God as the one who promised salvation and delivered on that promise is the basis for these humanitarian laws.

At the same time, the God who gave such commands and ordinances to the people of Israel is none other than their king. God was the sovereign who made a treaty containing such laws, promising blessings for obedience and judgment for disobedience. Only the Royal Person could make such provisions, such claims upon the people. God could make that claim because of the victory by which the Lord delivered Israel from Egypt.

"The LORD is king forever and ever."

12

Into Exile—and
the Herald of Victory

SHORTLY AFTER DEUTERONOMY was written, the document was apparently hidden somewhere in the Jerusalem temple, and it did not see the
light of day until 621 B.C. The king of Judah at this time was a young man
named Josiah. At his instructions some remodeling work was being
carried out in the temple, and during the course of this project someone
discovered the ancient Book of Deuteronomy. Immediately the scroll was
read to the king's secretary, who, in turn, took it to Josiah. When the king
heard the words of the ancient scroll, he was horrified, "for great is the
wrath of the LORD that is kindled against us, because our fathers have not
obeyed the words of this book, to do all that is written concerning us"
(2 Kings 22:13). The prophetess Huldah assured Josiah, however, that
God had heard his penitent lament (2 Kings 22:14–20).

Immediately the king summoned all the elders of Judah and Jerusalem
and read to them "the words of the book of the covenant which had been
found in the house of the LORD. And the king stood by the pillar and
made a covenant before the LORD . . . ; and all the people joined in the
covenant" (2 Kings 23:2–3).

With this ceremonial act Josiah began a reformation in the land of
Judah. Like Hezekiah a century earlier, he destroyed all the symbols of
Baalism. He removed all the priests who were misleading the people in
idolatrous ways; he broke down all the places where the people were
worshiping idols; he cast away all the symbols of Assyrian religion and
domination. The reform was religious and also political. The Assyrian
Empire was weakening badly under some kings who were not able rulers.
The powerful sovereign was no longer able to keep his vassals under
control. And so Josiah was able to extend his rule over some areas that

were not previously his. The people of Judah once again lived with the hope that they would finally be free from outside oppression and reexperience the glory of the days of David and Solomon.

Josiah centered all this hope in the city of Jerusalem and in its temple. According to the instructions in Deuteronomy which had been found in the temple, the king disqualified all other places of worship, so that the people would come to Jerusalem and with one voice worship one Lord. Because Josiah carried out almost every instruction and because he was faithful to the Lord, he was loved and respected by the people. "Before him there was no king like him, who turned to the LORD with all his heart and all his soul and all his might, according to all the law of Moses; nor did any like him arise after him" (2 Kings 23:25).

Unfortunately this good king was murdered at the city of Megiddo by the Egyptian pharaoh Neco (2 Kings 23:29) in 609 B.C. According to the principle of dynastic succession, Josiah's eldest son took the throne. He ruled briefly as Jehoahaz II. Neco showed, however, that he, Neco, was in charge by making a younger son of Josiah, named Eliakim, king. Neco's puppet, whom he renamed Jehoiakim, made Neco richer and richer, because the ruler of Judah taxed his people heavily in order to keep the pharaoh happy. Apparently, however, the people were allowed to worship the Lord without any difficulty and without any interjection of foreign religious influences from Egypt.

Within a matter of years the power over Judah changed to the hands of one Nebuchadnezzar, the king of Babylon. The people of Judah deceived themselves into thinking they could break loose from their new master. Apparently Josiah's reform strengthened an old idea in Jerusalem, to the effect that the city and its temple were invincible. The people felt that the Lord was present in the temple in a special way and that this presence was a lifetime guarantee against disaster.

JEREMIAH, PROPHET OF
DOOM AND REALISM

Along came the prophet Jeremiah whom the Lord had commissioned to preach his word. Against the false optimism of the people Jeremiah proclaimed the Lord's instructions and will. Yahweh commanded him,

> Stand in the gate of the LORD's house, and proclaim there this word, and say, Hear the word of the LORD, all you men of Judah who enter these gates to worship the LORD. Thus says the LORD of hosts, the God of Israel, Amend your ways and your doings, and I will let you dwell in this place. Do not trust in these deceptive words. . . . Will you steal, murder, commit adultery, swear falsely, burn incense to Baal, and go after other gods that you have not

known, and then come and stand before me in this house, which is called by my name, and say "We are delivered!"—only to go on doing all these abominations? Has this house, which is called by my name, become a den of robbers in your eyes? Behold, I myself have seen it, says the LORD. Go now to my place that was in Shiloh, where I made my name dwell at first, and see what I did to it for the wickedness of my people Israel. And now, because you have done all these things, says the LORD, and when I spoke to you persistently you did not listen, and when I called you, you did not answer, therefore I will do to the house which is called by my name, and in which you trust, and to the place which I gave to you and to your fathers, as I did to Shiloh. And I will cast you out of my sight, as I cast out all your kinsmen, all the offspring of Ephraim. (Jer. 7:2–4, 9–15)

According to this sermon by Jeremiah, God did not feel bound to the temple as the people thought. Centuries earlier, in the days of the judges, the ark of the covenant stood in the temple at Shiloh. Since God allowed that temple to be destroyed, the Lord would feel free to do the same to the one in Jerusalem where the ark stood now.

This temple sermon of Jeremiah, then, shows that the prophet was *not* on the same wavelength as Josiah, who made the temple the sole legitimate sanctuary for sacrifice and pilgrimage, in effect, for worship. The highly elevated position of the temple was regarded by Jeremiah as one more problem to be overcome in enabling the people to see the nature of true religion. In fact, there were a number of other points of contention between Jeremiah and Josiah's reform, one of which is reflected at Jer. 8:8–9. The prophet said,

How can you say, "We are wise,
  and the law of the LORD is with us"?
But, behold, the false pen of the scribes
  has made it into a lie.
The wise men shall be put to shame,
  they shall be dismayed and taken;
lo, they have rejected the word of the LORD,
  and what wisdom is in them?

These scribes, usually identified as the proponents and authors of Josiah's reform, pretended to have more wisdom than was obvious to Jeremiah. And so the prophet preached God's word that without a turning of the heart toward the Lord, nothing would save the people from disaster.

Still the people did not listen to the words of the Lord. They continued to feel that no real harm could come to them and foolishly rebelled against the mighty Nebuchadnezzar. Of course, there was no contest. In the year 597 B.C. the king of Babylon captured Jerusalem and carried off to exile Judah's king and many of the leading citizens.

Jeremiah continued his preaching over the years, but the people became more and more stubborn. And so, against the word of the Lord and his prophet, the people of Jerusalem rebelled again in 587 B.C. This time Nebuchadnezzar responded more emphatically. Not only did he carry off to exile more and more of Jerusalem's leaders; he now destroyed the temple and plundered its treasures, even the ark of the covenant.

Jeremiah was right after all. The Lord delivered the people into the hands of Babylon; the temple was destroyed; the king was gone; thousands of people were carried away as exiles to a foreign land. All of the high hopes that the people had experienced under the reign of Josiah were now completely destroyed because of their own faithlessness and deception.

Off in distant Babylon there were false prophets who spoke among the people that their exile would continue for only a short time. They were giving the people hope, but it was a false one. And so Jeremiah, who loved those very people on whom he had pronounced judgment, wrote the following letter to the exiles in Babylon.

> Thus says the LORD of hosts, the God of Israel, to all the exiles whom I have sent into exile from Jerusalem to Babylon: Build houses and live in them; plant gardens and eat their produce. Take wives and have sons and daughters; take wives for your sons, and give your daughters in marriage, that they may bear sons and daughters; multiply there, and do not decrease. But seek the welfare of the city where I have sent you into exile, and pray to the LORD on its behalf, for in its welfare you will find your welfare. . . . When seventy years are completed for Babylon, I will visit you, and I will fulfil to you my promise and bring you back to this place. For I know the plans I have for you, says the LORD, plans for welfare and not for evil, to give you a future and a hope. Then you will call upon me and come and pray to me, and I will hear you. You will seek me and find me; when you seek me with all your heart, I will be found by you, says the LORD, and I will restore your fortunes and gather you from all the nations and all the places where I have driven you, says the LORD, and I will bring you back to the place from which I sent you into exile. (Jer. 29:4–7, 10–14)

What is striking about this letter is its realism. The Lord sent the people away from their land because they had been unfaithful for many years. Now when they were in the foreign land, God did not apologize or brush it off as though it were nothing. Nor did God send messengers with false hopes, saying "Do not worry. This is merely a period of transition. We will not be here long!" On the contrary, those who water down God's will and judgment are the false prophets. The true prophet Jeremiah "tells it like it is": "You will be here a long, long time; settle down and make it your home." And, even more realistically, the prophet told the people to pray for their new home, because its welfare was their welfare (29:7).

There is an important lesson here. Life was not unimportant because the people were under punishment. Neither was life apart from the promised land devoid of meaning. On the contrary, Babylon was now the place where the people hung their hats. They must, therefore, live to the fullest the life they had in that place. This message which Jeremiah wrote to the people of Judah in exile speaks today to all who consider the world to be that evil place which people must avoid and escape in order to be "religious." Jeremiah's letter speaks against a distorted religious view that considers worldly concerns to be unimportant. It tells people everywhere that outside of paradise (the promised land in Israel's case) there is life *in* the world which deserves our attention and our prayers.

God cares about that life so much that, even in the midst of the exile which God brought upon the people, the Lord came to promise that after seventy years the exiles would be returned home. Even with those who stood under God's judgment, God planned for their ultimate good, giving them a future and a hope. This future and hope were such that only God could give them, and God did so through appointed messengers. Any messenger who happened along claiming he had an easier way or that the realities of life were just passing phases or that he himself could give salvation—that messenger was a false prophet. The true prophet is one who speaks God's word to people, taking seriously the conditions in which they live and holding out hope in God's faithfulness. Until all things are made new and the rule of God is fully established over everyone, God intends that people live *in* the world. And here people are to work to make this world a decent and just place in which to live. "In its welfare you will find your welfare."

EZEKIEL, PROPHET OF HOPE

The people to whom Jeremiah addressed his letter had difficulty accepting the hope he held out. And no wonder! Their hopes until now had been misplaced. They once had hope that their city of Jerusalem would never fall; now its walls were smashed and its people scattered. They once had hope that the land which God gave to their ancestors would be theirs forever; now they were in a foreign land, and someone else was in theirs. They once had hope that the temple was the center of all worship to God and was thus the place where God lived in a special way; now the temple was demolished. They once had hope that the ark of the covenant was the throne on which the Lord sat as king and where this Lord could be present in a particular way when the people needed him; now the ark was gone, apparently burned, and it seemed that God had gone up in smoke as well. To all appearances the God who had been so active and alive with their ancestors was now dead—and so was hope! If God, the source of life, were dead, then the people were dead too.

Into that situation came a prophet named Ezekiel. Trained as a priest, this man was one of the exiles in Babylon when God called him to be prophet. The nature of his calling was twofold. On the one hand, Ezekiel was to prophesy to the exiles that the worst was yet to come: the temple, still standing when he was called to be a prophet in 593 B.C., was about to be destroyed, and more people were to be brought to Babylon. On the other hand, as soon as news of the destruction of the temple and the city reached the people in Babylon (Ezek. 33:21), Ezekiel began to preach the return of the exiles to their homes.

One of the outstanding prophecies concerning this restoration takes place in the valley of the dry bones (Ezekiel 37). There the prophet is given a vision of the people's condition in exile. They are dried-up bones which are scattered over the valley. God commands Ezekiel to prophesy the word, so that the bones might be covered with flesh and skin and then enlivened with breath. The meaning of this imagery is made explicit in the words of the house of Israel:

> Our bones are dried up, and our hope is lost;
> we are clean cut off.
>
> (Ezek. 37:11)

From what are the people "cut off"? The particular form of the Hebrew verb used here occurs in three significant passages. (1) At 2 Chron. 26:21 King Uzziah was excluded (literally "cut off") from the temple because he was a leper and therefore unclean. (2) Psalm 88 describes a person so full of troubles that he considers himself among those who are dead and thus "cut off" from the presence of God (v. 5). (3) Likewise Isa. 53:8, part of the famous Suffering Servant song, depicts the servant as "cut off out of the land of the living." Thus the lament of the exiles as "clean cut off" at Ezek. 37:11 means they are separated from the presence of God and from life itself.

Finally, that the Israelites lament "our hope is lost" is further evidence of their despair. Hope is always directed toward God. Hope means that God will deliver and help in time of need (see Ps. 39:7; Jer. 14:8; 17:13). To complain "our hope is lost" is to lose all confidence that God will or can act to save them from their fate. In light of the misplaced hopes in

Jerusalem and the temple, it is understandable that many of the people of Israel considered themselves and their God to be dead.

Against that pessimism and defeatist frame of mind God sent Ezekiel to speak. God's word, issued through the words of Ezekiel, brought the people to "life," that is, to confidence in the Lord and to awareness of God's presence in their exile. This message to the people proclaimed that God is indeed alive and makes the people alive too. God lives not by what is always apparent to the eyes but by the word which is addressed by God to people through messengers. The temple is still in shambles; the ark is nowhere in sight; the city is a ruin; the people are still in Babylon. But God is alive, speaking and acting on behalf of the people and sending messengers to ignite the realistic hope that one day God will take them home.

And when God does take them back to Israel, the people "shall know that I am the LORD" (Ezek. 37:6, 13) and "that I, the Lord, have spoken, and I have done it, says the LORD" (v. 14). These loaded expressions make clear once again that God establishes lordship over the people of Israel by acting in history to give them new life and take them home. By this deliverance from bondage Israel will once again *know* God and God's lordship over their lives.

Other writers also addressed the people in their exile. The large Deuteronomistic history, which includes the Books of Joshua, Judges, Samuel, Kings, and additions to the Book of Deuteronomy found in A.D. 621, was composed about 560 B.C. Its purpose was to explain to the people the reason for their punishment as God's covenant curse, but also to indicate in many ways that God was very much alive even without all the old, apparent signs like the temple and the ark. In fact, the long history makes clear that God lives in heaven (cf. Deut. 26:15; 1 Kings 8:27–30, in particular), and so the destruction of objects and architecture does not affect either God's existence or ability to act.

THE SECOND ISAIAH, AS EXILE ENDS

Finally, toward the end of the long exile, sometime between 550 and 540 B.C. the Lord sent a new prophet whose name we do not know. His preaching is attached to that in the book of the eighth-century prophet Isaiah of Jerusalem, and so this latter prophet is called Second Isaiah or Isaiah of Babylon. Isaiah 40—55 contains his proclamation of God's word, and chaps. 56—66 of the same book seem to belong to a later period. (They nevertheless contain much material similar to that of our anonymous exilic prophet.)

At any rate, Second Isaiah's message was that the time of punishment in Babylon was over:

> Comfort, comfort my people,
>   says your God.
> Speak tenderly to Jerusalem,
>   and cry to her
> that her warfare is ended,
>   that her iniquity is pardoned,
> that she has received from the LORD's hand
>   double for all her sins.
> (Isa. 40:1–2)

Such a message of good news calls for public proclamations and jubilation, and so Jerusalem (perhaps Jerusalem in exile) is summoned.

> Get you up to a high mountain,
>   O Zion, herald of good tidings;
> lift up your voice with strength,
>   O Jerusalem, herald of good tidings,
>   lift it up, fear not;
> say to the cities of Judah,
>   "Behold your God!"
> Behold, the Lord GOD comes with might,
>   and his arm rules for him;
> behold, his reward is with him,
>   and his recompense before him.
> (Isa. 40:9–10)

Jerusalem is to serve as the messenger of good news that God comes triumphantly to rule over the elect people as king and to take them home. This is the beginning of Second Isaiah's message.

In another sermon the prophet makes the connection between good news and God's kingship even more explicit.

> How beautiful upon the mountains
>   are the feet of him who brings good tidings,
> who publishes peace, who brings good tidings of good,
>   who publishes salvation,
>   who says to Zion, "Your God reigns."
> Hark, your watchmen lift up their voice,
>   together they sing for joy;
> for eye to eye they see
>   the return of the LORD to Zion.
> Break forth together into singing,
>   you waste places of Jerusalem;

176

for the LORD has comforted his people,
  he has redeemed Jerusalem.
The LORD has bared his holy arm
  before the eyes of all the nations;
and all the ends of the earth shall see
  the salvation of our God.

(Isa. 52:7–10)

Here in dramatic fashion the publication of good news of peace and salvation is tied to the announcement "Your God reigns." Moreover, here, as we saw also in the parallels from mythology and in the Reed Sea event, this acclamation of God's kingship is based on victory in battle and on God's power. God "has bared his holy arm"; the Lord has "flexed his muscles" and has accomplished victory! This victory results not only in his own kingship but in peace, salvation, comfort, and redemption for God's people. In a sense, all these words contribute to the same image: life unrestrained by all external and internal factors. The Hebrew word for "salvation" (used twice in this passage at vv. 7 and 10) means essentially "to be wide." When God makes wide or spacious, therefore, barriers are removed that confine in narrow limits the lives of people— limits of bondage or exile or prison or anything else that restricts the freedom of participating fully in life's joys and responsibilities. Thus, "salvation" comes close to "peace" (Hebrew, *shalom*) which signifies essentially "completeness" or "wholeness," that is, life unencumbered by anything which prevents a person from full involvement in the life of the community. Likewise, when it said that the Lord "has *redeemed* Jerusalem" (v. 9), the image presented is that God played the role of the next of kin who pays the damages in a court case so that the indicted relative might go free.

Thus the "good tidings" announce that the death of the exiles (Ezek. 37:11) has been turned into life abundant by the victory of the Lord which establishes the divine kingship over the people of Israel. It is no wonder that Second Isaiah twice used this "herald of good tidings" idea to announce the release from Babylonian exile in terms of victory. The Hebrew word here meaning "announce good news" is a technical expression in the Old Testament used elsewhere to report the victory of a battle between armies (see 2 Sam. 18:19–31; 4:10; cf. Jer. 20:15, where the good news is that of a baby's birth). Thus the victory of the Lord is here acclaimed so that all the earth might know a new age has begun: God is king!

When the Old Testament was translated from Hebrew into Greek in the middle of the third century B.C., the words "herald of good tidings"

(Isa. 40:9) and "him who brings good tidings" (Isa. 52:7) were rendered in Greek by a participle of the same root which in the noun form is "gospel" (*euangelion*). The "gospel," in other words, is the good news. One might paraphrase the passage at Isa. 40:9 as

Get you up to a high mountain,
O Zion, evangelist....

or the one at 52:7 as,

How beautiful upon the mountains
are the feet of him who evangelizes....

How appropriate it is, then, that "Jesus came into Galilee, preaching the gospel ["good news"] of God, and saying, 'The time is fulfilled, and the kingdom of God is at hand; repent, and believe in the gospel" (Mark 1:14–15). Here too the good news is connected with the announcement that the kingdom of God is at hand—just as Second Isaiah related the two thoughts at 40:9–10 and more explicitly at 52:7–10. Indeed the anonymous prophet of the exile serves as fitting background for Jesus' own announcement of the good news of God's reign.

Isaiah 52:7 is quoted or alluded to several times in the New Testament. The most explicit reference is striking. It occurs at Rom. 10:15. This is in the context where Paul is urging the preaching of the message, the good news. Almost the entirety of Romans 10 consists of quotations from the Old Testament and their interpretations, and the chapter is loaded with profound and provocative insights. For example, when Rom. 10:13 quotes Joel 2:32, there is the New Testament's clearest illustration of how the gospel identifies Jesus with Yahweh (see Rom. 10:9 in this connection regarding "the name of the Lord"). The whole of Romans 10, drawing as it does so heavily from Leviticus, Deuteronomy, Psalm 19, Joel, and Isaiah, is a testimony to how Christian witnessing draws on long-established themes (see below, pp. 184–85).

AFTER THE EXILE:
THE PROPHET OF ISAIAH 56—66

Sometime after the return of the exiles from Babylon, a Jerusalemite was called by God to serve as a prophet to the people there. The report of his call at Isa. 61:1–11 explains his commissioning and the purpose of his role.

The Spirit of the Lord GOD is upon me,
because the LORD has anointed me

to bring good tidings to the afflicted;
   he has sent me to bind up the brokenhearted,
to proclaim liberty to the captives,
   and the opening of the prison to those who are bound;
to proclaim the year of the LORD's favor,
   and the day of vengeance of our God;
to comfort all who mourn; . . .

(Isa. 61:1–2)

This prophet has been commissioned to "evangelize" to the afflicted and brokenhearted. This task is further defined as "to proclaim liberty" as well as "to proclaim the year of the Lord's favor, and the day of vengeance of our God." In the Old Testament the "year" to "proclaim liberty" is the so-called Jubilee Year, the provisions for which are set forth in Leviticus 25. Essentially the importance of the event is summed up in verse 10.

And you shall hallow the fiftieth *year,* and *proclaim liberty* throughout the land to all its inhabitants; it shall be a jubilee for you, when each of you shall return to his property and each of you shall return to his family. (Lev. 25:10)

It seems that the prophet has been anointed to announce that the Jubilee Year and the Day of the Lord when God would establish the kingdom will coincide.

The situation to which he preached that message was a dismal one indeed. The prophet's predecessor and possible mentor had proclaimed that the return to Jerusalem from Babylon would inaugurate the reign of God (Isa. 52:7–10). When the people did return, however, they found nothing but rubble and ruin, despair and economic disaster—in short, everything the reign of God was expected to correct. In the midst of all that frustration of dashed hopes, this anonymous prophet announced that the reversal of bad times was yet to come. But come it would, and his call was already the beginning of the new and exciting future.

It is by no means surprising then that, according to Luke's Gospel (4:18–19), Jesus in the synagogue at Nazareth read this passage from Isaiah 61 and on it based his sermon (see above, pp. 106–10). He proclaimed in his hometown synagogue the good news that "Today this scripture has been fulfilled in your hearing" (Luke 4:21). The Day of the Lord when God would establish the kingdom, the time of the reversal of misfortune, is at hand in the very ministry of Jesus. This is the good news to be proclaimed, and it is addressed in this passage to the poor.

179

13

The Easter Victory:
Jesus as Lord

THE GOOD NEWS OF GOD'S victories that ran through Israel's history as gospel reaches its climax in the resurrection of Jesus Christ. Some interpretations locate that victorious climax even earlier, in his death. Here, in Jesus' cross and Easter morn, is God's victory over death.

What the exodus from Egypt was for the Old Testament, Jesus' resurrection is for the New. Just as God's triumph at the Reed Sea leads to acclamation as king and Lord, so Jesus' victory at Golgotha and the garden tomb lead to his being proclaimed Lord. It is true that in the New Testament the term "king" is almost always reserved for God. But by the events of Golgotha and the resurrection Jesus is so exalted that the very fabric of monotheism is strained to find ways of including this new experience of the victory in Christ. But ways are found, as the gospel of Jesus' lordship reiterates and builds upon many of the emphases found in the long history of Israel's gospel about the triumph of God (presented in chaps. 8–12, above).

"Jesus is Lord!" In that little phrase there is caught up much of what we have observed in the Old Testament in connection with God's victory. If the exodus from Egypt could be expounded there in mythic terms of a struggle in the world of nature, so too in the New Testament can the victory of the Lord Jesus be thus expounded. If God's victory of old could be expounded in terms of covenant relationships, so too can Jesus' triumph. Whether we think about "promise," or "imperatives," or even "advice for exiles," the New Testament has its counterparts to the Old.

Jesus of Nazareth had spent his months of public ministry proclaiming the kingdom of God (above, chaps. 6–7). His life ended on a cross, but he was raised, as Jews believed God had power to do, and as some Jews (the Pharisees) believed would happen some day to all the dead, or at least to all pious Israelites (Dan. 12:2–3; 2 Macc. 7:9, 11, 13–14, 23; John 11:24; Acts 23:8). What Ezekiel's magnificent vision about the dried-up bones that would be given flesh and breath of life (see chap. 12) promised to the nation (a "great host," "the whole house of Israel," Ezek. 37:10–11), later Jews applied to the individual, at least to individual Jews and sometimes to Gentiles. In other words, what had served to encourage Israel in exile came to encourage all kinds of people. Christians now proclaimed that this hoped-for resurrection had begun. The first example had occurred uniquely in Jesus. "He has been raised by God," they proclaimed, and added that therefore he is Lord.

This claim, that Jesus lives now with a new status from God summed up in the term "Lord," was destined to tear Israel asunder and lead eventually to two religions, Judaism and Christianity. It was to expand itself in turn through further assertions of faith. It would become, for Christians, a characteristic way of expressing all that they held most dear, so that in the twentieth century "the lordship of Christ" has become a touchstone of commitment for involvement ecumenically in the World Council of Churches. We are dealing here with what many regard as the oldest and most basic Christian confession. It is a way of stating the gospel about God's greatest victory.

The term "lord" is itself a more complex one than we might suppose. Ostensibly it addresses someone who holds the power of lordship. We might associate it in more modern times with a baron or earl in the British aristocracy or a member of the House of Lords. Or the term could be used to address a judge in court. For Christians it can denote "The Lord of my life" or the "Lord of all being, throned afar," as in the hymn by Oliver Wendell Holmes. Something of this same flexibility existed in Jesus' day. The Hebrew, Aramaic, or Greek term might be used as a polite term of address for someone like a rabbi who was regarded with respect and as having a certain authority. It was used by Mary Magdalene for the man she supposed to be a gardener in Jerusalem (John 20:15, "Sir").

On the other hand, the word had wide usage in the Hellenistic world for deities of various sorts (1 Cor. 8:5, "many 'gods' and many 'lords' "), and was claimed increasingly by the Roman emperors as a title (*dominus,* "Lord Caesar"). We have already seen how common the title is in the Old Testament. English translations often make it seem even more widespread by the device of rendering the four-letter sacred designation in Hebrew for God, *Y-H-W-H* (Yahweh), by the device of "Lord" (in small capital letters). (See above, pp. 115 and 129 n. 1. The RSV thinks the point important enough to comment on it in its preface [*Common Bible* edition, p. vii].) There is ancient precedent for this in that Christian scribes, in the translation of the Old Testament into Greek, regularly used the word for "lord," *kyrios,* at this point. The word *kyrios* thus had many connotations, but chiefly it became a word in the New Testament to express the exaltation of Jesus to new rank, power, and dignity.

EXAMPLES OF THE PRESENT
LORDSHIP OF CHRIST

We can see Jesus beginning to be acclaimed Lord by Christians in several vivid scenes in the New Testament. When about A.D. 50 Paul arrived in Corinth in the course of his missionary work, he went every Sabbath to the synagogue, according to Acts 18:4, and "argued . . . and persuaded" the Jewish members there and the Greeks who had embraced Judaism or were inquiring into it. But one version of the account is more specific. It says Paul did this by "inserting the name of the Lord Jesus." (This detail is found in the so-called Western text. Not all English translations include this variant, but that by the English Roman Catholic scholar, Ronald Knox, in 1944, has adopted it.) We may assume that Paul had developed a technique of calling out, "The 'Lord' is Jesus," at pertinent points in the sermon or during the reading of the lessons, as seems possible in the democracy of synagogue worship. (Recall how the synagogue rulers might invite a visitor to give a "word of exhortation," if he had any [Acts 13:15]. Jesus had commented on Isaiah 61 in the synagogue at Nazareth [Luke 4:21].) We know that the reading of Psalm 110 was one place that would prompt Christians to make such a comment:

Synagogue reader: "The LORD says to my lord:
'Sit at my right hand, till I make your enemies your footstool.' "
(Ps. 110:1)
Christian witness: "Jesus is lord! 'My lord' there means Jesus of Nazareth, not King David, as originally in the psalm."

Then the argument would be on in Corinth. See, further, Acts 2:34–35 and Heb. 1:13 and 10:12–13 for typical Christian use of Psalm 110, and Mark 12:35–37 for Jesus' own use of this verse as a conundrum to silence his enemies (Matt. 22:46) and delight the crowds.

A second example is reflected in 1 Cor. 12:3. "No one can say 'Jesus is Lord' except by the Holy Spirit." The phrase is a terse confession of faith and, according to this verse, the product of a heart filled with the Spirit of God. When one has yielded to the gospel, has been baptized and so "made to drink of the one Spirit" (1 Cor. 12:13), that person will express

Tomb in Jerusalem, its stone rolled aside, such as gospel accounts about Jesus' resurrection presuppose. This tomb, near the King David Hotel, may have been built for the family of Herod the Great.

his or her faith by acclaiming Jesus "Lord." Paul quotes the phrase here in this chapter in order to lead off a discussion of how "spiritual" or "charismatic" gifts are all in the service of the Lord Jesus Christ, given to build up his body, the church, and Christ the Lord is the Jesus who was crucified for us (1 Cor. 1:23; 2:2). The Old Testament knew its acclamations of God: "The Lord reigns" or "has become king" (Ps. 97:1). Here we have a Christian acclamation of Jesus as Lord, such as might have been shouted out in moments of confession and ecstasy at a service of worship.

A third illustration involving the phrase "Jesus is Lord" occurs in a more structured setting in the Epistle to the Romans where Paul is contrasting "the righteousness that comes from God" with "righteousness which is based on the law" which people try to establish on their own (Rom. 10:3–5). Then he makes his point about what the gospel is. Here he calls it the "word" (v. 8) that brings salvation to everyone who calls upon Jesus as Lord. Quoting Deuteronomy, he insists that the word (which he defines as the message Christians preach) is close at hand:

The word is near you, on your *lips* and in your *heart* [cf. Deut. 30:14]
(that is, the word of faith which we preach);
because, if you confess with your *lips* that
  Jesus is Lord
and believe in your *heart* that
  God raised him from the dead,
you will be saved.

(Rom. 10:8–9)

Here the acclamation "Jesus is Lord" is taken as the key confession for Christian lips, and the resurrection of Jesus as the basic item for believing hearts.

Paul's example leaves the possible impression that confession of faith could come before belief. That is due to his effort to expound the text from Deuteronomy in the order in which the words "lips" and "heart" there occur. So in order to prevent any misunderstanding he then goes on to sum up the logical and psychological sequence for faith and the confession of it:

Man believes with his *heart* and so is justified,
and he confesses with his *lips* and so is saved.
(Rom. 10:10)

The same passage then adds yet another example of how the application of the term "lord" was being changed in Christianity. Paul insists

(Rom. 10:12) that, for salvation, there is "no distinction between Jew and Greek; the same Lord is Lord of all and bestows his riches upon all who call upon him." Then, to support that point, the Old Testament is invoked (Rom. 10:13) "For 'every one who calls upon the name of the Lord will be saved' " (Joel 2:32 in the Greek translation). In Joel, "the Lord" was Yahweh. For Paul it is the Lord Jesus, confessed in Christian faith (Rom. 10:9; cf. 1 Cor. 1:2). The lordship of Jesus was, in such ways, coming to the confessed as the Christian gospel (cf. above, p. 178).

THE GREAT "CHRIST HYMN" OF
PHILIPPIANS 2:6–11

One of the fullest descriptions of Jesus' elevation to lordship comes at Phil. 2:11, as the climax of a grand poetic passage which many designate as an early Christian hymn. Some experts even feel that this hymn was originally composed in Aramaic and has been translated into Greek. The passage as Paul quotes it seems to fall into a pattern of at least two stanzas. The first is about Jesus' humiliation and death, the second about his exaltation and lordship. "Have this mind among yourselves," Paul writes the Philippians, "which is yours in Christ Jesus" (2:5), to introduce the first of the stanzas that follow:

H   ⁶Who, though he was in the form of God,
U   did not count equality with God
M
I   a thing to be grasped,
L   ⁷but emptied himself,
I   taking the form of a servant,
A   being born in the likeness of men.
T
I   ⁸And being found in human form,
O   he humbled himself
N   and became obedient unto death.

The phrase that occurs at this point, "even death on a cross," seems to intrude into the rhythmic pattern, and may be an addition by Paul to make absolutely clear that the hymn refers to "Christ crucified" (1 Cor. 1:23).

Then comes, in Phil. 2:9–11, the remainder of the hymn. This likely second stanza tells of the crucified Jesus' exaltation to lordship by God.

```
E     9Therefore God has highly exalted him
X        and bestowed on him the name
A        which is above every name,
L     10that at the name of Jesus
T
A        every knee should bow,
T           in heaven and on earth and under the earth,
I     11and every tongue confess
O        that Jesus Christ is Lord,
N     to the glory of God the Father.
```

This elaborate passage, however we arrange its powerful lines, tells of a godlike being ("in the form of God," yet who did not clutch tightly after deity) who became or was a human being ("in the likeness of men"), indeed a servant (the Greek is "slave," but some are reminded of the "suffering servant of God" in Isaiah 42—53). His fate was humiliation and death. But now, enter God! Note that in vv. 6—8 this godly servant is the subject. In vv. 9—11 God is the subject. The word "therefore" marks the transition. The resurrection is not mentioned by name but rather its results: Jesus is exalted and received the name above all names, the name of "Lord." This ascription of lordship is expressed in a phrase from Isa. 45:23 about how "every knee shall bow and every tongue shall swear," in the case of the Old Testament to Yahweh as Lord. But here is substituted the triumphant gospel of the early church, *"Jesus Christ* is Lord."

The term "Lord" at 2:11, particularly if interpreted in light of the background in Isaiah pointed out above, comes close to suggesting that Jesus now has the value and significance that Yahweh did in the Old Testament. The New Testament, however, even in this hymnic outburst, nonetheless holds Jesus' lordship within the bounds of the unity and oneness of God. There are not two deities. For, as v. 11 concludes, all this that God has done for Jesus was ultimately "to the glory of God the Father."

The hymn as we have outlined it above falls in simplest form into two stanzas. But some scholars have argued for other structures. For example, three stanzas:

I. Christ's preexistence

2:6   Who, though he was in the form of God,
            did not count equality with God a thing to be grasped,
2:7a, b but emptied himself,
            taking the form of a servant.

II. Incarnate life

2:7c   Being born in the likeness of men

2:8a, b and being found in human form,
he humbled himself
and became obedient unto death.

III. Exaltation

2:9   Therefore God has highly exalted him
and bestowed on him the name which is above every name,

2:10a   that at the name of Jesus every knee should bow

2:11a, b and every tongue confess that Jesus Christ is Lord.

In this analysis the phrases in verses 8c, 10b, and 11c that are not included above are termed later additions, perhaps by Paul. Yet others have found six short stanzas or have refused to commit themselves to much more than that there is a "poetic feeling" about the whole passage.

There are other points for debate in this so-called Christ hymn. When 2:9 says "God has *highly* exalted him," does that mean Jesus has been raised again to the exalted place he held before the events described in vv. 7 and 8, or does it mean he was elevated after his death to a greater dignity with God than that described in v. 6? The verb in question in v. 9 does have a prefix in Greek (hence "*highly* exalted," KJV, RSV), but does that suggest merely, "God raised him to the heights" (NEB), or imply rather "exalted him to the highest place" (NIV)? Such questions relate to how one decides about the precise sense of vv. 6–8 and their background. We spoke above of "a godlike being . . . who became or was a human being . . . , indeed a servant," and noted how some see behind v. 7 ("emptied himself") the thought of Isaiah about the servant, specifically of Isa. 53:12, that the servant of the Lord "poured out his soul to death." But is this Philippians phrase really a "servant" allusion?

One can also see a reference here in 2:6–8 to the figure of Adam in Genesis 1—3. Adam was made in the "likeness" and "the image of God" (Gen. 1:26–27); compare Phil. 2:6, 7, "the form of God . . . the likeness of men." More strikingly, the Adam figure in Genesis disobeyed God by grasping for "the fruit of the tree which is in the midst of the garden" which offered life and knowledge (Gen. 3:3–6; cf. 2:9); in contrast, the person "in the form of God" in Phil. 2:6–8—and Paul elsewhere does refer to "the last Adam" as a contrast to the first Adam (1 Cor. 15:45; cf. Rom. 5:14)—this person "did not count equality with God a thing to be grasped." That phrase in Phil. 2:6 could mean either something this

187

Adam figure already possessed but was willing to give up for others or something he did not yet possess but at which he refused to grasp selfishly for himself.

To take a final example of the discussions that swirl around this christological hymn, we have interpreted it above generally, though with caution, along widely held traditional lines that assume the person in v. 6 was "with God" at the start of the story but "became man" in vv. 7 and 8. The three-stanza interpretation noted above brings out the idea of an incarnation here even more sharply. But from time to time it has been argued that these verses do not describe the incarnation of a divine figure from above, but rather the existence and aspirations of a person Adam-like on earth from the outset. This view reads the lines in light of the description of the righteous man presented in the wisdom literature, as at Wisd. of Sol. 2:23,

> for God created man for incorruption,
> and made him in the image of his own eternity.

This "servant of the Lord" (Wisd. of Sol. 2:13, RSV note) is depicted there as set upon by enemies and condemned to a shameful death, but "in the hand of God" such a person will receive "great good" and will "govern nations and rule over peoples," the Lord reigning over all for ever (Wisd. of Sol. 2:12—3:9, esp. 2:18–20; 3:1, 5, 8).

We may diagram the possible interpretations of the course of this redeemer figure in Phil. 2:6–11 in three ways:

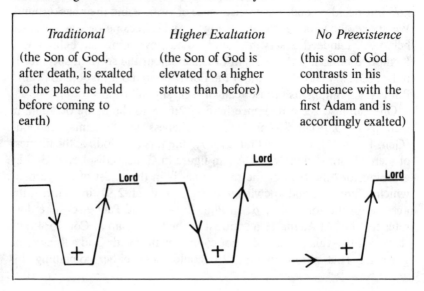

Traditional	*Higher Exaltation*	*No Preexistence*
(the Son of God, after death, is exalted to the place he held before coming to earth)	(the Son of God is elevated to a higher status than before)	(this son of God contrasts in his obedience with the first Adam and is accordingly exalted)

However we take this great hymn about Christ and however we interpret the "story of salvation" that it tells, it is necessary also to remember that Paul has quoted its tremendous tribute to Jesus Christ's obedience and subsequent lordship, in order, in the context in Philippians, to teach humility to Christians (2:1–5). As they serve others, they are to have, in their attitude of self-effacing service toward one another, the same attitude that Jesus had toward God. It is a Pauline way of saying what Jesus said, that in life "he who humbles himself will be exalted [by God]" (Luke 14:11). But what Paul gives us to illustrate that point portrays richly how Christians regarded Jesus as exalted over all the cosmos (heaven, earth, and subterranean regions) and how he reigns as Lord in heaven with the Father.

FUTURE LORDSHIP, VICTORY OVER DEATH AND DEMONIC POWERS, AND REFLECTIONS IN THE GOSPELS

All of the examples discussed above assert that the lordship of the resurrected Jesus is a present fact. He is Lord, at least ever since God raised him from the dead and exalted him with the name of *kyrios.* (The Greek word used here gives us in its direct-address form the liturgical phrase *Kyrie, eleison,* "Lord, have mercy".) But there are also places where Jesus' lordship is connected with his future coming. This is to accent another note, as if to say that, since his resurrection, he is simply waiting in heaven; he will become Lord only when he comes again. Acts 3:20–21, in a speech by Peter, reflects such a view. Jesus is "the Christ appointed for you" whom God will one day send but "whom heaven must receive until the time for establishing all that God spoke" through the prophets of old.

This picture of Jesus as future Lord also appears in the cry of the Aramaic church quoted at 1 Cor. 16:22, *Marana tha!,* "Our Lord, come." Revelation 22:20 has the same petition in Greek, "Come, Lord Jesus." Such an apocalyptic invocation is akin to an Old Testament aspect of the victory of God, for that victory was a future hope as well as a past historical event (see chap. 12, above).

The gospel of Jesus' lordship is, as we have seen, especially connected with victory over death, whether at Jesus' exaltation from the tomb at Easter or in the hope for our resurrection at the "last day." There are all sorts of links in the New Testament between Jesus' death and resurrection and Israel's exodus release from bondage in Egypt at Passover time. Jesus is called "our paschal [Passover] lamb" (1 Cor. 5:7). There is reference to the "exodus" (RSV, "departure") that Jesus was to accomplish in Jerusalem at the close of his ministry (Luke 9:31). Jerusalem is even once described as "Sodom and Egypt, where their Lord was crucified" (Rev. 11:8), in a metaphor that strikingly mixes symbols. For "Sodom" was a name applied to Jerusalem in Isa. 1:10 because of its sins. "Egypt" conjures up images of the exodus victory. The Lord Jesus' crucifixion there in Sodom-Egypt-Jerusalem is God's new victory.

The Old Testament, we saw (chap. 8), sometimes spoke of the victory of God in mythological terms, as surrounding cultures did with their gods' victories. One may note a touch of this in the description of Jesus' triumph in Phil. 2:10. Jesus is to become Lord over "every knee . . . in heaven and on earth and under the earth." This is the imagery of the three-story universe, inserted into the quote from Isa. 45:23. The point is not whether angels in heaven or demons on or under earth have "knees," but rather that all creatures, on any level of existence, are to bow and confess this Lord's reign. If we want a fuller reference to these enemies subdued in Christ's victory, Col. 2:15 gives this vignette: "He [God] disarmed the principalities and powers and made a public example of them, triumphing over them in him [Christ]." There is an alternative interpretation, however, for the pronouns are ambiguous. The meaning could also be: "He [Christ] disarmed the principalities and powers . . . triumphing over them in it [the cross]" (RSV note). In any case, the picture is of God's victory, at Jesus' cross and resurrection, over cosmic powers who are then led into subjection the way a Roman emperor paraded his triumph through the streets of Rome, with captives following. It is a picture of *Christus victor!*

Such passages describe the victory of the Lord Jesus in terms of defeat for demonic rulers. In a fuller list of these forces opposed to God, Col. 1:16 mentions "thrones, dominions, principalities, authorities." Ephesians 6:12 has a slightly different list: we fight not "flesh and blood" (human beings) but "principalities, powers, world rulers of this present darkness, the spiritual hosts of wickedness in the heavenly places"; and Rom. 8:38–39 gives still another list of what separates us from God.

It is sometimes assumed that these other-than-human creatures inhabited the underworld, and 1 Peter 3:18–19 has been interpreted to mean that Jesus descended into the underworld and bested the demonic forces there (the so-called harrowing of Hell).[1] But other passages locate these creatures in the heavenly realms between earth and God above. In this vein Satan is described as "the prince of the power of the air" (Eph. 2:2), and Eph. 4:8–10 can be taken to imply that it was when Christ ascended that he took a host of captives, that is, these demonic, cosmic forces. The whole idea can also be related to Jesus' victories during his earthly ministry over evil spirits and the demons of Beelzebub. Jesus exorcised them (see chap. 7) and frustrated their designs against God's world. The New Testament's message is that wherever such creatures exist, and however they oppose God's will, Christ has defeated them. That is the good news of his lordship. God's enemies are vanquished.

So pervasive is the theme of Jesus as Lord that it even casts its mantle over the gospel accounts of his life *prior* to the resurrection. We begin with an incident just after Easter. John 20:28 presents the high point in the whole Fourth Gospel. The scene is the one where Thomas, who had had doubts, confesses his belief in Jesus with the words "My Lord and my God!" This can be read as faith's reply to the claim of the Roman emperor Domitian, who ruled A.D. 81–96, to be *Dominus et deus noster,* "Our Lord and God." But it is better interpreted as Old Testament language, from Ps. 35:23, applied to Jesus. It is, incidentally, one of the rare but supreme moments in the New Testament when Jesus, in the language of praise, is called "God" (see also Rom. 9:5, RSV note; 1 Tim. 3:16, RSV second note).

When Jesus during his ministry was addressed as *mar* in Aramaic (Greek, *kyrie*), it need have meant no more than "sir" (see Mark 7:28). At times, however, during the ministry this term of address takes on a deeper meaning, as when the seventy return from their mission and report, "Lord, even the demons are subject to us in your name!" (Luke 10:17). On occasion there is ambiguity, probably deliberate, in an account. For example, when Jesus sends his disciples for an animal (and her colt) on which to make his "triumphal entry" into Jerusalem, he tells them that, if anyone objects, they shall simply say, "The Lord has need of them" (Matt. 21:3). That could refer to "the master of the animals" or "God," and even mean "their Lord has need." But when "the Lord" occurs in narrative as a designation for Jesus (e.g., Luke 10:1), then we know that the evangelist, in light of later usage, is describing Jesus with a title which reflects his ultimate elevation in authority. The victory of God at Easter which made Jesus Lord is now seen as already present in his lifetime.

John's Gospel goes especially far in pushing the good news of God's victory through Jesus back into his earthly career. John sees the cross, not simply the later resurrection, as this triumph. For this reason, he portrays Jesus as striding serenely, indeed masterfully, toward the cross. That is "the hour" when the Son of man will be glorified (John 12:23, 27), for what Jesus calls "my hour" is a reference to the cross (2:4; 7:30; 8:20; 13:1; 17:1). There is a similar and ironic meaning in the Johannine phrase "be lifted up" (3:14): it seems to refer to exaltation, but it is on a cross that the Son of man must first be "lifted up" (cf. 8:28; 12:32, 34).

Because the Fourth Gospel proclaims that the cross is a triumph, it alone of all the Gospels can have Jesus say, as he dies, "It is finished" (19:30). That is no cry of resignation but refers to his work in the plan of God. The crucifixion means that the victory of God is already complete.

MORE CONNECTIONS AND CONTRASTS

One could go on drawing out comparisons between "the gospel of God's victory in Israel" and its counterpart "in Jesus Christ." A prophet like Jeremiah condemned reliance on the temple (above, chap. 12). Jesus announced that in his ministry "something greater than the temple is here" (Matt. 12:6); he talked of its destruction (Mark 14:58; John 2:19–22), and his followers learned to live without such a cultic center. The Old Testament theme of "the covenant" is carried over, especially in its "grace" or "promise" form (see above, chap. 11, and compare Gal. 3:15–22; 4:21–31). Jesus brings to fulfillment Jeremiah's hope for a new covenant (Jer. 31:31–34; Luke 22:20, a verse which should not be relegated to a footnote as in some editions of RSV). "Covenant" is, however, not so prominent a theme in the New Testament as in the Old.

We may also note that just as God's victory and kingship imply a people in the Old Testament, so in the New the triumph that brings about Jesus' lordship leads to a new people, a fellowship or community called the church. These followers are, like Israel of old, exiles. Because Christians know exile and dispersion from their true home (which is with God; see Phil. 3:20), the epistles can address them as "aliens and exiles" (1 Peter 2:11; cf. also 1:1; James 1:1). An alert reader of the Bible will keep on discovering and exploring connections and contrasts between the two testaments along such lines.

Upon the importance of the good news of God's victory, however, the Old and New Testaments are united. Christians were the people who had experienced, beyond the exodus, a new liberating event by God which had made Jesus "Lord." On them rested the hope expressed in the benediction, "May the God of peace who brought again from the dead our Lord Jesus, the great shepherd of the sheep, by the blood of the eternal covenant, equip you with everything good that you may do his will, working in you that which is pleasing in his sight, through Jesus Christ; to whom be glory for ever and ever. Amen" (Heb. 13:20–21). This doxology suggests there would be even further implications of God's kingship and Jesus' lordship, in creation and the world, as indeed there are (cf. chap. 18, below).

NOTE

1. The "harrowing of Hell" was a popular theme in medieval English literature and art, inherited from the patristic view of "Christ the Victor." It depicted the overcoming of the powers of evil by Jesus during his "descent into Hades" between Good Friday and Easter. A thirteenth-century poem in the East Midland dialect describes the liberation of Adam and Eve, Abraham, David, Moses, and John the Baptist by Jesus.

IV

THE GOSPEL
OF GOD AS KING,
IN CREATION AND WORLD

The cedars of Lebanon, symbols of strength, splendor, and glory, were used in Solomon's temple as one means of glorifying God. Yet even such expressions of power yield before the power of the Creator (Ps. 29:5).

14

Yahweh Reigns—
in Israel's Worship

THE CONTRAST BETWEEN THE "natural" or cyclical understanding of life among Israel's neighbors and the "historical" basis of existence in the Old Testament does not mean that Israel had no interest in creation or the world. On the contrary, there are in the Book of Psalms and elsewhere in the Bible numerous hymns that demonstrate the acts of the Lord in creation. Some of these hymns bear striking similarities to hymns used by Israel's neighbors to extol their gods and their roles in creation and nature. Psalm 29, for example, culminates in an announcement that the Lord sits enthroned as king. Preceding this is a description of God which is parallel to that of the nature-god Baal in Canaanite poetry. Or again, Psalm 104, usually regarded as an Israelite adaptation of the early Egyptian hymn to the sun god Aton, describes the Lord's role over every aspect of creation.

Even such a strongly historically oriented prophet as Amos seems to have incorporated three stanzas of a creation hymn into his preaching, in order to proclaim the Lord's activity in creation as well as in history.

> For lo, he who forms the mountains,
>> and creates the wind,
>> and declares to man what is his thought;
> who makes the morning darkness,
>> and treads on the heights of the earth—
> the LORD, the God of hosts, is his name!
>> (Amos 4:13)

> He who made the Pleiades and Orion,
>> and turns deep darkness into the morning,
>> and darkens the day into night,

who calls for the waters of the sea,
  and pours them out upon the surface of the earth,
the LORD is his name. . . .

(Amos 5:8)

. . . he who touches the earth and it melts,
  and all who dwell in it mourn, . . .
who builds his upper chambers in the heavens,
  and founds his vault upon the earth;
who calls for the waters of the sea,
  and pours them out upon the surface of the earth—
the LORD is his name.

(Amos 9:5–6)

The use of these and other hymns (see Psalm 89; Jer. 31:35) demonstrates that, in the worship life of Israel, creation and God's role as creator played a significant part. The nature of such hymns leads one to believe that although confession of faith centered primarily in God's acts in history, his acts in creation likewise were an important subject of confession and praise.

THE LORD'S REIGN—
ENTHRONEMENT PSALMS

Significant in Israel's worship are those psalms that quite specifically announce the good news that God, *as creator,* is king over the world. The reference to God's reign or kingship is so explicit in Psalms 47, 93, 95–99 that many scholars have labeled them "enthronement psalms," used annually to celebrate the Lord's rule. There is some debate concerning whether the Hebrew words should be translated "The LORD has become king" (thus indicating that God is being crowned anew each year like the Babylonian Marduk) or "The LORD reigns/is king" (thus confessing a continuing situation rather than a yearly one). Nevertheless, the present reality of God's rule is indicated clearly. The kingdom of God was already present in the confession of Israel and in the people's worship.

To understand what was involved in this confession of the Lord's reign, we shall examine the various themes of the enthronement psalms which together give us an overall picture.

1. *"The LORD reigns/is king"* or *"The LORD has become king."* This assertion is an acclamation of God's reign which introduces Psalms 93, 97, and 99. The confession proclaims God's rule over both the worshiping community and the whole earth. Standing as it does in the first verses of these psalms, the announcement provides the motive or basis for all

198

that follows. In like fashion the same acclamation appears in the tenth verse of Psalm 96 and with the slight variation of "God" for "the LORD" in the eighth verse of Psalm 47. In 96:10 the announcement is to be made to the nations rather than simply to be contained in Israel's worship.

The Babylonian New Year Festival's liturgy included the story of creation where the god Marduk became the head of the pantheon. In the same story the other gods acclaim "Marduk is king." As a result, some scholars have made some rather direct connections between Babylon and Israel in this matter of enthronement. There are, however, a number of difficulties in making such a conclusion, particularly because there is no New Year Festival included in the major festival calendars of the Old Testament. Only in later Judaism does Rosh Hashana become an important celebration.

2. *"King."* Quite apart from the verbal form "become king" or "reign," the Hebrew noun for "king" is used in several of these psalms as a title for the Lord. Psalm 47 refers to "king over all the earth" (vv. 2 and 7) as well as "our [that is, Israel's] King" (v. 6). While the Lord is again called "king" at Pss. 98:6 and 99:4, the title is expanded at 95:3 to "a great King above all gods," thus indicating a time when the Hebrews still acknowledged the existence of other gods among their neighbors.

3. *"Maker."* In only two of these psalms is the Lord specifically called "our Maker" (95:6) or is the subject of the verb "made" (95:5; 96:5). In 96:5 the Lord is said to have "made the heavens" as a way of confessing who is true God while other "gods" are helpless idols who need to be served by people. Psalm 95 uses the "maker" idea in two ways. First, the Lord "made" the sea and "formed" the dry land, references to creation. Second, the Lord is "our Maker," followed by "he is our God, and we are the people of his pasture, and the sheep of his hand." In this second usage, the reference is not to the creation of the world but to the election of Israel as God's own people, God's own child. By using those two different ideas the psalmist confesses that for Israel God's kingship consists not only in a role as creator of the universe but also in the creation of a people who acknowledge Yahweh as Lord.

4. *Universal reign.* Twice in these psalms appears the belief that "the world is established; it shall never be moved" (93:1; 96:10). This confession asserts that since God has provided the world with stability and durability, the world is subject to him as king. Beyond this notion, the universal nature of God's reign appears in other psalms as "king over all the earth" (47:2, 7), or "most high over all the earth" (97:9), or "he is

exalted over all the peoples" (99:2). Moreover, these peoples or families of the earth will see his glory (97:6) and his victory (98:3), and they are called upon to praise the Lord (96:7–9), gather around him (47:9), and tremble at his glorious reign (99:1).

On the one hand, this universal reign seems to be patterned after the grandiose claims of earthly monarchs who described their kingdoms in terms beyond belief. An eighth-century B.C. king of Assyria named Sennacherib characteristically introduced the account of his military campaigns with this description of himself: "Sennacherib, the great king, the mighty king, king of the universe, king of Assyria, king of the four quarters [of the earth]." Likewise the Davidic king on Jerusalem's throne was promised at his coronation that the nations would be his heritage and the ends of the earth his possession (Ps. 2:8). Such universal claims then were typical of kings, and so the same stereotyped claim would have been extended to the Lord as king.

On the other hand, such a worldwide dominion under the Lord expressed the hope that one day in the future God would indeed be acknowledged as king by all peoples on the face of the earth. In many Old Testament passages, among them Isa. 2:2–4, the nations are portrayed as coming to Jerusalem to hear and learn the Lord's word and learn his will, and worship the only God. Thus, these "enthronement psalms" contain both confession of God's present reign and the hope or confidence that in the future God's rule will extend over everyone.

5. *Response of nature.* Since God's reign is universal, the whole universe responds before the throne of the king. The heavens are glad (96:11) and proclaim God's glory (97:6); the earth rejoices (96:11; 97:1) and quakes (99:1); the sea roars (96:11; 98:7); the floods clap their hands (98:8) and roar (93:3); the fields exult (96:12); and the trees and the hills sing for joy (96:12; 98:8).

In one passage (97:2–5) the natural forces have a different function. Here, as in Exodus 19, clouds, darkness, fire, lightnings, and earthquakes signify the presence of the Lord in coming to the people of Israel. In this sense these verses make up a theophany ("a God appearance"). But here—as elsewhere in the Bible—God's appearance is not described. It is not on what the worshiper sees that the psalm puts its emphasis, but on the impact of God's mighty and holy presence, which evokes awe and praise.

6. *Judge and justice.* One of the persistent themes running through these enthronement psalms is justice in judgment. The Lord the king comes as judge over Israel and over the peoples of the earth. The description of this role in the psalms is interesting to observe.

Thy decrees are very sure;
  holiness befits thy house,
  O LORD, for evermore.
              (93:5)

These decrees or testimonies are the divine and solemn charges which
the Lord makes on his people, similar to those explicit orders issued in
Deuteronomy (4:45; 6:17, 20) where the same Hebrew word (*'ēdōth*) is
used. That these testimonies are sure or confirmed means that they are
stable and secure like the dynasty of David (2 Sam. 7:16) or like a child
carried by an adult (Isa. 60:4). Thus they were regarded by the people of
Israel as a source of confidence and hope rather than as a burden. For this
reason the mention of the Lord's decrees is included in an expression of
praise to the Lord who is king and who established the world.

Then shall all the trees of the wood sing for joy
  before the LORD, for he comes,
  for he comes to judge the earth.
He will judge the world with righteousness,
  and the peoples with his truth.
              (96:12b–13)

That the Lord will judge all peoples with a true sense of what is right
and straight (see also 96:10, "The Lord reigns! . . . he will judge the
peoples with equity"), and that this role as judge will be executed on the
basis of faithfulness to responsibility (the meaning of "righteousness" in
the Old Testament) provided the motivation for nature to sing for joy (see
also 98:8–9). In like manner, because of such judgments,

Zion hears and is glad,
  and the daughters of Judah rejoice,
  because of thy judgments, O God.
              (97:8)

Thus the kingship of the Lord over Israel and all the earth points to the
divine role as judge and "lover of justice" (99:4). This in turn results in
joyful singing and glad celebration. God's execution of justice results
from the confession that he is king. That such judging is awaited with joy
and not fear shows the utter confidence and hope with which the faithful
worshiper trusts in the will of God and in God's faithfulness.

7. *"Victory."* We have seen previously that, in contrast to its neighbors
in the ancient Near East who acclaimed their gods as kings on the basis of
a victory in mythical combat, Israel confessed Yahweh as king because of
a victory over earthly enemies. Now, however, in "enthronement" Psalm

98, the Lord has acquired "victory" and made known "victory" in the sight of all nations. This "victory" provides the motive for the joy to be expressed "before the King, the LORD" (v. 6). What is interesting in this psalm is the lack of any reference to historical combat or Holy War; no allusion is made to any historical person or nation that Yahweh has defeated.

The word translated "victory" by the RSV in Psalm 98 is the same word which is usually rendered "salvation" (basically, "spaciousness, breadth"). The translation is justified on several grounds. First, at 1 Sam. 14:45 the word is used to refer to the victory which Saul's son Jonathan accomplished over the Philistines. Second, at Isa. 26:18 the same word is used in the phrase "no deliverance" as a synonym for the fall (or defeat) of the hostile forces in the world. Thus, there is ample reason for translating the Hebrew word "victory," but "victory" over whom? This victory of the Lord and Yahweh's kingship are celebrated only in rather general terms, and so we get the impression that the battle was one of a cosmic nature, quite similar to those many stories from Israel's neighbors.

There are at least two other pieces of evidence for such an impression. First, in these enthronement psalms there is lacking any serious mention of the acts of God in history. In all these psalms only two passages speak of historical persons or situations. Psalm 95:8–11 mentions the rebellion of the people of Israel at Meribah or Massah and the entire wilderness experience as one of complaining by the people against God (see Deut. 6:16). Because of this testing directed at God the people were not allowed to enter the "rest" Yahweh was going to provide (95:11), that is, the promised land. Psalm 99:6–7 enumerates testimonies and statutes spoken by the Lord to Moses, Aaron, and Samuel when they consulted him. In neither of these historical passages is the emphasis laid on God's saving deeds in Israel's encounters with hostile nations. Therefore, it is not in these historical references that the kingship of God is founded.

Second, Ps. 96:2 likewise contains the word "salvation," which should probably also have been translated "victory" in the RSV.

Sing to the Lord, bless his name;
  tell of his salvation from day to day.

The innocent little word "tell" is the same word which appeared at Isa. 40:9; 52:7; and 61:1 with the meaning "proclaim good tidings." In that context of the exile in Babylon and in reference to the announcement of victory in war at 2 Sam. 18:19–31 (seven times), we saw previously (under "The Second Isaiah, as Exile Ends" in chap. 12) that the word actually means "to report the good news of victory." In that case, Ps. 96:2 should be read as "proclaim good tidings of victory from day to day." Like Psalm 98, this psalm too celebrates the Lord's reign (96:10) over the earth which rejoices when he comes to judge—all on the basis of victory. But again, victory over what or whom? As in Psalm 98, so here in Psalm 96 no enemy is mentioned; thus it seems that in light of reference to God's making the heavens (96:5) and establishing the earth (96:10), the victory which marks the Lord as king is related somehow to creation and perhaps then to mythical combat.

Where in Israel—that is, in what geographical location—would the people have confessed their faith in Yahweh the king who is (was) victorious in mythical combat?

8. *"Zion."* Psalms 97 and 99 explicitly mention Zion, the temple mount in Jerusalem, as the setting for the enthronement psalms.

> *Zion* hears and is glad,
>   and the daughters of Judah rejoice. . . .
> (97:8)

> The LORD reigns: let the people tremble!
>   He sits enthroned upon the cherubim; let the earth quake!
> The LORD is great in *Zion;*
>   he is exalted over all the peoples.
> (99:1–2)

Yahweh sat enthroned as king upon the cherubim that stood beside the ark in the Holy of Holies, the most sacred part of Jerusalem's temple. It was in this temple on Mount Zion that the enthronement of the Lord was celebrated by the people in their confession and worship. This location might help to explain why it is that God's kingship is understood in these psalms in a way different from most of the Old Testament.

When David, in the tenth century B.C., selected Jerusalem as the capital of his new united monarchy, he accomplished an act of sheer political genius. The city had no ties to either the northern or the southern kingdom; no jealousies could arise over favoritism. But the same advantage also proved to be a disadvantage. The city of Jerusalem had no old Hebrew traditions connected to it, and as a result many of the ideas of the natives of Jerusalem stayed and became influential. Those natives were a branch of Canaanites called Jebusites, who worshiped a god named *El Elyon,* usually translated "God Most High."

The story was told that Abraham once had contact with this god and this city. In Gen. 14:17–24 the old patriarch was met by a certain Melchizedek who was priest of *El Elyon* and king of Salem (that is, Jerusalem). Abraham was blessed by Melchizedek in the name of *El Elyon,* and the patriarch responded by tithing everything he had to this Canaanite deity. This positive response of Abraham to the deity of Jerusalem served as a model for later generations of Israelites.

One of David's problems in his new capital city was to merge the native Jebusites and their traditions with the traditions of worshiping Yahweh. El was the chief god of the Canaanite pantheon, who revealed himself in various places as *El Roi* ("God of seeing"; Gen. 16:13); *El Shaddai* ("God Almighty"; Gen. 17:1 and often); *El Olam* ("the Everlasting God"; Gen. 21:33); and so forth. In time, as Baal became the chief god among the Canaanites, the veneration of El was decreasing. It seems that in many places, especially in Jerusalem, El, who was known there as *Elyon,* became identified with Yahweh the God of Israel.

This probable identification meant that many attributes of El were transferred to Yahweh. In Canaanite religion El was king over other gods and over the universe; he was the "creator of creatures," the father of humankind; he presided over a heavenly court (cf. 1 Kings 22:19; Isa. 6:1–8; Job 1); and his major function was to execute justice in this world. Although no such story has yet been found, it is likely that El had once vanquished some foe in order to assert his supremacy as king. The Ugaritic texts found in 1929 at Ras Shamra furnish much material on El and his attributes.

Now it is likely that the identification of *El Elyon* of Jerusalem with Yahweh of Israel is the reason that the enthronement psalms portray the Lord as king who accomplished victory and who executes justice in the earth which this God created. Thus a "foreign" god expanded the attributes of Yahweh in a positive way, and although Yahweh's own peculiar nature lies in his acting in history to create a people for himself, the Lord can also be worshiped in these terms:

> Clap your hands, all peoples!
>   Shout to God with loud songs of joy!
> For the LORD, *the Most High [Elyon],* is terrible,
>   a great king over all the earth.
>   (Ps. 47:1–2)

Or again,

> For the LORD is a great God *[El]*,
>   a great King above all gods.
>   (95:3)

Thus the understanding of Yahweh as the God of history came to include the confession of Yahweh as king over the world.

9. *Praise.* The enthronement psalms are unanimous in their expression of praise and worship for Yahweh the king. No element in these psalms is repeated in more forms than this call to worship this Lord. Let the psalms speak for themselves by random examples.

> Sing praises to God, sing praises!
>> Sing praises to our King, sing praises!
> For God is the king of all the earth;
>> sing praises with a psalm.
>> (Ps. 47:6–7)

> O come, let us sing to the LORD;
>> let us make a joyful noise to the rock of our salvation! . . .
> O come, let us worship and bow down,
>> let us kneel before the LORD, our Maker!
>> (Ps. 95:1, 6)

> Ascribe to the LORD, O families of the peoples,
>> ascribe to the LORD glory and strength!
> Ascribe to the LORD the glory due his name;
>> bring an offering, and come into his courts!
> Worship the LORD in holy array;
>> tremble before him, all the earth!
>> (Ps. 96:7–9)

> Extol the LORD our God,
>> and worship at his holy mountain;
>> for the LORD our God is holy!
>> (Ps. 99:9)

Thus did the worshiping community of Israel at Jerusalem recognize that the Lord was not the old familiar buddy down the street to be used at one's whim and desire. On the contrary, before the Lord the king, believers stand in awe, and in the midst of their confession praise him above all else. To acclaim the Lord as king was to announce the good news that he reigns over all, keeping the world secure and executing justice among all peoples. Such is the gospel of the enthronement psalms.

15
The Lord Reigns—
as Creator

APART FROM THOSE POWERFUL hymns which extolled God as creator and king in Israel's worship, the Old Testament bears witness to God's reign also in story form. In fact, the stories in Genesis 1 and 2 probably rank first among the favorite ones studied and debated even today. While we tend to argue and ponder over the manner in which the world took its present shape, the ancient writers were more interested in witnessing to God as the world's creator and by implication its king as well.

Throughout this book we have attempted to understand the purpose and the meaning of stories in terms of the word of God addressing people in their own times and places. That same approach enables us to gain some insights into the two creation stories which stand side by side at Gen. 1:1—2:4a and at Gen. 2:4b–25. These quite different witnesses to God as creator represent in their final forms the work of two old friends of ours: The Yahwist and the Priest whom we met in our discussion of the Reed Sea event of Exodus 14 (see above, chap. 9). That each of these writers was a particular witness to God's word will be seen as we study their creation stories by comparison and in isolation.

The following table will show at a glance both the similarities and the differences between these two accounts.

	P (Genesis 1)	J (Genesis 2)
Original State of Earth:	Watery chaos	Waterless desert
Name of Deity:	God (Elohim)	LORD God (Yahweh, Elohim)

	P (Genesis 1)	J (Genesis 2)
Scope of Story:	Universal	Local
Humans Over Other Creatures:	Have dominion	Give names
Order of Creation:	Light	Man (male)
	Firmament	Garden
	Earth, plants	Vegetation
	Sun, moon, stars	Rivers
	Birds, fish	Beasts, birds
	Humankind (male and female)	Woman
	Rest ("God rested")	

THE STORY OF EDEN

Because the J account is the older of the two, we shall discuss Genesis 2 first. The story begins by describing the condition of the universe before the Lord God went to work (2:4b–6). Since the Lord's creative activity does not begin until v. 7, the prior verses portray a pre-creation scene: no vegetation, no rain, no laborer—only a subterranean spring (RSV's "mist" is no longer acceptable as a translation) to water the ground. Obviously the picture presented here is one of a desert, and the author must surely have had in mind that vast, sandy, waterless area in southern Judah and beyond into the Negeb. From the author's point of view such an area is untouched by the Lord's hand and is thus representative of the time before the creation.

Out of this dry and dusty clay the Lord God made man—the male of the species—as a potter molds a vessel by trained hands. It remained a lifeless hunk of clay until the Lord God blew breath into his nostrils. Only then, with common, ordinary breath which originated from the Lord, did the creature come to life, and with that statement in v. 7 the writer confesses that there is no life apart from the Lord God, the creator.

This innocent little statement about the creation of the man is in one sense remarkably similar to the stories of "primal man" elsewhere in the ancient Near East, and in another sense it is completely different. Like some pagan stories, humanity is made out of clay. A tale known as "Creation of Man by the Mother Goddess"[1] from Mesopotamia at about 2000 B.C. records the discussion of the gods concerning the formation of humans. Apparently it is the mother goddess, appropriately named

Mami, who is responsible for the job, but other deities have their suggestions on how it is to be done. One deity suggests forming the figure out of clay and animating it with blood. Another suggests that the blood be obtained by killing another god and then mixing clay and blood. Precisely which method is used by Mami is not known because the clay tablet is broken here, but the suggestion of using a god's blood along with the clay probably prevailed, because another story about the creation of humans offers the same method. That other story is the famous creation epic known as the *Enuma Elish,* which reports the primordial battle between Marduk and Tiamat. After the victor had vanquished Tiamat, Marduk killed her general, Kingu, in order to make humankind out of his blood (see above, pp. 133–34).

In the story of Genesis 2, all this pagan gore is dismissed. True, the man is formed out of clay, but he is animated not by the blood of some murdered god; rather, he becomes a living being solely by the breath which the Lord puffs into his nostrils. Here the wild mythology is rejected by the Yahwist in favor of a sober statement about one God who alone is responsible for life.

The story goes on in Gen. 2:8–9, 15–17 (vv. 10–14 are probably a later addition to the story). Now that the Lord had this man on his hands, God had to put him somewhere, and so the Lord God planted a garden full of trees which were pleasant to the senses of sight and taste. It was a virtual oasis in the midst of the desert, and it was made just for the man. "The LORD God took the man and put him in the garden of Eden to till it and keep it" (Gen. 2:15), and then he instructed the man to eat freely of any fruit in the garden—with one exception: the fruit of the tree of the knowledge of good and evil.

In this respect the story is particularly striking. The man whom the Lord made was so important to God that the Creator planted a garden for the man's welfare. All the fruit, with that one exception, was his to enjoy. With that view the writer once again runs smack in the face of the pagan creation stories. In the *Enuma elish* Marduk says:

> I will establish a savage, 'man' shall be his name.
> Verily, savage-man I will create.
> He shall be charged with the service of the gods
> that they might be at ease![2]

Likewise in the "Creation of Man by the Mother Goddess," the motive for making humans lies in service to the gods. Humanity shall bear the yoke of creation and be a slave to the gods.

None of that is present in Genesis 2. The Yahwist portrays the man as the first act of the creation, and the garden is made for him. God even goes to work to plant a garden that the man might be comfortable and sustained. To be sure, the man is responsible for caring for this garden, but it is for his own well-being and not as a slave in a garden of the gods. In this way, the writer makes clear that work—even hard physical work—is part of man's original state. Indeed, work is part of the order of creation itself. This is important: work does not come as a curse after the rebellion of the man and the woman in Genesis 3; it is a blessing that God bestows on humankind, for whom the Lord created a livable earth.

All this was given to the man. He had freedom as a creature of God, but he did not have absolute freedom. The man was not free to do anything he pleased. There was one prohibition to make clear that the Lord God was still in charge: "Of the tree of the knowledge of good and evil you shall not eat, for in the day that you eat of it you shall die" (Gen. 2:17). Freedom and blessing were possible only with the recognition that the creature was not the Creator, and so the man was to obey. This distinction between Creator and creature is absolutely basic in understanding the Bible. In fact, any failure on the part of the creature to recognize this distinction leads to God's judgment. The threat of death is the manner of that judgment according to the author of Genesis 2.

It is striking that as soon as the Lord gave the man the sharp warning about imminent death for disobedience, God immediately expressed concern for the man's loneliness. In a very humanlike attempt to find him a companion, the Lord God made animals and birds and brought them to the man. The man named every living creature, and in this way—according to ancient Semitic thought—the man had control over all these creatures. The ancients believed that a person and his/her name were so closely related that knowledge of the name gave another person such intimate knowledge of the holder that one could control the other. But control over animals and birds did not satisfy the man's loneliness, and so now God put the man to sleep and made woman out of one of his ribs. Now finally creation reached its crowning glory: man and woman together establishing the first and primary relationship among persons in the form of marriage. "Therefore a man leaves his father and his mother and cleaves to his wife, and they become one flesh" (Gen. 2:24). God's desire that creatures be social beings rather than independent loners was thus achieved.

God achieved this creation of woman through one of the most perplexing methods the storyteller could devise for us twentieth-century readers. "So the Lord God caused a deep sleep to fall upon the man, and while he slept took one of his ribs and closed up its place with flesh; and the rib which the LORD God had taken from the man he made into a woman and brought her to the man" (Gen. 2:21–22). The deep sleep that God brought upon the unsuspecting man is probably not a divine anesthesia to prevent pain. In all probability "the deep sleep" here has the same function that it has in Gen. 15:12 where God hid his holy presence from Abraham's full vision as God passed between the dissected animals. Likewise, God made a deep sleep fall upon Saul and his men so that David could enter and leave Saul's camp without being seen (1 Sam. 26:12). Thus, in all cases where the word appears, the "deep sleep" prevents someone from seeing what God does not want seen. So it is when God made woman, the man was not allowed to be spectator of God's miracle; he was, however, fulfilled and blessed by the results of that miracle. For the creature that is sufficient!

As for "the rib trick" itself, it simply is not honest to repeat the old answer that men have one less rib than women as a result of creation. Such an answer is simply not true; men and women have the same number of ribs. What did the storyteller have in mind? Frankly, no one knows for sure, but the best solution advanced thus far is that the biblical storytellers had in mind some old creation stories from Mesopotamia where there often appeared a goddess named *Nin Ti*. Among the ancient Sumerians who inhabited Mesopotamia between 3000 and 2000 B.C., the word *Nin* meant "lady"; the word *Ti* could mean either "life" or "rib." And so, through many years of transmission both ideas were brought together in the Hebrew account of creation: Eve appears as "the mother of all *living*" at Gen. 3:20 and obviously as the lady of the "*rib*" at 2:21–22.

This entire creation story by the Yahwist thus includes many different elements that were characteristic of creation stories in the ancient world. At the same time the Hebrew storytellers and writers changed these stories and their punchlines to bear witness to the Lord God as creator— an informal, loving, and caring God who nevertheless insists unconditionally on the recognition of authority over all creatures.

THE STORY OF THE UNIVERSE

Genesis 1, the priestly account of God's creative activity, provides us with another perspective. In contrast to the casual storytelling style of the Yahwist, P's creation account is formal and programmatic. As was obvious in the priestly record of the Reed Sea event in Exodus 14, so here also are words and phrases repeated in rather monotonous fashion in order to build a well-defined system.

In order to clear the way for an understanding of God as creator in

Genesis 1, we must examine two issues that have caused much controversy over the years. The first is the picture of the universe as Genesis 1 portrays it, and the second is the matter of creation in "seven days." Perhaps it is safe to assume that most people tend to accept the portrayal of the universe and of nature, as described in the first chapter of the Bible. Yet many have difficulty with the seven days in light of what we know today about the age of the earth. An examination of the chapter might enable us to determine if these positions are justified.

1. The *picture of creation* in Gen. 1:1—2:4a is one that was typical of the ancient world and even persisted to the time of Copernicus in the sixteenth century. The reader will recall the reaction to Columbus's plan to find India by sailing westward from Europe. It is not necessary, therefore, to apologize or to defend the ancient biblical writers for their views of the universe. It is necessary, however, to understand what the writer of Genesis 1 meant by his description of the world.

Our examination will begin with the translation of the first words of the Bible which pave the way for understanding what follows. The usual translation, "In the beginning God created the heavens and the earth," has much to commend it, particularly a longstanding tradition. Yet good arguments can be raised for the translation offered in the footnote to the RSV and in some other, more modern translations such as the *New English Bible:* "In the beginning of creation, when God made heaven and earth, the earth was without form and void, with darkness over the face of the abyss, and a mighty wind that swept over the face over the waters. God said, 'Let there be light,' . . ." This reading suggests that the original state of things before God started working on creation was formlessness and waste, and the elements described contribute to that scene: darkness, deep, wind, and water—all unshaped, unformed substances. In other words, what existed before God began speaking his creative word was dark, watery chaos.

Then by God's fiat ("Let there be") order was brought about, step by step. First, in quite unscientific fashion, God called light into being to form the day—even though the sun was not made until the fourth day. Second, in the midst of all this chaotic water God placed a firmament, a hammered-out piece of metal which formed a vault and which was "hard as a molten mirror" (Job 37:18). This solid piece separated waters above from waters below.

Third, God pushed the waters to one side in order to let the dry land appear. On this land God placed vegetation containing seeds for the continuation of each species.

Fourth, God hung lights (actually the word means "tabernacle lamps")

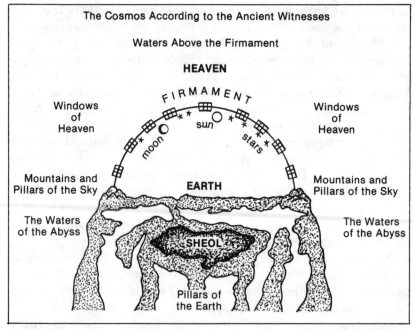

The Cosmos According to the Ancient Witnesses

Waters Above the Firmament

HEAVEN

FIRMAMENT

Windows of Heaven

Windows of Heaven

sun

moon

stars

Mountains and Pillars of the Sky

Mountains and Pillars of the Sky

EARTH

The Waters of the Abyss

The Waters of the Abyss

SHEOL

Pillars of the Earth

in the vault to serve as sun, moon, and stars. Fifth, God made birds to fly across the vault and sea creatures to inhabit the water. Sixth, God called into existence land animals and finally humankind (male and female together), and then God took a well-deserved rest.

On the basis of this description of the universe in Genesis 1 we can diagram the scene something like the one shown.

Such a tight system does not allow for rain or springs. Perhaps the inclusion of such details would have interrupted the symmetry of the Priest's description, and so he omitted them. Elsewhere in the Old Testament, however, provision is made for such necessities. At Gen. 7:11 the Noachic flood begins when "the fountains of the great deep burst forth, and the windows of the heavens were opened." Contrariwise, when they were closed, the flooding stopped (8:2). The windows of heaven are mentioned also at Isa. 24:18 and Mal. 3:10. Thus the diagram of the universe should also include grilles in the firmament and springs in the earth in order to present a complete picture of what the ancients, including the priestly writer, conceived creation to be. Such a view, of course, is unacceptable today, but we should not expect the ancients to have known what we do through the technological advances of telescopes, space journeys, and aerial photography.

2. The *seven-day pattern* is best discussed by delineating the days

exactly as the references to days are translated in the literal rendering of the RSV:

one day	(1:5)
a second day	(1:8)
a third day	(1:13)
a fourth day	(1:19)
a fifth day	(1:23)
a sixth day	(1:31)
on the seventh day	(2:2)

In the Canaanite poetry from Ugarit found in 1929, such a pattern appears again and again. One example will suffice to illustrate its use. In the story about Baal and his sister Anath, the bone of contention is that the god Yamm was given a palace but Baal was not. Finally, after Yamm had been vanquished, the chief god El granted permission for Baal to have a palace erected. Cedars from Lebanon and Sirion were brought to the place, and the construction is described like this:

Fire is set to the house,
    Flame to the palace,
Lo, a [d]ay and a second,
    Fire feeds on the house,
    Flame upon the palace:
A third, a fourth day,
    [Fi]re feeds on the house,
    Flam[e] upon the palace.
A fifth, a s[ix]th day,
    Fire feeds [on] the house,
    Flame u[pon] the palace.
There, on the seventh d[ay],
    The fire *dies down* in the house,
    The f[la]me in the palace.
The silver turns into blocks,
    the gold is turned into bricks.[3]

This and numerous other texts in Ugaritic poetry show that the pattern which begins with "one day" or "a day" and continues with the ordinal numbers "second" through "sixth" in sequence to culminate with the phrase "on the seventh day" is a common literary device. Its function is to record a continuing action that comes to its climax "on the seventh day."

This full pattern is taken up only in Genesis 1, but elsewhere in the Old Testament the pattern in abbreviated fashion serves the same function. "The glory of the LORD settled on Mount Sinai, and the cloud covered it *six days;* and *on the seventh day* he called to Moses out of the midst of the cloud" (Exod. 24:16). Or again, Joshua's siege of Jericho is described in these words: "And the second day they marched around the city once, and returned into the camp. So they did for *six days. On the seventh day* they rose early at the dawn of day, and marched around the city in the same manner seven times: it was only on that day that they marched around the city seven times. And at the seventh time, when the priests had blown the trumpets, Joshua said to the people, 'Shout; for the LORD has given you the city' " (Josh. 6:14–16).

Thus the climax to Moses' waiting on Mount Sinai came "on the seventh day" when God spoke to him; the climax of the siege of Jericho occurred "on the seventh day" and "at the seventh time" around the city when the walls fell down. And the climax of God's creative activity in Genesis 1 came when God rested "on the seventh day," thus establishing the Sabbath day as the high point in creation, according to the priestly writer.

Understood in this sense, the seven-day pattern in Genesis 1 is a literary device which frankly is not at all concerned with time per se. The pattern as a whole, by analogy with the stories about Moses and Joshua, indicates that God created until the work was finished, and the completion of creative work is celebrated by humankind on the Sabbath.

We have dealt with the issues of the picture of the creation and of the time involved in creation. We have seen that the picture presented in the Bible is one which is difficult to accept today, and we have concluded that the seven-day phenomenon is merely a literary device. What then is left for us in Genesis 1? What value does it have today?

Perhaps those questions can best be saved until we examine the issues which confronted the priestly writer in the sixth or fifth century B.C. Since the testimony to the word of God is always directed to particular situations, some of those particulars need to be seen.

GENESIS 1 IN ITS OWN TIME

The watery chaos which prevailed at the beginning of the account in Genesis 1 is similar to the description of the pre-creation state in the Babylonian *Enuma elish* and thus probably places the biblical writer in Mesopotamia.

> When on high the heaven had not been named,
> Firm ground below had not been called by name,
> Naught but primordial Apsu, their begetter,
> (And) Mummu-Tiamat, she who bore them all,
> Their waters commingling as a single body;
> No reed hut had been matted, no marsh land had appeared,

When no gods whatever had been brought into being,
Uncalled by name, their destinies undetermined—
Then it was that the gods were formed within them.[4]

In contrast to the Babylonian myth that proceeds from the watery chaos of Apsu and Tiamat to the creation (begetting) of the gods, Genesis 1 moves immediately from chaos to the created order of the universe. In this way the biblical writer makes emphatic the uniqueness of God, besides whom there is no other.

Moreover, in the *Enuma elish* heaven and earth are not created until later when the god Marduk defeats the monster Tiamat and uses half of her corpse to make the heavens. No such battle is mentioned in Genesis 1; in fact, the Hebrew word which corresponds to Tiamat, namely *tehom*, appears in Gen. 1:2 in reference to "the deep." This is in no way a personal adversary of God. In other words, the Genesis story allows the existence of no other god or godlike figure. It thus attests to the one God's uncontested and absolute supremacy over all of creation.

Likewise the heavenly luminaries are nothing other than the lamps that God set in the firmament for the purpose of distinguishing day and night, seasons and years. By contrast, in Babylon and Canaan, as well as in Egypt, the sun and moon and stars were deities who reigned over their realms and evoked worship and praise from the people. Thus, once again, the priestly version of creation demythologized the ancient notion of many deities, precisely at a time when the people of Israel were being tempted to fall down before the gods of their masters in exile.

The sea monsters that battled the chief god of Babylon (see above, pp. 133–34), and under "Monster-Hunting in the Bible" in chap. 8) are demoted in Genesis 1 to the creatures that God made and considered to be good. Far from being God's adversaries, the monsters of the sea are the Creator's own creatures.

In contrast to the Babylonian view that human beings were made as slaves of the gods, the author of Genesis 1 reaffirms and indeed exceeds the Yahwist's positive evaluation of humanity. There are two significant issues that come together at 1:26: "Then God said, 'Let us make man in our image, after our likeness; and let them have dominion over the fish of the sea, and over the birds of the air, and over the cattle, and over all the earth, and over every creeping thing that creeps upon the earth.' " That humankind is made in the image of God has given rise over the centuries and today to much theological debate, but what the author had in mind for his audience is our first concern. It is probable that this phrase was meant to portray humanity in royal terms, for it is known that in Egypt the god Amon, holding the sign of life toward King Amenhotep, said, "My beloved son, receive my likeness." That "the likeness" of the god was conveyed to the king of Egypt was probably well known in Israel, and so the phrase "image of God" seems to have pointed to the royal stature of humankind over against the slave image in Mesopotamia. Moreover, the divine fiat that humans should have dominion over the rest of creation further substantiates the high regard which the biblical writer had for Homo sapiens. People are to treat the creatures of the earth and the earth itself as a royal family cares for its realm. Therefore any ravaging of the earth or careless slaughter of its creatures or any despoiling of nature today is a denial of the royal task that God gave to humankind.

Again, in sharp contrast to the blood-spilling gore that characterizes creation in the *Enuma elish,* the God of Genesis 1 brings everything into being simply by speaking the word. This notion of the creative word of God appears in the Old Testament elsewhere only at Ps. 33:6 (see also 33:9, however),

> By the word of the LORD the heavens were made,
> and all their host by the breath of his mouth.

While such rarity of the idea is striking, the concept of God's creative word is a logical outcome of the effect of that word elsewhere. We have seen that God's word not only addresses specific situations but in numerous texts directs history itself to God's desired goals. That power which was so commonly confessed to be effective in Israel's history is here extended to the creation of the world, and in this sense the power of God is confessed to be supreme and uncontested in the face of pagan claims. God need only speak, and the divine will is accomplished.

Perhaps nowhere else in the ancient world is such a positive evaluation placed on created matter and earthly life as here in Genesis 1. In religions where aspects of nature are identified with the capricious gods and their whims, no such evaluation was possible. But the priestly writer portrays God as a master craftsman who examines each piece of work and declares "It is good!" (cf. Isa. 41:7). Seven times throughout the story in Genesis 1, God examines the product and sees that it is good. Thus, unlike those religions that regard the material world as evil and detrimental to the spiritual nature of humankind, the Bible asserts unequivocally the goodness of all that God made.

Moreover, against any view of divine capriciousness Genesis 1 becomes almost monotonous in its insistence that the Creator made things in such a way that each species continues its own kind by having within it its own seed. That an orange tree does not bear bananas attests to the continuing order that God brings out of chaos.

The various phenomena of nature are all created for a specific function. Light functions to distinguish between day and night. The firmament, we have seen, serves the purpose of separating waters from waters. The earth provides the soil for the plants to grow, and the heavenly luminaries serve as signs for festivals, for seasons, and for years—in addition to providing light. Thus, Genesis 1 is not so much a story of the origin of things as it is a description of the functions that each created phenomenon is to serve. As each aspect of the universe fulfills its designated purpose, the order intended by God will continue.

That God ordered all things in the universe makes abundantly clear that God is not identical to any part of the created world. God is distinct, and in this way reigns as creator over all that is. Like the author of Genesis 2, this writer asserts that distinction between Creator and creation which is basic to the whole Bible. But even more than the Yahwist, the Priest insists that the culmination of creation is the Sabbath when the creature worships God the Creator in a particular way.

THE NATURE OF HUMANS

Finally, this view of the Creator is quite directly related to an understanding of humanity, even of human sexuality. Both creation stories, that in Genesis 1 as well as the earlier one in Genesis 2, attest to the equality of male and female as part of the order that God established. The Priest saves the creation of humans for the sixth day, and his treatment of their creation is given considerable attention. There is, however, one verse which stands out as particularly significant for the issue of sexuality:

> So God created man in his own image,
>   in the image of God he created him;
>   male and female he created them.
>   (Gen. 1:27)

All three lines of this little poem have the same meaning: the image of God is portrayed in the world by the coexistence of male and female who, as the following verse indicates, are to participate in the creative action by being fruitful and multiplying and by ruling over the earth ("have dominion") on God's behalf. There is no possibility here of arguing that one sex has priority or mastery over the other.

Typical of the author of Genesis 2, the same view of sexual equality is described in story form. At first glance it appears that the male of the species is given priority, for he was created first. Only later was the woman made, and then only after "a helper fit for him" was not found among the animals. Perhaps it is no wonder that the Yahwist has been considered a male chauvinist. The story needs closer examination, however, in order to see the impact of the sexuality issue. In the first place, it is by no means certain that the author intended the woman to be sublimated to the man just because she was created second. (The ordering of things in Genesis 1 assumes the higher forms of life at the end.) Second, and more important, the translation of the RSV quoted above leaves a false impression. It seems to indicate that the woman was made in order to serve as an assistant to the man. A more literal translation of the words, however, gives a different impression: "a help [or strength] as his opposite." Such a rendering corrects a false view in two ways. First, it regards the woman not "fit for" the man but his counterpart, his partner, his equal. Second, the word "help" rather than "helper" draws attention to the use of the same word elsewhere in the Old Testament where it is used only to speak of God as Israel's "help" or "strength." Far from implying assistanceship or sublimation, the word describing woman seems to imply strength. Thus, the writer of Genesis 2 regards the sexes to be equal, just as does the author of Genesis 1. It is only due to the sin of Genesis 3 that the equality intended by God in creation runs askew (see Gen. 3:16). The restoration of that creation equality will wait the redemptive event in Christ, for by baptism into Christ's death "there is neither male nor female" (Gal. 3:28).[5]

To sum up, both the Yahwist and the Priest begin their stories of God's relationship with people by recounting their respective creation stories. In each case, however, a doctrine of creation does not stand alone; on the contrary, both these sources are essentially histories of the word of God. Their creation accounts are the first of the acts of God *in history* as God works out his purposes for Israel and for humankind. This context of history makes their creation stories unique among the myriad of stories in the ancient world. In using all the resources at their disposal, these two biblical writers assert in their own ways that the Lord reigns as creator as well as savior *in history*.

NOTES

1. "Creation of Man by the Mother Goddess," trans. E. A. Speiser in *Ancient Near Eastern Texts* (cited above, chap. 3 n. 1), 99–100 (Old Babylonian and Assyrian versions).

2. Trans. E. A. Speiser in *The Ancient Near East, Volume 1* (cited above, chap. 3 n. 1), 36.

3. "Poems about Baal and Anath," trans. H. L. Ginsberg in *The Ancient Near East, Volume 1* (cited above, chap. 3 n. 1), 104–5 (italics denote an uncertain translation; brackets, a restoration in the text).

4. "The Creation Epic," trans. E. A. Speiser in *Ancient Near Eastern Texts* (cited above, chap. 3 n. 1), 60–61.

5. See, further, Foster R. McCurley, *Ancient Myths and Biblical Faith* (cited above, chap. 8 n. 5), 87–88, 99–101, 102–3, 113–19.

16

Continuing
Creation in History

WHAT IS MOST STRIKING—even unique—about Israel's view of God as creator is the frequent use of creation thought and imagery to speak of God's actions in history. Whether it be the bizarre stories of monsters overcome at the time of creation or confessional statements about God the creator, these ideas bear witness to God's continuing activity on Israel's behalf and to God's reign over the universe. In other words, again and again in the Old Testament—especially in the preaching of the prophets—creation language of old provides the punch to proclaim the gospel of God's deeds in the present and in the future.

Without attempting to exhaust all the prophetic texts dealing with creation, we shall examine a number of examples from the major prophets Isaiah, Jeremiah, and Ezekiel, and then conclude with a lengthier study on Second Isaiah who brings the issue to its crowning glory.

CREATION AND HISTORY

In the latter half of the eighth century B.C. the prophet Isaiah criticized his fellow citizens of Jerusalem because they were attempting to ally themselves with Egypt against the Assyrian threat. In response to this reliance on the pharaoh, Isaiah cited the defeat of the monster named Rahab (see Pss. 87:4; 89:10; Job 9:13) as evidence that Egypt is as ineffective as the ancient monster before the Lord.

> For Egypt's help is worthless and empty,
>   therefore I have called her
>   "Rahab who sits still" [perhaps more accurately,
>   "Rahab who is conquered"].
>
> (Isa. 30:7)

The creation image of the defeated dragon is used to describe a forthcoming historical event: Egypt will be rendered as useless as the primordial monster.

The same prophet uses a different creation motif to describe his judgment on another nation, Edom:

> He [the LORD] shall stretch the line of *confusion* over it,
> and the plummet of *chaos* over its nobles.
> (Isa. 34:11b)

The words "confusion" and "chaos" are translations of the Hebrew words *tōhū* and *bōhū*, terms which appear in combination elsewhere only at Gen. 1:2 (and Jer. 4:23, yet to be discussed). In Genesis these terms are rendered, "without form and void." Their usage here in Isaiah must be seen as a reflection of the chaos that existed before God began the creative work described in Gen. 1:3—2:3. Their purpose here is to portray the land of Edom as in a state of desolation that will resemble the condition of the world before God formed the earth—all this is God's judgment as "recompense for the cause of Zion" (Isa. 34:8), a judgment that is accomplished in history.

Finally, Isaiah uses the doctrine of creation as evidence of the Lord's power to *save* Jerusalem from the siege of the Assyrians in 701 B.C. In a prayer offered by King Hezekiah there is contained the following allusion to Yahweh as creator and as king over the earth:

> O LORD of hosts, God of Israel, who art enthroned above the cherubim, thou art the God, thou alone, of all the kingdoms of the earth; thou hast made heaven and earth. . . . So now, O LORD our God, *save* us from his hand, that all the kingdoms of the earth may know that thou alone art the LORD. (Isa. 37:16, 20)

The gods of the Assyrians can be destroyed because they were merely the work of human hands; now the Lord, by acting to save from a historical enemy at a specific time, can show that he alone is creator of all and king of the whole earth. Thus in this prayer creation and salvation come together in an understanding of God and divine power.

A hundred years after Isaiah, at the end and turn of the seventh century B.C., the prophet Jeremiah preached in Jerusalem. Like Isaiah, Jeremiah used creation images to proclaim both the judgment and salvation of the Lord.

> I looked on the earth, and lo, it was *waste and void;*
> and to the heavens, and they had no light.
> (Jer. 4:23)

The Lord will come forth to bring on Judah such destruction that it will resemble the world before Yahweh began forming the earth. Even though the historical conqueror was the Babylonian army, nevertheless it was the Lord, the Creator, who commissioned powerful Nebuchadnezzar to return the land to its pre-creation condition of being *tōhū* and *bōhū*. (See also the same reasoning at Jer. 27:5–11.)

After the judgment had been accomplished by God in 597 B.C. and again in 586, when the city was destroyed and the people carried off as exiles, Jeremiah used the creation concept to assure the people of God's salvation. At Jer. 31:35–36, a hymnlike praise of God as creator assures Israel that they will be God's people as long as the sun and the moon are present in the sky to give light to the earth. Because the covenant God is the same as the creator God, Israel will never be forsaken by Yahweh. Again at 32:17–25, in a prayer of Jeremiah listing the wondrous deeds of Yahweh, the prophet praises God as creator for announcing that the siege of Jerusalem has now begun. At the same time, however, this creator-redeemer God has instructed Jeremiah to buy a field (32:8), by which action God intends to show that he will bring back the people and restore them to their land (32:44). Fields shall again be bought and sold. For the Lord, according to Jeremiah's prayer (32:17), "thou who hast made the heavens and the earth by thy great power and by thy outstretched arm," is the ruler of history. The same dual announcement of judgment and restoration in chapter 33 is introduced by a description of Yahweh as creator:

> Thus says the LORD who made the earth, the LORD who formed it to establish it—the LORD is his name: Call to me and I will answer you. . . . I will restore the fortunes of Judah and the fortunes of Israel, and rebuild them as they were at first. (33:2, 3, 7)

The prophet Ezekiel, who was carried off with the exiles in the first deportation of 597 B.C., twice speaks of God's judgment on the pharaoh of Egypt. Using all the imagery of the ancient creation myths, Ezekiel describes the pharaoh as a "dragon" who will be vanquished. The royal person of Egypt will be caught with "hooks" in his jaws (Ezek. 29:3–5), just as the serpent Leviathan was captured (see Job 41:1). The same king will be ensnared in a net (Ezek. 32:2–8), just like the helpers of Tiamat in the *Enuma elish*. Moreover, the land of Egypt will be covered with blood and the lights of heaven will be darkened so that the land will resemble the earth before God set the lights in the firmament. This destruction upon Egypt will be Yahweh's doing, but again earthly instruments—the Babylonian army (cf. 30:25; 32:11)—are used to carry out these plans.

CREATIVE REDEMPTION

Finally, the prophet known as Second Isaiah stresses more than any other prophet the view that God is creator. In his sixteen chapters (Isaiah 40—55) this "Isaiah of Babylon" proclaims his gospel that the time of exile is coming to an end, that the period of punishment is over, and that the exiles will soon be free to go home (see under "The Second Isaiah, as Exile Ends" in chap. 12). In order to get his message across, he uses every means at his disposal, especially the view of Yahweh as creator. This emphasis is probably due to the clear acknowledgment in Babylon that Marduk is creator. In that context it is interesting to see how Second Isaiah used creation themes.

> The LORD is the everlasting God,
>> the Creator of the ends of the earth.
>>> (Isa. 40:28b)

This verse is only a small part of a section (vv. 12–31) dealing with the sovereignty and incomparable nature of God. The purpose of these verses is to tell those who have opportunity to return to Judah that Yahweh is unlike the gods with which the exiles had come into contact in Babylon. Those gods are nothing; but Yahweh is so great that nothing and no one can be compared to him and his mighty works, the most important of which is creation. Such a confession is directed against the claims that the god Marduk is the creator.

This claim that Yahweh is the Creator of the universe is repeated at Isa. 45:18–19. Here the prophet announces that, since the Lord created the earth as a place of dwelling for all people, the end of his actions will not be destruction. Moreover, the relationship of Israel to the Lord, just as that of creation to the Lord, is not chaotic but true and right, faithful and constant. It is an orderly world, not one of confusion, in which humankind is to dwell. And it is an orderly way in which Israel is to have a relationship with the Lord.

> Hearken to me, O Jacob,
>> and Israel, whom I called!
> I am He, I am the first,
>> and I am the last.
> My hand laid the foundation of the earth,
>> and my right hand spread out the heavens;
> when I call to them,
>> they stand forth together.
>>> (Isa. 48:12–13)

This image of God as universal creator introduces an announcement that Yahweh is about to bring this might to bear upon Babylon and its people. God the Creator will bring judgment on the Babylonians, and the people of Israel will be freed to go forth from Babylon.

The Lord's instrument for destroying Babylon and freeing Israel is the Persian king Cyrus, whose armies are moving toward the land of captivity. To describe the Lord's commissioning of Cyrus (Isa. 44:24—45:13) the prophet employs creation themes twice. At 45:7 the Lord's power to "form light and create darkness" expresses divine sovereignty and the effect of creation power. Then vv. 11 and 12 show that, as creator, God and his ways should not be questioned. Apparently, what is meant in this text is that God's use of Cyrus as an instrument of deliverance should not be questioned since it is the sovereign creator God carrying out divine plans.

This universal aspect of God as creator is used again at Isa. 40:12–17, 21–24 as a demonstration of power to save in history. Here Yahweh is described as having established heaven and earth in order to show superiority over powerless nations and useless idols. The Lord is portrayed as a king who continues his creative power that brings rulers of the earth to nothing. This long discussion of Yahweh's power follows immediately upon the initial announcement that he is coming to gather them as a shepherd does his flock and take them home (40:9–11).

Alongside this testimony to the Lord as Creator of the universe in Second Isaiah's preaching is the confession that the Lord is the Creator of Israel.

> But now thus says the LORD,
>   he who created you, O Jacob,
>   he who formed you, O Israel:
> "Fear not, for I have redeemed you;
>   I have called you by name, you are mine."
>   (Isa. 43:1)

The continuing nature of God's creation of Israel is here emphasized in two ways. (1) The words "who created you" and "who formed you" are participles in Hebrew; thus they denote continuation ("he who keeps creating you, . . . keeps forming you"). (2) The reference to the creating of Israel is intimately connected with God's act of redeeming and electing Israel ("you are mine") in the midst of its bondage in Babylon.

> I am the LORD, your Holy One,
>   the Creator of Israel, your King.
>   (43:15)

The verses which precede this quotation introduce Yahweh as the

"Redeemer, the Holy One of Israel," and speak of releasing the people from captivity in Babylon. The verses which follow seem to allude to the Reed Sea event where Yahweh delivered the people from bondage in Egypt. Undoubtedly the purpose here is to inspire confidence in the Lord to accomplish this *second* exodus. In the midst of this entire passage Yahweh is called "the Creator of Israel," and so here—as in 43:1—the creation of Israel is tied up closely with deliverance. On this basis of the Creator who redeems, Yahweh reigns over Israel as king.

The ideas of Yahweh as creator of Israel and creator of the universe are combined at Isa. 44:24.

> Thus says the LORD, your Redeemer,
>   who formed you from the womb:
> "I am the LORD, who made all things,
>   who stretched out the heavens alone,
>   who spread out the earth—Who was with me?"

Verses 24–28 again tie together the idea of creation and deliverance (specifically in terms of restoration to the land of Judah). God, who is the Father of Israel and the Creator of all things, is active in the world frustrating human knowledge (v. 25), announcing hope to the exiles (v. 26), commanding "the deep" (v. 27), and raising up Cyrus through whom God will fulfill his purpose and restore Jerusalem (v. 28). This proclamation begins with creation—of Israel and of the whole earth—and concludes with the restoration of Jerusalem by the redeemer God.

Finally, Second Isaiah combines the mythology of creation imagery with the deliverance at the Reed Sea.

> Was it not thou that didst cut Rahab in pieces,
>   that didst pierce the dragon?
> Was it not thou that didst dry up the sea,
>   the waters of the great deep;
> that didst make the depths of the sea a way
>   for the redeemed to pass over?
>   (51:9–10)

The mention of Rahab, the dragon, the sea, and the great deep shows clearly that the author of these verses had in mind ancient creation myths. With that obvious demonstration of the Lord's power, the prophet combines the act of God in freeing Israel at the first exodus. *Now* the same creator-redeemer God is called upon to awake and put on strength so that "the ransomed of the LORD shall return, and come to Zion with singing" (v. 11). The God "who stretched out the heavens and laid the foundations

225

A view of Jerusalem looking west from the Mount of Olives across the Kidron Valley. The large dome to the right of center is the Islamic Dome of the Rock, which stands on the site of Solomon's temple.

of the earth" (v. 13) is the same one who comforts the exiled people and restores them to their land.

The use of creation themes in Second Isaiah to announce the gospel of freedom from exile is so prominent that one scholar has referred to his message as "creative redemption."[1] Indeed this prophet, above all others, actually proclaims that creation takes its present and continuing form in redemption. In other words, God's redemption of the people from exile is the form which creation took at that present moment. Second Isaiah's message then was this: God the creator is active now. God's creative work did not end with the structuring of the universe, as though God "retired" after Genesis 1. On the contrary, God the creator was creating salvation from exile. As a result, Israel came into being as a new creation, and the Lord was acknowledged as its king.

Thus prophetic preaching did not seem to emphasize creation for its own sake. It was creation for the benefit of Israel—for its judgment and for its salvation—that was proclaimed by the prophets. To accomplish this powerful message the prophets used various and sundry creation themes to announce the word of God to the people of their day.

226

NOTE

1. See Carroll Stuhlmueller, O.P., *Creative Redemption in Deutero-Isaiah* (Analecta Biblica 43; Rome: Biblical Institute, 1970), or, more briefly, his treatment of "Deutero-Isaiah" in *The Jerome Biblical Commentary,* ed. R. E. Brown, J. A. Fitzmyer, and R. E. Murphy (Englewood Cliffs, N.J.: Prentice-Hall, 1968), 22:4, 17, 18, and elsewhere; or J. Reumann, *Creation and New Creation: The Past, Present, and Future of God's Creative Activity* (Minneapolis: Augsburg Publishing House, 1973), 73–79, 102–8.

17

Creation and Wisdom

As we have seen, much of the Old Testament tells of God's creative power taking the form of redemption and judgment. In order to tie together such actions of God in history and the concept of creation, the Old Testament writers used bizarre imagery from the ancient creation myths. Yet there also exists in the Old Testament a more reflective approach to creation and creator. It seems that *reason* replaces *drama* in an attempt to deal with nature and God's continuing world rule.

Such a recognition is important for a holistic understanding of the Old Testament. While so much of the biblical impact is achieved by means of storytelling, there does exist alongside those dramatic pieces a contemplative spirit. In other words, while the ancient Hebrews are noted for their stories, they were likewise people of reflection.

Such reflection about God as creator of the universe appears in a sublime hymn known to us as Psalm 8.

> When I look at thy heavens, the work of thy fingers,
>   the moon and the stars which thou hast established;
> what is man that thou art mindful of him,
>   and the son of man that thou dost care for him?
> Yet thou hast made him little less than God,
>   and dost crown him with glory and honor.
> Thou hast given him dominion over the works of thy hands;
>   thou hast put all things under his feet.
>
>   (vv. 3–6)

The psalmist is awed by his observation and thinking about the wonders of God's created world. The galaxies of stars and the moon above present the miracle of the whole cosmos in all its majestic splendor. It is

228

no wonder that humanity seems so small and insignificant in contrast to the vastness of the universe. (Today, of course, we know it to be even greater than the ancient poet did.) And yet this contemplation of human-kind's role in the world's expanse leads the psalmist to realize the royal nature which God bestowed on Homo sapiens, under whom God placed the world. It seems that God's providential care and ordering of all creation for continuance is the motive for the repeated expression of praise:

O LORD, our LORD,
   how majestic is thy name in all the earth!
                    (Ps. 8:1, 9)

This type of reflective thinking had its home in the so-called wisdom movement which spread throughout the ancient Near East but was concentrated especially in Egypt and in Mesopotamia. But what is this "wisdom"?

In effect, wisdom is a prephilosophical attempt to understand life. It includes the human and natural worlds as one realm. One believed it was possible by observation to gather together all the characteristics that make up life. By so accumulating such data about the whole created world, a person comprehended and acknowledged the order of the universe. Understanding and participating in this order was the goal of wisdom. All such order was and is created by God and belongs to God, but people can discipline themselves in order to play their proper role in the order of things and thus be wise.

By its very definition wisdom is the concern of everyone regardless of his or her nationalistic loyalties. Thus wisdom is international. And so the wise teaching of foreigners could be taken over into the Old Testament— sometimes, but not always, modified by the Israelites. In the Old Testament there is contained *Egyptian* wisdom, especially the "Instruction of Amen-em-opet,"[1] incorporated almost wholesale into Prov. 22:17– 24:22; *Aramaic* wisdom of "The Words of Ahiqar"[2] is scattered throughout Proverbs; *Ishmaelite* wisdom in "the Words of Agur" and in "the Words of Lemuel" appears at Proverbs 30—31, respectively. That the Israelites were also familiar with (and probably also somewhat influenced by) the wisdom of still other peoples is also clear: Babylonian (Jer. 50:35; 51:57); Canaanite (Ezek. 28:3, 17); Edomite (Jer. 49:7; Obadiah 8; Job 2:11).

OLD TESTAMENT WISDOM BOOKS

While there are many wisdom influences throughout the Old Testament—even in the Psalms and prophetic books—there are only three

writings that are classified as wisdom books: Proverbs, Job, and Ecclesiastes. These books, while quite different from one another, are strikingly similar in several ways: they are completely without nationalistic
interest; they contain no mention of Israel's worship system; they make
no allusions to the history of Israel or of any other nation. The three are
therefore consistent with the characteristics of "wisdom."

Yet different they are indeed. The Book of Proverbs is a collection of
proverbial sayings that have as their aim to teach the ardent student the
way to find life and to avoid the snares of death. These maxims teach that
in order to become wise, a young person must listen to the advice of the
teacher, remain cool in the midst of adversity, maintain an even temper,
avoid the advances of loose women, keep good company, never cheat in a
business transaction, behave according to the expected protocol in the
royal court, and so forth. Such characteristics, best illustrated in the
story about Joseph (Genesis 37—50), were common in wisdom teaching
throughout the ancient Near East.

Yet the Book of Proverbs, while consistent with the general approach,
demonstrates at the same time some important examples of Israelite
piety. In the first place, the compiler of the present book includes in his
introduction the true basis for wisdom.

> The fear of the LORD is the beginning of knowledge;
>> fools despise wisdom and instruction.
>> (Prov. 1:7)

This same teaching—that the basis of wisdom lies in a person's "fear,"
that is, obedience and awe, of the Lord—is repeated in various ways
throughout the book. One such example picks up typical wisdom terms:

> The fear of the LORD is a fountain of life,
>> that one may avoid the snares of death.
>> (Prov. 14:27)

A second emphasis in the Israelite approach to wisdom is an insistence
on the limitations of human wisdom in the face of God's having "the last
word."

> The plans of the mind belong to man,
>> but the answer of the tongue is from the LORD.
>> (Prov. 16:1)

> A man's mind plans his way,
>> but the LORD directs his steps.
>> (Prov. 16:9)

This teaching, repeated at 19:21 and 21:31, prevents humans from becoming overly confident about their own abilities to reason.

Along with such precautions against wisdom, there arose in Israel a stronger reaction to the basic premise that by being "wise" a person can expect to be rewarded with health and wealth. The Bible contains two books—Job and Ecclesiastes—which indeed challenge that claim of the wisdom teachers.

The Book of Job is a combination of at least two levels of writing. The first and older level is a story of loss and restoration. Job 1:1 through 2:10 tell that one of the sons of God, a certain Satan ("Adversary"), stood in the heavenly court along with the other sons of God and challenged the faith of Job. Given permission by God to test Job's faith, Satan caused the loss of the man's children and possessions. Yet Job stood fast in his faith and would not curse God. The restoration occurs at the very end of the book when God blessed Job with more than he had at the beginning. This story, as is clear even in English translation, is told in prose. It is a common story told over and over again in the ancient world where the sufferer is usually unnamed.

With the exception of single paragraphs to move the reader out of and into this story, the rest of the book is written in poetry. This large block of material consists mostly of a series of dialogues between Job and his three friends, Eliphaz, Bildad, and Zophar (plus another named Elihu). It is in these dialogues that the Israelite writer makes his point. The friends who advocate the typical wisdom teaching claim that, since the good are rewarded and the wicked punished, Job's suffering must be due to his having committed some sin. The poet's own position, which comes out in Job's refusal to accept that "doctrine of divine retribution," is vindicated in the story by the restoration at the end. No answer is given for the question, "Why do people suffer?" Yet the book's teaching is that, even without such "wisdom," people are called to hold on to their faith.

The Book of Ecclesiastes ("The Preacher") adopts an even stronger tone against typical wisdom. This author writes with a degree of pessimism, even cynicism, against such a human attempt to have all the answers. Such an approach is striking from the pen of an author who himself is highly learned—as his own arguments demonstrate. While it seems at first glance that this author is an agnostic, what really bothers him is that mechanical view of God that believes in the simplistic punishment-reward theory of justice. This book is written, therefore, both to correct a certain view of God and to put a limit to human knowledge.

These three books—Proverbs, Job, and Ecclesiastes—no matter which position they take on the issue of reward and punishment, no matter how optimistic or pessimistic they are about human wisdom, nevertheless share in wisdom's approach to life and learning. They base no arguments on history (contrary to the rest of the Old Testament), and they pay no attention to cultic matters. They argue strongly, however, on the basis of creation and on the view of God as creator. Such a universal approach to life's questions, no matter what they are, is the way of wisdom.

The "Preacher" offers us a few examples of this concern for God's ordering of the universe.

> I have seen the business that God has given to the sons of men to be busy with. He has made everything beautiful in its time; also he has put eternity into man's mind, yet so that he cannot find out what God has done from the beginning to the end. (Eccles. 3:10–11; see also 7:13–14)

Simultaneously, he points to God as the creator of persons: "Remember also your Creator in the days of your youth" (Eccles. 12:1). While not developing an understanding of creation any further, the "Preacher" does not allude to God in a way other than creator, for such is the means by which he addresses his "wise" audience.

The Book of Job makes frequent reference to God as the maker of an individual (see 4:17; 10:8–9; 31:13–15; 33:4; 36:3). But more pronounced is the use of creation themes in order to stress the wisdom of God over the foolishness of humans. In answer to the rhetorical question, "Whence then comes wisdom?" Job declares:

> God understands the way to it,
>   and he knows its place.
> For he looks to the ends of the earth,
>   and sees everything under the heavens. . . .
> He established it, and searched it out.
> And he said to man,
> "Behold, the fear of the Lord, that is wisdom;
>   and to depart from evil is understanding."
>   (Job 28:23–24, 27–28)

Thus humans can attain wisdom only by fearing, that is, obeying, the Lord who created everything and continues to control nature. This same wisdom of God connected with his providential care over creation occurs also at Job 37:1–13 and all of chaps. 38—39.

That playing one's role in the order of things has a profound effect on ethics or behavior can be seen at Prov. 17:5.

> He who mocks the poor insults his Maker;
> he who is glad at calamity will not go unpunished.

This notion that rewards and punishment are based on a belief in the Creator probably has its home in Egyptian wisdom, but the idea is perfectly consistent with the goal of wisdom in general.

Perhaps the most interesting wisdom passage that deals with creation is Prov. 8:22–23, 27–31, a speech by Wisdom in personified form.

> The LORD created me at the beginning of his work,
>   the first of his acts of old.
> Ages ago I was set up,
>   at the first, before the beginning of the earth. . . .
> When he established the heavens, I was there,
>   when he drew a circle on the face of the deep,
> when he made firm the skies above,
>   when he established the fountains of the deep,
> when he assigned to the sea its limit,
>   so that the waters might not transgress his command,
> when he marked out the foundations of the earth,
>   then I was beside him, like a master workman,
> and I was daily his delight,
>   rejoicing before him always,
> rejoicing in his inhabited world
>   and delighting in the sons of men.

The passage affirms the antiquity of Wisdom; there is no part of the universe that is older than she. (In Hebrew the noun "wisdom" is feminine in gender.) Indeed, she was present alongside God at the time of creation itself and played delightedly among the things God had made. Wisdom is portrayed here as a person who works and rejoices in the created world.

IN THE APOCRYPHA AND BEYOND

A later wisdom book called Ecclesiasticus, or The Wisdom of Jesus the Son of Sirach, was one of a number of works not accepted into the Old Testament canon. Written in the early part of the second century B.C., this book is included in the Apocrypha. Similar to Proverbs 8, the first chapter of Sirach mentions that "wisdom was created before all things" (v. 4). But the author of this book develops the personality of Wisdom even further. Wisdom speaks thus:

> I came forth from the mouth of the Most High,
>   and covered the earth like a mist.
> I dwelt in high places,
>   and my throne was in a pillar of cloud.
> Alone I have made the circuit of the vault of heaven

and have walked in the depths of the abyss.
In the waves of the sea, in the whole earth,
   and in every people and nation I have gotten a possession.
Among all these I sought a resting place;
   I sought in whose territory I might lodge. . . .
In the holy tabernacle I ministered before him [God],
   and so I was established in Zion.

(Sir. 24:3–7, 10)

This Wisdom that has settled in Jerusalem has now become one of the means by which (or whom?) God relates to the people of Israel. She typically invites people to approach her.

Come to me, you who desire me,
and eat your fill of my produce.
(Sir. 24:19)

Or again at the conclusion of the entire book, Wisdom speaks:

Draw near to me, you who are untaught,
   and lodge in my school.
Why do you say you are lacking in these things,
   and why are your souls very thirsty?
I opened my mouth and said,
   Get these things for yourselves without money.
Put your neck under the yoke,
   and let your souls receive instruction;
   it is to be found close by.
See with your eyes that I have labored little
   and found for myself much rest.
(51:23–27)

With this invitation to "come/draw near to me," the command to bear the yoke, the ease of labor, and the finding of rest, it seems that Wisdom speaks anew in the words of Jesus at Matt. 11:28–30.

Come to me, all who labor and are heavy laden, and I will give you rest. Take my yoke upon you, and learn from me; for I am gentle and lowly in heart, and you will find rest for your souls. For my yoke is easy, and my burden is light.

When the author of Matthew puts these words into Jesus' lips (this speech is missing in the parallel section at Luke 10:21–22), the evangelist seems to be announcing that Jesus himself *is* wisdom, for he speaks the way Wisdom does in Sirach. Such an equation is by no means foreign to the New Testament. In Luke 11:49 "the Wisdom of God" speaks. An

234

equation of Jesus with this Wisdom can be seen by looking at the parallel passage at Matt. 23:34, where Jesus says what "the Wisdom of God" is quoted as saying in the Lukan verse. But more important is the first chapter of 1 Corinthians were Paul calls Christ "the power of God and the *wisdom of God*" (1 Cor. 1:24) and him "whom God made *our wisdom,* our righteousness and sanctification and redemption" (1:30). This "wisdom of God" is "Christ crucified" (v. 23), and so this man is our redemption.

To sum up, while "wisdom" was commonly considered to be a body of knowledge that humans could acquire through instruction, other groups in Israel regarded "wisdom" as so closely related to God alone that it was said to have been the "first of his acts of old" (Prov. 8:22). As such, "wisdom" was considered to be, like the word of God, that means by which God created the heavens and the earth (Prov. 3:19; compare Ps. 33:6). From there the idea of "wisdom" developed in the apocryphal books to be, like the law, that revelation of God which resided in the Jerusalem temple and which invited all people to learn (Sirach 24 and 51). Finally, according to some New Testament writings "wisdom" (or word) became incarnate (compare John 1:1–14 with Sirach 24) and was crucified for the redemption of all humankind (1 Corinthians 1). As a result of that new understanding of "wisdom" Paul carried out his ministry of witness among the Corinthians.

> Yet among the mature we do impart wisdom, although it is not a wisdom of this age or of the rulers of this age, who are doomed to pass away. But we impart a secret and hidden wisdom of God, which God decreed before the ages for our glorification. (1 Cor. 2:6–7)

That "wisdom" is Jesus Christ and him crucified!

NOTES

1. "The Instruction of Amen-em-Opet," trans. John A. Wilson in *The Ancient Near East, Volume 1* (cited above, chap. 3 n. 1), 237–43, where, in the margin, references are cited to similar verses in the Book of Proverbs.

2. "The Words of Ahiqar," trans. H. L. Ginsberg, in *The Ancient Near East, Volume 1* (cited above, chap. 3 n. 1), 245–49.

18

Jesus Christ and Creation, in New Testament Witness

THE EARLY CHURCH MIGHT have rested content simply with the magnificent portrayal of creation and God's reign as creator which the Old Testament had developed (see chaps. 14–17, above). There, in worship and in creed, in relation to a gospel of redemption and to universal wisdom, so much that is so significant had already been said that Christianity could have spent decades and centuries in working out for itself the implications of Israel's faith. In point of fact, however, the Apostles' Creed goes no further than Old Testament phraseology. This creed says simply:

> I believe in *God the Father Almighty* [*Pantokrator*, "all-ruling, all-sovereign,"
>> a term from the Greek Old Testament, found at 2 Cor. 6:18 and Rev. 1:18;
>>> 4:8; among other passages in the New],
> *Maker of heaven and earth* [Gen. 14:19, 22].

Even the more elaborate Greek-sounding phrases in the Nicene Creed, "and [Maker] of all things, visible and invisible" (cf. Col. 1:16), are but expansions of the basic Old Testament doctrine. The fact is that creation was never part of the New Testament kerygma, whether in Jesus' basic preaching (above, chaps. 6—7) or the proclamation of the apostles (see chap. 25).

But Christianity in the New Testament period did not remain silent about creation. This is the more remarkable because there were powerful factors which pulled it in the direction of ignoring God's world. These factors included an eschatological expectation that, since Jesus was risen, the "end of all things" might soon be at hand, with the resulting implication, "Never mind the world"; and a type of piety found especially in the Greek mind which tended to concentrate on "spiritual" things like "the soul" and to ignore the body and the world. These factors sometimes combined in an apocalyptic outlook, eagerly awaiting "the Day of the Lord" (see chaps. 19–20), an attitude which saw the present world as so evil and corrupt that only an action of God could suffice, destroying this "old" world together with the people in it, followed by a "new creation" of the "age to come." This pessimistic attitude about the world is vividly expressed in a document in the Apocrypha called 2 Esdras: opponents are trodding down God's promises and covenants (5:28–29); Zion, like all other nations, has sinned (3:23–36); the result is that faith questions God's creation and even his promises (6:55–59; 7:46[116]–56[126]).

Fortunately for us, the New Testament did speak on creation—fortunately, since Christianity has often been very vulnerable here. On the one extreme has been the danger of ignoring the world as too crass and material for believers to be bothered about; this "spiritualistic" approach is as old in Christianity as Marcion, a second-century heretic, who attributed creation to an inferior, secondary craftsman-deity, and not to "the Father of our Lord Jesus Christ." At the other extreme has been a tendency sometimes in Christianity to equate the world and God. This confusion of the Creator and the creation existed in Greek thought, and all idolatry is based on it. Romans 1:19–32 protests against such a view. In a modern form, God may be philosophically identified with the world system or process so that, again, God is an amalgam of the universe.

Between these two extremes has often been a Christian tendency in practice to misuse the resources of creation. Genesis 1:28, the command to humans to "subdue" the earth and "have dominion over" all creatures, has been mistaken as a license to rape and waste the world. (Hence the slaughter of some 100 million buffalo and the extinction of the passenger pigeon in the nineteenth- and twentieth-century U.S.A., and hence all that is summed up by that word "ecology," which became popular in our language two decades ago—"ecology" and the crisis in the "world household.") In terms of justice, it is precisely those sinners, according to another apocryphal passage, who oppress the righteous man, who also say, "Come, therefore, let us enjoy the good things that exist, and use the freshness of creation avidly" and in effect insist, without regard for others or for the future, either, "Gather ye rosebuds while ye may" (Wisd. of Sol. 2:6, RSV and NAB; the phrase in Robert Herrick's poem derives from 2:8). This is to use up the world with no awareness of our human stewardship under God.

Christ depicted as *pantokrator* ("almighty") and creator in the apse mosaic of
Cefalù Cathedral, Sicily, twelfth century. The Greek inscription reads, "I am the
light of the world . . ." (John 8:12).

GENERAL TEACHING ABOUT CREATION
IN EARLY CHRISTIANITY

The New Testament assumes, of course, all the Old Testament has said about creation. This includes belief that "God is king" over all the world (1 Tim. 6:15), that God made everything (Acts 4:24), that God's reign is universal over all peoples (Acts 17:24–27), and that nature does the bidding of the Lord (Acts 14:15). Judgment, justice, and victory are expected from God, just as in the Old Testament (see chap. 14), and praise for this Lord is the right response (Eph. 1:6, 12, 14; cf. Rev. 19:1–2, 5). The New Testament can say, "The earth is the Lord's, and everything in it" (1 Cor. 10:26) just as the Old Testament could (Ps. 24:1; 50:12).

A significant link from the Old Testament and Judaism to post-Easter Christianity is, of course, to be found in the teachings of Jesus. During his ministry he naturally carried over some of these emphases about God and creation from the Old Testament Scriptures. The term "creation" is not itself very common on the lips of Jesus, though there is reference in his apocalyptic teaching to "the beginning of the creation which God created" (Mark 13:19).

More important is the way Jesus argues from God's creation to draw a conclusion for his own day. When some Pharisees asked him if divorce of a woman by her husband was lawful, he rejected the teaching from Moses (which said that it was, Deut. 24:1–4). Instead, Jesus appealed back prior to Moses to the time of creation, back from the Book of Deuteronomy to the first book in the Bible, Genesis: "From the beginning of creation 'God made them male and female,' and 'for this reason a man shall leave his father and mother and be joined to his wife, and the two shall become one'" (Mark 10:6–8, citing Gen. 1:27; 2:24; au. trans.). Jesus' appeal is away from the later law, given after the "fall" of humankind (Genesis 3), to God's original will expressed at creation.

Most important is the way Jesus' teachings and life constantly reflected his personal trust in God the creator, and his joy in the things of God's creation. Unlike John the Baptist, who was quite ascetic, Jesus enjoyed wine and food (Luke 7:33–34). He broke bread and celebrated festivals with thanksgiving (recall the meal in the upper room and the Feeding of the Five Thousand). Fasting is not called for when he is present (Mark 2:18). His teachings echoed trust in God's care for even the birds and the grass in the field, let alone the people on the earth (Matt. 6:25–34). Jesus had a way of interpreting the law stemming from creation about the Sabbath (Exod. 20:8–11) in such a manner that it served human needs rather than restricted people: the Sabbath was made for man (Mark 2:27). God's creation is *for* people. Jesus did not lecture on creation. He lived loving it as God's good gift for God's children.

The particular concern of the New Testament after Easter is to reiterate all this and apply it to its new situation. That means, above all, to speak about creation in relation to Jesus Christ, the new object of faith. Just as, in light of his resurrection from the dead, Jesus was confessed to be exalted as Lord, with a lordship that would extend until the end of all things (see chap. 13), so also the Lord Jesus Christ was confessed, looking back in the other direction, to have had a role in creation, eons of time before. We may have difficulty in seeing how a teacher from Nazareth who died on the cross could be associated with a creation that had occurred centuries before Abraham and even prior to Adam, but once the leap was made by faith to declaring Jesus to be "in the form of God" (Phil. 2:6) and one who was "with God" before he became a human being (John 1:1–3), it was inevitable to connect him with creation. Old Testament faith had already done something similar in speaking of Wisdom as a personified figure who was present at the creation. Cf. Prov. 8:22–31; as in chap. 17, above.

Of course, the New Testament does not boldly associate the man "rabbi Jesus" directly with creation. Usually some title of exaltation is employed, at the least the title "Christ" and more commonly "the Word" or "Word of God" (John 1; Heb. 11:3; 2 Peter 3:5). Unusual is the way Jesus speaks in the Fourth Gospel, "Before Abraham was, I am" (John 8:58). That solemn statement, as it now stands in John, is an assertion of preexistence. But "I am" is also an allusion to the divine Name of Exod. 3:14, and could have once meant nothing more than " 'God' was before Abraham." For all this, however, God the Father is never shoved out of the picture, as in the ancient Near Eastern pattern of a younger deity deposing an older one (see above, pp. 133–36, 203–4, 207–8). Rather, here the Father remains the "faithful Creator" (1 Peter 4:19), in whose image the human being was made and must be remade (Col. 3:10, reflecting Gen. 1:26–27). A role is found for Jesus Christ, but generally it is subordinate to God's; Christ is presented as vicegerent or agent (note the careful use of prepositions in 1 Cor. 8:6, discussed below).

Three other general remarks may be made before examining passages. (1) The first is to remind ourselves that, while the New Testament speaks of "creation at the *beginning* of the world" (what many people think of as "the" creation), the apostolic writings also make reference to the idea of *continuing* creation, or the exercise of God's sovereignty throughout the ongoing centuries since the world began. Jesus applies God's care to the grass of the field (Matt. 6:30) and to the commonest kind of sparrows (Matt. 10:29; humankind had gotten more ruthlessly efficient when the time of the passenger pigeon came!). Consider also John 5:17, "My Father [God] is working still [God did not "retire" at creation], and I am working," Jesus Christ said.

(2) A second observation is that the idea of *"creation out of nothing,"* which never quite came to expression in the Old Testament, is found in the New. Ancient Near Eastern myth envisioned the world as being shaped from existing materials, often from the parts of some former god (cf. chap. 15). Genesis 1:1–2, which reflects the notion of prior existing "stuff," is best translated (see above, p. 211), "When God began to create the heavens and earth, the earth was without form and void" (RSV note). But what is not stated in the Old Testament comes to be expressed in the Old Testament Apocrypha: one is admonished "to look at the heaven and the earth and see everything that is in them, and recognize that God did not make them out of things that existed" (2 Macc. 7:28). Paul reflects this idea in Rom. 4:17, and also in Heb. 11:3, "By faith we understand that the world was created by the word of God, so that what is seen was made out of things which do not appear." In classical terms, *creatio ex nihilo,* "creation out of nothing." The effect of such a statement is to enhance the miracle of creation, although it is also a possible reflection of the "wisdom movement" where "reason replaces drama" in dealing with creation.

(3) It may have been noted by alert readers that none of the passages in the New Testament relates the Holy Spirit to creation. It is Jesus Christ the Word who is the agent of God in creating. Contrary to later views, in the Bible the Spirit is seldom connected with creation.

Somewhat surprising is the range of situations and literary forms in which there is reference to creation in the New Testament, not only carrying over the Old Testament theme of God reigning as creator but also developing a place in God's creative activity for Jesus Christ. Just as in the Old Testament, there are *hymns* in the New Testament, like Col. 1:15–20 (see below), dealing with creation (and redemption). Underlying the first chapter of John is what many consider to be a hymn about creation and redemption (the *Jerusalem Bible* prints it as such), most likely in vv. 1–5, 9–14, and 16–18. There are *confessions of faith* about creation, such as 1 Cor. 8:6 (see below) or Rom. 4:17, where it is said that Abraham believed in God,

who gives life to the dead [resurrection]
and calls into existence things that do not exist [creation].

Paul applies the phrases to the miracle of God raising up descendants from Abraham, from his "dead" body and Sarah's barren womb, to inherit the promises of God.

Creation imagery can be hooked up also with *apocalyptic expectations* about the "last times." Thus, 2 Peter 3:5–14 parallels the work of the word of God in creating "an earth formed out of water and by means of water" (v. 5) and in destroying the heavens and earth by fire (vv. 6–7; cf. vv. 10, 12)—though there is then a promise of "new heavens and a new earth" (v. 13) beyond all this. Romans 8:18–23 is another passage about creation, its bondage and future liberation. Both of these sections really use "creation eschatology" as the basis for an *ethical appeal,* to live "lives of holiness and godliness" (2 Peter 3:11) and to wait patiently with hope (Rom. 8:24–25). Thus, 1 Peter 4:19 calls upon Christians to trust a faithful Creator. What obtained "from the beginning of creation" is the basis for Jesus' rejection of divorce and his stance for permanence in marriage (Mark 10:6–9).

There was, further, a particular tendency in early Christianity to describe *baptism* as a kind of new creation. In addition to 2 Cor. 4:4–6, where Paul compares his own "enlightenment" (v. 4) with the command at Gen. 1:3, "Let light shine out of darkness" (2 Cor. 4:6), and the famous reference in the same epistle to "any one in Christ" as a "new creature" (or "creation") (2 Cor. 5:17), the following passages should be pondered as reflecting the baptismal experience:

> Put on the new nature, which is being renewed in knowledge after the image of its *creator.* (Col. 3:10; cf. Eph. 4:24)

> We are [God's] workmanship, *created* in Christ Jesus . . . that he might *create* in himself one new man [or race] in place of the two [Jews and Gentiles]. (Eph. 2:10, 15)

> Of his own will [God] *brought us forth* by the word of truth, that we [Christians] should be a kind of *first fruits of his creatures;* therefore . . . receive . . . the implanted word, which is able to save your souls. (James 1:18, 21)

As in the Old Testament (see chap. 16), creation language serves the gospel of redemption.

Thus far we have said that creation entered into early Christian thinking in a surprising variety of ways. But how did it come about that creation was a topic of theology, even though the basic proclamation of Jesus and the apostles did not include it? The obvious answer is that both Jesus and the early church *assumed* what the Old Testament had said about the subject. What is more, God as creator had been a major theme in Jewish teaching of the day, and we may be sure that Jewish missionaries such as Matt. 23:15 describes included "the world as the creation of the One God" in their stock missionary preaching to Gentiles. Accordingly, when Christian missionaries began to venture into the Greco-Roman world, they no doubt used some of the same terms and arguments as Jewish missionaries and apologists had, in order to convince Gentiles that the God they proclaimed was the One who had made the world in which we live. Paul's address at Athens (Acts 17:22–31) is an example of such a reasoned appeal, as is the little speech at Acts 14:15–17, at the Temple of Zeus in Lystra.

On such occasions, the missionaries for Christ could draw upon what Jews before them had said in their propaganda efforts. It is likely that even some parts of Paul's letters reflect such materials used by Jews in their missionary work; perhaps Rom. 1:18–32, with its indictment of the pagan world for its corruption and sin and therefore the need for a new faith in the creator God, comes from such a background. It may be noted too that early Christians could make use of phrases and ideas from Greek poets and philosophers in their effort to show that the world is a work of God. In Acts 17:28 there are quoted, though not by name, Epimenides ("In him we live and move and have our being") and Aratus ("for we are indeed his offspring"). Epimenides was a religious teacher and wonder-worker in Crete about 500 B.C.; Titus 1:12 calls him a prophet and cites a derogatory comment by him about the natives of Crete. Aratus, who lived from about 315 till 240 B.C., was a native of Paul's home area, Cilicia. The citation in Acts is from Aratus's poem *The Phaenomena,* a versified version of a handbook on astrology, which was extremely popular in antiquity.

Early Christian preaching (which we shall examine more fully in chap. 25) thus fell into two types, with or without reference to creation, depending on the audience addressed. For those who already knew about God as creator—for example, the Jewish audience such as we encounter in Acts 2—the proclamation dealt especially with Jesus' death and resurrection. For non-Jews or any audience unfamiliar with the biblical view of God as creator, the basic proclamation would also include something about this topic and about God's kingly rule and care of the earth and for its peoples, now also connected with Jesus Christ. Such an approach, or approaches, proved valuable for subsequent Christian witnessing, post–New Testament. For it provided an illustration of how one must pay attention to where people are and to the world, creation, and God's rule, before, or as, one sets forth Jesus as savior.

A NEW TESTAMENT CREED AND A
HYMN ABOUT CREATION

A good illustration of even more specifically Christian talk concerning creation can be seen in the single verse at *1 Cor. 8:6,*

> For us there is one God, the Father, from whom are all things and for whom we exist, and one Lord, Jesus Christ, through whom are all things and through whom we exist.

At the heart of this verse is the good Old Testament phrase, "There is one God," a thought also asserted in v. 4, "There is no God but one." That, of course, is a paraphrase of Israel's greatest confession of faith, the so-called *Shema* (named from its opening word in Hebrew), "Hear, O Israel: the Lord our God, the Lord is one" (Deut. 6:4, RSV note). This phrase had become a battle cry and slogan for Jewish existence, "One God!" The descriptive clause that follows in 1 Cor. 8:6 could have been used in any synagogue in the Greek-speaking world: "from whom are all things and for whom we exist." It asserts God's creation of the universe and also of Yahweh's own people. The rhetorical language is similar to that which Paul uses in Rom. 11:36 about God ("from him and through him and to him are all things"), which is typical of Roman Stoic philosophy.

So far we have an assertion about God as creator which could have been confessed in any synagogue. But alongside it, in deliberate parallelism, has been placed a reference to the "Lord Jesus Christ." We are reminded here of those acclamations with which early Christians broke forth, "Jesus Christ is Lord" (see chap. 13). Perhaps even as a synagogue gathering was confessing its faith in God as creator, some Jewish Christian boldly inserted his testimony to the lordship of Jesus—and this led to Christ's being assigned a role in creation. As the verse now stands, the parallelism is absolutely symmetrical: "one" has been added before "Lord" to balance "one God"; the title "Father" has been placed after "God" to balance "Jesus Christ" (it can mean both "Father of the world" and "Father of our Lord Jesus Christ"); and the prepositions describing Christ's role have been chosen with great care, so as to give him a place as agent in creation and yet subordinate in function to God. In structural form, literally, the creed ran, "[We believe in]

> One God, the Father,
>   from whom [are] all things, and we [exist] for him,
> and one Lord, Jesus Christ,
>   through whom [are] all things, and we [exist] through him.

God is the source and goal of being, Jesus Christ the means for life.

The amazing thing is that this carefully structured four-line assertion of faith had taken shape by the early fifties. For Paul quotes it in a letter about A.D. 55 to the Corinthians, quite casually, in the course of a discussion about whether Christians were free to eat meat that had first been part of a pagan sacrifice (as almost all meat for sale in Corinthian butcher shops was). Paul's answer was yes, we have liberty to eat any such food (1 Cor. 8:8), since the whole earth is the Lord's (10:25–26). But he did condition this freedom of creation by concern for those weaker in faith who might be offended by such actions (8:13). In asserting his argument from creation he shows us how early and how fully Christian belief in Jesus' place in creation had developed.

Hymning Christ as Creator

A fuller example of the early church's confession of Christ's role in creation of the universe occurs in the hymn at *Col. 1:15–20*. This time we shall begin with the verses in rhythmic form, arranged in two stanzas, the one about creation and the second about redemption. This is the structure that many scholars find in the passage.

I. Creation

[15]He is the image of the invisible God,
    the first-born of all creation;
[16]for in him all things were created,
    in heaven and on earth,
      visible and invisible,
Whether thrones or dominions
    or principalities or authorities—
all things were created through him and for him.
[17]He is before all things,
    and in him all things hold together.
[18a]He is the head of the body,
      the church.

II. Redemption

[18b]He is the beginning,
    the first-born from the dead,
      that in everything he might be preeminent.
[19]For in him all the fulness of God was pleased to dwell,
      [20]and through him to reconcile to himself all things,
    whether on earth or in heaven,
    making peace by the blood of his cross.

The poem clearly falls into two halves, as the phrases *"first-born* of all *creation"* and *"first-born* from the *dead"* suggest. Some familiar biblical ideas occur. Creation and redemption are brought together, as in the Old Testament (cf. chap. 16). Creation concerns "all things . . . through him and for him" (v. 16), which is language reminiscent of 1 Cor. 8:6. There is the stock phrase "heaven and earth" (vv. 16, 20), used to sum up the whole of cosmic reality, but there is also a reflection of the current world view about "cosmic powers"—namely, "thrones, dominions, princi- palities, and authorities," which are included in what he created.

It must also be said that the passage is more christological than any material on creation that we have looked at thus far. There is no reference to God the Father as creator; in fact, there is no reference to God at all except that Christ is "the image of the invisible God" (v. 15). At the same time, for all this concentration on a creator who is other than God, there is no reference to Jesus Christ by name. In Greek the verses begin with the relative pronoun "[he] *who,"* with the identity inferred only from the context (in this case, from v. 14, "his beloved Son"). (That is a normal way for New Testament hymns to begin, however.) The point stands that except for references to "the church" (v. 18a) and "the blood of his cross" (v. 20), one would have a pretty hard job identifying who this creator- redeemer figure is. A final perplexity is that, oddly, the church is men- tioned in connection with stanza I, on creation, rather than under II, as a result of redemption.

Some scholars think we have here an early Christian hymn that took shape in the Hellenistic world. It may have originated in those enthusiast groups of Christians who, caught up in the experience of the lordship of Jesus, expanded their praises of him to highest heaven and back into the origins of time. Their kudos for Christ was expressed in a very Greek way, and that may account for the puzzling detail in v. 18. In Hellenistic thought, the world was sometimes known as "the body of Zeus." (Here was a case in Hellenistic religion where the creation and its supposed creator were identified.) At an early state, the poem may simply have ended the first stanza with the words,

He is the head of the body [i.e., of the world].

But in Pauline thought the body of Christ is *the church* and not the world (1 Cor. 12:12–27), made up of believers, not of every pagan and Jew. To be truer to Pauline thought, the Epistle to Colossae has added a reference to "the church," thereby spoiling the structure but improving the the- ology. In stanza II the reference to "the blood of his cross" may also be an addition to specify that the agent of creation here described is none other than Jesus Christ who made atonement by his blood.

There is much more that could be said about this richly suggestive passage. "That in everything he might be preeminent" (v. 18) is a way of talking about Christ's lordship. The phrase in v. 19, ". . . in him all the fulness of God was pleased to dwell," is traditionally taken as a reference to the incarnation, but when Colossians takes up the theme of "fulness" it is to stress the life in him to which we have access (2:9–10). The reconciliation wrought by Christ is regarded as cosmic (1:20), though 2:15 is more detailed in describing "the principalities and powers" not as being reconciled but as defeated. In the "creation" section, one feature especially catches the eye: Christ who is preexistent (v. 17a) is also one who "holds things together" (v. 17b). This introduces us to the theme of "providence."

ONGOING CREATION—AND CONCERNS

In the Old Testament, we have seen, God not only creates the world, but also rules it. God's providential care watches over nature and history. Jesus reflected this belief in God's providence when he spoke of God's care for his children and for the birds of the air and the lilies of the field (Matt. 6:24–34). The "nature miracle stories" narrated about Jesus, like Mark 4:35–41, the Storm at Sea, are in many ways "creation miracles," reflecting God's control over the forces of nature.

Not surprisingly, when Jesus is given a place in creation, according to assertions of the early church, he is also seen to rule continuingly as a part of ongoing creation. In addition to Col. 1:17, Heb. 1:3 says the same thing: the Son, through whom God created the world (Heb. 1:2), who reflects the glory of God and bears the stamp of his nature (cf. Col. 1:15), upholds "the universe by his word of power."

What has happened here is in line with Old Testament developments. God the deliverer was spoken of as creator. His reign was extended into the world. Poetical, mythical language and reason both were employed to set forth God's greatness. In the New Testament, Jesus the Lord comes to be spoken of in connection with creation too. His role includes, in christological language, sustenance of the universe. He becomes, for faith, a cosmic Christ, celebrated in hymns and creeds, with mythic language sometimes drawn in. The wisdom tradition crops up here too, portraying Jesus as a teacher of wisdom in what he says, and eventually as "the Wisdom of God" (see under "In the Apocrypha and Beyond" in chap. 17)—a link to what the Old Testament had said about "wisdom" in creation. The New Testament has less of "wisdom literature" than the Old (but compare the Book of James, with its aphorisms, as a reflection of this tradition). But it offers Wisdom incarnate, in God's Son.

Over the years a tug of war threatened to develop for the hearts and minds of God's people. Too much emphasis on the world as God's creation and on common-sense wisdom could cause them to settle down in that world, complacent, and to conform to it. That they could not, with complete comfort or a good conscience, was due to another strand found in the Old Testament and heightened in Christianity: the future aspect of God's reign and the apocalyptic "Day of the Lord," which implied certain reservations about this world (see part 5, below). But for times when God's people were tempted to be too future-oriented and apocalyptically inclined, the New Testament had spoken, positively and christologically, of the creation.

That is why God's people have always been *in* the world, but *not of* the world (cf. 1 John 4:4–6, 17). They are formed by God, through Christ, as is his world. But since it is a world of sin, rebellion, disobedience, and decay, they must not be conformed to this world but transformed to God's Son (Rom. 12:2).

Theses on Creation

What both testaments say about creation can be fittingly summed up, as a conclusion to these last four chapters, in a series of propositions for modern-day consideration.[1]

1. What the Bible says in both Old Testament and New about creation is a statement of *faith*. In light of an experience of redemption, faith goes on to speak about the origin of things.

2. The mood or environment of such faith-statements is one of *praise* for God, in hymns, confessions, and other expressions of the doxological stance of faith.

3. The language and even some of the ideas in these faith-statements, however, often come from the science and philosophy of the author's day. Faith-statements about creation use the *vocabulary and insight of the times.*

4. The New Testament early gave *Christ* a role in creation as well as in redemption. One implication is that we dare not too rigidly compartmentalize the first two articles of the Apostles' and Nicene Creeds.

5. There is concern throughout the Bible to see creation as an *ongoing* activity, concerning existence now and not just origins in the past.

6. In some situations it was necessary for early Christians to *witness*

about their beliefs concerning *the world,* its creation and its care, along with testimony to their having experienced salvation.

7. Christians are concerned about the world because it is God's and Christ's by creation as well as by redemption. There is thus a *"stewardship of creation."* Such an idea is shared, in their own ways, by Jews, followers of Islam, and all who reckon with a creator God.

NOTE

1. There is a fuller discussion of these propositions in J. Reumann, *Creation and New Creation: The Past, Present, and Future of God's Creative Activity* (cited above, chap. 16 n.1), 100–108; and on 1 Cor. 8:6, see pp. 24–31.

V
THE GOSPEL
AS HOPE—
GOD'S FUTURE REIGN

The tel ("mound") of Megiddo, a city rebuilt twenty times between 3000 and 400 B.C. Frequent battles here caused Mount Megiddo (Hebrew *har Mĕgiddôn*) to become the symbol for the last battle (Armageddon, Rev. 16:16).

19
"The Day of the Lord"

THE REIGN OF GOD in Israel's history seemed at times to be incomplete. Undoubtedly that view was due in part to such tragedies in Israel's life as the division of the monarchy following Solomon's death, and later the destruction of the northern kingdom and the subjugation of the southern one at the hands of the Assyrians. Yet perhaps it was these very tragedies that enabled Israel to see even more clearly than before that it had no monopoly on God. The Lord's reign, the Israelites realized, must surely extend far beyond the recognition and confession of Israel to include the whole universe. Their own views of creation enabled them to confess that reign in the first place. Yet, since it was clear that other nations at the time did not acclaim the Lord as king, the biblical prophets looked beyond their own situation into the future when God would be established as king and creator of a new world.

This new time to which the prophets pointed was not to come about as a result of gradual growth. It was in no way conceived to be the end of a process in which the world would evolve into a golden age. Indeed, if anything, the Old Testament portrays history as a downhill slide. Instead of the old glory of the Davidic-Solomonic Empire, there was tragedy; in place of freedom, there was confinement—political, economic, and moralistic.

Hope, though it waned at times, never died, because the mediators of God's word preached in various ways that *one day* the Lord would execute some dramatic event that would usher in the divine kingship over everyone. Indeed, this expectation must have existed quite early in Israel's history and prevailed among the folks of the marketplace, the fields, the washing wells, and the court. By a mighty act they believed the Lord would come *one day* rightfully to claim everything as his own. Such a claim, of course, meant God would destroy by their own claims the evil forces that were in opposition. In the minds of the people, those forces were primarily Israel's enemies.

A DAY OF JUDGMENT AND THREAT

The first preacher among the prophets to address this idea of "the day of Yahweh" was Amos. Though a southerner from Judah, Amos preached exclusively, it seems, in the northern kingdom Israel in a time of national optimism (about 760–750 B.C.). His message was essentially one of judgment, and in this context he interpreted "the day of Yahweh" in a manner quite different from his audience.

> Woe to you who desire the day of the LORD!
>> Why would you have the day of the LORD?
> It is darkness, and not light;
>> as if a man fled from a lion,
>> and a bear met him;
> or went into the house and leaned with his hand against the wall,
>> and a serpent bit him.
> Is not the day of the LORD darkness, and not light,
>> and gloom with no brightness in it?
>>> (Amos 5:18–20)

The following verses go on to explain that the Lord takes no pleasure in the formalities of religious expression if there is no meaning from the heart that results in justice and righteousness (Amos 5:21–24). For this reason God will make "the day" one of darkness for those optimistic Israelites who had thought that, because God was "on their side," they could simply sit back and watch divine judgment on everyone else. Not so, said Amos, God's judgment comes on you as well when he acts "on [or "in"] that day."

> ". . . he who is stout of heart among the mighty shall flee away naked *in that day*," says the LORD. (Amos 2:16)

> "The songs of the temple shall become wailings *in that day*," says the Lord GOD. (8:3)

> "And *on that day*," says the Lord GOD,
> "I will make the sun go down at noon,
> and darken the earth in broad daylight."
>> (8:9)

> *In that day* the fair virgins and the young men shall faint for thirst. (8:13)

Or, with a turn of the phrase, the prophet again spells out another reason for such judgment on Israel.

"Hear this word, you cows of Bashan,
  who are in the mountain of Samaria,
who oppress the poor, who crush the needy,
  who say to their husbands, 'Bring, that we may drink!'
The Lord GOD has sworn by his holiness
  that, behold, the days are coming upon you,
when they shall take you away with hooks,
  even the last of you with fishhooks.
And you shall go out through the breaches,
  every one straight before her;
and you shall be cast forth into Harmon,"
says the LORD.
(4:1–3)

Thus, while the precise expression "the day of Yahweh" occurs only sixteen times in the Old Testament, the same future and decisive act of the Lord is meant by the substitute phrases "that day" or "the days are coming." Amos, first to introduce these terms into his prophetic preaching midway through the eighth century B.C. in order to announce judgment in Israel (along with other nations), was by no means the last to employ such terminology. For example, Isaiah:

In that day men will cast forth
  their idols of silver and their idols of gold . . .
  to the moles and to the bats,
to enter the caverns of the rocks
  and the clefts of the cliffs,
from before the terror of the LORD,
  and from the glory of his majesty,
  when he rises to terrify the earth.
(Isa. 2:20–21)

Indeed, later prophets, following Amos's lead, preached about the Lord's Day in ferocious battle terms in order to announce God's judgment. A passage from the end of the Babylonian Exile (about 538 B.C.), inserted into the Book of Isaiah, contains this oracle concerning Babylon:

Hark, a tumult on the mountains as of a great multitude!
Hark, an uproar of kingdoms, of nations gathering together!
The LORD of hosts is mustering a host for battle.
They came from a distant land,
  from the end of the heavens,
the LORD and the weapons of his indignation,

255

to destroy the whole earth.
Wail, for *the day of the LORD* is near;
    as destruction from the Almighty it will come! . . .

Behold, *the day of the LORD* comes,
    cruel, with wrath and fierce anger,
to make the earth a desolation
    and to destroy its sinners from it.
For the stars of the heavens and their constellations
    will not give their light;
the sun will be dark at its rising
    and the moon will not shed its light.
                              (Isa. 13:4–6, 9–10)

Likewise, the prophet Jeremiah includes in his preaching the oracle concerning the army of Pharaoh Neco, king of Egypt:

"Prepare buckler and shield,
    and advance for battle!
Harness the horses;
    mount, O horsemen!
Take your stations with your helmets,
    polish your spears,
    put on your coats of mail!
Why have I seen it?
They are dismayed
    and have turned backward.
Their warriors are beaten down,
    and have fled in haste;
they look not back—
    terror on every side!"
        says the Lord. . . .

"Advance, O horses,
    and rage, O chariots!
Let the warriors go forth:
    men of Ethiopia and Put who handle the shield,
    men of Lud, skilled in handling the bow.
That day is *the day of the Lord GOD of hosts*
    a day of vengeance,
    to avenge himself on his foes. . . ."
                          (Jer. 46:3–5, 9–10)

This day of the Lord as one of disaster and bloody judgment occurs also in the preaching of Ezekiel in the early sixth century B.C. (Ezekiel 7; 30:1–5) and earlier in that of Zephaniah between 630 and 625 B.C. (1:7–18): "*the day of the LORD* is at hand" (cf. Mark 1:15).

The imagery of the Lord doing battle as a mighty warrior who causes the enemy to panic and flee in the midst of terror (Jer. 46:5) and who uses the heavens above to cause darkness on the unfortunate enemy (Isa. 13:10) calls to mind the ancient holy wars of Yahweh that took place in the days of the judges in Israel. In the days of Joshua, the Lord fought against the five kings of the Amorites, throwing them into a self-destructive panic and pelting them with hailstones from heaven (Josh. 10:1–11). In Samuel's battle against the Philistines, the Lord "thundered" and thus caused the enemy to panic and flee (1 Sam. 7:10–11). At the Reed Sea, we have seen, God used wind, water, and darkness to destroy the Egyptians (Exod. 14:10–31). What is striking about those and other battles of old, those wars of Yahweh, is that repeatedly the phrase "on that day" appears in their telling: "Thus the Lord saved Israel [on] that day from the hand of the Egyptians" (Exod. 14:30; see also 1 Sam. 7:6, 10; 14:23, 24, 31). In other words, when the prophets described the battle to come in the future, they looked back to Israel's past not only for details of battles but even for the key term "on that day." God's actions in the past was Israel's clue for envisioning what the new day would be like.

A DAY OF RESTORATION AND *SHALOM*

What was to happen "on that day" was not, however, judgment alone. After the judgment the Lord would bring restoration, at least for a remnant of the people. Even the Book of Amos, filled with prophecies of doom, concludes with two "day-of-Yahweh" passages that promise restoration in the land.

> "Behold, *the days are coming*," says the LORD,
>   "when the plowman shall overtake the reaper
>   and the treader of grapes him who sows the seed;
> the mountains shall drip sweet wine
>   and all the hills shall flow with it.
> I will restore the fortunes of my people Israel,
>   and they shall rebuild the ruined cities and inhabit them;
> they shall plant vineyards and drink their wine,
>   and they shall make gardens and eat their fruit.
> I will plant them upon their land,
>   and they shall never again be plucked up,
>   out of the land which I have given them,"
>   says the LORD your God.
>   (Amos 9:13–15)

Here the promise given is for the rebuilding of ruined cities, vegetation and fruit so plentiful and fast-growing that the farmers will hardly keep up with the harvesting, abundant wine from fertile vineyards, and no more destruction and exile.

Another benefit in the kingdom to be established is promised in a text from Isaiah that hits upon the remnant issue as well.

> *In that day* the branch of the LORD shall be beautiful and glorious, and the fruit of the land shall be the pride and glory of the survivors of Israel. And he who is left in Zion and remains in Jerusalem will be called holy, every one who has been recorded for life in Jerusalem, when the LORD shall have washed away the filth of the daughters of Zion and cleansed the bloodstains of Jerusalem from its midst by a spirit of judgment and by a spirit of burning. Then the LORD will create over the whole site of Mount Zion and over her assemblies a cloud by day, and smoke and the shining of a flaming fire by night; for over all the glory there will be a canopy and a pavilion. It will be for a shade by day from the heat, and for a refuge and a shelter from the storm and rain. (Isa. 4:2–6)

Again, like so many passages dealing with the day of salvation, this one contains the picture of a fruitful paradise. (Cf. also Isa. 30:23–26; Jer. 31:12; Ezek. 34:29; 47:12; Isa. 41:17–20; Zech. 9:16–17; 14:8; Mal. 3:11.) But beyond the response of nature, the old signs of the Lord's presence among the people—namely, cloud by day and smoke and fire by night (see Exod. 13:21–22)—will become protective instruments for the temple built and the congregation assembled there for worship. Thus the temple of Jerusalem plays a central role in the kingdom of God that will be inaugurated "in that day."

Such broad-sweeping portrayals of the "paradise life" lead directly to the conclusion that the day of the Lord when God is established unequivocally as king is the beginning of *shalom*. *Shalom* is that condition in which men and women are free to live life unrestrained and unhindered by forces of confinement. *Shalom* means living life to the fullest, participating without difficulty in the life of the community, and experiencing a devout and close relationship with God. All this seems to fit the descriptions of restoration which will occur on "the day of the Lord" and beyond. Thus, the kingdom of God or new age for which people waited would take place amid all the material goods of the world. It would be a time of plenty, of joy, of protection, of long life, and so it was indeed believed to be part of this world rather than of heaven.

Moreover, this state of *shalom* in the new age to come reached out to include nations other than Israel. To be sure, Israel—specifically Jerusalem—was the focal point for God's relationship with the Gentiles, but all peoples would indeed come to learn his will.

It shall come to pass *in the latter days*
  that the mountain of the house of the LORD
shall be established as the highest of the mountains,
  and shall be raised above the hills;
and all the nations shall flow to it,
  and many peoples shall come, and say:
"Come, let us go up to the mountain of the LORD,
  to the house of the God of Jacob;
that he may teach us his ways
  and that we may walk in his paths."
For out of Zion shall go forth the law,
  and the word of the LORD from Jerusalem.
He shall judge between the nations,
  and shall decide for many peoples;
And they shall beat their swords into plowshares,
  and their spears into pruning hooks;
nation shall not lift up sword against nation,
  neither shall they learn war any more.

                                (Isa. 2:2–4)

This beautiful and powerful passage, repeated at Micah 4:1–3, expands the earlier descriptions of "the latter days" to include a universal pilgrimage to Mount Zion where all nations would learn God's law (that is, instruction), submit to God's judgments, and abolish war. Peace among nations! Harmony among the peoples! Worship of the Lord in every land! Even the concept of *shalom* has become larger. This is what the reign of God will be like.

So different, in fact, will life be in the future kingdom that no other term would suffice but "new creation."

For behold, I create new heavens and a new earth;
  and the former things shall not be remembered or come into mind.
But be glad and rejoice for ever in that which I create;
  for behold, I create Jerusalem a rejoicing,
    and her people a joy. . . .

                             (Isa. 65:17–18)

The passage goes on to describe the lack of distress, the long life of children (but not eternal life), fruitful vineyards and enjoyment thereof, meaningful labor, abundant posterity, and even harmony among known hostile animals. Now the picture of *shalom* is so vast that a new heaven and a new earth will be required to contain it. Again, this hope to come does not call for the ruination and dismissal of all things material; on the contrary, along with the new heavens, a new *earth* will appear at God's doing, and material blessings will abound! Again, God the creator will reign!

The prophets expected this or that event in history was God's means of bringing about the Lord's "day" and resulting reign. Judgment on the Egyptians or on the Assyrians or the Babylonians or a list of others, including Israel and Judah, was expected to be the end time. Sometimes, even often, the prophesied judgments occurred, but life went on much as before. And so the people looked forward to the next big event on the world scene, and when that was over, to the next and the next. In other words, "the day of the Lord" was constantly being identified with this or that forthcoming historical occasion, and thus was pushed time and again into the future because the expected results were not fulfilled.

Thus it is striking that this promise of God to reign in the future over a kingdom of universal *shalom* persisted among the prophets. Such was the confidence of Israel that the reign of God that was confessed would *one day* include all people. Such a time would come only at God's own doing!

20

The Birth of Apocalyptic

THE LONGING FOR THAT glorious day of Yahweh which the Lord would bring about in order to fulfill, but not end, history became more and more a remote dream in many segments of Israel. And no wonder! Hundreds of years of history did not seem to lead to the conclusion that things were getting any better. On the contrary, it seemed that history was leading Israel on a downhill path of oppression and disaster. The longer history continued, some thought, the worse life would be.

The glorious days of the Davidic-Solomonic Empire were short and long gone. Ever since the monarchy split into two nations near the end of the tenth century B.C., that glory was only a memory. In the eighth century Assyria overpowered the people, bringing an end to the state of Israel in the north and subjecting the state of Judah in the south to vassalhood. At the end of the seventh century, Judah had a few years of unexpected glory under Josiah, but soon it was a vassal of Egypt and, within short order, of Babylon. Then, due to a rebellion in 597, Judah was devastated by the exile of its leading citizens to Babylon. Ten years later, after another rebellion, the city of Jerusalem was leveled, and the sacred temple reduced to a pile of rubbish. In 538 the Persians took control and offered the exiled Judahites opportunity to go home, but few were interested. As beneficent as the Persians were, Judah was nevertheless a vassal once again. That allegiance ended in 331 B.C. when Alexander the Great made the territory of Judah part of his Greek Empire, and for a century and half various factions warred for control of the land, only to give way eventually to the powerful Roman Empire which exercised authority and demanded allegiance.

How could the people of Israel continue to hope in God's plan to unfold into fulfillment in history? History seemed to be one disaster after another, and nothing more. Without confidence in history and God's action in history the people resorted to a different kind of theological expression: apocalyptic.

CHARACTERISTICS OF APOCALYPTIC
COMPARED WITH PROPHECY

"Apocalyptic" is a Greek word that basically means "to unveil." It has to do with unveiling the secrets of the cosmos that were revealed only to a select few. This revelation came in various forms but most commonly through bizarre visions that could be interpreted only by those individuals who had been given the secrets. This is the first and major characteristic of apocalyptic.

And here is a second. Apocalyptic writings describe the future as the time when God would suddenly intervene into history, destroy virtually everything that now exists, and establish a heavenly kingdom. Those so inspired were thought to be able to describe vividly the fate of the wicked and the bliss of the righteous and, beyond that, to determine *when* the end is coming on the basis of a divine world plan which had been foreordained.

Third, in this view history becomes very mechanical as it follows the "game plan," and so people are rather passive as they wait to see *what will happen* next. In other words, it is not a personal God who acts in history; rather things occur—by fate—and people simply wait for the terrible day.

Fourth, the world and people in it are regarded as evil and are increasingly becoming more evil. Since people do not act but passively wait, the world becomes progressively worse. No one acts to better the situation.

Fifth, there thus arises a dualism of two worlds or ages that are directly opposed to each other: the present evil age and the time of bliss to come. That future scene is otherworldly rather than earthly, and it will be filled with the children of light rather than the children of darkness—another dualistic view.

These major characteristics of apocalyptic show the sharp contrast between this type of thinking and the more typical view of the prophets. A comparison of the two types throws the strangeness of apocalyptic into a clearer light.

1. The prophetic view of history testified that Israel saw itself as saved, elected, and made a covenant partner in the unfolding of God's activities in the past. Each generation, by identifying itself with the past commu-

nities who were delivered and chosen, took on an identity as a people with whom God continued to act as a covenant partner. There was nothing mechanical about the relationship: God acted to judge and to save the people in the midst of whatever situations the people found themselves. This view stands in sharp contrast to apocalyptic where the emphasis is not on the personal dealing of God with Israel but rather on the divine plan for world empires which would work itself out according to a cosmic clock. Apocalyptic's concept of history as a world plan depersonalizes the Lord of history known in the preaching of the prophets.

2. The prophetic view of history saw the activity of God unfolding a purpose or plan in which the Lord would move history toward the desired goal: a time when all people on earth would come to the focal point, Mount Zion, giving praise to Yahweh and seeking to learn God's law. Even in the wild-eyed new creation of Isaiah 65—66, the new will be earthly: people will still die, but they will live longer (one hundred twenty years); justice will prevail for all; food will be abundant *on the earth.* But the goal of apocalyptic is the destruction of the world that is becoming more and more evil with each passing day, and with that obliteration a new spiritual age will result.

3. The prophets *spoke* to and about the situation of their audiences, telling it "like it is." They portrayed the facts in all candor and honesty, naming the villains, describing the problems, and publicly announcing the will of God. In apocalyptic, by contrast, the inspired *wrote* about their own situations in veiled terms by speaking in images of animals, statues, or even past times and long-dead people. It was only the gifted few who could interpret the message concerning what would happen next according to God's mechanical plan, and they often did this by use of obscure allegories.

Thus it is clear that for apocalypticism history was not the arena of God's activity with the people. There was no positive value to history at all; it served only as the arena in which evil evolves into destruction. And so, in ancient Israel (and in modern times as well) apocalyptic flourished whenever times were bad and confidence in history and in humankind was lost.

APOCALYPTIC IN THE
BOOK OF DANIEL

Although there are small sections of various Old Testament books that contain apocalyptic style and thought, only one book is classified as apocalyptic—the Book of Daniel. While the story is set in the time of the

Babylonian Exile in the sixth century B.C., the book was written to
address the situation of persecution under the Seleucid king Antiochus
IV Epiphanes (175–163 B.C.). More specifically, the author started his
writing sometime after 167 B.C. when the Maccabees rose up against the
Syrians (see above, pp. 79–80, 82–83). The reference to the "little help"
received by the faithful in their time of testing is probably an allusion to
unenthusiastic response given by the people as a whole to the Maccabean
leaders (Dan. 11:34). Moreover, the reign of Antiochus IV is rather
accurately described, with the sole exception of his death—an error
which probably indicates the book was finished before he died in 163 B.C.
Therefore, it was sometime between 167 and 164 B.C. that the Book of
Daniel was composed.

The book consists of two parts. Chapters 1 through 6 contain stories of
Daniel and his friends in Babylon; chaps. 7 through 12 report the visions
of Daniel concerning the future of the kingdom of the earth. Thus, only
half the book contains apocalyptic features, but the two halves are
connected by the insertion of Nebuchadnezzar's dream in the first section
at chap. 2.

With the exception of chap. 2, the first part of the book is concerned
with one fundamental point: the faithful and pious Jew in danger of
temptation and harm will be protected by holding firm in faith in God
and by not compromising allegiance to God's requirements. This point is
demonstrated in the first chapter when Daniel and friends refused to eat
the king's delicacies but flourished nevertheless by eating only kosher
food. In chap. 3 the friends were tossed into a furnace that was so hot the
attendants died from standing too close, but the three friends were
unharmed because of their refusal to indulge in idolatry. In chap. 4, when
Daniel reported to the king that his dream foretold loss of kingship
accompanied by insanity, no harm came to Daniel; on the contrary, he
received a promotion. The handwriting-on-the-wall episode in chap. 5
gives evidence of that same fearless allegiance to God on Daniel's part.
And in chap. 6, Daniel, thrown into the lions' den, emerged unharmed,
but the guards were mauled to death. Thus every chapter contains one
more episode which testifies that Yahweh will protect those who remain
faithful. Those who remained pious in Israel had nothing to fear from
Antiochus IV and his hatchet men. God would deliver the steadfast.

It is the dreams and visions, however, that illustrate the method and
message of apocalyptic. The dream of Nebuchadnezzar in chap. 2 and the
vision of the four beasts in chap. 7 serve as examples of the way apocalyptic works.

Because King Nebuchadnezzar was troubled by dreams, he summoned the magicians, the sorcerers, the enchanters, and the Chaldeans to tell him the dream and its interpretation. When they admitted that they were unable to comply with his wish, the king ordered all the wise men throughout Babylon to be killed. One of those about to be murdered was an exile from Judah named Daniel. He stepped forward and announced to Nebuchadnezzar both the contents of the dream and its meaning.

In his dream the king saw a mighty image standing before him. Its head was gold; its breast and arms, silver; it had a belly and thighs of bronze and legs of iron. Its feet were partly clay and partly iron. Here is how Daniel explained its meaning:

> You, O king, . . . are the head of gold. A kingdom of silver shall follow you, then a kingdom of bronze, finally a kingdom of iron. But the last kingdom shall be divided—part clay and part iron—and thus brittle. Then God in heaven will set up his kingdom; it will shatter all the others and last forever. (2:37–44, paraphrased)

The dream, therefore, had to do with four world empires. Thus we have here a clear and simple presentation of history: events will take place in a succession of world empires that will become increasingly inferior until the coming of God's kingdom puts an end to the series.

The first empire was clearly that of Nebuchadnezzar, the Babylonian (or more properly, Neo-Babylonian) Empire: "You, O king, are the head of gold." The fourth seems clearly to point to the Greek Empire of Alexander and his successors, which was a divided empire. The second and third, therefore, must be the empires of the Medes and the Persians. Daniel 5:28 tells us that the Neo-Babylonian Empire was given to the Medes and Persians, and 8:20–21 that the Medes and Persians were overthrown by the king of Ionia, that is, Greece.

According to the author of Daniel, then, the end of the succession is near his own time (167–164 B.C.), for he and his audience are living in the period of the fourth and last empire. Such a realization allows two observations: (1) the coming end is not due to the nature of the Greek, or Seleucid, Empire; it is simply that the cycle has run through its mechanical and foreordained course; (2) the question of the precise time of the end is left open here, but it is near at hand.

The vision of the four beasts at Dan. 7:1–28 portrays the same series of empires and their fate. Daniel had a vision in which he saw four beasts come up out of the sea. The first, which looked "like a lion," was the Neo-Babylonian Empire; the second, "like a bear," was the Median Empire; the third, representing the Persian Empire, looked "like a leopard"; and the fourth, horrible beyond description, was the Greek Empire. This last beast had ten horns, representing various kings, and then "a little one" was added to the others as a description of Antiochus IV Epiphanes. Then "one that was ancient of days" appeared (the royal figure of God the judge), and soon the fourth beast was slain, and the dominion of all the others was taken away. As the vision continued, "one like a son of man" appeared before the Ancient of Days, and to him was given dominion over all peoples and nations. His kingdom was eternal and indestructible.

The interpretation of this vision is offered in the following vv. 15–18, and in different form in vv. 23–27. The "one like a son of man" is a corporate figure representing "the saints of the Most High." These saints are apparently those faithful and pious Jews who withstand the persecution under Antiochus IV and who will be rewarded with dominion in the kingdom to come. That villain will prevail "for a time, two times, and half a time" (7:25), thus for three and a half times—a number used elsewhere in Daniel (12:7) and in the New Testament Book of Revelation (12:14) as a time of trial and of waiting for the coming of God. At any rate, the end is near, and the people wait in hope for God to establish the expected kingdom.

These visions must be interpreted historically. That is to say, the writer had in mind not events in our day of the twentieth century but events in his own time which he tried to address with his understanding of the word of God. It was persecution and trouble between 167 and 164 B.C. that caused the Book of Daniel to be written, and it was to that situation that he addressed his message with all the methods of apocalyptic literature. Seen in this way, neither Daniel nor any other book can be used today to predict the end on the basis of forced analogies between the "secrets" of apocalyptic and contemporary events. To do so is to deny that the word of God was spoken to a specific audience at a certain time and place.

SOME EARLIER OLD TESTAMENT EXAMPLES

The seeds of apocalyptic were sown long before 167 B.C., and so it is important to recognize that apocalyptic-type sections appear in other books of the Old Testament. For example, during the exile of the sixth century B.C. the prophet Ezekiel and his disciples used images and concepts that introduced apocalyptic to the people of Israel. The famous prophecy against Gog of Magog is one such example (Ezekiel 38—39). The leader of a powerful army will come up against Israel after the people of Israel are dwelling securely in the land. Gog will bring his forces out of the far north to conquer Israel, but in the manner of the holy wars of old, the Lord will cause the earth to quake, thus causing Gog's army to panic and destroy itself. By this victory, which will occur "on that day," "the nations shall know that I am the LORD, the Holy One in Israel" (Ezek. 39:7).

This passage, like the later apocalyptic visions, must be interpreted historically rather than as a prediction for "the late great planet earth" to be fulfilled in our time. While the name of the long-gone Magog remains a mystery, Gog himself is probably to be identified as the seventh-century king Gyges of Lydia (known in Semitic writing as Gugu and Gug) who warred in Asia Minor against the powerful Cimmerians ("Gomer" of Ezek. 38:6). The terror of this mighty Gog became legendary, and it is thus in legendary fashion that the author of this passage speaks to his audience about the day of the Lord on which he will defeat the overwhelming enemy (just as in the old holy wars). To suppose, as some modern interpreters do, that the Meshech of 38:2 is contemporary Moscow, that the Hebrew word *rōsh* meaning "chief" prince in the same verse should be changed to *rūsh* for Russia, and to further identify that country by its "northern" location in relation to Israel—all in order to argue that an imminent Russian invasion of Israel will mark the end of the age—is not only without evidence; it is based on pure conjecture and coincidence of sound similarity. But worse, it assumes that the prophecy had no real meaning for the people of Ezekiel's day; if it did not, then it was no proclamation of the word of God at all. The word is always addressed to a particular situation in the life of people.

Several centuries after Ezekiel, sometime in the fourth or third century B.C., a poet of apocalyptic bent composed a series of songs, poems, and sayings, which are incorporated as a block in Isaiah 24—27. This little "apocalypse of Isaiah," inserted into the preaching of the eighth-century prophet, has many of the characteristics discussed at the beginning of this chapter. The overriding message is that the present world of distress will be replaced through Yahweh's cosmic catastrophe by a new age of bliss for Israel and for all people. Several individual units stand out in this apocalypse, one dealing with a banquet.

> On this mountain the LORD of hosts will make for all peoples a feast of fat things, a feast of wine on the lees, of fat things full of marrow, of wine on the lees well refined. And he will destroy on this mountain the covering that is cast over all peoples, the veil that is spread over all nations. He will swallow up death for ever, and the Lord GOD will wipe away tears from all faces, and the reproach of his people he will take away from all the earth; for the LORD has spoken. (Isa. 25:6–8)

This banquet celebrating the day of the Lord includes the nations far and wide who will come to Israel for the festival (see Zech. 14:16). Through this fellowship of the meal God will bring together all peoples into the kingdom "on that day" (see also Matt. 8:11). In addition, the celebration meal marks the end of death itself and of the utter disdain for Israel which the peoples hold for that ever-persecuted nation.

That hope for the end of death is sharpened somewhat by a promise of resurrection from the dead, a notion which, apart from here and Dan. 12:1–3, is lacking elsewhere in the Old Testament:

> Thy dead shall live, their bodies shall rise.
> O dwellers in the dust, awake and sing for joy!
> For thy dew is a dew of light,
> and on the land of the shades thou wilt let it fall.
> (Isa. 26:19)

The day of the Lord, in this poet's preaching, will clearly come with God's victory over enemies. In highly mythological fashion the apocalyptist announces:

> In that day the LORD with his hard and great and strong sword will punish Leviathan the fleeing serpent, Leviathan the twisting serpent, and he will slay the dragon that is in the sea. (Isa. 27:1)

This passage is particularly striking because of its similarity to one of the ancient Canaanite poems of Baal found at the city of Ugarit.

> Since you smote Lotan, the fleeing serpent,
> Destroy the twisting serpent,
> Shalyat of the seven heads. . . .[1]

Without doubt Lotan and the biblical Leviathan are the same. So are the first two descriptions of the serpent as "fleeing" and "twisting" (in the two Semitic languages involved, the words are identical). But the biblical writer used the mythological image in a new way: no longer does the destruction of Lotan/Leviathan belong in the pre-creation past or in the natural cycle of the seasons—as did the Baal stories in ancient Canaan. In the biblical writer's view, the victory of God over the symbol of evil, that fearsome monster, will occur in the future, specifically "on that day." This is the apocalyptist's description of the last battle in history.

One more battle description clearly identifies the result of the Lord's victory.

> On that day the LORD will punish
> the host of heaven, in heaven,

and the kings of the earth, on the earth.
They will be gathered together
    as prisoners in a pit;
they will be shut up in a prison,
    and after many days they will be punished.
Then the moon will be confounded,
    and the sun ashamed;
for the *Lord of hosts will reign*
    on Mount Zion and in Jerusalem
and before his elders he will manifest his glory.
                   (Isa. 24:21–23)

The cosmic victory of God over all opposition will provide the basis for reigning *as king* and for the glorious manifestation of God. Thus just as in those historical victories over foes at the Reed Sea (Exodus 14) and in Babylon (Isa. 52:7–10), just as in the hymnic victory or salvation in creation (Psalms 96 and 98), so now in the apocalyptic victory over the forces of evil, God will reign as king. This is the gospel of apocalyptic: that God's kingdom will come *soon!*

Pro and Con on Apocalyptic

Now a final word about apocalyptic. It is important for us today to realize that only a fraction of the many apocalyptic writings of late Judaism are present in the Old Testament—only one book, a few chapters in prophetic books here and there, mostly in the time of the exile and beyond. That realization enables us to see that the negative attitude toward history and the lack of confidence in God's work in history was *not* the *normal* attitude in the Old Testament. That view of an impersonal God with a mechanical notion of history was different from the rest of the Bible.

But these apocalyptic writers had their good points too, especially those moderate apocalyptists in the Bible. They saw that God's kingdom was not identifiable with the kingdoms of the earth. They understood that the history of the world would not evolve into the kingdom of God, and that the kingdom would come only by God's own hand, intervention, and will. Thus the writers of apocalyptic saw that the kingdom of God was *not of* this world. What they failed to realize was that the kingdom would take place, however, *in* the world. They lost the idea that God's rule was present as well as future, and so they really could not have understood a carpenter from Nazareth announcing, "The time is fulfilled, and the kingdom of God is at hand; repent, and believe in the gospel" (Mark 1:15).

NOTE

1. Author's translation. There is a slightly different translation by H. L. Ginsberg in *The Ancient Near East, Volume 1* (cited above, chap. 3 n. 1), 108, in fuller context of the Ugaritic "Poems about Baal and Anath."

21

The Kingdom and the "Messiah"

THE REIGN OF ISRAEL'S first king, Saul, had little significance religiously for the tribal confederacy of Israel. In fact, in many ways Saul was more of a charismatic leader like the judges (Gideon, Samson, and others) than a king. Nevertheless, king he was indeed acclaimed in a purely political way, so that Israel would be like the nations around it (1 Sam. 8:5). The move to kingship came so quickly that cultic or religious ideas could not catch up to it. Israel had religious rites within the old tribal structure to take care of the appointments of various personnel, but at the accession of Saul to kingship no such rite was available. The new monarch along with his kingdom could not really be harmonized with the old tribal traditions.

Kingship for Israel's first man on the throne was a matter of political necessity quite separate from cultic or religious institutions and thinking. As a result, Saul's potential as king was undermined from the very beginning. Whenever he stepped out of his political bounds and presumed to disregard distinctions between cult and monarchy, he was promptly rebuked by the prophet/seer/judge Samuel and, of course, by Yahweh, who eventually withdrew the spirit from the unfortunate Saul (see 1 Sam. 15:10–35; 16:1–14).

In effect, Saul was a failure as king—not because of his own shortcomings, but because kingship itself rested on no religious foundation. If this kind of kingship had prevailed in Saul's successors, Israel would probably have returned to the tribal organization and have relinquished kings entirely.

It was the very earthy, military, and political genius of David that brought him to the throne of Judah and eventually also to the rule of

Israel in his new capital city of Jerusalem. At first David's power existed solely in his own exceptional ability to arrest political decline and disorder. He fortified his city; he built a palace with the help of foreign craftsmen; he soundly defeated the Philistines; and he brought the sacred ark into his capital (see 2 Samuel 5—6).

THE DAVIDIC COVENANT

When David had rather firmly established himself, the Lord promised through the court prophet Nathan that David's dynasty would endure forever.

> And your house and your kingdom shall be made sure for ever before me; your throne shall be established for ever. (2 Sam. 7:16)

Thus did David's kingship acquire what Saul never knew: a religious or theological foundation on which his government was constructed. The Lord thus chose or elected David through the powerful voice of a prophetic spokesman, Nathan, and for this reason gave David's reign religious sanction. Kingship was no longer a separate political institution but an integral—if not major—part of the religious understanding of the people of God.

This religious significance of Yahweh's election of and promise to David cannot be overstated. In David's farewell speech, recorded at 2 Sam. 23:1–7, the failing king describes his relationship with Yahweh thus:

> Yea, does not my house stand so with God?
> For he has made with me an everlasting covenant,
> ordered in all things and secure.
>
> (23:5)

It was a *covenant* which the Lord made with David, the content of which was God's promise of an enduring dynasty. This covenant of Yahweh's grace provided the foundation of David's kingship over Judah and Israel.

This covenant is the essential difference between the kingship of David and that of Saul, his predecessor. Saul's rule was a matter of immediate necessity in the face of the Philistine threat, but David was appointed to a permanent covenant of royal authority by the oracle of Yahweh's prophet. This new covenant, however, provoked a radically new understanding of Yahweh's relationship with his people. In the old tribal confederacy Yahweh was the ruler of the people of Israel; in the new royal covenant, David exercised the function of an elect representative of divine rule. In the old confederacy of tribes Yahweh's relationship with the people was quite direct; in the new royal covenant Yahweh related to the people through a specific dynasty.

In some texts of the Old Testament, the continuance of a Davidic heir seems to be dependent on a king's faithfulness to Yahweh's ordinances.

> If your sons keep my covenant
>> and my testimonies which I shall teach them,
> their sons also for ever
>> shall sit upon your throne.
>> (Ps. 132:12)

The apparently conditional statement, however, is preceded by one which demonstrates that the promise of God is unconditioned.

> The LORD swore to David a sure oath
>> from which he will not turn back:
> "One of the sons of your body
>> I will set on your throne."
>> (Ps. 132:11)

Another psalm makes the point even more explicit. After repeating the oath to David in vv. 3–4 and again in vv. 28–29, Psalm 89 continues,

> If his children forsake my law
>> and do not walk according to my ordinances,
> if they violate my statutes
>> and do not keep my commandments,
> then I will punish their transgression with the rod
>> and their iniquity with scourges;
> but I will not remove from him my steadfast love,
>> or be false to my faithfulness.
> I will not violate my covenant,
>> or alter the word that went forth from my lips.
> Once for all I have sworn by my holiness;
>> I will not lie to David.
> His line shall endure for ever,
>> his throne as long as the sun before me.
> Like the moon it shall be established for ever;
>> it shall stand firm while the skies endure.
>> (Ps. 89:30–37)

It is Yahweh's promise, not conditions placed on the kings and met by them, that is the overriding element in this election of and covenant with David. Here, as in the case with God's covenant with Abraham (Gen. 15:7–21), the promise is unconditioned.

That promise was tested severely in the eighth century B.C. At this time

the Assyrian Empire was stretching itself westward toward the Mediterranean Sea. In order to attempt blocking King Tiglath-pileser's advance,
the king of the northern kingdom Israel and the king of Syria plotted to
replace King Ahaz, the Davidic king of Judah, with their own crony, a
"son of Tabeel" (Isa. 7:6). But speaking through the prophet Isaiah, the
Lord gave Ahaz a sign: a young woman, pregnant with child, will bear a
son who will be named Immanuel; by the time he is old enough to
distinguish good from bad (moral decisions? taste of food?), the lands of
the two plotting kings will be deserted. That sign, addressed to Ahaz as
"house of David," assures even this faithless king (see the evaluation at
2 Kings 16:1–4) that the coup will not succeed. Yahweh will keep the
Davidic king on Jerusalem's throne (see Isa. 10:10–17).

Such an interpretation based on the historical events described at Isa.
7:1–9 does not by any means render vv. 10–17 unimportant for Christianity. While the author of Matthew's Gospel (Matt. 1:23) uses Isa. 7:14
in the context of a virginal conception in Mary, the mother of Jesus, the
context in the time of Isaiah was a historical-political crisis in 735–734
B.C. Nevertheless, the point of the story is to demonstrate the faithfulness
of the Lord to the promise made to David, that God would keep a
Davidic king on Jerusalem's throne. The story asserts God's faithfulness
to rule universally through a king of Davidic descent. That promise is
fulfilled once and for all in the life, death, and resurrection of Jesus who is
called by the Greek translation of the Hebrew word *messiah:* Christ.

PSALMS FOR A CORONATION

As one would expect, such a religious or theological understanding of
kingship provided the basis for writing a number of psalms. An entire
collection of "royal psalms" appears in the Psalter, covering such a range
of royal matters as coronation, marriage, warfare, and duty. This collection includes Psalms 2, 18, 20, 21, 45, 72, 110, and, as we have already
seen, 89 and 132. Most interesting are the two that were composed for
the occasion of the kings' coronations on Jerusalem's throne: 2 and 110.

Psalm 2 begins with a description of the chaotic political and international scene that ensued when an ancient monarch died: the hostile
neighboring rulers and vassals plot.

> The kings of the earth set themselves,
>   and the rulers take counsel together,
>   against the LORD and his anointed, saying
> "Let us burst their bonds asunder,
>   and cast their cords from us."
>
> (Ps. 2:2–3)

While the action described here is important, the title given to the king is most significant for our purposes: "his [God's] anointed." To put the title back into its Hebrew form is to spell out the word *messiah*. In other words, an "anointed" one is a *messiah*. While the word is used as a verb to describe the anointing of prophets, priests, and kings, the noun is used primarily of kings. Furthermore, kings of the northern kingdom Israel never receive this title in the Old Testament writings; indeed with only two exceptions the noun *messiah* is used for Davidic kings: Saul (1 Sam. 24:6) and Cyrus, king of Persia (Isa. 45:1). The term, therefore, is virtually a technical word for the kings who ruled over Judah from the time of David in the tenth century down to the time of restoration from Babylonian Exile in the sixth century B.C.

The plotting of the neighboring kings against the Lord and the "anointed" one on Jerusalem's throne causes only uproarious laughter from God. The Lord need only speak, and the kings will destroy themselves in panic. The security of the Jerusalem king is assured when the cultic priest (or prophet) speaks on behalf of God.

> I have set my king
>   on Zion, my holy hill.
>   (Ps. 2:6)

The king then describes the relationship between the Lord and himself.

> I will tell of the decree of the Lord:
> He said to me, "You are my son;
>   today I have begotten you."
>   (Ps. 2:7)

This report of God's words sets forth the relationship in two ways. First, the divine announcement, "today I have begotten you," indicates that on coronation day itself (not on the day of the physical birth of a child) the king becomes the son of God. "Today" provides the key to understanding when and how this relationship takes place. Second, the short declaration "You are my son" was a formula used throughout the ancient Near East as a technical and legal means of adopting a child. A man or woman needed only say these words to a child in order to make the adoption binding. Thus Yahweh's election of and covenant with David takes the form of a parent-child relationship by virtue of adoption.

This relationship, by no means confined to Psalm 2, provides one of the basic clues for understanding the "messiahs" of Jerusalem.

> He shall cry to me, "Thou art my Father,
>   my God, and the Rock of my salvation."
> And I will make him the first-born,
>   the highest of the kings of the earth.
>   (Ps. 89:26–27)

Even the oracle of Nathan which announced to David the promise of

Yahweh for an everlasting dynasty identifies the Lord's relationship to David's successor with these words: "I will be his father, and he shall be my son" (2 Sam. 7:14).

The belief that the very human kings were adopted by Yahweh on the day of their coronation stands in sharp contrast to the view of ancient Egypt that the king was himself divine. It is also contrary to the Mesopotamian notion of a divine birth. For Israel those who came to the throne were humans, and humans they remained, during and after the coronation. Now, however, their relationship with, and thus their responsibility to, Yahweh, the true king, was intimate and intense, for they were the means by which the Lord related to the people as a nation.

Beyond this adoption of the king, the coronation rite described in Psalm 2 goes on to include God's promise of universal domain and victory, and finally a warning to those unruly kings who conspired against the Lord and the *messiah*. Thus, the king has been crowned and has received his status as son of God. But another psalm, 110, may contain other earlier parts of the coronation ceremony.

Psalm 110, a difficult one to read because of a problematic Hebrew text, contains at the outset the Lord's command to take the throne.

Sit at my right hand,
till I make your enemies your footstool.
(v. 1)

Like Psalm 2, Psalm 110 goes on to describe the reign of this Jerusalem king (note "Zion" in both psalms) over his enemies (v. 2). There is some reference to the king's leading an army to victory (v. 3a), and then occurs a very strange sentence.

From the womb of the morning
like dew your youth will come to you.
(Ps. 110:3b)

The Septuagint, the Greek translation of the Old Testament, has a reading which tries to make sense out of the difficult Hebrew text.

From the womb of the Morning Star
I begat you.

This translation, just as likely as that preferred in the RSV, repeats the view of Psalm 2 that the king is God's son. In this case, however, the sonship is acquired not by adoption but by the highly mythological notion that the king is the son of God through "Morning Star." That the king of Babylon was so conceived is clear at Isa. 14:12 where he is called "Day

Star, son of Dawn [Morning Star]!" In any case, the poet has here introduced a strange and foreign element into the picture, but perhaps such is a poet's right in order to describe the king's relationship to God in intimate terms.

Further, Psalm 110 announces to the Davidic king,

You are a priest for ever
after the order of Melchizedek.
(Ps. 110:4)

Apart from this verse there is no clear notion that Israel's king was a priest as well. But the only other time Melchizedek appears in the Old Testament he does play a dual role: at Gen. 14:17–24, Abraham meets Melchizedek who is king of Salem (that is, Jerusalem; see Ps. 76:2) *and* also priest of God Most High (the Canaanite god *El Elyon*). Apparently when David conquered and took Jerusalem from the Jebusites, their Canaanite ways and ideas strongly influenced the nature of David's court and its accompanying images. The reference to "a priest for ever after the order of Melchizedek" might then be an influence from the earlier rulers of the city.

The coronation psalm goes on to repeat the king's victory over his enemies (110:5), rule and judgment among the nations (v. 6), and then a drink from the brook (v. 7). This last verse describing a drink is usually understood as a ceremonial drink of purification in which the prospective king indulged before he entered the temple to be crowned. It could, however, have been a sacramental drink after the crowning had taken place. In any case, some type of drink by the brook was part of the coronation ritual.

THE CORONATION PSALMS AND
JESUS CHRIST

This somewhat detailed discussion of Psalms 2 and 110 is intended to demonstrate that these two psalms, so often quoted in reference to Jesus in the New Testament, had their own meaning and their own specific use in the Old Testament. They were used as parts of the liturgy for crowning the Davidic kings who, by the principle of dynastic succession, came to the throne of Jerusalem. In all probability they were used for hundreds of years for that situation in the life of Israel.

At the same time, in that present setting the psalms express a *future hope*. They express a promise, in fact, that the Davidic king will rule over a universal kingdom and that he will accomplish this by glorious victory with the Lord (at his left hand). That God "will make the nations your heritage, and the ends of the earth your possession" (Ps. 2:8) was a hope of which the people of Israel were very much aware. As they looked around them in the days of David and Solomon, such a hope was at least a wild possibility. Things were headed precisely in that direction, so it must have appeared. But as time went on, that glorious hope became less and less a reality. When the kingdom split and the two halves were subjected to outside dominion, that longing for "the day" took more and more the form of a distant future hope. It was precisely this longing for fulfillment that became the source of expectation for a messianic king of the last days who would come from the house and lineage of David.

The formula of sonship at Ps. 2:7 was used repeatedly for Jesus in the New Testament (see Matt. 3:17 and pars.; Acts 13:33; Heb. 1:5; 5:5; and 2 Peter 1:17). Likewise, Jesus refers to himself as Lord by quoting Ps. 110:1 at Matt. 22:44 and pars., and the same verse is quoted at Heb. 1:13 to show Jesus' superiority over the angels. Moreover, the notion in that verse of "the right hand of God" where the king sits occurs repeatedly in the New Testament as the enthronement place of the resurrected Christ. Finally, the reference to Melchizedek at Ps. 110:4 is applied to Jesus in the Epistle to the Hebrews (5:6, 10; 6:20; 7:11, 15, 21).

It becomes quite clear that the New Testament witnesses used these quotations from the coronation psalms in order to demonstrate that Jesus Christ was the messianic king of the last days. It now becomes our task to investigate the *prophecies* concerning a messiah to see how they related to Jesus.

22

The Kingdom
and Messianic Prophecies

THAT EXPRESSED HOPE THAT the Davidic king on Jerusalem's throne would lead to worldwide dominion took form not only in the coronation psalms from Israel's court but also in the prophetic preaching on Jerusalem's streets. It was the Jerusalem prophets who were intimately involved with that promise of an enduring dynasty, and so it was they who announced the ideal king to come as well as the nature of his rule. Isaiah, Micah, Jeremiah, and Zechariah—these are the major prophets in whose collections of sermons are contained the so-called messianic prophecies.

Before we examine several of the important texts from these Jerusalem prophets, some general comments are in order. (1) Some of the passages we shall discuss are highly debatable in regard to authorship. Whether it was Isaiah or Micah or Jeremiah or Zechariah, or one of their followers, or even a much-later preacher who composed these passages is very difficult to determine in some cases. To spend a great deal of time and space on that question, however, leads to little benefit except when the passage itself addresses an obvious historical situation. Therefore, the question of authorship need not occupy a major portion of our time. (2) In *none* of the "messianic" prophecies is the word *messiah* used. In other words, contrary to the coronation psalms (particularly Ps. 2:2) where the word "anointed" is used for the reigning Jerusalem king, the prophecies about the ideal king to come do not use that term. The most explicit title in such prophecies is the word "king" itself, but most often the allusion is made simply to the Davidic family.

Without the term "messiah" itself, however, the notion of an ideal ruler to come was known in Israel, at least from the time of Isaiah in the eighth century B.C. and continuing until the time of the New Testament and beyond. It is our task in this chapter to examine the major prophecies concerning this future ruler and the relationship of this king to the kingdom of God.

Because of its usage at Matt. 1:23, the prophecy at Isa. 7:10–17 concerning the Immanuel child is usually listed among the messianic texts. Our study of that passage in the previous chapter (p. 274) indicated that the passage is indeed "messianic" in the sense that the Lord promises the continuation of the Davidic dynasty in Jerusalem and the removal of the Syro-Ephraimite threat of deposing the king in favor of their own crony (see above, pp. 273–74). The child to be born is already well along the way in his mother's body, and so the immediate threat against the Davidic house will immediately be removed. Thus the text is not so much a prediction of a distant future event as it is a prophecy of God's faithfulness to overcome the impending crisis of 735–734 B.C.

TWO KEY PASSAGES:
ISAIAH 9 AND 11

Isaiah 9:1–7 presents a more interesting portrayal of the hoped-for kingship of a Davidic ruler. The lands of Zebulun and Naphtali had been conquered and subjugated by the Assyrian Tiglath-pileser III in 734 and 732 B.C. This disaster was a time of gloom and anguish, of distress and darkness for the people in that section of Israel. Over against that dismal scene Isaiah preaches a promise of contrast.

> The people who walked in darkness
>   have seen a great light;
> those who dwelt in a land of deep darkness,
>   on them has light shined.
>
> (Isa. 9:2)

The plight of the people, resembling that of a description of the mythological nether world or "land of the dead," will be turned into a scene of joy and life when the Lord comes to set them free.

> Thou hast multiplied the nation,
>   thou hast increased its joy;
> they rejoice before thee
>   as with joy at the harvest,
>   as men rejoice when they divide the spoil.
> For the yoke of his burden,
>   and the staff for his shoulder,
>   the rod of his oppressor,
>   thou hast broken as on the day of Midian.

For every boot of the tramping warrior in battle tumult
   and every garment rolled in blood
   will be burned as fuel for the fire.
               (Isa. 9:3–5)

In powerful battle imagery God is addressed as the one who causes rejoicing by removing the burden of foreign control over the people. Insofar as victory will result for Naphtali and Zebulun, the battle will resemble that described in Judges 6:33—7:25. In that story the judge Gideon summoned Asher, Zebulun, and Naphtali to join him against the Midianites and Amalekites who were invading the land. In the ensuing battle, "the Lord set every man's sword against his fellow and against all the army" (Judges 7:22), and so in typical holy-war fashion God caused the enemy to destroy itself in panic and then flee. Thus the reference to the battle at Isa. 9:4–5 as similar to the one "on the day of Midian" implies that the Lord will bring about victory by means of a holy war. In this sense, namely, that by holy war God will accomplish victory in the future, the passage becomes a "day-of-Yahweh" prophecy when God will establish the kingdom. It is God alone, in other words, who will fight the battle, gain the victory, and thus acquire the right to rule. How does the Davidic ruler to come fit into this picture?

For to us a child is born,
   to us a son is given;
and the government will be upon his shoulder,
   and his name will be called
"Wonderful Counselor, Mighty God,
   Everlasting Father, Prince of Peace."
Of the increase of his government and of peace
   there will be no end,
upon the throne of David, and over his kingdom.
   to establish it, and to uphold it
with justice and with righteousness
   from this time forth and for evermore.
The zeal of the LORD of hosts will do this.
               (Isa. 9:6–7)

This hymn, sung by the people (note the phrase "to us") after the victory has been accomplished, celebrates the accession of a Davidic king to the throne. The words "a child is born . . . a son is given" might refer not to the birth of a baby but to the adoption of a king by the Lord on the day of his coronation. This announcement, in other words, might have the same meaning as the formula "You are my son, today I have begotten you" at Ps. 2:7. The joy expressed, therefore, is that there will come to the throne in God's kingdom a Davidic ruler who will receive the throne names "Wonderful Counselor" (he needs no advisors to attain his plans), "Mighty God" (as in Ps. 45:6–7, he is the legitimate representative of God on earth), "Everlasting Father" (his rule will be enduring and fatherly; the kings in Mesopotamia were each called "Father of the land"), and "Prince of Peace" (the one who will rule with such righteousness to the Lord that all creatures will experience life to the fullest, that is, *shalom*).

Finally, there is added that this king will rule with justice and righteousness (see the "coronation" Pss. 45:6–7; 72:1–2) and that his rule will be eternal (see 2 Sam. 7:16) on the Davidic throne. What will bring about his rule and the peaceful time is not that king himself but "the zeal of the Lord of hosts." In other words, the king's function is to rule justly and righteously in the kingdom of God that God sets up for him by holy war. That rule will extend to the northern territories of the former Davidic-Solomonic Empire and will thus be a time of glory over against the gloom of the present scene for Zebulun and Naphtali.

The prophecy at Isa. 11:1–9 must be understood against the background of 10:33–34 in which Isaiah announces the destruction by Yahweh of Judah and the king. While judgment is inevitable because of the sin of people and king, judgment is not the last word.

> There shall come forth a shoot from the stump of Jesse,
> and a branch shall grow out of his roots.
>
> (Isa. 11:1)

Immediately it is clear that the hope following destruction lies in the accession to the throne of a Davidic ruler, for Jesse was indeed the father of David himself to whom God made the enduring promise. On this future ruler God will bestow his spirit just as he gave it to David originally (1 Sam. 16:13), the spirit through which God spoke by David (2 Sam. 23:2). This gift of the spirit will make the future ruler a wise one—as is clear from the words to describe the gift: wisdom, understanding, counsel, might, knowledge, and fear of the Lord. As a wise king this Davidic descendant to come will ably exercise his appointed function: justice.

> He shall not judge by what his eyes see,
> or decide by what his ears hear;
> but with righteousness he shall judge the poor,
> and decide with equity for the meek of the earth;

and he shall smite the earth with the rod of his mouth,
   and with the breath of his lips he shall slay the wicked.
Righteousness shall be the girdle of his waist,
   and faithfulness the girdle of his loins.
                                        (Isa. 11:3b–5)

As in Isa. 9:6–7, the duty of this king who will come is to rule with justice and righteousness. In this case, he will act as judge in the land not by means of advisors or even by his own perceptions but by righteousness, that is, by faithfulness to the duties imposed on him in his relationships to the Lord on the one hand and to the people on the other. It is his relationships that determine his judgments, and so as God's representative he will protect the poor and the needy and thus do the work of God (see Pss. 9:9; 68:5; Prov. 22:22–23; 23:10–11). Such care for those unable to care for themselves was a primary function of Davidic kings (see the "coronation" Ps. 72:12–14) and of kings elsewhere in the ancient world. The wicked and ruthless will experience the king's judgment as anything but benign, for he will slay those who oppose the will of Yahweh.

This reign of righteousness and faithfulness would stand in sharp contrast to the present situation in which someone like Ahaz or Manasseh was king in Jerusalem. Indeed, the effect of such a king's rule would extend to all of God's creation as a golden age.

The wolf shall dwell with the lamb,
   and the leopard shall lie down with the kid,
and the calf and the lion and the fatling together,
   and a little child shall lead them.
The cow and the bear shall feed;
   their young shall lie down together;
   and the lion shall eat straw like the ox.
The sucking child shall play over the hole of the asp,
   and the weaned child shall put his hand on the adder's den.
They shall not hurt or destroy in all my holy mountain;
for the earth shall be full of the knowledge of the Lord
   as the waters cover the sea.
                                        (Isa. 11:6–9)

All creatures will be affected by the king's righteous rule in God's kingdom. Animals that are now hostile to one another shall dwell and feed together. Children will play around the habitats of serpents without harm. The reason for all this harmony in creation is that the whole earth under the king's rule is "full of the knowledge of the Lord"—not intellectual knowledge, not mental discipline, but a personal, even intimate, relationship like that which exists between a husband and wife. "Adam *knew* Eve his wife, and she conceived and bore Cain" (Gen. 4:1). It is that close relationship of personal knowledge that characterizes the kingdom to come. Such is the responsibility of the king who will judge with righteousness in that kingdom and thereby effect *shalom*.

THREE MORE TEXTS, IN MICAH, JEREMIAH, AND ZECHARIAH

Isaiah's contemporary in Jerusalem was the prophet Micah. The two prophets differed in their preaching in one significant respect: for Isaiah, Jerusalem and its institutions were invulnerable to the onslaught of outside invaders; for Micah, however, Jerusalem and everything in it would be leveled to the ground. Nevertheless, Micah too looked beyond the destruction of the Lord's judgment to a new Davidic king.

> But you, O Bethlehem Ephrathah,
>   who are little to be among the clans of Judah,
> from you shall come forth for me
>   one who is to be ruler in Israel,
> whose origin is from of old,
>   from ancient days.
> Therefore he shall give them up until the time
>   when she who is in travail has brought forth;
> then the rest of his brethren shall return
>   to the people of Israel.
> And he shall stand and feed his flock in the strength of the LORD,
>   in the majesty of the name of the LORD his God.
> And they shall dwell secure, for now he shall be great
>   to the ends of the earth.
>
> (Micah 5:2–4)

Out of the birthplace of David, that is, out of the Davidic line, will come a ruler who will represent the Lord. His origin goes back to the days when God promised to David the enduring dynasty (2 Samuel 7). Until this new Davidic ruler comes to the throne, however, God will judge the people in the form of exile to a foreign land. Like a woman in the pain of childbirth will Jerusalem be carried away to Babylon (see Micah 4:9–10), but during that laborious pain the king to come will arise, and the people will return home. This king is portrayed as a kindly shepherd (as were kings in the ancient Near East as early as 2000 B.C.), and as such he fits the description of Ezekiel's view of the restoration of the Davidic dynasty after return from exile (see Ezek. 34:23–24). The king's function here is not to redeem Israel from exile; the Lord will accomplish that (Micah 4:10). Rather it is to "feed" the people when they return by ruling with the strength and power of the Lord and by giving glory to that God who established the kingdom. By so doing, the people "shall dwell secure," that is, experience *shalom,* in a universal kingdom over which the king rules in fame.

Jeremiah, too, looked beyond the present kings of Jerusalem to the new Davidic ruler to come. In a passage which is repeated in almost identical fashion at Jer. 34:14–16, the prophet of the early exilic period announces the king of the day of Yahweh.

> "Behold, the days are coming," says the LORD, "when I will raise up for David a righteous Branch, and he shall reign as king and deal wisely, and shall execute justice and righteousness in the land. In his days Judah will be saved, and Israel will dwell securely. And this is the name by which he will be called: 'The LORD is our righteousness.'" (Jer. 23:5–6)

The portrayal of the king here is no different from the other passages we have discussed: Davidic descent; wisdom, justice, and righteousness as marks of his reign; *shalom* as the result for the people of the once-again-united monarchy of Judah and Israel. This king's (throne) name will be *Yahweh Tsidqēnū,* "the Lord [is] our righteousness." This throne name might have a quite specific historical meaning.

In 598/597 B.C. when Nebuchadnezzar quieted Jerusalem's rebellion and carried off the first exiles to Babylon, he took with him King Jehoiachin. For some reason the Babylonian ruler replaced Jehoiachin with the latter's uncle (also of the Davidic family) Mattaniah (see 2 Kings 24:17). Uncle Mattaniah was given a new name when he took the throne: Zedekiah ("my righteousness is Yahweh"). It happened that Zedekiah's followers were attaching all kinds of illusory hopes to that king. It might be that Jeremiah's message about the king to come was intended to announce that the hopes for the future lay not in "*my* righteousness is Yahweh" but in a "Branch" established by the Lord who will be called "*our* righteousness is Yahweh." He will be raised up on the day of the Lord and will reign in God's kingdom.

Several hundred years later, probably in the fourth or third century B.C., an anonymous prophet proclaimed this song which was recorded in the Book of Zechariah:

> Rejoice greatly, O daughter of Zion!
>   Shout aloud, O daughter of Jerusalem!
> Lo, your king comes to you;
>   triumphant and victorious is he,

> humble and riding on an ass,
>> on a colt, the foal of an ass.
> I will cut off the chariot from Ephraim
>> and the war horse from Jerusalem;
> and the battle bow shall be cut off,
>> and he shall command peace to the nations;
> his dominion shall be from sea to sea,
>> and from the River to the ends of the earth.
>> (Zech. 9:9–10)

At first, this song seems to announce the arrival of the Lord into the midst of Jerusalem. A similar song at Zech. 2:10, in fact, announces "for lo, I come and I will dwell in the midst of you, says the LORD." Likewise, at Zeph. 3:14–20, a hymn with a similar beginning announces the presence of "the King of Israel, the LORD" in Israel's midst, and it goes on to announce the Lord's victory and rescue of the people. This image of Yahweh who ends all war is attested in our passage as well: God eliminates from existence chariot, war horse, and sword.

That the passage in Zechariah 9, however, surprisingly turns to a Davidic king's coming is clear from the last lines of the song. The reference to the king's universal dominion is a direct quotation from Ps. 72:8, a coronation psalm that wishes for the Davidic ruler on Jerusalem's throne precisely that vast range of rule. Moreover, the use of the ass in his triumphal and victorious entrance into the city recalls the coronation of Solomon, David's first successor. As part of the coronation itself, it seems,

> Zadok the priest, Nathan the prophet, and Benaiah ... went down and caused Solomon to ride on King David's mule, and brought him to Gihon. There Zadok the priest took the horn of oil from the tent, and anointed Solomon. Then they blew the trumpet; and all the people said, "Long live King Solomon!" (1 Kings 1:38–39)

Thus the passage looks forward to the imminent arrival of the long-expected Davidic king who will rule universally after God has established a condition of peace.

This text is important for Christians, of course, because in the New Testament the writer of Matthew uses it (21:1–9) to describe the entry of Jesus into Jerusalem on Palm Sunday. While Matthew gets two animals into the picture instead of the one in Zechariah's poetic parallelism and while he omits the reference to "triumphant and victorious is he" in order to emphasize the humble entry of Jesus, the point the author wants to make comes to focus in the question of Matt. 21:10: "Who is this?" It was Matthew's purpose to explain who Jesus is, and one of the key elements in that regard was to show that Jesus is Messiah. Matthew accomplished this task by quoting Old Testament texts about the future ruler. Thus, here as elsewhere in his gospel, Matthew looks back to the Old Testament witnesses in order to proclaim to his community the identity and the work of Jesus.

A SUMMARY ON SUCH PROPHECIES

In conclusion, then, all these so-called messianic prophecies are in essential agreement. Yahweh was to deliver the people and establish the kingdom. When it had been set up "on that day," the Lord would then raise up the new Davidic king to rule over that universal domain with justice and righteousness and wisdom.

It is somewhat striking that this hope for an ideal Davidic *messiah,* though references are scattered over a number of centuries, was really of rather limited concern in the Old Testament. Beyond the five passages we examined here, one must strain to find many more that clearly look forward to the future king.

It is also a startling realization to see that if one were to draw an image out of these Old Testament messianic prophecies, one would never envision a man born in an animal's stable, working in a carpenter's shop with sawdust on his clothes and callouses on his hands, crucified like a common thief on two pieces of wood, and buried in someone else's tomb. Indeed these passages do not predict the life and times of Jesus of Nazareth, but they do testify to Israel's hope that one will come to rule in God's kingdom with justice and righteousness. In Jesus Christ, God fulfilled this hope of Israel—not in the way expected, to be sure. But such a divine surprise shows that God is not limited even to the testimony of inspired witnesses.

23

Jesus, Who Preached God's Kingdom, as Messiah

THE COMBINATION OF THE two words "Jesus Christ" comes so routinely to mind for us that we are apt to miss its origin, richness, and complexity.

"Jesus," of course, denotes the historical person from Nazareth who appeared in Galilee in the days of the emperor Tiberius and proclaimed the good news of the coming kingdom of God (see above, chaps. 6–7). Behind "Jesus" is a Hebrew name, *Yĕhôšûʿâ,* meaning "Yahweh is salvation" or "Yahweh saves." In Matt. 1:21 it is said by an angel of the Lord, with reference to the name given to the son of Joseph and Mary, "he [that is, either Jesus or God] will save his people from their sins." Many Jews in antiquity bore this name; today, one stands out, Jesus of Nazareth.

"Christ" is derived from an adjective "anointed [one]," in Hebrew *messiah.* This term was used in a variety of ways in Israel, especially from the time of King David and his successors. It referred above all to the Davidic king, a ruler on the throne of Israel, who was descended from David, regarded as "the Lord's anointed" (see chaps. 21–22). But by the time Jesus of Nazareth lived, the term "messiah" had taken on a bewildering array of meanings in the light of expectations about God's future reign. This was especially so in those apocalyptic expressions of the good news that developed in Israel's periods of despair and hopelessness.

How did Jesus of Nazareth fit into and fulfill all of these Old Testament longings and Jewish expectations about "the day of the Lord" (chaps. 19–20, above)? How did he react to the age-old notions of an anointed ruler with a universal kingdom? In what ways does he bring to fruition what pious Jews were waiting for, and in what ways does he contradict their hopes and represent a new turn in the revelation of God's kingly rule?

We have already seen (chaps. 6–7) that Jesus preached, taught, and introduced by his deeds the kingdom of God. Jesus' message was about God and thus not about himself. But Jesus' followers began to hail him as "lord," using that pregnant title of such striking ambiguity. During Jesus' own ministry the word might have suggested nothing more than "sir" or "master." But after Easter the title conferred upon Jesus a name "above every name" (Phil. 2:9). Thus Jesus received lordship in a higher sense, under the kingship of God (chap. 13). This lordship of Jesus was proclaimed by Christians not only with regard to the future, when he would be Lord of all, but also in connection with the present and the past. Jesus was acclaimed as Lord now and therefore also as God's agent at creation in the past and the one who "upholds the universe" today (Heb. 1:2–3; chap. 18).

Something of the same course of development holds true with the term "Christ" ("messiah, anointed one"). The early church clearly employed it as a title for Jesus. That "Jesus is the Christ" became a test for true believing and even for being recognized as a child of God (1 John 2:22; 5:1). Most likely this confession about Jesus made most sense in an Aramaic-speaking church, or at least in a Christian community steeped in knowledge of the Old Testament and Jewish messianic expectations. The title was characteristic enough that followers of Jesus as the Christ were nicknamed "Christ-ians," initially at Antioch (Acts 11:26). But it is hard to guess what "Christ" and "Christian" meant to pagans who did not know much about the Old Testament, or about the ancient Near Eastern practice of "anointing." Indeed the Greek term *christos* would literally mean "smeared" or "perfumed."[1]

It would appear that what began as an adjective in Hebrew usage and became a technical term in Jewish expectations and a title for Jesus ended as a proper name for the man from Nazareth. For to many people, since the second half of the first century, "Christ" has seemed to be "Jesus' last name," so to say, and no longer a title. Compare the phrase "Jesus Christ is Lord" (Phil. 2:11), where "Christ" has become part of his name, and the honorific title is "Lord."

But, given all this unfolding history for the words "messiah" and "Christ," how did Jesus look upon this term? Three factors make it difficult to answer this question.

First, we must be careful to distinguish Jesus' own attitude during his lifetime from later acclamation of him by his disciples after Easter. The developed sense of Phil. 2:11 ("Jesus Christ is Lord") or of 1 John 5:1 ("Jesus is the Christ") should not be retrojected into his historical ministry.

Second, the variety of views about "messiah" abounding in Jesus' day must be reckoned with also. A Jew could say, "We have found the messiah (which means Christ)," as did Andrew (John 1:41), and mean Jesus of Nazareth. A Samaritan woman could declare, "I know that Messiah is coming (he who is called Christ)" (John 4:25), but she probably had in mind not an anointed king from the house of David but "Taheb," "the one who returns," as a Samaritan figure presumably similar to the "prophet like Moses" hoped for on the basis of Deut. 18:15. Still different from either of these was use by the Jewish rabbi Akiba, early in the second century A.D., for whom "messiah" meant the leader of a Jewish revolt against the Romans, a nationalist and a revolutionary—specifically a man named Simon bar Kochba (meaning "Simon, son of a star"). With such a variety, we must always ask, What could the term "messiah" have meant when someone used it in Jesus' day?

Finally, we need to look at what the several gospel texts actually say, and not just how tradition has harmonized them. People often think there was a single clear view of messiah in the Old Testament and that Jesus took it over lock, stock, and barrel. Chapters 21–22 have shown how involved the Old Testament story is at this point, especially as viewed against the future hopes of Israel. In the discussion that follows, we shall be looking at the gospel passages that view Jesus as messiah, one who brings the gospel of God's victory and the day of the Lord. We shall often have to scrutinize them in some detail.

One final preliminary is necessary. It pertains to the word "fulfill," which has already been noted several times with regard to Jesus and the Old Testament (above, chaps. 6 and 7). The Gospel of Matthew especially emphasizes how Jesus fulfills the Scriptures. Matthew does this through many Old Testament quotations, often introduced by the formula, "This happened in order that it might fulfill what was spoken by the prophet, saying. . . ." But this term "fulfill" can mean not merely "accomplish," "bring to pass," or "comply with that which was promised or predicted before." It may also have the sense of "fill full of new meaning," or "make complete by bringing to an end," and thus it may even mean "annul" or "destroy"! All sorts of twists and turns can take place as part of God's surprises in the course of "fulfillment."

FULFILLMENT AND ESCHATOLOGY

In antiquity, varied meanings for a word like "fulfill" were not regarded as strange at all. There is, for example, the story about Croesus, king of Lydia, in Asia Minor, who ruled during the sixth century B.C. In a quandary over whether to invade Persia or not, Croesus asked the famous oracle of the Greek god Apollo at Delphi for advice. Back came the answer that if he sent his army against Persia, he would destroy a great empire. So he invaded. And the Lydians were defeated. When he protested to Delphi that he had been deceived, the oracle answered that, on the contrary, its prediction was fulfilled: a great empire was destroyed—his own! People marveled at the dexterity of Delphi's answers, and Croesus was reported to have been so pleased that he sent further gifts.

To illustrate what "fulfillment" means in the New Testament, we turn to Matthew's Gospel, which especially emphasizes the theme. In Matthew, as evidence, we have first of all a series of "formula quotations" where Jesus is said to "fulfill" what a prophet had spoken (Matt. 1:23; 2:6, 15, 18, 23; 4:15–16; 8:17; 12:18–21; 13:35; 21:5; 27:9–10). We have already seen (in chap. 7, p. 114) that the use of Isa. 53:4, "He took our infirmities and bore our diseases," at Matt. 8:17 is, to say the least, an application we would not expect. The "day-of-Yahweh" passage at Isa. 9:1–2, with its related verses about a Davidic king (9:6–7, see above, p. 281), is associated by Matthew at 4:14–17 with Jesus' relocation in Capernaum in a way that gives the passage a christological sense it never had before. The text at Isa. 7:14, about a young woman conceiving during the Syro-Ephraimite crisis of 735–734 B.C., is given new meaning through the Greek rendering of the term more specifically as "virgin," and then by application to Mary's conception of Jesus through the Holy Spirit (Matt. 1:20–23). And when Matt. 2:15 says the return of Jesus from Egypt "fulfills" Hosea 11:1, "Out of Egypt I called my son," we have a case where what the prophet spoke originally was not prediction of a future event, though so taken by Matthew, but was rather a simple description of the exodus. That is, it referred to that past time when Yahweh called his "son" Israel out of slavery in Egypt. (One should examine Hosea 11:1 in its Old Testament context.) Fulfillment here makes sense only if we see Jesus as a figure parallel to the people of God, or Israel, in the Old Testament. Surely this is to fill the Hebrew Scriptures with new meaning.

We have a second important insight into what the New Testament means by fulfillment when we look at Jesus' teachings in Matthew. Jesus warns those who might think his purpose is to set aside all prior expressions of God's will, "Think not that I have come to abolish the law and the prophets; I have not come to abolish them but to fulfil them" (Matt. 5:17). But how does Jesus in his teachings "fulfill" them? In some cases it is by heightening and radicalizing what the Old Testament had said:

You have heard that it was said to the men of old, "You shall not kill" [Exod. 20:13]; and "whoever kills shall be liable to judgment." But I say to you that every one who is angry with his brother shall be liable to judgment. (Matt. 5:21–22)

You have heard that it was said, "You shall not commit adultery" [Exod. 20:14]. But I say to you that every one who looks at a woman lustfully has already committed adultery with her in his heart. (Matt. 5:27–28)

Again you have heard that it was said to the men of old, "You shall not swear falsely, but shall perform to the Lord what you have sworn" [Lev. 19:12; Num. 30:2]. But I say to you, "Do not swear at all. . . ." (Matt. 5:33–34)

These are three of the six "Antitheses" in the Sermon on the Mount. (The term denotes sharply contrasting statements where Jesus sets in antithesis his own word over against what the Old Testament says. Quoted above are the first, second, and fourth Antitheses.) Jesus here takes the old scriptural principle and fills it with further meaning, extending its application to thoughts as well as overt acts or, in the case of 5:33–34, carrying the concern of the Old Testament for truthfulness to an undreamed-of degree: Jesus looks for personal relationships where no oaths are needed to affirm one's honesty.

When, however, we look at the other three Antitheses in this same chapter, the pattern changes. How is the law being "fulfilled" there?

It was also said, "Whoever divorces his wife, let him give her a certificate of divorce" [Deut. 24:1–4]. But I say to you that every one who divorces his wife . . . makes her an adulteress. (Matt. 5:31–32)

You have heard that it was said, "An eye for an eye and a tooth for a tooth" [Exod. 21:23–24]. But I say to you, Do not resist one who is evil. (Matt. 5:38–39)

You have heard that it was said, "You shall love your neighbor [Lev. 19:18] and hate your enemy" [an admonition not found in the Old Testament, or the Jewish rabbis, but reflected in the Dead Sea Scrolls]. But I say to you, Love your enemies. . . . (Matt. 5:43–44)

In each of the above cases, in Antitheses three, five, and six in Matt. 5:21–45, the old command is abolished. (Not radicalized or heightened, as was the case with the first three cited; but abolished!) No divorce, no vengeance "eye for eye," no hatred of enemies. Here the law is "fulfilled" by being set aside. The effect is to put an end to these particular laws. Jesus, of course, did the same thing with Old Testament food regulations (Mark 7:15) and in effect did the same with all the cultic regulations about the temple and its priestly life. The result is well summed up in

Rom. 10:4, "Christ is the end of the law." Here "end" must be taken not merely as "goal of the law" but as its termination. Christ is the one who puts an end to the law as a way of salvation and life (NEB has "Christ ends the law"). And so we have "fulfillment" also in this sense of putting an end to something.

Jesus and Eschatology

Aware that "fulfillment" comes about in many ways, we may now ask how Jesus of Nazareth fulfilled the Old Testament hope of God's future reign, its messianic dreams, and its expectations about a Davidic ruler to come. How did he fit with the eschatology of a coming kingdom?

With regard to the ancient hope for the day of Yahweh, for a time when God would fulfill his promises and reign as king, intervening to defeat the forces of evil, it may be said that Jesus did proclaim and inaugurate the eschatological kingdom of God. This he preached, announcing its dawning and drawing out its implications for daily life. "The kingdom is at hand; repent! believe!"

If one asks, "How near is this kingdom?" the answer is, "Near as never before." The first rays of the new day's dawn are to be seen in Jesus' activities, fulfilling the promises of the prophets: "The blind receive their sight and the lame walk, lepers are cleansed and the deaf hear, and the dead are raised up, and the poor have good news preached to them" (Matt. 11:5; see also Isa. 35:5–6; 61:1–2). His wondrous deeds were part of God's "Holy War" now waged against Beelzebub and his demons (Matt. 12:27, par. Luke 11:19). God's kingship is drawing nigh, through and in Jesus. What prophets and kings in ages past longed to see and hear, but did not, is now taking place. Blessed are those who do see and hear! See Matt. 13:16–17, parallel Luke 10:23–24, for a beatitude to this effect.

Yet for all this evidence that in Jesus' own message about the gospel of God's future reign the kingdom is irrupting into human life here and now, there are also occasions in Jesus' words when the future aspect still shines through. On the one hand, the kingdom is here, growing, at work like leaven (Matt. 13:33, par. Luke 13:20–21). Or it is increasing like a mustard seed into a shrub and tree in which "the birds of the air can make nests" (Mark 4:30–32, par. Matt. 13:31–32; see also Dan. 4:41). On the other hand, the kingdom is nonetheless described as future. To pray "Thy kingdom come" means it is not yet here for me. Jesus' solemn pledge in the upper room, "I shall not drink again of the fruit of the vine until that day when I drink it new in the kingdom of God" (Mark 14:25), implies that even on the eve of his death he does not regard it as present yet. Jesus even warns against people who make the claim "Lo, the kingdom is here" or "Lo, there"; rather, he says "on that day" when the Son of man comes, there will be lightning flashes lighting up the sky and the normal routines of life will come to an end (see Luke 17:22–37, esp. vv. 23–24, 26, 30, 31).

Readers with an alert ear or eye for Old Testament phrases will note in the last two passages echoes of the "day-of-Yahweh" theme: "that day" (Mark 14:25); and "on that day" (Luke 17:31; cf. also vv. 24, 30, 34). This apocalyptic outlook does appear in the sayings of Jesus, including the note of impending judgment found in Old Testament "day-of-the-Lord" passages. True, Jesus does not refer to the "day of Yahweh" as Paul does, for example, in 1 Thess. 5:2: "The day of the Lord will come like a thief in the night." But Jesus does speak of "the day of judgment" (Matt. 10:15; 11:22; 12:36), and he even uses the same comparison to a thief that Paul employed:

> Watch therefore, for you do not know on what day your Lord is coming. But know this, that if the householder had known in what part of the night the thief was coming, he would have watched. . . . (Matt. 24:42–43)

(It is possible that Paul used the phrase with the words of Jesus in his mind.)

"The days are coming" is a formula on Jesus' lips to introduce an apocalyptic warning, just as in the Old Testament (Luke 17:22; 21:6; 23:29). So is the phrase "in those days," referring to the dark, foreboding "last times" ahead (Mark 13:17, 19, 24). There are also examples of "on that day," just as in the Hebrew prophets and apocalyptists, referring to a time of judgment by God:

> On that day many will say to me, "Lord, Lord, did we not prophesy in your name, and cast out demons in your name, and do many mighty works in your name?" And then will I declare to them, "I never knew you; depart from me, you evildoers." (Matt. 7:22–23)

See also Luke 17:31; Mark 13:32; Matt. 24:50.

It may be noted that some of these New Testament statements have, in effect, interpreted "the day of the Lord" ("Yahweh" in the Old Testament) to refer to the Lord *Jesus* who now will serve as judge (as in the Matthew 7 passage just cited). As a transition to this usage one may also observe references to the "coming of the Son of man" (Matt. 24:37, 39; cf. v. 42) or in a phrase uniquely Lukan, "the days [plural] of the Son of man" (Luke 17:22, 26; cf. v. 24).

"Son of man" was an Old Testament term denoting a human being or humankind (cf. Ps. 8:4; Ezek. 2:1, 3, 6, 8, and many more verses in that book). The phrase came to be used in apocalyptic also. There it was employed both for a corporate representation of the people of Israel, and also for a supernatural figure who comes from heaven to earth. For the former usage, see Dan. 7:13 in the context of 7:9–22. For the latter, we must go outside the usual canon to writings like 2 Esdras in the Old Testament Apocrypha and *Enoch* in the Pseudepigrapha.

Whatever its background, "Son of man" was a term frequently found in the sayings of Jesus, and Jesus is himself identified in the Son-of-man sayings cited above as coming in the future to deliver and to judge (see the Matthew 24 and Luke 17 passages). Luke's verses seem to think of a series of such "days of the Son of man."

The most succinct section in the teachings of Jesus about this future aspect of God's reign is the major apocalyptic discourse preserved for us in Mark 13, with parallels in Matthew 24—25 and Luke 21:5–36 and 17:22–37. These three (or four) versions—of what is often called the "Little Apocalypse," in distinction to the Book of Revelation or the "big" apocalypse—differ so much from each other that it would seem each evangelist has edited the genuine sayings from Jesus in a particular way. But all the passages have in common a future reference to impending troubles for Jerusalem, persecution for Jesus' followers, the need for watchfulness, and the "second coming" of the Son of man at the close of the age.

(Actually, no gospel passage uses the phrase "second coming," but the term—like the Greek word *parousia,* which means "arrival," "coming," or "being present"—is a convenient one to designate this promise of a divine event bringing normal history to an end, with judgment, rewards and punishments, and fulfillment of promises. The only New Testament passage to come close to the phrase occurs in Heb. 9:28, Jesus will "appear *a second time*)."

That not every last statement about the future attributed to Jesus goes back to him historically is, of course, a possibility. Biblical scholars wrestle with a saying like Mark 9:1 and its parallels in Matt. 16:28 and Luke 9:27 (respectively)—

> Truly, I say to you, there are some standing here who will not
>   taste death before they see that the kingdom of God has come
>   with power;
> Truly, I say to you, there are some standing here who will not
>   taste death before they see the Son of man coming in his
>   kingdom;

> But I tell you truly, there are some standing here who will not
> taste death before they see the kingdom of God—

to try to ascertain which version of it, if any, goes back to the historical Jesus during his ministry. But such difficult passages aside, sufficient solid evidence exists to make quite clear that Jesus taught both that the kingdom would be fulfilled in the future and that it was present during his ministry. How shall this double position be explained?

The solution is not to claim that Jesus' views about the kingdom "developed" or "matured" over the years and that first he believed it was immediately present but later changed his mind and viewed it as future. Or the other way around—first future, then in later life, present. The gospel verses do not fit any such pattern of development. Nor will it help to claim that Jesus vacillated, believing one thing one day and the opposite the next. Our gospels do not yield a "psychological profile" of Jesus. Nor can either part of the data be thrown out as not genuinely from Jesus.

We must recognize that Jesus, who pronounced the kingdom imminent, breaking in, and even present, also assigned to it a future aspect. People do not have it at their beck and call or under their control. It is *God's* kingship, and present though God may wondrously be in the ministry of Jesus, God is also always above, beyond, and ahead of us, God's kingly reign in human lives not yet at the full. All this is true to the Old Testament experience where God's past victory and present activity begot future promises and hopes about what was yet to come.

We may put it very simply. Jesus' appearance, actions, and message, great as was the gospel that they brought for his own day, pointed beyond themselves. God's revelation in Jesus generated further promises, to be fulfilled later on. God had surprises even after Jesus' day!

This future aspect to the gospel of the kingdom may be illustrated by reference to the Gentiles or pagans, all the non-Jews of Jesus' day. Old Testament prophetic teaching about the day of Yahweh had looked for a universal pilgrimage to Mount Zion (Jerusalem) where all nations would learn Yahweh's will and ways (see chap. 19, pp. 258–59). Jesus, in his own ministry, dealt by and large with Jews only (Matt. 15:24). Experiences with Samaritans (John 4:7–43), "Canaanites" (Matt. 15:22–28), and Roman army officers (Matt. 8:5–13, par. Luke 7:1–10) were at best rare. Jesus seems to have spread his good news before an immediate audience of Jews, in Galilee and Jerusalem. He trusted to God that any further spreading of the message would come in God's own time and way.

It may well be that Jesus, like the Old Testament prophets, looked for a day of Yahweh when God would be manifested, call the Gentiles, and lead them to the "holy mount" where there would be a great banquet (cf. Isa. 56:6–8; 25:6–9). But God did not work it out that way. The hope that "many will come from east and west and sit at table with Abraham, Isaac, and Jacob in the kingdom of heaven" (Matt. 8:11) did not materialize in the first century through any divinely led pilgrimage to Mount Zion as the world came to an end. Rather, the invitation to God's table was spread by missionary, evangelistic endeavor, going out from Jerusalem (as in the Book of Acts) to the ends of the earth (Matt. 28:19–20). Jesus fulfilled the Old Testament hope by bringing near, in a way that had never happened before, the good news of God's reign. But this gospel created in turn its own future of further promises.

JESUS AND THE TITLE OF "CHRIST"

But now, in light of what we have said about eschatological hopes and fulfillment, what of the messianic prophecies and dreams?

Chapters 21 and 22 have previously traced the usage of *messiah* (Greek, "Christ") in the Old Testament. In the centuries immediately preceding the time of Jesus, speculations about "messiahs" multiplied. Some people still hoped for a descendant of the old royal house of David who would restore the national kingdom. But the failure of Zerubbabel in his attempt to gain power as anointed king about 520 B.C.—he was a Davidic "light that failed," about whom we know all too little (cf. Hag. 2:20–23; Zech. 4:1–6, 10–14; 3:8–10; 6:12)—led others to look elsewhere. Once there was no Davidid (a descendant of the house of David) on the throne or Davidic scion waiting in the wings to be king, some put their hope in an anointed priest. Indeed, the Hasmonean dynasty in the second century B.C. brought to the fore a priestly family that claimed royal power and then later high-priestly prerogatives. Qumran looked for both an eschatological high priest and a subordinate kingly messiah. Still others awaited a preexistent, heavenly deliverer, like the Son of man, perhaps. A militant revolutionist leader was the desire of Zealot groups. Some pious circles hoped for God to come.

Such was the gallery of "messianic" figures in Jesus' day. The pages of the first-century Jewish historian Josephus are dotted with men who claimed to be "chosen by God" or "anointed" to bring in the kingdom.

How, then, did Jesus respond, amid this welter of messianic claims? Warily, and with reticence. That would seem to have been good sense on his part, and the gospel accounts show Jesus treading with caution on those rare occasions when the term "messiah" was introduced. Even if he were himself fully convinced that he was the Lord's anointed, the situation suggested that he go easy until the term could be redefined, in the way he wished.

Two passages in particular show how Jesus dealt with the messianic hope, when applied to him. One concerns his trial, the other Peter's confession.

At the trial, the Jewish high priest asks finally: "Are you the Christ [= Messiah], the Son of the Blessed?" (Mark 14:61). The parallels, Matt. 26:63 and Luke 22:67, have variant forms of the same question. Jesus' reply, in Mark, is simple and direct, followed by an additional statement about the future:

> I am; and you will see the Son of man seated at the right hand of Power, and coming with the clouds of heaven. (14:62)

But the reply in Matthew and in Luke is not quite so clear:

> You have said so. But I tell you, hereafter . . . [it goes on with the words about the Son of man]. (Matt. 26:64)

> If I tell you, you will not believe; and if I ask you, you will not answer. But from now on . . . [goes on with the Son-of-man passage]. (Luke 22:67b–68)

Matthew's version can be interpreted to mean, "That is correct," or it can be taken to imply "*You* said that, *I* do not!" Luke gives the answer as a counterstatement, "If . . . , if. . . ." In any case, all three Gospels agree that Jesus then went on to speak about not the Christ but the Son of man. He spoke of the Son of man, to be seated at God's right hand, to come with or on the clouds of heaven. We today might wish that some disciple had been there with a tape recorder. But such was not the case. Critical scholars question whether we possess any sort of accurate account or even if a Jewish trial took place.[2] At the very least one must say that Jesus does not emphasize the title "Christ" when he is asked about it at his trial.

A similar situation occurs when we turn to Peter's confession of Jesus as messiah, at Caesarea Philippi. It comes as the climax of Jesus' ministry in Galilee. In light of all the popular opinions that Jesus is some sort of a prophet (Matt. 16:14), Simon Peter answers Jesus' question, "Who do you say I am?" (16:15) with the words,

> You are the Christ, the Son of the living God. (Matt. 16:16)

Jesus then goes on to praise Peter for this truth, which has come to him not by human insight but by divine revelation (16:17):

> You are Peter [*Petros*], and on this rock [*petra* in Greek, referring either to Peter's confession or Peter himself] I will build my church. . . . (16:18)

(Protestants traditionally have taken *petra* to refer to the confession, Catholics take it to refer to Peter himself, though both interpretations antedate the Reformation.) In Matthew's account, in any event, Peter is a great hero of faith to perceive who Jesus really is.

Attractive as that emphasis is, one must also reckon with the fact that Matthew's account goes on to describe how Peter immediately misunderstands Jesus' goal in life, that Jesus must go to Jerusalem and die. Peter would dissuade him from the cross. Hence, Jesus must reprimand Peter by saying,

You are a hindrance [literally, stumbling block] to me. (Matt. 16:23)

Peter ends up on the side of men, not of God! All this suggests an overall portrait of Peter as a typical disciple, one minute capable of great insight, the next of satanic misunderstanding. Like ourselves! Jesus' church can be built upon such a person when that person confesses Christ, but the same building stone becomes a stumbling block when he or she opposes the Lord. There is even a suggestion that the title "Christ" must be understood in light of going to Jerusalem and the cross.

But it is the parallel account in Mark (8:27–30) that really raises questions about the widespread, traditional understanding of Peter's confession, that found in Matthew. In Mark, after Peter's statement "You are the Christ" (8:29), there is no commendation of Peter for using the title "messiah." On the contrary, Jesus enjoins silence on the disciples. They are not to use the term "Christ" with any one. Jesus begins instead to talk about "the Son of man" being rejected, killed, and how he will "after three days rise again" (8:31). (This is the same pattern that appeared at Jesus' trial. Someone uses the term "Christ," but Jesus goes on to talk about the "Son of man.")

In Mark, Jesus rebukes Peter as a Satan, opposed to "the side [or program] of God" (8:33). For Peter had apparently had in mind by the term "Christ" a glorious, national, perhaps militaristic hero, a new Davidic claimant to the throne. Mark 8:27–33, read as it stands without Matthew's additions, has with some justice been called "Peter's Satanic Misunderstanding of Jesus," not "Peter's Heroic Confession of Jesus." (Mark's version, we may remind ourselves, is generally accounted the one first written down, on which Matthew's version is based. And Luke's terse version, 9:18–22, is closer to Mark's than to Matthew's.)[3]

What does all this add up to? Our accounts of Jesus' trial and of the Caesarea Philippi experience clearly suggest that Jesus did *not* uncritically accept the title "messiah"! He is reserved about it, because of the current danger of its being misunderstood. It is even likely that he was positively opposed to using it. His attitude combats the kind of mentality described in John 6:14–15, when the crowd, after the feeding of the five thousand, wanted "to come and take [Jesus] by force to make him king." That is, they wanted to make him an anointed ruler, leading, quite likely, a revolt against the Romans. That mentality was so deeply ingrained in the disciples that even after Easter they asked Jesus, "Lord, will you at this time restore the kingdom to Israel?" (Acts 1:6). Jesus again refused such a program.

The kingdom implied an anointed ruler. Jesus proclaimed God's kingship. But because Jesus made no pretense to becoming an earthly ruler himself, he had to be very chary about accepting the title "messiah" during his earthly ministry. In fact, a case can be made, as suggested above, that he rejected the term "Christ" during his lifetime. Things were not so blatant with Jesus as in the chorus in *Jesus Christ Superstar* where people went around singing that he was "the Christ, the great Jesus Christ." In the Synoptic Gospels, Jesus never says, "I am the Messiah"; in the Fourth Gospel, such a claim (cf. John 4:26) seems a post-Easter reflection. It remained for the cross and resurrection to show who Jesus really was. Then men and women could confess "Jesus is the Christ," giving the Old Testament concept new meaning, in light of the life that he had actually lived, the death he died, and the new dignity that God conferred on him.

In summation, Jesus did not adopt any predetermined mold of messiahship and conform to it. Because of the misuse of the term "messiah" in his own day, Jesus found it about as unusable as the term "covenant" (see above, chaps. 10 and 11). Jesus chose to speak of God's kingdom, frequently; and of covenant, only rarely. Instead of "Christ," Jesus favored other terms, like "Son of man" or "the Son [of God]" or aspects of the "servant of Yahweh" concept. What Jesus did do was to provide new contours for the usage, after his earthly work, of the term "messiah." He gave a shape to Christ-hood that sent followers scurrying to the Old Testament to see what prophetic hopes had been fulfilled, and hastening to the creation of new categories in which to confess who Jesus is for faith, as the good news marched on.

"SON OF DAVID" AS A
TITLE FOR JESUS

Every title used of Jesus in the New Testament deserves to be explored in something of the way we have examined "Lord" (in chap. 13 and also pp. 288–89, above) and "Christ" (in this chap., pp. 289–90 and under "Jesus and the Title of 'Christ' "). Space, unfortunately, scarcely permits treatment here of the many other names given to him, except for one. That term is "son of David," and we take it up because it is so closely related to "messiah."

In chapter 21 we learned how God covenanted with David that David's throne would be "established for ever," with Davidic offspring upon "the throne of his kingdom for ever" (2 Sam. 7:12–16). Historically, the Davidic line on the throne ended abruptly with Zerubbabel around 520 B.C. But hope sprang eternal that a new descendant of David would arise as anointed king. Thus, the *Psalms of Solomon,* a Pharisaic composition from the first century B.C., recall how God had chosen David as king, and these psalms then recount the calamities that had recently befallen Israel. These included the conquest of Jerusalem by the Roman general Pompey in 63 B.C. Then comes a devout prayer for Israel, "Behold, O Lord, and raise up to them their king, the son of David" (*Pss. Sol.* 17:23). It may be added that the same psalm, however, also prays in other sections to God as "our King" (17:1, 38, 51), thus not just for a Davidic monarch. The *Eighteen Benedictions,* a synagogue prayer, asks in a spirit akin to *Psalm of Solomon* 17 for mercy "on the kingdom of the house of David," with the petition, "May the shoot of David [cf. Isa. 11:1] sprout quickly forth."

As is well known, the New Testament confesses Jesus to be the Christ, son of David. According to Rom. 1:3–4, the gospel concerns God's son,

who was *descended from David* according to the flesh
and designated Son of God in power according to the Spirit of holiness by
   his resurrection from the dead.

Christians are reminded by Paul, in one of the Pastoral Epistles, to

remember Jesus Christ,
   risen from the dead,
      descended from David, as preached in my gospel.
                           (2 Tim. 2:8)

In each instance the reference to Davidic descent refers to Jesus' ministry and time on earth in contrast to that since the resurrection.

During his earthly ministry, according to the gospels, Jesus was occasionally addressed as "Son of David," that is, as a person descended from Israel's great anointed king. Bartimaeus, for example, cried out, "Jesus, Son of David, have mercy on me!" (Mark 10:47). The title is especially common in Matthew (see 9:27 and 15:22, and compare 12:23).

It is in the stories about the birth and infancy of Jesus that the Davidic theme comes to the fore. The hymn by Zechariah, father of John the

Baptist, hopes for redemption through a savior in the house of David (Luke 1:68–69, from what we liturgically call the "Benedictus"). The angel Gabriel tells Mary that her son Jesus "will be great . . . ,

> and the Lord God will give to him the throne of his father David,
> . . . and of his kingdom there will be no end. (Luke 1:32–33)

Luke stresses that Joseph was "of the house of David" (1:27); that is why he went to "the city of David," Bethlehem,[4] to be enrolled at the census (2:4). Matthew also stressed Joseph's Davidic descent (Matt. 1:20). The Book of Revelation also refers to Jesus' Davidic connections (5:5; 3:7).

No doubt the tour de force linking Jesus to David comes in the genealogies of Matthew 1 and Luke 3. While modern readers often regard these lists of "who begat whom" as pretty dull or obscure and irreconcilable in details, both evangelists assigned a fair amount of precious papyrus space to these tables, Matthew at the very beginning of his book.

Matthew 1:1–17	*Luke 3:23–38* *(in reverse order)*
(40 or 42 names, 14 + 14 + 14)	(77 names, in groups of 7)
See 1 Chron. 1:1–27 for a genealogy from Adam through Abraham; Gen. 5:3–32 for a genealogy, Adam through Noah.	(1) Adam, the son of God (2) Seth, the son of Adam (3) Enos (4) Cainan — From Adam to (5) Mahaleleel — Abraham, 21 (6) Jared — names, 3 x 7 (7) Enoch
	(8) Methuselah (9) Lamech (10) Noah
See Gen. 11:10–26 for a genealogy from Shem to Abraham.	(11) Shem (12) Arphaxad (13) Cainan (14) Shelah
	(15) Eber (16) Peleg (17) Reu (18) Serug (19) Nahor (20) Terah

Jesus, Who Preached God's Kingdom, as Messiah

Matthew 1:1–17	Luke 3:23–38 (in reverse order)	

(1) Abraham	(21) Abraham	
(2) Isaac	(22) Isaac	From Isaac to
(3) Jacob See 1 Chron. 2:1–15	(23) Jacob	David, 14
(4) Judah + for a genealogy of	(24) Judah	names, 2 x 7.
Tamar Jacob through		See 1 Chron.
(5) Perez David; cf. Ruth	(25) Perez	1:28–34 for a
(6) Hezron 4:18–22 for a	(26) Hezron	genealogy of
genealogy from	(27) Arni	the sons of
(7) Ram Perez through David.		Abraham and
	(28) Admin	Isaac.
(8) Amminadab	(29) Amminadab	
(9) Nahshon	(30) Nahshon	
(10) Salmon + Rahab	(31) Sala	
(11) Boaz + Ruth	(32) Boaz	
(12) Obed	(33) Obed	
(13) Jesse	(34) Jesse	
(14) David the king +	(35) David	
(Bathsheba), the wife of		
Uriah (the Hittite)		
(15) Solomon Cf. 1 Chron.	(36) Nathan	From Nathan
(16) Rehoboam 3:10–19	(37) Mattatha	to Shealtiel
(17) Abijah	(38) Menna	(end of the
(18) Asa	(39) Melea	Babylonian
(19) Jehoshaphat	(40) Eliakim	Exile), 21
(20) Joram	(41) Jonam	names, 3 x 7.
(21) Uzziah	(42) Joseph	
(22) Jotham	(43) Judas	
(23) Ahaz	(44) Symeon	
(24) Hezekiah	(45) Levi	
(25) Manasseh	(46) Matthat	
(26) Amos	(47) Jorim	
(27) Josiah	(48) Eliezer	
(28) Jechoniah	(49) Jesus	
(deportation to Babylon,		
586 B.C.)	(50) Er	
	(51) Elmadam	
	(52) Cosam	

303

Matthew 1:1–17		Luke 3:23–38
		(in reverse order)
		(53) Addi
		(54) Melchi
		(55) Neri
Jechoniah		
(29) Shealtiel or	Cf. 1 Chron	(56) Shealtiel or Salathiel
Salathiel	3:17.	
(30) Zerubbabel		(57) Zerubbabel — From
(31) Abiud		(58) Rhesa — Zerubbabel to
(32) Eliakim		(59) Joanan — Jesus, 21
(33) Azor		(60) Joda — names, 3 x 7.
(34) Zadok		(61) Josech
(35) Achim		(62) Semein
(36) Eliud		(63) Mattathias
(37) Eleazar		(64) Maath
		(65) Naggai
		(66) Esli
		(67) Nahum
		(68) Amos
		(69) Mattathias
		(70) Joseph
		(71) Jannai
		(72) Melchi
		(73) Levi
(38) Matthan		(74) Matthat
(39) Jacob		(75) Heli
(40) Joseph + Mary		(76) Joseph
(41) Jesus called Christ (42)		(77) Jesus

Many features and difficulties in these genealogies will be apparent from even a few moments of study. Matthew traces Jesus back to David and Abraham, as is emphasized in 1:1, through three periods of fourteen names each (1:17). Technically the second section has only thirteen names, unless we count Jechoniah as was done above; but in that case the third section is one short, unless we count "Jesus" as a name for his earthly life and "Christ" as separate, a title given later. Luke, with a more universal interest, traces the genealogy all the way back to Adam, son of God. (Luke also sees Jesus as son of God, 1:35.) Luke's seventy-seven names can be arranged in multiples of seven, though Luke's mathematical pattern is not so obvious as that in Matthew, nor does Luke call attention to such a structure.

Some of the difficulties stem from the Old Testament genealogies with which the evangelists are working (references cited above, in the margin). Others come from translation variants as one moves from Hebrew to Greek. Some differences are accounted for by different lines of family descent. After David, for example, Matthew—see his number 15— follows the line through Solomon, David's successor to the throne. Luke, on the other hand, traces the line through Nathan, his number 36, who was David's third son born in Jerusalem (2 Sam. 5:14), representing a branch of the family that never came to the throne (Zech. 12:12). Both evangelists agree on tracing Jesus' line through Joseph, even though they assume the virgin birth (Matt. 1:20–25; Luke 1:26–38). Luke even "covers" this by stating Jesus to be "the son *(as was supposed)* of Joseph" (3:23, italics added to RSV rendering). Their genealogies seek to trace Jesus' *legal* parentage back to David, rather than his physical paternity.

Matthew, oddly, mentions four women in his genealogy (numbers 4, 10, 11, and 14), in addition to Mary (1:16). Each woman can be said to have been either not Jewish (so Jewish tradition states) or to have had some irregularity that marked her marriage or her motherhood. Tamar was accused of harlotry when impregnated by her father-in-law Judah (Genesis 38—though she was more righteous than he); Rahab was a harlot (Joshua 2); Ruth turned up "at the feet" of Boaz and got him to marry her (Ruth 3); David's sin with the wife of his brave Hittite army officer, Uriah, is well known (2 Samuel 11).

Why include the names of these women, and how do they relate to Mary (Matt. 1:16)? Some have suggested Matthew is responding to Jewish charges that Jesus was illegitimate (just as, in 28:11–15, he responds to Jewish charges or "explanations" that the empty womb was a case of body snatching). In this case Matthew would be replying, "There was *plenty* of irregularity in King David's ancestry!" Others think Matthew is stressing human sinfulness and that Jesus, whose very name means "he saves," will deliver even all such sinners (1:21). Still others stress the pagan background of these women and that therefore Matthew's aim is to show the universal nature of Christ's work (see also 28:18–20). Yet another theory is that Matthew reflects inner Jewish debate on the ancestry of the promised Davidic messiah and emphasized Jesus as the true anointed one.[5]

One thing looms clearly: Matthew and Luke see Jesus as a descendant of David. And it is quite likely that Jesus, at least on Joseph's side, *was* of the house of Israel's greatest king.[6] Genealogical lines were taken very seriously in the Jewish world. Especially for the priestly families, careful records were kept. For lay folk, like Joseph and Mary, there was perhaps an oral tradition in family circles. Of course, the two varying lists we have may reflect differing family oral accounts, plus different readings of the fragmentary Old Testament records (as in Chronicles), plus varying concerns of the evangelists in putting together Matthew 1 and Luke 3. But in these several forms there existed what later was called a "Jesse tree"—a family tree tracing Jesus' ancestry back to David and his father Jesse and beyond ("Jesse windows" depicting the genealogy are found in cathedrals like Wells and Chartres and in Dorchester Abbey near Oxford).

The likelihood that Jesus really was a "son of David" makes his handling of the "messiah question" even more intriguing. Of course he really was in many ways "God's anointed." There was an anointing with the Spirit at baptism; he was Davidic and anointed by his birth (and conception), and through Joseph's Davidic descent. But "messiah" had so many misleading connotations that Jesus, we have argued, was cool to the title, until he, by his death, and God, by raising him from the dead, could show what it really means to be the Lord's messiah. He fulfilled prophecies by repudiating some current ideas and filling other older ones with new meanings. There were surprises here because of the great surprise that reversed so many human expectations on Easter day.

And so, as a result, the Christian faith down through the centuries has let all these bewildering details fall into the background. In the foreground is the simple, powerful phrase:

Jesus Christ.

NOTES

1. Cf. Morton S. Enslin, *Christian Beginnings* (New York: Harper & Brothers, 1938; Torchlight ed., Parts I and II, 1956), 192.

2. Cf. Gerard Sloyan, *Jesus on Trial: The Development of the Passion Narratives and Their Historical and Ecumenical Implications* (Philadelphia: Fortress Press, 1973), on such issues.

3. In addition to treatment in J. Reumann's *Jesus in the Church's Gospels: Modern Scholarship and the Earliest Sources* (Philadelphia: Fortress Press, 1973), 264–65, see also on Caesarea Philippi, *Peter in the New Testament: A Collaborative Assessment by Protestant and Roman Catholic Scholars*, ed. Raymond E. Brown, K. P. Donfried, and J. Reumann (New York: Paulist Press; Minneapolis: Augsburg Publishing House, 1973), 64–69, 83–101.

4. The term "city of David" normally in the Old Testament refers to Jerusalem and particularly to Zion, a triangular hill in the southeast part of the city, which

David took from the Jebusites and made his capital (2 Sam. 5:6–10). Luke has in mind Bethlehem, south of Jerusalem, as David's home town (1 Sam. 16:1; 17:12–15; cf. Micah 5:2).

5. Cf. Raymond E. Brown, K. P. Donfried, J. A. Fitzmyer, J. Reumann, eds., *Mary in the New Testament: A Collaborative Assessment by Protestant and Roman Catholic Scholars* (New York: Paulist Press; Philadelphia: Fortress Press, 1978), 77–83.

6. Cf. R. H. Fuller, *The Foundations of New Testament Christology* (New York: Charles Scribner's Sons, 1965), 111; E. Stauffer, *Jesus and His Story,* trans. Dorothea M. Barton (London: SCM Press, 1960), 22–23. Further, F. Hahn, *The Titles of Jesus in Christology: Their History in Early Christianity,* trans. H. Knight and G. Ogg (Cleveland: World Publishing, 1969), 240–46. Indirect but ancient evidence is also provided by a reference in Eusebius, *Ecclesiastical History* 3.11.19–20, about how the emperor Domitian had arrested the grandsons of Jude, the brother of Jesus, on the suspicion that, as Davidic descendants, they might represent a threat to the Roman state.

VI
The Gospel in the Early Church

The New Testament is a story of the gospel's advance from Jerusalem (top: temple area, Mount of Olives beyond) to Rome (bottom: here represented by its forum; Arch of Titus center rear, Colosseum beyond).

24

Jesus Christ, the Kingdom, and More Good News

JESUS OF NAZARETH, WHO had preached the coming of the kingdom of God as good news, had come—and gone. In the spring of A.D. 30 not only did he depart from his familiar haunts in Galilee, but at Passover time he also was removed from the places where he had taught and preached in Jerusalem. His life had come to an end, in a shameful way, upon a Roman cross.

After the events of Friday, 7 April, his followers were in deep gloom. They scattered, disheartened—some to Galilee, others into hiding locally. Only a few faithful women went about the necessary tasks of preparing to embalm the corpse that had been buried hurriedly before the beginning of the Sabbath.

Then, in the midst of this sadness, began to come reports on the first day of the new week that someone had seen him, alive! Peter had such a report. So did other disciples, a pair of them on Emmaus Road; eventually, all eleven as a group. (Judas, ruing what he had set in motion, had committed suicide.) Stories came to the fore about how some of the women had found empty the tomb, which belonged to Joseph from Arimathea, where Jesus had been buried. What had been dismissed as female fantasy—that they had gone to the wrong place, or that these women were making up "an idle tale" (Luke 24:11), even claiming that they had seen him vibrant and radiant—now began to make sense.

Thus began "the Easter Gospel," the good news that Jesus lives. This Easter Gospel proclaimed not only that he was now alive but also that he was exalted by God to life and lordship as a result of the triumph over death. Assertion of the lordship of Jesus was thus, in light of Old Testament precedent about God's lordship shown in the exodus, the result of this newest victory of God (see above, chaps. 8–13, esp. 13, "The Easter Victory: Jesus as Lord").

THE DEVELOPING ROLE
OF "CHRISTOLOGY"

It was also inevitable, in time, that acknowledgment of Jesus as Lord led to new titles of honor being bestowed on him by those who hailed this latest and supreme manifestation of God's kingly power. Jesus was never declared king in place of God, though the idea of him as king-regent within God's whole dominion occasionally does appear in the New Testament (cf. Matt. 25:34, 40). But he was designated now as "messiah" or, in Greek, "Christ" (see chap. 23), and a host of other titles followed honoring him. Indeed, in time, as the magnitude of what God had done in and through Jesus dawned on people, new understandings of his functions and role in the plan of God emerged, both in regard to creation (see chap. 18) and to the future, eschatologically (see chap. 21).

Jesus as the Christ, Lord of the church, who was confessed to have played a role in creation and who would reign even more fully at the end as judge (2 Cor. 5:10), loomed larger and larger. He became himself the good news. And who he really was, now viewed in the light of Easter dawn, was reflected in confessions and accounts of his life and ministry and origins. This process of applying new and greater titles to Jesus is called "Christology" because of the prominence of the term "Christ" in it.

OLD TESTAMENT REFLECTIONS

A good illustration of such developments is the way an Old Testament verse from Ps. 2:7 was applied and reapplied to Jesus. In an example of what may have been the starting point for this process, reflecting the Easter Gospel, Paul in a sermon at Pisidian Antioch applied this verse to the fact that God had raised Jesus from the dead (Acts 13:32–33):

> We bring you the good news that what God promised to the fathers, this he has fulfilled to us their children by raising Jesus; as also it is written in the second psalm,
> "Thou art my beloved Son;
> Today I have begotten thee [Ps. 2:7]."

Quoting an old psalm verse originally used when an Israelite king was enthroned, Paul insisted that Jesus has now been enthroned, as Son of God, by the resurrection on Easter Day. The same view is reflected at the sermon in Acts delivered on the day of Pentecost when Peter declared the resurrection to mean that God had designated Jesus "Christ" and "Lord" (2:32–36).

But this note of fulfillment, where "today" in the Old Testament passage denotes the day of resurrection, need not be confined to Easter. We have already examined (in chap. 6) the scene in the synagogue at Nazareth where the "today" when Scripture is fulfilled was equated with the beginning of Jesus' ministry (Luke 4:21). Hence, it is not surprising that in the account of Jesus' baptism we should also have this same psalm verse quoted in some versions. In Luke 3:22, according to some manuscripts (RSV footnote), the heavenly voice says,

> Thou art my beloved Son;
> Today I have begotten thee—

as if the point at which Jesus was elevated to sonship was his baptism.

The very phrase "I have begotten thee" points us to an even earlier incident in the earthly course of Jesus when God designated him as "Son": namely, at his birth or at his conception. This is what eventually became "the Christmas Gospel." Luke 1:31–35 reflects the idea of the begetting of Jesus by the Holy Spirit: he will be called "Son of the Most High" (God), and he is depicted as one who will reign on David's throne, "and of his kingdom there will be no end." "Today" here refers to Jesus' birth, or properly his conception (celebrated in church calendars as "The Annunciation of Our Lord," 25 March, nine months before 25 December).

It remained for the Fourth Gospel to project back to the ultimate degree possible "the day" from which Jesus is God's Son: John 1:1–14 makes his sonship stem from eternity (cf. also Col. 1:15). Christian faith eventually came to say, "There never was a time when the Son was not." So speak the later confessions of faith against the opinions of Arius.

CHRISTOLOGY AS GOOD NEWS

After Easter the New Testament was thus rapidly on the way to asserting Jesus' lordship to the nth degree, and this was regarded as good news or gospel in itself:

> I bring you good news of a great joy . . . a Savior, who is Christ the Lord (Luke 2:10–11);
> I would remind you . . . in what terms I preached to you the gospel. . . . Christ died for our sins . . . he was raised on the third day (1 Cor. 15:1, 3, 4);
> . . . the sufferings of Christ and the subsequent glory . . . the things which have now been announced to you by those who preached the good news to you . . . (1 Peter 1:11–12).

The gospel, or good news, was thus destined to take new shapes after

Easter, in view of what Jesus had said and done, and reflecting what the Old Testament had said. We will thus find many more ways of stating the good news than ever before (see also above, chap. 5). But as we explore these in the following chapters, we must ask what became of Jesus' own gospel emphasis on "the kingdom of God," in the development of the "Jesus movement" into the church during the rise of Christianity. Yet overall the emphasis will be on Jesus as the Christ. In the New Testament only at 1 Thess. 3:6 is the verb "to proclaim good news" applied to a current happening among Christians. The good news is regularly Jesus himself, the Christ.

25

The Easter Gospel
the Apostles Preached—in the
Book of Acts and Beyond

THE NEWS THAT JESUS was alive and reigned was enough to send anyone forth rejoicing—and preaching. You wanted to share the latest and most momentous story of all that God had done. Especially was this true of Jesus' closest friends, the eleven and the others who had been with him during the Galilean ministry and who had followed him to Jerusalem, to his death and unexpected victory. Furthermore, the resurrection appearances that we find recounted in our gospels regularly include a command from the risen Lord to go and share the news: "Go, tell his disciples and Peter ..." (Mark 16:7); "Go therefore and make disciples ..." (Matt. 28:19); "as the Father has sent me, even so send I you" (John 20:21).

THE "LITTLE CREEDS"

The most succinct form of this "new news" was regularly a brief slogan, much like an auto's bumper sticker nowadays in terseness, which summed up in a nutshell what had occurred. These very early statements, which are almost little creeds, are today embedded in our New Testament writings, especially the epistles. Paul and others liked to quote them, as reminders of the essence of the faith that had been preached from the outset. They often cite them in the course of an argument to direct hearers to "first things" and to bedrock priorities. In a letter like that to Rome, to a place where he had never been, Paul quotes such summaries (as in Rom. 1:3–4) as a means to confirm their bond of common identity. In many cases, if you simply put the words "I believe that . . ." in front of such statements, you have a mini-creed.

Typical is the statement, "God raised him from the dead" (Rom. 10:9).

Sometimes the emphasis is not simply on the past event but on the present implication, "Christ has been raised [by God]" and therefore, "he is risen" (1 Cor. 15:12, 13, 14, 16, 17, with v. 15 using the past tense about Paul's missionary preaching in Corinth, "we testified of God that he raised Christ"). In New Testament thought, it may be noted, the emphasis is on God as the one who raised Jesus. Even when 1 Thess. 4:14 says "Jesus died and rose,"[1] it is still understood that God raised him (1 Thess. 1:10); the focus at 4:14 is on Jesus who died. The same is true of slogans like 2 Tim. 2:8, "Remember Jesus Christ, risen from the dead. . . ." God is the one with power and ability to raise the dead (Heb. 11:19; 1 Peter 1:21); so Christians believe (Rom. 4:24). They also believe that God who raised Jesus will raise them up also (1 Cor. 6:14; 2 Cor. 4:14). The Easter Gospel is about this glorious work of God.

As can be seen from some of the examples cited above, the news of Jesus' resurrection is often coupled with some other event in his career, for example, his death (1 Thess. 4:14); cf. also 1 Cor. 15:3–4,

Christ died for our sins in accordance with the scriptures, . . .
he was raised on the third day in accordance with the scriptures. . . .

In 2 Tim. 2:8 his death is coupled with his descent from David (this is not so much a reference to his nativity as to his messianic lineage); cf. also Rom. 1:3–4, the gospel concerns God's Son,

who was descended from David according to the flesh
and designated Son of God in power . . . by his resurrection.

There, in a phrase omitted above, the resurrection is also specifically connected with the Holy Spirit (the full phrase reads, ". . . designated Son of God in power according to the Spirit of holiness by his resurrection"), as is also suggested by Rom. 8:11. On occasion Jesus' resurrection can be linked with his future return also, as at 1 Thess. 1:10; the Thessalonians are henceforth to serve God and "wait for his Son from heaven,

whom he [God] raised from the dead,
Jesus who delivers us from the wrath to come.

Even more elaborate is a passage like 1 Peter 3:18–19, 22:

Christ also died for sins once for all,
  the righteous for the unrighteous,
  that he might bring us to God,
being put to death in the flesh
but made alive in the spirit;

in which he went and preached to the spirits in prison . . . ,
who has gone into heaven and is at the right hand of God,
with angels, authorities, and powers subject to him.

Here surely is the language of the victory of God.

It will be noted that, while resurrection is coupled with Jesus' death, messianic descent, and future return, as well as his present exaltation, there are no passages that couple resurrection with Jesus' teachings, parables, or even miracles. These confessions of the Easter Gospel linked God's victory over death with the person of Jesus (he is "Messiah," or "Lord") or his work (he "died for our sins"). What was of first importance was the work of salvation, as gospel, not moral instruction. The implications of the Easter victory for the ethical life will follow, that is true, but they are not at the heart of the Easter Gospel. First, what God has done; then, in this case even separately, what we do in response.

THE KERYGMA IN ACTS

Much the same thing is true of the sermons that are reported in the Book of Acts. There, in the fullest reflection within the New Testament of early Christian preaching, the accent is on how God has raised Jesus from death. This is regularly coupled with his death, which is described in some detail. Since these sermons are longer and more detailed than the little credal slogans and are narrative in form, rather than abstract statements concentrating on only one or two facets of Jesus' work, the proclamation in Acts often tells more about the ministry of Jesus; for example, it is added that he taught or that he worked miracles. But even here there is almost never any content from his teaching reflected. Specific miracles are not recounted. We even look in vain for any reference to Jesus' theme, the kingdom of God, when these sermons summarize his career. Contrary to the credal slogans, the sermons in Acts do incorporate a call for response: they usually conclude with an admonition to repent and believe (as did Jesus' own kerygma, according to the summary in Mark 1:15) and also an appeal to be baptized. But of ethical imperatives, to do this or that worthy thing in daily life, there is nothing; that sort of admonition comes later in the unfolding of believers' lives.

Most of these points can be seen if we analyze a typical sermon. In Acts 2, Peter, speaking in Jerusalem fifty days after Easter (on the Jewish festival of Pentecost), begins, after catching his audience's attention (2:14), with a reference to what has just happened. He refers to the phenomenon of Jesus' Galilean followers being able to speak about "the mighty works of God" in a way that people of a dozen or more nationalities can understand them in their own languages (Acts 2:1–13).

This, Peter says, is not due to too much alcohol (for, after all, it is only 9 A.M.!) but represents fulfillment of a prophecy by Joel about the "last days" (Acts 2:15–20). Then comes the real message, the Easter Gospel: "Jesus of Nazareth . . . crucified and killed . . . God raised up" (vv. 22–24, 32). There is brief description of his ministry: he was "a man attested to you by God with mighty works and wonders and signs which God did through him in your midst" (v. 22). There is strong emphasis, for an audience in Jerusalem where he had been crucified, on how God's "having loosed the pangs of death" (v. 24) and not abandoning Jesus to Hades (vv. 31, 27) fulfills the Old Testament. Indeed, what may seem unusual expressions to us come directly out of Psalms passages, which Peter sees fulfilled in Jesus, a descendant of David. (It must be remembered that people then held the view that David wrote the Psalms.) Acts 2:25–28 quotes Ps. 16:8–10 (in a Greek version). Verses 29–31 explicate how the words could not apply to David but must speak of the messiah (Christ, whom Peter identifies as Jesus). The phrase in v. 24 about "the pangs of death" reflects Psalms language (cf. Ps. 116:3).

Here, for the first time, at least so overtly, we meet the important New Testament idea of God's plan to save, "the definite plan . . . of God" (Acts 2:23). The sermons in Acts claim that even Jesus' death was no mere human contrivance, but, for all its tragedy, part of God's overall design to save his human creatures, something God had thought out in advance (hence the word "foreknowledge," v. 23). Compare Acts 4:28, or 13:36 and 20:27, where RSV translates the exact same Greek word as "the counsel of God." The sermon in chapter 2 also speaks of Jesus' exaltation (v. 33), in accord with the Old Testament (v. 34), and the titles of honor that have now been given him (v. 36, "Lord" and "Christ").

When the crowd is moved to ask, "What shall we do?" Peter concludes with what is a standard answer in these sermons: "Repent, and be baptized," each one, for the forgiveness of sins; inherit the promise of God (2:37–39).

The outline suggested above for Peter's Pentecost sermon is rather typical of several other sermons in Acts that proclaim the Easter Gospel. Examples occur in Peter's sermon to Cornelius, the Roman army officer at Caesarea (Acts 10, in what is sometimes called "Pentecost for Gentiles"); Paul's long sermon at Antioch in Pisidia (Acts 13); and the briefer declarations involving Peter in Jerusalem (3:12–26; 4:8–12; 5:27–32). All these speeches may be outlined as follows:

The Easter Gospel the Apostles Preached

Pentecost	Gentile Pentecost	Other Speeches

(1) The *situation*. (Sermons in Acts may have an Old Testament "text" very near the beginning, but there is an even stronger tendency to pick up and reflect the local scene and situation in the face of which the preacher speaks.)

Pentecost	Gentile Pentecost	Other Speeches
2:14–21	10:34–35	Cf. 3:12; 4:9

(2) What was prophesied has been *fulfilled*, the "last times" are here.

2:16–18	10:43	13:27–29, 33

(3) This has come to pass in the ministry, death, and resurrection of *Jesus*,

    (a) Who was born of the seed of David

2:29–31		13:22–23

    (b) went about doing good (a brief reference to his ministry);

2:22	10:38	

    (c) He died on the "tree" (the cross),

2:23	10:39 (wording from Deut. 21:22)	13:27–29

    (d) but God raised him up and manifested him to witnesses.

2:24–32	10:40	13:30–31

(4) Now Jesus is *exalted*, at God's right hand.

2:33–36 (use of of Ps. 110:1)	Cf. 10:36	Cf. 13:30, 34

(5) A sign of Jesus' present messianic dignity and power is the presence of the *Holy Spirit*, now poured out.

2:33	Cf. 10:38, 44	Cf. 5:32; 13:52

(6) *Further fulfillment* will come at the last judgment by Jesus (10:42) and the "establishing all that God spoke" when Christ comes again (3:21).

(7) Of all this we are *witnesses*.

2:32	10:41	13:31

(8) Therefore, you should *repent*, be *baptized*, receive *forgiveness* of sins and the gift of the *Holy Spirit*.

2:38–39	Cf. 10:47	13:38–39

Clearly these sermons in Acts share a common outline. Indeed, their very sameness is not without its difficulties, since Peter and Paul are made to speak almost exactly alike, and Paul in such addresses (Acts 13, above; cf. 17:22–31; 20:18–35) does not use many of the ideas and terms found in his epistles to established congregations. In any case, Luke, by the very massiveness of the structure in these sermons, is seeking to show us what evangelistic preaching in the early church was like. We meet here the apostolic kerygma or proclamation by those "sent forth" to confront Jews and Gentiles with the Easter Gospel. Its heart was Jesus, crucified and risen.

THE KERYGMA AND THE KINGDOM

In this way, after Easter, the emphasis on Jesus was changed. He had been the one who himself proclaimed good news (about the kingdom of God); now he became the one who, risen and exalted, is proclaimed as himself the good news that brings forgiveness of sins and freedom (Acts 13:38–39). The gospel message thus took a new shape, as was inevitable after the Easter victory of God.

What happened, however, in this process, to Jesus' own emphasis on God and God's kingship? The supremacy and power of God, of course, remain. God, we have seen, it is who raised Jesus. Exalted as Jesus was, it is to God's "right hand"—that is, at a place of honor but in relation to God the Father. The term "kingdom" continues too, but with diminished frequency. Although the Gospel of Luke employed it forty-six times, "kingdom" occurs in Acts on just eight occasions. Those eight examples are enough, however, to show that Jesus' theme of the kingdom was continued after Easter in the early church, but with inevitable changes.

Jesus himself is depicted in Acts by Luke as continuing to speak of "the kingdom of God" to his eleven disciples throughout the forty days between Easter and his ascension (1:3). The disciples, alas, still continued to misunderstand it in the old nationalistic sense of a kingdom that would be restored to Israel (1:6). Just as some of them had hoped during Jesus' lifetime for positions of honor in an earthly kingdom (cf. Mark 10:35–45; Luke 22:24–27), so now, in the flush of Easter enthusiasm, they looked for restoration of Israel's old prerogatives. But Jesus directed them instead to missionary witnessing, under the Spirit (1:7–8).

"The kingdom of God," understood as Jesus had taught it, could in their witness still form the theme of Christian missionary preaching, however. Luke uses it as a kind of shorthand expression for what was preached, for example, by Philip the Evangelist or Paul and others:

> 8:12—in Samaria Philip "preached *good news about the kingdom of God and the name of Jesus Christ*";
>
> 14:22—Paul and Barnabas, in what is today southern Turkey, exhorted the disciples in Lystra, Iconium, and Antioch of Pisidia "to continue in the faith, and saying that through many tribulations we must *enter the kingdom of God*";

19:8—in a synagogue at Ephesus Paul spoke boldly, "arguing and pleading about *the kingdom of God*";

20:25—to the elders from Ephesus, who come to meet with him at Miletus, Paul describes himself as having "gone *preaching the kingdom [of God]*";

28:23—to Jews at Rome who visited his lodgings, Paul expounded his position, "testifying to *the kingdom of God* and trying to convince them about *Jesus* both from the law of Moses and from the prophets";

28:31—the closing words in Acts that echo in our ears, as Paul resides for a two-year period in Rome, are that he "welcomed all who came to him, *preaching the kingdom of God* and *teaching about the Lord Jesus Christ.*"

It can be observed that often "the kingdom" is the theme when the audience is Jewish (19:8; cf. 20:25; 28:23, 31) or a group related to the Jews (cf. 8:12). "The kingdom" could thus still be kerygma or the topic of post-Easter preaching (at 20:25 and 28:31 the Greek verb is "preach kerygma"). It could be "the good news" (8:12). But usually in these passages the kingdom is future (cf. 14:22); it is not yet (1:6–8). First comes a missionary interim. A final significant feature in the Acts references is the way now, as never in Jesus' lifetime, the kingdom of God is paralleled with Jesus himself (who since Easter is crucified and risen); cf. 8:12 (where "the name of Jesus" is equivalent to his person), 28:23 and esp. v. 31. Jesus himself, the new form of the gospel, can henceforth stand in tandem with the kingdom, or, as we shall see, supersede it, especially for preaching among non-Jews.

A vivid insight into what was happening in these exciting decades in the forties and fifties can be gained from a scene in Acts 17. At the Greek city of Thessalonica Paul and Silas have been engaged in giving their gospel witness in the synagogue, no doubt testifying to Jesus Christ and the kingdom. They make converts, but there is also opposition, an uproar; a mob attacks the home of Jason, Paul's host. In the confused scene that follows, the charge against Paul and Silas is this: "These men who have turned the world upside down have come here also, and Jason has received them; and they are all acting against the decrees of Caesar, saying that there is *another king, Jesus*" (17:6–7). We can guess what the confusion must have been. People heard the missionaries proclaim the kingdom (of God) and a new Lord, Jesus. They must have taken him to be a king, like Caesar, and concluded this Jesus was a revolutionist threat to

321

the Roman government. Paul and Silas would then be seditionists, "acting against the decrees of Caesar."

At Thessalonica the charges did not stick (17:9), but Paul and Silas did have to leave town (17:10). A few experiences like this would have been enough to convice early Christians that they must present their message with a clarity that would avoid such misunderstandings, and that, for a non-Jewish audience that did not know the Old Testament background to the kingship of God (that Jesus had preached), new ways must be found to express the good news. God's power, sovereignty, love, and rule could be expressed in other ways than by "kingdom."

The Easter Gospel which God had created in raising Jesus from the dead was now the new good news. But proof of the fidelity with which the early church (for that is what was taking shape, almost without knowing it) preserved Jesus' message about the kingdom is the way the Christian preachers in Acts preserved "the kingdom" as a theme at times—and the way the four evangelists preserved it as Jesus' theme in the gospels (which were written even later than the incident in Thessalonica), and the way Paul reflects it too. The kingdom of God will continue as a theme, but in light henceforth of the gospel about Jesus Christ.

NOTE

1. The rendering "rose *again*," found in many translations, does not mean Jesus rose twice, but is a traditional attempt to do justice to a Greek verb that means literally "rose up" or came back to life after death.

26

Paul and
the Gospel He Received

THE "EASTER GOSPEL" WAS the good news that Paul received from those
who had been followers of Jesus Christ before him. It was this gospel
which he in turn passed on to new converts, both Jew and Gentile, in the
Mediterranean world. In Paul and his work, this message and the messenger intertwined.

So influential was the "apostle to the Gentiles," as Paul is called (Rom.
11:13), that it has often been assumed he was a kind of "second
founder," after Jesus, of Christianity. Some have even argued that this
man from Tarsus in Asia Minor perverted the simple religion *of* Jesus
into a religion *about* Jesus, foisting upon it the notions of "church,"
"sacraments," and "ministry." True, Paul did find new and amazingly
fruitful ways of restating the gospel (see chap. 27). But the fact is that
many of the features often credited to Paul (or that he is blamed for) were
in reality the common property of apostolic Christianity, as it developed
in the thirties and forties.

If Jesus died and rose in A.D. 30, and Paul was converted in A.D. 33 or
36 but did not begin his missionary career until the year 47 or so, then we
have a period of almost two decades of Christian development quite apart
from Paul before his letters began to appear in the fifties. The evidence
for this development, within the apostolic church, of a common Christianity that Paul inherited can be read in the Book of Acts (written
perhaps in the nineties). It can also be ferreted out from pre-Pauline
passages quoted in the epistles (written in the fifties and later) by Paul
and his circle of helpers. From such New Testament material we learn
that Paul received much more than a bare-bones message that "Jesus
lives" from the Christian church then taking shape.

Paul himself had been born "Saul" (a name which stuck until it was changed during his first missionary journey in Cyprus, Acts 13:9; cf. vv. 2 and 13). He, as a zealous Jew devoted to the law, had once persecuted the church (Gal. 1:13–14). Jesus, to him, was an unrighteous rebel who deserved the cross; his followers should be stamped out (Acts 9:1–2). As a Pharisee, Saul believed in a future resurrection, but that Jesus, of all people, should be risen and exalted now, was preposterous.

Yet God was at work on Saul. Perhaps it was through a process of conscience, or by reflection about the Hebrew Scriptures, or from the impression Christian martyrs made on him (cf. Acts 7:59—8:1). At any rate, there was brought about a sudden change. Luke provides three separate accounts of how Saul was dramatically converted on the road to Damascus (Acts 9:3–22; 22:6–16; 26:12–20). From the importance given the incident in the Book of Acts, Paul's has become the classic prototype of Christian conversion, though it is seldom noted it was not conversion from worldliness and sin to faith but from one religion to another faith.

Great as Paul's experience was, he, while suffering loss of much that had been precious in his past (Phil. 3:8), carried over much also from his Jewish heritage. This inheritance included the Hebrew Scriptures, rabbinic ways of interpreting them, high Jewish moral standards, and even practices from the synagogue. Paul himself explains his new experience with Christ as nothing short of a "revelation." He used such language to describe how God, who had set him apart by grace—as with the prophet Jeremiah—"from [his] mother's womb" (KJV), was "pleased to reveal his Son" to him, and through Paul to reveal Christ to countless others thereafter (Gal. 1:15–16, cf. NEB; reflecting Jer. 1:5). Too many people have tried to imitate Paul's conversion experience, too few his Christian fervency and obedience.

WHAT PAUL RECEIVED FROM
EARLIEST CHRISTIANITY

What did Paul inherit as gospel in the fellowship or community of Jesus Christ into which he entered? First and foremost, there were those *little creeds that summed up the Easter Gospel with its note of Old Testament fulfillment,* "creedlets" such as we have already examined (see chap. 25). These, as in the case of 1 Cor. 15:3–5, served in turn as "building blocks" for further Christian thought. As we have the verses today, 15:3–5 are part of a complex argument about the resurrection of Christians. The Corinthians had problems either with the Semitic idea that the resurrection involved *bodies* (and not just "immortal souls") or with the promise

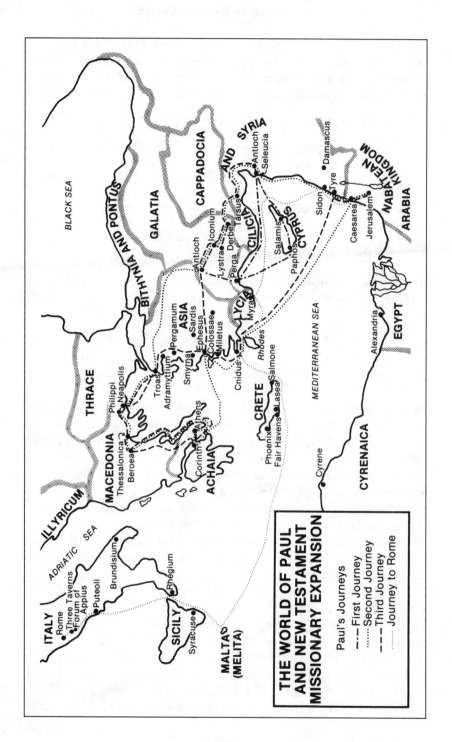

BLACK SEA

ILLYRICUM

ADRIATIC SEA

ITALY

Rome
Three Taverns
Forum of Appius
Puteoli
Brundisium

Rhegium

SICILY
Syracuse

MALTA (MELITA)

THRACE

MACEDONIA
Thessalonica
Beroea

Philippi
Neapolis

ACHAIA
Corinth Athens

BITHYNIA AND PONTUS

GALATIA

CAPPADOCIA

AND SYRIA

NABATEAN KINGDOM

ARABIA

Damascus

Antioch
Seleucia

Sidon
Tyre

Caesarea
Jerusalem

Antioch
Iconium
Lystra
Derbe
Perga

CILICIA
Tarsus

Salamis
Paphos

CYPRUS

ASIA
Pergamum
Sardis
Ephesus
Colossae
Miletus

Troas
Adramyttium
Smyrna

LYCIA
Myra

Rhodes

Cnidus

CRETE
Phoenix
Fair Havens Lasea
Salmone

MEDITERRANEAN SEA

Cyrene

CYRENAICA

Alexandria

EGYPT

THE WORLD OF PAUL AND NEW TESTAMENT MISSIONARY EXPANSION

Paul's Journeys

--- First Journey
.... Second Journey
–--– Third Journey
·········· Journey to Rome

that they would rise *in the future*. Some of the Corinthians may have thought they were already raised. Paul begins to untangle these complex problems by patiently reiterating something they and he alike all accepted, a little four-line creed found in vv. 3b–5a.

> 1 Now I would remind you, brethren, in what terms I preached to you the gospel,
>> which you received,
>>> in which you stand,
>>>> 2 by which you are saved, if you hold it fast—unless you believed in vain. 3 For I delivered to you as of first importance what I also received,
> that Christ died for our sins in accordance with the scriptures,
>> 4that he was buried,
> that he was raised on the third day in accordance with the scriptures,
>> 5 and that he appeared. . . .

Then follows a list (or lists) of resurrection appearances, to which Paul adds his own revelatory experience: Christ appeared

<table>
<tr><td>to Cephas,</td><td>to James,</td></tr>
<tr><td>then to the twelve,</td><td>to all the apostles;</td></tr>
<tr><td>then to 500 plus;</td><td>last of all, to Paul</td></tr>
<tr><td>(vv. 5–6)</td><td>(vv. 7–8)</td></tr>
</table>

It is possible that even vv. 3 and 4 originally consisted of separate little acclamations, "Christ died for our sins" (cf. 1 Peter 3:18) and "Jesus was raised" (cf. Rom. 4:25); here they have been put together with perfect balance. Lines 1 and 3 of the little creed each have the phrase "in accordance with the scriptures"; perhaps Isa. 53:5–12 and Hosea 6:2 or Ps. 16:10 are meant. Each line has a distinctive prepositional phrase: in line 1, "for our sins," which makes the death an atoning one, and in line 3, "on the third day," which fulfills scripture as well as gives chronology. Each of the major parallel lines has a supporting clause; the burial in line 2 reinforces the reality of Jesus' death, and the appearances in line 4 undergird the resurrection.

This kerygmatic credo, Paul says, is what he inherited and faithfully preached when he came to Corinth. The Corinthians accepted it and lived by it. The rest of the chapter draws out the implications of what they are to believe: if Christ has been raised, so too will they who are in Christ. There will take place a resurrection of the dead. It will be in bodily form, Christians bearing the image of "the man from heaven," Jesus (1 Cor. 15:49). And Paul, in good Old Testament fashion, then draws ethical implications from all this, as to how we ought to live (15:58) and even how his converts should give to a collection for the relief of Jewish Christians in Jerusalem (16:1–3). The Easter Gospel in credal slogans thus helps build further good news and commands for the people of God.

Apostolic Teachings

What Paul inherited included, second, *teachings of Jesus and of the early church* that served to direct the life of Christians in worship and daily existence.

A good example is a passage also in 1 Corinthians, at 11:23–25. It begins with the same formula found at 15:3. (The words "received" and "delivered" were technical terms from rabbinic use for passing on intact the teaching of some earlier authority; hence Paul employs them here.)

> 11²³ For I *received* from the Lord what I also *delivered* to you, that the Lord Jesus on the night when he was betrayed, took bread, ²⁴ and when he had given thanks, he broke it and said, "This is my body which is for you. Do this in remembrance of me."
>
> ²⁵ In the same way also the cup, after supper, saying, "This cup is the new covenant in my blood. Do this, as often as you drink it, in remembrance of me."

This time there is not the same precise parallelism as in 15:3–5, but the two "words of institution" do balance each other: "This is my body . . ." balances with "This cup is . . . ," and twice repeated are the words is "Do this . . . in remembrance of me." The reference to an actual happening is clear: the "Lord" is named as Jesus, his words are quoted; a date is given, and a setting provided, at a "supper." That refers to a meal at Passover time. Some other details in the wording, like the reference to "new covenant" (Jer. 31:31), reflect Old Testament background, as does the idea of "remembering" (cf. Exod. 12:14).

We are accustomed to recite such words at celebrations of the Lord's Supper. That is quite likely how these words were being used by Christians in the thirties and forties, and indeed why Paul had passed them along to the Corinthians in the first place as part of his gospel teaching. They were words, Paul could say to the Corinthians, "in which you stand" (15:1) every time there is participation in the cup and bread that actualize the body and blood of Christ (1 Cor. 10:16), that is, his presence. The words announce his death and all its benefits, like the forgiveness of our sins, as the verse which is added at 11:26 makes clear: "As often as you eat this bread and drink the cup, you proclaim the Lord's death until he comes." The proclamation made by the Lord's Supper thus concerns the cross and the subsequent victory of God at Easter, made vivid here and now, and the promise the Lord will come in the future and fully reign.

Paul has quoted all this in 1 Corinthians 11 because of a problem in that troubled but gifted congregation. There was trouble at the communal meal (11:17–34). When Christians assembled in what should have been a time of fellowship and unity, factions had emerged. The structure of the service originally seems to have included an actual meal, eaten *between* the sharing of the bread (body) and the sharing of the cup (blood) (cf. v. 25, "after supper"). This structure was later changed to one where there was a meal first and *then* the bread and cup. This latter arrangement was apparently the practice in Corinth at the time Paul was writing (cf. 11:20–22, 33–34). (The meal, or "love feast" [Jude 12], was eventually dropped from early Christian worship, precisely because of abuses such as occurred in Corinth. For centuries Christians have been accustomed just to bread and wine as the sacrament, and that development occurred already in the New Testament.)

Some of the Corinthians had gotten into the habit of greedily eating the food and even getting drunk at the meal before the blessing over the bread and cup. Paul seems particularly angered that some Christians who "have nothing" (11:22) and go hungry (11:21)—likely slaves or believers from the lower classes who perhaps could not get to the service as early as others, until after their daily work was done—were being discriminated against by other Christians. (If this seems hard to believe, that there was discrimination at the Lord's Supper, even worse things apparently could happen at Corinth. Paul at 10:1–12 had to warn Christians there that sacraments were not a kind of magical rite that let us behave however we want.)

To the problems at Corinthian communion services Paul addresses the "words of institution" (11:23–25) that he had shared with them from the beginning of their faith. It is a *Lord's* Supper that they eat (v. 20), not a private party of their own. The Lord is Jesus who died for them and who will come again, and who will be and is Judge. Therefore "discern the body" (v. 29). By that Paul means not simply, "Be aware that you receive the true body and blood of the Lord" (cf. vv. 27–28 which some Christians stress as a reference to perceiving Christ in the "elements"), but, more important, discerning the body of the Christ as the Christian community (cf. 1 Cor. 12:12, 27), even in those poor slaves who came late to the assembly. Here, as in 1 Cor. 15:3–5, a piece of traditional teaching that comprised part of the gospel Paul had received (11:23–25) is being used to speak as further gospel, and as warning, in a new situation in Corinth.

Ethical Instructions

What Paul inherited thus included teachings about faith, worship, and daily life which could be used the way the Lord's Supper account was employed in 1 Corinthians 11. It also included a number of *instructions quoted from Jesus* and *a common body of ethical admonitions* that could be passed along to new Christians as a norm or guide.

Examples can be briefly listed, first of Jesus' teachings. When Paul says, "The Lord commanded that those who proclaim the gospel should get their living by the gospel" (1 Cor. 9:14), he has in mind presumably the saying of Jesus, "The laborer deserves his wages," a saying now found at Luke 10:7 and Matt. 10:10. When Paul writes, "I know and am persuaded in the Lord Jesus that nothing is unclean in itself" (Rom. 14:14), the pertinent teaching of Jesus is Mark 7:15 or Matt. 15:11. Paul seems to know something of what we call the Sermon on the Mount; compare Rom. 12:14 and 17 with Matt. 5:44 and 39–42. Paul's Greek writings still retain the Aramaic word for father, *Abba,* which Jesus no doubt used in the Lord's Prayer (see above, pp. 119–21); compare Gal. 4:6 and Rom. 8:15 with Luke 11:2. There could even have been a collection of such teachings in the first decades of Christianity which Paul and others used.

As to common *ethical admonitions,* we know that there were teachers in the early church who instructed converts more deeply in the truths of faith and the ethical implications of their new commitment. Galatians 6:6 refers to such teachers and to those being "taught the word"; the Greek expression is one from which we derive our terms "catechist" and "catechetical instruction." There are also New Testament references to "the traditions Paul taught" (cf. 1 Cor. 11:2; 2 Thess. 2:15) and even to "the standard of teaching to which you were committed" (Rom. 6:17). In reading the New Testament epistles one cannot but be struck by a common pattern of ethical admonition in letters by Paul and his helpers, by Peter, and by James. These admonitions are often built up around some key verb, as the following table makes clear:

"Put off" (bad habits; KJV)	Col. 3:8	Eph. 4:25–31	1 Peter 2:1–2; James 1:21
"Put on" (good characteristics)	3:10, 12	4:24	cf. Rom. 13:12
"Be watchful, pray"	4:2–3	6:18–19	1 Peter 4:7; 5:8

"Stand" or "withstand"	Col. 4:12	Eph. 6:11–14	1 Peter 5:8–12; James 4:7
"Be subject to . . ."			
husbands/wives	3:18–19	5:21–33	1 Peter 3:1–7
fathers/children	3:20–21	6:1–4	
masters/slaves	3:22—4:1	6:5–9	1 Peter 2:18–20

The imagery of "putting off" and "putting on," while natural with regard to ethical habits, also reflects the practice of baptism. There the candidate would disrobe ("put off" outer garments) and then, according to later practice, dress in white ("put on") after being baptized. The "subjection" theme came into Christianity from the Old Testament (cf. 1 Peter 3:6) and the contemporary world. (In chap. 32, p. 424, we shall see how Christianity modified and reshaped some of its dangerous features, including the subjection of women.) The command "Be subject to . . ." could also be applied with regard to our relation to God and for relations of those who are younger to elders (1 Peter 5:5–6) and with regard to the citizen and the state (1 Peter 2:13; Rom. 13:1–7).

All this evidence points to a pattern of ethical instruction for people entering the Christian faith, particularly those entering the church from paganism, who needed rudimentary lessons in a type of life that followed the gospel call. Paul and other writers sometimes reflect this material. Thus we begin to see a church that, in connection with its good news, had from earliest days credal announcements of the gospel, teachings from Jesus and teachings of a general ethical nature, and a sacramental life. For, in addition to the Lord's Supper, *baptism* existed as the great rite of entrance, as response to the good news, what one does upon hearing the kerygma (Acts 2:38). John the Baptist had used a water rite (Mark 1:4–5), and his disciples (Luke 11:1) no doubt continued the practice (cf. Acts 19:1–3). Jesus could have baptized during his ministry (cf. John 3:22; 4:1), though one passing reference (at John 4:2) says it was his disciples, not he, who engaged in the practice. It was really after Easter, in the early church, that the practice became the norm for entrance into the Christian community. Paul can even assume that Christians in Rome, a place where he had never been when he wrote Romans, know all about baptism, for he argues *from* the practice (Rom. 6:3–11) and need not argue *for* it.

Early Christian Hymns

In addition to all these components in the gospel that Paul received out of the rich heritage of the apostolic church in its first twenty or thirty years, one other item deserves to be singled out. That is the *hymnody* of early Christians. Whether they did so in Aramaic or in Greek, Christians praised God. They could, of course, from the outset have used psalms from the (Old Testament) Scriptures. But since there are New Testament references to "psalms and hymns and spiritual songs" that they sang with thankfulness in their hearts (Col. 3:16), we are safe in supposing there must have been a growing collection of such hymnody. These songs must have been sung at times of celebration, particularly baptisms and communion services and Sunday worship.[1]

It is likely that 1 Peter 3:18–22 reflects such a hymn about Jesus' death, resurrection, and exaltation (see above, pp. 316–17). Colossians 1:15–20 is commonly regarded as a hymn about Jesus' role in creation and redemption (see under "Hymning Christ as Creator" in chap. 18). Philippians 2:6–11 is an elaborate poetic composition concerning Jesus' descent to death and exaltation as Lord (see under "The Great 'Christ Hymn' of Philippians 2:6–11" in chap. 13), certainly composed prior to the time of Paul's letters and perhaps originally going back to the Aramaic-speaking segment of the church. We may cite here, as a portion of a baptismal hymn, Eph. 5:14,

Awake, O sleeper, and arise from the dead,
And Christ shall give you light,

and the longer composition now quoted at 1 Tim. 3:16 about Christ:

He [literally, "Who"] was manifested in the flesh,
Vindicated [or justified] in the Spirit,
    Seen by angels,
Preached among the nations,
Believed on in the world,
    Taken up in glory.

We seem to have references here to Jesus' incarnation, resurrection, and ascent; to the missionary advance of the kerygma into the world of the Gentiles; and to Jesus' glorious exaltation. There is a neat rhetorical pattern contrasting the two spheres of earth and heaven that many people of the day found natural in their thinking: flesh/Spirit, nations/angels, world/glory. Such passages are notoriously hard to pin down as to precise meaning, and one reason is because they are, as hymns, in the language of poetry.

PAUL'S INHERITANCE AND USE
OF KINGDOM-LANGUAGE

In such an emerging church, with its creeds, kerygma, teachings, ethical concerns, sacraments, and songs, what happened to Jesus' message about the kingship of God? We have already suggested (above, pp. 321–22) good reason why other ways had to be found to express God's sovereignty and Jesus' lordship in the Greco-Roman world than through the "kingdom of God." Nonetheless, in addition to the "kingdom" references in Acts that we have explored, a number of verses about God's kingdom occur in the Pauline epistles that were being written in the fifties and later. Some of these references are part of the gospel material that Paul received, though in other cases the use of kingdom terminology is his own, employed out of Paul's loyalty to Jesus and in fidelity to the Old Testament background.

A half dozen of the Pauline verses refer to the kingdom as a future phenomenon, yet to come—just as in the Old Testament and sometimes in Jesus' teachings. Some of these occur in what must have been part of that inherited body of ethical instructions in the early church. For example, Paul writes to the unruly Corinthians (1 Cor. 6:9–11),

> 6⁹ Do you not know that the unrighteous will not *inherit the kingdom of God?* Do not be deceived; neither the immoral, nor idolaters, nor adulterers, nor sexual perverts, ¹⁰ nor thieves, nor the greedy, nor drunkards, nor revilers, nor robbers will *inherit the kingdom of God.*
> ¹¹ And such were some of you. But you were washed, you were sanctified, you were justified in the name of the Lord Jesus Christ and in the Spirit of our God.

The list of types of sinners need not be a biographical profile of Corinthian converts, but simply a stock ethical list found in early Christian teachings. More important, Paul says these people, however once bad, were now baptized ("washed"), justified, and sanctified in Christ. Note also the verb "inherit" and its future tense—the kingdom will be a gift to come.

The same verb, "inherit," is used with regard to a list of vices that Paul quotes at Gal. 5:19–21.

> 5¹⁹ The works of the flesh are plain:
> fornication, impurity, licentiousness,
> ²⁰ idolatry, sorcery,
> enmity, strife, jealousy, anger, selfishness, dissension, party spirit,
>   ²¹ envy,
> drunkenness, carousing, and the like.
> I warn you . . . that those who do such things *shall not inherit the kingdom of God.*

After the corresponding list of "virtues" in vv. 22–23, one might expect to read, "Those who do these things *will* inherit the kingdom of God." But there is there no reference to any "salvation by good works"—simply a reference to living a life in conformity with the cross of Christ Jesus, v. 24.

Early Christianity thus certainly connected the kingdom with a morally responsive life, just as Jesus did in his words about "fruit" from a good tree, fruit suitable for the kingdom (Matt. 7:16–20; 21:33–41). Paul in 1 Thessalonians makes the point well: we exhort, encourage, and charge you "to lead a life worthy of God, who calls you into his own kingdom and glory" (2:12). This process may even involve suffering for the future kingdom of God (2 Thess. 1:5). It is clear that a person as he or she is by nature, that is, as "flesh and blood," in the Semitic phrase, "cannot inherit the kingdom of God" (1 Cor. 15:50); there must be change brought about by God at the second coming. Paul even preserves a highly apocalyptic little account of how Christ will, at the end, hand over the kingdom to God, who will then be all in all (1 Cor. 15:22–28). This implies the possibility of a "kingdom *of Christ*" for a time, and occasionally there is reference to that (cf. Eph. 5:5, "any inheritance in the kingdom *of Christ and* of God").

All these references make the kingdom seem so much a future thing that one is moved to ask if the early church, as reflected in the epistles, did not lose sight of the kingdom of God as a present fact, now breaking in, as Jesus had proclaimed. While the future aspect was so very much emphasized in the epistles, the present side of the kingdom was, however, not lost. Paul makes a reference to it in a discussion about "strong" and "weak" Christians and their scruples over what a believer could or could not eat. "The kingdom," he writes at Rom. 14:17 with reference to this situation, "is *not* food and drink." He then goes on to offer three equivalent terms that may reflect the mind of the early church on what the kingdom is; positively, the kingdom can be summed up by "righteousness and peace and joy in the Holy Spirit." These are God's eschatological gifts, given now—rejoicing, thanks to the Holy Spirit's presence (cf. Romans 8); peace (*shalom,* cf. Rom. 5:1); but above all, God's gift of justifying righteousness. In that latter theme Paul was to find yet another way to express the gospel, and to deepen its meaning (see chap. 27).

From this background in the gospel which he received, Paul's own vocabulary continued to include "kingdom" as a theme. He used it in a warning to the Corinthians: "the kingdom of God does not consist in talk but in power," present now, for the gospel is "the power of God" expressed as "righteousness" and in "Christ crucified" (1 Cor. 4:20; cf. Rom. 1:16–17 and 1 Cor. 1:23). Just as in 1 Cor. 11:27–32, the presence of this Lord can mean judgment. There Paul was speaking to some in Corinth who thought they were already in the kingdom and already "reigned as kings," triumphantly (cf. 1 Cor. 4:8). It would appear that some Corinthians overdid the present aspect of the kingdom. Perhaps that is why Paul spoke instead so often of its future side (cf. 1 Cor. 15:49–50).

Other writings in the Pauline corpus pick up both aspects. Colossians 1:13 speaks of Christians as having been "transferred . . . to the kingdom of [God's] beloved Son." The imagery reflects the Old Testament exodus: transfer from Egypt to the promised land. But Colossians has reinterpreted these two physical kingdoms as "the dominion of darkness" (from which we have been delivered, 1:13) and as "the inheritance of the saints in light" respectively (1:12). Lest anyone mistake this metaphorical application, the kingdom of God's Son is further defined as "redemption, [i.e.,] the forgiveness of sins," which believers share in now (1:14). This idea of the kingdom as a present fact may also be reflected in the description of several of Paul's Jewish Christian companions as "my fellow workers for the kingdom of God" (Col. 4:11). In 2 Timothy, on the other hand, the kingdom is spoken of as future. It is coupled with the judgment and Christ's parousia (or future coming), and is God's "heavenly kingdom" for which Paul and others will be saved (2 Tim. 4:1).

Paul in his own writings and the reflections of early church usage in epistles by him and by other apostolic writers therefore preserved the "kingdom" theme, seen now in light of the Easter Gospel. Like Jesus, Paul and his co-workers in the faith regarded it as present and future, as a gift and as the basis for ethical demands (1 Cor. 6:9–10; Eph. 5:5; cf. Mark 1:14–15). The tendency, as he gave new expression to the good news (see below, chap. 27), was to move toward an accentuating of the gospel as a joyous, liberating present reality, while still holding fast to its future promises.

NOTE

1. By the time Paul wrote 1 Corinthians in the mid-fifties, there seems to have been a shift from the Jewish Sabbath (the seventh day of the week) to the first day of the week (Sunday) as the particular time for Christian worship. Compare 1 Cor. 16:2 and Rev. 1:10. Sunday worship celebrated the central fact of Jesus' resurrection on the first day of the week (Mark 16:1–2).

27

The Gospel Paul Advanced

THE MISSIONARY CAREER OF PAUL coincides with and, according to the New Testament, spearheads the greatest period of missionary advance in the first-century church. The Book of Acts begins in Jerusalem, the center of Israel's hopes, where Jesus had died and been raised, and ends with Paul preaching the gospel in the imperial capital, Rome. Paul's three "journeys" in Acts—actually, a continuing campaign of incessant labors with long periods in key cities like Corinth and Ephesus, whence the gospel spread to the surrounding countryside—and his many epistles[1] serve to document the progress of the gospel from Palestine north and west into Asia Minor, Greece, and Italy.

Of course, there must have been hundreds of other unnamed missionary witnesses, plus the several dozen of Paul's friends and other apostles mentioned in the New Testament. These unheralded men and women, often in the course of their daily work, spread the gospel to Rome long before Paul got there and carried it east and south as well. (See chap. 5, above, on this early history of the missionary church.) But Paul it was who is singled out, by the New Testament generally and in Acts chapters 13—28 particularly, to symbolize this great advance. One gets the impression that after his death, which occurred between A.D. 60 and 67, the Christian movement, partly because of the upheaval caused by the fall of Jerusalem in A.D. 70, and partly because of sporadic persecutions and internal problems, had to devote more and more effort in the last thirty years of the century to coming to a new self-understanding before there could be much further advance.

Paul, we have already seen (chaps. 25–26), inherited from the early church Jesus' message about the kingdom and the Easter Gospel with its rich amplifications. He preached the same basic good news as the other apostles (1 Cor. 15:11). His witness he even checked with Cephas (Peter), James (the brother of Jesus), and John in Jerusalem (Gal. 2:2, 7–10), and it was endorsed by them. Their agreement was that Paul should concentrate on Gentiles and the Jewish Christian apostles on Jews ("the circumcised") and that Paul should "remember the poor" (at Jerusalem), as Gal. 2:9–10 reports, perhaps, it has been suggested, from actual minutes of their meeting. Paul carried out that pledge faithfully. A great deal of his energy in each congregation went into raising money for "the saints" at Jerusalem (cf. 1 Cor. 16:1–4; 2 Corinthians 8—9; Rom. 15:25–29).

Thus Paul was a loyal churchman, and he is particularly so portrayed in Acts. He speaks there in his sermons very much as Peter (see chap. 25). He, like other missionaries, seems indeed subservient to "headquarters" in Jerusalem (Acts 9:26–30, contrast Gal. 1:16–21; similarly Acts 11:27–30; 12:25 RSV note; chap. 15; and 18:22, assuming "the church" mentioned there that Paul "went up and greeted" means the one at Jerusalem). Luke, because he held a view that there were twelve apostles and twelve only[2] therefore hesitates to call Paul an "apostle" in the Lukan sense of the word (as defined at Acts 1:21–22, namely, one who was with Jesus from his baptism until the ascension and who is "a witness to the resurrection"). Indeed, Paul is called "apostle" in Acts only in one story (14:4, 14), but Paul himself defended vehemently in his own letters his apostolic authority (cf. 1 Cor. 9:1; 2 Cor. 11:5; 12:11–12; much of Galatians is a defense of Paul's apostolic office and apostolic gospel).

One gets the feeling that Luke, in order to fit certain things into his own theological view of history (see below, pp. 448–51), has shaped the picture of Paul so as to maximize certain features. The "real Paul," as seen in his own writings, was even more dynamic than in Acts, indeed almost volcanic. This point is important in understanding what the gospel was for Paul. For while he received and transmitted the Easter message, he also developed, amplified, deepened, and extended this good news so that it would speak to peoples who could not read a line of Hebrew or think in Semitic terms, to peoples who had not been shaped from childhood by the high morality of Judaism, and who might likely think that "the kingdom of God" meant an earthly state and that the word "Christ" ("anointed") was a proper name or meant the "smeared" or "perfumed one" (which indeed the Greek could mean; see above, p. 289).

Hence Paul was almost forced to recast the gospel he had received, in order to make it comprehensible to his audiences and to fit the new

Paul's apostolic mission took him to Ephesus where, according to Acts 18—19, he labored for two years. Foreground: theater ruins. A great street ran to the harbor beyond (now silted up).

situations that he faced. When he speaks about "my gospel" (Rom. 2:16; 16:25), he does not mean one that he had invented, but the gospel he had received, though now developed along fuller and new lines. To be true to the gospel and to his Lord (who was working in Paul through the Holy Spirit), he had not simply to repeat, but to proclaim anew. In Paul the gospel comes to take new shapes, loyal to the earlier traditions and not entirely unpredictable, given his Old Testament roots and the world in which he labored, but new and destined to become themselves the norms for subsequent centuries.

"JUSTIFICATION" AS GOOD NEWS

What is the gospel, according to Paul? It is, of course, always the good news about Jesus Christ, crucified and risen (cf. Rom. 1:3–4, 9). It reveals God's power, at work to save. And first and foremost it takes for Paul the form of *righteousness* or *justification*. The Pauline gospel is, as the Reformation often formulated it, the message of "justification by grace alone, for the sake of Jesus Christ, received through faith." Paul himself makes it the subject of his most formal epistle, to the Christians at Rome: the gospel, he wrote at the outset in a definition,

is the power of God for salvation to every one who has faith,
    to the Jew first and also to the Greek.
For in it *the righteousness of God* is revealed through faith for faith; as it is written,
    "He who through faith is *righteous* shall live."
                    (Rom. 1:16–17, quoting Hab. 2:4)

It has to do with the twin facts "that [God] himself *is righteous* and that he *justifies* him who has faith in Jesus" (Rom. 3:26).

Yet even how to translate the Greek words involved (and the Hebrew behind them) causes English translators to squirm. We have the choice of an Old English root, "rightwise," and a Latin root "*justitia*":

	From Old English	*From Latin*
Noun	righteousness	justice
Adjective	righteous	just
Verb	declare or render righteous or rightwise(n)	justify
Noun	_____	justification

Each set of terms has its connotations and limitations, and translators often shift from one to another. Note Rom. 3:26 above, where the RSV shifts from "is righteous" to "justifies." *The Living Bible* paraphrases very freely, as a few examples show: ". . . makes us ready for heaven—makes us right in God's sight" (1:17); "a different way to heaven" (3:21); and at 3:26 seemingly gives up the terms entirely! We must, however, let the Bible set the meaning for us. Basically the sense is that of "a relationship to what is right or just." But accurate English renderings are difficult.

This difficulty comes in part because the basic relationship is with God. It is "the righteousness *of God*" that is involved. God sets the norm for what is right and just. But "God's righteousness" can mean (1) "a quality which belongs to God," one of his attributes (rendered as "justice" at Rom. 3:5). Or (2) it can mean "the righteousness which is valid before God," that is, the quality in a person which lets that person stand in the judgment by God (as at 2 Cor. 5:21, perhaps). Or the same phrase can suggest (3) "a righteousness from God" (Phil. 3:9), the God-given righteousness which saves or judges and helps the believer stand in the judgment.

The matter is clarified in Paul only when we consider the Old Testament background on which he is drawing. References are plentiful in the Hebrew Scriptures to justice and righteousness as a demand from God for human conduct that conforms to the divine standards (Micah 6:8; Jer. 22:3; Ps. 11:7), for "righteousness and justice are the foundation of [God's] throne" (Ps. 97:2). Yet there was also in Israel an awareness that it was not the righteousness of the nation or the justness of the people that accounted for God's blessings on them (Deut. 9:4–6). And so at times there is assertion of the fact that God's righteousness means his redemptive activity, his actions which bring righteousness and salvation. This emphasis comes to the fore especially during the exile in the words of the Second Isaiah (see under "The Second Isaiah, as Exile Ends" in chap. 12), where "righteousness" becomes synonymous with God's saving work. Note the parallelism, when God says

> I bring near my *righteousness* [NAB, justice]; it shall not be far off,
> and my *salvation* shall not tarry. (Isa. 46:13, KJV)

Many modern translations render what is literally "righteousness" here by the word "deliverance" (so RSV; cf. also Isa. 46:12; 51:5, 6). For "righteousness" in parallel with "salvation" in RSV see 59:17; 61:10.

Thus Jewish (and early Christian) thought knew of "righteousness" (or "justification") as an action of God, bringing "salvation" (cf. Isa. 45:8). Furthermore, "salvation" in the same chapters in Isaiah can be equated with the good news that "your God reigns" (52:7). The links were there to make the equation, good tidings = salvation = your God reigns = righteousness of God. In New Testament terms this becomes,

gospel = salvation = kingdom = justification.

We may add that the context of the Old Testament references is often that of (1) judgment or a law-court scene, where God enters into a lawsuit with his people (cf. Isa. 41:1, 21; 43:9) and the hope is for a vindication which can come only from God (Isa. 50:8–9); or (2) that of the judgment at the "last day." In particular, there is a hope that "the servant of the Lord" will bring justice/righteousness in that day (Isa. 42:1–4).

It is quite likely that Christians, long before Paul himself wrote a line of his epistles, had begun to speak of God's victory at Easter in terms of the long-expected establishment of God's righteousness. The second line of the little creed or hymn at 1 Tim. 3:16, which speaks of Christ as "vindicated in the Spirit" (see above, p. 331), means literally *"justified* in the Spirit" (KJV; RSV note), so that the resurrection was a kind of "justification of Jesus." Jesus is therefore "the *Righteous One"* (1 Peter 3:18, au. trans.) who was God's servant (Acts 3:14, 26) and who is "our *righteousness"* (1 Cor. 1:30). His death-resurrection means atonement for sins and therefore salvation, as is stated in what is likely an early Christian slogan which Paul quotes:

[We believe in God who] raised from the dead Jesus our Lord,
who was put to death for our trespasses
and raised for our justification.

(Rom. 4:24–25)

Perhaps the most elaborate of these early Christian statements about righteousness or justification that Paul inherited is embedded in Rom. 3:24–26, about how we are *"justified* . . . through the redemption which is in Christ Jesus," redemption achieved when God set him forth and he died on the cross as an "expiation" or bloody offering for sin, like the temple sacrifice on the day of atonement (cf. Leviticus 16, esp. vv. 11–16). In the complicated language of Rom. 3:25–26, this death served to show that, although God seemingly passed over sins in former times, he still is righteous: Jesus' blood provides a "covering" or makes "atonement" for sins. Paul declares that the cross shows God *is just* and *justifies* those who believe in Jesus (v. 26). Here we have the nucleus of Paul's theme about justification by faith: people are "set right with God," not by anything they do but solely through what God has done, in Jesus' cross and resurrection; by accepting this in faith, you receive salvation (cf.

Rom. 10:9–10). Paul's shorthand expression for this is "the righteousness of God . . . through faith" (Rom. 1:17; 3:22).

To grasp Paul's meaning, one cannot underscore too much the three salient points Paul emphasizes as he uses this version of the gospel, especially in writing Galatians and Romans.

1. We said the Judaism of Paul's day did not minimize an eventual judgment to be based on the good works people had done in life. Their deeds, particularly those of prayer, fasting, and giving alms, in accordance with the law, would deliver them, it was believed. Paul, on the other hand, denies that a person can ever get right with God by what she or he does (Gal. 2:15–16; Rom. 3:20). At this point Paul is in tune with Jesus' demand for a righteousness beyond human means, beyond the letter of the law (Matt. 5:21–48). What Paul proclaims is that in the judgment presided over by God salvation can come only by "grace as a gift" from God (Rom. 3:24). Justification is thus by *grace.*

2. Judaism saw the judgment by God as coming in the future. It was an experience to come in the "day of Yahweh." But for Christians the last times had already begun. Jesus was risen from the dead, the first fruits of what was to come. Therefore Paul moves up the judgment to the present—for the Christian. The verdict of "justified" at the "last day" has already been pronounced, Paul says, for those who believe. "*Now* God's righteousness *has been revealed*" (Rom. 3:21, au. trans.). "Since we are justified by faith, we *do* have peace with God" (5:1, au. trans.). Paul can even speak of the Christian's situation as "a new creation" and as "the day of salvation"—now (2 Cor. 5:17—6:2). And in this too he was true to Jesus who announced a kingdom breaking in, with meaning here and now.

3. In conformity with Old Testament usage and Jesus' own demands, Paul also calls on justified Christians to live righteously. There are to be "fruits of righteousness" (Phil. 1:11), as part of Christian existence. In the terse slogan at Rom. 14:17, the definition of the kingdom as "righteousness and peace and joy" could even mean "righteous actions" by Christians. It is more likely the reference is to righteousness in the sense of God's saving gift of redemption to us, but we must not lose sight of the ethical aspect that righteousness always includes. Christians are in every way "slaves of righteousness" (Rom. 6:18), made what they are by God's righteousness and dedicated to the service of justice.[3]

OTHER WAYS TO PUT THE GOSPEL: RECONCILIATION

Almost in the same breath, however, that he says the gospel is righteousness, Paul can also say that the gospel is *reconciliation.* This second way of stating what the good news is occurs statistically not too often, being clustered in two chief passages, in Romans 5 and 2 Corinthians 5. Both, however, are magnificent examples of presenting the message of God's grace in a gripping way. If "justification" impressed itself upon the Protestant Reformation as the chief way of expressing the gospel, "reconciliation" has commended itself to many moderns as the best way of telling people what God has done. The "Presbyterian Confession of 1967" has for that reason made reconciliation central.

Reasons for such significance are not hard to seek. If "justification" is a figure drawn from the law court and judgment, "reconciliation" is a metaphor derived from the experience of "making up" within a personal relationship. Though justification requires a certain understanding of Old Testament thought, reconciliation is instantly apparent to everyone who has ever suffered even a lover's quarrel. Unlike "righteousness/justification," this word presents few difficulties in translation. At Rom. 5:11, where the KJV had translated, "we have now received the atonement," the Greek phrase can literally be rendered "we have now received our *reconciliation,*" as in the RSV; the KJV phrase means to be "at one" with God, that is, reconciled. In an age of anxiety and estrangement, like ours, the term "reconcile" speaks the gospel in language that is meaningful, especially because of ethical implications about reconciling fragments of a world divided socially, racially, economically, and in countless other ways.

To grasp Paul's meaning on reconciliation, one should read and ponder Rom. 5:9–11 and 2 Cor. 5:17—6:1. The Romans passage paints a picture of us separated and alien from God, "enemies" toward him. The great news is that we have been, and shall be, reconciled to God by the death of his Son, who also lives henceforth to intercede for us (cf. Rom. 8:34). That is how "atonement" or "reconciliation" has been made, and we can rejoice in it. Further, 2 Corinthians adds that the whole new life we have, as new creations of God (cf. also 2 Cor. 4:6), is God's work, through Christ who reconciles us to himself. Our task is to proclaim this message to a sinful world: "Be reconciled to God" (5:20). We have a "ministry of reconciliation."

The theme occurs in two other epistles briefly. Colossians 1:21–22 comments on the phrase in the early Christian hymn at 1:19–20, "God was pleased . . . through [Christ] to *reconcile* to himself all things" (see under "Hymning Christ as Creator" in chap. 18). The comment is that God has reconciled to himself, through Jesus' death, people who were estranged and hostile. Ephesians 2:16 says the same thing: Jesus' blood on the cross reconciled Jews and Gentiles to God. But the Epistle to the

Ephesians develops the further idea that the reconciliation was also *between* Jew and Gentile so as to create a new humanity, or "one new man" on earth, "in one body," the church (cf. 2:11–16).

It is possible that some of these phrases were used prior to Paul. If so, they likely arose in the Greek-speaking church as ways of describing what Christ means. For "reconciliation" is a rare term in the Old Testament. In Paul there is often a corporate, cosmic, or universal touch to the term. One may compare Col. 1:20 or Rom. 11:15, where the fact that the Jews in Paul's day by and large were rejecting the gospel was a reason why he turned to the Gentiles, thus bringing about what is called "the reconciliation of the world." Finally it needs to be noted that these passages that speak of reconciliation usually relate it so closely to "justification/righteousness" (cf. Rom. 5:9; 2 Cor. 6:20) that later theology, as in the Lutheran Confessions, rightly says "justification is reconciliation." And when later theologians add that the two terms also imply the "forgiveness of sins" (cf. 2 Cor. 5:19, which speaks of how "trespasses" are not "counted"), we are brought back to the world of the historical Jesus who declared, "Your sins are forgiven." That is to be reconciled.

LIFE "IN CHRIST" AS GOOD NEWS

In addition to justification and reconciliation, Paul had a third way to present the gospel: it also means to be "*in Christ.*" The phrase "in (Jesus) Christ" or some form of it is ubiquitous in the Pauline corpus, occurring over 160 times. There is nothing quite like it in Old Testament religion and even in the Gospels or Acts. The closest thing is the idea of "in the name (or person) of Jesus" (cf. Acts 2:38; 3:6; Matt. 18:20). Paul himself may have been the one who created this "relational" concept.

To call the "in Christ" relationship "mystical," as has often been done, serves only to confuse the issue, since "mystical" is notoriously hard to define and is itself scarcely a biblical term. To describe "being in Christ" by a kind of material analogy, like a fish being "in water," or Christ being "like the air we breathe," as commentators once were prone to do, is even more unfortunate, since the Christ-relationship is with a living person, not with a thing like water or air.

Some uses of the phrase by Paul are natural enough, such as "to be justified *in Christ*" (Gal. 2:17); there the sense can be simply "by Christ." Likewise with Romans 6, we have been "baptized *into Christ Jesus*" (v. 3) and so are "alive to God *in Christ Jesus*" (v. 11); that need mean nothing more than "through Christ." Certain other cases are to be explained by the fact that Paul did not apparently have the term "Christian," for the first recorded use of the Greek word for Christian(s) is at Acts 11:26, and

Paul never uses the adjective. His equivalent sometimes is the phrase "in Christ." To speak of "a man *in Christ*" (2 Cor. 12:2) may therefore simply denote "a Christian man" (as NEB actually renders it). Thus, "in the flesh and in the Lord" (Philemon 16) means "both as man and as Christian" (NEB).

But the meaning deepens when we begin to explore Paul's use of this and related prepositional phrases, and recall that no one in Paul's day would ever think of talking about being "in Moses" or "in Socrates." Combining the evidence, we get the following picture. Sometimes there is a reference to what happened "in (the case of the historical) Christ Jesus," who died on the cross (cf. Rom. 3:24; Phil. 2:5). Yet because he is a living figure, larger now than history, one can also speak of him in the present tense, as a figure in whom we live (cf. Rom. 6:11; 1 Cor. 1:30). This Christ-figure is therefore related to the church (1 Cor. 1:2), with which he so identifies that this body of believers is "the body of Christ" (1 Cor. 12:27). What is more, this Christ will come again, and so "in Christ shall all be made alive" (1 Cor. 15:22). In this way the "in Christ" theme overarches all Christian existence. As it has been put, "We follow Christ 'in Christ' "—and dare not overlook this vital relationship with him which is also a social relationship with other Christians in the church, his body. For this theme, 1 Corinthians 12 and Ephesians 1—3 are the great passages.

THE GOSPEL AS SALVATION (HISTORY)

What is the gospel in Paul? Fourth, some would suggest that it is *salvation* or *salvation history,* a theme to sum up all these other gospel emphases. Paul certainly does talk of the gospel as "the power of God for *salvation*" (Rom. 1:16) and of "now" as the "day of *salvation*" (2 Cor. 6:2). Jesus is the savior (Phil. 3:20). Christians are people who can say "We were, are being, and shall be saved" (Rom. 8:24; 1 Cor. 15:2; Rom. 5:9–10). Justification, reconciliation, life in Christ are stages, then, that make up "salvation," according to this view.

Others go further and try to construct a "history of salvation" in Pauline thought. Such a history can be built around certain key figures whom he mentions. These include **Adam** (Rom. 5:14, 18; 1 Cor. 15:22), whose trespass brought death to all; **Abraham** (Romans 4; Galatians 3), who "believed God, and it was reckoned to him as righteousness" (Gen. 15:6) so that Abraham becomes a prototype of justification by faith; **Moses** (1 Corinthians 10; 2 Corinthians 3), who introduced the law that served only to bring out human sin, and not to get us right with God; **Christ,** who put an end to the law of Moses (Rom. 10:4), who fulfills the

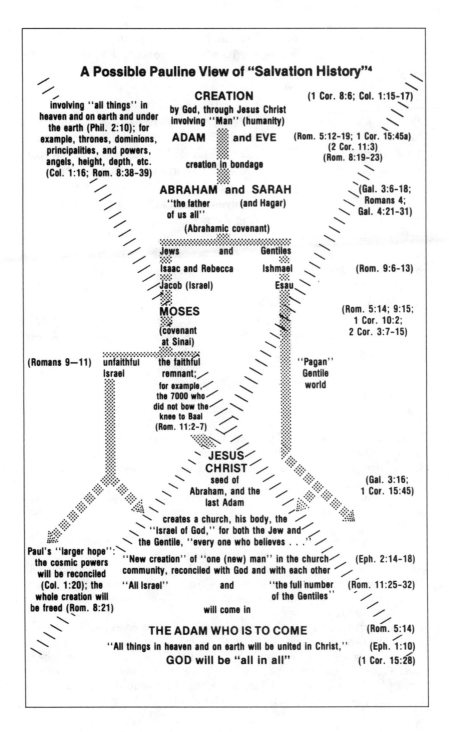

A Possible Pauline View of "Salvation History"[4]

involving "all things" in heaven and on earth and under the earth (Phil. 2:10); for example, thrones, dominions, principalities, and powers, angels, height, depth, etc. (Col. 1:16; Rom. 8:38-39)

CREATION
by God, through Jesus Christ
involving "Man" (humanity)

(1 Cor. 8:6; Col. 1:15-17)

ADAM and **EVE**

creation in bondage

(Rom. 5:12-19; 1 Cor. 15:45a)
(2 Cor. 11:3)
(Rom. 8:19-23)

ABRAHAM and SARAH
"the father   (and Hagar)
of us all"

(Abrahamic covenant)

(Gal. 3:6-18;
Romans 4;
Gal. 4:21-31)

Jews   and   Gentiles

Isaac and Rebecca   Ishmael

Jacob (Israel)   Esau

(Rom. 9:6-13)

MOSES

(covenant
at Sinai)

(Rom. 5:14; 9:15;
1 Cor. 10:2;
2 Cor. 3:7-15)

(Romans 9—11)   unfaithful
Israel

the faithful
remnant;
for example,
the 7000 who
did not bow the
knee to Baal
(Rom. 11:2-7)

"Pagan"
Gentile
world

**JESUS
CHRIST**
seed of
Abraham, and the
last Adam

(Gal. 3:16;
1 Cor. 15:45)

creates a church, his body, the
"Israel of God," for both the Jew and
the Gentile, "every one who believes . . ."

Paul's "larger hope":
the cosmic powers
will be reconciled
(Col. 1:20); the
whole creation will
be freed (Rom. 8:21)

"New creation" of "one (new) man" in the church
community, reconciled with God and with each other

(Eph. 2:14-18)

"All Israel"   and   "the full number
of the Gentiles"

will come in

(Rom. 11:25-32)

THE ADAM WHO IS TO COME   (Rom. 5:14)

"All things in heaven and on earth will be united in Christ,"   (Eph. 1:10)

GOD will be "all in all"   (1 Cor. 15:28)

promise to Abraham (Gal. 3:16) and is the life-giving "last Adam" (1 Cor. 15:45); and finally, "the **Christ who is to come**" (cf. Rom. 5:14), the second Adam (1 Cor. 15:45–49) at the end.

Such patterns can also be bound up with "covenants" (Rom. 9:4; Eph. 2:12), for Paul did think at times in terms of two covenants (Gal. 4:24). We can also spot passages where Paul reflects the age-old idea of a "victory of God," this time through Christ, over cosmic, demonic powers (cf. 1 Cor. 2:6–8; Col. 1:16; 2:15; Eph. 1:21). But no sustained treatment of these themes, it must be added, is offered by Paul's letters.

Hence we can only guess or debate whether Paul operated with some sketch of the "whole sweep of salvation history" such as some scholars credit to him, such as is shown in the sketch on p. 345.

Did such a pattern of salvation history or understanding of "the plan of God" stand behind what Paul wrote on certain occasions? We cannot prove it, but many feel that such a sketch of salvation history may be another possible way of spelling out his gospel, alongside justification, reconciliation, and life "in Christ."

No wonder, with so many ways of stating the good news according to Paul, that Ephesians refers to "wisdom of God in all its *varied forms*" (3:10, NEB). It is a many-splendored gospel that Paul developed.

NOTES

1. Thirteen letters in the New Testament are attributed to Paul. About half a dozen of these are held by critics to be the work of Paul's pupils. Some of the Pauline letters may consist of portions of several letters of his; 2 Corinthians, for example, likely contains parts of three separate letters. Even the most radical of critics count as genuine, however, segments of ten or more separate letters by Paul.

2. According to Luke, Judas, when he died, was replaced, but for no one thereafter in the "apostolic college" was a successor chosen (cf. Acts 1:15–26; 12:1).

3. For more on the topic in ecumenical discussion, see J. Reumann, *"Righteousness" in the New Testament: "Justification" in the United States Lutheran–Roman Catholic Dialogue*, with responses by Joseph A. Fitzmyer and Jerome D. Quinn (Philadelphia: Fortress Press; New York: Paulist Press, 1982), sections 77–222 and 376–408, with attention to the other Pauline ways to put the gospel in sections 192–216.

4. Such charts have especially been stimulated by the conceptualizations presented by Oscar Cullmann, notably in *Christ and Time: The Primitive Christian Conception of Time and History*, trans. Floyd V. Filson, rev. ed. (Philadelphia: Westminster Press, 1964). See further the chart on "Paul's Conical View of History" in W. D. Davies, *Invitation to the New Testament: A Guide to Its Main Witnesses* (Garden City, N.Y.: Doubleday & Co., 1966), 302, and his more

specific chart on "Paul's View of History," 303. The chart here is a fuller development of that found in *Word and Witness: Understanding the Bible II* (Philadelphia: Lutheran Church in America, Division for Parish Services, 1980), 96–97. The biblical references in the margins should be examined to see how Paul refers to the figures noted in boldface capital letters. The selection of these five seminal figures is justified in C. K. Barrett's *From First Adam to Last* (New York: Charles Scribner's Sons, 1962).

28

Apocalyptic Anew:
Jesus, Easter,
and in Paul's Letters

It SHOULD COME AS NO surprise that apocalyptic appears in the New Testament. But it may occasion some surprise that apocalyptic can be used to set forth "good news" and that apocalyptic therefore does have a place in "the history of the gospel."

For apocalyptic writings have often led to some strange aberrations in history, none more so than that weird last book in the Bible, The Revelation of Saint John the Divine (KJV). Controversies over some of its features stretch from the "chiliasts" of antiquity (who believed in some form of literal thousand-year reign on earth for resurrected martyrs, such as is spoken of in Rev. 20:1–6) to many sect groups of today. One commentator on the book once said that Revelation either found a man cracked when he began to study it or left him so afterward! Martin Luther had his doubts about whether the Book of Revelation even belongs in the canon. Moreover, Revelation is a writing full of bad news and judgment.

Yet apocalyptic appears in several other places in the New Testament too and can, especially in certain situations, speak the gospel of Christ powerfully, even though it employs some tricky techniques in style and content that demand study. The whole thing ought to be labeled "Handle with Care" or "This May Be Hazardous for Your Spiritual Health!"

Apocalyptic, we have already seen (p. 27, and chap. 20), is one of the several main types of literature found in the Bible. The term covers both the writings that "unveil" God's will and plans for the future and also the mood or outlook that underlies such literature.

In chapter 20 we explored how apocalyptic arose in dark times. It appeared as a way of looking at life, history, and God during those cheerless years of Israel's exile and persisted during the even drearier days that followed exile. Everything was going downhill. Things were so far gone, the world so bad, that God, it was held, God personally must intervene to set life right. Such an outlook contrasted very much with the prophetic view that was illustrated in Jeremiah's letter to the exiles (above, pp. 172–73). For Jeremiah had said, even of the exile: live where you are in the world; come to terms with it. Apocalyptic said: the world is very evil; look to its destruction. So people waited passively for the "day of the Lord," dreaming dreams and seeing visions, often with symbolic imagery, about how the evil would be wiped out and good rewarded.

There thus emerges in apocalyptic a far-reaching "dualism," a sharp distinction between good and evil, between "this age" and "the age to come," between light and darkness, between God and Satan. This dualism would be resolved only by God's ending "the present evil age" (as Gal. 1:4 puts it, using a characteristic Jewish phrase) and by ushering in of the promised "age to come." In dark times, contrasting gloomy present and bright hereafter, apocalyptic thus kept alive the hope that God's kingdom would come victoriously, in spite of all present evidence to the contrary, and come *soon* (another characteristic word in apocalyptic).

THE APOCALYPTIC STRAND IN JESUS' TEACHING

Jesus' own message, we have seen (chap. 6), was sometimes couched in apocalyptic terms. For he talked about "fulfillment" of earlier dreams: "Now the 'kingdom of God' *has come*" (au trans.; cf. Mark 1:15; see above, pp. 1–2, 96–101). He talked of the kingdom breaking in and urged people to live in light of it; one felt the presence and power of God's kingly rule (above, pp. 115–16). All this can only be described as realization of some of Israel's future apocalyptic hopes.

Yet in his teaching Jesus also sometimes employed the language and mood of apocalyptic in its own right. For the kingdom he announced had a future side (see above, p. 115, and under "Jesus and Eschatology" in chap. 23). His teachings are streaked with coloring from the fact that the kingdom is "not yet," at least "not quite yet" here, not fully as yet. In particular there runs through the good news of Jesus certain echoes of Old Testament apocalyptic about "that day." Jesus could still look forward to "those days" when the sun would be darkened, the moon would not give its light, the stars would fall, and the "powers" in heaven would be shaken, when the Son of man shall come (Mark 13:24–27; above, pp.

293–95). The very fulfillment that Jesus brought about indeed created new apocalyptic hopes for an imminent consummation.

EASTER AND APOCALYPTIC

Nowhere is this truer than with the resurrection of Jesus himself and the Easter Gospel that proclaimed him now as living Lord (see chaps. 13 and 25), for they generated new apocalyptic expectancy. Any Jew of that day who heard that someone had been raised from the dead could only conclude that the promised general resurrection must not be far behind, and that all the other events of the "last days" must soon be upon the world. The Easter experience therefore triggered hopes, inevitably, that the end was at hand. The mood of the first Christians must have been one of "enthusiasm" in the technical sense of that word: they were "full of God" and of God's Spirit. They expected great things; they boldly witnessed to their "new news" and shouted the praises of Jesus Christ in cosmic terms. We see them caught up in the fervor of apocalyptic enthusiasm, which gave birth to new expressions of the gospel.

Examples of such "apocalyptic anew" meet the reader at many points in the New Testament. The early preachers, for instance, boldly asserted that what people of the day were seeing was nothing less than fulfillment of what apocalyptists in the past had prophesied. Hear the words of Peter's first reported sermon. It is Pentecost. The Holy Spirit has just come. What is happening, he claims, fulfills "what was spoken by the prophet Joel:

> In the last days . . ., God declares,
> I will pour out my Spirit. . . .
>   (Acts 2:16–21, quoting
>   Joel 2:28–32)

That apocalyptic fulfillment, where sons and daughters "prophesy" and men old and young "dream dreams," set the mood for declaring Jesus "Lord and Christ" (Acts 2:36). The enthusiasm of the new faith led to hymning Jesus as lord of the universe (Col. 1:15–20; Phil. 2:6–11; cf. above, chaps. 13 and 18). Everything from the creation to apocalyptic expectations about the impending "last times" (see 2 Peter 3; above, p. 242) could be caught up in a vision of life that owed much to the impact of apocalyptic. We all owe a great debt to this apocalyptic outlook—hopes fulfilled, new expectations. For it mothered a great deal of Christian theology.

The apostle Paul well illustrates the point. Before becoming a follower of Jesus, Saul, as a Pharisee, had already believed that there would be a resurrection, some day. For Pharisees believed in the future raising of the dead by God (Acts 23:6). They had a hope that the good would rise and that their oppressors would not (cf. Ps. 16:10; Isa. 26:13–14, 19), or if they did, that the wicked would be raised only to be punished. A Jewish writing in the Pseudepigrapha, *2 Baruch* (or the Syriac *Apocalypse of Baruch*), dated in the last part of the first Christian century, declared that

> all who have fallen asleep in the hope of him [the Messiah] shall rise again.... The souls of the righteous ... shall come forth ... and ... rejoice.... But the souls of the wicked ... shall then waste away the more. (30:2–4)

(Sometimes these texts speak only of the resurrection of Israelites, sometimes of all people in the world. Sometimes only the resurrection of the good is mentioned, other times the resurrection of the evil too—for punishment, as in Dan. 12:2.)

Now for anyone like Paul, reared in such an environment, to accept the resurrection of Jesus implied that if one man (Jesus) has been raised, then the resurrection of all persons (in Israel, or perhaps from all the human race) must follow soon. Such is the background for Paul's phrase about Christ as "the first fruits" of the dead (1 Cor. 15:23; see also Col. 1:18, "the first-born from the dead"): Jesus is the harbinger of the coming harvest. His resurrection guarantees a "good crop" to come. (See 1 Cor. 15:35–42, where Paul even compares burial to planting a seed which will be raised in glory at God's harvest time.)

Apocalyptic, then, helped shape Paul's whole outlook. The cornerstone for his new outlook was, of course, the gospel that "Christ died for our sins [and] that he was raised," in fulfillment of past promises, that is, in accordance with the Scriptures (1 Cor. 15:3–4). But the gospel Paul received also included a future side, about the kingdom as an inheritance yet to be given (1 Cor. 6:9–11; Gal. 5:19–21; cf. chap. 26, pp. 332–33). What was thus part of the message that was transmitted to Paul, about the future and apocalyptic hopes, was especially brought to the fore in his encounters with Christians, such as those at Corinth, who thought the kingdom was already completely present and fully realized. But Paul always had some reservations about making Christianity here and now a complete and finished product. He believed God always has yet more to come, even though the decisive God-given event has already taken place, namely, the death and resurrection of Christ.

Thus, in Paul's own gospel as he advanced the good news, the accent is on justification here and now, on reconciliation with God now, on life in Christ today. But there always remains a future side. Likewise, Paul's

sketches of salvation history—the broad sweep of God's plans through-
out past, present, and future—stretch beyond one's present blessings in
Christ toward a "larger hope" (see under "The Gospel as Salvation
[History]" in chap. 27).

In general, we must therefore say that the New Testament, whether in
Jesus' teachings or in Paul's letters, stresses the good news of what has
been done, but never lets go of the good news for the future about what
God yet will do. Both these sides of the gospel may employ apocalyptic
categories: on the one hand, about promises already fulfilled (the present
emphasis); on the other hand, about promises yet to be fulfilled (the
future emphasis).

The line of development for apocalyptic thus runs from the Old Testament, through Jesus, to Paul and other New Testament writings, and goes
on into future centuries. We may diagram it like this:

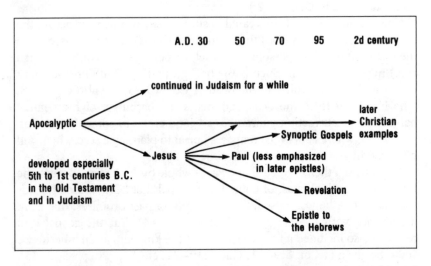

Something has already been said of Old Testament examples and Jesus'
own use of apocalyptic. Jewish examples continued at least into the
second century A.D. There are many Christian specimens also outside the
Bible. These include *The Apocalypse of Peter* (in the New Testament
Apocrypha), *The Shepherd of Hermas* (in the Apostolic Fathers), and *The
Apocryphon of John* (from among recent finds of Gnostic literature at
Nag Hammadi). These latter examples do not concern us here.

The Synoptic Gospels have material of this type in the so-called Little
Apocalypse (see above, p. 295, on Mark 13 and pars.). Hebrews 12:22–
29 can be cited as an example from a different sort of book; in reading
the passage, note the gift of the kingdom at v. 28, and of a new covenant

mediated through Jesus at v. 24, but then the warning that God will shake the heaven and earth "yet once more" in v. 26, which quotes Hag. 2:6. Christians frequently took over Old Testament passages about apocalyptic signs in the heavens. Mark 13:24–25 provides an example from Isa. 13:10 and 34:4. But Christians did not always make very much of the stock-in-trade details of apocalyptic writing. Witness the total absence in Acts 2 of any application of the "signs" of blood and fire cited in vv. 19–20 from Joel 2:30–31. The Old Testament writer had made reference to "portents" or wonders in the heavens, and on earth "blood and fire and columns of smoke." These very verses are quoted in Acts 2:19–20—but nowhere in Peter's sermon is there any emphasis upon such details, only on the Spirit. Hebrews 9:27–28 should also be recalled, since that is the closest the New Testament ever comes to employing the phrase "second coming" when it describes the sequence of death, judgment, and how Christ will appear "a second time" to "save those who are eagerly waiting for him." In the pages that follow we shall concentrate on a few examples of apocalyptic from Paul and then in chapter 29 on the Book of Revelation itself.

THE THESSALONIAN LETTERS

When Paul arrived in Thessalonica, just before A.D. 50, the common missionary gospel he was setting forth included proclamation of the "living and true God" and his Son, Jesus, "[risen] from the dead," whom we await from heaven, "who delivers us from the wrath [or judgment] to come" (1 Thess. 1:9–10). This message included an apocalyptic side to preaching; the gospel had an orientation toward the future. Thus the Thessalonians came to expect that Christ would come soon and that they themselves would be raised to the full life of the promised kingdom (2:12). But in the few months between the time when Paul left the city and the time when he wrote to them the letter we now call 1 Thessalonians, a couple of members of the little congregation must have died. Their deaths raised questions that Paul sought to answer by invoking apocalyptic and other materials from the arsenal of Scripture and faith.

In 1 Thess. 4:13–18 Paul takes up the problem from the standpoint of Christian hope (cf. v. 13). The discussion begins with the kerygmatic truth that all Christians professed, "Jesus died and rose again," and its corollary that believers who died, God will bring to life through Jesus (v. 14). But when? and how? Paul assures the anxious Thessalonians, as a "word of the Lord," that the Christians who are alive at Christ's coming will not have any advantage over believers who have died in the interim (v. 15). Nor, vice versa, will the dead have any advantage over those then alive. Neither group, the living or the dead, will have any head start on the other in getting into the kingdom of God. Then Paul uses a vividly apocalyptic picture of what will happen (vv. 16–17): the Lord (Jesus) will descend, the dead in Christ will be raised up, and Christians who are living at the time will be "caught up together with them in the clouds to meet the Lord in the air." Paul then leaves the scenario literally hanging in midair, concluding simply with the comment, "So we shall always be with the Lord" and the admonition to "comfort one another with these words" (vv. 17–18). There is, it is to be underscored, no speculation about what things will be like after we are "with the Lord." Paul's use of apocalyptic stops short of such concerns.

From this passage in 1 Thessalonians 4, it may be noted in passing, has come the later idea of "the rapture," derived from the Latin word behind the verb translated in RSV as "be caught up together with them in the clouds." Actually, "rapture" is not a biblical term, so it will not be found in Bible dictionaries. It is variously used, by sectarian groups, to refer to the sudden rendezvous of all Christians, dead and living, with the returning Christ; or for a "secret coming" of Christ when, prior to the "great tribulation" (cf. Rev. 7:14), he will waft "true believers" to security, out of the unparalleled troubles to afflict the world for the next seven years. At times, 1 Thessalonians 4, the only passage of its kind in the Bible, has been linked in such constructs with other passages like Matt. 24:40–41 and details in Revelation so as to create a series of dramatic events for the end time. Such speculation is not Paul's point, however, in 1 Thess. 4:13–18, and the "doctrine of the rapture" is an innovation developed by certain interpreters only in the nineteenth century.

Plainly Paul did use apocalyptic in 1 Thessalonians 4. But his purpose must be kept in mind: to comfort Christians concerned about whether they who live or their loved ones who had died would get into the kingdom first. The answer is, neither group will be at a disadvantage. The basis for the hope of all believers is the Lord Jesus who died and was raised, and the goal is simply to be "with him." There is no speculation about what things will be like after we are "with the Lord."

But some people in Thessalonica did speculate about precise chronological details, or to use the biblical phrase, about "the times and the seasons." This happened even though Paul had earlier taught them as much as they needed to know. Nonetheless, in 1 Thess. 5:1–11 he goes over again what he had taught them before. The tone is markedly catechetical. The entire passage should be read with the background of each unit (as noted below) kept in mind:

5:1—The topic, "Times and Dates," has already been the subject of instruction at Thessalonica.

5:2—"The Day of the Lord will come like a thief in the night." Cf. Jesus' saying at Matt. 24:43–44 parallel Luke 12:39–40; and Rev. 3:3.

5:3—Its suddenness and inevitability are like the birth of a child. The analogy to a woman's labor pains is common in the Bible; cf. Ps. 48:6; Isa. 13:6–8; and John 16:21.

5:4–5—The moral implication is that we ought not be "of the night or of darkness" (when thieves operate) but "children of light and . . . of the day" (KJV). The comparison between night and light is found both in Scripture and in the Dead Sea Scrolls. For the New Testament, see Rom. 13:11; Eph. 5:8–14.

5:6–7—Hence the exhortation to keep watch and be sober. Cf. Rom. 13:11–13.

5:8—As daylight people, arm yourselves with faith, love, and hope. Here Paul employs the imagery of defensive armor, from Isa. 59:17 (breastplate, helmet). But Paul works in the Christian trilogy of these three leading features in any believer's life; cf. also 1 Thess. 1:3 and 1 Cor. 13:13.

5:9–10a—The grounding and goal for this eschatological admonition lies in God and the salvation granted through Jesus. Note the use of the little credal phrase, "Christ . . . died for us"; cf. 1 Thess. 4:14 and 1 Cor. 15:3.

5:10b–11—Awake or asleep (referring to the problem of 4:13–18), we belong to the Lord Jesus, and the aim is to "live with him." (See also 1 Thess. 4:17 and Rom. 14:8–9 where the argument is similar.) Therefore, not only "comfort one another" (4:18) but "encourage one another" (5:11; the Greek verb is the same in each instance) and "build one another up."

Many modern sectarians must be disappointed to get eleven verses on the theme of the "times and seasons" (suggesting for them the second coming and "the rapture"), only to discover that Paul avoids all timetables and speculations. There *is* a day of the Lord to come, but do not try to guess God's plans. Instead, give yourself, all the more, to living the life of faith, love, and hope, affirming and helping others. Christian existence now is what matters, based on the cross and resurrection of Christ in the past and on a future hope that shapes life for the better. But no speculations, please, about the rapture or the date. Paul is a pastoral theologian, not an apocalyptic alarmist.

There is further evidence, though, that the congregation in Thessalonica had troubles with those who misread and wrongly applied Paul's teaching on apocalyptic eschatology. In 2 Thess. 3:6–13 Paul says that some Christians were living undisciplined lives of idleness. They were "busybodies instead of busy" (3:11, Moffatt's translation; cf. also v. 6). Perhaps they had quit their usual work and had stopped well-doing in the world because they thought it was soon to end (cf. v. 13). Paul's advice is to keep on with the daily round, and more drastically he commands, "No work, no eats" (vv. 12, 10, au. trans.). In chapter 1 of this same letter the point is made again, using a host of apocalyptic details about the judgment to come (vv. 6–10): Paul cites this apocalyptic passage to encourage the Thessalonians to "fulfil every good resolve and work of faith by [God's] power," and thus be worthy of God's calling and kingdom (vv. 11 and 5). Eschatology here serves ethical exhortation.

In contrast to the passages above where the danger among the Thessalonians was so future an orientation that life and service in the present world were ignored, 2 Thess. 2:1–12 takes up a problem at the opposite end of the spectrum. Here we deal with those who were claiming that "the day of the Lord has come" already (2:2; see also 2 Tim. 2:18, where heretics are teaching the same sort of "overrealized eschatology"). The implication would be that the kingdom has already arrived in its fullness. Apparently a letter, purporting to be from Paul, had been circulating to this effect, shaking up the Thessalonians about "the coming of our Lord Jesus Christ and our assembling to meet him" (2:1–2). (The reference is to the parousia of Christ and the gathering of Christians for Christ, though there is no reference to meeting him in midair, as if at some "rapture.") Paul holds fast to the future side of Christianity in this case. He insists that the day of the Lord will come, but that it has not occurred yet, as anyone can see. And it will not occur until certain "signs" happen first. There then follows an elaborate compendium of apocalyptic materials, giving such "signs," in vv. 3–4, 6–12.

The gist of these verses in 2:3–12 is that "the rebellion" (perhaps a cosmic one) and the appearance of a mysterious figure opposed to God, variously called "the man of lawlessness" or "son of perdition" (vv. 3–4), must come *before* the day of the Lord. Since these things have not occurred as yet, the day of the Lord surely is not already here!

The imagery of the passage has received many interpretations through the centuries, often to fit current needs. In Paul's day the reference intended by the phrases "he who now restrains [the mystery of lawlessness]" (2:7) and "that which restrains the man of lawlessness" (see 2:6) may have been either to the Roman emperor and empire, respectively, who and which did hold back lawlessness and chaos; or to Paul and the preaching of the gospel, as having certain goals to attain before the end could come (compare Mark 13:10). But we do not know precisely Paul's interpretation. And, indeed, 2 Thessalonians may even have intended to use the phrases without precision. For the important thing about the passage is that apocalyptic of the most intensive kind was being employed, but with the purpose of cooling off some extremist eschatological speculations as to whether the end had already come.

The prevalence of so much apocalyptic material in the two relatively brief letters to the Thessalonians raises, incidentally, some much debated questions for students of the Bible. One is how 1 and 2 Thessalonians relate to each other, if the problem in the one is the *delay* of the parousia (for, according to 1 Thess. 4:13—5:11, Christians are dying, but Christ has not come) and the problem in the other is that people are saying that the day of the Lord is *already present* (2 Thess. 2:1–12). One solution is to claim that a change has taken place within the congregation between the letters, even perhaps that 2 Thessalonians was written before the document we term 1 Thessalonians (so that the shift is from "realized" to "imminent" eschatology). But in either case, would a change in situation have been so sudden, within a few weeks or months? Another is to claim that 2 Thessalonians was written to a different audience than 1 Thessalonians, either to a Jewish Christian segment of the congregation (as opposed to a Gentile Christian one) or even to some other place like Philippi. But most scholars have not been convinced by either of these proposals. A more widely accepted "solution" today is that 2 Thessalonians is the work of some disciple of Paul, facing a different situation, perhaps some years later, writing in the master apostle's name.

Such a decision about 2 Thessalonians points to another question: did Paul's own views on the second coming change over the years? His early letters make much of it. His later epistles, especially Colossians and Ephesians, virtually ignore the theme. Some scholars think that Paul's views evolved or "progressed" so that he gave up apocalyptic thought in his later years. A view with more to commend it, whatever one decides about the genuineness of this letter or that, is that Paul always preserved a "future side" to Christianity. But how much he emphasized this, and whether in apocalyptic terms or not, depended on the particular circumstances in which he wrote.

Always, however, the point stressed above must be kept in mind: Paul employed apocalyptic, but his aim in so doing needs to be taken into account. Just as "the devil can cite Scripture for his purpose," contrariwise an apostle can use apocalyptic for purposes that are nonapocalyptic. Two brief examples will further illustrate how Paul could employ patches of apocalyptic in his letters.

HOW PAUL USED APOCALYPTIC— FURTHER EXAMPLES

In 1 Corinthians 15 Paul is discussing the resurrection of the dead, perhaps speaking against people in Corinth who think they are already raised up into the life of the kingdom (above, pp. 333–34, 351). He begins with the article of faith about Jesus' death and resurrection (1 Cor. 15:3–5) as the heart of the gospel he received (15:1–11). Then he goes on to apply it to our resurrection, concerning which there had been some dispute among the Corinthians. First, Paul asserts *that* the dead do rise (15:12–34), and second, he discusses *how,* or with what sort of body, the resurrection life will occur (15:35–58).

In vv. 20–28 there is a rather apocalyptic picture of the "last things" in salvation history. The resurrection of Jesus is the starting point. He is the "first fruits" from the dead. At his parousia (coming), those who belong to Christ will rise. After "the end" (v. 24), following Christ's victory over all cosmic powers and enemies of God (including death), the kingdom will be turned over to God the Father.

Occasionally commentators have wanted to interpret v. 24 to mean "the end" of the resurrection, in the sense of its completion through a raising up of all dead persons, Christians and non-Christians alike. In that case, the order of events (in regard to the raising), would be,

1. Christ (already occurred);
2. "those who belong to Christ" (at the parousia, v. 23); and
3. the rest of humankind, after that.

(The translations by Ronald Knox and in *The Amplified Bible* may tend in this direction by reference to "the end" as "the [full] completion" of the resurrection.)

Some other commentators have sought to read into the sequence a period supposed to fit between Christ's "coming" and "the end," when Christ and Christians reign in a kingdom on earth. This would be a sort of "millennium" or "interim kingdom of Christ," of the kind found in Rev. 20:4–6. But the linguistic evidence for such a view in 1 Corinthians is slender, and the sense of the text is against it. Thus the vast majority of scholars see here Paul's usual teaching: Jesus was raised, those in Christ will be raised also—and the whole point of the passage is to stress

Christ's resurrection victory as the basis for the hope of our own future life in the kingdom. And that is good news, indeed.

Paul's most sweeping and majestic passage dealing with such a hope occurs in Rom. 18:19–22. It concerns the whole cosmos, groaning in bondage and waiting for deliverance to come at a time when we, the children of God, will enter into our heritage of liberty. Surely these four verses (possibly from an apocalyptic source) provide a glorious expression of concern and hope for the nonhuman, even the inanimate, world. (Luther presumably had Rom. 8:21 in mind when he said to his dog, "In heaven you too shall have a golden tail"!)

But the climax of Paul's paragraph says nothing whatsoever about our pets or animals, or about trees or any part of creation except the human part. The climax is, indeed, in express terms, limited to us "who have the first fruits of the Spirit" (v. 23), that is, us Christians. Paul's interest in citing this immense apocalyptic hope was to encourage Christian people in their present sufferings to live in hope, expectantly (vv. 18, 23–25).

Here we have a very important clue for the interpretation of apocalyptic materials. Paul used apocalyptic to express the future side of the gospel, as hope, and as exhortation to persevere in the world in hope, with faith and love. We may now test this insight on that most apocalyptic of all New Testament books, the Revelation of St. John.

29

The Apocalypse of John: Preaching in Times of Persecution

THE BOOK OF REVELATION has had a checkered history. In the ancient church it suffered from both friends and enemies. From enthusiastic friends, because it was often in heretical circles, like those of the Montanists, that the book was popular. (The Montanists were a group that claimed new revelations from the Spirit and the gift of prophecy, especially through a man named Montanus and his female assistants, shortly after A.D. 150.) And from enemies, because the chiliasts, who stressed a thousand-year reign of Christ and of the Christian martyrs between Christ's return and final victory (20:1–7), often caused church leaders, especially in the West, to oppose and reject the entire book. ("Chiliasm" comes from the Greek word for "thousand." "Millennium" is from the Latin word for the same number. Hence the proponents of such ideas are "chiliasts" or "millennialists" or "millenarians.")

Moreover, the contents of Revelation seemed to contradict other parts of the New Testament. The detailed signs for the end, cited for example in 8:7–11, appeared inconsistent with the teaching that the day of the Lord would come suddenly, "like a thief in the night" (1 Thess. 5:2). It was, therefore, only with difficulty that Revelation won a place in the New Testament canon. One result of this has been poor transmission of its Greek text. Revelation was less frequently copied by scribes, so its text has been more poorly preserved than most other books of the New Testament.

Luther speaks for many when he said that his spirit could not "accommodate itself to the book"; it seemed to him neither apostolic nor prophetic, and not to "teach Christ" the way most of the New Testament does. But Luther went further than most disgruntled readers: he relegated Revelation to a lower rank in the New Testament than most other books and did not even assign it page numbers in his 1522 German New Testament!

APPROACHING A MYSTERIOUS BOOK

It is possible, however, to strip away some of the mystery about the book. A significant first step is to put the book squarely in its likely historical setting. The time is about A.D. 95. The Roman emperor Domitian was claiming to be Lord and God and was thus coming into conflict with the Christian movement. Persecution loomed. The place where Revelation took shape is an island called Patmos, off the coast of Turkey. Here the author of Revelation is in exile for his witness to the kingdom (not of Caesar but) of God (1:9). His audience consists of Christians in seven representative churches on the mainland of Asia Minor (1:11). The writer's name is John (1:1, 4, 9; 22:8). Although later tradition has identified him with John the son of Zebedee, to whom also the Fourth Gospel has been traditionally credited, this claim is dubious, for the styles and thought of Revelation and of the Fourth Gospel are quite different. The author of this apocalypse was probably an otherwise unknown Jewish Christian prophet, of local authority, whose name was a common one, John.

A second helpful step toward understanding is to remind ourselves that the book is an apocalypse, with all the usual features of such literature (see above, p. 27, and under "Characteristics of Apocalyptic Compared with Prophecy" in chap. 20). Clearly this book reflects these characteristics, as Christians, under pressure of persecution, look for God's supernatural redemption to come soon, bringing them life in the new heaven and the new earth. Other features typical of apocalyptic literature are abundantly present: the symbolic use of colors (especially gold, red, and white), sounds, dramatic actions, and even numbers. (Note the code use of the number "666" for "the beast" at 13:18, *six* denoting all that is sinister and evil; and the use of the sacred number "7" to indicate totality and perfection, as in Rev. 1:20; 3:1; 5:1–6.)

A third necessary step is to get an overview of the book's contents. Opinions differ among interpreters, but there is broad agreement on a basic outline for the book in eight sections:

    I.   Prologue, chap. 1
    II.   Letters to the Seven Churches in Asia Minor, chaps. 2—3
    III. The Vision of Heaven, chaps. 4—5
    IV. The Three Series of Judgments, chaps. 6—16

    V.   The Destruction of Babylon (Rome), Oppressor of God's People, 17:1—19:10

   VI.   The Victory of the Word of God, including Christ's thousand-year reign and Satan's final defeat, 19:11—20:10

  VII.   The New Heaven and Earth, a New Jerusalem, the city of the Lord God and the Lamb, the place of life after the last judgment, 20:11—22:5

 VIII.   Epilogue, closing warnings, beatitudes, and exhortations, 22:6–21

We may fill in some of this structure with more detail and then offer some comments about it.

    I.   Prologue
       A. Title and introduction, 1:1–3
       B. Salutation and praise to the risen Christ, 1:4–8
       C. John's vision of the risen Christ, 1:9–20

   II.   Letters to the Seven Churches
       Two are praised unreservedly, Smyrna and Philadelphia. Three are approved but criticized—Ephesus, Pergamum, and Thyatira. One, at Sardis, is severely rebuked, and the church at Laodicea is utterly condemned.

  III.   The Vision of Heaven
       A. Vision of God in majesty, 4:1–11
       B. Vision of the Lamb and the scroll with seven seals, 5:1–14
       The Lamb, Christ, who was slain to ransom people from every tribe and tongue to make them a kingdom, is the one who opens God's plan for the world and who indeed has carried it out.

  IV.   The Three Series of Judgments

7 Seals (chap. 6)	7 Trumpets (chaps. 8—9)	7 Bowls (Plagues) (chaps. 15—16)

1. Conquest, 6:1–2
2. War, 6:3–4
3. Famine, 6:5–6
4. Death, 6:7–8
5. Souls crying for judgment, 6:9–11

6. *Earth*quake, with signs in the heavens, the great day of wrath, 6:12–17	1. Hail, fire on *earth*, 8:7 2. Fire on the *sea*, 8:8 3. *Rivers* poisoned, 8:10–11 4. *Sun*, moon, stars darkened, 8:12	1. On *earth*, sores on men, 16:2 2. *Sea* becomes like blood, 16:3 3. *Rivers* become like blood, 16:4 4. *Sun* scorches men, 16:8–9
7. Silence, 8:1	5. Invasion by locusts from the underworld, 9:1–12 (= the first woe) 6. Slaughter by four angels from the *Euphrates* and their cavalry, 9:13–19	5. Pain, sores, darkness on the throne of the beast, 16:10–11 6. *Euphrates* River dried up; three demonic spirits, 16:12–14 7. "It is done," earthquake, Babylon destroyed, 16:17–21; cf. chaps. 17—18
	7. "The kingdom of the world has become the kingdom of our Lord and of his Christ," 11:15	

As these three series of judgments stand, they give the impression of one disaster following another, as if twenty-one steps in all. There is, however, also a certain parallelism in parts of the sequences (note the italicized words). One further gets the impression that repetition is being used to heighten the effect, the feeling of judgment.

Moreover, other patterns are imposed and additional materials added to this threefold repetition of seven judgments. For while this fourth section of Revelation covers chapters 6 through 16, only a part of these chapters is used for listing the twenty-one judgments. One obvious

One of the seven churches addressed in the Book of Revelation was Sardis
(3:1–6), northeast of Ephesus. Amid the towering columns of a pagan temple a
small Christian church was later built.

subpattern is that of the "three woes" (cf. 8:13). These woes comprise
Trumpet 5; plus apparently Trumpet 6, with related catastrophes in 9:20
through 11:13 (cf. 9:12 and 11:14 for reference to "the second woe");
plus perhaps Trumpet 7 or chapter 13, about the dragon and the beast
from the sea. The patterns coalesce and become hard to follow.

Complicating this structure with its catalogue of disasters even more
are the efforts of the author to provide relief from these grim prospects by
some upbeat scenes. The writer inserts a number of "parenthetical
interludes," as if to say, "Here is hope amid all the suffering and gore."
There are four such interludes interspersed in these chapters:

A. the marking of the saints with God's seal and their ultimate
triumph, chapter 7;

B. the angel and the "little scroll" (chap. 10), and the resurrection and exaltation of two martyred witnesses (11:1–13), as harbingers of victory;

C. the woman, the child, and the dragon, a way of describing in code language Christ's victory for the church, chapter 12;

D. the Lamb and his redeemed on Mount Zion, chapter 14.

Our hope kept alive by those appended scenes (which offer glimpses of good news), we move on to the denouement in sections V through VIII, chapters 17—21, final victory and vindication.

All in all, though at times confusing, the details of this masterful construction never cease to amaze, even if some of the author's plans (like the "three woes") were not finally and precisely carried through. There are many subtle inner relationships. Thus, the "mark of the beast" on his followers (13:16–17) is a devilish parody of the seal God places on the forehead of his chosen ones (7:3–4). The grisly "supper of God" in 19:17–21, feeding on the flesh of rebel kings, is a grim counterpart to the Lord's Supper (3:20; 22:17). The bride of the Lamb (21:9) is a contrast to the great harlot (17:1).

Throughout the book there is a general movement from "things as they are" (persecution, apathy, apostasy within the churches, as well as some bright spots of faithful witnessing, chaps. 1—3) to "things as they will be" in the future apocalyptic plan (chaps. 6—22). The link between the present and the future is God and his Son, the Lamb, whose blood redeemed those to be saved. This is depicted in the magnificent visions of chapters 4 and 5. God and Christ will bring about the promised victory, and his people must stand firm in faith.

SOME CHRISTIAN FEATURES

"Apocalypse" means "revelation" or "unveiling." The Book of Revelation is an apocalypse, not "of John," as we conventionally call it, but *"of Jesus Christ ..."* (1:1; Paul used exactly the same phrase at Gal. 1:12). It is an apocalypse, a revelation, which God gave Christ to show to his servants through John (1:1–2). While the Book of Revelation conforms to many apocalyptic conventions, this Christian apocalypse has some singular features of its own.

We note three distinctive characteristics. One is the way the Old Testament is used; another is the emphasis upon Jesus Christ; and the third is the inclusion of much liturgical material from the early church.

The author of Revelation employs the Old Testament extensively, and his book is more saturated with such references, usually from the Hebrew, than any other book in the New Testament. Of its 404 verses, some 278 have been said to refer in one way or another to the Old Testament. But the references are not formal citations, as with Matthew's "formula quotations" or even as in Paul. Rather they are phrases, ideas, and allusions, often with a twist that gives them new meaning.

For example, the calamities poured forth from the bowls of the angels in chapter 16 remind us of the plagues of Moses' day in Egypt (Exodus 7—10). Boils on man and beast in Egypt become here sores on all persons who have the mark of the beast! Locusts, frogs, and water-turned-to-blood occur in both lists (see above, pp. 144–47, for Moses' plagues in Egypt). Of course, the parallel is not quite exact, for there were ten plagues, and only seven bowls or vials of wrath. But decoded, and in terms of biblical theology, the hint is that Yahweh who defeated Pharaoh god will also through Christ overcome the Dragon (a significant term in ancient Near Eastern mythology) and his beast. (To let the secret out of the bag, the beast-with-the-seven-heads-and-ten-horns, 17:7–14, represents Rome and its emperors, most likely from Augustus to Nero or Domitian.) Even the place, according to Rev. 16:16, for the last climactic battle, "Armageddon," comes from the Old Testament. In Hebrew, *har Mĕgiddôn,* is the "mount of Megiddo," the site of several decisive battles in Israel's history, including Josiah's defeat by Pharaoh Neco of Egypt (2 Kings 23:29; cf. 9:27; Judges 5:19). Hence from the Greek form of a Hebrew place name, "Armageddon" entered English (without an initial "h" as in its Latin form).

Another striking illustration, which introduces an important shift of meaning, is the use of the phrase "I am the first and the last." In the Old Testament, Yahweh speaks thus at Isa. 41:4; 44:6; and 48:12. In Revelation it is the risen Christ who says this (1:17). There is an equivalent phrase, "I am the Alpha and the Omega," associated with God (1:8; 21:6), but Christ appears to say this also (22:13). The shift in meaning is profound: what Yahweh alone could say in the Old Testament comes from the lips both of God and of the risen Christ in the New Testament. In Rev. 2:8, "the first and the last" is also used of Christ.

This last example leads to the next distinctive and even more significant feature in Revelation, namely, the way the author uses the Old Testament to describe Jesus Christ. We expect that Revelation 4, with its picture of God enthroned, will draw from the Old Testament (it especially employs Ezek. 1:26 and Isaiah 6). But we do not necessarily expect that Revelation 5, with its picture of Jesus, should do this. Yet it does so repeatedly. We have Jesus there described as "Lion of the tribe of Judah" (cf. Gen. 49:9), "Root of David" (Isa. 11:1, 10), and a lamb with seven eyes (compare Rev. 5:6 with Zech. 4:10). There is a concatenation of phrases from the Hebrew Scriptures, christologically applied.

Things go a step further when we observe the number of times Revelation applies to Jesus Christ certain Old Testament phrases originally used of Yahweh. We have already noted the use of "first and last." There are further examples in the almost surrealistic description of Jesus Christ in Rev. 1:12–16. Here we have the images of hair "white as white wool," eyes "like a flame of fire," and a voice "like the sound of many waters." These were originally Old Testament phrases to describe God (see Dan. 7:9–10; Ezek. 1:24 and 43:2). By transferring these Old Testament images for God to Jesus Christ, the author of Revelation is making the common confession of the New Testament, "Jesus Christ is Lord."

One final example of such "reverse English" (or, properly, Hebrew and Greek). At Rev. 19:13 Jesus the Word of God is described as coming "clad in a robe dipped in blood." This is properly identified as an allusion to Isa. 63:1–2. In Isaiah it is God coming from Edom in garments crimson with blood. But there is a twist. In Isaiah it is the blood of enemies; in Revelation, since Jesus is the one who ransomed us by his blood (5:9 and 1:5), it is his own blood poured out for those who were once enemies that stains his robe. The Old Testament is here being used christologically.

Finally, as to the third distinctive feature, Revelation embodies much liturgical material, such as its wealth of hymns. For example, at 4:11 and 5:9–10 there are songs about the Lamb's worthiness. These inspired Horatius Bonar's later lines,

Blessing and honor and glory and pow'r,
Wisdom and riches and strength evermore,
Give ye to Him who our battle hath won,
Whose is the kingdom, the crown, and the throne!

There are also 15:3–4 (a new "Song of Moses," to celebrate God's mighty deeds), and 19:1–3 and 6–8 (a "Hallelujah Chorus"). These hymns likely come out of early Christian worship and are inserted by the author to convey the mood of triumph amid scenes of despair. This usage is a further Christian touch, which departs from the normal pattern in apocalyptic.

Another element in Revelation that makes the book more than just an apocalypse is the collection of seven letters in chapters 2—3. These owe more in their structure and content to the early Christian epistle form than to the apocalyptic heritage. What is more, they depict the church and speak to it in a remarkably frank way. Each letter has the same structure:

1. Address to the church's "angel" (either its pastor or more likely its guardian spirit with God);
2. The authoritative assertion, "The words of him who . . .," and then some appropriate description of Christ;
3. The "body" of the letter: praise, exhortation, or reproof for the church in its situation;
4. Conclusion: admonition to give heed, and the promise of reward.

In style, these letters have nothing in common with the rest of Revelation. But in content, they speak the same message. For they too address Christians in the current crisis, where they are threatened with persecution so great that believers may fall away; there is warning of judgment to come and encouragement to stand firm. We see also in these letters why some of the extreme forms of apocalyptic will be needed later on in the book: certain churches are in a bad way, for sin and indifference abound. Christians need to hear the full measure of God's message for the day. They must hear both judgment and grace.

These letters, like the three distinctive features noted earlier—the use of the Old Testament, the emphasis upon Jesus Christ, and the presence of liturgical materials—constitute an important clue for assessing the whole Book of Revelation. They help to answer the question, What was the author trying to do?

THE PURPOSE: REVELATION TO WHAT END?

Quite simply, for all the devices and techniques employed, John of Patmos was seeking to preach God's message to a very specific situation, in his own day and to congregations he knew. Revelation is not a secret plan for subsequent centuries of history. Attempts by some to apply it to predict current events have regularly failed. It is not a literary garden to be allegorized to fit our own meanings, as others have often attempted. The book addressed its own day. It deals with what "soon" must come to pass (1:1; cf. 1:3, "The time is near"). It thus refers to the impending crisis caused by demands that Christians in western Asia Minor, about A.D. 95, worship Domitian, instead of, or along with, Jesus Christ. Jesus' lordship was thus at stake, God's sovereignty threatened.

John took all sorts of material at hand—the letter form; beatitudes (cf. 1:3; 14:13; 16:15; 19:9; 20:6; 22:7 and 14—the seven promises in the book that begin with "blessed"); the Old Testament; hymnody; and apocalyptic from the past—plus visions of his own, and wove these all together to speak artfully to his day. "Stand fast," he says, "God will soon intervene."

John was wrong, of course, in terms of looking for an immediate end to human history. He was right that Rome would fall, eventually, and that God's cause would triumph in the present crisis of his audience. In such a time one sees more intently, even if the long-term perspective may be blurred. The permanent value of the book is that it preaches God's victory in Christ in the face of an imminent and specific danger. "Hold on!" Christians in subsequent crises have found strength in the book and its cryptic imagery.

The Book of Revelation found the most urgent message for its day to be "Stand fast and wait for the Lord's deliverance." It used apocalyptic devices to deliver that message. But for all the visions, numbers, sounds, colors, and sevenfold sequences of disasters, it possessed and continues to set forth an "eternal gospel." (See the vivid summary scene in 14:6–7, even if the gospel there is put in somewhat negative terms.) At its heart is Christ, crucified, our deliverer, judge, and Lord. That he has won the victory and will triumph again, the book never tires of saying. The mysterious chapter 12 describes Jesus' victory in the language of myth— first in terms of a child (Christ), born of a woman (Israel as God's people, 12:1–6); then (12:7–12) in terms of a "war in heaven," where the dragon is also bested. But in each case the real victory was won "by the blood of the Lamb" (12:11). That is, it was won at the cross. And God's people will prove victorious through Christ in the present struggle with Satan's minions on earth, if only they hold true to Christ.

In this version of the gospel, is there any room for "the kingdom"? Decidedly. Good news is several times put in "kingdom" terms. For example, there is the assertion that Christ, by his blood shed on the cross, out of love, to free us from our sins, has "made us a kingdom, priests to his God and Father" (1:6 and 5:10, echoing the hope of Exod. 19:6). To be a Christian means to "share . . . in Jesus the tribulation and the kingdom and the patient endurance" (1:9). Over against God's kingdom stands a devilish parody, the kingdom of the beast and his earthly emperors. (This does not refer to all governments or even Rome for all time, but rather to Rome of the day, where the ruler sought to be worshiped in God's place; cf. 16:2; 17:12, 17, 18.) The Apocalypse can triumphantly, however, assert, "Now . . . the kingdom of our God and the authority of his Christ have come, for the accuser . . . has been thrown down" (12:10). The message reverberates,

The kingdom of the world has become the kingdom
   of our Lord and of his Christ,
and he shall reign for ever and ever.

(11:15)

He shall reign! That is good news; that is "kingdom" news.

Revelation makes the tidings of the Old Testament new (21:5). God reigns, has reigned, and will rule—in Christ.

30
The Gospel as Life: John's Writings

IN THE GOSPEL AND three epistles of John we move into a different world from anything noted thus far in Scripture. In John's situation we hear the gospel being proclaimed as "eternal life."

True, there are links and associations with other parts of the Bible, but the Johannine writings present us with "the word of life" (1 John 1:1) in a way in which no other portion of the Bible does. The First Epistle of John was written to "proclaim to you the eternal life which was with the Father and was made manifest to us" (1:2). The Fourth Gospel was written

> that you may believe that Jesus is the Christ, the Son of God,
> and that believing you may have life in his name.
> (John 20:31)

Traditionally the Fourth Gospel, the medium-length letter we call 1 John, and the two little notes which follow it in the canon (2 and 3 John) have been associated with the Apocalypse of John (see chap. 29, above). This association rests on the theory that John, the beloved disciple, one of the Twelve, wrote them all. But the mood and content of the other Johannine writings are manifestly different from the Book of Revelation. For John's Gospel and the epistles nowhere reflect a series of impending catastrophes, with the end of the world about to come, as in the Apocalypse. The mood is rather one of calm. Christ is in command throughout, and not just at the parousia. Attention is directed inward, to the community of believers, more than to the world raging outside.

We have already seen that the man who wrote Revelation was a Jewish Christian prophet, with considerable authority in the parts of Asia Minor around Ephesus (see above, p. 361). We shall see in the discussion below

371

that there are grave questions about identifying the beloved disciple with John the son of Zebedee and as the author of the Fourth Gospel. So while there are some themes common to Revelation and the other Johannine writings, there are good reasons for emphasizing the differences in contents between them and the Apocalypse. Thus we suggest for the Johannine Gospel and epistles an authorship other than John the seer or prophet who wrote the last book in our New Testament collection.

These Johannine writings (minus the Apocalypse) also have affinities with Paul and the Easter Gospel he received and in turn advanced (see above, chaps. 26–27). All these documents emphasize the death of Jesus and his lordly status. Indeed, John, in telling of the life of Jesus on earth, seems to impart to the whole ministry something of the glory and power of the risen Lord. John's Gospel could be called a meditation on Paul's words, "You know the grace of our Lord Jesus Christ,

> that though he was rich, yet for your sake he became poor,
> so that by his poverty you might become rich.
>
> (2 Cor. 8:9)

John's Gospel reflects such an experience with Jesus Christ: "from his fulness have we all received, grace upon grace" (1:16). Yet Jesus strides through the pages of this Gospel by John as anything but "poor" and in "poverty." For while he can be weary and thirsty (John 4:6–7) and can even cry with people who are hurting from the tragedies of life (11:35), Jesus always remains in command of situations (cf. 4:10, 13–14, 16–19, 25–26). His own death is no tragedy, but represents life laid down according to God's will and plan (10:17–18). To the crucifixion Jesus carries his own cross; he does not need someone to help him (19:17; compare Mark 15:21). His death is a triumph because God's work for him on earth is successfully finished (19:30).

There are other features in John that have their counterparts in Paul, besides this emphasis on the crucified and risen Lord. We must note, however, that certain key Pauline ideas are lacking, or at least not stressed, in John. Thus, for example, "justification" is not prominent in the Fourth Gospel ("righteousness" or "justification" occurs only in 16:8–11). (We shall see, however, that the courtroom setting at the judgment, which Paul assumed, is reflected in John.) "Grace" occurs only in the passage already noted above (1:14, 16–17). "Faith" is mentioned as a noun only at 1 John 5:4 (though the verb "believe" is common). "Justification by grace through faith" is thus not a Johannine way of expressing the good news. Perhaps, however, one of Paul's alternate ways of expression, to be "in Christ," does have a counterpart in John 15, in

Jesus' words about the disciples as branches who must abide in Christ, the true vine. All in all, however, the Johannine writings betray no direct dependence upon Paul. They represent a different way of expressing the gospel.

Finally, there are also links between the Fourth Gospel and the Synoptics. As in the cases of the Apocalypse and Paul, we are here again in John, for the most part, in a world which differs from that of Mark, Matthew, and Luke. True as it is that all of the first four books in the New Testament are "gospels" so far as literary type is concerned, John is a different sort of gospel. It is separated from the first three in the canon in structure, style, and themes. This does not mean that John and the Synoptics do not overlap often; they do. They share an emphasis on the passion of Jesus, for example, and report some of the same miracle stories such as the Feeding of the Five Thousand (John 6:1–15; cf. Mark 6:32–44; Matt. 14:13–21; Luke 9:10–17; this is the only miracle story in all four Gospels). But it does mean that John, even when telling of the same event, will do it in his own way, as witness to Jesus for the situation in John's own day.

OUTLINES, GEOGRAPHICAL
AND THEOLOGICAL

Nowhere can this difference from the Synoptics be seen more clearly than in the basic outline for the story of Jesus. The structure in Mark and Matthew is familiar to us: introduction (in Matthew's case, some nativity stories too); Jesus' ministry in Galilee; the journey to Jerusalem; then the passion, death, and resurrection of Jesus. Luke's sequence (after introduction and infancy material) is Galilee, the Samaritan or travel section, and Jerusalem. Thus, the Synoptic Gospels picture Jesus going just once to Jerusalem during his ministry, for the festival of the Passover, at which time he is put to death. (Luke 2:41–51 describes also how Jesus went to Jerusalem as a twelve-year-old boy.) But John has a completely different outline. It sees Jesus in Jerusalem four or five times in the course of his ministry, so that there is a shifting back and forth between Judea and Galilee. What is more, all of these trips to Jerusalem seem timed to coincide with a Jewish festival, and what Jesus says or does sometimes relates to that festival and its themes.

The following passages should be consulted to see John's geographical (and festival) outline:

John 2:13, 23—"Passover." After an initial ministry in *Galilee* (1:43—2:12) Jesus cleanses the temple in *Jerusalem* and engages in dialogue with a member of the Sanhedrin, named Nicodemus.

This is followed by a period of baptizing in Judea (3:22; 4:1–2) and of witnessing in Samaria (4:3–45), then return to *Galilee* (4:46–54).

5:1—"a feast of the Jews" (Passover, scholars suggest, or Tabernacles or New Year's in the fall). Jesus heals a lame man at the Pool of Bethzatha (or Bethesda, or Bethsaida—manuscripts have different spellings), near the Sheep Gate, in northeast *Jerusalem*. After a controversy about his authority to heal on the Sabbath, we find him at 6:1 again by the Sea of Tiberius or of *Galilee*. The Feeding of the Five Thousand, which is now narrated, together with a discourse by Jesus on the bread of life, is dated by a reference to "the Passover, the feast of the Jews," which was "at hand" (6:4). This would be the second Passover during Jesus' public ministry.

7:2—"Tabernacles," a feast in September or October. Jesus, after first saying he will not go to *Jerusalem* for the feast, does go up in private (7:10), and on the last day of Tabernacles speaks publicly about "living water" (7:38). In spite of opposition from the chief priests and Pharisees (7:45–52), he speaks about himself as the light of the world (chap. 8)[1] and heals a blind man (chap. 9), still in Jerusalem, as the reference (9:7) proves when it refers to the Pool of Siloam (in the southeast section of the city). The discourse about the Good Shepherd (chap. 10) must take place also in Jerusalem, as no change of place is indicated. John 10:22 finds him still in Jerusalem at the time of the December feast which commemorated the rededication of the temple in 164 B.C. (At that time Judas Maccabeus had recovered it from the Syrians. This celebration is known today as Hanukkah.) Because the Jews sought to stone Jesus for his claims to be "one" with the Father (10:30), Jesus withdrew "across the Jordan," to the other side of the river, into *Perea*, near where John had baptized (10:40; cf. 3:23).

11:55; 12:1, 12; 13:1; 18:28; 19:31—"the Passover of the Jews." After a visit to Bethany, east of Jerusalem, where Jesus raised from the dead Lazarus, the brother of Mary and Martha (chap. 11), Jesus withdrew to a wilderness town "called Ephraim" (11:54). The location of Ephraim we do not know, though the reference may be to a place some fifteen miles north-northeast of Jerusalem. He comes back to Bethany (chap. 12), makes his entry into *Jerusalem*, hailed by festival crowds (12:12), but is crucified before the citizens of Jerusalem eat their Passover meal. According to John, Jesus died just as the Passover lambs were being slain at the temple for the feast that night. He is thus literally "the lamb of God" (1:29).

This analysis of John yields four festival trips to Jerusalem, five if we count Tabernacles (7:2) and the feast of the Dedication (10:22) separately. To this pattern of "Galilee-Jerusalem" can be added two more instances. Jesus first appears on the scene in his ministry in Judea (1:19 refers to Jerusalem; 1:29, 35–42) and then moves to Galilee (1:43). At the end of the Gospel, the resurrection takes place in Jerusalem, of course (chap. 20), but there is an added chapter (21) about how Jesus also revealed himself in Galilee.

Overlaying this geographical outline, which shifts back and forth between Galilee and Jerusalem, can also be seen a "theological outline." The Fourth Gospel is, like Synoptics and Paul, concerned with declaring who Jesus is. It accomplishes this by a structure that runs like this:

Prologue about the Word (in Greek, *Logos*), Jesus Christ (1:1–18).

I. *The Work of Jesus* as he comes from the Father, into the world (1:19—12:50). The ministry of Jesus, as John tells of it, stresses his deeds or miracles as "signs" and his words in terms of long discourses (see below).

II. *The Return of Jesus to the Father* (13:1—20:29).

The passion-resurrection account is expanded with discourses, especially about "the Paraclete" who is to come when Jesus goes away (see below).

Epilogue in Galilee (chap. 21), a postresurrection appearance in Galilee, after the three appearances in Jerusalem in chapter 20.

This sequence witnesses to Jesus as one who was with God, who came in the flesh (1:14), among us, in Galilee and Jerusalem; as the Son of man who is lifted up (3:14), not only upon a cross but also in exaltation; and as the Lord who goes away but sends the Paraclete or Comforter in his stead (16:7). In all this, John's Gospel is often closer to the thought of the early church and Paul than to the picture of Jesus in the Synoptics.

This different way of looking at Jesus, set within the broader spectrum of God's glory, has over the centuries become a favorite of many Christians. John gives us a witness to Jesus as the Christ in a way that is all-encompassing. But alert readers frequently are aware of problems in relating John to the other Gospels. For example, was Jesus' public ministry just one year long (as in the Synoptics) or did it cover three Passovers or more (as in John)? When was the temple cleansing? Was the raising of

Lazarus (John 11) the event which sealed Jesus' fate, or was it Jesus' disputes with the scribes and Pharisees (Mark 2:1—3:6; 11:27—12:40)? John and the Synoptics leave different impressions at these points.

JOHN'S DISTINCTIVE STYLE

John differs in style too. In the Synoptics, Jesus speaks in parables or in short memorable sayings. His words often have a parallelism typical of Hebrew poetry or the repetitiveness typical of the Old Testament wisdom style of literature. (See, for example, the Antitheses of the Sermon on the Mount, Matt. 5:21–48; above, pp. 291–93.) Only on occasion does Jesus give a longer speech (Mark 13; the five discourses in Matthew). Even so, these Synoptic collections of his teachings differ in tone from the discourses in John (cf. 3:5–21; 5:17–47; 6:22–59; chaps. 10 and 15). In John, Jesus' tone seems more elevated, less earthly. His words soar majestically, they strike some as almost mystical. He is a revealer in the way the Jesus of the parables never is.

To illustrate this matter of style in the Fourth Gospel, we may begin with the fact that, whereas in Mark, Matthew, and Luke "parables" are Jesus' characteristic way of communication, in John's Gospel the term "parable" is never used of him.[2] Not only is the word missing, but in John there are no examples of story-analogies that begin, "the kingdom of God is like. . . ."

Another curious fact is the usage of the Hebrew word *amēn*. In the Synoptics, Jesus uses it, as no one else of his day did, at the start of an important declaration, "Amen, I say to you . . ." (usually rendered in English, "Verily" or "Truly I say to you . . . ," cf. Mark 10:15; Matt. 6:2). In John, however, the Hebrew word is regularly doubled, "Amen, amen, I say to you . . ." (cf. 1:51; 3:3: "Truly, truly . . .").

We can therefore readily recognize as characteristically "Johannine" in style the discourse in chapter 10, which begins "Truly, truly I say to you . . ." and goes on to develop a "figure" of speech about the sheepfold and the true or good shepherd. Read John 10:1–6, then 7–18; this passage is as close as John's Gospel comes to a parable. Yet it seems to many readers to be verging on an allegory, where many details take on literal significance: Jesus is the Good Shepherd, the sheepfold is the church, his flock; there are false teachers which threaten it.

This last example introduces us to the fact that in the Fourth Gospel Jesus' discourses are about himself in a way his teachings never are in the Synoptics. In the other Gospels Jesus proclaims, above all else, the kingship of God. In John he speaks of himself and his mission in relation to the Father.

Nowhere in John is this emphasis on who Jesus is clearer than in the "I am" sayings. Seven times he speaks of himself in the first-person singular with some descriptive noun in the predicate:

6:35	"I am the bread of life" (cf. 6:51, "the living bread")
8:12	"I am the light of the world" (9:5 also)
10:7, 9	"I am the door [of the sheep]"
10:11, 14	"I am the good shepherd"
11:25	"I am the resurrection and the life"
14:6	"I am the way, and the truth, and the life"
15:1, 5	"I am the [true] vine"

There is an extent to which these amazing statements—and one cannot help noting how often they speak of life or a source of life—are paralleled in the Synoptics by statements beginning with "I came . . ." (for example, Mark 2:17, "I came not to call the righteous, but sinners," or Mark 10:45, especially if the phrase there, "Son of man," is a way of saying " 'I' also came not to be served but to serve . . ."). But there is no parallel in the Synoptics to these sevenfold claims on Jesus' lips which appear in John.

Further, there are some nine examples where Jesus employs "I am" without any word in the predicate. That is, simply, "I am." Sometimes this means nothing more than "it is I," as when, to the frightened disciples on the boat in a storm at sea, Jesus, walking on the water, says, "It is I [literally, "I am"]; do not be afraid" (John 6:20). Such usage can be found in the Synoptics (cf. Mark 6:50). But when Jesus says, in John's Gospel (8:58), "Truly, truly, I say to you, before Abraham was, I am," we seem to have a claim that he antedates Abraham and takes priority over him. But there is more.

In the Old Testament the "I am" formula was used as a self-identification of Yahweh. Compare Exod. 3:14–15, ". . . I AM has sent me to you," Moses was to say to Israel. In Deutero-Isaiah the phrase is especially prominent: "I, I am the Lord"; "I am He"; God is the great "I am" (Isa. 43:11; 41:4; 43:13). Against this background, Jesus is claiming nothing less than deity when he says, "You will die in your sins unless you believe that I am he" (John 8:24). See also 8:28 and 13:19 with reference to his passion. In 18:5 occurs a stunning incident. Here what seems a simple self-identification to the soldiers who come to arrest him in the garden of Gethsemane, "I am [Jesus]," has a deeper implication. It causes the soldiers to fall back in awe (18:6), as if before the divine.

Putting all these observations together, we can see in John a series of "revelation discourses" where Jesus reveals primarily that he is the revealer of God! There is often a pattern: an "I am" saying, followed by a call and some promise or warning. To illustrate:

Chapter 10	*Chapter 15*
"I am the door" and "the good shepherd" (vv. 7, 9, 11, 14);	cf. 15:1, 5, "I am the true vine";
Warning against false shepherds (vv. 8, 10, 12, 13);	cf. 15:2, 6, branches that bear no fruit are taken away;
Promise: "I lay down my life for the sheep ... there shall be one flock, one shepherd" (vv. 15, 16).	cf. 15:3–4, 7–9, "if you abide in me ..., ask ..., and it shall be done for you."

The Johannine discourses, moreover, heighten the place of Jesus christologically. John may even call him "the only God." See 1:18 in the textual variant in the RSV footnote, or in the NEB note, "himself God, the nearest to the Father's heart." This reading is supported by the earliest papyrus copies of John recently discovered. The climax of the Fourth Gospel comes when Thomas confesses Jesus as "My Lord and my God" (20:28).

John's discourses thus mix warnings and promises in presenting the message of the Son who reveals God. These warnings and promises are distinct in style from the teachings of Jesus in the other Gospels.

THE KINGDOM OF GOD AND
ETERNAL LIFE

John's themes also differ considerably from those of the Synoptics. John's is the Gospel of life, proclaiming Jesus as the one who reveals the Father. What happens, then, to the theme of the kingdom of God, which was so prominent in the Synoptics as the central message of Jesus?

The kingdom as a subject does not disappear in John, but it is muted. An example occurs in Jesus' nighttime conversation in chapter 3 with Nicodemus, a ruler of the Jews, a member of their Sanhedrin (governing council), who eventually became enough of a disciple to stand up for Jesus (7:50–52) and who helped bury Jesus (19:39). In their first dialogue Jesus tells him, in an "Amen-saying," that

unless one is born anew [the Greek can also mean "from above," from God], a person cannot see the kingdom of God. (3:3, au. trans.)

Two verses later Jesus enlarges upon the thought:

> Truly, truly, I say to you, unless one is born of water-and-the-Spirit [a reference to baptism], a person cannot enter the kingdom of God. (3:5, au. trans.)

These verses remind one of the Synoptic sayings about entering the kingdom (see Matt. 18:3). John 3:3 is a call for radical renewal. Its expansion in 3:5 tells how one is born "from above" (or anew), namely by water-baptism and the gift of the Spirit that accompanies it. All this ties in with the detail in John that Jesus' disciples engaged in water-baptism (3:22; 4:2). But when we add the Johannine teaching that the Spirit would not be given until Jesus was "glorified" (i.e., on the cross, see 7:39), then 3:5 seems more to refer to baptism accompanied by the coming of the Holy Spirit after Easter in the early church. These verses would be evidence that the Johannine community or church viewed baptism as grounds for seeing, and entering into, God's kingdom. But they are the only two places in John where the precise phrase "kingdom of God" occurs.

The one other cluster of references to the kingdom comes during the trial of Jesus before Pilate in chapter 18. Jesus speaks of *"my* kingship" three times, meaning a "kingdom of Jesus Christ." Connected are references to Jesus as a king. Pilate asked, "Are you the King of the Jews?" (18:33). Jesus eventually answers, "My kingship is not of this world; if my kingship were of this world, my servants would fight . . .; but my kingship is not from the world" (18:36). When Pilate muses, "So you are a king?" Jesus does not quite accept his use of the term: "You say that I am a king. For this I was born, and for this I have come into the world, to bear witness to the truth. Every one who is of the truth hears my voice" (18:37). Pilate breaks off the dialogue with his famous retort, "What is truth?" and goes back to calling Jesus "the King of the Jews" (18:39).

Scattered throughout the Fourth Gospel are other references to Jesus as a king (1:49; 12:13, 15; 19:3, 12, 14–15, 19, 21) and even to an attempt to make him an earthly king by force (6:15). This attempt Jesus rejected. Underlying these passages in chapter 18 and elsewhere is a feeling that Jesus truly is a king, but not in a human, physical sense. Pilate misunderstands, as do all who want to make of Jesus an earthly ruler.

All in all, sufficient references exist to convince us that John knew of the Synoptic theme of the kingdom of God and that he was also aware of the tendency after Easter to give Jesus a share in God's kingship. But ultimately John shied away from kingdom-language, just as Paul did and the preachers in the Book of Acts, for "kingdom of God" or the idea of "King Jesus" could too easily be misunderstood as worldly, political rule like Caesar's (cf. Acts 17:7, and the discussion above in chap. 25, pp. 321–22).

What does John then employ as his basic term to express the gospel? Life, eternal life. And that equation of "life" with "the kingdom," as the center of the Gospel, is one already found in the Synoptic Gospels. Note the parallelism in the following warning to disciples in Mark:

> If your hand causes you to sin, cut it off;
>> it is better for you to *enter life* maimed
>>> than with two hands to go to hell,
>>>> to the unquenchable fire.
> And if your foot causes you to sin, cut it off;
>> it is better for you to *enter life* lame
>>> than with two feet to be thrown into hell.
> And if your eye causes you to sin, pluck it out;
>> it is better for you to *enter the kingdom of God* with one eye
>>> than with two eyes to be thrown into hell.
>>>> (Mark 9:43–47; cf. also Mark 10:17 with 10:23–25)

The kingdom of God means life. Martin Luther reflected this connection when he wrote that the purpose of Christ's work is that we might *"live under him in his kingdom."*[3]

MIRACLES AS SIGNS

What of the miracles in John? Miracle stories in the Fourth Gospel there are. They are fewer in number than in the Synoptics. The Johannine accounts often, however, heighten the miraculous (e.g., when Lazarus is raised, he has been dead four days, 11:39, and not just a few minutes as in the case of Jairus's daughter). Structurally, John's miracles are often related to a discourse, as an occasion for it:

Five thousand fed—"I am the bread of life" (chap. 6);

Man born blind healed—"I am the light of the world" (chaps. 8—9).

Most interesting, and baffling, however, is the fact that we seem to have the remnants of yet another outline in the miracle stories. This outline stands in addition to the geographical and theological outlines already described. For after the wedding feast at Cana where Jesus changed a hundred gallons of water into wine, it is stated, "This, the *first* of his signs, Jesus did at Cana in Galilee, and manifested his glory" (2:11). Then, after the healing of an official's son, it is stated at 4:54, "This was now the *second* sign that Jesus did. . . ." Yet, in between what seems an enumeration of the first two "signs" Jesus did are references to other signs or miracles (cf. 2:23; 3:2; note the plurals).

Many students of the Fourth Gospel think there was once a source that presented a total of seven miracles by Jesus as signs. (The very word "sign" is an Old Testament term for the wonders wrought during the exodus and Israel's pilgrimage in the wilderness; cf. Deut. 7:19; 34:11.) "The Book of Signs" or even "Signs Gospel" is a term suggested for this supposed collection, the contents of which are now incorporated into John's Gospel. A possible list of these miracle-signs would include:

1. Wedding feast at Cana (2:1–11);
2. The official's son healed (4:46–54);
3. The lame man at the Pool of Bethzatha cured (5:1–9);
4. The Feeding of the Five Thousand (6:1–13);
5. Jesus walks on the waters of the Sea of Galilee (6:16–21);
6. The man born blind receives sight (9:1–34);
7. The raising of Lazarus from the tomb (11:1–44).

However, stories 2, 4, and 5 in the list above have counterparts in the Synoptics (see Matt. 8:5–13 and Luke 7:1–10 as analogues to number 2, and Mark 6:32–44 and 45–52 and parallels for numbers 4 and 5). Therefore, these stories need not have come from a "signs" source. And other scholars would suggest the Miraculous Draft of Fishes (21:2–14; cf. Luke 5:1–11) belongs in the list.

Regardless of where the Fourth Gospel got these stories, and regardless how many of them there were, far more important is the concept of "signs." It is obviously an important term throughout; cf. 6:2; 7:3; 11:47; and above all 20:30, which is part of the concluding paragraph of the book. (This paragraph is the original conclusion of the Gospel if chap. 21 is an epilogue added later.) This verse at 20:30–31 sums up the purpose of the Gospel book thus:

> Now Jesus did *many other signs* . . . which are not written in this book; but these are written [the seven, or however many John includes] that you may *believe. . . .*

The purpose of the signs would thus be to promote faith. That is the very thing said about the first sign at Cana (2:11): "This, the first of his signs, Jesus did . . ., and his disciples believed in him." There are occasions when miracles promote faith, and through the ages many Christians have held miracles dear because they thought a miracle would produce faith.

It is therefore all the more surprising that, in the very midst of this emphasis on signs as promoting faith, we find in the story of the official's son a striking statement by Jesus, "Unless you see signs and wonders you will not believe" (4:48). He is thus critical of those who want faith to depend on something miraculous like a healing! The important thing in the story about the official is that he believed Jesus' promise before the healing occurred. He first believed, then went his way (4:49–53). There is here an implied criticism of faith based on miracles, in favor of faith based on nothing but promise. A strange book, this Gospel of John!

SETTING AND DEVELOPMENT OF
JOHN'S GOSPEL

Who could have written such a Gospel? Why and when? This Fourth Gospel has long been an enigma to those who study it. Fifty years ago there was a strong tendency to advance its date well into the second century. A tiny papyrus fragment from Egypt, recording parts of five verses from John, which was published in 1935, helped push that dating back into the first century, for this fragment, stemming from the second century, showed that John's Gospel was already in circulation by that time in a remote Egyptian village. Therefore, John's Gospel must have been written A.D. 90 to 100.

From the 1800s on, many tended to locate John in the Greco-Roman world outside Palestine, because of its seemingly metaphysical discourses and on the grounds that reference to Jesus as the Logos (or Word, 1:1–18) reflected philosophy such as was taught at Alexandria, Egypt. But there were those who championed an Old Testament, Jewish background, even for the Logos theme. The idea of the Word could have roots in Prov. 8:22–31, about Wisdom personified helping with the creation; see above, p. 233, 240. This position in favor of Jewish backgrounds also found support in the Dead Sea Scrolls. It thus became plausible to think of a Palestinian setting for much of the Fourth Gospel; some even argued that John was the earliest of the four Gospels to be composed, a supposition not supported in further research.

The widely held, current consensus is that John's Gospel appeared in the nineties, somewhere in the eastern Mediterranean, perhaps Syria or Asia Minor, as the result of a long process of theological refinement of materials about Jesus. Very likely the situation in which the Gospel was put together included certain definite opponents or options to Christianity as an influence. One such opponent appears in John's references to "the Jews." The Fourth Gospel does not pick out just the Pharisees or Sadducees as opposition to Jesus, as in the Synoptics, but lumps them all together simply as "the Jews" (cf. 9:22; 19:7, 12, 14, 16–17). It is even said, "They will put you out of the synagogues" and kill you in God's name (16:2). Such statements no doubt reflect the break that had taken place between the Jewish synagogue and the Christian community in John's own day.

Jesus cured a lame man in Jerusalem (John 5:2) at Bethzatha ("twin pools") with "five porticoes." A site excavated near the Antonia fortress has remains from the healing god Serapis.

Because, however, John's statement about divisions of his time, as synagogue and church were developing separate identities, has all too frequently led to anti-Semitic tendencies among Christians, it is well to bear in mind the suggestion that John is likely using the term "the Jews" to refer to *all* representatives of unbelief. This includes Gentiles, indeed *all* who boggle at the claims of Jesus Christ. Thus at 6:41 "the Jews" who murmur against Jesus as "the living bread which came down from heaven" (6:51) are to be equated with "the people" (6:24) or the "multitude" (6:2) who misunderstand Jesus, and ultimately equated with "the world" which lies in darkness and unbelief (1:5, 10).

The Gospel of John may also be directed against the "Gnostic" movement (Greek *gnosis,* "knowledge"), a religion which stressed revealed knowledge, and more especially against a particular breed of Gnostics called the "Docetists." This group taught that Jesus had merely "seemed" or "appeared" (Greek *dokein*) to be a human being and that the Lord had not come incarnate, that is, "in the flesh." That may be why the Fourth Gospel never uses the noun "knowledge," though it does stress dynamically the verb "to know," and insists Jesus came *in the flesh* (John 1:14; 1 John 4:2).

Similarly, there may at times be comments directed against those who still thought John the Baptist was God's promised one. In a way that the Synoptics never do, the Fourth Gospel makes the Baptist a witness to Jesus (1:19–27), but he is a witness who must diminish while Jesus increases in importance (3:22–30). Only the Christ, Jesus, matters; the forerunner pales to insignificance, except as a pointer to him.

Who was responsible for this Fourth Gospel? Clearly, a community of Christian believers is involved. "*We* have beheld his glory" (1:14; cf. 1:16), they testify (cf. also 19:35 as part of their certification of the truth). It would be a community such as speaks in First John ("that which *we* have seen and heard *we* proclaim," 1:3). But there is also an individual involved, called "the disciple 'whom Jesus loved' " (John 13:23–25; 19:26–27; 20:2–8), also referred to as "another disciple" or "the other disciple" (18:15–16), and "the other disciple, the one whom Jesus loved" (20:2; cf. vv. 3, 8). He is the only disciple who was an eyewitness at the cross, the Fourth Gospel says:

He who saw it has borne witness—his testimony is true, and he [God? Christ? the evangelist? or, most likely, the eyewitness?] knows that he tells the truth. (19:35)

The first twenty chapters of John do not identify this beloved disciple any further. It has been speculated that he represents an idealization of discipleship—staying close to Jesus, remaining with him at the cross, quick to believe the resurrection (20:8). Others suggest that Lazarus (chap. 11) is the beloved disciple, since he was the one person concerning whom the Fourth Gospel says Jesus loved him (11:3).

Chapter 21 offers further clues. At 21:7 the beloved disciple is the first in Galilee to recognize the risen Jesus and call him Lord. Of the seven followers mentioned in the scene by the lake—Simon Peter, Thomas, Nathanael, "the sons of Zebedee [James and John], and two others of his disciples" (21:2)—he is not Simon Peter, for the beloved disciple is distinguished from him (vv. 15–19, 22). Apparently this disciple whom Jesus loved is now dead, by the time of the writing of chapter 21 (see v.

23). But the community (v. 24, "*we* know") certifies he is the one who bore witness and wrote the things in the Fourth Gospel. Tradition has equated him with John, the son of Zebedee.

Modern scholars have spent much time putting together all this evidence. The result runs something like this, in their view. There was an eyewitness, perhaps indeed one of the Twelve, John the son of Zebedee, who knew a great deal about Jesus' teachings and career. This person passed on what he knew. Over the decades his observations were cast and recast by him and his pupils in certain distinctive patterns. Under the Spirit of the living Lord, these traditions about Jesus took on ever-deeper significance, as people preached and meditated on these words. Perhaps this growing Johannine material was even cast at one time into the form of a gospel built around a series of signs. Later on, the evangelist or final editor revised this story of Jesus to meet further needs of his day. The finished Gospel, by the end of the first century, also reflects the comments of the community of Christians who treasured the Johannine witness (1:14; 19:35). This Johannine community, which had for a long time remained within the framework of the synagogue, did not stress structure or organization. Its identifying feature, a high Christology, arose especially from the supreme worth its members, in their alienation from the world and expulsion from the synagogue (9:22; 16:2), experienced in Jesus.

ETERNAL LIFE—AND LOVE

However John's Gospel came about, its message is life, life from God, through Jesus Christ. When the Johannine writings call it "eternal life," they do not mean existence strung out everlastingly, as if a person should go on living indefinitely. It is rather life of a particular quality—from God, characteristic of the new age for which apocalyptists of the period longed. It is life marked by God's promises fulfilled. The good news according to John is that this life of the coming age is available *now*—not just at the resurrection of the dead in the future (John 5:28–29) but *now,* with the implication that one has already passed through the judgment and been accepted by God (5:24). This life means knowing God, here and now, and Jesus Christ whom God sent (17:3). It means to be born from above (3:3, 5), by baptism, and to abide in God and Christ. Assumed is that what people call "life" in the present world is merely existence, actually a kind of death (5:24). Christians are people who know that they "have passed out of death into life" (1 John 3:14). The gift of God is eternal life in Jesus Christ, and if we spell it with a capital letter, Life, that distinguishes it from all other forms of "mere living."

The thought is added in 1 John that "regeneration," to be "born anew" (John 3:7), lies at start of this process—note how often the verb *"born* (of God)" is used (1 John 4:7; 5:4, 18). Rebirth through baptism makes one a child of God, but never in isolation. The stress is on fellowship with other Christians as well as with God (1 John 1:4, 7). Indeed, "family fellowship" in God's community is essential. Yet the fact must be noted that even "born-again [or "born-from-above"] believers" in the Christian community still sin (1 John 1:8, 9, 10); they are not yet perfected until the future fulfillment at the parousia, concerning which the letter says:

> We are God's children now; it does not yet appear what we shall be, but we know that when he [Christ] appears we shall be like him. (1 John 3:2)

But the call is to Christlikeness in love, to become what they already are, as children of God, to live without continuing to sin all the time (as the Greek of 3:6 and 9 and 5:18 implies, and the *Good News Bible* [TEV] accurately translates, "Whoever is a child of God does not continue to sin," 3:9).

Changed persons, though not yet perfect ones, sinners who abide in Christ—such is the picture of Christians in the Johannine writings. So powerful is this concept that people sometimes have misread John as saying a person's very substance is changed by the new birth and that "in . . . regeneration God creates . . . a new man in such a way that the substance and essence of the Old Adam . . . are completely destroyed."[4] But no, John says, the tendency to be a murderer like Cain or to close one's heart to people in need (3:11–18) is always threatening even the best Christians. That is why God's people, even as they abide in Christ, need the "new commandment" (John 13:34) to keep on loving one another; love must be in deed and truth (1 John 3:18). Regeneration, renewal, for the Johannine writings, is moral, and the writer never tires of urging love, in things great and small (1 John 3:16–17). One writer[5] has, indeed, suggested that 1 John is constructed around three everyday "tests" for life—righteousness or doing right; loving; and believing. The tests may be outlined thus:

The Christian life (eternal life),

as fellowship with God and walking in the Light (1:5—2:28)	as divine sonship (2:29—4:6)	as a closer correlation of righteousness, love, belief (4:7—5:21),

is tested by our attitude toward

(a) righteousness/sin
  1:8—2:6, esp. 1:9   2:29—3:10a, esp. 3:7, ⎫
(b) loving   love, 4:7—5:3, esp. 4:7,
  2:7–11, 15–17,   3:10b–24, esp. 3:14 ⎬
  esp. 2:10
and (c) belief   belief 5:4–21, esp. 5:4.
  2:18–28, esp. 2:23   3:25—4:6, esp. 4:2 ⎭

Of course, the thoughts of 1 John so intertwine that no outline ever is sufficient, but this one makes the point that moral earnestness in everyday living is one of the emphases of this epistle. Bluntly put: "We know that we have left death and come over into life; we know it because we love our brothers" (1 John 3:14, TEV).

THE HOLY SPIRIT OR PARACLETE

What emboldened the Johannine writer (or writers) to speak thus confidently in Jesus' name? What helped them take teachings that went back to Jesus' days on earth, amplify them over the succeeding decades, and preach to new situations? The clue to Johannine achievements here lies in the final theme in the Fourth Gospel that we must emphasize. This is the Holy Spirit or, in John's terms, "the Paraclete" (Greek *paraklētos*).

For John, "God is spirit" (4:24). "Life" is a result of the Spirit (6:63). Rebirth comes via the Spirit (3:5–8). In all this, the Fourth Gospel is reflecting the experience of the early church as seen in Paul and Acts more than the Synoptic picture of the historical Jesus. But the five "Paraclete sayings" in chapters 14—16 go beyond anything even in Paul, let alone the other Gospels.

The term "paraclete" means literally someone "called to the side of" someone else, called to help. For example, the term could be used for a lawyer in a court case—hence the rendering "advocate" (in the NEB, for example, at John 14:16). Less legalistic in sound (though the term may ultimately reflect the courtroom setting in Paul's image of justification) is the translation "counselor" (RSV, 14:26) More consoling is the old *King James Version,* "comforter" (14:26). Others have used the translation "helper" (TEV) or "one . . . to stand by you" (Phillips, 14:26).

The First Epistle of John uses this almost untranslatable term to describe Jesus Christ as our "advocate with the Father" (1 John 2:1): he is in heaven pleading our case with God. But the Fourth Gospel employs this same word for the Holy Spirit as God's advocate or spokesperson with us. Five short statements, unparalleled in the other Gospels, expound the Spirit's functions. The verses deserve to be read and pondered:

14:15–17—the Father will give you the Spirit of truth to be with you.

14:25–26—the Paraclete will "teach you all things, and bring to your remembrance all that I have said to you," Jesus promised.

15:26–27—the Counselor will bear witness of Jesus, for you who are witnesses.

16:5–11—Jesus must go away before the Spirit can come to carry out a mission of setting the world straight about sin, righteousness, and judgment.

16:12–15—this Spirit will guide you into all truth, glorifying Jesus, taking what is from Jesus and declaring it to you.

We may add that this Spirit/Paraclete who takes the place of Jesus when the latter departs is a personal indwelling presence. When first granted on Easter Day by the risen Christ (20:22), the Spirit became the basis for Christian witness and life, in the face of persecution (15:26—16:4), in conjunction with sorrow, joy, and prayer (16:16–24).

This Christ-figure, the Spirit, who dwells within the Christian community, has, among other things, three significances in Johannine thought. (1) The Paraclete takes Jesus' teaching and develops it to meet new needs (16:14). *Not* new revelations, but that which was once revealed in Jesus of Nazareth is now carried to new heights. No better example can be seen than the Fourth Gospel itself, the Paraclete's achievement of taking, in Jesus' words, "what is mine and declaring it to you." (2) Here is John's answer to the problem of a second coming to Jesus. While the Johannine writings still include that future note of parousia, resurrection, and judgment (1 John 3:2; John 5:28–29), the emphasis is far more that "another Paraclete," like Jesus, *has already come.* With the Spirit present, one need not worry apocalyptically about a parousia, and the Fourth Gospel does not. (3) When 14:15–21 talks of this Paraclete coming whom the world cannot see or know, yet bringing life and love to disciples who keep the commandments, we are coming close to a Johannine version of the kingdom of God. It is God's reign, realized here and now, in the Spirit.

There is much more to explore in John's lush, verdant world of thought. Different, deep, enduring, the good news according to the Johannine Gospel and epistles is like a river, appropriate for a child to wade in and for an elephant to swim. Yet at its heart it remains the truth we have long known and treasured—

God loved the world so much he gave his only Son,
so that everyone who believes in him may . . . have eternal life.

(John 3:16, TEV)

The testimony is this: God has given us eternal life.
We have seen and tell others. . . .

(1 John 5:11; 4:14; TEV)

John would ask, Have you this life? Do you share it?

NOTES

1. John 7:53—8:11, concerning Jesus and the woman caught in the act of adultery, is rightly removed at this point by most modern Bible translations. Only some Greek manuscripts insert it here; others have it at the end of John's Gospel, and still others between Luke 21:38 and 22:1. It is, thus, a widely told story about Jesus in the biblical manuscripts, completely in his spirit of forgiveness and his call to lead a new life. The story also reflects a view of women and their rights in advance of many of the laws in Jesus' day, and takes a sly dig at the sinfulness of men's imaginings (8:7; cf. Matt. 5:27–30). Significantly, at 8:9, it is shown that the longer one lives, the more one sees the truth of Jesus' point that the one "without sin," if such a person exists, should "cast the first stone." Even if the story is read at this point in John, it plainly assumes a setting in Jerusalem (8:1–2).

2. The *King James Version* once uses the term in English for the "parable" of the sheepfold, at John 10:6. But the Greek has a different word from that usually translated as "parable" in Mark, Matthew, and Luke. This term in John the *Revised Standard Version* better renders as "figure" every time it occurs (10:6; 16:25, 29).

3. *The Small Catechism by Martin Luther, in Contemporary English* (Minneapolis: Augsburg Publishing House; Philadelphia: Board of Publication of the Lutheran Church in America; and St. Louis: Concordia Publishing House, 1968), 12, Explanation to the Second Article of the Apostles' Creed.

4. Such was the contention of one of the most polemical but theologically conservative of the later, "second generation" figures in the Protestant Reformation, Flacius Illyricus. His opinion, quoted above, is rejected in the Lutheran *Formula of Concord, Solid Declaration,* 2.81. Though people today do not commonly employ such language about "essence," Flacius obviously has modern counterparts who stress "total regeneration" to the believer's "very core."

5. See Robert Law, *The Tests of Life: A Study of the First Epistle of St. John* (Edinburgh: T. & T. Clark, 1909; reprinted, Grand Rapids: Baker Book House, 1979), 21–24, for his outline.

31

The Church:
God's People of
the Gospel in Pilgrimage

BIBLE STUDY ALL TOO FREQUENTLY overlooks the church as a theme in the New Testament. But, then, the churches, all too frequently through the centuries, have overlooked what Scripture has to say about that institution we call the church. In this chapter we shall survey something of what the Bible says about the community "in Christ," as the gospel people of God.

In order to accomplish this, we shall have to range over a number of biblical books, just as will also be the case in dealing with ethics (chap. 32), for the biblical teachings about the church are not concentrated in just one place or two. Rather, they run through almost every book in the New Testament. We shall concentrate here on four glimpses at the church, in Paul, James, 1 Peter, and Hebrews. Inevitably, too, we shall encounter other related themes, including ethical concerns, in studying these authors and books.

In this study process, we shall also uncover a course of development in the New Testament idea of the church. We shall see God's churchly, Christian people on the move in pilgrimage, in the world of the first century. That pilgrimage stretches on to our own day. From what these first Christians experienced of God's program for the church, people today can gain direction for their own pilgrim path and for the churches in which they, in turn, worship and work, and into which they may seek to win others. (For general background see under "Jesus and the Rise of Christianity" in chap. 5.)

Cynics have said, "Jesus came preaching the kingdom of God, but the church resulted instead." Jesus, we have seen (in chaps. 6 and 7), did cast his gospel primarily in terms of the kingship of God. It is, moreover, true that a church, where Jesus Christ was Lord, later emerged (see chap. 13 on Jesus as Lord). But we have also already seen something of the continuity in this development. For when God raised Jesus from the dead and made him Lord, the good news inevitably took a new form, the Easter Gospel. As the witnesses to Jesus spread their story about him, the message about the kingdom tended to be misunderstood in the Gentile world (see above, pp. 321–22), and so new ways of presenting the gospel of the goodness of God the king had to be found. Such is what Paul and John achieved. They viewed the gospel as justification, reconciliation, or eternal life, in Christ (chaps. 27 and 30).

The course of development for the church itself runs something like this.

1. According to the Gospel records, *Jesus of Nazareth did not during his lifetime establish* what we think of as *a church.* There is no passage where he does that prior to his death, and only two Gospel verses where the term "church" is used at all. Both are in Matthew, and will be provided with a fuller context in discussion in chapter 33, below (see pp. 442–43, 445–46). Matthew 18:17 deals with rules for discipline in a community, and 16:18 envisions a worldwide church built on the rock of Peter and his confession of Jesus as Christ. Quite apart from any polemics over Peter, both verses have been questioned as sayings of the *historical* Jesus. In any case, in 16:18 it is the future tense that is used: Jesus says, "I *will* build my church . . . ," that is, later, after the resurrection.

2. Although overt founding of a separate church outside Judaism is thus not asserted before Easter, there are clues to an *intention of Jesus.* It does seem he expected a religious community to result from his ministry and work. The whole background of Israel as a people points in this direction: one bands together with those who have had a similar experience of God's lovingkindness and rescuing actions. In choosing twelve from among his followers (Mark 3:13–19), Jesus seems to have been echoing the idea of the "twelve tribes" in Israel. When he taught his disciples a prayer of their own (Luke 11:1–4), he was marking them out as a specific group. In identifying with the baptism by John, Jesus and his followers, some of whom had been a part of the Baptist's movement, were stamping themselves as a "remnant" within Israel. When Jesus, in the upper room in Jerusalem, at Passover time, before he died, gave new meaning to the bread and wine they ate and drank, he was constituting his little group as a fellowship that viewed God and the ongoing actions of God in new ways. Thus seeds were sown, out of which would grow the church.

3. *After Easter, the Jesus movement took further shape,* at first within

Judaism. Initially this movement was scarcely conscious of beginning what would become a worldwide church. The Jerusalem converts still frequented the temple for prayer, and they continued Jewish customs and ways (cf. Acts 2:46; 3:1, 11–16; 4:1–4). But the impact of the fact that "they had been with Jesus" (Acts 4:13) and the power of the resurrection message caused these disciples to draw some further conclusions. "The sect of the Nazarenes" (Acts 24:5), as it came to be called, grew and expanded. It became "the way (to life and God)" for increasing numbers within Israel. Paul speaks of it as "the Way, which they [in official Judaism] call a sect," and testifies of himself as a Jewish follower of Christ, "According to the Way ... I worship the God of our fathers, believing everything laid down by the law or written in the prophets, having a hope in God ... that there will be a resurrection of both the just and the unjust" (Acts 24:14–15).

Others of these earliest followers drew consequences from some of Jesus' teachings about God as Father (*Abba*) and from his actions in eating with publicans and sinners: they began to share the good news with Jews who spoke Greek and who followed Greek customs ("the Hellenists," mentioned in Acts 6:1). When persecution drove these Hellenists from Jerusalem, they shared their message in Samaria (with Samaritans! Acts 8) and then with people from far off who had embraced Judaism. An example would be the Ethiopian court official in Acts 8:26–39. Eventually the step was taken of bringing Gentiles into the fellowship of Jesus Christ. According to Acts 10, it was Peter who first took this step, when, guided by the Holy Spirit (10:44), he preached to and baptized a Roman centurion and all his household. In this way the gospel about Jesus spread, to Jews and to Greeks (Acts 11:19–20).

4. Thus, long before Paul wrote any epistles and even before his own missionary career began (see Acts 13), there were *small groups, cells, fellowships,* and *house-churches of "Christians"* (as they came to be called, Acts 11:26) throughout the eastern Mediterranean. By sometime in the forties, the movement had reached Rome. Sometimes these "Jesus-chapels" or conventicles (which must have met in private houses or in the open air) took the Jewish name of "synagogue" (literally, a "gathering together") or "assembly" (in Greek *ekklēsia*, giving our word "ecclesiastical"). They adopted patterns of social organization. Often this pattern included elders or presbyters so that a kind of ministry and leadership was developing. These Jesus groups began to take over from elsewhere and create for themselves forms of worship and communal life. We know all too little (compared with what we would like to know) about their structure, liturgies, habits of prayer and Bible reading, and

works of mercy and witnessing, but in the thirties and forties such things were already coming into practice.

5. While we have thus traced the emergence of local groups, each "church" in its local situation must have had some knowledge of other Christian groups elsewhere and at least at times *a vision of a universal fellowship.* This more-than-local aspect was fostered by travel and personal contacts but above all by the concepts of God as a universal king and of Jesus as Lord of the universe. Naturally, some New Testament writings, like Colossians and Ephesians, reflect this larger sense of Christianity more than other documents do. But even in so early a letter as 1 Corinthians, devoted to local problems in Corinth, Paul touches on the "ecumenical" or universal aspects of the Christian movement. Note the salutation, "To the church of God which is at Corinth . . . together with *all those who in every place* call on the name of our Lord Jesus Christ, both their Lord and ours" (1:2); see also the references to "the churches of God" (plural, 11:16; also 4:7; 7:17; 14:33). Given a universal Lord, a universal fellowship could not help but result, in spite of all the pulls from local or regional concerns.

6. It is well to remind ourselves that *all books in the New Testament come from or through this church which was emerging* in the first century. Obviously that is true of the epistles or even Revelation with its letters to the seven churches of Asia Minor. It is also true with the Gospels. Mark, Matthew, and Luke (especially when we consider Acts) reflect to greater or lesser degrees a "doctrine of the church," as we shall see in chapter 33. There is also "ecclesiology" or a doctrine about the church in the Fourth Gospel, although in a different key. When it is said of the Word of God, "*we* have beheld his glory" or "from his fulness have *we all* received" (John 1:14, 16), that is the Christian community offering its testimony. What is the figure of the vine and the branches (John 15) but a metaphor about the church? And no passage in the New Testament lays more emphasis on "oneness"—involving Christ, the disciples, those who will believe through them, and the Father—than John 17, the prayer of Christ for unity.

7. *There is a connection between the kingdom of God and the church,* of which that cynical comment with which we began this section scarcely dreams. Yes, out of the kingship of Yahweh that Jesus proclaimed, there arose a church of Jesus Christ the Lord. But this church is precisely a place where God's kingship is confessed, centered, and in halting ways realized as nowhere else in the world! The church becomes, indeed, a prelude to that final kingdom where God's rule will be "all in all" (1 Cor. 15:24–28).

The Epistle of James illustrates this point. James speaks not only of a "royal" (or sovereign" or "kingly") law, to love one's neighbor as oneself (2:8), but also of how God has "chosen those who are poor in the world to be rich in faith and heirs of the kingdom which he has promised to those who love him" (2:5). (This last-mentioned verse, about a promised kingdom for the poor, is very reminiscent of Jesus' first beatitude in Matt. 5:3, when he promised that to "the poor [in spirit]" will belong "the kingdom of heaven.") The Second Epistle of Peter likewise talks of a future kingdom: "Be the more zealous . . . so there will be richly provided for you an entrance into the eternal kingdom of our Lord and Savior Jesus Christ" (1:10–11); such is the promise for which the Christian community waits (3:12–13). Christians, in 1 Peter, are addressed as "a royal priesthood," literally, a "kingly body of priests" (2:9), implying an association with kingship here and now. Hebrews, which contains routine references to Old Testament kingdoms (11:33) and to the scepter of God's kingly power in the hands of Christ (1:8, using a quotation from Ps. 45:6), goes furthest in seeing the kingdom as a possession of God's people in Christ here and now. That book says, "Let us be grateful for receiving a kingdom that cannot be shaken"—and then adds as the proper response, "and let us offer to God acceptable worship" (12:28).

All this is evidence from these epistles that the kingdom message was not forgotten in the church, and that it was treasured as a future hope and, to some degree, a present reality. It is the Pauline epistles, however, that make the connection closest between the kingdom of God and people in the church. According to the Pauline epistles, evil, unrighteous persons will not inherit the kingdom of God (1 Cor. 6:9–10; Gal. 5:5). It is those who have heard the gospel of God, about Christ, whom God calls into his kingdom (1 Thess. 2:12), whom God makes worthy of the kingdom (2 Thess. 1:5). It is a kingdom of "righteousness and peace and joy in the Holy Spirit" (Rom. 14:17)—which is not a bad description of the church! Paul can speak of Christian missionaries as "fellow workers for the kingdom of God" (Col. 4:11).

Perhaps the most significant phrase in these epistles is the reference at Col. 1:13 to "the kingdom of [God's] beloved Son" into which God has "transferred us" by calling us out of "the dominion of darkness" through the gospel and baptism. This identifies the church as the kingdom of the Son, implying both a link to, and some distinction from, the kingdom of God which is to be our full inheritance later on. More of this theme will appear below in chapters 33 (on Matthew) and 35 (on later church history). *The point is, the kingdom of God finds expression precisely in the church of Jesus Christ.* But how does the church understand itself in the New Testament, if it is, at least in some way, "kingdom come"?

PAULINE IDEAS ABOUT THE CHURCH

For clarification we turn above all to the letters of Paul. They are early, they reflect many different situations, they are all marked with a strong sense of the church. What stands out first, to any reader, is a strong sense of continuity with Israel in the past. Yet there is also an idea Israel never had, of being the "*body* of the Messiah." Finally, there is a sense of divine purpose for the church in the world, according to Paul.

We begin with what might be called "Israel terms." These are terms that Paul applies to the community that believes in Jesus Christ, but they are all vocabulary that referred originally to Israel in the Hebrew Scriptures. Once Paul has a reference to "the Israel of God," in Gal. 6:16. Many take this to mean the church, though others believe it refers to the Jews. "People of God" is not a phrase Paul uses of the church as 1 Peter 2:10 does, nor is the related Old Testament term "covenant" as common in Paul. But listen to the phrases that he does employ about the church: "Abraham's offspring" and "sons of Abraham" (Gal. 3:29 and 3:7, emphasizing the promise to Abraham); "commonwealth of Israel" (Eph. 2:12); "Jerusalem" (Gal. 4:26); the "remnant, chosen by grace" (Rom. 11:5); and such common terms as "the saints" and "the elect," both ideas going back to Old Testament usage. All the figures of speech at Rom. 11:16–24 have Old Testament backgrounds, about the dough offered as first fruits (Num. 15:20–21) and the root and branches of the olive tree (see Hosea 10:1 and Zech. 4:3). Even the reference to the church as God's "garden" or "field" (1 Cor. 3:9, NEB, RSV) reflects the Old Testament and not just an agricultural figure of speech: the "remnant" of Israel is "the planting of the LORD" (Isa. 61:3).

This identity with the Israel of the past must have served to give early Christians both roots and a heritage. It also allowed the Hebrew Scriptures to speak to them afresh. You are Israel!

Yet Christians did not simply think of their community as a continuity with God's people of the past. There was a newness also about their self-understanding. The impact of Jesus and the Easter Gospel had changed things. The church's consciousness was centered in Jesus Christ, and no phrase makes clearer what was involved than that central one in the Pauline epistles, the "body of Christ." Indeed, at times people have made it appear to be the *only* figure used in Paul to describe the church, and at times it seems to be not a figure at all but a statement about reality, indeed in terms of actual being. Before looking at what is said about the church as the body of Christ, it is worth pointing out that this is but one of over eighty expressions describing the church in the New Testament,[1] and it is an extremely fluid one, with varying meanings. We must be careful not to overdo even this favorite figure in Paul.

The term "body of Christ" seems to burst upon us for the first time in an analogy in 1 Corinthians 12. Paul is seeking to stress the oneness of the Christian community, in the face of a tendency among the Corinthians to fragment into splinter groups by support of favorite leaders (1:12–13; 3:3–21) or along lines of their differing spiritual gifts (12:4–11). Appealing to the common experience of baptism, Paul writes, "We were *all* baptized into one body . . . , and *all* were made to drink of one Spirit" (12:13). Then comes his famous analogy, one well known from use in Roman history. For Menenius Agrippa had once persuaded the plebeians to end a revolt by explaining to them how each group has a role in society, just as different organs do in the human body. So Paul compares the differing talents and gifts of Christians to the functions of hands, ears, eyes, the nose, and other parts of the body—each has a function and cannot get along without the others. The head (v. 21) is just another part of the body, like the feet; neither can say, "I do not need you."

The biggest surprise in 1 Corinthians 12 comes at the conclusion where we might expect Paul to say, "You all are *like* the parts of a body and must work together." Instead he says, "You *are* the body of Christ and individually members of it" (12:27). This goes together with a surprising statement at the beginning of the passage. There, instead of "Just as the many members of a body are one, so also with *Christians*," Paul has written (v. 12), "Just as the body is one and has many members, and all the members of the body, though many, are one body, so it is with *Christ.*" These two remarkable statements suggest that the church and its members are intended to be pulled together as a body and be ruled by Christ, who permeates the totality. The presence of the risen Jesus in the community makes "body of Christ" more than metaphor.

The sense of this phrase shifts, however, when we turn to the "imprisonment epistles" of Paul (those which state they were written while he was in prison). These are Philippians, Colossians, and Ephesians. In the latter two letters the "members" of the body are rarely mentioned. Instead the stress is now on Christ as the *head* of the body, while the *body* is defined as the church. Colossians 1:18 is a good example of this sense and represents a transition from the earlier use in 1 Corinthians 12 (and also Romans, see 12:5) to the later usage which is found also in Ephesians (see 1:23; 5:23). We may graphically depict the difference in the earlier and later Pauline use:

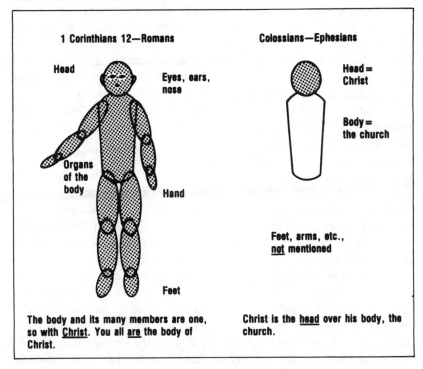

1 Corinthians 12—Romans

Head

Eyes, ears, nose

Organs of the body

Hand

Feet

The body and its many members are one, so with <u>Christ</u>. You all <u>are</u> the body of Christ.

Colossians—Ephesians

Head = Christ

Body = the church

Feet, arms, etc., <u>not</u> mentioned

Christ is the <u>head</u> over his body, the church.

What the two figures have in common, of course, is that Christ *rules* the body, the church. He works *in* all its members. The Corinthians passage suggests his presence, with each and every man, woman, and child in Christ. The imprisonment epistles stress his lordship *over* all of us in the church. There is clear indication, especially when Rom. 12:5 is considered, of the mutual interdependence and cooperation and coordination with which Christians are to work, under their Lord. One can hardly overlook what must have struck the first readers of Paul in Corinth with force: those who *are* the body of Christ are precisely those who *participate in* "the body of Christ," that is, who partake of the one bread and the one cup in the Lord's Supper (1 Cor. 10:16–17; 11:26). And those nourished by this sacrament were to go and *be* the body of Christ in the world, using their gifts to serve (Rom. 12:1–8).

But what do the members of the body of Christ *do* in the world? What is the *purpose* of the church, according to the Pauline epistles? So many different ways of putting it are employed by Paul that it is almost presumptuous to suggest a summary. One oft-heard answer that we ought *not* to accept is to claim the purpose of the church is to be "an extension of the incarnation" in the world—if by that is meant that the church on earth is all that Christ was and is. (This opinion could even imply the church has a savior's role.) That would fail to recognize that the church, like all its members, is sinful as well as redeemed. True, the church belongs to the Lord, but still is Christ's only in an imperfect way. Christ rules the church, but is not identical with it. He is always over it as Lord. But what we can say is that the church continues the "incarnational principle," in the sense of humble service in the world, like the ministry of its Lord (Phil. 2:6–11).

Another way to express this would be to say the church is called upon to proclaim and convey God's work in Christ as good news to and in the world. The church here offers praise to God for this glorious opportunity to serve. *Proclamation,* first of all. The church is the *missionary* body of Christ, making the word of God fully known to all the world (Col. 1:21–29). Its gospel is what God has done in Christ. *Conveying God's work,* second. This means not only witnessing and making available God's forgiveness and justifying grace, but serving (a) as a workshop or arena where God is especially at work, transforming lives, and (b) as a voice crying out for justice and decency in the world. (This *social-ethical* function of the church, admittedly, is one which has become more prominent in later times than in Paul's day, but the heritage from the Old Testament prophets and certain New Testament dynamics—including the Book of James, as we shall see—call for the church's involvement here.) "No man is an island," the Anglican priest and poet John Donne wrote. In the solidarity of humanity, the church is God's spokesperson for the poor, the suffering, and those treated unjustly. "If one member suffers, all suffer together" (1 Cor. 12:26). The church is that part of humanity whose eyes God has opened to see the vision of the promised new heavens and earth "in which righteousness dwell," as 2 Peter 3:13 phrases it. Our definition above also adds that the purpose of the church is to *offer doxologies about God,* to sing God's praise for mercies granted and opportunities bestowed. It was characteristic of Paul to break out in thanks to God in the midst of his highest theological thoughts; see, in Romans, for examples, 7:25; 9:5; 11:36; 16:25–27; and the rhapsodic 8:31–39.

To proclaim, to be a place for God to work, to be a conscience for the world for good, to praise the Lord—in addition, to this list we must add, finally, as part of the purpose of the church: *to be a spearhead of God's plan for humanity.* Ephesians, that great epistle about the church, is full of expressions concerning this function for those who are "in Christ." We may paraphrase 3:7–12 thus: God's eternal purpose is that, as the church proclaims "the unsearchable riches of Christ," people may see God's plan for their salvation, and even the angels in heaven look on to see how the ministers of the gospel are advancing the wisdom revealed to them. Or more specifically: the church is the full expression of Jesus Christ—he fills the church, and the church is meant to give full expression to Christ (1:23). Or finally, in more personal terms: the goal of the church is to have every person grow up into Christ, its head, who fills the whole body and gives it growth, working through his various ministers and in all the saints (4:11–16).

The good news here *includes the church.* The church is not only a vehicle for the gospel, but is itself *part* of it.

A VIEW FROM JAMES ABOUT THE CHURCH: SOCIAL JUSTICE

This sublime Pauline picture of what the church of Jesus Christ is meant to be is almost too grand for us to comprehend. It is the more significant because it was worked out by no ivory-tower theologian but a missionary, in the midst of hard work and growing pains in troublesome little congregations around the Aegean Sea. Much more down-to-earth are the glimpses of the church provided by the Epistle of James. Perhaps the outstanding impression from this little sermon or address which has been made into a letter is the blunt concern for living the faith in its social-ethical implications. James undergirds what we called above the task of the Christian fellowship to cry out in behalf of justice and decency in the world and especially within its own ranks.

The five chapters in James may be called a New Testament example of "wisdom literature." Just as in ancient Israel (see pp. 228–33, above), so here in the "Christian Israel," there is room for expression of the proverbial, common-sense, plain person's outcry, underscoring in simple terms what God wills. In so saying, the Epistle of James reflects little of the message that the kingdom of God is breaking in, or of the Easter Gospel, but a good many parallels occur to teachings of Jesus. Among these echoes are verses about perfection (1:4; see Matt. 5:48), hearers and doers (1:22–27; see Matt. 7:24–27), and peacemakers (3:18; see Matt. 5:9). The Sermon on the Mount lives on here, as straightforward, practical morality.

The author has traditionally been identified with Jesus' own brother James (who did not follow Jesus during the earthly ministry and who became a believer only after Easter). But the book itself calls the author simply "a servant of God and of the Lord Jesus Christ" (1:1). There is little of Christology beyond that verse and 2:1 (the only places where Jesus is mentioned by name). The parousia is alluded to, however, at 5:7–8, and baptism is assumed at 1:8, 21, and probably 2:7. The Greek style is excellent. The outline is helter-skelter, however, jumping from topic to topic often via word-links. For example, the same word is used to mean "trials" in the sense of testings (which can have good effect) in 1:2–4, and "temptations" to sin (which are bad) in 1:13–18. We seem to have polished paragraphs, such as might have been used in a sermon or sermons, to which a vague salutation has been added. "To the twelve tribes in the Dispersion," 1:1, would be a way of addressing Jews scattered throughout the world; a Christian author using it of Christians must be paralleling the church's experience with that of Israel.

The average reader has little trouble absorbing and applying the terse statements and examples about enduring under temptations (1:2–18); profession and practice (1:19—3:18); condemnation of current abuses (4:1—5:6); and the closing exhortations (5:7–20). The attack on those who trust in "faith" and do no works (2:14–26) is what has frequently caught the eye. James has often been taken as contradicting the Pauline teaching of "justification by faith alone." James calls for works, not faith alone (2:24). But a careful reading will show that what James is attacking was a kind of faith that was just a "head trip," mere intellectual belief, the kind even demons can have (2:19). That was never what Paul meant.

What James is pleading for is the kind of faith that goes deeper and expresses itself in a life that is committed and responds in deeds. With that, Paul would have agreed, though he would have been more careful to underscore that such works cannot save—and that the "faith" described as being "apart from works" is unworthy of the name. It has been argued that James was combating people who had learned Paul's terminology but never understood it or practiced what Paul meant. In that case, James could actually be defending Pauline ideas that have "gone to seed." James would be doing this by using different terms to get at Paul's meaning.[2]

What does all this tell us about the church or "assembly" known to James (2:2; the word is, literally, "synagogue")? Obviously, that some people in it were prating formulas about faith but not practicing the thing itself. Frank churchman that he was, James comes out swinging against these opponents. Those who teach are admonished (3:1–5). There are warnings about how we use our tongues (3:6–12), practice wisdom (3:13–18), and get along with others (4:1–12; see 2:8–13). There are words of warning for people who plan this or that without counting God in (4:13–17), especially the rich (5:1–6).

Of all the hortatory material in James, the most revealing is the scene about how the rich oppress the poorer folk, even in church. One may read and reread 2:1–7 as a perpetual indictment of any congregation that allows discrimination by one class or group over another. The words in 5:4–6 are reminiscent of an Old Testament prophet, inveighing against the privileged who oppress the poor in Samaria or Jerusalem. And now it was happening in the church! When James says of them, "You have condemned, you have killed the righteous man" (5:6), he may be thinking of past martyrs from Abel to Zechariah (see Matt. 23:35), and maybe also of Jesus Christ. Formal persecution in James's own day is unlikely. Dare we today include all the martyrs, down through the Nazi Holocaust against the Jews, or blacks in Namibia and South Africa?

The message we thus get is a forceful one—practice justice! Do God's will! Be a church lining up with the impoverished and the oppressed. This, too, is part of the New Testament picture of the church. It tells us there were failings among members in this local assembly or that. And there were voices to speak out, to warn, and to condemn—and also to remind Christians of the promise of the kingdom (2:5).

FIRST PETER: THE CHURCH IS FOR THOSE WHO FACE SUFFERING

The "First Epistle General of Peter," as it is sometimes called, presents us with another aspect of the church in the first century. This is the element of witness in the face of persecution and possible suffering, an element in Christian identity that has armed many for the struggles of life over the centuries.

This letter, 1 Peter, is one of the General Epistles or Catholic Letters, so-called because they are addressed not to a single church like Corinth or even an area like Galatia, but to a more general audience, the church at large. In this case those addressed are described as "the exiles of the Dispersion in Pontus, Galatia, Cappadocia, Asia, and Bithynia" (1:1), that is, the Christians in pilgrimage in this world, who reside in what is modern Turkey. (James, 2 Peter, 1 John, Jude, and possibly 2 and 3 John fit into this same category of general epistles, also termed "church epistles." These epistles are all addressed to the church at large or a more-than-local segment of it.) As author is mentioned here "Peter, an apostle of Jesus Christ" (1:1), "a fellow elder and a witness of the sufferings of Christ as well as a partaker in the glory that is to be revealed" (5:1). (A second, shorter letter, dealing with false teachers in the church and the delay of the second coming, also appears in the New Testament over Peter's name. A majority of scholars today agree that 2 Peter is not by

401

Peter himself, and some question 1 Peter as well.) The date for 1 Peter would fall in the sixties, unless it is by someone other than Peter himself, in which case a date as late as A.D. 110 has been proposed.

One reason for the amount of questioning about 1 Peter rises from the theological thought in the book: 1 Peter is, in content, really a Pauline letter! That is, much that is said in it is akin to what Paul's letters say. Is it, therefore, likely to have been composed by the apostle to the Jews (Peter, or Cephas, who according to Gal. 2:9 directed his efforts to "the circumcised"), whose ideas historically differed from Paul's (see Gal. 2:11–21)? One answer may be that both 1 Peter and Paul's letters reflect, in their points of agreement, what must have been *common* apostolic Christianity.

The other reason for doubts about the date and authorship of 1 Peter has to do with the persecution of Christians reflected in the book. Was it a persecution under the emperor Nero, A.D. 64–67, which seems to have been limited to Rome? Or was it the more severe persecution about A.D. 96 under Domitian, which we know included the areas mentioned in 1 Peter 1:1 (see the Book of Revelation, pp. 361, 362, 367–68, above)? Or was it the persecution that is documented for Bithynia (mentioned in 1:1) in the time of Trajan, about A.D. 111? Scholars frankly differ in their judgments. And since Peter was traditionally martyred by A.D. 67 at the latest, any date assigned after 67 means Peter could not have written the document as we have it.

The matter is exacerbated by the fact that the epistle seems to reflect *two* somewhat different situations in different chapters:

1:3—4:11, persecution, *threatens* (see 1:6; 2:20; 3:17). But, 2:13–17, Christians are urged to be loyal to the state and even to the emperor.	4:12—5:11, persecution *is present* (see 4:12, 14, 19; 5:6, 8); 4:16, they are now being persecuted as Christians for "the name" (of Jesus).

In the section up to 4:11 there is less the tone of a letter than after 4:12, and more the note of an address to the newly baptized. In fact there have been attempts to construe 1:3—4:11 (or till even 5:11) as a homily or even reflections of a liturgy at a Christian service of baptism. It has also been proposed we have two versions of the same letter, one part to be read (2:11—4:11) for those not yet persecuted, the other section (4:12—5:11) for those already suffering; other sections, like 1:1—2:10 and 5:12–14, could apply to both situations.

Such speculations, interesting as they are, prove unnecessary to under-

Rome was the goal of Luke's missionary account in Acts. Paul arrived there in chains. At times the authorities persecuted Christians. The Colosseum (left center) was the site of martyrdoms.

stand what 1 Peter says about the church. Believers face suffering. To be a witness for Christ opens up the possibility of reproach, slander, opposition, and even suffering. How do the five chapters of 1 Peter encourage and equip the suffering saints for their stewardship of God's "varied grace" (4:10)?

One avenue of appeal is to stress the future hope. Christians have a great hope for the future (1:3–9). "Set your hope fully upon the grace that is coming to you at the revelation of Jesus Christ" (1:13). Judgment looms (4:17–19), but after suffering will come glory (5:10). This theme of suffering and future glory will also be found in the Gospel of Luke (e.g., 24:26 and 46).

Another avenue is to underscore baptism, which has united believers to Christ, and thus not only to his suffering but also to his resurrection and the salvation which awaits us (1:3–21). There is baptismal language in 1 Peter, especially at 1:23, "You have been born anew . . . through the living and abiding word of God." Some even think we have reflections of a service, a liturgy where the baptism would have taken place between 1:21 and 1:22. In 3:20–21 there is also an elaborate comparison of baptism with Noah's ark: baptism saves us "through water" (that is, by means of it); the ark saved eight persons "through water" (that is, when the flood threatened).

In addition, 1 Peter also appeals to the common faith of the Christian church. This is done by weaving in phrases from early creeds:

> Christ "was destined before the foundation of the world,"
> he "was made manifest at the end of the times" (1:20).
> Christ "suffered for you" (2:21),
> "he himself bore our sins in his body on the tree,
> that we might die to sin and live to righteousness" (2:24).
> Christ "died for sins once for all, the righteous for the unrighteous,
> that he might bring us to God,
> being put to death in the flesh but made alive in the spirit;
> in which he went and preached to the spirits in prison";
> Christ, through the resurrection, "has gone up into heaven
> and is at the right hand of God,
> with angels, authorities, and powers subject to him" (3:18–22).
> He "is ready to judge the living and the dead" (4:5; see also 4:17);
> Christ's glory will be revealed, "when the chief Shepherd is manifested" (4:13; 5:4).

Here we have God's eternal plan, Christ's passion, atoning death, resurrection, ascension, the judgment, and his parousia. The epistle reminds us of what has been done for us in Christ, and also of how Jesus himself was an exemplar for us in suffering (see 2:21–25).

Christians for centuries have found real comfort amid their vicissitudes from these emphases on hope, baptism, and Christ. There is something else they ought not overlook. After giving that magnificent picture of the church in 2:4–9a, so filled with Old Testament or "Israel" terms, 1 Peter goes on to state the purpose for the people of God in the church: "that you may *declare the wonderful deeds of [God]* who called you" and from whom "you have received mercy" (2:9–10). In other words, the church, for all its trials and troubles, is to be a *missionary* fellowship. Witness there is to be, to and in the world—even when the world persecutes the people of God.

HEBREWS: A PILGRIM PEOPLE
"ON THE WAY"

Once when the author of Hebrews wanted to go on and give more examples of what faith had accomplished in the past, but found he was running out of space, he remarked that "time would fail me to tell of Gideon, Barak, Samson, . . ." etc. (Heb. 11:32). (He then, nonetheless, listed over a dozen more examples.) The same is true of talking about the church in the New Testament: time fails us here to tell of much more. It would be helpful, for example, in a day when managerial style and "organizational development" have been both stressed and deplored and when fresh attention is given to titles and job descriptions for church leadership, to explore 1 and 2 Timothy and Titus, the Pastoral Epistles. For in them pastoral advice is given on structuring the church, including the office of overseer-superintendent or bishop, and/or that of elder or presbyter, plus deacons and widows. But we must move on to that anonymous document called "To the Hebrews" as even more significant.

Hebrews consists of twelve closely knit chapters arguing the superiority of Jesus Christ, and a thirteenth chapter consisting of admonitions of a variety of sorts. Chapters 1—12 are like a majestic sermon; chapter 13 is more like the conclusion of a letter, including greetings from "those who come from Italy" (13:24). Commonly Hebrews has been called an epistle, but it lacks the salutation found even in a general epistle like James. It may be best to call it what 13:22 does, a "word of exhortation." No author is mentioned, and there is no consensus about the guesses of scholars over the centuries. Luther suggested as author Apollos (cf. Acts 18:24–28 and 1 Cor. 3:1–9, 21–23); some think a woman, Priscilla, along with her husband, Aquila (see Acts 18:2, 26; 1 Cor. 16:19), wrote it (note the use of "we" at Heb. 5:11 and 6:3). But we do not know. The date could be anywhere between A.D. 55 and 95, most likely 80 to 90.

Again the most important thing for interpreting the book is to grasp its setting. Hebrews is addressed to Christians who, though veterans in the faith, are nonetheless in danger of drifting away from their Christian commitment. That they are at least second-generation Christians is shown by references to their glorious past experiences and "former days" (10:32–36; 13:7). But now they have become lethargic and "dull of hearing" (5:11), on the verge of lapsing back into what they were before they accepted Christ, and so they need not be instructed afresh (see 2:1; 10:23; 12:3, 12–13). Hence the writer argues, cajoles, and threatens, even to the point of saying that once you fall away from Christ, *no* renewal ever is possible again (see 6:4–6; 10:26; and 12:17, citing Esau as an example). This idea of "no second repentence," an example of rigorism in early Christianity, shocked Luther (who knew no such limits to God's love). Actually the author of Hebrews does not go quite this far with regard to his hearers, for his tone assumes they will return to Christ and hold fast with faith unshakable and inherit the promises (see 6:9–12; 10:35–39; and the admonitions of 11:1—12:2).

Hebrews thus is directed, with great confidence, to a problem that has afflicted the church in every generation from the A.D. 80s to the 1980s and no doubt beyond: the lack of excitement which sets in among some Christians after a while, so that they grow slack in faith.

If we knew exactly who the people were whom the epistle addresses, we could understand its method of argument even better. Traditionally the audience has been taken to be Jewish Christians who seem to be drifting back to Judaism as a way of life. More recently there have been attempts to link the book with Christians who had once been part of the Dead Sea Scrolls community at Qumran and had an intense interest in priesthood. Yet the book also reflects a very Greek way of thinking, such as is found in Plato and Philo. In this kind of thinking there is a heavenly world above, to which the earthly realm corresponds as "shadow" does to "substance" (see 8:5; 10:1). That is, the heavenly world is the real one.

Regardless of these varied possible cultural-religious backgrounds, our author has undertaken to address his hearers in a way relevant to them, so as to stress the superiority of Christ and thus urge allegiance to him in the face of apathy, persecution, or whatever. Note the basic outline:

The Supremacy of Jesus, Mediator of the New Testament Revelation—
   A. He is *superior to the angels,* through whom the law was given—chaps. 1—2;
   B. *Superior to Moses,* mediator of the law (3:1–6) *and to Joshua* ("Jesus" in Greek)—3:7—4:16.
   As great High Priest (see 5:1–10 on his qualifications), Jesus is
   C. *Superior to the priests* of the Old Covenant—chaps. 5—7;
   D. *Superior to the tabernacle and sacrifices* of the Old Covenant—chaps. 8—10.
   Hence *the admonitions:* loyalty to the great High Priest (10:17–39); faith (chap. 11); endurance and holiness (chap. 12); and various injunctions (chap. 13).

Interwoven into the argument are a good many early Christians creeds (e.g., 1:3 on Christ in creation, atonement, and exaltation). There is also a method of argument that reflects a dualistic view of two worlds, above and below. Nowhere is this better seen than in the way the meaning of Christ's death or the work of atoning for human sin is described. He "made purification for sins, he sat down at the right hand of the Majesty [God] on high" (1:3). Regarding his death, it is said Jesus "suffered outside the gate in order to sanctify the people through his own blood" (13:12). Jesus tasted suffering and death for everyone (see 2:9, 14). These phrases reflect cultic language from the Old Testament. In 13:12 "outside the gate" reflects not only the fact that Jesus died outside the gate of Jerusalem (see John 19:17, 20) but also the fact that ritual sacrifice for the day of atonement was to take place "outside the camp" (see Leviticus 16, esp. v. 27; and Heb. 13:13).

Hebrews then goes on to argue that Christ, the great High Priest, after his sacrificial self-offering on Golgotha, was exalted to a place of honor with God, having passed through the heavens to a true "sanctuary . . . set up not by man but by the Lord" (8:1–2; see also 1:3; 4:14; 5:8–10; 6:19–20). There he ministers, for us and to us (see 8:6; 9:11–12; 10:19–22). But while Christ is alive and serving as mediator for his people, today and for all time, the author of Hebrews is very careful to say that the work of Christ in the heavenly sanctuary is not a new duplication of the cross outside Jerusalem. That sacrifice occurred "once and for all" (to quote one of the great Greek words of the New Testament, rendered by a phrase in English, found several times in Hebrews, at 7:27; 9:12; 10:10). What the High Priest does is to continue to intercede for sinners, *on the basis of* the atoning cross (see 7:25; 9:24). All this is enough to make people cry out in thanksgiving and praise, do good, and share themselves and all they have with others (see 13:15–16) sacrificially. Christ emboldens us to "draw near" to God and to live in faith (10:22–25).

The emphasis on Christ and his sufficiency and superiority to all prior arrangements for salvation can also be seen in the way Hebrews handles the theme of "the covenant." Seventeen of the thirty-three New Testament uses of this word occur in this document. The contrast is between the "first covenant" given under Moses at Sinai (9:18–22; see also Exod. 24:6–8) and the "new covenant" for which Jeremiah hoped (Jer. 31:31–34, cited and interpreted at Heb. 8:8–13). The first covenant has become obsolete (8:13), its offerings and priesthood abolished (10:9).

Christ is superior to Moses (3:1–6). He is superior to the Levitical priesthood (the author makes this point by linking Jesus to a mysterious priest-king, Melchizedek, who had appeared in Genesis 14, in the story of Abraham; see Hebrews 7). Christ has a tabernacle, in the heavens, superior to the Israelite one on earth (Hebrews 8—10, esp. 9:24). In every way the covenant in Christ supersedes the old. Again, as in Paul, the real pattern is one of "promise (to Abraham) and fulfillment in Christ." But here there is the added dimension of a heavenly world, where God has designed all and perfects all. The pattern on p. 408 shows the thought of Hebrews. We should add that the epistle uses this conceptual framework as a basis regularly to exhort Christians to live more confidently and faithfully (e.g., 4:14–16; 10:23; 12:1–2).

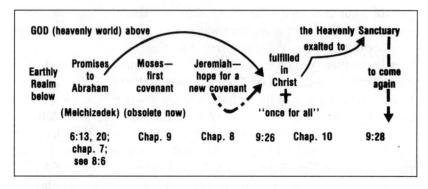

It needs to be noted that when Hebrews speaks about the Old Testament tabernacle or tent (8:5; 9:2–21) it is referring to the portable sanctuary used during the years of wilderness wanderings after the exodus, not to the later temples in Jerusalem. This underscores a final theme important to note in this book and the Bible as a whole.

The traditions of Israel about the wilderness go back to the very roots of God's people. They are preserved especially in Exod. 15:22—17:16 and Numbers 11—36. Two different understandings emerge. According to the one, the wilderness was a place of great intimacy for Israel with Yahweh, where God cared for his people as almost never before or afterward. These were halcyon days to which later generations looked back for a paradigm of the ideal religious life. This positive estimate seems to have been found especially in the literature of the northern kingdom (see Hosea 2, esp. vv. 14–15; Jeremiah 2; Deut. 8:1–10).

The other understanding of the wilderness years was negative: Israel had *not* obeyed God, but instead murmured, and in spite of the exodus miracle desired to return to Egypt (see Exod. 14:11–12; 15:24; 16:2–3; 17:2–3). Numbers 21:4–9 suggests the Israelites became impatient not merely *on* their journey but *at* the journey. Psalm 78, it has been suggested, is a polemic from Judah against the northern view that everything had been rosy back in those days in the desert. The truth was that the Israelites in the wilderness had been "a stubborn and rebellious generation" (78:8), who "did not keep God's covenant" (78:10).

Judaism has long been aware of the importance of this wilderness period for Israel. To remind members of the wanderings in the desert after the exodus, a synagogue in the U.S. Virgin Islands has sand on the floor, to recall the years of pilgrimage.

Against this background, the striking thing is that the early Christian church sometimes saw itself very much like ancient Israel during the wilderness period. It has passed through the sea in its exodus and now finds its experience parallels Israel's in the wilderness. The best example is 1 Cor. 10:1–11, where Israel's experience is used as a warning for the church. Even "sacraments" (to which ancient Israel had counterparts) do not save those who presume too much. (The verses should be read in this light, looking for parallels to the Old Testament for the Christians in Corinth. The Old Testament, in its own right, thus takes on meaning for the church.)

The Epistle to the Hebrews takes up this same understanding of the church paralleled to Israel "on the way" in the wilderness. The church is the people of God between the exodus (Christ's death and resurrection) and the "promised land" (Hebrews 4 even speaks of a promised "rest" for the people of God). En route in life, they too, like ancient Israel, are likely to grumble and complain (Heb. 3:7–19 quotes Old Testament verses about rebellion in the wilderness as a warning to Christians). But now, as then, God is faithful, who has given us his promises (19:23), and we are to walk by faith until we arrive at "the city of the living God," the "kingdom that cannot be shaken" (12:22, 28).

Here we see a picture of the church as God's pilgrim people, on march toward a goal but not having as yet attained. They are "the wandering people of God,"[3] kept by him and empowered by God with a vision of the city they seek (11:10, 16; 13:14). This picture has been brought into new prominence in recent years, for one thing through recovery of it as a theme in biblical scholarship. But the Second Vatican Council of the Roman Catholic Church also made telling use of it. Vatican II, in its "Dogmatic Constitution on the Church," entitled *Lumen Gentium* (from its opening words, "The light of all nations is Christ"), deliberately stressed this theme from Hebrews, about the church as the pilgrim people of God. It is a healthy counterbalance to all stress upon the institution and its organization and hierarchies (possibly already foreshadowed in the Pastoral Epistles), to say that the church, in Augustine's words, " 'like a pilgrim in a foreign land, presses forward amid the persecutions of the world and the consolations of God,' announcing the cross and death of the Lord until He comes (see 1 Cor. 11:26)."[4] The biblical image has helped renew the concept of the church for many Catholics, and can do so for other Christians as well. The church is part of God's good news for humanity.

NOTES

1. Cf. Paul Minear, *Images of the Church in the New Testament* (Philadelphia: Westminster Press, 1960; paperback, 1970).

2. See J. Reumann, *"Righteousness" in the New Testament* (cited above, chap. 27 n. 3), sections 266–83.

3. The phrase comes from Ernst Käsemann's dissertation, published in German in 1939, Eng. trans. Roy A. Harrisville and Irving L. Sandberg, *The Wandering People of God: An Investigation of the Letter to the Hebrews* (Minneapolis: Augsburg Publishing House, 1984). For the people of God in Hebrews as Israel in the wilderness, see 3:7—4:13 esp.

4. *Lumen Gentium* 8, in Walter M. Abbott, S.J., ed., *The Documents of Vatican II* (New York: Guild Press, America Press, Association Press, 1966), 24, quoting Augustine, *Civ. Dei* xviii, 51, 2, *Patrologia Latina* 41, 614.

32

Living "in Christ"; Ethics for Families, Church, Society, World

THE JOHANNINE MESSAGE, dealt with in chapter 30, impels believers, in light of God's love for them in Christ (John 3:16; 1 John 4:11), to a life of loving. Christians are to "love not the world" (1 John 2:15, KJV) but one another, totally, sharing their goods and giving of themselves (1 John 3:16–17). Rooted in the true Vine, Jesus Christ, disciples are to bear "much fruit" (John 15:1–9).

The gospel message of Paul dealt with in chapters 26 and 27 likewise calls on all brothers and sisters in the faith, in response to God's mercies set forth above all in Jesus and his cross, to present themselves in a living, sacrificial service to others in the world. They are not to be conformed to a world that is passing away. (Rom. 12:1–2; cf. 1 Cor. 7:31) but to be attuned to an age to come that God promises (1 Cor. 2:9–10), an age already upon believers, where Life is at work (2 Cor. 5:17; cf. 4:10–12). Christians are therefore to love and "do good to all, especially to those who are of the household of faith" (Gal. 6:10, au. trans.). There is to be "fruit produced by the Holy Spirit," virtues in which their lives are to abound (Gal. 5:22–23, au. trans.), and they are to express love in dozens of practical ways each day (Rom. 12:9–21).

This emphasis on Christian living existed from the outset in the entire early church. It appeared among the churches addressed by Paul, in the Johannine community, among congregations facing persecution in Asia Minor and Italy, and within the groups of disciples in Jerusalem and Galilee. An ethical concern, for personal conduct, family life, church fellowship, and actions in society and the world of the day, is manifest in virtually every New Testament writing. Hence followers of Jesus Christ— justified, forgiven, hoping in God's promises—had to work out what "life in Christ" meant, as citizens or slaves in Caesar's empire, as a minority in Palestine or a scattering across the cities of the Gentile world. "Church" (see chap. 31) and "ethics" go together.

Those "in Christ" of the first few Christian generations knew they possessed a living Lord, whose word touched upon them every moment of existence. But *how* were they to live and act in a hostile world? This world often had its own contrary styles of life and denied the Christians' faith and questioned their practices as folly or as overly stern and fantastic, inherited from a Jewish God called Yahweh. (Gentiles were often intrigued by the God of the Old Testament and at times repelled; they even made attempts in Greek to pronounce his Hebraic name.) To carry out the will of Yahweh and express the lordship of Jesus Christ in daily life was one of the toughest assignments early Christians had. And it is a task that is not any easier in our day, to live a witness and a life of love here and now.

Bible study does not always tackle this area of morality or ethics in the New Testament. Indeed, there are reasons for avoiding it. The passages that deal with the subject are often scattered. This may in turn lead to treating verses in isolation, without the context the New Testament writer has given them. More practically, one suspects people often react with less than burning interest here because they assume they already "know all about it." They may decide what Scripture says is "old hat," too old-fashioned, for example, on sexual morality or divorce. Or they exclaim, disinterestedly, "Another lesson on love," assuming they already know everything the Bible has to say on the topic, and then some. (To talk of "love," without explanation of what the Bible means by *agape,* can sometimes lead to merely reinforcing our own human, secular impressions and experiences.) On the one hand, therefore, bored disinterest. A particular menace for many Christians, on the other hand, is the tendency to take isolated Bible verses and make of them a new law code, about love! That, too, is misuse of the Bible. Yet while to say "love—or perish" may be literally true in some cases, and good advice psychologically, theologically it threatens to turn the response of loving into a means for seeking to earn salvation.

A further difficulty in studying what the New Testament includes under "life in Christ" is the sheer variety of material and emphases, just as we have seen in studying "the church" in the New Testament. Some documents, like the Epistle of James, seem to have little reference to Christ (cf. above, pp. 399–400), while others abound in christocentric passages. James is closer to the wisdom tradition; Paul draws his inspiration more directly from the impact of Christ as crucified and risen Lord.

Each document addresses a specific situation, aiming to apply the gospel to a set of needs. But this very variety of settings makes it hard for us to systematize New Testament teaching about Christian living. The same point holds true for people today in the variety of settings where they seek to be Christian.

A related problem is eschatology, the relation of expectations about the end of the world to ethical actions. The two Epistles of Paul to the Thessalonians are shaped under the expectation that Christ is coming soon (see under "The Thessalonian Letters" in chap. 28); therefore one lives with a rigor that can be sustained for a short time because the end is about to come. Paul has even been interpreted at times as advising Christians to avoid marriage completely because "the appointed time has grown very short" (1 Cor. 7:8, 29, 32–35). Yet the Pauline corpus also provides wholesome advice on the relation of husbands and wives analogous to the relationship between Christ and the church (Eph. 5:21–33); in Ephesians the parousia is barely a factor, if mentioned at all.

Even the social-economic-political situation varies from book to book in the New Testament. The Book of Revelation confronts a scene of impending persecution. The world, one finds, is a place of evil, under Satan, soon to pass away. The government is a menace to faith. On the other hand, Luke takes a keen interest in showing Roman governmental officials in the best light, especially in Acts. Or, again, James condemns the rich (cf. 5:1–6; 2:17), but Luke's writings show a positive interest in the well-to-do. Patches of the New Testament sound downright revolutionist (cf. Luke 1:51–53; Acts 5:29); other sections can be read as an appeal to support the status quo (1 Peter, e.g., 2:17). The Pastoral Epistles, 1 and 2 Timothy and Titus, in the pains they take to describe details about living in church and society, seem solidly middle-class— others would say "bourgeois" or even "square."

All this is to suggest that we must take seriously the variety of settings in which the New Testament talks about life in Christ. *Existence shaped by the Lord Jesus can take many forms.* Christian life styles in the early church varied. This is so not only because of the situation in which the gospel was being applied and lived, or the type of eschatology, but also because of what each convert brought to his or her new existence. A bourgeois Christianity became inevitable as middle-class people embraced the faith. (Just as in many American churches today, to be "middle class" is not salvation in itself or a barrier to being saved, but a milieu in which one practices one's faith, within the structure of society—though not uncritically.) In the early church, eschatologies that related to ethics inevitably waxed and waned, as conditions heightened expectation that

413

Jesus would come soon, or the hope for fulfillment took new forms (as with the theme of the Paraclete in the Fourth Gospel). Faith had to come to terms with order for life and the world. Such mundane things as how to care for "real widows" and regulate possible cases of fraud in the welfare rolls (see 1 Tim. 5:3–16) demanded a place on the church's agenda. Christian faith, in the New Testament, was coming to new self-understandings in the worlds of varying sorts where Christians lived. Hence it came to terms with realities like family, church, and social life.

How Christian life and witness worked out here will be tackled in this chapter by looking at some resources the first Christians had available, including certain emphases theologically from the gospel. Then, more briefly, we shall note a few specific passages for study, to illustrate how their ethical patterns for "doing the truth" of the gospel worked out in certain New Testament writings. In seeing how our ancestors in the faith worked out their life and witness here, we may find some gospel imperatives that still hold for us, and ways of working out our witness in life here, different as some conditions may be.

DIVINE DIRECTIVES IN DAILY LIFE
FROM THE GOSPEL

Jesus Christ

At the heart of any Christian endeavor to live in Christ was, of course, the vibrant, vital experience of a *living Lord.* Jesus of Nazareth, who ministered among Galileans and others for a short time before his death, now was alive and reigned as Lord. He was an influence, a presence, a means to life, for all his followers.

We dare not underestimate the impact of this resurrection faith upon ethics. One famous teacher at Cambridge University, Sir Edwyn Hoskyns, always began his lectures on New Testament ethics, it is said, with the remark, "We shall begin, of course, with the passages about the resurrection." That Jesus lives, and rules as one's Lord, is the starting point for working out one's manner of life. "I live; yet not I, but Christ lives in me," wrote Paul (Gal. 2:20, KJV).

Jesus, thus, is the *agent* of the new life. He mediates it. Paul rarely speaks of being "in *God.*" Much more commonly he talks of being "in *Christ.*" Seldom does he refer to "Christ *in us.*" Much more commonly it is a matter of us being "in Christ." (To that extent Gal. 2:20 is an exception.) That does not imply that something of Christ is in each one of us, but rather that we individuals are united in him, in his body the church, by baptism, and are caught up into his purposes. John's Gospel is similar. "Abide in me, and I in you," Jesus says (15:4; "you" is plural). Yet the Johannine writings go on, in a way Paul does not, to speak of the mutual indwelling of the Father and the Son, and of believers in both of them: Jesus prays that "even as thou, Father, art in me, and I in thee, they also may be in us" (John 17:21, au. trans.). The First Epistle of John, in describing the life imparted by the word, goes even further in an emphasis on "abiding in God" (cf. 4:16).

Yet this Jesus, who relates people to God in an abiding way, is not only the instrument "so that we might live through him" (1 John 4:9); he is also a *model* for the life to which God would lead us. To have Jesus Christ as a pattern is, of course, almost inevitable, because "no one has ever seen God" (John 1:18). In that the Son has made him known, the Son becomes the expression of what God the Father is (John 1:18; the whole Johannine prologue means God has expressed himself definitely in Christ; see also Heb. 1:3). We know self-giving love, as the core of the divine, because Christ laid down his life for us (1 John 3:16).

A term in Paul's thought for this role of Jesus as exemplar of the heart of God is *"imitation."* "Be imitators . . . of Christ" (1 Cor. 11:1). It is a term that often worries some Christians, especially when it gets hooked up with other human beings as models to be imitated ("be imitators of *me*," Paul wrote, 1 Cor. 4:16). Even more daring is the imitation of God (Eph. 5:1); who can do that? Is there not a danger of thinking too highly of ourselves and our possibilities and of making other people idols for our lives?

Yet Paul does use such expressions in speaking to baptized, believing Christians. If we take careful heed of what he says, the dangers diminish, and "imitation" becomes a flesh-and-blood way of spelling out the divine intent for human life. For one thing, when Paul speaks of Jesus Christ in this way, it is never of incidents in Jesus' earthly life, like his mannerisms or habits of piety, to be duplicated by us. (In fact, Paul's letters tell us very little about incidents in the earthly career of Jesus.) It is rather the *preexistent* Christ who is held up as example and the way in which Jesus, in a spirit of self-sacrifice, gave himself to the cross. Read again Phil. 2:5–11, and note what is mentioned, especially in vv. 6–8, as to the "mind of Christ" that is to obtain in our relations with each other. Humility, not conceit; willingness to forego rank in order to serve—these are the characteristics of Christ's obedience commended to us. Consider also 2 Cor. 8:9, in an appeal to be generous in giving a gift of grace in the appeal for relief funds: "You know the grace of our Lord Jesus Christ, that

though he was rich, yet for your sake he became poor,
so that by his poverty you might become rich.

For another thing, when the apostle does speak of imitating Paul, it is always with reference to the way he himself seeks to imitate Christ—who in turn is a reflection of God. Note the progression:

1. Paul:	"Be imitators of me, as I am of Christ."	Cf. 1 Cor. 11:3, woman, man.	Cf. also 1 Cor. 4:16; 2 Thess. 3:7–9; Phil. 3:17.
2. Christ:	(1 Cor. 11:1). See also 1 Thess. 1:6–7.	Christ.	
3. God:	Eph. 5:1.	God.	

To reverse the sequence, when it is said "Be imitators of God" (Eph. 5:1), the context is ethical ("walk in love," 5:2), and the real example is Christ. If Paul is spoken of as example, it is in connection with the way he reflects and radiates his Lord (see esp. 1 Thess. 1:6). When Paul says "Become as I am" (Gal. 4:12), it refers to his freedom and humility in Christ, freedom to be a servant for his Lord. If Paul dares to hold up as example "my ways in Christ" for a congregation (1 Cor. 4:17), the reference may be to what he teaches, but is more likely to his Christian "way of life"—which, when we look up 4:9–13, turns out to be a life marked by weakness and disrepute in the world's eyes and a style of returning blessing for insults and patience for hostility. What Paul has captured here is the spirit of Jesus Christ; for Paul reflects the way Jesus had conducted himself during the passion as well as what Jesus taught (cf. Matt. 5:39, 44).

Indeed, the whole theme of imitation—of Paul, or Christ, or God (or of other Christians and whole churches, according to 1 Thess. 2:14)—is nothing more, and nothing less, than further development of Jesus' words about a heavenly Father whose sun and rain are gifts to all alike, a God like whom we are to be. Can we imitate this beneficence and love, of which we so lavishly receive? Imitation of this sort is ethical application of God's love. "Freely you have received, freely give" (Matt. 10:8, NIV). Dare we today appeal to a godlike generosity shown by our lives as witness to the love from God we know? The New Testament suggests it is a test of Christianity, that our lives reflect the generosity we have experienced.

The Will of the Father

In discussing the living Christ and imitation of God's love, we have inevitably come into contact with *God and his will* as a further factor in

Christian life. Just as the Father and the Son could not be separated in considering love, so in the New Testament's discussion of love the will of God cannot be left out of the picture. For God's will is a loving one, and it is spoken of not only in connection with a plan to save humankind but also with regard to believers and their daily lives.

"Thy will be done," Jesus prayed (Matt. 6:10). In the Fourth Gospel he speaks again and again of doing "the will of him who sent me" (John 4:34; 5:30; 6:38–40). According to Paul, God's will is to save humankind through Christ (Gal. 1:4). God's "purpose," to use another word, was effected through the cross. It expresses itself in a call to individuals, and behind it is an eternal purpose of love (read Rom. 8:28–39 in this light). God's will and purpose therefore uphold us amid all vicissitudes, in this world and the judgment to come!

For Paul this meant in particular that his call to be an apostle and to witness for Christ was by the will of God (see 1 Cor. 1:1 and also the opening verse of 2 Corinthians, Colossians, and Ephesians). As a missionary, he learned to say (imitating Jesus!), "The will of the Lord be done" (Acts 21:14; see Mark 14:36). He regularly announced his plans with the qualification, "by God's will" (Rom. 1:10; 15:32; 1 Cor. 4:19). The most famous example of Christian conduct being circumscribed by the phrase "if the Lord wills" occurs, completely in line with Pauline thought, in the Epistle of James. See James 4:13–17, for a warning for affluent businessmen who so plot out their lives that they forget God may have other plans. Jesus' story about the foolish farmer who left God out of his plans (Luke 12:16–20) has here been restated in terms of advice to qualify future plans with the phrase that pious Christians for centuries have appended to their statements: *D.V., Deo volente,* "God willing."

Curiously, Paul in his personal plans sometimes speaks without any reference to divine guidance or God's will, even at points where some people might expect it. His hope to go to Spain to preach (Rom. 15:24) and his travel plans after Corinth (1 Cor. 16:1–9) are not put under the specific umbrella of "This is the will of God," nor does he add "If God wills." He was here quite flexible. There were plans and dreams, but God's program for him was not "cast in concrete," as if he had "telegrams from heaven" about every step of the way. Nowhere is this openness more beautifully expressed than when Paul contemplates his possible death in prison:

> For me to live is Christ, and to die is gain. . . . My desire is to depart and be with Christ, for that is far better. But to remain in the flesh is more necessary on your account. (Phil. 1:21, 23–24; all of vv. 19–26 should be read.)

Paul saw his call and the overall work of salvation as God's will; that colored what he did day by day. But even this great apostle did not claim divine guidance for every little detail; indeed some of his big decisions seem to reflect common-sense planning, not revelations.

There is, however, a most important area where God's will dominates and it is what especially concerns us here, namely, the ethical aspects of daily life. Paul was strong on emphasizing the growth of Christians toward what God wills. Some aspects of God's will, and application of it to daily life, can be seen in the following verses:

Rom. 12:2, Let your minds be renewed, your whole self transformed, in order that you may discern God's will, that is, that you may know what is good, acceptable, and the perfect thing to do in life. (This rich verse has been paraphrased here, on the basis of several English translations of the Greek.) More specifically, using the RSV terms:

"good" means that which is morally good and beneficial to others (see 1 Thess. 5:15);

"acceptable" means "pleasing to God" (cf. Eph. 5:10);

"perfect" means "mature" (as Phillips renders it; see Col. 4:12), not just "good intentions" but carrying a thing through consistently.

The sentiments of this verse are put into the form of a prayer for Christian growth at Col. 1:9–10, which should be made the content of our prayers for others.

1 Thess. 5:16–17, The will of God for us is to rejoice, pray, and give thanks.

1 Thess. 4:3, "This is the will of God [for you], your sanctification." The content here in vv. 3–8 is very much down-to-earth and deals with sex life. The old 1611 translation was sometimes subject to misinterpretation with regard to "each one" knowing "how to possess his vessel in sanctification and honour" (v. 4, KJV). Modern translators suggest it deals with taking a wife (RSV). The passage as a whole touches on God's will as abstaining from immorality (v. 3) and acting in holiness in marriage (vv. 4–5), and, indeed, all of life, even in business affairs (v. 6, RSV footnote). It is a part of God's call (v. 7). But it needs to be added that God's is not only a commanding will, but also an *enabling* one—God gives his Holy Spirit to you (v. 8) as power.

The Spirit Who Sanctifies

That brings us to the role of the *Holy Spirit* in ethics as part of the early church's emerging trinitarian faith. Christ the Lord is agent and a model for the new life. God's will abides in, and shapes, that life. But the Spirit also plays a part. This is so because in the New Testament the Holy Spirit regularly is the force and person linking the risen Christ to those in the world who believe. This is true for Paul, for John, and in other parts of the Christian Scriptures. Recall 1 Thess. 5:8, just cited, or the work of the Paraclete described in the Fourth Gospel (John 16:12–13; 14:26).

The particular function of the Spirit in connection with living ethically is *sanctification*. God's will is "your sanctification" (1 Thess. 4:3). That is something Christians pray God has done, is doing, and will do with them, that he make them "holy." Paul must often have prayed for his people, "May the God of peace himself sanctify you wholly . . ." (1 Thess. 5:23). Christians rejoice because God chose them "to be saved, through sanctification by the Spirit and belief in the truth" (2 Thess. 2:13).

But what does "sanctification" mean? The root idea in the Old Testament implied both "holiness" and "separateness" (cf. above, chap. 10, p. 156). What is sanctified to Yahweh has been separated from ordinary usage and dedicated to God. It passes from the realm of the profane to that of the holy. Thus, for Israel, there were holy times (like the Sabbath), holy places (like the "holy land" or Palestine, and the "holy city," Jerusalem; see Exod. 15:13; Isa. 11:9; 52:1), and holy persons. These include the priests (Exod. 30:30–32) and all Israelites (Exod. 19:6; Lev. 19:1–2). There were also holy objects, like the temple, its sanctuary, and its offerings (Exod. 30:25–29; Lev. 27:30–33; for example). Behind it all stood, of course, a holy God, Yahweh (cf. Isa. 6:1–5), the "Holy One of Israel" (Isa. 5:16, 19). He demanded, "You shall be holy, for I the LORD your God am holy" (Lev. 19:2). Therefore the nineteenth chapter of Leviticus is a code enjoining a pattern of behavior on the people of Israel, a holiness code for various aspects of life.

The New Testament carries over this passion for sanctification or holiness as part of God's will for his people. The demand for holiness continues after Christ has come. God's will is still "your sanctification." The divine command still holds, "You shall be holy, for I am holy"— 1 Peter 1:15–16 quotes and applies it. Those in Christ are declared to be "a royal priesthood," just as Israel was to have been (1 Peter 2:9, citing Exod. 19:6). So it is that all Christians addressed in an epistle are called "saints," literally "holy ones" (Rom. 1:7; 1 Cor. 1:2; etc.). If we ask where this sainthood, holiness, or sanctification comes from, the answer is Christ, "the source of your life . . . , whom God made . . . our righteousness and sanctification . . ." (1 Cor. 1:30). If we ask how this comes about, the answer is through baptism that unites us to Christ. As

Paul puts it at 1 Cor. 6:11, reflecting what was common practice by the
year A.D. 50,

(RSV) "You were washed,	(NEB: You have been through the purifying waters;
you were sanctified,	you have been dedicated to God and
you were justified	justified)

in the name of the Lord Jesus Christ and in the Spirit of our God."
Baptism, as the entry into Christian life, is here described as justification and
sanctification that every Christian possesses.

If sanctification (holiness) is a gift every believer has been granted, it
can also be the basis for an appeal to live in sanctified (holy, God-
pleasing) ways. Romans 6:19 and 22 ring out with the appeal for
Christians to yield themselves "to righteousness for sanctification"—"a
holy life" (NEB), "for holy purposes" (TEV). The imperative of
sanctification follows hard upon the indicative of God's gift.

But the New Testament is realistically aware that sanctification, though
it is God's gift and is something we are called to and toward, is never an
achievement clinched, wrapped up, and fully accomplished in this life.
One prays for it all through life, expects it fully at the future parousia,
and knows sanctification comes only from God (1 Thess. 5:23–24).
"Perfection" comes only at the end. Part of the good news, however, is
that, according to the Epistle to the Hebrews, "he who sanctifies [that is,
Jesus Christ] and those who are sanctified [we, and all who believe in
Christ]" are one family, and Christ has, by his suffering and blood,
already "perfected for all times" and sanctified a people who strive for
holiness (Heb. 2:10–11; 10:10; 12:14; 13:12).

It should be added that, for all the carryover and parallels from the Old
Testament with regard to sanctification, the New Testament does also
differ considerably. No longer were holy times like the Sabbath exalted
over human needs (cf. Mark 2:27–28; Col. 2:16). The concept of a "holy
city" or holy land was replaced by the idea of the whole earth as the
Lord's, indeed the Lord Jesus Christ's (1 Cor. 10:26; Col. 1:16). No
Jerusalem temple matters any more, for there is a universal church (Eph.
2:19–22). The priesthood is universalized, too, to include all Christians
in their ministry of service and witness (1 Peter 2:4–9). What matter are
the holy God, his holy servant Jesus (Acts 4:27), and Christ's people
dedicated to sanctification.

To sum up what we have seen thus far about divine directives for daily
life from the gospel, there are in the New Testament trinitarian dynamics
for ethics in Christ:

the living Lord, Jesus Christ—agent and model, for "imitation";
God the Father—his "will" calls and guides;
the Holy Spirit—enables and deepens a life of "sanctification."

But the New Testament provides even more in resources that helped shape the ethics of the early church.

ADDITIONAL RESOURCES FOR LIFE IN CHRIST AND WORLD

In a world where Christians faced all sorts of daily dilemmas—like responses to the state and society, or whether they could eat foods that bore the stamp of pagan gods, or whether holiness demanded they should separate from social activities of the day, like banquets at a Corinthian temple (1 Corinthians 8; 10:14–30)—more direction was needed even than the dynamics of the gospel.

Very often direction was found in the *Hebrew Scriptures,* interpreted now to fit new situations and in light of Christ. We have already seen, with regard to the will of God and holiness, how the New Testament could quote from the Old Testament on these points. Thus, Paul reiterates four of the Ten Commandments dealing with relations to the neighbor as incumbent upon Christians (Rom. 13:9); Paul cites what in one enumeration (the Roman Catholic–Lutheran; see above, p. 158) are the Sixth, Fifth, Seventh, and Ninth Commandments, and he cites them in that order. The whole law of God is seen as summed up in the words of Lev. 19:18, "You shall love your neighbor as yourself" (Gal. 5:14). Even on matters of church discipline, the Old Testament can be quoted to undergird an argument (see 1 Cor. 5:13, which cites Deut. 17:7).

The Old Testament Scriptures, of course, had not come down to the early church in isolation. They were accompanied by Jewish interpretations, especially from the rabbis. Inevitably, within the New Testament we have reflections of some of these *Jewish insights.* Jesus himself at times accepts them, and other times, as is well known, rejects them. Consider Mark 10:2–9, where Jesus teaches that a man should not divorce his wife. Here Jesus is expressing the viewpoint of Rabbi Shammai, rather than the more liberal one of Rabbi Hillel, in interpreting the law in Deut. 24:1–4. When Paul teaches that the body is a temple from God (1 Cor. 6:19) or that we are to bear God's "image" (1 Cor. 15:49; Col. 3:10), he is reflecting a thought found in Hillel: "See what care is bestowed on the statue of the emperor to keep it bright and clean; ought we not likewise keep God's image, our body, clean and free from every blemish?"

Jewish teachings, which had been developed to help converts in the synagogue apply the Old Testament law to their situation as Gentiles now following the God of Israel, must often have been helpful to Christians too. The very name used for such teachings, *halacha* or how one "walks" (before the Lord, in life), is reflected in certain places in the epistles; see Rom. 6:4 or 13:13 in the KJV, though modern translations may render it "conduct ourselves."

There existed, in the first century, ethical teaching not only from Judaism but also from the *Greco-Roman world*. The various philosophical movements of the day had their canons of morality. Sometimes the New Testament takes up this wisdom from the world of the day and quotes it as an aid to Christians. To illustrate, 1 Cor. 15:33 endorses a line from the play *Thaïs* by the Attic Greek poet Menander, "Bad company destroys good morals." When Phil. 4:8 talks about "whatever is true, whatever is honorable, whatever is just, . . . whatever is gracious . . . ," as the object for Christian meditation, it is employing phrases used by Stoic philosophy. The emphasis at times on "what nature teaches" (1 Cor. 11:4; Rom. 2:14–15) also reflects good Stoicism.

Particularly striking as examples of teachings about morality from the world of the day, which the New Testament has taken over, are the "lists of vices and virtues" and "tables of household duties." The latter are collections of instructions from groups within a household, like husbands and wives, parents and children, or masters and slaves. Appropriate admonitions are given for each group. See, as examples, Col. 3:18—4:1; Eph. 5:22—6:9; and 1 Peter 2:18—3:7. The former, the virtues-and-vices lists, are a string of good practices and bad about which Christians are encouraged or warned.

The point to be noted about the lists and tables is that they often reflect current morality which has been more or less Christianized and is offered to guide believers in their "walk" in the world. They may be termed "sanctified common sense," viewed from the perspective of the Christian dynamics.

We illustrate from the list of *virtues and vices* in Galatians 5. Paul's thought may be outlined as follows:

Vices (vv. 19–21)	*Virtues (vv. 22–23)*
Now the works of the flesh are plain:	
fornication, impurity, licentiousness;	
idolatry, sorcery;	love, joy, peace;
enmity, strife, jealousy, anger, selfishness, dissension, party spirit, envy;	patience, kindness, goodness;

Vices (vv. 19–21)	*Virtues (vv. 22–23)*
drunkenness, carousing, and the like.	faithfulness, gentleness, self-control;
I warn you, as I warned you before, that those who do such things shall not	against such, there is no law.
inherit the kingdom of God.	

We can readily impose on this structure the following headings, to bring out the contrasts:

1. *Theme,* contrasting "works" with "fruit," and "flesh" with "Spirit." The vices result from human inclinations, but the virtues are a result of growth prompted by the Holy Spirit.

2. *Fifteen vices* are then listed, probably in the sequence of, first, sexual transgressions (three of them); then sins involving religion (two are mentioned); third, eight violations against brotherly love; and finally, two examples of intemperate excess ("drunkenness, carousing"). The *nine virtues* may fall into three groups of three. Perhaps we are to see some contrasts between these groups of three virtues and the vice-groupings in the left-hand column. For example, "patience, kindness, and goodness" are antidotes to the kind of poison in a community brought about by "enmity, strife," etc.

3. Finally there is a *closing contrast:* those who practice these vices "shall not inherit the kingdom of God" (a classic understatement, probably stemming from Christian catechetical instruction about the kingdom as an inheritance and yet as a demand; see above, pp. 332–33). In contrast, Paul remarks to the Galatians who were being tempted to desert the gospel for a religion of legalism, "Against such [virtues] there is no law"! But such hallmarks of Christian living are to be heeded.

Now the fact of the matter is such virtue-and-vice lists were common in the ancient world. There are rough parallels in the Old Testament (compare Deut. 27:15–26 or Psalm 1). Closer analogies occur in Greek literature, especially from the Stoic philosophers. Philo, the Jewish philosopher in Alexandria, has lists of evils that run as high as 160 items! Attempts have also been made to trace such contrasts back to Qumran and even Persian thought.

Noteworthy for us to realize is that ethical material of this sort is not uniquely Christian, but comes out of the best of the insights of the day. True, Christians have often introduced new touches into such directions. For example, in Gal. 5:22, Christians would surely understand "love" against the background of God's love for us, and the word for "faithfulness" is the same one that Paul uses in discussing "justification *by faith.*" But the implication is, Christians need not "reinvent the wheel," but are free to accept insights for moral action and ethics from the world and from other religions—provided the dynamic from which such materials are viewed and with which they are used is always that of the gospel.

"Subjection" in the Haustafeln

Perhaps Christians today will wish to keep this background in mind as they wrestle through the meaning of certain passages in the Bible and look for family applications today. For the *"tables of household duties"* in the New Testament (called by the German word *Haustafeln* in Luther's Catechism and in modern scholarship) are not without their problems in an age of women's liberation. Some, indeed, would reject the New Testament completely at the point where it admonishes "Wives, *be subject* to your husbands" (Col. 3:18; Eph. 5:22; 1 Peter 3:1) and puts women in a category with slaves and children in relation to husbands, masters, and parents.

To be sure, the words about subjection are part of the New Testament, but it may help to remember they are also reflective of a social attitude of the day, one widespread in the pagan and especially the Jewish world. They are part of a pattern that runs thus: God is the head of Christ, who is the head of every man, who is the head, as husband, of a wife (1 Cor. 11:3). Yet Christian theology has seen fit to hold that ultimately Christ is not inferior to God but, as later Christology puts it, "is everything the Father is." That could imply that woman too is "everything man is," as part of humankind. One can also argue that Paul actually softens the harsh subordination of women generally held in his day by applying the analogy only to the *married* woman in relation to her husband (as in 1 Cor. 11:3). Colossians 3:18 talks, moreover, about being "subject to your husbands, as is fitting *in the Lord.*" And if we want to know what that means, we should look at Ephesians 5, where two points emerge.

1. "The husband is the head of the wife *as Christ* is the head of the church," and that means in a loving, self-sacrificing way (5:22–33).
2. Both husband and wife are to be subject "to *one another* out of reverence for Christ" (5:21). That means a mutual subordination, equality, and respect (cf. v. 33).

These New Testament ethical admonitions thus still have significant meaning, provided they are not read out of context, with no regard for their background. Perhaps what they tell us most of all with regard to ethics for home, society, and world, is that, like the New Testament writers, we need to listen to the best insights of our day and then think through, with the mind of Christ, our own answer of faith, as baptized believers—under the impact of the gospel dynamic.

It remains to add—whether or not we like such virtue-and-vice lists, whether or not we find it easy to work with such tables of familial duties—that there is a fondness, not to say a craving, for such patterns to guide behavior, to this day. The Boy Scout laws are an example. Religious groups which stress rigid discipline, indeed even mind-control, had great vogue with some young people in the 1970s and early 1980s. We even have modern approximations of Paul's list of virtues in Gal. 5:22–23 in the philosophical code of an athletic coach.

John Wooden, coach of many famous basketball teams at the University of California at Los Angeles, developed what he called a "pyramid of success," listing the virtues that lead to a winner in basketball—and life. Since his teams won the national collegiate championship seven straight times, in ten out of twelve years at the time he retired in 1975, and had once had eighty-eight victories in a row, his views merit attention. As featured in the *New York Times Magazine* for December 2, 1973, Wooden's "pyramid of success" includes among its over twenty-five key terms three of the nine items in Paul's list in Galatians, namely "self-control," "faith," and "patience." Others like "team spirit" (cf. Phil. 2:2) and "honesty" (cf. Phil. 4:8, KJV) fit Paul's thought well. We are dealing with perennial characteristics here of the human spirit at its best. Christianity recognizes such characteristics as important for life. Without making them into a law to be obeyed (whereby we can earn salvation), or confusing them with the good news, Christianity can allow them a role as resources for shaping life in the world, under the dynamic of the gospel.

SOME CASE-STUDY PASSAGES

The gospel of the triune God thus provides the basic dynamic in the church for Christian ethics. Scripture, the traditions surrounding it, and the best insights of the world of the day, all help Christians work out their appropriate patterns of ethical response.

Within the pages of the New Testament—in spite of all the difficulties that the young church was facing in an age of growth, and in spite of an often considerable uncertainty about how soon the return of Christ might be, a return that would, of course, put an end to the need for any and all ethics—there are signs of Christians hard at work on patterns of faith, for life. Husbands, wives, and children, in their mutual relationships, are all objects of concern in the endeavor to create Christian families and homes. Love and fellowship within the Christian community are emphasized in almost every writing. Increasingly a problem was the question of how to relate to the society around them. The proper response to the changing face of the Roman government therefore is an issue in Rom. 13:1–7, in the Book of Revelation (see above, chap. 29), and for the church as depicted in Acts (see 5:29, but also 16:35–39, and Paul's other experiences with Roman officials).

A *Panegyric on* Agape

A high spot of New Testament teaching about living the Christian life is surely *1 Corinthians 13*. Often called Paul's "Hymn to Love," it is not so much a hymn as a rhythmic exhortation to Christians, about love toward one another. It assumes God's love toward us in Christ, and goes on to show what is "a still more excellent way" for congregational upbuilding in Christ. This loving way is more excellent than any of the other charismatic gifts the Corinthians possessed (see 12:31 and 14:1). One should read the chapter, if possible in several translations, keeping its outline in mind; 1 Corinthians 13 falls into three verses or strophes:

Strophe I, vv. 1–3, a series of "if" clauses, "if I do thus and so but fail to exhibit love, then I am [or gain] nothing." Note the progression from speaking in tongues to sacrificing self or property. None of it matters without love.

Strophe II, vv. 4–8, some fifteen things are predicated of love. Some like to say these qualities describe what Jesus Christ was like; others, that they mirror the divine nature and will that we ought to imitate.

Strophe III, vv. 9–13, the imperishableness of love, enduring even after hope is fulfilled and faith turns to sight.

A further exercise might be to read through the entire First Epistle to the Corinthians, examining how love is brought to bear upon the various problems, chiefly ethical, faced by Paul in that congregation. For the Christian today who lives "in Christ," the principle and dynamic of love for others is still the guiding star.

Slavery

A second case study in New Testament ethics is found in the little *Letter to Philemon*. One reads this twenty-five-verse book anxiously to see what it recommends about a runaway slave. The traditional reconstruction is that Onesimus, a slave belonging to Philemon, a Christian of Colossae, had escaped from his master but, while free, in a distant city, encountered Paul. The apostle converted Onesimus to

Christianity. After being helped during his own imprisonment by Onesimus, Paul nonetheless insisted that Onesimus go back to his owner. But Onesimus, though still a slave, goes now as a brother in Christ.

Some people today may be impatient with Paul for not striking harder against the inhumane and cruel institution of slavery. Paul, of course, was expecting the world to end soon and probably thought slaves and others should therefore stay as they were until God intervened to set things straight (1 Cor. 7:20–24). We need to remember, although we did eventually free those who were literally, physically slaves—in the United Stated only during a civil war in the 1860s—that there are other forms of economic and social slavery, about which Christians today are doing all too little. The fact that we opted to end the subservience of slaves to masters ought also to embolden us to draw some implications regarding women and men in the similar passages on "household duties." Perhaps more than a century after seeing that the slave-master relationship found in the ancient world need not be continued any more, now we are becoming aware that the subjection-of-women theme is not all there is to biblical teaching about male-female relationships.

Mission in Society

A final topic worth examining in the pages of the New Testament has to do with the development of the church's understanding of its role in *society and the world.* Throughout much of the first century the church seemed on the defensive, a tiny movement struggling to exist, scarcely able to touch, let alone influence, society at all. But the Epistle to the Colossians begins to set forth that concept of the church as mission that the Book of Acts so artfully dramatizes. The church is the *missionary* body of Christ, seeking "to make the word of God fully known, . . . to make known . . . Christ . . . , the hope of glory; him we proclaim, warning every one, teaching every one . . . , that we may present every person mature in Christ" (Col. 1:25–28, RSV, adapted). The Epistle to the Ephesians raises this outreach to the most exalted level, with a vision of the church growing and expanding in the world, on the basis of the witness of Paul and the ministries of countless others (see Ephesians 1—3, esp. 2:13–22 and 4:11–16).

SUMMARY—AND APPLICATION

The New Testament thus has a healthy interest in the principle and practice of love among peoples, its application to the knottiest problems of life, and its spread through Christian witness in the world. In tackling the complexities of ever-changing family life, community relationships, and social issues, it listens for the newest wisdom and the old insights from any and all sources. But throughout, the New Testament is motivated by the gospel dynamic.

In this way the Christian church began an involvement in God's world that has gone on from New Testament times to our own day. Sometimes the church has retreated from the world and ethical concerns, other times it has plunged in all too recklessly. But to live in Christ, where it as a community is, facing situations there and applying the gospel as well as common sense, it knows to be its calling. So, too, for every Christian.

Perhaps what we need as much as anything is the gift to read the Scriptures with new sensitivity, about ourselves and our world, with ethical concern. To illustrate: the parable about the Good Samaritan (Luke 10:30–36) is so familiar that we seldom appreciate any more the shock it must have been for the Jewish audience of the Jewish preacher, Jesus, to have heard coupled with the hated term "Samaritan" the possibility that such a person might be "good."

Traditionally the tale of the Good Samaritan has been read as an "example story": as *he* did, "Go and do *thou* likewise" (v. 37, KJV). Well and good. That interpretation has inspired much noble, not to say heroic, conduct. But what if we let the story have the power of drawing us in as participants? For it compels us at the outset to identify, not heroically with the fourth person coming along the road, the Samaritan, but with the first one, the victim who was thrown into the ditch, beaten up, left half dead (10:30). Can we not then sense keenly, from his ditch-level, the failure of all too many (religious people!) who pass by, from whom one might have expected help? And then would we not recoil, as surely as a good Jew would have, from the help and touch, from receiving the aid needed, from a Samaritan? What a reversal of values! It lets one see life anew, this story does, and challenges one to "take it from there." The coming of the kingdom upsets our usual values, disturbs our normal views, and liberates us to venture new things—once we have been ministered to by Jesus or by his Samaritan.[1]

Christians are people who have been ministered to by God and by the people of God in so many ways. Their eyes are opened by the coming of the kingdom to look for new ways and manners in which to serve, shaped by the gospel dynamic of love. Individually and corporately, they are bidden to live for others, ministering to them.

NOTE

1. Cf. Robert W. Funk, "The Good Samaritan as Metaphor," *Semeia* 2, *The Good Samaritan* (Missoula, Mont.: Scholars Press, 1974), 74–81.

33

Three Proclamations
of Jesus: The Witness
of the Synoptic Evangelists

TELLING THE STORY OF JESUS never ceased in the early church. We have already seen in part 2 how Jesus himself had appeared, preaching the gospel of God (see above, chaps. 6 and 7). For knowledge of his actual ministry we are, of course, dependent on later reports, accounts, and books. This story of Jesus took a new turn with his resurrection: he is Lord (see above, chap. 13). The good news henceforth became an Easter Gospel (see above, chap. 25). Jesus Christ is spoken of by faith as mediator of creation (see above, chap. 18). But the story of Jesus went on. It kept being retold. We have seen how the Gospel of John appeared, sometime in the 90s, to address the good news to a particular situation and circumstances (see above, chap. 30). We now turn to the other three Gospel accounts of the Jesus story in the New Testament, which return us to the heart of Christianity, Jesus Christ. These are the "good news books" that go under the titles (in the early manuscripts), "According to Matthew," "According to Mark," "According to Luke."

The term to be supplied at the head of all these titles is "The Gospel." For each evangelist assumed he was presenting the one and only gospel. Luke, we have seen, added a second volume, Acts, to carry on the story of the actions of the risen Christ through his church (see above, pp. 86–88, 104–5, and chap. 25). Matthew will tend to incorporate this emphasis on the church and its development in the one volume he writes about Jesus.

But while each evangelist presents the one and only gospel, he always does so writing in a particular time and place. Hence the situation and needs addressed will account for a good many differences when we compare the books of Matthew, Mark, Luke, and John. Actually, the modern reader has an advantage that no ancient Gospel writer ever had: today we can read all four Gospels; but there is no evidence or likelihood that any evangelist had before him the works of his three colleagues in the Christian canon.

John's Gospel we have already examined, and it stands out as a high point in New Testament development. But the other three, which are so alike in many ways that they have traditionally been called the "Synoptics,"[1] should not be overlooked, for they are significant theological presentations in their own right. Too often Matthew, Mark, and Luke have been regarded as totally overshadowed by Paul and John. Biblical studies in recent years have helped us appreciate as never before the meaningfulness of the work of each evangelist as a witness to Jesus Christ in his own day.

Generally Mark is conceded to have been the first Gospel book to be written down, though for many centuries it was assumed (and still is in the opinion of some scholars) that Matthew was composed first. Usually Mark is dated around A.D. 70, and Matthew and Luke ten to twenty-five years later. Matthew seems to many observers to be earlier than Luke and both of them prior to John, but one should not be dogmatic about such matters. What seems "earlier" or "later" about a particular Gospel may simply reflect the degree of development in that community for which the evangelist writes or the sources he employs.

More important is the whole idea of writing a gospel book. So far as we know, Mark was the pioneer who first took this momentous step. Prior to that time there had been lots of isolated stories circulating about Jesus, sayings of his, collections of teachings, passion accounts, creeds, and hymns, as we have seen, and these may have been in oral or written form, but no one had put this material together as an organized whole, so as to provide an account of Jesus' ministry, passion, and resurrection. Mark led the way in this new direction of telling the Jesus story.

The Gospels, of course, are not biographies, for who could tell a person's life and omit (as Mark does) his birth, childhood, education, family (cf. 6:3 as the only hint in Mark) and psychological aspects, let alone the final climax of the story, his resurrection appearances, his becoming Lord? Even in Matthew, where something of Jesus' infancy is recounted, and in Luke, where there is more attention to biography and psychology, we do not have a "life" in the strict sense, such as Suetonius wrote of the twelve Caesars or Plutarch provided about famous Greeks and Romans. No, the New Testament Gospels are witness literature, written "through faith for faith" (Rom. 1:17)—that is, by persons who believed, in order to convert others and deepen Christian life within the church.

It is often said that Mark, in writing the first Gospel, created a new literary form different from biographies, intended to awaken and nurture faith in his Lord. There were rough analogies in the Greek world in writings about wandering philosophers like Apollonius of Tyana, who traveled about, teaching, and who were credited with working miracles. There existed in the Jewish world lives of the prophets, who were credited with speaking in the name of Yahweh and with performing extraordinary deeds. Within the Old Testament, even the cycle of stories about Elijah and Elisha (cf. 1 Kings 17—2 Kings 10) can be claimed as precedent. But Mark—or some predecessor, if we want to assume there were earlier efforts prior to Mark or behind the Fourth Gospel, for the "many" of whom Luke 1:1 speaks as having "undertaken to compile a narrative" about Jesus could include more than Mark and Matthew—Mark is the first one whose work is preserved, the pioneer retelling of the fuller Jesus story as good news.

One other preliminary matter deserves note before looking at the three Synoptics individually. While our evangelists were persons of theological insight and amazing ability, we should not suppose too much creativity on their parts, as if they were inventing materials. In most cases they had sources, oral or written, and these they used by shaping them to fit the situation of their day. To this extent each Gospel is a preaching of the good news to needs about A.D. 70 or 90, but each evangelist works with materials he has received from earlier decades, going back to the time of Jesus.

An illustration or two will help to show how the evangelists worked, both with fidelity to traditions they received and, in preaching to their own day, with a certain freedom that may surprise us. A case in point involves two obvious collections of materials in Mark. Mark 1:21–39 can be described as "a day in the life of Jesus." Directly after the Markan prologue, 1:1–15 (see above, pp. 95–96), and stories about the call of the first disciples (1:16–20), we see Jesus, in Capernaum on a Sabbath, heal in the synagogue (1:21–28), then heal in Simon Peter's home (1:29–31), heal after sunset (when good Jews feel they can move about, now that Sabbath is over, 1:32–34), and in the morning pray alone and then move on in his ministry (1:35–39). Then, after an isolated story about a leper (1:40–45, there is no indication of time or place), there follows a collection of stories about Jesus in controversy with opponents. See 2:1—3:6; its subsections, 2:1–12, 13–17, 18–22, 23–28, and 3:1–6, give us five incidents where Jesus faces opposition from scribes (2:6, 16) and Pharisees (2:24; 3:6), leading to a breach between them and Jesus so great that the opponents are ready to kill him (3:6).

We are shocked to see, in reading Matthew, how the neat chronological Markan sequence in 1:21–39 is broken up and distributed as part of a new arrangement. The details work out thus (though they will be most convincing only if one takes time to look up the verses or to examine them in a synopsis of the Gospels):

	Mark	Matthew
Jesus heals in the synagogue at Capernaum	1:21–28	cf. 7:28–29, otherwise omitted
Jesus heals in Simon's home	1:29–31	8:14–15
Jesus heals at evening	1:32–34	8:16
Jesus moves on next day to pray	1:35–38	omitted
Jesus goes throughout Galilee (preaching and exorcisms)	1:39	cf. 4:23

Whatever Matthew may have thought of Mark's "typical day" in Jesus' ministry, he had reason to use the stories otherwise. One good reason we have already seen (cf. above, pp. 113–14): Matthew likes to collect materials in a neat and orderly way. The two healings thus become part of his collection of ten miracle stories in Matthew 8—9. The other verses he uses as part of his concluding comments on the Sermon on the Mount at 7:28–29 and to frame in 4:23 (and 9:35) the whole section of chapters 5—9; see above, p. 112. (To be sure, someone might want to argue that Matthew's Gospel came first, but then we face the problem of how Mark managed to put together "a day in the life of Jesus" with chronological correctness from such random materials in Matthew 4, 7, and 8.)

The other block of material, in Mark 2:1—3:6, about how Jesus handled opposition, is similarly reworked by Matthew. Without going into detail, the table provided shows the parallels (Luke is included to indicate that Luke here follows the sequence in Mark, as indeed he also does for Mark 1:21–39):

	Mark	Matthew	Luke
Jesus heals a paralytic	2:1–12	9:1–8	5:17–26
Criticism of Jesus for receiving and eating with tax collectors like Levi	2:13–17	9:9–13	5:27–32

Three Proclamations of Jesus

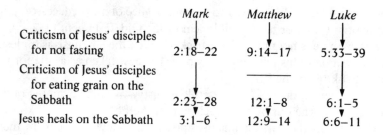

	Mark	Matthew	Luke
Criticism of Jesus' disciples for not fasting	2:18–22	9:14–17	5:33–39
Criticism of Jesus' disciples for eating grain on the Sabbath	2:23–28	12:1–8	6:1–5
Jesus heals on the Sabbath	3:1–6	12:9–14	6:6–11

Here again readers can see that Matthew has a different pattern, and they can discern, indeed, what it is: Mark 2:1–22 is used in Matthew's collection of ten miracles (Matthew 8—9, specifically at 9:1–17). The reader of Matt. 9:18—11:30 will find Matthew then brings in other miracles also, for example, from Mark 5:21–43, cf. 10:46–52, Jairus's daughter, the woman with the hemorrhage, and a blind man, to fill out his collection. Matthew 9:35 rounds out his structure in 4:23—9:35 (see above, pp. 112–14). Matthew 10 and 11 present material from other sources than Mark about the mission of the Twelve and about Jesus himself (see esp. 11:25–30), before picking up Markan material again (Matt. 12:1–21 = Mark 2:23—3:12).

It can be fascinating to explore such passages, and scholars take great pains to search out the possible meaning of these agreements and varieties within Mark, Matthew, and Luke. Very likely Mark 1:21–39 and 2:1–3:6 were collected units of material before Mark put his book together. We could also spend time exploring the history of each story during the years of its oral transmission and use (as form criticism does). Or we could trace the same story through its use by each evangelist, or speculate about differences in meaning the same saying has in different contexts. Cf. Matt. 10:26 in the context of v. 27, and Luke 12:2 in the context of 12:1–3; the former application suggests " 'Truth will out'; proclaim it boldly," whereas the latter uses the same figure of speech to warn that dark, hidden deeds will one day be found out.

All these explorations could be carried out, behind and among the Synoptics, but we mean here to look at each Gospel as it stands, in order to get at the particular message of each evangelist.

MARK: GOOD NEWS IN DARK AND CHANGING TIMES

"The beginning of the Gospel of Jesus Christ, the Son of God," as Mark heads his book (1:1), can refer, we have already seen (pp. 95–97, above), to Jesus' initial public appearance, preaching the gospel about the kingdom, in Galilee (1:14–15); or to the appearance of his predecessor, John the Baptist (1:4); or to the fulfillment of the Old Testament (1:2–3). In any case, there is not much about backgrounds; the emphasis is on Jesus and the action in his ministry. Perhaps 1:1 is best taken as a title for the entire book (as in the RSV).

That understanding of Jesus' earthly ministry, as "the beginning of the Gospel," is borne out by the conclusion of the book. As is well known, Mark ends, in the earliest manuscripts, and, following them, in most modern translations, at 16:8. The final scene is of Easter morn, when three women go to the tomb in order to anoint Jesus' crucified body, but find the tomb empty and are told by "a young man . . . in a white robe," that Jesus is risen; "Go, tell his disciples and Peter that he is going before you to Galilee; there you will see him, as he told you" (16:7; cf. 14:28 for Jesus' promise).

The underlying assumption of this scene at the empty tomb and indeed of the whole Gospel is that this Jesus, of whom Mark tells, is risen and exalted as "Christ" and "Son of God." The good news for Christians begins with this story of how, in fulfilling Old Testament promises, God "anointed Jesus of Nazareth with the Holy Spirit and with power; how he went about doing good and healing all that were oppressed by the devil"; how God was with him, even after his death at Jerusalem, and raised him up to be Lord and Christ (Acts 10:36–40; 2:32–36). What the sermons in Acts tell in a few proclamatory phrases, Mark depicts in more detail quite vividly, with stories, dialogue, and drama. What the witnesses in Acts tell with their mouths (10:39), Mark the evangelist relates in his own way with pen and papyrus.

Mark's version of the gospel has a certain "pell-mell" quality about it. One event follows hard upon another. "Immediately" is a favorite word (1:10, 12, 18, 20, 21, for example). There are only a few efforts at precise chronology; 1:21–39 has already been mentioned as a time sequence, but just when that momentous Sabbath and Sunday occurred is not precisely specified. The dating of the transfiguration (9:2) as occurring "after six days" is unusual (only the passion chapters have such chronological concerns); but even here we are left to guess, "Six days after what?" (Presumably, Peter's "confession," 8:27–33.) Geography is often just as vague. A classic example has involved the efforts of geographers to trace the route of 7:31 (where RSV is more possible than KJV in its translation had been) and 8:10 ("Dalmanutha" is unknown to us; some manuscripts substitute other names).

All this suggests that Mark's chief concern is to concentrate on Jesus and his story as the beginning of the gospel and to tell it with a certain excitement and urgency. The contents of the book in outline runs like this. (For a theological outline see below, p. 441.)

1. *Prologue* (1:1–15), telling us who Jesus is, what his message is about (1:15), and that God is with him. See under "Beginning the Good News in Mark" in chap. 6.

2. *Jesus Ministers in Galilee and Beyond (1:16—9:50)*
Students of the Bible debate exactly how these chapters are structured. There are different ways of dividing up the material. References to excursions outside Galilee are limited—just enough to assure Gentiles reading or hearing "the Good News according to Mark" that inclusion of them in the kingdom was foreshadowed in the ministry of Jesus. The following sections and units stand out:
   a. Call of the first four disciples to become "fishers of men" (1:16–20). The phrase seems to mean here "evangelize people," not snare them for the judgment (as in Jer. 16:16).
   b. "A day in the life of Jesus"—teaching and working miracles (1:21–45; see above, pp. 431–32).
   c. Controversy with opponents (2:1—3:6), see above, pp. 431–33.
   d. Jesus' growing ministry (3:7–35), involving twelve specially appointed disciples (3:14–19) and the opposition of friends (3:20) and family (3:31–35).
   e. A collection of three parables about the kingdom (4:1–34).
   f. Two cycles of stories, about sea-, healing-, and feeding-miracles by Jesus:

(1) Stilling the storm at sea (4:35–41)	Walking on the sea (6:45–52)
(2) The Gerasene demoniac (5:1–20)	Blind man of Bethzatha (8:22–26)
(3) Jairus's daughter raised, and the	Syrophoenician woman (7:24–30)
(4) Woman with a hemorrhage healed (5:21–43)	Deaf mute (7:31–37)
(5) Feeding of the 5000 (6:34–44)	Feeding of the 4000 (8:1–10)

   g. Intertwined with these miracle stories are references to the Twelve sent forth to witness (6:7–13, 30–33) and, more ominously, the rejection of Jesus in his home synagogue (6:1–6) and the martyrdom of the forerunner John the Baptist (6:14–29).

h. Of Jesus' ministry, there are brief summaries (6:6b, 53–56) and one long discourse, on freedom from Pharisaic and Mosaic laws (7:1–23), almost in the spirit of Paul (or is Paul in the spirit of Jesus on this point?). Verses 8:11–21 sum up the "signs" (miracles) that Jesus has been performing and the disciples' lack of understanding. He will give "no sign ... to this generation" (8:12). They "do not yet understand" (cf. 8:17–18, 21).

i. All the more surprising therefore is Peter's confession of Jesus, "You are the Christ" (8:27—9:1, esp. 8:29). Since Jesus turns the conversation in the direction of "the Son of man" and suffering (8:31), there is reason for calling Peter's use of the term "Christ" at this point a misunderstanding that Jesus must correct (see above, p. 299). There thus unfolds a pattern of which Mark is fond:

    (1) Christology—having the right view of Jesus as suffering Son of man (8:27–33)

    (2) Discipleship—getting a right view of what it means to follow Jesus: denying self, confessing Jesus, bearing a cross (8:34–37)

    (3) Eschatology—understanding the times: the kingdom is near, our fate when the Son of man judges will depend on our response to Jesus (8:38—9:1)

j. The transfiguration, where Jesus appears transformed, together with Elijah and Moses, and God bears witness again to him (cf. 1:11), is another pointer as to who Jesus is and will be—God is with his Son (9:2–8).

k. The dialogue "on the way" (a Markan phrase, 8:27; 9:33) intersperses teachings with another healing story (9:14–29). The Twelve still do not understand about discipleship (9:33–50) or about Jesus' coming death (9:9–13, 30–32).

l. Throughout this section there are occasional references to or for Gentiles. There is, for example, the bold teaching that it is the things within the heart of a person that defile, not the foods we eat (7:14–23). The excursion by Jesus into the region of Tyre and Sidon and healings of a Greek woman (7:24–30) as well as of Legion (5:1–20) and of a deaf man (7:31–36)—thus fulfilling the dream of Isaiah for restoration during the exile (cf. 7:37, which reflects Isaiah 35:5–6)—to mention nothing of the fact that the important events of 8:27–30; 8:31—9:1; and perhaps 9:2–13 occur on a pagan site north of Israel, all suggest this Jesus will be important for other peoples besides the Jews.

3. *Jesus Goes Up to Jerusalem* (chaps. 10—13)
   a. "On the way" (apparently Jesus goes down the east bank of the Jordan, 10:1) there is opportunity for more ethical teaching (10:2–31). There is a final miracle (10:46–52), where the man healed then follows Jesus "on the way" (10:52). The disciples still do not understand (10:35–44). Again the passion is emphasized (10:32–34, 45).
   b. In Jerusalem, after Jesus enters and next day cleanses the temple, we have a series of controversies with chief priests, scribes, elders, Pharisees, and Sadducees. The stage is set for his death. "Have faith in God," Jesus counsels (11:22). In some ways the controversy stories and teaching materials in chapters 11—12 remind one of Mark 2:1—3:6.
   c. Chapter 13, the "Little Apocalypse" (see above, pp. 295, 349–50), seems to many readers an intrusion. It must have been very important to Mark to spend so much space on the fall of Jerusalem (13:1–2, 14–23), persecution (13:9–13) for the gospel's sake, and apocalyptic signs of the end of the age (13:3–8, 24–27). However these words spoke to his own day, Mark was also employing them, just prior to the story of the death of Jesus, so as to provide a ray of hope: beyond all the suffering and catastrophe stands God, who is in control (v. 20) and who will care for the elect (v. 27) and bring salvation (v. 13). Hence the closing admonition is to watchfulness (13:33, 37).

4. *Jesus' Passion, Death, and Resurrection* (chaps. 14—16)
   Now follows the familiar story of the cross. The plot is set in motion by Judas Iscariot (14:10–11, 43–46) at the behest of the chief priests and scribes (14:1–2, 53–65). Since Jesus could not be anointed for burial when he was placed in the tomb (cf. 16:1) or on Easter morn, Mark tells a story about a symbolic anointing beforehand (14:3–9)—which is itself made part of the preaching of the gospel "in the whole world" (14:9). The woman who "has done what she could"—her name not recorded, as in so many gospel stories—is thus immortalized.
   Step by step the events unfold of the upper room (14:12–31), Gethsemane (14:32–52), the Jewish trials (by night, 14:53–65; and by day, 15:1), Peter's denial and remorse (14:66–72), the Roman trial (15:2–20), crucifixion (15:21–41), burial (15:42–47), and the empty tomb (see above, pp. 298, 311). The enigmatic close to Mark's Gospel, that the women were afraid at the news of Jesus' resurrection (16:8), has been

variously interpreted. Most likely it is a final stoke of irony—"afraid," before the best news ever about Jesus? To understand the outcome, one must go back and read the prologue once again and the underlying confession in Mark's witness that Jesus is risen Lord!

If such are the contents of Mark, what do we make of the book as a whole? A number of fascinating interpretative clues have been suggested. One revolves around the term "Son of God" employed in the title verse, 1:1. Three times there are significant confessions of Jesus using this title, and an attempt has been made to line each up with "enthronement rituals" known from the ancient Near East (cf. under "Psalms for a Coronation" in chap. 21, esp. p. 276):

1:11	The voice from heaven says, "Thou art my beloved Son; with thee I am well pleased," as the Spirit descends on Jesus.	"Adoption" by God announced.
9:7	The voice out of the cloud testifies, "This is my beloved Son; listen to him," at the transfiguration.	Proclamation to the disciples.
15:39	The centurion, on behalf of all Gentiles, confesses, "Truly this man was the Son of God."	Enthronement, acclamation.

Surely "Son of God" is a significant title for Jesus in Mark's witness, but there is no suggestion in the text of this threefold progression in the references. He is also called Son of God at 3:11 and 5:7 by demon(iac)s and, in effect, at the trial (14:61–62). So these three stages are not the central structure of Mark.

Another pattern can be found in the parallelism involving the forerunner, Jesus, and the disciples:

John the Baptist preached (1:4) and was "delivered up" (1:14, to prison and death);

Jesus came preaching (1:14), and was "delivered up" (9:31; 10:33; cf. Mark 14—15);

The disciples preach, Christians are to preach (3:14; 13:10; 14:9), and they, as Jesus' followers, will be "delivered up" (13:9–13).

The suggestion here is that discipleship involves trodding the way that Jesus and his predecessor went (cf. 8:34–37).

Still another possible inkling of Mark's thought lies in the word "gospel." Again it is a word in his title (1:1) and prologue (1:14–15). We have, in citing 13:10 and 14:9, noted that the gospel is something that Mark assumes will go on being preached (by disciples, the Christians), after Jesus' death and resurrection. Two further references suggest what Mark means by the gospel: when Jesus talks of "losing one's life" or giving up things "for my sake and the gospel's" (8:35; 10:29), plainly the gospel is being paralleled with Jesus himself. In Mark, Jesus Christ is the gospel. Mark's book, which tells the Jesus story, is "the beginning" of the gospel. The witnesses are to go on telling it!

What situation prompted Mark to put together the good news for his day in the manner he has presented it? Clearly his endeavor is to present miracle stories, parables, apocalyptic, and the passion materials in a way that makes Jesus the Son of God who was delivered up for us and who is himself good news in that very death and ensuing lordship. A great deal depends on the date and place for which we assume Mark was written.

It has been traditional, since the second century, to hold that Mark was written for Christians in Rome during the persecution under Nero, around A.D. 66 to 70. The aim, therefore, would be to offer hope, amid suffering, to Christians in Rome.

Others have preferred to relate the book to the war going on in Palestine A.D. 66 to 70, where the Jews had rebelled against Rome. If circulated among Christians there, the book could have encouraged them amid their tribulations (cf. 13:7–8, 14–23). In that case, chapter 13 would have special meaning for readers of Mark.

A related view depends on a particular interpretation of 16:7 (cf. 14:28). The words, Jesus "is going before you to Galilee; there you will see him," need not be taken as a reference to a resurrection appearance (which Mark does not report) but could apply to the parousia, in Galilee. In that case the book would be a fervent appeal to flee Jerusalem and get to Galilee where the second coming will occur at any moment. But why write a book about "the beginning of the gospel" if the world is soon to come to an end?

All these interpretations make of Mark "good news for dark times."

A more theological interpretation suggests the heart of the book is the passion story in chapters 14—16, toward which the "passion predictions" (8:31; 9:31; 10:33–34) point, as do the controversies in 2:1—3:6 and in chapter 12. Mark then wishes to stress the "theology of the cross" in contrast to any view of Jesus simply as a miracle worker or teacher. Even the disciples when they "do not understand" his impending death are guilty of a wrong or one-sided view of Jesus.

Finally, if we were to date Mark *after* A.D. 70, rather than before the fall of Jerusalem, then the message would take on still another dimension. When the war against Rome began, many Christians (just as many Jews) must have seen signs of "the end of the world." There had been giddy hopes of victory and an independent Jerusalem. Instead the city lay in ashes now and Yahweh's temple was destroyed. Did that mean all hope was lost and God was dead? No, says Mark, go back to your roots, in Galilee, where it all began. Think again about Jesus' message that God is king, recall the power shown in his ministry. Faith still asserts that Jesus is Lord and Son of God. And go, share this good news with the Gentiles, throughout all the world.

In these last two cases, Mark's book speaks as a gospel not just for evil days but for changing times, pointing us to what matters in Christianity as a new day begins, in Galilee, where the mission spreads forth to preach Jesus as crucified and risen Lord.

Whatever the precise circumstances when he wrote—and Mark lets us read these only between the lines, not telling us even his own name (the designation "According to Mark" is a traditional one)—Mark has left us a powerful pioneering effort at telling the Jesus story in a holistic way. Both Matthew and Luke were to follow his basic outline.

MATTHEW: STRUCTURING THE TEACHINGS OF JESUS AND THE CHURCH

To grasp what Matthew has done, creatively, as a preacher and witness, it is interesting to compare his larger book with that of Mark. The Markan outline is reflected in the other Synoptic Gospels, but especially in Matthew.

Mark	*Matthew*	*Luke*
		Historial Preface, 1:1–4
	Infancy, chaps. 1—2	Infancy, chaps. 1—2
1. Prologue, 1:1–15	Preparation for the Ministry, 3:1—4:11	Preparation for the Ministry, 3:1—4:13
2. Ministry in Galilee, 1:16—9:50	Ministry in Galilee, 4:12—18:35	Ministry in Galilee, 4:14—9:50
3. To Jerusalem, chaps. 10—13	To Jerusalem, chaps. 19—20	To Jerusalem, 9:51—19:44
4. Passion, Death, Resurrection, 14:1—16:8	Passion, Death, Resurrection, chaps. 21—28	Passion, Death, Resurrection, 19:45—24:53

We shall see that Luke varies most from Mark, but the Markan outline shaped both the Gospels of Matthew and Luke, in considerable detail.

The same thing holds true if we venture a "theological outline" of themes in the first two Gospels (Luke will be treated later below). Mark, the pioneer Gospel, presents his story in two sections, with only a bit appended about backgrounds in the past or about the church:

THE GOSPEL OF MARK, A THEOLOGICAL OUTLINE

Old Testament	*Galilee* *(chaps.1—9)*	*To and in* *Jerusalem* *(chaps. 10—16)*	
Old Testament fulfillment seen in John the Baptist (1:2–3); occasionally through Jesus, cf. 14:18, 34; 15:24; etc. Little on "Israel."	"The place of beginnings, revelation, and salvation."	"The place of hostile powers and of the death of Jesus."	Church and mission cf. 13:10, 11–13.
	Public Ministry Jesus preaches, teaches, does miracles, on "the kingdom of God." The disciples respond at first but "do not understand." Controversy stories (2:1—3:6). Passion predictions (8:31; 9:31; 10:33–34).	*Private Ministry* Fewer miracles, Jesus speaks more about himself and the future. The disciples still misunderstand and deny and desert Jesus. Controversy stories (chap. 12). Passion narrative. Resurrection announced, but no appearances.	

Matthew carries over a great deal of these emphases, but augments them at a number of places. We shall outline three of Matthew's favorite emphases first and then chart the resulting "theological outline" for Matthew.

1. Matthew puts a far greater emphasis on *teaching* than Mark ever did. All too often Mark had said "Jesus taught" but failed to report what he said (e.g., Mark 1:22, 27). Matthew is determined to remedy that by giving us more content here. But that is not all. Matthew stresses teaching, ahead even of preaching and healing (cf. 4:23), for Jesus and the disciples both (see pp. 112–13, above). His must have been a teaching

church where scribe-like teachers were prominent (cf. 13:52) and the Great Commission was to spread the gospel by teaching (28:20). Matthew exhibits his emphasis on teaching by concentrating what Jesus said in five great discourses, only two of which have parallels in Mark:

Matthew 5—7, the Sermon on the Mount;

chapter 10, missionary instructions, when the Twelve are sent out (cf. Mark 6:7);

chapter 13, parables about the kingdom (the three in Mark 4 have here become a collection of seven parables);

chapter 18, discipline in the community of disciples (or church, 18:17);

chapters 24—25, eschatology; compare Mark 13, and note the closing verses at 24:42–51, where the emphasis is not only on watchfulness (24:42) but also on good stewardship in the interim (24:45–51).

Some would add as a sixth discourse chapter 23, a collection of "woes" against the scribes and Pharisees.

2. Matthew is concerned to exhibit a *continuity with the past,* particularly with the Old Testament Scriptures, as he writes his Gospel. This can be seen in the way he has Jesus and John the Baptist announce exactly the same message (3:2; 4:17). But, then, disciples are to preach that message too (10:7), and so the resulting continuity is a further example of the sequence of "John-Jesus-disciples" that Mark had presented. But Matthew goes further by beginning his Jesus story with a genealogy stretching back to Abraham (1:1–17) and by his stress on Jesus as "son of David" (see above, pp. 101–2, and under " 'Son of David' as a Title for Jesus" in chap. 23). The very title of his book suggests a link to the initial book in the Old Testament, for while we translate 1:1 "The book of the genealogy of Jesus Christ," it means literally "the book of the *genesis* of Jesus. . . ." Finally there are to be mentioned the use of Old Testament verses introduced by the formula, "This happened [in Jesus' life] to fulfill what was spoken by the prophet in the Old Testament" (see above, pp. 102–3, 114, 291), and the way Matthew employs allegorical details in parables to reflect Israel's past history. For examples, read 21:33–44 (in light of Isa. 5:1–7) and 22:2–10 as suggestions that Israel has rejected God's messages from the time of the earlier and later prophets to the Christian missionaries, right down to the fall of Jerusalem in A.D. 70 (cf. 22:7).

3. Matthew has a particular interest in *the church* (see above, p. 391). His is the only Gospel to use the word (16:18; 18:17). He closes with Jesus sending forth his church to preach in all the world (28:16–20). Those discourses in chapters 10 and 18, to say nothing of 5—7 and

23—25, can be read as pertinent to the church of Matthew's day. Above all, some of the parables of chapter 13 (see below) weave in a "doctrine of the church." If all of that is true, Matthew has considerably expanded the range of view found in Mark to something like this:

THE GOSPEL OF MATTHEW, A THEOLOGICAL OUTLINE

Creation   Parousia

Background in Israel	*The Period of Jesus*	*The Time of the Church and of Mission*
Genealogy, stressing Abraham and ——→ David (1:1–17)	Jesus is son of David, son of Abraham (1:1)	28:16–20, go to all the world, Gentiles included
Old Testament promises are now fulfilled ——→ (cf. 1:23; 2:6, 4:15–16, etc.)	Jesus = the Servant (8:17 = Isa. 53:4) who fulfills Scripture	New promises made: "I am with you always" (28:20)
The law, the prophets, until ——→	John the Baptist (11:12–13), find continuity with Jesus,	as with the disciples also
Israel's past history points to rejection (21:33–44; 22:2–10)	Jesus calls for righteousness (6:33; 5:20; 5:6; 13:43)	The church likewise is always under judgment, and its members face God's ethical demand (22:11–13; 5:20)
	Galilee (chaps. 4—18) Jerusalem (chaps. 19—28)	

Matthew sees continuity between the past and the present. He imposes a view of the church and a message for the community of his day on the Jesus story as he tells it, rather than write a second volume about the church as Luke does. Of course his main section, on Jesus' ministry, follows Mark's outline, as indicated above, with its Galilean and Jerusalem sections, and the teaching discourses are built into that structure.

What sort of situation can have prompted Matthew to tell his story thus? It is commonly conceded that he writes some ten to twenty-five years after the fall of Jerusalem, A.D. 85 to 90 more specifically. That means Jerusalem has fallen and a period of reflection has set in. It also means that the intense mood of expectancy for the parousia of Christ, such as had characterized Mark's day and Pauline letters (like those to Thessalonica), was past and it was not yet a time of apocalyptic expectancy such as would rise again about A.D. 95 under the threat to the faith presented by the emperor Domitian (see above, chap. 29). In eschatology Matthew's job is to sustain the future hope but not to fan the flames of unrealistic timetables for the end. In that light, one ought to read 24:12, 26–28, 37–51, and chap. 25, all of it material that Mark does not include.

Matthew's situation some fifteen to twenty years after Mark also means that there has come to be an increasingly sharp demarcation between Judaism and the Christian church. Matthew can speak of *"their* synagogues" (4:23; 10:17; 12:9), that is, of the Jews, in distinction to the local assemblies of Jesus' disciples. After A.D. 80, as Judaism was reconstituting itself following the fall of Jerusalem, there was added to the standard synagogue prayer a petition that no follower of Jesus could pray, because it said, "let . . . the Nazarenes and the *minim* [apparently references to Jewish Christians, the latter term meaning "sectarian" or "infidel"] perish . . . and be blotted from the book of life." As the "parting of the ways" came, Christians, including the author of the Gospel of Matthew, responded with equal vehemence. Sections like 23:1–36 and verses like 27:25 and 22:7–8 reflect such feelings. (Twentieth-century Christians, no longer in that same situation in which Matthew's community lived, dare not let these passages become a basis for allowing the anti-Semitism always latent in the world to become a new attack on Jews or Israelis.)

Matthew also faced a different situation than Mark on one other score. His church community was strongly Jewish Christian in background (Mark composed for Gentiles primarily; note Mark 7.) Matthew's group has often been described as a kind of Jewish Christian enclave within the Jewish ghetto in some city like Antioch in Syria or in some large town in northern Palestine. Yet because of the hardening of the lines between Judaism and the emerging Christian church, to gain new members from those of Jewish background was increasingly unlikely. And the rest of the Christian movement was becoming more and more Gentile—Greek and Roman members who knew little of the Hebrew Scriptures, the ethics of the law, God's past promises, and who indeed could not even read Hebrew! The conditions in Matthew's day were much like those of an old German or Swedish Lutheran church in a downtown urban area in the

1960s: boats with North European immigrants had ceased coming, the blocks around the church were crowded with blacks and Hispanics; will old Emmanuel Church die?

The answer that Matthew gives is "No!" Mission will go on. True, Jesus himself never during his earthly ministry evangelized Samaritans or Gentiles (cf. 10:5). Only rarely did he have contact with "foreigners" (cf. 8:5–13; 15:21–28). But now, after the resurrection, the wraps are off: go everywhere, to *all* peoples (28:19–20).

But that dare not mean severing ties with the past. Hence Matthew underscores continuity between ancient Israel and the church. Hence the "formula quotations," to point up how past promises were being fulfilled.

Above all, this new situation dare not mean "cheap grace" where "anything goes" when you become a Christian. Jesus' teachings are laid out clearly and in detail. "The kingdom" is a gift, but you must seek its "righteousness" (6:33). Indeed, "righteousness" is a thematic word often denoting God's righteous will, which Matthew seeks to spell out as presented by Jesus. At times Matthew makes him sound more legalistic than the other Gospels do, but the aim is to make sure converts see that responsibility follows upon conversion. The "indicative" is there, but the "imperative" which follows more so.

Two points in Matthew's well-wrought presentation deserve final note. He stresses the church as no other evangelist does. He also links it to the kingdom as almost no other New Testament writer does. While Matthew speaks a great deal of "the kingdom *of heaven*" (e.g., 4:17; 13:24, 31, 33, 44, 45, 47) and occasionally of "the kingdom *of God*" (e.g., 12:28; 19:24), its equivalent term (see above, p. 104), Matthew also introduces, in the explanation to the parable of the Weeds in the Wheat, a distinction between "the kingdom *of the Father*" and "the kingdom *of the Son of Man.*" The parable (13:24–30) should be read, and then its explanation (13:36–43), noting the closing verses:

> The *Son of man* will send his angels, and they will gather out of *his kingdom* all causes of sin and all evildoers. . . . Then the righteous will shine like the sun in *the kingdom of their Father.* (13:41, 43)

The kingdom of the Son of man is something now existing, out of which those who do evil will be gathered before the kingdom of the Father comes. It is attractive to suggest that Matthew means by "the kingdom of the Son of man" nothing other than the church where God's rule and Jesus Christ are acknowledged and obeyed. The church is that sphere where the kingdom already holds sway, though Matthew warns that its members will be subject to a judgment too (cf. 22:11–13; 16:27;

13:47–50). He thus associates the kingdom with Jesus Christ in a way paralleled by only a few other passages like 1 Cor. 15:24; Col. 1:13; and Rev. 1:9.

Finally Matthew stresses the presence of Christ himself with that community and each and every believer. The promise of "Emmanuel" or "God with us" (Isa. 7:14) is very precious to Matthew, and he sees it fulfilled in Jesus Christ. That point is made at the very conclusion of the book: "Emmanuel" is brought to completion when Jesus makes a new promise (28:20), "Lo, *I* am with you always, to the close of the age" (or "ends of the world"), a promise echoed at 18:20, "Where two or three are gathered in my name, there am *I* in the midst of them." This presence of Jesus with his people in mission is what has enabled Christians for centuries to move on and advance the gospel to all who will hear and obey.

LUKE: THE BEAUTIFUL STORY OF SALVATION FOR THE ENTIRE WORLD

A good deal has been said already concerning this "good news book" about Jesus traditionally attributed to Luke, a Gentile and a physician (Col. 4:14; Philemon 24; 2 Tim. 4:11). He is not mentioned by name in the Gospel according to Luke, but tradition assumes he is the author of the passages in the first-person plural ("we") in the Book of Acts, perhaps quoted from a travel diary (cf. Acts 16:10–18; 20:5–15; 21:1–18; 27:1—28:16). But others argue the author of both volumes is an otherwise unknown Greek Christian.

Reference to Acts reminds us that this author had the opportunity, perhaps through the generosity of Theophilus (1:3; Acts 1:1), if the man mentioned in his dedications was his patron, to write also a second volume on the beginnings of the church. In this way this author is responsible for 28 percent of the New Testament. That means also that in "Volume 1," his Gospel, Luke is free to concentrate on the account of Jesus' life, from before his birth to the ascension into heaven, without having to weave in a view of the church as Matthew had. The result of Luke's craftsmanship has been called "the most beautiful book ever written."

For Luke is a literary master. His basic outline, already given above (p. 440), follows Mark to a considerable degree, but it also incorporates a historical preface, worthy of a Hellenistic historian of the day (1:1–4); extensive infancy and childhood accounts (chaps. 1—2); and unique teachings and parables and resurrection appearances (e.g., 10:29–37, the Good Samaritan; 15:11–32, the Prodigal Son; 24:13–35, the risen

Christ on the Emmaus Road). Sections of the first two chapters are studded with hymns and songs, like 1:46–55, 68–79; 2:29–32, which Christians still sing, and which sometimes echo in Luke's later chapters (cf. 2:14 with 19:38).

Behind his work lie sources, which he says he was diligent to trace out, and the example of the "many" who had "undertaken to compile a narrative" of the events "which have been accomplished among us," by God through Jesus and in the church (1:1). Besides Mark, Luke had before him as he wrote, if not Matthew (as a few people think), a collection of Jesus' sayings reflected also in Matthew (i.e., the Q source, as a great many more think), and the Old Testament in its Greek form. Above all he had a source unique to himself, with many incidents and sayings from Jesus' ministry, which no other evangelist uses. This material is often called "Luke's special source" or "L."

While conventionally it is assumed Luke took over Mark and added other source materials to it, there is some basis for supposing that he actually began with L and Q and came upon Mark only later, adding Markan material to what was already a "first edition" of his Gospel. Such a theory is especially attractive to explain the fact that the middle section and the passion sequence in Luke's Gospel differ so much from Mark. The section of his gospel from 9:51 to 18:14, which we referred to above simply under the heading "To Jerusalem" and which some commentators call the "Samaritan section"—it *mentions* Samaritans several times (9:52; 10:33; 17:16) but does not describe much of the action as occurring *in* Samaria—consists almost entirely of material found only in Luke or Matthew, almost never from Mark.

Even better evidence for Luke "going his own way," on the basis of accounts he prefers over what is in Mark, is the passion story, particularly the Jewish trial(s). It is well known that Mark speaks most of a trial before the Sanhedrin at night (14:53–64), followed by a brief reference to a second council meeting of the Sanhedrin in the morning (15:1). It is also well known that such a sequence violates what we know of rules for the Sanhedrin, about night trials and the power to pronounce and execute a death sentence. Luke has a far superior outline: there is only one Jewish trial session, and it comes by day (22:66–71). He specifies the charges against Jesus (22:3), and adds a hearing before Herod Antipas (23:6–12). Of course, Luke could have simply "rewritten" Mark with "improvements" in each instance, but the case is strong for supposing he had a different source at his disposal.

It has sometimes been observed by students of the Bible that stories in Luke have affinities with passages in the Gospel of John. Compare the two anointing stories, in Luke 7:36–50 and John 12:1–8, in contrast to the ones in Mark (14:3–9) and Matthew (26:6–13). Only in Luke and John do the names "Mary and Martha," "Lazarus," and "Annas" occur (Luke 10:38–42 and John 11:1 and 12:1–3; Luke 16:20 and John 11:1, 2, 5, 11, 17, 43; Luke 3:2, Acts 4:6, and John 18:13, respectively). These are the two Gospels where Satan leads Judas to betray Jesus (Luke 22:3; John 13:2, 27), where we are told it was a *right* ear which was cut off from a servant of the high priest by a disciple in Gethsemane (Luke 22:50; John 18:10) and where a miraculous catch of fishes occurs (Luke 5:4–9; John 21:5–11). What interplay must have existed among the Gospels, in light of such evidence, has always intrigued scholars and everyday readers. Likely John knew Luke's Gospel, or at the least they shared some common traditions.

It is the situation in which Luke writes, however, that affects his way of telling the story of Jesus, as much as the rich sources he had available. As with Matthew, the time is after the fall of Jerusalem. (Luke even uses a different section of material about "Jerusalem surrounded by armies," 21:20–24, in place of the Markan verses on "the desolating sacrilege" standing in the holy place, Mark 13:14 par. Matt. 24:15). The date is somewhere around A.D. 90. But the mood is more akin to that in John than to the apocalyptic "dark days" reflected in Mark or the confrontations with Judaism sensed in Matthew. In particular, Luke is addressing his story of the good news of Jesus to the Greco-Roman world.

Accordingly, as a Gentile writing for Gentiles, Luke eliminates a good many Semitic expressions. The only "foreign" word retained is *amēn*, when it occurs at the start of a saying by Jesus (often translated "verily" or "truly"). Even so, "amen" is eliminated in Luke's Greek, except on six occasions. By comparison, Mark had "amen" thirteen times, Matthew thirty, and John twenty-five (always in the doubled form, "Verily, verily, I say to you . . ."). After an initial use at 4:24, on Jesus' rejection in Nazareth and how the gospel will go to non-Jews, Luke seems to use "amen" to call attention to the significance of things Jesus says for future Christianity. This small example suggests Luke was quite conscious of the audience he wanted to reach, exemplified by Theophilus who needed to be buttressed by a clear, orderly account of the things about which he is already somewhat informed.

Luke thus writes to set forth, in narrative, the "Jesus story" for a church that was increasingly universal in its outlook. *All* women and men in the world are targets for its message. Unlike Matthew, he does not have to worry, in his setting, about Jewish rivalry. Debates over the law, as in Paul's day, are a thing of the past. If there is any concern, it is to convey to the Roman government (some even think Theophilus was an official of the state) the impression that Jesus and Christianity are no threat to an orderly society. So it is, according to Luke, that the Roman governor Pilate gave sentence only at the demand of the Jews (23:24), that the Roman centurion at the cross says "This man was innocent" (23:47), and that later in Acts the Roman officials deal fairly and kindly with Paul (cf. Acts 13:12; 16:38–39; 27:42–43).

But the main emphasis in Luke is to lay a groundwork, in Jesus' ministry, for a gospel that will reach out to all, universally. Luke shows special interest in women (8:1–3; 10:38–42—his book has been called "The Gospel according to Thirty-One Women" who are referred to in it), an interest in Samaritans, the poor (4:18; 6:20—chaps. 15—19 have been called "The Gospel to the Outcast"), and all humankind. Note how the genealogy goes back to Adam, 3:38, and how at 3:4–6 only Luke adds the words of Isaiah that "*all* flesh shall see the salvation of God."

In a very real way Luke's theme is "salvation," for all. The frontispiece scene in 4:16–30, which we have already examined, makes that clear (see pp. 106–10, above). Perhaps in line with this interest Luke features "gospel" even more than "the kingdom of God" as theme for Jesus' ministry. His consciousness of how Jesus' followers are to spread that gospel of salvation also prompts him to lay more emphasis on prayer and the Holy Spirit than Mark or Matthew does. Prayer and the power of the Spirit are two resources that witnesses possess for working in the world (cf. 18:1; 11:13; 24:49, for example, and throughout the Acts of the Apostles).

Because of his interest in salvation and in telling his story historically, Luke has probably done more than any other New Testament writer to give us an overall sweeping view of God at work in history to save. Some of his theological ideas can be profiled as seen on p. 450.

A great many implications can be drawn from Luke's theological view of history, where God has been at work in Israel, through Jesus, and now in the church. Three of these are especially of interest at this point.

1. "The kingdom of God" continues to be a Lukan theme, from 4:43 on. Luke seems to view it as many Christians ever since have thought of it (perhaps under Luke's influence). The kingdom is that rule of God which drew marvelously near when Jesus was on earth. In line with such a view, Luke alone reports the saying, "Behold, the kingdom of God is in the midst of you" (17:21)—meaning not so much "in your hearts," spiritually, as "among you," in Jesus and his mighty deeds—unless the emphasis is on how it is given as a gift, suddenly, without "signs to be observed," during his ministry (17:20). But the kingdom, according to

THE GOSPEL OF LUKE, A THEOLOGICAL OUTLINE

Creation   Parousia

The Age of Israel
From creation,
through law and
prophets, to
John the Baptist.
(See 3:23–38
or above,
pp. 302–4.)
Note 16:16.

The Age of Jesus as "Salvation Time"
Nothing like it has ever been
known: Jesus was on earth,
ministering!
He had Satan under control;
he did miracles; he taught; he
received the poor, women,
Samaritans, and died a martyr's death,
to show God to be the loving father.
When Jesus says " 'Today' fulfillment
has come" (4:21, au. trans.), he is
referring to that unique time of the
earthly ministry,

in

Galilee	Travel to	Jerusalem
4:14—9:50	Jerusalem	19:28—24:53
	9:51—19:27	(*not* Galilee)
	(Samaria)	

These three sections provide something of a parallel to the outline in
Acts (cf. 1:8):

R e s u r r e c t i o n — A p p e a r a n c e s
T h e   A s c e n s i o n   i s   o f   J e s u s

The Age of the Church
until the parousia
Jesus sits
enthroned at God's
right hand (Acts
7:55). Holy Spirit
given (Acts 2). The
church, though often
hard pressed by
enemies, bears
witness and seeks to
evangelize all
peoples.

The word of God
grows and spreads.
(Acts 6:7; 12:24;
19:20, etc.)

Jerusalem (Acts 1:12—8:3)	Judea, Samaria, neighboring parts (8:4—12:24)	Paul goes to Rome (12:25—28:31)

Luke, is also a reality to come only in the future; 21:31 suggests that it
will come only after certain signs enumerated apocalyptically in vv. 25–
30 have taken place. We have already seen that this present/future
kingdom was continued as good news in the early church; indeed, the
closing words of Acts have Paul preaching the theme in Rome. But talk
about a "kingdom" or "Jesus as king" (Acts 17:7) could be misunderstood in Roman circles (see above, pp. 321–22). All in all, Luke's view
seems to be that the kingdom was here, as never before, when Jesus was
on earth, and it will come in its fullness at the future coming of the Lord
in glory.

2. Luke's "eschatology" or view of the "last things" thus becomes
crucial for understanding his thought. He recasts the theme of Mark 13
into two separate discourses, 17:22–37 and 21:5–33. He indicates the

fall of Jerusalem was *not* the end of the world (21:20), for there are "the times of the Gentiles" (21:24) to be fulfilled: life will go on (17:26–30), people eating, drinking, marrying, and so forth; there are "days of the Son of man" to be lived through (17:22–30). God's people in the church should continue their life and witness, prayer and watchfulness (21:34–36), until their "redemption" (21:28) comes. Keep on, with faith and trust, bearing testimony, you are in God's hands (21:12–19).

3. By the way he has thus treated Jesus' message about the kingdom (and related it to other gospel themes) and by the way he has helped Christians live over the long haul since Jerusalem's fall (but without giving up the hope for a future return of Christ), Luke has, perhaps more than any other New Testament writer, set the lines of development for future Christianity. The later "church year calendar" (with the ascension and the festival of Pentecost forty and fifty days after Easter, and a Christmas nativity event implied) is a contribution from Luke to us. So are his understanding of Jesus' place in the history of salvation, and the eschatology of a kingdom that came and will come. Luke's two volumes thus have become a norm for a great deal of Christianity, enabling believers in ensuing centuries to keep on living and applying the good news in church and world.

NOTE

1. The term "synoptic" implies both that a similar overall view pervades all three works so that we see Jesus in them in much the same way, and also that, if the three books are printed side by side, the sequences of stories and even the actual words line up closely in parallel ways. A good "synopsis" of the Gospels helps one see many such details and variations; cf. Burton H. Throckmorton, Jr., ed., *Gospel Parallels: A Synopsis of the First Three Gospels,* 4th ed. (Camden, N.J.: Thomas Nelson & Sons, 1979), or Reuben J. Swanson, *The Horizontal Line Synopsis of the Gospels* (Dillsboro, N.C.: Western North Carolina Press, 1975).

VII
THE ONE GOSPEL
IN ITS MANY FORMS

The good news over the centuries centers in Jesus and his cross. On these ancient steps in Jerusalem to the Kidron Valley Jesus may have trod the night before his death, and pilgrims may still walk.

34

The Bible's Witness
to Good News
in Old Testament and New

THE GOOD NEWS FROM GOD to humanity in the Scriptures has, as we have seen, taken many forms. So many, in fact, that some readers who have worked through the first thirty-three chapters of this book may now wish, in the final part, that "the real gospel would stand up and identify itself!" How nice if one fixed formula of *the* good news could appear, with God's "imprimatur" to serve for all times and situations. But God has not chosen to work that way, in giving us the Bible. There is no single résumé of which it is said, "This is the one and only way of stating the gospel."

What we can now do, after surveying the seemingly bewildering array of ways to put the glad tidings for Israel and the early church, is to sort out some of these forms of the gospel in the Scriptures. Then in chapter 35 we can look at how the gospel message has resounded through the centuries from New Testament times to our own day. In doing these two things we can look also to see how these varied forms of the gospel may have an impact on us, and how some of the good news may be carried further into God's world today, perhaps even by us.

REVIEWING THE CENTRAL MESSAGE OF
GOOD NEWS IN SCRIPTURE

The kingdom of God we have found to be a recurring theme in many parts of the Bible. It came into prominence in our analysis because we started with Jesus. For Jesus came "preaching the gospel of God, . . . 'The kingdom of God is at hand . . .'" (Mark 1:14–15). God's kingship, as it was breaking in during Jesus' ministry, was the central message on Jesus' lips. In so speaking, he was playing with dynamite, for to talk of Yahweh's kingship was potentially explosive during the Roman occupation. Jesus had to make clear he was no zealot revolutionist, but was proclaiming the justice, love, and concern for which God calls and which God brings, especially among those who were outcasts even amid his own people.

Chances are the same theme, that "Yahweh has become king and reigns," would have emerged as prominent, if not clearly central, if we had started with most portions of the Old Testament. Only if we had begun with New Testament books beyond the first three Gospels would we have found the kingdom to be a more peripheral theme in contrast to some other subjects.

So it was, in light of the Synoptic Gospels and much of the Hebrew Scriptures, that we traced the kingdom/kingship of God as a basic theme. It turned out to be a subject reflected in the whole range of Israel's faith, marking the nation's life as a people under God the Lord, a people who are constituted by God's actions and pledged to obedience to God's will. "God is king" of Israel by virtue of the deliverance from slavery in Egypt, in view of the covenant that God gave, on the basis of promises the Lord made that carry even into the dark days of exile. "God has been king," since creation, and becomes king again each new year, enthroned on Israel's praises, king over all the world. "God will be king," in the future too, Israelite faith said, in looking hopefully toward the future.

One way, therefore, of expressing the good news has been to speak of God's sovereign rule, as king:

in the past—at the exodus, at creation, and dozens of other times and places;

in the present—over the believing community and, according to their assertion, throughout the world;

in the future—when he "redeems" his people from misfortunes into which they periodically fall, and he finally winds things up, with justice and judgment, at the "day of the Lord."

Of course, we also saw how this pervasive theme took a back seat after Easter to other expressions of good news, because the ancient Near Eastern idea of God as king could become politically touchy and even dangerous for Jews and Christians alike to use. The Roman Empire was likely to view as a revolutionary threat to the state Jewish prayers for restoration of "the throne of David" in Jerusalem, for "the horn of freedom," and for "the arrogant kingdom to be rooted out in our days" (perhaps meaning Rome's rulers), as a synagogue liturgy put it. The Romans likewise viewed any talk of kingship connected with Jesus as a menace. Under Roman rule and with the rise of Christianity, would therefore the age-old theme of the kingdom of God drop from sight? That it did not, we shall see below in chapter 35.

In exploring the kingship of God in Scripture we have also come across related themes that sometimes were elevated front and center as "the gospel." Historically two events have been supremely important for Jews and Christians, both celebrated at the same time of the year, at what the Bible calls "Passover time":

the exodus from Egypt—God delivers his "son," Israel, from bondage;
the resurrection at Jerusalem—God raises his son, Jesus, from the dead.

These were two ways, some twelve centuries apart, of speaking of *God's victory.* This "victor" theme proved a popular one, especially in the early centuries of Christianity when the church fathers loved to speak of Christ as "Victor over death," and it continued the Old Testament motif of Yahweh's victory in the "Holy War."

We have also uncovered other related themes that appear and reappear in both testaments, themes which have meant good news to countless thousands over the centuries. One is surely *the covenant,* though we have seen that this is less pervasive in the New Testament than in the Old, where indeed it took a variety of forms. Another is the idea of *lordship,* first of God and later of Christ. To many people today to have an (over)lord may seem like bad news, but for biblical peoples this was a comforting message. To know that there was a God pledged to Israel, or that someone called Jesus, whom they had come to know and rely upon as a companion in Galilee, was now "Lord of all," implied security and a basis for confidence. Related, too, is the notion of *promise*—life can rest upon pledges made by one whose word is reliable.

"Kingship" and such related topics may have seemed strange to some readers before they began the in-depth study of these last thirty-three chapters. Their premise may have been that "Christianity is Christ," and that Jesus is himself the gospel. This expectation has surely not been disappointed in our survey. For we have examined Jesus during his ministry, Jesus exalted by his resurrection as Lord, Jesus the Lord affirmed by faith for his role in the creation and preservation of the world, and the Lord Jesus as messiah or Christ. If that is not enough, we have also looked at him in the sermons and faith the apostles preached and in each one of the gospels. If anyone wants to say, highlighting the New Testament, that the gospel is *Jesus Christ,* the evidence is there for that.

Still other ways have been found, however, to put the good news. *"Justification"* or "the righteousness of God" has been accorded its place, not only in the epistles of Paul, but also prior to that, in the Old Testament and earliest Christianity. *Eternal life* as a theme has been noted, especially in John, but elsewhere as well. What else can be better news for a prisoner on trial than to get the verdict "acquitted" (or "justified")? Or for a person in the midst of a dying society, soured relationships, and shriveled personhood to receive the gift of "true life" from beyond? To take a final example that we explored, it also turned out, in some segments of the Bible, that the message from God was that the Almighty, the Holy One, is with his people in their greatest needs or perils, or that God sustains them in their *pilgrimage* and witnessing.

Readers probably can recall other expressions of good news that surprised and delighted them in working through the scriptural witness. To mention two others that moderns might not think can be part of the gospel, we recall the insistence of both testaments that ethics and the community can be designated as good news too.

As for *ethics*, it may come as a surprise that exhortation and commands can be good news. Too often such things seem to us to be "law," "bad news"—requirements to convict people of their sinfulness or "no-nos" to which we can never conform. Biblical religion reasoned, however, that God's will for us is a good thing, and to know its contents from God is even better, and to put it into practice as an obedient response to his delivering us is best of all. Not that people save themselves thereby, but their response is part of that "obedience of faith" that follows when we have been transformed by the gospel (cf. Rom. 12:1–2). Statements about what God wants us to do are thus part of the good news.

Examples of "good news ethics" have been seen frequently. Forms of the covenant may include stipulations for Israel to obey. Paul's letters regularly include an ethical section about "what God wills" for us, on the basis of what God has already done (Rom. 12:1, "I appeal to you therefore . . . by the mercies of God . . . ," marks the transition point in that epistle). Matthew, in his situation, builds the imperative from God plainly into his Gospel. Luke provides a startling example when he writes of John the Baptist, "So, with many other *exhortations*, he *preached good news* to the people" (3:18). If one reads the previous verses, they turn out to sound like anything but good news, for John mentions judgment (3:7, 17), repentance (3:8), and principles of conduct. Some interpreters suggest Luke's verb means nothing more than "preached" in a broad sense, but it is the same expression used at 4:18 and 43. At 3:18 the TEV therefore rightly renders it, "In many different ways John . . . preached the Good News to them." What is at stake is that the gospel includes a pattern from God for people's lives in the new age.

The *church* too, or the community, must be accounted part of the good news, and not just an adjunct, let alone a barrier to it, as some moderns may think. Very often, earnest students of the Scriptures have opposed the Bible to the church. (Sect groups especially made "the organized church"—as if there were a "disorganized one"!—a favorite whipping boy.) The Bible itself shows us that the community of Israel ranks high throughout the Old Testament—Yahweh created it, delivered and sustained it time and time again, ordained its worship, sent prophets to renew the community, and sought to sustain a remnant out of it or to create new shoots and life from "the vine" that was Israel (Ps. 80:8–19). In the New Testament, "the church of God [or of the Lord]" is something "he obtained with his own blood" (Acts 20:28, RSV note—the reference is probably to "the blood of his Own [Son]," meaning "Christ died for the church," but some commentators think "the blood of God himself" is meant!). Christ, the true vine, has "branches" (church members) who "bear fruit" (live ethically) (John 15:1–17). Thus the church not merely preaches the good news, but must, through its members in Christ, live it and be a part of the gospel.

VARIETY, YET UNITY

The result of finding so much variety within the Bible, so many ways of experiencing good news, should not be a cause of despair but of joy. God is speaking to people in different situations. There are many facets of God's truth to convey.

Even the tensions discovered biblically within a single theme, like the kingdom of God, have, each of them, their purpose. Is the kingdom present or future? When a scriptural passage stresses the presence of the kingdom, that is to let people know that God is doing something then and there. When another passage speaks of it as still to come, that is to remind people that even as baptized Christians they do not yet have everything at their disposal, all of God at their beck and call.

There have, of course, often been concerted efforts to make one theme from the Bible more central than others. Often these endeavors have cut across denominational lines and have reflected the spirit of an age, as a theme whose time had come. Thus, for example, the nineteenth and early twentieth centuries saw a mission impulse to evangelize the world sweep through much of Christendom. Samuel Wolcott reflects it in these lines:

> Christ for the world we sing;
> The world to Christ we bring
>   With loving zeal.

Countless missionaries set out "to evangelize the world in this generation." The mission movement arose partly from biblical injunctions, partly from revivalist preaching, and partly because the time was right.

Another example: in America in the 1960s social justice became the central thrust of many for their faith. Episcopalians, Baptists, Catholics, clergy, nuns, lay people, of countless backgrounds, marched, preached, and prayed together for civil rights for blacks and other minorities.

More frequently, perhaps, denominations or churches have been formed around some particular emphasis, and sometimes this has involved an effort to make a particular biblical teaching the norm. The Reformation is a case in point. Generally there was an effort among the Reformers, not only to return to Scripture, but to make its great truths central. Lutherans in particular stressed "the gospel" and defined it in terms of the theme of "justification by grace through faith." It may be admitted that this way of putting the good news reflected especially Luther's own personal struggle to find a gracious God. But the theme is a major one in many parts of the Bible, in terms of "the righteousness of God," and probably the chief and central way in Paul's writings, certainly in Romans, of expressing what God is doing for us, as gospel. Lutherans thus remain that confessional church within the Christian family, or that theological movement within the church catholic, that perpetually proposes "justification" as the article in which a church stands or falls, as the organizing theme for theology, as the gospel basis for life.[1]

Not all Christians, of course, come out at the same point on the centrality or exclusivity of justification as a touchstone for Christianity. In light of their own experiences and heritage they read Scripture differently and may wish to use some other theme or themes as the primary way to express the good news. Each group should be concerned, ecumenically, as witnesses, not to insist that every formulation of the gospel must agree verbally with their own wordings, but to examine whether the other possible formulations being proposed, ancient or modern, express that message from and about God which what they call central includes. Such concerns ought to involve the following:

1. Is God seen here as working salvation, a right and renewed relationship with God, for humankind?
2. Is this action of God a matter of grace, without salvation somehow becoming dependent on human actions or intents?
3. Is a trusting, obedient, loving human response being called forth?
4. Is Christ's cross seen as the means for effecting this renewal?
5. Is sin, as human selfishness, self-love, disobedience, and lack of fear for God, taken as seriously as, say, Genesis 1—3 and Romans 1—3 take it?
6. Yet is there hope that transformation, growth, and ultimate fulfillment will result from what God is doing here?

7. Some would add, are both the personal and cosmic dimensions seen here?

If these emphases—which Reformation Christians, for example, will recognize as ways of expressing what classical dogmatic language meant (1) by justification, (2) by grace above, (3) through faith, (4) for Christ's sake, plus (5) the factors of sin and the human condition (anthropology), (6) future eschatology, and (7) the aspects of justification that go beyond what happens in an individual's heart and life—are somehow involved, then one has a proper expression of the gospel. It ought not to be implied that the good news can be expressed only in the language of justification/righteousness, or using the law-court setting (see under " 'Justification' as Good News" in chap. 27), but rather that any expression of gospel must preserve what justification makes so clear to those espousing it.

Similarly with those who champion "reconciliation" as a theme. Or "election." Or "the work of the Holy Spirit." Can Roman Catholics with their more sacramental system of salvation, Methodists with their emphasis on "sanctification," or the Orthodox with their traditional view of "the divinization of humanity" speak similarly today, as part of biblical theology?

Thus, the spirit of an age and one's denominational heritage help shape how people over the centuries have expressed the gospel. It should also be noted that, while we have tried, in this study, to keep separate the different biblical ways of expressing the good news, Christians through the ages have often mixed and combined them. At times these combinations have seemed almost promiscuous. Biblical scholars nowadays feel that the easy interpretation of a verse in Isaiah or Matthew by one in John, and of both by a theme from Paul, may be a disservice to all four biblical writers and keep us from hearing God's word in its original situation. Yet later theology systematically seeks to combine their ideas. Poets, of course, especially take license in interrelating images. Consider, for example, the variety of themes (italicized) in just one verse of a Pentecost hymn by the American, Samuel Longfellow:

Holy Spirit, right divine,
King within my conscience *reign:*
Be my *law,* and I shall be   ("Holy Spirit, truth
Firmly bound, for ever *free.*   divine," stanza 5)

Interpretation that is fair to this author ought to begin by seeing what scriptural and other ideas he had in mind, in his situation, including what is expressed in the other verses of the hymn. Then, taking into consideration liberties allowed for artistic creativity, and only then, should one consider how this holds together as a poetic expression of good news, to be sung at Pentecost.

Thus, to our multiplicity of biblical expressions of good news, there must be added subsequent expressions of the gospel in different periods of history, as various churches may have emphasized and as Christians have combined images and themes.

But, then, whoever said the noun "good news" is singular? We often pause, in everyday speech, to question whether to use a plural or singular verb with "news." While we may say, "The news is good," the word is literally a plural form of what is "new," and for several centuries was used as a plural or singular. The fact is that in the Bible "good news" is decidedly plural in the forms it takes. The variety is rich. And how could it be otherwise, if God was to speak to so many different situations? What folly to limit our gospel to just one mode of expression when there are so many needs to which to speak! The Bible is thus an inexhaustible well for witnessing, and a perpetual source for reading good news (plural) from God.

Yet no matter what form that news from God took, readers have been conscious of certain common concerns or emphases running through it, if it really is *good* news. Above all these include that God is at work, graciously, in this situation, for good. We have found that to be so, whether "kingdom," "Christ," "justification," or "covenant" language was involved. And the shorthand way Christians have often used to sum up what is involved is to speak of "the gospel," thus reflecting the fact that the Greek and Hebrew terms, *euangelion* and *bᵉsorah*, are both singulars.

"Gospel" is preeminently a New Testament term. The RSV translation employs it indeed *only* in the New Testament. But the Old Testament speaks of "good tidings" of "good" (Isa. 52:7; see above, pp. 176, 177–78). The Christian Scriptures specify these tidings as "the gospel of God" (Mark 1:14; Rom. 1:1), "the gospel of the kingdom" (Matt. 4:23), "the gospel of the grace of God" (Acts 20:24), "the gospel concerning his Son" (Rom. 1:3), "the gospel of Christ" (Rom. 15:19), "the gospel of your salvation" (Eph. 1:13), and "the gospel of peace" (Eph. 6:15). It is an "eternal" message (Rev. 14:6), which, in the form of the justification theme, is "the power of God for salvation to every one who has faith" (Rom. 1:16). The gospel of which the Bible speaks is something to be very personally appropriated and to be expressed, for all its objective content, as "my gospel" (Rom. 16:25; 2 Tim. 2:8; see above, pp. 336–38). It is the good news than which there is no other; a "different gospel" than that about God's saving work in Christ for us, is no gospel at all,

Paul insists, but only a devilish parody and "bad news" (Gal. 1:6–7). "The gospel" is "the word" (Acts 15:7; Col. 1:5) and truth (Gal. 2:14; Col. 1:5).

"Gospel," then, is what gives unity to the many themes and ways of expressing the good news, in the Bible and beyond. Inevitably it takes many forms, but gospel as good news is the unifying thread.

"The story" (the big story for people), God's story in Scripture, then, is the gospel. In witnessing and life, our stories, each individually, are meant ultimately to be under God's story and conform to it, if they are to be authentically gospel. But to know the richness of how the gospel has been expressed scripturally is a help for our testimonies in the variety of life situations that modern believers face.

NOTE

1. E. W. Gritsch and R. W. Jenson, *Lutheranism: The Theological Movement and Its Confessional Writings* (Philadelphia: Fortress Press, 1976), 6, 36, 207. In ecumenical discussion, and in comparison with alternative possibilities, cf. J. Reumann, *"Righteousness" in the New Testament* (cited above, chap. 27 n. 3), esp. sections 326–30, 336–51, with the response by J. A. Fitzmyer in sections 422–26; and "Lutherans and Catholics in Dialogue, VII," *Justification by Faith* (Minneapolis: Augsburg Publishing House, 1985), 13–74 (Common Statement), and 77–81 (J. A. Fitzmyer, "Justification by Faith and 'Righteousness' in the New Testament").

35

Kingdom and Gospel
Through the Centuries—
from the New Testament to
the Waning Twentieth Century

Since the close of the New Testament canon (see above, pp. 32–34), the gospel has continued to be told, proclaimed, and spread in many forms. The good news has had an ongoing history that continues to our day, every time a sermon is preached, each time a witness evangelizes someone for Christ, or whenever people tell their own "God stories," under the overarching spread of the Scriptures as experienced by each believer and church.

In his book, *Evangelical Witness*, Ralph W. Quare has a chapter intriguingly titled, "Where Has All the Good News Gone?"[1] Some groups have, of course, implied it disappeared for centuries, until their sect recovered it in modern times. However, Christians who take history as an arena of God's activity and who treasure the promise that God's Spirit has ever been at work and who believe that no age is left without God's witness (cf. Acts 14:17) must reckon more seriously with these intervening centuries. Protestants cannot exclude the presence of the gospel in the church in the period before the Reformation reawakened people to what Scripture said. Catholics cannot overlook what the Reformers said or life in the Protestant denominations since the sixteenth century.

And so the answer to the question about the gospel is that the good news has gone out into the world for centuries, in many forms. The varied scriptural contents of the good news have multiplied and taken on the colorings of Europe, Asia, Africa, and the Americas, and the trappings of the years, as the gospel moved on. Needless to say, we do not have time or space here to indicate the numerous variations with which Christians have expressed themselves, though it has been hinted above (pp. 89–90, 459–62) how different decades and denominations bring new ways of telling the God story. To detail the entire history would be to recount nothing less than the history of the church, the development of theology and of evangelization and witnessing.

What we can do here is describe some highlights of how that particular way of asserting the gospel that Jesus used—namely, as good news about "the kingdom of God"—has gone on inspiring people through the centuries and taking ever new and exciting ways, as gospel, of capturing imaginations and lives for Christ and God.

Whatever became of the gospel about the kingdom, after Jesus' death and resurrection? We have seen that, while other ways of stating the gospel tended to replace it after Easter and as the church advanced into the Roman Empire, the kingdom of God remained a theme in Paul (see under "Paul's Inheritance and Use of Kingdom-Language" in chap. 26), in John (see under "The Kingdom of God and Eternal Life" in chap. 30), and elsewhere (see under "The Kerygma and the Kingdom" in chap. 25, and pp. 369–70, 393–95, 445–46, and 449–50). At times the kingdom was placed in tandem with the lordship of Jesus Christ (Acts 28:31), and on occasion there was reference to the kingdom of Christ as a future, intermediate age (1 Cor. 15:24; see above, pp. 358–59), or to "the kingdom of the Son of man" as the church, an intermediate stage now, before the future "kingdom of the Father" (Matt. 13:41, cf. above, pp. 445–46; Luke 22:29). In the statement of Acts 1:6–8, that it is not for mortals on earth to know when the kingdom would be restored to Israel, but that Christ was now empowering "apostles" to be his witnesses, some people were later to see authorization for an apostolic governance in the church as the reign of God. And the equation, at Col. 1:13–14, of the kingdom of God's beloved Son with "redemption" and "forgiveness of sins" was to provide the groundwork for interpretation of the kingdom as the rule of God in redeemed, forgiven human hearts.

In all these ways, the New Testament contained seeds for later flowerings of the kingdom theme, reinforced by the innumerable Old Testament references to God as king. Even though the epistles and other writings apart from the Synoptics in the New Testament failed to stress the kingdom of God (or of Christ), the idea was one that would continue to occur in Christian thought and life. It was a theme that for twenty more centuries would warm hearts and minds. In the "Te Deum" it even became a way of stating the Easter Gospel:

> You, Christ, are the king of glory,
> . . . You overcame the sting of death,
>   and opened *the kingdom of heaven* to all believers.

PATRISTIC TEACHERS: AUGUSTINE AND
THE "CITY OF GOD"

If we were to put on parade the references to the kingdom in the second, third, and fourth Christian centuries, the most prominent place would go to those concerning "a visible reign of Christ on earth between his second coming and the Last Judgment"—the kind of millennial kingdom that some infer from Revelation 20. True, there are references in this period to the kingdom as "the perfect reign of God in heaven after the Last Judgment" or as "the Visible Church on earth between the first and the second coming of Christ."[2] But the notion of a thousand-year kingdom on earth, perhaps especially involving martyrs, exercised the greatest attraction on the Christian mind, particularly in a period of persecution and speculations about "the end." Millennialism or "chiliasm" (see above, p. 360) was a widespread eschatology.

The figure who changed this direction and gave the kingdom new meaning as "the city of God" was Augustine, bishop at Hippo in North Africa (A.D. 354–430). A Numidian, akin to the Berbers, he may have had Negro blood in him. Augustine's own story is dramatic. In spite of the prayers of his mother, Monica, a Christian, he avoided baptism and lived a sensuous life, fathering a son out of wedlock, drifting spiritually from one religion and philosophy to another. A brilliant teacher of rhetoric, he was moved by the sermons of Ambrose, bishop of Milan in Italy, and then was converted when a voice told him "Take up and read" the Bible and he opened to Rom. 13:13–14, "Not in rioting and drunkenness, not in chambering and wantonness, not in strife and envying. But put ye on the Lord Jesus Christ, and make not provision for the flesh to fulfil the lusts thereof" (KJV). He was baptized at age thirty-three, ordained by popular demand, and then served as bishop of Hippo Regius, a town west of Carthage in modern Tunisia, from 395 until his death.

Augustine was a deep thinker in an age when much was changing. There were opposition religious sects, competing Christian groups (especially the Donatists, who stressed personal purity and opposition to the world), and rival theological ideas. In particular Augustine took a stand against the optimistic views of a monk, Pelagius, who claimed Adam's sin affected no one but Adam, that people are born with powers uncorrupted and only later fall into sin, and so children do not need infant baptism. Augustine opposed Pelagius on all three points (cf. Genesis 1—3; Romans 1—3 for Augustine's idea of the power of sin) and set the future pattern for Christian theology generally.

It is with what he said about the kingdom of God that we are here concerned. Early in his career, Augustine held to the prevailing millennial view that the kingdom would come as a thousand-year reign of Christ on earth. This he came in time to repudiate as an apocalyptic misunderstanding. He knew of the view that the kingdom would come only after the last judgment, and also of statements that linked (but did not identify) the present church with the kingdom, such as Cyprian's dictum, "A person cannot hope to reach the kingdom who deserts the church which is destined to reign." What Augustine did was to stake out the church and the whole sweep of its history as the reign or kingdom of God. Of course, he qualifies it, so that distinctions are kept between "the church as it now is" and "the church as it will be," but church and kingdom were identified as they rarely had been before.

Augustine's greatest exposition of the theme came in a twenty-two-volume work which he began in 410 when Rome fell to the Visigoths, and which he finished in 426, just before the Vandals lay siege to his own city. Pagans had been charging that the fall of Rome was due to the abandonment of the worship of the ancient Roman gods under Christian influence. As a historian, Augustine sought to show that the seeds of decline had come prior to, and quite apart from, the rise of Christianity. As a Christian, he went on to ponder all history philosophically and theologically. There exist, he became convinced, two "cities." (His Latin word could mean "state" or "commonwealth," but the rendering "city" has become traditional.) The "city of God" stands opposed to "the earthly city" or the kingdom of the devil. Augustine traces the city of God from creation, through Abraham, Israel, Christ, and the church. The "earthly city" or kingdom begins with the fall of the angels (cf. Gen. 6:4) and of the man and the woman (Genesis 3), and then is traced through Cain (Genesis 4), the tower of Babel, and the great but sinister empires of Nineveh, Babylon, Persia, Macedonia, and Rome.

In this "tale of two cities" we may contrast:

	for the city of God	for the city of the world
the foundation:	love of God	love of self
purpose:	heavenly peace	merely earthly peace
resource:	justice	justice borrowed from the city of God

Augustine saw two distinct classes of people: the elect or citizens of the city of God, and those "disapproved," outside, in the kingdom of the devil. In his system, election and grace reign supreme. The Augustinian synthesis went beyond the biblical imagery to combine elements of the gospel into a new pattern. Its results were to be felt in Luther's day and beyond. More important, Augustine had given new life to the kingdom theme. The church is the kingdom of God, made up of redeemed humanity, on pilgrimage until the final promised reign of God. The secular power, insofar as it can be reclaimed from the devil, becomes an instrument of the church. The stage is thus set for the church to reign supreme.

THE KINGDOM IN THE MIDDLE AGES:
JOACHIM OF FLORA

That is what happened in the Middle Ages: the kingdom of God was identified not simply with "the city of the saints" but with the church and specifically its hierarchical structures. Pope and bishops ruled God's kingdom, the church, to which the state and earthly kings should be subservient. Of course, this shift in interpretation had some basis in historical, sociological facts. Already in Augustine's day, as the Roman Empire broke up and went under, it was the church that became the dominant institution in society. In the Middle Ages all the more was the papal hierarchy an ecclesiastical embodiment of order and rule in society, an embodiment that was equated with the kingdom.

Even in the Middle Ages, however, quite apart from the rumblings of national rulers and princes (which would lead to the rise of modern secular states), there were voices of protest and alternative views. One of the most interesting, as a type presaging an interpretation of God's rule that keeps appearing in our own day, lies in the writings of Joachim of Flora (or Fiore), a monk in southern Italy. In his view, all history is divided into three periods:

1. The age of the Father, from Adam to John the Baptist, as described in the Old Testament, when people lived under the law; it was the time when the married predominated.
2. The age of the Son, from Jesus Christ to the year A.D. 1260, as set forth in the New Testament, when people lived under grace; it was a time of the clerics. (Joachim, who died just a few years after 1200, got the figure of 1260 by taking the biblical figure of "42 [generations]" [cf. Rev. 11:2 and 13:5] times the average of thirty years to a generation; cf. the 1260 days assumed in Dan. 7:25 and 12:7. All such references have long been a happy hunting ground for apocalypticists.)
3. The age of the Spirit, when the new religious orders (such as the one that Joachim founded) would evangelize the world, and the people would live under the freedom of the Spirit. It would be the age of the monks!

Joachim thought he was writing "an eternal gospel" (cf. Rev. 14:6). Like so many apocalyptic timetables, his called for the end or for a decisive new stage just after the "prophet" made his predictions. Like all such timetables, it proved wrong. But Joachim, in designating his second period as "the middle age," gave us our term "Middle Ages." What is more, his approach is exemplified in many subsequent groups, like the Millerites and the Rutherfordites (connected respectively with nineteenth-century Adventist and twentieth-century Jehovah's Witnesses movements), who seek to fix the date of the parousia or of "Armageddon" (Rev. 16:16). Joachim's scheme of three "dispensations" is the grandparent of modern attempts, such as are found in *Scofield Reference Bible* notes, to fix a whole series (usually seven) of "dispensations."

IN REFORMATION TIMES:
THE "TWO KINGDOMS"

Reformation treatment of the kingdom of God represents a refreshing return to biblical categories after speculations like those of Joachim and the institutional development after Augustine whereby the reign of God was identified with the rule of the church hierarchy. John Calvin's well-known emphasis on "the sovereignty of God" can be said to be an effort to put the Old Testament "kingship of Yahweh" into other terms. The Calvinistic attempts to translate "theocracy" (or "rule by God") into city government, as at Geneva beginning in 1541, were less successful. The aim was to have a consistory of clergy and lay people govern all of life according to a strict moral code. Puritan life style in New England and blue laws in many U.S. states owe much to this approach of building the kingdom of God on earth by religious control through the civil government. Recall the Eighteenth Amendment to the United States Constitution, on prohibition of alcoholic beverages, or legal efforts of the "Moral Majority" in the 1980s toward morality by law. The "Geneva experiment" thus left its mark, but, for all its laws and even execution of heretical opponents like Michael Servetus in 1533, did not succeed.

The Lutheran Confessions, reflecting Augustine, relate the kingdom of God to the church, in contrast to "the kingdom of the devil" (Apology of the Augsburg Confession, VII and VIII, section 16; cf. Eph. 2:2). But these confessional writings are careful to add that the church is not to be equated with the hierarchy but with all believers, and that in this world the true church and its members are "hidden under the cross" (Apology, VII/VIII, 18).[3] That is, there is no reign in glory as yet, but life is discipleship, perhaps marked by suffering (cf. Mark's view of Christ and discipleship, above, p. 438). In particular, in the church there are admittedly mingled together "good seed" and "weeds" (Matt. 13:38); who "the wicked" are and who "the saved" will not be seen until God's final judgment. The implication would be: seek to witness to all, let all grow in the church, Christianity may involve suffering, let God be the final judge.

Perhaps the best-known use of kingdom imagery for Lutherans occurs in the Small Catechism, when Luther explains the Second Article of the Apostles' Creed. He describes the purpose of Christ's work in very personal terms, with the triple phrases,

in order that I might be his [Christ's],
live under him *in his kingdom,*
and serve him in everlasting righteousness, innocence, and blessedness.

There one has a host of biblical ideas: "in Christ," the kingdom, a response of service, righteousness, and life. The kingdom is where those who belong to Christ live and work, that is, in church and the world.

This brings us to one of the most significant proposals from the Reformation period for conceptualizing God's rule, the doctrine of the "two kingdoms." After all we have seen in the Bible and the developments since Augustine, the concept is not strange. Luther and theologians following him worked out an understanding about God's reign that has proven useful with regard to social-ethical matters, even though many (Lutherans included) have misunderstood and abused it, and others have rejected it (or at least what they understood it to mean).

At the heart of the two-kingdoms view is the understanding of faith that God rules not only in his church (where his kingship is confessed) but also in his world (where it usually is not acknowledged but which world he made as creator and still preserves). The trick, however, is to grasp that God rules in two different ways or styles in these two realms. In the kingdom on the right (to use language from Matt. 25:33, 34, 41) God rules through love and the gospel; in the kingdom on the left, the world or state, in contrast to the church, God rules through justice and law. The two ways of governing should be distinguished and not confused. One does not try to run the state, therefore, on the basis of the Sermon on the Mount (which is intended for disciples of Christ, not civil servants who may be of all sorts of religious persuasions). At the same time the church and its function are to be distinguished from the United Nations or from a corporation like General Motors.

God rules all the universe

on the left	on the right
the world, the state,	the church,
through justice and law,	through love and the gospel,
as God's creation.	as God's redemption.

This way of thinking frees Christians to participate fully in "worldly" concerns for justice and human betterment with people of all religions or of no religion. Christians carry their motivation from the gospel into activities in and for all creation. But they do not expect others to have to "join their church" or believe as they do, in order to work together to get things done in society. A shared concern for justice is what matters here. At the same time, the church is allowed to be the church—living for the gospel, for redemption, proclaiming word and sacrament, without losing its soul, in order to serve the world. People generally can witness for justice on all sorts of bases. Christian believers witness to Christ as Lord and savior on the basis of the Bible's God story which they have heard. Evangelism, then, is winning lives to Christ, becoming committed in his body, in order to serve there and in the world—where, believers can see, God reigns also as king.

MODERN INTERPRETATIONS: THE SOCIAL GOSPEL; APOCALYPTIC; EXISTENTIALISM

Coming closer to our own times, we find the kingdom of God has received still other interpretations. Perhaps the one most congenial to and favored by many Americans has involved "the Social Gospel." It was popularized by Walter Rauschenbusch (1861–1918), the son of a German Lutheran who became a Baptist. Rauschenbusch began his ministry in the "Hell's Kitchen" section of New York City, with people "out of work, out of clothes, out of shoes, and out of hope,"[4] yet living in the shadow of vast accumulated wealth. He became convinced that God was at work in the social struggle and that the kingdom is "the energy of God realizing itself in human life." Christians must, therefore, join the struggle for justice, to bring about the kingdom on earth. With passionate conviction Rauschenbusch, as preacher and seminary teacher in Rochester, New York, put forth the plea to get involved, to put faith into action, through settlement houses, urban causes, and the improvement of working conditions. His followers called, in later decades, for involvement in civil rights and crusades against multinational corporations.

Many traditionalist Christians (usually among "the haves," not the "have nots") react against such efforts as unworthy of the church or sense in the Social Gospel a human scheme to build what only God can bring, the kingdom. Undoubtedly many who supported the Social Gospel naively felt they were creating utopia on their own. But Rauschenbusch showed how the age-old symbol of the kingdom could fire the imagination anew. It no doubt functioned similarly for freedom riders in the 1960s, and those who have thought of the church as politically activist, a kind of "avant-garde of the new regime."[5]

Resorting to biblical texts, in the face of all these interpretations about the kingdom, some New Testament scholars about 1900 set a new current in motion by stressing the apocalyptic or eschatological side of the kingdom of God in Jesus' teachings. The nineteenth century had pretty well been given over to views of the kingdom (or "dominion of God," as they liked to call it) in an ethical sense. The kingdom, as Albrecht Ritschl says, "consists of those who believe in Christ, inasmuch as they treat one another with love without regard to differences of sex, rank, or race, thereby bringing about a fellowship of moral attitudes and moral properties extending through the whole range of human life."[6] Similarly Harnack in 1899: the kingdom is "the rule of the holy God in the hearts of individuals," a matter of "God and the soul, the soul and its God."[7] Given an ethical interpretation, or an individualist one, the kingdom became something to build, develop, or cultivate. On this view, even Transcendental Meditation could achieve the reign of God!

While certain of the Pietists had always kept alive a more apocalyptic view of the kingdom as God's work, not humankind's, it was the achievement of New Testament critics, often of a radical bent, to turn the tide. These scholars began to see that the New Testament did not support what their age was saying about the kingdom of God. Ritschl's own son-in-law, Johannes Weiss, wrote in 1892 that the kingdom in Jesus' preaching is not a gradual evolutionary achievement, but solely and only the activity of God. No one, "not even Jesus can bring, establish, or found the Kingdom of God; only God can do so." Weiss saw that such a conclusion from the Bible might make Jesus' view of the kingdom irrelevant for Europe (and America) in his day, so he simply admitted that "this conception of ours [of the kingdom as the highest Good and the supreme ethical ideal] parts company with Jesus' " own eschatological view.[8].

The scholar who carried this finding to its logical outcome, and whose name became almost a household word and his fame legion, was another German, Albert Schweitzer, at the University of Strassburg. Schweitzer applied this apocalyptic understanding of Jesus' view of God's kingdom not only to the preaching but to everything Jesus did or said. The result was a Jesus who believed at first that God would inaugurate his kingdom during his own lifetime, probably while the Twelve were on a mission tour (Mark 6:7–13; Matthew 10, esp. v. 23). But that proved wrong. No Son of man appeared on the clouds of heaven. Jesus then decided, according to Schweitzer, that he himself must die—then the Son of man and the kingdom would come. He did die. But no Son of man, no kingdom came. Jesus thus, in Schweitzer's view, died a disappointed eschatologist, and Jesus' teachings, which were for only that brief interval before the kingdom comes, have no lasting value. (Schweitzer himself subsequently went off to French West Africa, to labor heroically as a medical humanitarian—"missionary" may be too strong a term—his ethics and life view increasingly informed by Stoicism and oriental religions.)

Schweitzer did, however, recapture the eschatological side of the kingdom which no one since his day has been able to ignore. But he made it so one-sidedly apocalyptic that the kingdom would have little value after Jesus' death, according to Schweitzer's analysis, save as a noble idea to be filled with new content, primarily ethical.

Whither the kingdom now? The story of its interpretation is not over. Other expositors have frankly faced the fact that all predictions of the end of the world, even in the New Testament, proved wrong, and so they have gone back to Jesus' words to find some other abiding value in the kingdom. One suggestion comes in the approach of Rudolf Bultmann (1884–1976). For Jesus, he says, the kingdom was a future power that was already determining the present. What it did was force people to come to a decision, about God and the rule of God, about themselves and life. What matters is thus the way human existence is conceived of here and now. Announcement of the kingdom is a call for people to turn, repent, and come to "authentic existence," as life lived in faith. More radically the kingdom proclamation is a summons to live depending on God as a power outside ourselves. This is an "existentialist" interpretation, that is, applying to human existence and employing the language of existentialist philosophy.

Thus, in the long history of its use, over a millennium in the Bible and two thousand years since Christ, the kingdom of God has had dozens of interpretations and new twists of meaning. We can view it as

otherworldly and future; or
as this-worldly and present—individually or via social action;
   a path through history, opposed to the devil's earthly kingdom,
     leading to a heavenly realm;
   a stage or dispensation in history;

the area, the church, where God's rule is confessed, as opposed
to the world where God also rules in other ways but
unacknowledged; or
as this-worldly but future—to be achieved by God or us or both;
or any combination of the above!

THE KINGDOM AS SYMBOL

A much-debated symbol! Needless to say, all the chapters in this book, about Jesus' view, or Paul's usage, or Matthew's, have been written with an awareness of this history of interpretation. (The reader might wish to review the biblical passages now with subsequent interpretations and turns in mind!) And the debate goes on. We have suggested some of the biblical content involved in God's kingdom (chaps. 1–33). We have also seen some subsequent interpretations (chap. 35). Clearly what is apparent is the staying power of this theme as a symbol for something central in the Bible and in Christianity.

Yet one must admit it has been a symbol with levels of meaning—not one fixed sense, exhausted when its time has come and gone, but a set of meanings, never exhausted, which continue to project new senses on ahead to inspire and lead the people of God.[9]

This pervasive symbol of the kingdom has thus had a tremendous history, from the ancient Near East and its mythological usage (chap. 8) to Jesus (chaps. 6–7) and beyond. The psalmist caught the vision of what the kingdom of God means in these words:

All thy creatures praise thee, LORD,
    and thy servants bless thee.
They talk of the glory of thy kingdom
    and tell of thy might,
they proclaim to their fellows how mighty are thy deeds,
    how glorious the majesty of thy kingdom.
Thy kingdom is an everlasting kingdom,
    and thy dominion stands for all generations.
                    (Ps. 145:10–13, NEB)

Anonymous writers, between the Old Testament and the New, kept the hope alive during dark days, as when the author of the *Assumption of Moses* wrote: Then shall God's kingdom appear, "throughout his creation, and then shall Satan be no more, and sorrow shall depart. . . ." Then came Jesus, and the kingdom was at hand. Ever since believers have been trying to let the promise come to fulfillment, for which they pray, "Thy kingdom come." Luther explained this petition very existentially, "To be sure, the kingdom of God comes of itself, without our prayer, but we pray . . . that it may also come to us." Then he added that this happens when "the heavenly Father gives us his Holy Spirit so that by his grace we may believe his holy Word and live a godly life, both here in time and hereafter forever."[10]

The meanings of the symbol march on. Perhaps a Christian in the second century summed things up well in a succinct phrase: "In the gospel, the kingdom of God is Christ himself."[11] Or as a later theologian put it in the next century, "Christ is himself the kingdom."[12] The symbolism of the kingdom, that God is Lord and breaks into human life, supremely in Jesus Christ, has been set in motion by Scripture in a rich way. The gospel is the norm that defines the kingdom as good news. Jesus is, increasingly since Easter, its content. God's rule in every life and land and age is the goal. To express the kingdom meaningfully, as gospel, in Christ, is the task of those who witness to Christ.

The Bible provides abundant ways to grasp hold of the message about the kingdom. The kingdom of God is but one way of expressing the gospel. Witnesses for true life must experience the kingdom, justification, Christ, and gospel as their own, before they can talk much about these things, but as they speak and live, they will also find God and Christ, the kingdom and the gospel making them *their* own! In telling the God story, one not only comes to know God better but is known, one finds, also by God (Gal. 4:9; 1 Cor. 13:12).

A Hassidic tale tells how Rabbi Zusya of Hanipol once remarked, "In the coming world they will not ask me, 'Why were you not Moses?' They will ask me: 'Why were you not Zusya?' "[13] Christians too are accustomed to the need to be themselves, and witness where they are, developing their own gifts and talents. But there is a sense in which they must also answer differently, for they and their story are never just of themselves, but of their Lord. They are "in Christ" and must live in him.

The zenith of Bible study comes when we know the God story of Scripture and the Christ reports so well that they are told with our own accents, comfortably and familiarly; when our stories, individually, are subordinated to God's deeds, glory, and might; when we listen to others to detect what God is saying or will have said here. Then we are beginning to have eyes and ears of faith, to see and hear the kingdom of God and Christ taking shape in human existence, as good news. Word has become witness for us, and our witness word of God.

NOTES

1. Ralph W. Quare, *Evangelical Witness: The Message, Medium, Mission, and Method of Evangelism* (Minneapolis: Augsburg Publishing House, 1975), 67–94.

Built around study of Paul's Epistle to the Romans and on "law and gospel" as a key to effective evangelism, the book reflects experiences of a professor at Wartburg Seminary, Dubuque, Iowa. As a church historian, Quare divides the twenty Christian centuries into eleven stages, from the Docetists (see above, pp. 383–84) to *Jesus Christ Superstar,* around the questions:
  A. Who saves us? questions on Christology in the first four centuries;
  B. How are we saved? grace, predestination and free will, and sacraments, from Augustine to the Reformation;
  C. Says who? the questions of authority, revelation, and the church.
The book may be read with profit as a theologically oriented treatment of Romans considered as "An Evangel for Evangelists."

2. Archibald Robertson, *Regnum Dei* (New York: Macmillan Co., 1901), 119.

3. *The Book of Concord,* ed. T. G. Tappert et al. (Philadelphia: Muhlenberg Press, 1959), 170–71.

4. Benjamin E. Mays, ed., *A Gospel for the Social Awakening: Selections from the Writings of Walter Rauschenbusch,* intro. by C. Howard Hopkins (New York: Association Press, 1950), 14.

5. Harvey Cox, *The Secular City* (New York: Macmillan Co., 1965), 127.

6. Albrecht Ritschl, *Rechtfertigung und Versöhnung III,* 3d ed. (Bonn, 1888), 271 (au. trans.). Cf. the official Eng. trans., *The Christian Doctrine of Justification and Reconciliation: The Positive Development of the Doctrine,* trans. H. R. Mackintosh and A. B. Macaulay (New York: Charles Scribner's Sons, 1900), 285.

7. Adolf von Harnack, *What Is Christianity?* trans. T. B. Saunders, 3d rev. ed. (London: Williams & Norgate, 1904), 57, 58.

8. Johannes Weiss, *Jesus' Proclamation of the Kingdom of God* (1892), trans. and ed. R. H. Hiers and D. L. Holland (Philadelphia: Fortress Press, 1971), 129–30, 134–35.

9. Cf. Norman Perrin, "The Interpretation of a Biblical Symbol," *Journal of Religion* 55 (1975): 348–70, and his book, *Jesus and the Language of the Kingdom: Symbol and Metaphor in New Testament Interpretation* (Philadelphia: Fortress Press, 1976), esp. 15–88. His conclusion is that "in the proclamation of Jesus 'Kingdom of God' was used as a tensive symbol," that is, with a set of meanings never exhausted (in contrast to a one-on-one "stenosymbol"); it evoked "the myth of God acting as king" (p. 196).

10. Luther, Small Catechism, III, Explanation to the Second Petition; in *The Book of Concord,* ed. Tappert et al., 346.

11. As quoted in Tertullian, *Against Marcion* IV. 33.

12. Origen, *Commentary on Matthew* 14.7, "Christ is himself the king of the heavens, just as he is absolute wisdom, righteousness, and truth, and absolute kingship."

13. As quoted by Victor Gollancz, *A Year of Grace* (1950; reprinted, Harmondsworth, Eng.: Penguin Books, 1955), 402 (the rabbi involved died in 1800), from Martin Buber, *Tales of the Hasidim: The Early Masters,* trans. Olga Marx (New York: Schocken Books, 1947; paperback, 1961), 251.

APPENDIX:
A CHRONOLOGICAL TABLE

From Abraham to Saul

	EGYPT	PALESTINE	HITTITES	MESOPOTAMIA	
				MARI	BABYLON
				Zimri-Lim	Hammurabi
				1730–1697	1728–1686
2000 B.C.	XII *Dynasty*	Middle Bronze II	City-States		
1750	Hyksos	Beginning of Patriarchs			
1650	XV *Dynasty*		Old Kingdom		
1550	Hyksos expelled	Hebrews in Egypt			
	New Kingdom				
	Amenophis I				
	Thutmosis I				
	Thutmosis II				
	Thutmosis III				
	Amenophis II	Late Bronze	Hittite Empire		
1400	Amenophis III		Shuppiluliuma		
	Amenophis IV	Amarna Period			
	(Akhenaten,				
	Tutankhamen,				
	XIX *Dynasty*				
1300	Sethos I	The Exodus			
	Rameses II				
	Merneptah				

478

	EGYPT	PALESTINE	HITTITES
1200	XX *Dynasty* Rameses III Rameses IV–XI	Beginning of Iron Age Joshua T J h u e d g e s	End of Hittite Empire
1100	End of Egyptian Empire		
1050	XXI *Dynasty*	Fall of Shiloh Samuel Kingship of Saul	

From David to Alexander

UNITED KINGDOM

KINGDOM **DIVIDES**

B.C.	KINGS OF JUDAH	PROPHETS	UNITED KINGDOM	KINGS OF ISRAEL	EVENTS	EASTERN EMPIRES and RULERS
1000 B.C.			David			
961			Solomon		Temple built	
922	Rehoboam			Jeroboam I		Assyrian Empire
915	Abijam					
913	Asa					
901				Nadab		
900				Bassah		
883				Elah		Ashurnasirpal II
877				Zimri		
876				Tibni		
				Omri		
873	Jehoshaphat					
869				Ahab		
858		Elijah				
850				Ahaziah	Battle of Qarqar	Shalmanezer III
849	Jehoram			Jehoram		

	KINGS OF *JUDAH*	*PROPHETS*	KINGS OF *ISRAEL*	EVENTS	EASTERN EMPIRES and RULERS
842	Ahaziah	Elisha	Jehu		
	Athaliah	Amos			
837	Jehoash				Shamshi-adad
815			Jehoahaz		
810			Jehoash		Adad-nirari III
801					
800	Amaziah				
786		Hosea	Jeroboam II		Shalmanezer IV
783	Uzziah	Isaiah			Ashurdan
746			Zechariah		Ashurnirari V
			Shallum		
745			Menahem		
742	Jotham	Micah			Tiglath-pileser III
738			Pekahiah		
737			Pekah		
735	Ahaz				
732			Hoshea		
726					Shalmanezer V
721				Fall of Samaria Deportation to Assyria	Sargon II

481

B.C.	KINGS OF JUDAH	PROPHETS	KINGS OF ISRAEL	EVENTS	EASTERN EMPIRES and RULERS
715	Hezekiah				
704					Sennacherib
687	Manasseh				Esarhaddon
668	Amon				Ashurbanipal
642					Ashuretililani Sinsharishkin Ashurubalit
640	Josiah				
626		Jeremiah			BABYLONIAN EMPIRE Nabopolassar
609	Jehoahaz Jehoiakim			Fall of Ninevah Fall of Haran	
605		Ezekiel		Battle of Carchemish	Nebuchadnezzar
598	Jehoiachin			1st deportation	
597	Zedekiah			Fall of Jerusalem	
587				2d deportation 3d deportation	

482

BABYLONIAN EXILE

Date	Events	Eastern Empires and Rulers
		BABYLONIAN EMPIRE
559		Amel-Marduk
555		Nergal-shar-usur
		Nabunaid
		PERSIAN EMPIRE
538	First return of exiles	Cyrus
529		Cambyses
520	Rebuilding of temple resumed	
521		Darius I
515	Completed	
485		Xerxes I
464		Artaxerxes I
458	Ezra arrives	
445	Nehemiah arrives	
423		Xerxes II
		Darius II
404		Artaxerxes II
336		Darius III
333	Alexander the Great defeats the Persians	

WESTERN EMPIRES

KINGDOM OF MACEDON
Philip
Alexander

PTOLEMAIC EMPIRE
323–283 B.C. Ptolemy I

285–246 Ptolemy II

246–221 Ptolemy III
221–203 Ptolemy IV
203–181 Ptolemy V

181–146 Ptolemy VI

170–164 Ptolemy VII
   (co-ruler)

145–117 Ptolemy VII

116–108 Ptolemy VIII
116–107 Ptolemy IX
   (co-regent)

88–80 Ptolemy VIII

PALESTINE

High Priests at Jerusalem

Onias II
(200 Antiochus takes Palestine)
Onias III
Jason

HASMONEAN RULERS
166–160 Judas Maccabeus
160–142 Jonathan
142–135 Simon
135–104 John Hyrcanus I

104–103 Aristobolus I
103–76 Alexander Janneus

76–67 Alexandra

EASTERN EMPIRES

SELEUCID EMPIRE
312 Seleucus king at Babylon
301–280 Seleucus king at Antioch
280–262 Antiochus I
261–247 Antiochus II
247–226 Seleucus II
226–223 Seleucus III
223–187 Antiochus III
187–175 Seleucus IV
175–163 Antiochus IV
   (Epiphanes)
163–162 Antiochus V
162–150 Demetrius I
150–145 Alexander Balas
145–139 Demetrius II
145–142 Antiochus VI
139–129 Antiochus VII
129–125 Demetrius II (cont.)
125–96 Antiochus VIII
115–95 Antiochus IX

EASTERN EMPIRES

PTOLEMAIC EMPIRE

80–56 Ptolemy XIII

51–30 Cleopatra

HASMONEAN RULERS

66–63 Aristobolus II
(63 Pompey takes Jerusalem)
63–40 Hyrcanus II
40–37 Antigonus

HERODIAN RULERS

37–4 Herod the Great
(4 B.C. Kingdom divides)

ITUREA
4 B.C.–A.D. 34 Philip

37–44 Agrippa I

48–100 Agrippa II,
king of Chalcis

53–100 King of
former tetrarchies
of Philip and Lysanias

56 Agrippa II rules parts
of Galilee and Perea

GALILEE
4 B.C.–A.D. 39
Antipas

JUDEA
4 B.C.–A.D. 6 Archelaus
6–41 Roman governors
(26–36 Pontius Pilate)
41–44 Agrippa I king over Judea, Galilee, and Perea
44–66 Roman governors
(52–60 Felix)
(60–62 Festus)
66 Jewish Revolt
70 Fall of Jerusalem

ROMAN EMPIRE

27 B.C.–A.D. 14 Augustus

A.D. 14–37 Tiberius
37–41 Caligula
41–54 Claudius

54–68 Nero

68–69 Galba/Otho/Vitellius

69–79 Vespasian
79–81 Titus
81–96 Domitian

Indexes

SCRIPTURE REFERENCES

Indexes

Scripture References

NAMES AND SUBJECTS

Page references to photographs and captions are in *italics*.

Names and Subjects

Israel, Israelite, xv, xvi, 2, 4, 11, 13, 17, 32, 39, 40, 41, 51, 52–53, 57, 60, 71, 73, 74–76, 82, 91, 107, 113, 124, 133–43, 151, 152, 153, 156, 159, 164, 168, 171, 173, 174, 180, 181, 197–205, 206–19, 220, 222, 224, 225, 230, 234, 236, 244, 253, 255, 257, 258, 259, 261, 262, 266, 268, 271, 277, 286, 295, 300, 301, 339, 349, 369, 385, 395, 399, 408–9, 419, 436, 480–82
   northern kingdom, 42, 75, 76, 161–62, 164, 260, 274, 275, 285

"J" source, 148–51, 165, 206–10, 217, 218. *See also* Yahwist
Jacob, xxiv, 67, 72, 124, 126, 143, 153, 156, 165, 166, 223, 224, 259, 297, 303
Jenson, Robert W., 463 n. 1
Jeremias, Joachim, 129 n. 2
Jerusalem, 19, 42, 44, 52, 74, 75, 76, 83, 84, 86, 88, 101, 103, 115, 129, 156, 166, 169, 170, 172, 173, 175, *183*, 189–90, 200, 203–4, 205, 220, 221, 222, 225, 234, 235, *238*, 258, 259, 261, 269, 272, 274, 275, 276, 277, 279, 283–86, 296, 299, 305, 306 n. 4, *310*, 311, 317, 335, 336, 373, 374, 395, 407, 437, 440, 444, *454*, 482, 484, 485
Jesse, 42, 282, 303, 306
Jesus, xvi, xvii, 1–4, 15, 16, 25, 39, 40, 41, 42, 43, 54, 57–58, 69, 81, 82, 85–86, 92–129, 147, 178, 179, 180–93, 234–35, 236, 240, 269, 286–87, 288–307, 311–14, 316, 317, 319, 320, 321, 324, 331, 335, 340, 342, 365–66, 377, 380, 393, 431–32, 440, 446
   and apocalyptic, 293–95, 348–50
   and bad news, 57–58
   "Christ," response to title, 297–300
   and coronation psalms, 277–78
   death, 40, 46, 58, 180, 185, 293, 306, 316, 317–19, 342, 351, 372, 406
   death and resurrection, 4, 48, 86, 97, 104, 110, 180–93, 243, 274, 300, 312, 315, 316, 317, 318, 319, 323, 326, 334, 340, 350, 351, 353, 355, 437, 438–39
   and eschatology, 293–97
   future, in teachings of, 293–97
   and the Gentiles, 296–97
   as king (regent), 312, 321–22, 379
   law and, 291–93
   message, 95–110, 289
   ministry of, 82, 86, 96, 103, 105–6, 108, 111–29, 179, 180, 191, 313, 317, 318, 319, 375, 407
   miracles, 107, 113–14, 123–25, 431–32
   parables, 54, 122, 126–28
   as Son of David, 301–6
   Son of man and, 294–95
   teaches, teachings, 42, 57–58, 106, 111, 112, 113, 115–23, 125–28, 239–40, 247, 327, 349–50, 378, 441–42
Jesus Christ, xvii, 1, 2, 13, 39, 44, 59, 69, 71, 81, 86, 90, 96, 97, 100, 186, 192, 235, 236–49, 277–78, 287, 288, 301, 306, 311, 320–21, 368, 375, 382, 395, 414–16, 421, 439, 457, 468
Jewish Christian(s), 16, 87, 101, 105, 327, 334, 335, 406
Jews, Jewish, 1, 7, 13, 16, 32, 58, 77–79, 86, 180, 242, 243, 264, 288, 290, 296, 305, 320, 321, 323, 336, 342, 374, 382–83
Joachim of Flora, 468–69
John the Baptist, 1, 86, 96, 97, 100, 102, 104, 105, 113, 121, 193 n. 1, 239, 301–2, 330, 384, 438, 458

Joseph, husband of Mary, 102, 107, 288, 304, 305, 306
Joseph (OT), 143, 230
Josiah, King, 76, 169, 170, 171, 261, 303, 482
Judah (tribe, nation), 75–76, 91, 161–64, 169, 170, 176, 221, 223, 254, 260, 261, 275, 282, 285, 480–82
Judaism, 12, 32, 33, 88, 89, 106, 157, 181, 182, 199, 269, 341, 391, 448
Judas (betrayer of Jesus), 346 n. 2, 448
Judas (Maccabeus), 79, 82, 374, 484
Judgment(s), xx, 1, 42, 46, 47, 56, 57, 60, 68, 166, 168, 173, 209, 221, 222, 226, 228, 239, 254, 255, 256, 260, 282, 283, 284, 294, 319, 334, 340, 341, 348, 361, 362–63, 385, 445, 466
Justice, 167, 168, 200–201, 237, 239, 263, 282, 283, 285, 287, 399–401, 470
Justify, justified, justification, 49, 90, 101, 331, 333, 338–41, 342, 343, 346 n. 3, 351, 372, 400, 457, 461

Käsemann, Ernst, 410 n. 3
Kazantzakis, Nikos, 10
Kerygma, 98, 100, 109, 113, 236, 317–22, 330, 331
King, 52, 53, 74, 159, 172, 199, 274–77, 279–87, 301, 374. *See also* David; Saul
   God as, 98, 122, 133, 136, 142, 143–51, 155, 157, 168, 174, 177, 180, 198–99, 201, 205
   Jesus as?, 312, 379
Kingdom of God, xvi, xvii, 1–3, 8, 9, 15, 47, 57, 85, 90, 96, 97, 98, 101, 110, 111, 114, 115, 119, 121, 123–25, 153, 154, 156, 178, 179, 180, 258, 269, 281, 284–85, 287, 288, 289, 293, 311, 314, 317, 320–22, 332, 333, 334, 335, 336, 356, 378–80, 388, 394, 409, 423, 433, 445, 455–56, 474–75. *See also* Kingdom of heaven
   in Acts, 320–22
   and church, 390, 393–95, 468
   future, to come, 98, 115, 321, 333, 334, 349–50
   and gospel through the centuries, 464–76
   interim, of Christ, 358
   interpretations of, 473–74
   Jesus' views on, 127–28, 285–96
   language in Paul, 331–34
   in Luke, 450
   and messiah, messianic promises, 271–78, 281–87
   presence of, present, 98, 115, 121, 122, 333, 334, 349
   in Revelation, 369–70
   why deemphasized in early church, 321–22
Kingdom of heaven, 3, 103, 104, 111, 115, 121, 124, 175, 189, 297, 445, 465
Kingdoms, two, 16, 67, 161, 470–71
Kingship
   of David, 271–74
   of God, xvi, 85, 86, 97, 98, 111, 127, 137, 198, 201, 289, 296, 300, 332, 455
   and good news, 176
Knox, Ronald, 182, 358
Kubo, Sakae, 36 n. 9

Law(s), 14–15, 27, 35, 38, 40, 43, 58, 77, 79, 81, 83, 85, 87, 88, 89, 152, 156, 157, 159, 167–68, 171, 235, 259, 340, 341, 342, 394, 412, 421, 425, 444, 448
   apodictic and casuistic, 158, 159
   Christ the end of, 293, 345, 346
   and gospel, 14–15, 41

Indexes

Wooden, John, 425

"Word and Witness" program, vi, xx–xxiii, 347 n. 4

Word of God, of the Lord, xvi, xxiv, 1, 2, 9, 38–50, 96, 105, 125, 133, 171, 175, 184, 200, 235, 240, 241, 242, 259, 266, 353, 362, 403, 463, 475

World(s), 17, 68, 122, 228, 233, 237, 242, 248, 249, 262, 269, 331, 383, 411

Worship, xvi, 74, 139, 164, 171, 173, 197–205, 230, 236, 258, 259, 331, 334 n. 1, 392–93, 394

Yahweh, xvi, xvii, 11, 73, 85, 115, 137, 138, 143–51, 155, 164, 170, 178, 185, 186, 197–205, 222, 223, 224, 225, 254, 255, 257, 261, 263, 264, 271, 274, 281, 282, 283, 287, 288, 291, 294, 365–66, 367, 408, 412

Yahwist, the, 206–10, 217, 218

Zion, Mount, 42, 51, 52, 76, 115, 176, 178, 201, 203, 221, 225, 234, 237, 258, 259, 263, 269, 296, 297, 306 n. 4, 365

DATE DUE

SEP 24 '96			
OCT 8 '96			

DEMCO 38-297